WHEN THE IRON BIRD FLIES

WHEN THE IRON BIRD FLIES

China's Secret War in Tibet

JIANGLIN LI

Translated by Stacy Mosher
With a Foreword by the Dalai Lama

STANFORD UNIVERSITY PRESS
Stanford, California

STANFORD UNIVERSITY PRESS
Stanford, California

A previous version was published in Chinese under the title *Dang tieniao zai tiankong feixiang: 1956–1962 qingzang gaoyuan shang de mimi zhanzheng* ©2012 by Lianjing chuban gongsi.

Printed in the United States of America on acid-free, archival-quality paper

Library of Congress Cataloging-in-Publication Data
Names: Li, Jianglin, 1956– author. | Mosher, Stacy, translator.
Title: When the iron bird flies : China's secret war in Tibet / Jianglin Li; translated by Stacy Mosher.
Other titles: Dang tie niao zai tian kong fei xiang. English
Description: Stanford, California : Stanford University Press, [2022] | "A previous version was published in Chinese under the title Dang tieniao zai tiankong feixiang: 1956–1962 qingzang gaoyuan shang de mimi zhanzheng ©2012 by Lianjing chuban gongsi." | Includes bibliographical references and index.
Identifiers: LCCN 2021026174 (print) | LCCN 2021026175 (ebook) | ISBN 9781503615090 (cloth) | ISBN 9781503629790 (epub)
Subjects: LCSH: Tibet Autonomous Region (China)—History—1951–| Tibet Autonomous Region (China)—History—Uprising of 1959. | China—Relations—China—Tibet Autonomous Region. | Tibet Autonomous Region (China)—Relations—China.
Classification: LCC DS786 .L4619313 2022 (print) | LCC DS786 (ebook) | DDC 951/.505—dc23
LC record available at https://lccn.loc.gov/2021026174

LC ebook record available at https://lccn.loc.gov/2021026175

Cover design: Rob Ehle

Cover photo: © Ian Dikhtiar | Dreamstime.com

Text design: Kevin Barrett Kane

Typeset at Stanford University Press in 11.5/15 Arno Pro

When the iron bird flies,
And horses run on wheels,
The Tibetan people will be scattered like ants across the world,
And the Dharma will come to the land of the Red Man

Prediction attributed to Padmasambhava, 8th century

CONTENTS

FOREWORD

By His Holiness the Dalai Lama

In her 2010 book entitled *Tibet in Agony: Lhasa 1959*, the Chinese historian Li Jianglin presented conclusive research on the Tibetan popular uprising, the circumstances that led me to leave Lhasa for exile in India, the emergency situation in Tibet at that time, the attitudes of senior Chinese leaders, and so on. Presenting an honest and detailed account of the situation at that time, and informing historians in China especially, and the general reader, about the real situation, it was most beneficial.

Here, in Li Jianglin's second book, *China's Secret War in Tibet*, we have for the first time a Chinese historian presenting conclusive research on Tibet's recent history and the facts about China's military suppression of Tibet in the 1950s, in an unbiased and genuine manner. She has consulted a great many books and documents, public, private, and secret, as well as interviewing many persons involved in that history, in order to clarify many things about the events of that time. As I always say, "China's 1.3 billion people have a right to know what really happened, and I believe that if they could get an understanding of the real situation, they would be able to distinguish good from bad and truth from falsehood," and it is my hope that through this historical documentation establishing the truth of what happened, Chinese intellectuals, and all other readers, will come to understand the real situation and be able to deepen their approach to and understanding of the Tibet problem in the spirit of seeking truth from facts.

With my praise and admiration for the author on the fruition of her many labors.

The Dalai Lama
Tibetan Royal Year 2139
Water Dragon
March 30, 2012

PREFACE TO THE ENGLISH EDITION

1

While I was researching the March 1959 "Lhasa incident,"[1] the descriptions and information that I found scattered across large quantities of sources, along with the recollections of participants on both sides of the conflict, shifted my gaze toward a broader scope of time and space: the events that took place in the three traditional Tibetan provinces[2] in the years from 1956 to 1962.

A large amount of written material shows that intense military conflicts occurred in China's southwestern and northwestern regions from the mid-1950s through the early 1960s, covering all three of the traditional Tibetan provinces, which today are known as the Tibet Autonomous Region (TAR) and the Tibetan prefectures of the four peripheral provinces. On one side of the conflict were the Chinese People's Liberation Army (PLA) Field Armies and regional units with their modern weaponry, as well as trained militia; on the other side were Tibetan farmers, herders, and monks, along with a handful of government officials and some Tibetan soldiers, armed mainly with homemade muskets, rifles, knives, and spears. This military conflict lasted six and a half years, from the early spring of 1956 through the summer of 1962. Of the PLA's twelve military commands at that time, seven participated in this conflict to varying degrees,[3] drawing on infantry, artillery, cavalry, air force, armored and motor vehicle, and anti-chemical divisions, among others.

This was a military operation "under the unified command of the Central Military Commission (CMC) and the leadership of local party committees,"[4] and its policy-makers and commanders were key figures in modern Chinese history, including Mao Zedong, chairman of the Chinese Communist Party (CCP) and CMC; Zhou Enlai, premier and deputy chairman of CMC; as well as Deng Xiaoping, Yang Shangkun, Peng Dehuai, Su Yu, and Zhang Aiping.[5] From a military perspective, the CCP's military operation in the Tibetan regions was a complete success, but it is the least publicized of the CCP's military engagements: The military operation was and has continued to be carefully avoided and covered up, both during the conflict and in the decades that followed. The *Complete History of the Chinese People's Liberation Army*, an authoritative ten-volume source published by China's Academy of Military Science in 2000, refers to this conflict as a PLA "elite-force" military operation, summing it up in two sentences: "(March 1959) The Chinese People's Liberation Army troops stationed in Tibet began pacifying an armed rebellion in Tibet on the 20th. The battle to suppress the rebellion ended in victory in March 1962."[6] These sentences hide a crucial fact: that in addition to the "troops stationed in Tibet" at that time, one of the main forces engaged in the battle in Tibet was the elite 54th Army, which had fought in the Korean War. This omitted information hints at a vastly complex reality whose violence and devastation were enormous both in their scale and in their impact on the modern history of the region. For instance, one of the facts not recorded there is that the air force dispatched two Tupolev Tu-4 aircrafts to strafe and bomb an armed rebellion at the Lithang (Litang) Monastery on March 29, 1956.[7] Nicknamed the Bull, this type of aircraft was a Soviet-made long-range heavy bomber, the most advanced that the Chinese military owned at that time.

The total number of Tibetan casualties in this 6-year campaign may never be made known to the public. In 1961, the CCP held a "Northwest Ethnic Minorities Work Conference," which partially redressed the "over-amplified pacification of the rebellion" in Qinghai and Gansu provinces, but what has been made public up to now omits key information.[8] In the

1980s, the CCP finally acknowledged that it had "committed the error of over-amplification" in its war in the Tibetan regions and was compelled to provide some redress by releasing prisoners still in jail, rehabilitating large number of accused "rebels," and providing small amounts of monetary compensation to the families of people "wrongly executed,"[9] but the specifics remain classified to this day, and the information recorded in local gazetteers is confusing and incomplete. In short, after more than half a century, this military conflict remains a closely held secret.

After the Chinese edition of my book *Tibet in Agony: Lhasa 1959*[10] was published, in 2010, I immediately began researching this broader military conflict and its background, process, and aftermath.

2

For readers who may not have in-depth knowledge of the history of modern Tibet, I would like to provide a brief geographic and historical background.

First, regarding the definition of "Tibet": The Chinese term *Xizang* has a specific meaning in China's modern history, and is not equivalent to the traditional three Tibetan regions. Geographically, traditional Tibet included the three regions of Ü-Tsang and Ngari (Weizang Ali, central Tibet, and western Tibet), Kham (Kang, eastern Tibet), and Amdo (Anduo, northeastern Tibet), together covering approximately one fourth of today's China, while *Xizang* refers to central Tibet, which is more or less the area of today's Tibet Autonomous Region (TAR).

Traditional Tibet had internal differences, not only in geography and customs but also in politics and administration. In his book *Tibet: Past and Present* (1924), the British diplomat Sir Charles Alfred Bell (1870–1945) elaborates this point. He refers to the regions where Tibetans live as "ethnographic Tibet" and calls the realm of the Lhasa government "political Tibet." He adds, "While attempting to define the former, let us not neglect the latter."[11]

"Political Tibet," i.e., the Ü-Tsang region plus Ngari, western Kham, and the Hor states, had a stable political system with a central government, the *Kashag* (cabinet) government in Lhasa, or *Dewa Shung*, formally known as *Ganden Potrang*, which lasted for about three hundred years until it was abolished by the Chinese government on March 28, 1959. The rest of Kham was divided into a number of kingdoms and principalities, administrations that Chinese historical materials typically refer to as a "local chieftain (*tuci*) system,"[12] emphasizing a subordination to imperial control that was often exaggerated or even fictitious.[13]

The agricultural areas of Amdo also supported several established kingdoms and principalities. For example, before the People's Republic of China (PRC) was established, kingdoms such as Choné (Zhuoni)[14] and the Gyalrong (Jiarong) states[15] had endured for centuries. Pastoral areas were often governed by the headmen of tribal confederacies, called *shokka*, and their constituent units, called *tsowa* or *dewa*. These communities are referred to uniformly in official Chinese sources as "tribes" (*buluo*), although this term ignores the complex and specific character of the variety of social and political relations in different Tibetan regions. In English, as in Chinese, there are no simple terms to accurately describe the variety of polities and forms of social organization in traditional Tibet, and as the details are not the subject of this book, I have freely used the words "tribe" (in its loosest sense), and "clan" (which has a nearly identical meaning in English), for the sake of readability, along with the Tibetan *shokka* and *tsowa*, where they are known to apply, especially to describe the more independent pastoral groups of the Golok grassland and other areas of eastern Tibet.

The relation between Tibet and China also went through different stages. After the downfall of the Qing dynasty in 1911, the Nationalist government established in the following year attempted to extend its rule to "political Tibet," but without meaningful success. In 1917 and 1918, a military conflict broke out between the Tibetan and Chinese armies, resulting in a Tibetan government successfully taking back Chamdo (Changdu) and part of Kham. Drichu (the Jinsha River) remained the border between central Tibet and China, and Chamdo was ruled by Tibetans until 1950. In the 1920s and 1930s, the Nationalist government successfully incorporated Kham and Amdo into its political system by establishing new provinces. Qinghai Province was established in 1928, bringing a large part of Amdo and part of Kham into its jurisdiction. Xikang Province was formally established in 1939, covering most of Kham. This process did not proceed without Tibetan resistance. Three military clashes collectively known as the Sino-Tibetan War took place in the 1930s between Tibetan forces and the Chinese army in Qinghai and Sichuan. The conflicts ended with ceasefire agreements and a reclarification of the borders between central Tibet and China. However, in many regions, especially pastoral areas, the Chinese government was unable to establish administrative power. Tibetan nomads and farmers in many areas kept their way of life until it was forcefully changed by the events described in this book.

It is worth noting that the period when the Nationalist government expanded its power to the Tibetan regions corresponded to the era when the Communist movement led by the CCP was underway. Due to their remoteness and cultural differences, the majority of Tibetans had not participated in the revolution. During the Long March (1935–1936), the Red Army, including most of the top CCP leaders, passed through Ngawa (Aba)[16] and Garzê (Ganzi).[17] It was not a happy encounter for either side. The Red Army leaders and soldiers found themselves penetrating an utterly alien region. In their desperate effort to find provisions, Red Army soldiers looted monasteries and villages and were ambushed by Tibetan tribesmen, resulting in quite a few military clashes. Due to the language barrier, CCP propaganda was minimally effective in wooing Tibetan support, and only five Tibetan youths followed the Red Army all the way to Yan'an to be groomed as communist cadres. When Mao Zedong announced the founding of the PRC on October 1, 1949, the PLA occupied only half of the country. It soon advanced toward regions inhibited largely by ethnic minorities, including the traditional Tibetan regions of Amdo and Kham. One year later, central Tibet was occupied by the PLA. Details of this process are presented in chapter 7 of this book.

3

After taking power, the CCP immediately launched a series of political campaigns to remold China into a socialist country. In the first ten years of the PRC, political movements such as land reform, the Campaign to Suppress Counterrevolutionaries, the establishment of state-private partnerships (SPPs) in industry and business, the Anti-Rightist Campaign, the Agricultural Cooperative Movement, and the Great Leap Forward swept across the country, resulting in the largest famine in Chinese history and millions of deaths by execution and starvation. The events described in this book took place within this general time frame.

Even though most of the political campaigns mentioned above also took place in the ethnic minority regions and caused the same catastrophic results, as described in various chapters of this book, in those areas the CCP was somewhat flexible in implementing its policies based on local social and economic conditions. For example, land reform, referred to as "democratic reform" in minority areas, started a few years later there than in inland China. In the Tibetan regions (areas where Tibetans live, known after 1951 as "the-four-province-one-region Tibetan areas"), it was launched in different years in different provinces: in Yunnan in 1955, Sichuan in 1956, Gansu and Qinghai in 1958, and the TAR in 1959. Nor was the Great Leap Forward necessarily a driving force in all of the Tibetan regions. In fact, reform in the Tibetan regions of Yunnan and Sichuan provinces began prior to the Great Leap Forward. However, it was a main factor in pushing land reform and the cooperative movement in certain Tibetan regions, particularly in the pastoral areas of Qinghai. Other political campaigns, such as the Campaign to Suppress Counterrevolutionaries, the Anti-Rightist Campaign, the Agricultural Cooperative Movement, and the Great Leap Forward, took place in the Tibetan region as well, sometimes in a different variation. For example, in pastoral regions, cooperatives had two forms: Public-Private Partnership and communes.

As we will see in the book, both the goal and the methods of land reform in Tibet were essentially the same as in inland China. The same vocabulary was used as well, including "land reform work team," "struggle meeting" (*douzheng hui*), "spitting bitterness rally" (grievance-venting) (*suku hui*), and dividing society into different classes. On the other hand, some initiatives, such as the so-called Religious System Reform Movement, were much more destructive in Tibetan regions than in inland China.

The modern Chinese administrative divisions of traditional Tibet are essentially colonial in nature and conception, often cutting across traditional boundaries and inevitably blurring the historical identity of these places, while the Tibetan concept of the "three regions" does not describe current administrative reality. In order to provide a clearer account of this segment of history, this book will use the term "Tibetan regions" to refer specifically to the "Tibetan regions of the four provinces," i.e., the traditional Tibetan regions of Kham and Amdo, and will use the term "Tibet" to specifically refer to the Tibet Autonomous Region, i.e., Ü-Tsang, Ngari, and the Nagchu (Naqu) and Chamdo regions. I must emphasize that this book uses these designations purely for the sake of narrative clarity and to facilitate the citation of sources, and not based on my personal views regarding Tibet's history and politics.

The CCP's process of establishing grassroots government in Tibet produced the administrative place names in use today, which are usually but not always based on Chinese-language pronunciations of the Tibetan names. This book uses the Tibetan place names by default, with their Chinese equivalents on first occurrence and in direct quotations from Chinese sources. A bilingual conversion table is appended to relieve any confusion. Regrettably, because I was unable to conduct field research, it was sometimes difficult to determine the locations of some smaller places that don't appear on maps. In such cases, I have done my best to identify major landmarks, such as mountain ranges, monasteries, lakes, and rivers, in order to give readers a better idea of where events occurred.

4

For many years, modern Tibetan studies have mainly focused on central Tibet. I must point out that the events described in this book are not limited to what is now the Tibet Autonomous Region, and my focus is not limited to the fate of the Tibetan elites. Most events presented in this book took place in Kham and Amdo, in remote pastures or villages little known to outsiders, and are intimately connected with the fate of ordinary people, including nomads, farmers, monks, and merchants. Their stories run through the entire book. Apart from the story of Aten, recounted by the exiled Tibetan author Jamyang Norbu,[18] the personal experiences of relevant persons in the book are all drawn from my interviews in Tibetan refugee settlements in India and Nepal. All of the details provided by the interviewees were cross-referenced against official Chinese materials.

The vast majority of the figures, photos, and maps in this book come from Chinese-language sources, including more than 200 county, prefectural, military, population, and CCP historical and organizational gazetteers for the Tibetan regions; hundreds of internal reports on the Tibetan regions published in the Xinhua News Agency periodical *Internal Reference (Neibu Cankao)* from 1949 to 1962; around 200 biographical essays by frontline PLA officers and soldiers as well as biographies of and memoirs by high-ranking commanders; and dozens of situation reports relating to PLA battle units. Primary sources also include records of interviews with more than 100 Tibetans, a portion of which are listed in the bibliography of this book.

I need to point out that the official Chinese sources include classified and "semiclassified," i.e., "*neibu*" or "internal" publications, most of which have never been formally made available to researchers and general public. The Chinese government system is comprised of three branches: the party, the military, and the administration, with the party above the other two. Depending on the importance of their contents, documents are categorized as "top secret" (*juemi*), "classified" (*jimi*), or "internal" or "semiclassified" (*neibu*), and each level has a restricted range of circulation. Normally, documents marked "top secret" circulating among leaders at the provincial level and above; "classified" documents are available to leaders all the way down to the county level; and "semiclassified" *neibu* documents are usually restricted to party members and cadres, not to be viewed by the general public. Given the large number of officials and party members, however, many classified and semiclassified documents have to be printed in considerable quantities. At the same time, each province also produces its own document collections for its own internal use. As a result, keeping all the historical documents secret is not an easy task.

Since the 1980s, many historical documents have found their way into used bookstores and/or been sold online by used-book sellers. Some collections have appeared in electronic databases, and some have been collected and sold by print-on-demand companies. Over the years, I have been able to find thousands of pages of documents that have not been formally declassified in libraries, archives, and used bookstores. All of the classified documents cited in this book have been verified by comparing them with other sources or with censored open publications.

The Chinese edition of this book was published in 2012 by Taiwan's Linking Publishing Company (*Lianjing chuban gongsi*). For the English edition I have made many revisions and added some details that I discovered more recently, and I have also corrected some figures based on newly discovered military documents. The events described in this book took place over a vast area, so it is quite a challenge to present them in a coherent and accessible way for readers who might not be familiar with China's recent history. I have opted to break this complicated and little-known history into smaller scenes, interwoven with personal experiences. At the end of the book, statistics that I have worked out from many volumes of official publications provide readers with a fuller picture of what happened in the Tibetan regions in those years.

This book can only serve as a starting point, providing a general picture of this hidden war. I look forward to more memoirs by those who experienced this period, as well as the declassification of and public access to files, more researchers taking an interest in this period of history, and the use of multi-faceted research to fill in the details of this blank space in the modern history of both Tibet and China and to correct any errors and omissions in my account.

While I was researching and writing this book, Tibetans in all three Tibetan regions began a new round of resistance against Chinese Communist rule. This time they protested with self-immolation, using their lives to draw the world's attention to their situation. Perhaps history can tell us why one generation of Tibetans after another has continued to resist, and why their resistance is so absolute.

ABBREVIATIONS

CCP	Chinese Communist Party
CIA	Central Intelligence Agency
CMC	Central Military Commission
CPPCC	Chinese People's Political Consultative Conference
NPC	National People's Congress
PLA	People's Liberation Army
PRC	People's Republic of China
SPP	state-private partnership
TAP	Tibetan Autonomous Prefecture
TAR	Tibet Autonomous Region
TMC	Tibet Military Command
TWC	Tibet Work Committee

WHEN THE IRON BIRD FLIES

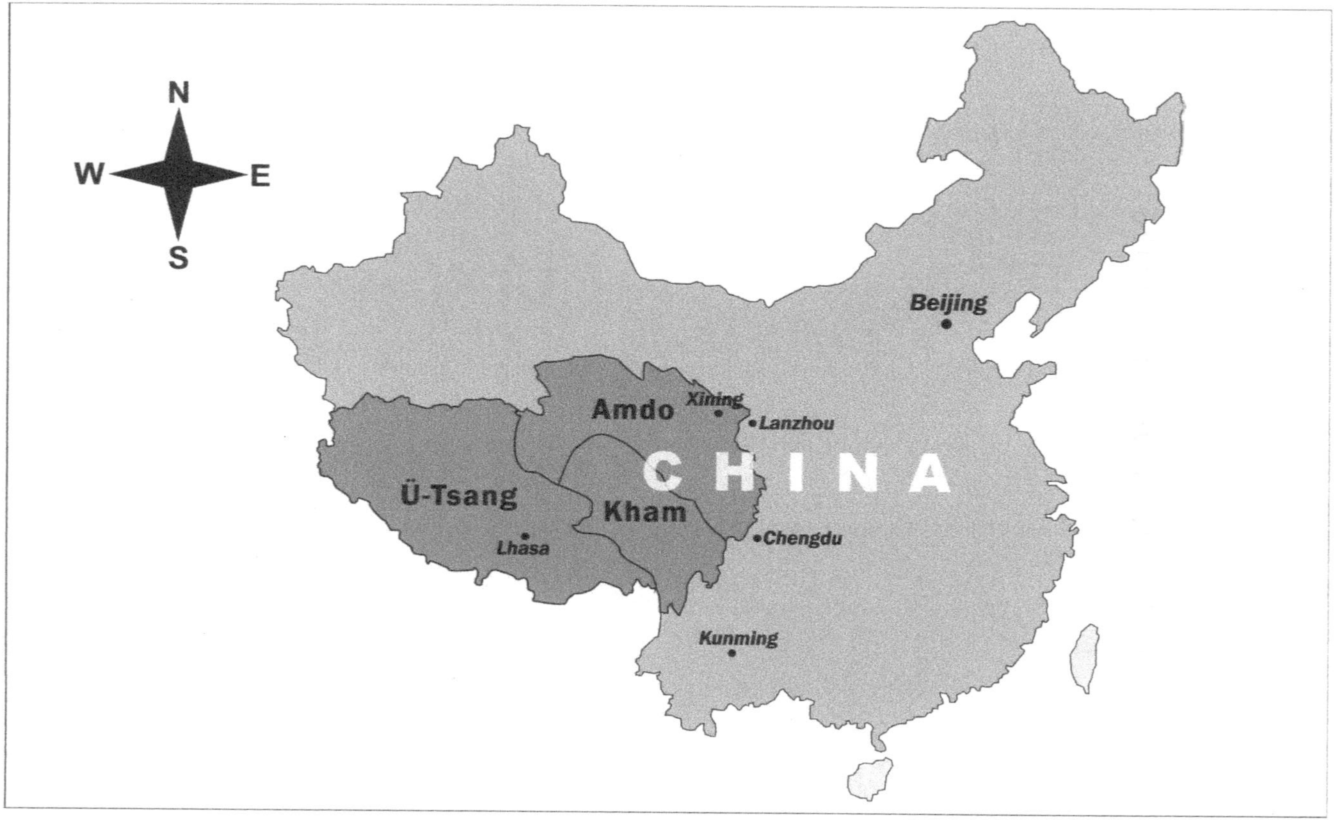

MAP 1. Traditional Tibet, overlaid onto China. Source: Marvin Cao.

MAP 2. Traditional Tibet, comprised of the three provinces of Kham, Ü-Tsang, and Amdo, in current Chinese administrative divisions. Source: Marvin Cao.

Chapter 1
THE STORM RISING IN THE MOUNTAINS

1

Early autumn 1955.

In the Yellow River source region of Lakes Gyaring (Zhalinghu) and Ngoring (Elinghu),[1] a highland pastural area 4,294 meters above sea level, Ngolo, a 22-year-old herder girl, prepared to move her herd to winter pasture, as she always did at this time of year. Ngolo's family of six owned more than 100 yaks and 200 sheep, which made them a moderately well-off family. As a part of the large nomad group, Ngolo's family had lived in this region, known as "Upper Golok,"[2] for many generations. The area was far away from the outside world, and Ngolo knew nothing about events beyond her part of the world; she had no idea that her homeland had been "liberated" by "Red Chinese" a few years back and had already become part of the Golok Tibetan Autonomous Prefecture in Qinghai Province. However, there were rumors that the "Red Chinese" had arrived. Sometimes while fetching water from the river, she would see unfamiliar armed horsemen off in the distance, but they had not come to her area.[3]

The Yellow River flowed from Upper Golok down through the Bayan Har (Bayankala) Mountains and snow-capped Mount Amnye Machen (Animaqing) into the grassy hills of southeastern Golok. At the foot of a sacred mountain called Nyenpo Yutsé (Nianbaoyuze)[4] lay a vast pastureland where the Khangsar (Kangsai), Khanggen (Kanggan), and Drasar (Wasai) tribes grazed their flocks and which was known as "Middle Golok."[5]

One day in early autumn, in a small *tsowa* under the Khangsar tribe, 8-year-old Damcho Pelsang heard a sheepdog howl outside his tent. Running out, he saw several armed Chinese cadres striding toward his tent, and he dashed toward them with excitement, no longer afraid of these "outsiders."

Damcho Pelsang's *tsowa* had only 20-odd households, totaling a little more than 100 people. His father had died when he was very small, leaving his mother, older sister, and himself. For as long as he could remember, his mother had used the "outsiders" to scare him when he was naughty. The elders said the outsiders were Ma Bufang's soldiers. Ma was a Muslim warlord serving as governor of Qinghai at that time. Between 1921 and 1941, his army had suppressed the Tibetans of Golok seven times for resisting heavy taxes, killing thousands, plundering a large number of livestock, and taking more than a thousand women and children captive.[6] The elders told Damcho Pelsang that Ma's soldiers would kill or kidnap little boys to feed to their horses. Back when the "outsiders" were at war in Golok, Ma's troops would kill any little boys they saw, so when the elders heard that Ma's troops were coming, they would quickly hide all the boys. These newer outsiders said they were the people's army and not Ma Bufang's troops, but even so, the first time Damcho Pelsang saw them, he trembled with fear and hid in the corner of the tent, not daring to breathe lest he be discovered and carried away.

Then one day a yak trod on Damcho Pelsang's foot, and the outsiders put ointment on the injury and bandaged it, and gave him some candy as well. From then on, the outsiders would bring candy to pass out to the children whenever they came. Damcho Pelsang gradually came to know them; the lack of a common language is not so important for a child, and the smiling faces and candy-filled hands of the outsiders communicated goodwill. Damcho Pelsang and his mother never imagined how quickly this would change.[7]

On the south side of the Bayan Har Mountains, a small river flowed southeast from Qinghai to Sichuan, collecting numerous streams on its way down the plateau. After winding hundreds of miles through rugged land, it became a large river the Tibetans called the Drichu (Jinsha River), the upper reach of the Yangtze River. Natural barriers formed by precipitous mountains cut off the upper reaches from the multitudes who lived along the river's lower course. Few of those below knew that the upper region was part of traditional Tibet and was inhibited by Khampas,[8] once famous for their martial prowess. For centuries the Khampas had lived in the vast region where the Yangtze source waters[9] and the Drichu and Nyagchu (Yalong) rivers converge, covering most of the Yangtze's upper basin.

Khampa tillers and shepherds flourished among the region's mountains and valleys, the jurisdiction of their kings and hereditary chieftains.[10] Among the region's "four great kings," the Dergé (Dege) Gyalpo ruled over a territory that extended across five of today's counties and at its prime had 70,000 households totaling more than 200,000 people.[11] In the late Qing, Zhao Erfeng,[12] with his mighty army, forcibly abolished the hereditary social structure through a massive slaughter in Kham, earning himself the nickname "Zhao the Butcher." After Zhao Erfeng died in the revolution that overthrew the Qing dynasty in 1911, most chieftains returned to power, but they never reclaimed their previous glory. When Xikang became a province in 1939, most of Kham was nominally included in China's Republican government system. Yet while many districts established county governments, their administrative power didn't reach to the grassroots level, and without adequate military strength to protect it, a county government might be unseated at any time and some officials even lose their lives.[13] In some districts the local chieftains were simply appointed heads of the neighborhood administration (*bao-jia*), and the local militia was renamed the "peace preservation corps." Government taxes were collected by local headmen and paid in Tibetan rather than Republican currency.[14] For that reason, the social structure and lifestyle of Tibetans hadn't significantly changed by the time the Communists came to power.

While Ngolo and the other herders around Ngoring Lake prepared to move to their winter pastures in 1955, Aten, the headman of Dhunkhug (Dunku) Village in Nyarong (Xinlong) along the Nyarong river, was notified by the local district head, a Chinese cadre, that he was being sent to Chengdu's Southwest National Minorities Institute to study for one year. Dhunkhug was a small village of only six households that earned their living through both farming and herding. Aten's father had once been the settlement's headman, but in the traditional system, the headman of a small settlement had no salary or privileges and just did all the legwork. The family's financial situation was unexceptional, and in years when the harvest was poor, they had to borrow grain to get by. Aten was in his thirties when the CCP arrived, and since his father had taught him to read and write, local cadres selected him to run their errands, and he became a go-between for the CCP and Tibetans. Aten had two wives, and his only daughter had just turned five. He was reluctant to spend a year studying in Chengdu, leaving his family behind with no one to look after them, but the higher-ups wouldn't take no for an answer. Aten had no choice but to bid his wives farewell and ride his horse to Garzê, then ride by truck to Dartsedo (Kangding), where he could catch a long-distance bus to Chengdu. No one told him what he'd be learning in Chengdu, nor did anyone tell him that this was part of a much larger plan to transform Tibetan society.[15]

Around the same time, at the Zhichen (Xiqing) Monastery along the Nyichu (Niqu) River in northern Kham's Garzê County, the son of the headman of Drangtsa (Zhangzha) village, 11-year-old Yetan, was studying scripture as usual. His home on the edge of the Sertar (Seda) grasslands was a small village of fifteen households. Most were farmers, but each family also had yaks and sheep, and while by no means wealthy, they lacked for nothing. The small village was buried deep in the mountains, and apart from Muslim traders who occasionally came through to trade salt, needles and thread, and other small items for the villagers' wool and hides, outsiders didn't come in and the villagers didn't go out; the only reason to leave the village was to visit the monastery or ask lamas to perform Buddhist rituals.

Yetan's father was a Horpa,[16] and his mother came from the Washul *shokka, the* largest tribe in Sertar.[17] Yetan had two sisters, and his parents had sent him to the monastery when he was small. Studying at the monastery, Yetan lived a simple and carefree life. He had never seen Chinese people, and had no idea that heaven and earth had changed places beyond the mountains.

2

When Mao Zedong declared the establishment of the People's Republic of China in Beijing on October 1, 1949, the CCP occupied most of the major cities and about half of the country. The PLA had yet to enter many parts of the southwest and northwest, especially regions mainly occupied by minority peoples. By the end of April 1950, the PLA had occupied the whole country except Taiwan, and was making military preparations to take Tibet. Following the advancing PLA troops, Chinese cadres, many of them hastily recruited in newly occupied cities, began entering minority regions.

Throughout history the Chinese had never mingled to a great extent with the minority peoples, differing from them as they did in language, religion, and lifestyle. In order to prevent ethnic minorities, with their large quantities of handmade weapons, from turning into hostile forces, the newly established CCP regime adopted a "prudent policy," striving to gain a footing in those regions and foster cadres among the ethnicities so they could implement social transformation programs once a "mass foundation" was prepared.

On November 14, 1949, Mao Zedong sent a cable to Peng Dehuai and the Northwest Bureau directing them to "organize a coalition government, that is, a united front government" in the ethnic minority regions and to cooperate with people in the upper strata with the objective of "fostering large numbers of ethnic minority cadres." Mao observed that "thoroughly resolving the problem of ethnic minorities, and completely isolating ethnic minority reactionaries, will be impossible without a large number of Communist cadres from among these minorities."[18]

In a speech on June 6, 1950, Mao expounded on the CCP's strategic policy at that time. Regarding the issue of social reform in ethnic minority areas, he warned cadres to be cautious: "Without popular support, without the people's armed force and without the minority nationalities' own cadres, no reforms of a mass character should be attempted," and he called on the entire party to "earnestly and painstakingly make a success of its united front work."[19]

Twenty days later, on June 26, Zhou Enlai repeated Mao's warning: "the matter [land reform] cannot be handled with undue haste. For example, land reform can be postponed for three to five years and then reconsidered. If conditions aren't ripe, it can be carried out after ten years or eight years."[20] Two days after Zhou Enlai made these remarks, the CCP promulgated the "Land Reform Law of the People's Republic of China," which explicitly stipulated that this law was "not applicable to ethnic minority areas."[21]

In October, the CCP won the Battle of Chamdo, and the Tibetan government was forced to send a delegation to Beijing for negotiations that resulted in the signing of the "Seventeen-Point Agreement for the Peaceful Liberation of Tibet" on May 23, 1951.[22] The PLA 18th Army's advance force entered Lhasa on September 9 of that same year, at which point the three traditional Tibetan regions were all occupied by the CCP.

In accordance with the policy stated by Mao, when the CCP first entered the Tibetan regions, it strove to build good relations with local communities and religious leaders, channeling influential people in the upper ranks into a "coalition government" and using their influence to gradually approach the masses and groom "activists" to become ethnic minority cadres. In January 1952, Mao agreed to the Northwest Bureau's suggestion "not to carry out land reform for the time being in the interior regions occupied by Tibetans, and not to touch any of the land of Lamaist temples at present; in particular, taking over the land of Buddhist monasteries too early will be detrimental to us."[23]

Land reform in the minority regions was not postponed for long, however. Once land reform in the Chinese interior was completed, in 1953, the Yunnan provincial party committee immediately began arranging for it to start in minority regions in the border area. Two methods were adopted in Yunnan's land reform campaign. In areas where "class polarization was already very evident," it adopted the method of a top-down "land reform through peaceful consultation." This was a buy-out policy toward members of the upper strata of ethnic minority communities. In areas where "class polarization was not evident," it skipped the land reform and pushed for "direct transition into socialism."[24] However, both methods proceeded with the backing of military force. In 1955, the Yunnan "ethnic minority joint defense armed forces numbered 57,515 personnel and took part in 711 battles, resulting in the death, wounding, or capture of 524 enemies."[25] More armed conflicts were to take place in the following years.

In Xikang province, where Tibetans were the largest population group, preparation for land reform began in late 1954. On November 7, 1954, the CCP's Kangding (Dartsedo) prefectural party committee notified all counties under its jurisdiction to begin preparing for land reform.[26] By that time, nearly 2,500 ethnic minority cadres had been groomed in Xikang Province, and 450 Communist Party members and 1,200 Communist Youth League members had been recruited. There was also a regular army unit made up mainly of Tibetans, the Tibetan Thirteenth Regiment of the Chinese People's Liberation Army.[27]

A few months later, during the CCP's National Party Congress, held in Beijing from March 21 to 31, 1955, the party put forward its first Five-Year Plan, which included "building socialist industrialization" and "carrying out socialist transformation of non-socialist economic sectors." By then, land reform had been completed in the Chinese interior, and the agricultural mutual aid and cooperative movement was in progress. Socialist transformation in industry and commerce was nearly completed, and it was only in the regions mainly occupied by ethnic minorities that the transformation of "non-socialist economic sectors" had not yet begun.

It was at this time that the Xikang provincial party committee submitted its plan for land reform in the Tibetan regions to the Central Committee. According to this plan, Xikang would take the lead with land reform in the farming areas and begin "socialist transformation by launching a mutual aid and cooperative movement" at the same time.[28]

On July 30, 1955, the First National People's Congress (NPC) passed a resolution that eliminated the province of Xikang, which covered most of Kham and in which Tibetans made up the majority, merging a large part of it with Sichuan Province. Sichuan, governed by the provincial CCP first secretary Li Jingquan, became the largest Tibetan-inhabited region outside of Tibet. Most of the province's Tibetan population of around 680,000 lived in the Garzê and Ngawa autonomous prefectures and in the Mili (Muli) Tibetan Autonomous County of the Liangshan Yi Autonomous Prefecture.[29] At that point, the traditional Tibetan region of Kham was divided into several portions. The portion east of the Drichu came under the jurisdictions of Qinghai, Sichuan, and Yunnan provinces, while the portion west of the river came under the jurisdiction of the "Chamdo Liberation Committee" directly under the State Council.

On July 31, Mao called a meeting of provincial, municipal, and autonomous region party secretaries demanding that the agriculture cooperative movement be accelerated throughout the country, because "large amounts of funds are needed to accomplish both national industrialization and the technical transformation of agriculture, and a considerable portion of these funds must be accumulated through agriculture."[30]

Apart from the capital raised through agricultural taxes, Tibetan regions had rich mineral, water, forestry, and other natural resources that China needed for industrialization.[31] Consequently, the socialist transformation of the Tibetan regions proceeded apace.

3

Just as the Chinese government was preparing for the socialist transformation in Tibetan regions, Beijing began performing a piece of United Front theater.

At 5:30 in the afternoon on September 4, 1954, a chartered train carrying the Dalai Lama, the Panchen Lama, and their retinues arrived in Beijing from Xi'an, the capital city of Shaanxi Province. Chinese Premier

Zhou Enlai and Vice-President Zhu De, along with more than 800 other dignitaries from all walks of life, were at the Beijing train station to receive them in grand and buoyant style.

The next day, Zhu De hosted a banquet for the two lamas at Zhongnanhai's Purple Light Pavilion, after which the lamas embarked on an itinerary arranged by the Central Committee.

On the afternoon of September 11, Mao Zedong received the Dalai Lama, then only 19 years old and on his first trip outside Tibet, at Zhongnanhai's Diligent Hall. The officially published photo shows the Dalai Lama, wearing the saffron robe of a traditional Tibetan official, bowing slightly and with both hands presenting a *khata* to Mao, ramrod-straight in his gray tunic suit and stretching out his hands to receive it. Neither performs the standard courtesy of bowing to the other.[32] The meeting of two faiths and two eras against the backdrop of the Chinese communists' successive victories seemed to presage the inevitability of intense conflict.

The young Dalai Lama attended the First National People's Congress from September 5 to 28 and was elected vice-chairman of its standing committee. He and the 16-year-old Panchen Lama became "China's youngest national leaders."[33] At a celebration marking the fifth anniversary of the founding of the PRC on October 1, the Dalai Lama mounted the Tiananmen gate tower in his new official capacity.

After that, the Dalai Lama and his entourage made a tour of several cities. In accordance with the Central Committee's instructions, wherever the Dalai Lama went, he was received with the highest protocol, personally met by party secretaries, and feted at lavish banquets, to ensure that he and his officials felt honored to the greatest possible extent and to show that his new government position was no empty title. Even so, the party secretaries all knew very well what the title meant. The Central Committee's instructions obliged provincial officials to be respectfully attentive, but that didn't mean they really held this young "national leader" in any regard.

In Tibet's neighbor, Sichuan Province, First Secretary Li Jingquan made it clear that he wasn't buying this line. In March 1955, accompanied by the central government representative in Tibet, Zhang Jingwu, and the United Front Department deputy director, Liu Geping, the Dalai Lama and his retinue left Beijing for Tibet, stopping over in Chengdu on April 20. Yan Hongyan, the provincial deputy secretary and vice-governor, hosted a welcoming banquet for them that night. Ignoring the interpreter, Yan read off his speech without stopping. The vast majority of the guests were Tibetan government officials and religious leaders who didn't understand Mandarin and had no idea what Yan was saying. The atmosphere became strained.

The Dalai Lama and his group stayed in Chengdu for several days, but First Secretary Li Jingquan never showed his face. According to the Communist Party's ranking system, the Dalai Lama, as vice-chairman of the NPC standing committee, was a Class 2 official, and Liu Geping, as United Front Department deputy director, was Class 3, while Li Jingquan was only Class 5,[34] so in theory, the Dalai Lama and Liu Geping both outranked Li Jingquan. However, by then the Dalai Lama understood that in China's political system, the party always outranked the government, and a party leader was always higher than a national leader. Even so, a party leader should still show superficial respect to a national leader, and Li Jingquan's snub was obviously a public expression of the fact that he didn't consider the Dalai Lama a genuine national leader. This raised doubts among the Tibetan officials, who discussed among themselves whether Li's attitude implied a change in the central government's policies.

The Dalai Lama was also despondent. Before arriving in Sichuan, he'd returned to his hometown to visit relatives, but surrounded by officials the whole time, he had been unable to have a private conversation. When he asked about their living conditions, his relatives replied "very good," but tears glistened in their eyes as they spoke. The village where the Dalai Lama was born[35] had both Tibetan and Chinese residents, and land reform had been carried out there in 1951. The Dalai Lama's parents had once owned 40 *mu*[36] of land that they farmed themselves. When he was sent to Lhasa at the age of four as the reincarnation of the 13th Dalai Lama, the entire family went with him, and the family's land and house were given to the Dalai Lama's female cousin. During land reform, his cousin was designated a landlord, and her land and home were confiscated and redistributed to others. The Dalai Lama's brother-in-law's family were also designated landlords and all their assets confiscated.[37] One relative was jailed for "transferring assets for a landlord." The famous Jachung (Xiazong) Monastery near the Dalai Lama's home village, where the Gelug sect's fourteenth-century founder Jé Tsongkhapa was ordained as a monk, was badly damaged during land reform.[38] The Dalai Lama was depressed after the brief meeting with his relatives. He began to have doubts about the CCP's "reforms" and had increasing misgivings about the prospects for the party's Tibet program.[39]

Xu Danlu, the head of the liaison office for the political department of the Tibet Work Committee (TWC), learned that Li Jingquan had refused to receive the Dalai Lama. Worried that the Central Committee's United Front efforts had fallen short, he reported the matter to the Central Committee.

The report reached Zhou Enlai, who was in Jakarta for the Bandung Conference.[40] After the May 1st International Worker's Day, Zhou Enlai and Vice-Premier Chen Yi flew from Guangzhou to Chengdu to "see the Dalai Lama off" in a special effort to redeem the poor impression that Li Jingquan had created. During their three days in Chengdu, Zhou and Chen had several significant but somewhat cryptic private conversations with the Dalai Lama.[41]

Puntsok Wangyal,[42] deputy director of the politics and law department of the State Minority Nationalities Affairs Committee, who accompanied the Dalai Lama back to Tibet, recalls that during two conversations, Zhou Enlai suggested that "it would be best not to begin reforms immediately," because "in Tibet the conditions for carrying out reforms are not yet sufficient." He suggested that the Dalai Lama wait until "the thoughts of the leaders and the masses are matched."[43]

Article 11 of the "Seventeen-Point Agreement" states: "In matters related to various reforms in Tibet, there will be no compulsion on the part of the Central Authorities. The Local Government of Tibet should carry out reforms of its own accord, and when the people raise demands for reform, they must be settled through consultation with the leading personnel of Tibet."[44] This provision only mentions "matters related to various reforms in Tibet," but the content, methods, and timing of these "reforms" were not explained or delineated, only that "the Local Government of Tibet should carry out reforms of its own accord." That is what the Dalai Lama did.

From the day he took over the reins of government, the Dalai Lama knew very well the responsibility he bore for reforming Tibetan tradition. In 1952, the Dalai Lama had established a fifty-member Reform Bureau,[45] headed by ministers Ngapo Ngawang Jigmé and Surkhang. The Reform Bureau included a standing committee that was responsible for investigating and proposing reform projects. With the Dalai Lama's permission, the government had on January 17, 1954, promulgated the "Notice Regarding Reforming of the Tibetan Social System in Accordance with the 'Agreement.'"[46]

The "Notice" included five provisions, making detailed stipulations regarding taxes, agriculture, corvée labor,[47] education funds, and so on, and stating that

> beginning in the Wood Horse year (1954), nobility who illegally extend their territory will be investigated and their affairs settled, and the territory occupied in excess will revert to the integrated management of the local government. Tsé Lekung and Shol Lekung[48] treasurers must carry out their duties according to the document's stipulations. Corvée labor or taxes are not to be imposed over and above the amount stipulated, in order to benefit the people's livelihood.

The Notice also stipulated, "If district governors, *dzong* officials [a *dzong* being a subdivision of a district], or heads of estates break the law and cause harm to the affairs of the people, all monks and laypeople are empowered to report their misdeeds."

This reform plan, which limited the power of the nobility and the monasteries, could be considered the Tibetan government "carrying out reforms of its own accord." If not for the interference of outside forces, the reforms led by the Dalai Lama would have continued to develop gradually. However, it can be seen from the conversations that Zhou Enlai had with the Dalai Lama in Chengdu that the CCP was opposed to the Dalai Lama's reform plan.

4

While the Dalai Lama was in Beijing, a massive operation was being planned for the Tibetan regions. In the following months, after he returned to Tibet, the plan was put into action.

On March 9, 1955, three days before the Dalai Lama left Beijing, he, the Panchen Lama, and Ngapo Ngawang Jigmé were invited to attend the State Council's seventh plenum, which passed a resolution to establish a Preparatory Committee for the Autonomous Region of Tibet (PCART). This "Preparatory Committee" was Tibet's highest *de facto* administrative organ until the Autonomous Region was formally established. Yet the CCP's policy on Tibetans living in the four provinces was not bound by the Seventeen-Point Agreement, and at the time that the PCART was being set up, land reform was about to begin there. It was during this month that the Xikang provincial party committee submitted to the Central Committee its preliminary plan for implementing land reform among the province's ethnic minorities.[49]

In mid-August, then-Vice-President Liu Shaoqi and Deng Xiaoping, who had been promoted into the CCP's politburo in April, summoned the Xikang provincial party secretary, Liao Zhigao, and other cadres, instructing Sichuan and Xikang to formulate reform plans and jointly report to the Central Committee.[50] One month later, the two provincial party committees submitted a report and a preliminary plan to Beijing requesting that land reform be carried out in minority regions in order to avoid "separation from the masses." The plan laid out the specifics of the reform and decided that the reform would begin in agricultural areas first, leaving the pastoral regions for the next stage.[51] No specific reason was given for this arrangement; it was likely a way to stabilize the pastoral regions in order to reduce possible resistance.

Meanwhile, in the interior of China, the agricultural cooperative movement was underway. In mid-October, the CCP passed a resolution[52] that pushed the nationwide movement to a new level. Party committees in the Tibetan regions of Sichuan, Qinghai, Gansu, and Yunnan immediately leapt into action. The Yunnan provincial party committee held a conference for cadres at the prefectural, county, and township levels, during which it was decided that land reform in minority regions would be completed by 1957, along with agricultural cooperative pilot schemes.[53] By then, Tibetans in Yunnan had already risen up in protest. In fact, it was the first region where Tibetans began protesting, but the effect was limited.[54]

Qinghai began promoting cooperatives in the pastoral areas and set about organizing cooperative animal husbandry pilot projects in Malho (Huangnan) and Tsolho (Hainan) prefectures.

Gansu Province's Kanlho (Gannan) Prefecture decided to launch straight into agricultural cooperatives throughout the prefecture.

In the winter of 1955, Mao directed Zhang Guohua, head of the TWC, to tell TWC cadres to prepare for "democratic reform," emphasizing that it was "necessary to prepare for fighting; if the nobility resist, we should be prepared to destroy some of them, and chase away some others. Having a few more people cursing us in Kalimpong or Hong Kong doesn't matter." Zhang Guohua used a top-secret telephone line to transmit that directive to Fan Ming, who was in Tibet directing the TWC's work.[55] This directive shows that less than five years after the Seventeen-Point Agreement was signed, Mao was prepared to resort to war in order to impose reforms on Tibet.

In December, Sichuan held its first provincial people's congress. During the congress, the delegate from Garzê Prefecture proposed that land reform be carried out in the Tibetan and Yi minority regions (as had already been decided within the party), and the congress discussed and passed that motion as well as four plans for implementing land reform drafted by the prefectural party committee.[56]

From December 26, 1955 to January 5, 1956, the CCP Kangding prefecture committee held an enlarged conference. It was at this conference that specific land reform methods and locations were decided and arranged.

This is how the top-down social transformation movement referred to as "democratic reform" began to unfold and shatter all of Tibetan society. The Red Tempest soon swept across the plateau, throwing the lives of Ngolo, Damcho Pelsang, Aten, and Yetan into turmoil. Each of them, like countless others among their people, was forced to take a life-or-death journey.

Chapter 2

REBELLION SPARKED IN THE YEAR OF THE FIRE MONKEY

1

1956, the year of the Fire Monkey in the Tibetan calendar.

Shortly after the New Year, the "democratic reform" was set in motion.

As in the rest of China, reform in the Tibetan regions was to be carried out in four stages. In the first stage, groups of specially organized Chinese cadres and Tibetan activists, known as "land reform work teams," would be dispatched to villages, using propaganda to mobilize the masses and raise their "class awareness."

A document formulated by Garzê Prefecture's Gyesur (Jiulong) County party committee on February 20, 1956, shows the actual methods used for propaganda and social mobilization in land reform:

> Integrate classic examples of peasant suffering, stimulate laboring people's hatred of the landlord class, attack and expose rumors and the landlord class's intimidation and bribery, explain the contrast in power between landlords and laboring people, teach and establish confidence in struggle against the enemy; explain the brutality and reactionary nature of the landlord class's use of rent, usury, etc. to oppress and exploit the peasant class so everyone understands the necessity and justice of the reforms; incorporate enlightening the masses on the reasons for their

> own backwardness and poverty; launch a grievance-venting campaign involving detailed accounting, excavating the roots of poverty, and "spitting bitterness" (grievance-venting).[1] First arouse individual enmity among the peasants and then gradually induce class hatred and the realization of why it is necessary to organize and unite to topple the feudal system and the landlord class, then go a step further by enhancing the class consciousness of the masses to the level of the party's policy line.[2]

"First arouse individual enmity among the peasants and then gradually induce class hatred" was not a new invention. It was widely used in the CCP's land reform programs in the rest of the country. The CCP's long-term, repeated practice of using personal grudges for social mobilization was gradually solidified into an established process and became the CCP's basic method in the land reform movement, which was also used in the Tibetan regions.

The so-called grievance-venting campaign referred to mass rallies to "vent grievances" and denounce the "ruling class"; this kind of rally was called "*douzheng hui,*" or "struggle meeting," in Chinese. It was one of the CCP's powerful and widely used tools to mobilize the masses. It served two purposes: first, it destroyed the dignity and reputation of the targets of the grievances and crushed their willpower; and second, it incited and magnified the hatred of the masses and ripped apart any spirit of community between the masses and the targets. This second objective was even more important. To this end, the denunciation rally always used a variety of inducements to encourage people to inflict verbal and physical violence on the people being denounced. In many cases, cadres had trained "activists" to set an example by inflicting violence on the targets of the struggle meeting. The resulting bloody spectacle had an intense psychological effect on others, while at the same time creating terror among the participants.

In the recollections of Tibetans, the denunciation rallies arouse fierce indignation. The Tibetan language doesn't even have a word for "struggle," and the Chinese term *douzheng* (struggle) was simply transliterated as *thamzing*. Tibetans found it especially intolerable when senior monks, who were widely respected at all levels of society, were humiliated and dishonored. This was one of the major factors that drove people to revolt, and also a major reason why the activists and land reform work teams bore the brunt of the attacks during these revolts.

This first stage also involved organizing militia comprised of selected Tibetan men who were armed with weapons seized from well-to-do families, a process referred to as "trading carrying-poles for guns" and during which "rural leadership stalwarts" could be discovered and groomed.

The second stage divided the populace into classes according to the criteria set by the State Administrative Council.[3] Completion of this stage immediately led to the third: confiscating the land and other assets of landlords and rich peasants, distributing land and farming implements to peasant households, and dividing up houses, some for government use, referred to as "distributing the fruits of democratic reform." After these three stages were completed, the final and most important stage was establishing party and youth league organizations and a grassroots government in the villages.[4]

Both in interior China and in the Tibetan regions, land reform was accompanied by a campaign to "suppress counterrevolutionaries" that also involved arresting and killing local elites. For example, the work plan for Sichuan's Gyesur County stated, "Combined with democratic reform work, after feeling out the situation of concealed counterrevolutionaries, carry out the formalities of reporting and approval and in April begin arresting those who should be arrested."[5]

As stated in the preliminary plan drafted in the previous year, at this time, reform was limited to the agricultural areas, where the CCP had much more experience. To avoid large numbers of livestock deaths caused by potential social turmoil, another set of policies, mainly increasing salaries for hired herders, was adopted in pastoral regions.[6]

The Sichuan provincial party committee believed that reform could be implemented smoothly in Ngawa Prefecture, since most parts of this area had already been "liberated" in 1950 and preparations for reform had been quietly carried out as early as 1953. The prefectural party committee had gained an understanding of who all the people were who were held in high regard in local communities by using Tibetan activists to conduct door-to-door investigations. In the coming reform movement, those people would become targets for the populace to vent their hatred of the ruling class. For the provincial party committee, these areas had better "mass foundations" for success.

Garzê, however, would present difficulties, especially the "six counties of southern Kham,"[7] where the political situation was more complex. The Sichuan provincial party committee therefore decided to leave that area alone for the time being, but would increase the military presence there on the pretext of "assisting the local government in strengthening unification and production work"; if conflict arose, it could be promptly suppressed.[8]

On January 16, sixty-nine influential Tibetan leaders from various parts of Garzê were summoned to Dartsedo (Kangding) for a conference to be "consulted" about land reform issues. This conference was to last more than three months. However, only one week later, on January 23, the Sichuan provincial party committee submitted to the Central Committee a draft plan for land reform in Sichuan's Tibetan regions.[9]

In February, the party committees in the counties where the reform was to proceed summoned local Tibetan leaders to the county seat for a meeting, thereby separating religious and community leaders from the people. Then, in mid-February, "land reform work teams" composed of more than 7,700 cadres and activists set off for the villages to launch the "democratic reform movement."[10] They were instructed that the reform must be completed in four months. This meant carrying out the entire process in an intense and forceful manner.

In this way, the hurricane of land reform swept down from the highest levels and sped its way through Garzê and Ngawa. With their leaders away, people were confused and frightened by the activities forced upon them by outsiders. They did not understand such concepts as "class struggle," "exploiting class," and "oppressed class" and were offended by the violent denunciation rallies, which violated their religious beliefs.

Shortly after land reform began, Tibetans in several localities rose up in armed revolt against the CCP's "democratic reform." At this time, the

40-year-old Khampa headman Aten was still in training at the Southwest National Minorities Institute and had no idea of these unexpected events in his homeland. He was soon to be sent home to participate in the reform as a trained activist, and learn with horror what the "reform" meant for his people.

In February, Yetan, the 11-year-old monk at Zhichen Monastery, heard the shocking news that his mother's clansmen had begun fighting the Chinese on the Sertar grasslands.

2

The Sertar grassland is in northern Garzê, on the border between Sichuan and Qinghai. At more than 4,000 meters above sea level and ringed by mountains, Sertar had natural defenses that made it impervious to outsiders. During the Republican era, Sertar remained outside the jurisdiction of Qinghai and Sichuan Provinces, and its herders paid no taxes; no external political authority had ever been established there. In the 1930s and 1940s, the Muslim warlord Ma Bufang attempted to subjugate Sertar, but failed.

The Washul were Sertar's largest tribe, who according to oral tradition, had migrated to the area during the Qing dynasty and established their herds on the vast pastureland. After the CCP entered the Tibetan regions, the headmen of Sertar's tribes gradually became aware of the situation in neighboring areas and engaged in piecemeal contact with the PLA. The PLA demonstrated a friendly attitude by giving them used clothing and rides in their vehicles and by inviting them to meals, and these initial contacts left a good impression on the Sertar headmen, who felt that "liberation" might not be so bad after all. The headmen asked lamas to carry out a divination over whether they should be "liberated," and the answer they received was, "Liberation is good, but deaths will be unavoidable."[11] Perhaps that is why the CCP work teams encountered no resistance when they entered Sertar in August 1952 and declared the area "liberated."

The operations of the work teams in Sertar proceeded smoothly from then on, and within a few years they had established a series of government organs and had convened several meetings of tribal headmen. With the approval of the State Council, Sertar County was formally established in November 1955—the first government in Sertar's history.[12]

Following the establishment of Sertar County, the Washul chieftain Rigzin Dondrup became county head and a delegate to the Sichuan Provincial People's Congress, as well as vice-chairman of the Garzê Prefectural People's Political Consultative Conference. According to official sources, however, on February 15 and 16, 1956, Rigzin Dondrup sent more than thirty herdsmen on horseback to surround the frontier sentry post, demanding that the government work teams withdraw from Sertar. The situation developed into an armed conflict, with one herdsman killed and another wounded. In the official historical narrative, this was referred to as the "Sertar incident" and the "first shot in the Khampa armed rebellion."[13]

Two days later, the Sichuan provincial party committee called an urgent meeting of prefectural party secretaries in all ethnic minority areas to study the problem of land reform in Garzê. The result of the study was a demand that all of these areas "to the greatest extent possible compress the timespan for mobilizing, organizing, and arming the masses." It also required that "within twelve days, peasant association membership should reach 80% of all adult peasants, and self-defense corps membership should grow to around 10% of the total population."[14] That meant that in the face of popular resistance, Sichuan's party bosses demanded that the local cadres speed up land reform rather than slowing it down. That ensured an escalation of the situation.

The counties of eastern and northern Kham responded by speeding up their work. This resulted in demands of guns and grain from middle peasants, the levying of taxes on monasteries, public denunciation rallies, the humiliation of lamas and attacks on Buddhism, and forcing monks to take part in the killing of rats and insects in violation of the Buddhist tradition of reverence for all living things.[15] At least 10% of the population, and in some districts as much as 20%, was classified as "landlords" or "rich peasants."[16] In other words, 10 to 20% of the population consisted of "class enemies," and according to the Land Reform Law, their land and other assets would be confiscated.

Some headmen in Lithang, Nyarong (Xinlong), Bathang (Batang), Palyul (Baiyu), and other counties of Garzê decided to resist. Conflicts between them had been unavoidable throughout history, but in the face of a shared crisis, they put aside their old grudges and made a stand together.[17]

Armed uprisings broke out in Garzê and Ngawa prefectures in February and March of 1956. By the end of March 1956, eighteen of Garzê Prefecture's twenty counties and forty-five of its seventy-seven townships had experienced full-scale or localized insurrections involving a total of 16,000 people and more than 8,000 firearms. During this time, fourteen land reform work teams came under attack, and ten county seats were besieged or encircled. More than 200 land reform cadres were killed, and the PLA suffered more than 300 casualties.[18]

Urgent telegrams asking for reinforcement besieged the Garzê prefectural party committee like a snowstorm.

3

What caused the sudden outbreak of armed resistance in Sichuan's Tibetan regions in 1956? For decades, the uprisings in Kham have been attributed to the incitement and plotting of the Tibetan government, particularly to the Dalai Lama's junior tutor, Trijang Rinpoché, as they returned to Tibet from Beijing the previous year.

For the spring 1955 inland tour of the Dalai Lama and Panchen Lama, the Tibet Work Committee allocated a retinue of cadres and guards, and established a party group led by Zhang Jingwu himself. Three party branches were also established to accompany the two lamas.[19] The Dalai Lama was therefore trailed by journalists and "security personnel" throughout the time that he toured the inland regions and on his journey back to Tibet. The Xinhua News Agency's *Internal Reference* published many detailed reports on the movements of the Dalai Lama.

According to the internal report, Trijang Rinpoché and the others had "frequent contacts with leading personages in all localities and regularly had closed-door secret talks." However, the report showed that all Trijang Rinpoché had actually done was to mediate local disputes, in accordance with time-honored tradition. In fact, although Beijing's plan for land reform in Garzê and Ngawa was brewing in May 1955, it was limited to discussions within the party. The decision was not issued until the end of 1955, and plentiful documents serve as evidence of the timetable for this clear policy shift.[20] It would therefore have been impossible for the Dalai Lama to know about the CCP's plans while he was on his way back to Tibet, and it's hard to imagine that Trijang Rinpoché and others had gotten wind of it at that time.

The 1956 uprisings in Kham mainly centered on people's opposition to the forcible imposition of land reform, their refusal to hand over guns,[21] their protest against taxation,[22] their defense of their religion, and their demands for the withdrawal of Chinese cadres who were coercively changing their way of life. Currently available CCP documents and the recollections of participants from both sides all indicate that the Tibetan revolt in early 1956 was spontaneous, and that rebel groups were only in contact with each other and received no aid from anyone.

One government source mentions the discovery of "a secret agent, Bangdacang, who had close contact with British imperialist spies, and who took part in plotting the insurrection in Batang County,"[23] implying that the British government was involved in what happened in Bathang. However, "Bangdacang" is the Chinese transliteration for Pangdatsang, the name of a rich and influential merchant family with commercial connections in India. The source does not specify who this "Bangdacang" is, nor does it provide any details about the alleged plot.

Puntsok Wangyal went to Kham to investigate the situation in June, and Jago Topden, Pangda Dorjé, one influential figure from the Pangdatsang clan, and many other Tibetan leaders all told him the same thing: "The reforms in Kham had been done poorly and in a rush. There was inadequate planning and no careful discussion with upper-strata Tibetans."[24] Zhang Xiangming, head of the Tibet Work Committee Policy Research Office, who at the time was leading a group of people on a study trip to Garzê, recalls:

> They divided the work teams into three levels: one level held meetings with the upper strata, one level with middle peasants, and one level

> with poor peasants and hired farm laborers, holding meetings level by level. Their class divisions were not the same as those of Tibetans but were the same as those used in the inland regions, and the division of land was also carried out according to the inland land reform methods. I heard that when they began land reform, they basically had not done any consultation work. When they held meetings in Chengdu, they called in the headmen from Xikang and announced that they were going to carry out democratic reform, but there was no real discussion and no careful work. Some Tibetan cadres said there wasn't even the most rudimentary consultation, and in effect they just straight-out announced their decision.[25]

Large-scale uprisings occurred in Sichuan's Tibetan regions at almost the same time in February and March 1956, but there is no evidence that the Tibetans had coordinated these incidents in advance. Tibetan sources show that in some areas, such as southern Kham, and in the Tsakhalho (Yanjing), Dzayul (Chayu), Gonjo (Gongjue), Tengchen (Dingqing) counties under the administration of the Chamdo Liberation Committee where uprisings occurred in summer 1956, there was contact among the local militias, who fixed dates to take action at the same time,[26] but nothing like a unified agreement. It is more likely that these uprisings were people's direct response to the land reform movement that had suddenly been sprung on them, and to the violence of the land reform work teams. Since land reform occurred around the same time in these areas, it's only natural that people would have responded with uprisings around the same time. There were also cases of different responses. In Middle Village (Zhongzhai) and Lower Village (Xiazhai) in Ngawa's Trokyab (Chuosijia) County,[27] land reform was completed in about three months without conflict. But when the work team proceeded under order to Upper Village (Shangzhai) to launch land reform, it came under attack, and almost all of the thirty land reform work team members were killed.[28]

The CCP's levying of high taxes on people and monasteries was another reason for the revolt. There is very limited material available concerning taxation in the Tibetan regions in the 1950s, but scattered documents show that once the CCP entered the Tibetan areas, it greatly increased grain taxes year by year. Furthermore, when the CCP began "land reform" in February 1956, it began controlling grain supply at the same time: "The prefecture has decided to provide food staples to villages in the areas where democratic reforms are carried out, covering 36% of the population for three months, with a monthly provision of 13.5 kilograms per person."[29] The government's substantial increase in grain levies while controlling the provision of food staples was bound to lead to food shortages. This may have been the reason for many instances of Tibetans looting grain stores during the uprisings.

During land reform, the work teams not only appropriated a great deal of grain but also forced households with higher living standards to hand over their "superfluous foodstuffs" in the name of "donating grain."[30] In actual practice, foodstuffs were subject to "confiscation," "procurement," or "donation" at the complete discretion of the work teams and activists. The work teams' categorization of 10–20% of the population as "landlords or rich peasants" was closely related to this; the more "landlords and rich peasants" there were, the more goods could be confiscated, and the greater the "fruits of land reform."

Meanwhile, the CCP levied taxes on monasteries. Resistance by the Hor Drango (Shouling) Monastery in Drango (Luhuo) County was suppressed in March 1956. After Communist troops "annihilated[31] more than 700 people," "the Shouling temple's eighty-member council sent representatives to the county's Work Committee to deliver a written assurance that they would not resist taxation again." This indicates that taxation was the direct reason for the Drango monks' resistance.[32]

4

What kind of people took part in the uprisings? Chinese and Tibetan sources both indicate that participants in the uprisings in all regions spanned class divisions but mostly came from the lower middle class, including farmers, herders, monks, and traders.

Around 1,000 of the most influential monks and laypersons in the Kham region had by then been given places in the NPC, the Chinese

People's Political Consultative Conference (CPPCC), or provincial and prefectural governments.[33] After the uprisings, the CCP absorbed upper and mid-level community leaders into work groups and sent them into rebel areas with the military[34] to help the government win over rebel leaders. This meant that most of the organizers of the uprisings in the various localities were local leaders at the county level or below, or local figures who had the capacity to rally support.

Since the late Qing era, the social structure in Kham had undergone significant change, and generalizing it as a "feudal serf system"[35] would be an oversimplification. According to a social survey in June 1954, in most parts of northern Kham, *tralpa*,[36] who leased land and cultivated their own crops, made up 60% of the population, while *gepa*,[37] who cultivated land or worked as servants for landowners, headmen, or monasteries, made up 40%. In most parts of southern Kham, *tralpa* composed 90% of the population, and *gepa* less than 10%. In eastern Kham, where most of the land and pastures no longer belonged to headmen or monasteries, and ordinary people were no longer forced to undertake unpaid labor for headmen, *gepa* made up only 2–3% of the peasant population. That is to say, the vast majority of peasants in these regions cultivated their own fields. *Tralpa* were not necessarily poor, and families with surplus laborers could engage in trade or hire themselves out. As a result, when the Tibetan regions were divided into class categories, the landlords, rich peasants, and middle peasants were mainly *tralpa*, whom the CCP classified as "serfs."[38]

Kham's villages typically had land for common use, including pastures, wasteland, cultivated land, and mountain forests. In the communally owned mountain forests, villagers could hunt, collect medicinal herbs, and cut lumber, and on the communally owned pastures, they could graze their livestock. Communally owned cultivated land was jointly tilled by villagers, and the harvests were used for religious ceremonies or stored against natural disasters.[39] The economy of Kham consisted mainly of agriculture and herding, and the majority of peasants engaged in a mixture of the two. The *tralpa* didn't own their land, but they owned their livestock, and the amount of livestock one possessed was an important standard in determining wealth. For this reason, communally owned pastureland was extremely important. But the land reform transformed the mountain forests and pastures into state-owned land, and the communally owned fields and wasteland were also requisitioned or "adjusted"; wasteland and communal pastures that had earlier been transformed into farmland through official campaigns was distributed to farmers.

As was the case in the villages of the inland regions, very few people in the Kham region owned absolutely nothing, and most people qualified as middle strata to a greater or lesser extent. Land reform mobilized the lowest class of people in a designated population to expropriate the assets of that population's relatively well-off social strata. Since land reform was first and foremost a political movement, every village and settlement was obliged to designate a certain quota of people as landlords and rich peasants and to make these people targets for "mobilizing the masses." The conditions differed in each locality, so the standard for being "wealthy" was completely relative; in terms of assets, one district's "landlord" might be nothing more than a "middle peasant" in another district. Under these circumstances, the fate of people in the middle stratum was very uncertain; when the policy was applied strictly, they could be classified as "rich peasants," but if the policy was applied leniently, they would be "middle peasants." Sometimes it depended on whether a locality had enough "landlords and rich peasants"; if the quota couldn't be met, people in the middle stratum were used to top it up. However, because the majority of people were in this stratum, their production and management capacity was strong and they made up the bulk of taxpayers, so during land reform there was an emphasis on protecting middle peasants in order to avoid "antagonizing too many people."[40] A district designating 10 to 20% of its people as "landlords and rich peasants" meant that a relatively large portion of the middle stratum had their assets confiscated; this caused many of them to join in uprisings.

Every stage of the land reform process in Kham, from its preparations to its implementation, demonstrated the arrogance and high-handedness of the CCP regime, as well as the ignorance and brutality of its cadres. Land reform was launched just as the spring plowing was about to begin, which meant that it was certain to encounter serious difficulties from the outset. The wholesale abolition of debt and ordering the monasteries to cease lending exacerbated the grain shortages that typically occurred at this time. Farming families who needed to borrow had nowhere to go, and the government had no way to provide them with foodstuffs, so some faced the threat of going hungry.

Traditionally, in the Tibetan regions, peasants who tilled the fields of monasteries or headmen had a plot of land corresponding to their corvée or rent obligation. Once corvée was abolished, this land was confiscated. According to tradition, seed grain was provided by the landowner, but once land was redistributed, those who had formerly owned the land naturally no longer provided seeds. This meant that peasants who were provided with land had no seeds to plant on it.

Kham's mountainous landscape provides very limited arable land, and the promise of "two portions of land to each monk, one portion to each family and one portion to the monastery" could not be honored in practice. The only way to allow peasants with "little or no land" to "enjoy the fruits of victory" was to "adjust" the assets of the monasteries. Ostensibly, the government would provide seeds and grain to peasants who lacked them, but vehicular roads had yet to be built, and with the spring plowing imminent, there was no way to transport grain from outside within a short time. The Garzê prefectural party committee therefore adopted the method of "mobilizing landlords to donate grain," which actually amounted to confiscation. Furthermore, not all of the confiscated grain was given to the peasants; a considerable portion of it became "grain tax" that was provided to the land reform work teams. These were important reasons why peasants from all levels resisted land reform.[41]

5

After the uprisings broke out, the Garzê prefectural party committee made urgent political and military arrangements. On the political front, it "vigorously strengthened upper strata united front work" by hastily arranging positions for some upper-level figures who had not been previously appointed, and strove to stabilize the pastoral areas. At the same time, it "vigorously mobilized and organized the arming of the masses and organized joint defense to defend the fruits of victory," urgently recruiting young Tibetans into the army and expanding the Tibetan civil corps, as well as planning and organizing upper-class individuals in military operations in order to "rapidly divide the enemy."[42] On the military front, it requested reinforcements from the higher levels.

At the time, PLA units stationed in the Garzê Prefecture included three infantry regiments and one battalion of the Ganzi Military Sub-Region, with some 5,000 personnel, plus 700 cavalry troops. Adding in more than 1,200 in the police force, there were nearly 7,000 armed personnel.[43] Facing sudden widespread rebellion, however, the Ganzi Military Sub-Region feared it would be short on manpower and urgently sent cadres to each county to organize military service bureaus, demanding that they mobilize new combatants for the Tibetan regiment before March 20, 1956.[44] These new recruits were sent to the battlefield after being rushed through only one or two months of training. In the hastily assembled Tibetan regiment, reinforcements suffered the heaviest casualties of all of the troops participating in the fighting.[45]

From March to April, the CCP quickly transferred five regiments and one battalion of reinforcements from parts of Sichuan Province and the adjacent Yunnan Province to Garzê, and the militias were expanded to 19,055 personnel.[46] The PLA's regular army totaled around 13,000 troops,[47] versus around 16,000 Tibetans who took part in the resistance,[48] but only about half of the Tibetans had any kind of firearms, including hunting rifles and muskets.

In accordance with the battle deployment of the Chengdu Military Command, the first battle in Kham was to be fought in Lithang. The plan was to employ military force to push through the land reform in Lithang's farming areas, and then use Lithang as a base area to forcibly extend land reform to other counties of southern Kham.[49]

But the biggest battle had yet to begin.

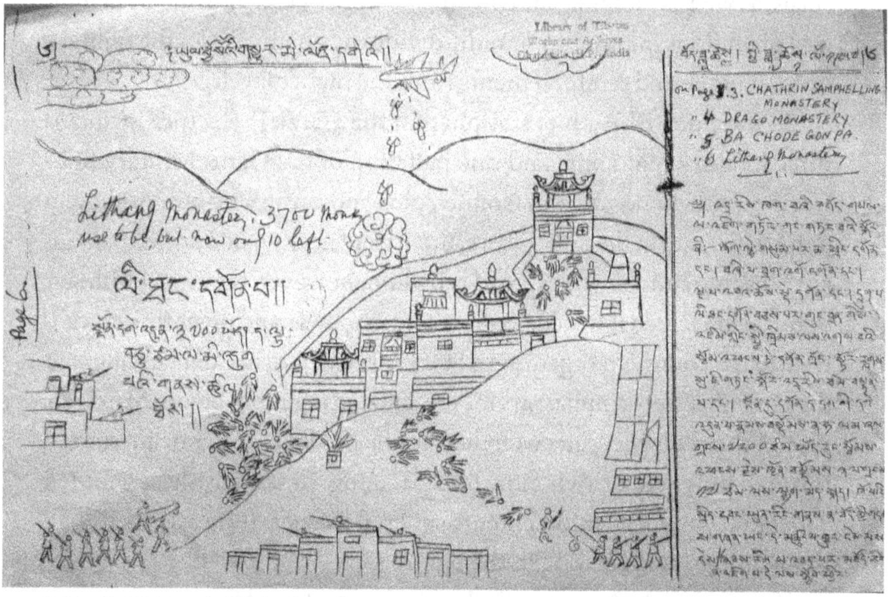

FIGURE 1. The bombing of Lithang Monastery, originally printed in the *Tibet Mirror*, July 1, 1957. Translations of the text across the top and to the left and right sides:

Top line: *Tibet Mirror* newspaper, 4th day of 5th Tibetan month [July 1, 1957].

Left side: (in English): "Lithang Monastery, 3700 monks used to be, but now only 10 left."

(In Tibetan): "Lithang Monastery, formerly had 3700 monks, now reportedly only ten."

Right side: "These pictures show the destruction: on page three, Chatreng Monastery, four, Drakgo Monastery, five, Ba Choede Monastery, six, Lithang Monastery, shows how the Communists dropped bombs on monasteries and villages against international law. Previously there were a total of 7,200 monks at these monasteries, and after the bombing, no more than a total of 17 are left. If their power lasts for a longer time, the same is sure to happen to other great Tibetan monasteries. Please render assistance! Save us from this destruction . . ."

Source: Office of Tibet, Washington, D.C. Used with permission. English translation: Matthew Akester.

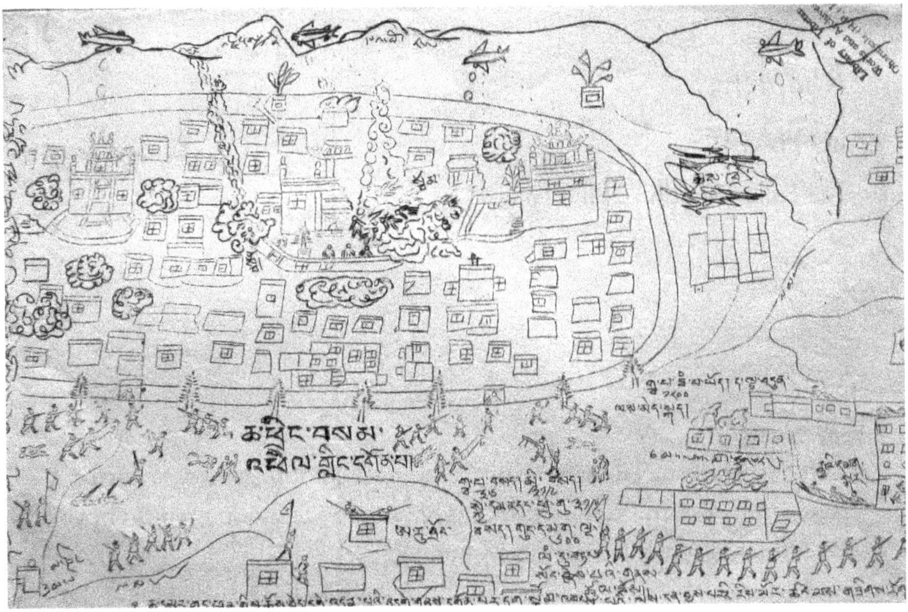

FIGURE 2. The bombing of Chatreng Monastery, originally printed in the *Tibet Mirror*, July 1, 1957. Translation of the text at the bottom of the picture: "Everyone look at this drawing of the Chinese Communists bombing a place of religion."
Source: Office of Tibet, Washington, D.C. Used with permission. English translation: Matthew Akester.

Chapter 3

LITHANG

The Fallen Buddha of the Future

1

Lithang, which in Tibetan means "a meadow smooth as a brass mirror," is in southwestern Garzê, most of it lying 3,600 to 4,600 meters above sea level. It is inhabited mainly by herders.

Historically, southern Kham mainly fell under the jurisdiction of the Lithang Gyalpo and Bathang Gyalpo. In the late Qing, Zhao Erfeng killed off the southern Kham chieftains one by one and established three counties[1] in what had once been the Lithang Gyalpo's territory. Afterwards, during the Republican era, the Nationalist government installed officials in the county seat of Lithang, called Lihua at that time. However, Nationalist rule was never more than nominal. The county government could only govern the few Chinese families living there, and everything regarding local administration had to be done in consultation with the Lithang Monastery, formally known as the Jamchen Choekhor Ling Monastery. The Nationalist government appointed the headmen of various localities to postings in the grassroots government, but these headmen were also under the control of the monastery's *khamtsens (in Chinese, kangcun)*. Being the basic organizational unit, a *khamtsen* is usually organized according to the place of origin of the monks, thus keeping close ties with the local community. Through these connections, the monastery maintains its influence over the people.

The CCP entered the area in 1950 and the following year changed its name from Lihua to Lithang. For local people, this change in the "Chinese officials" brought no change to the "dual administration," and "liberation" only burdened them further with the CCP's steadily increasing taxes.

Lithang consists mainly of the Bumyak grasslands. The family of the Bumyak chieftain, who bore the title Yorupon, came from Amdo at the time of the Qing incursion and had been in Lithang for ten generations.[2] When an advanced detachment of the PLA 18th Army marched toward Bathang, the Bumyak herdmen ambushed and killed a PLA officer.[3] In 1952, their leader, the last Bumyak chieftain, Yorupon Sonam Wangyal, was given the position of chairman of the Lithang County People's Congress, but he never accepted that position. The CCP likewise never set foot in the Bumyak grasslands until August 1955.

In January 1956, all of the high-ranking Tibetans in Lithang County were summoned to Dartsedo for the conference on land reform, as mentioned earlier, except for the Bumyak chieftain Sonam Wangyal, who flatly refused to cooperate with the CCP.[4]

Meanwhile, the CCP's Lithang County Work Committee began arranging for preliminary land reform work in the farming areas. The first step was to groom local activists, and based on past experience, initial mobilization targeted the socially marginalized—the poor, beggars, and the unemployed. Individuals of the appropriate type were called to the county seat for training and "class education," during which they were encouraged to vent their grievances. Once "class consciousness" had been reinforced, the leaders of the Lithang Monastery were summoned for a meeting, during which they were made to listen to the accusations of the activists as evidence that "the masses were demanding reform." In mid-January, the Lithang County Work Committee announced that Tibetans were to hand over their weapons for the implementation of "peaceful reform."[5] At the same time, the county work committee and garrison began constructing defense fortifications and formulating battle plans.[6]

Although remote, Lithang wasn't closed off from the surrounding territory. The Lithang Monastery was Garzê's largest monastery and possessed abundant capital, with commercial ties that extended east to

Shanghai and west to Calcutta (now Kolkata), and with quite a few business representatives in Lhasa and Kalimpong.[7] Although the Tibetan regions were initially exempted from land reform, news had made its way from the inland regions, and Tibetan leaders knew very well what this "reform" involved.[8]

In addition to the formal army that was maintained under the *Kashag* government, other Tibetan regions maintained a tradition of civil-military integration; most men of appropriate age would become soldiers in times of conflict, but usually without formal military training. Households were assigned to classes based on their economic situation; the higher the class, the heavier the corvée imposed on them. Since members of those families were required to go to battle when a conflict arose, they had to possess a certain number of guns and horses. A lighter corvée was imposed on lower-class households, and in times of war the headmen would usually distribute guns to them or require them to contribute manpower. For this reason, those who possessed guns in the Tibetan regions were mostly in the middle stratum or higher.[9] According to the CCP's official statistic prior to 1956, the Ganzi and Aba prefectures had a total of 80,000 guns, of which 70% were "owned by the masses."[10]

Monasteries also held a certain number of weapons; these were usually guns stored there for the defense of the monastery and the community, or "divine guns" donated by people who had vowed never to use them again or as an act of repentance. These weapons were hung in the Dharmapala (Dharma protector) temple, and most were rusted beyond repair.

Apart from guns, knives were common personal possessions. Small knives were used by young and old, male and female alike in the pastoral areas to cut meat at meals, and for slaughtering livestock. Herders had to be armed with a hunting gun or at least a sharp sword to fight off wolves. During the land reform, all firearms, knives, and swords were confiscated from individuals and monasteries.

After receiving the order to hand over their weapons, Yorupon Sonam Wangyal, the Bumyak chieftain, and some individuals from middle or upper-strata families who remained at the Lithang monastery[11] held a meeting to discuss the situation, and they decided that they would rather resist. Sonam Wangyal was the only Lithang chieftain who had refused to go to Dartsedo for the consultant meeting, so, at the age of 25, he became the main leader of the Lithang uprising. The leaders sent messengers to Chatreng (Xiangcheng), Palyul, Nyarong, Barkham (Ma'erkang), and other places calling on everyone to rise in revolt together, and also sent people to Lhasa to request aid and weapons from the Kashag government.[12]

Sources from both sides indicate that there were multiple rounds in the Battle of Lithang, and several small-scale battles had occurred by the time PLA reinforcements rushed to the scene. At the time, the PLA garrison in Lithang consisted of less than one regiment. The Tibetans had the numerical advantage, but they lacked heavy weapons such as machine guns or cannons. The PLA, meanwhile, had fewer troops but superior weapons and plenty of ammunition. The result was substantial casualties on both sides.

In February, more than forty villages in Lithang and neighboring districts rallied their manpower, and more than 3,000 men from various places rushed to the monastery.

On March 7, Tibetans constructed a dam on the river to cut off water to the downstream areas. Two days later, Tibetan snipers fired on five PLA soldiers digging through the embankment to release the water, killing two and wounding one.[13]

The Battle of Lithang had begun.

2

The Lithang Monastery, situated about one kilometer north of the Lithang county seat, was the leader of all of Lithang County's forty-one monasteries. Initially built in 1580, it had undergone several expansions, and as of 1950, it extended 550 meters north to south and 300 meters east to west, containing 428 buildings with a total of more than 1,500 rooms and 4,371 monks.[14] Its formal name, Jamchen Choekhor Ling, means "Dharma wheel of Jampa," Jampa being the Tibetan name for Maitreya, the Buddha of the Future, whose image dominated the monastery's main temple hall.

Since the elimination of the Lithang Gyalpo, the area had become divided among multiple and mutually insubordinate major and minor headmen, and the Lithang Monastery had gradually taken over as the supreme authority acknowledged by all parties. The monastery had eight *khamtsen* through which it exerted its influence. If a dispute arose between headmen, they would usually ask the monastery to uphold justice; if a villager was unhappy with a punishment imposed by a headman, he could also "appeal" to the monastery, whose arbitration was considered final. The most powerful position at the monastery was that of Lithang Kyabgon Rinpoché, and the third Kyabgon Rinpoché, born in 1949, was in his minority at that time.[15]

It was the PLA's first major battle in Garzê, and the CCP took it very seriously. If the resistance of Lithang's Tibetans could be crushed and the monastery brought under control, this would wipe out the power center of southern Kham. Viewed from this perspective, the Battle of Lithang was not a mere suppression but actually a power seizure; this is why the CCP deployed more than two regiments of troops in a blitzkrieg strategy against Lithang.

On March 16 and 17, a PLA regiment stationed in Dartsedo's Rangakhar (Xinduqiao) township,[16] and three companies stationed in Yidun (Lieden) County,[17] were dispatched to Lithang from east and west. They were ordered to converge there by March 22. Together with the Lithang troops, they formed the main force to capture the monastery. After arriving at Lithang, the Yidun troops secretly gathered in an undisclosed location and sent a company to evaluate the situation. This is what they discovered:

> There were about 2000 people in Litang lamaist temple, Minle village,[18] and Caizixi; over 70 people headed by the Maoya (Bumyak) chieftain Sonam Wangyal were stationed in Reshuitang (Hot Spring)[19] and inside the small lamaist temple; over 400 people headed by the Tsosum headman and Molake headman were located in the area of Litang's east hill and the airport on the south side of the town. [Rebels] were building bunkers and laid siege to the county seat.[20]

Based on the situation, the task was divided among the PLA troops as follows:

> The 65th Regiment (minus one battalion) was responsible for encircling and annihilating more than 2,000 people entrenched in the lamaist temple, and would deploy one company to the east hill to wipe out the enemies there. The First Battalion of this regiment took a detour from Minle village toward the north, then turned east to the small temple on the east side of the lamaist temple. The 3rd Battalion (minus one company) was to complete the encirclement from the small temple [on the east side] to Caizixi.
>
> The 68th Regiment stationed in Litang would deploy its main force to coordinate with the 65th Regiment and detour from Minle village to the south side of Litang monastery to Caizixi, forming an encirclement to block the enemy's escape route on the south, and would send a small troop to prevent armed rebels in the airfield area[21] from attacking and harassing.

At dawn on March 22, PLA troops completed the encirclement of the monastery. The command post occupied the mountain east of the monastery.[22]

As soon as the encirclement was complete, the two regiments staged an attack on the Tibetan forces, intercepting more than three hundred Tibetans trying to break through and killing or wounding about eighty of them. Unable to withstand the onslaught, the Tibetans retreated, most of them concentrated within the monastery and the small temples around it.

At 9 a.m., the PLA command post held a battle conference for its officers and decided that the main force of the 65th Regiment would storm the small temples outside the monastery and then move in to capture the monastery's highest point, the main assembly hall. The 68th Regiment would immediately move from the hot spring to the west hill of the monastery, blocking the western escape route and protecting the flank of the main attacking troops. Other troops would press forward to tighten the siege.

At 2 p.m., the PLA launched a fierce artillery attack and occupied the outer temples, after which soldiers pressed on toward the monastery under fire cover. Using explosives, they blasted a hole in the boundary wall, and a company of soldiers poured into the monastery through the gap, heading straight to the main assembly hall.

They were immediately trapped in crossfire.

The monastery was situated on the slope of a hill, with hundreds of buildings stacked upward, row upon row. Dozens of narrow passageways extended in every direction like a giant maze. With thick, battered walls and flat roofs, traditional Tibetan monastic buildings formed natural fortifications.

Occupying a favorable terrain with a commanding position, the Tibetans fired from all directions, forcing the invading PLA soldiers into narrow alleys as their casualties mounted. When the first company entered and didn't return, the PLA commander sent in another company, but a three-wave offensive by a battalion of soldiers was repulsed every time and forced to retreat. The PLA attack had failed, exhausting artillery shells and explosives. With "80 casualties, loss of a 60 mm mortar and sixty-eight guns of various types, and the depletion of more than 53,000 bullets, the thwarted attack entailed painful losses and had an adverse effect";[23] the attack was called off for the time being.

On March 23, the PLA held another battle conference and adopted "delaying tactics," sending Tibetan cadres into the monastery for "political win-over" while awaiting the replenishment of their ammunition and drilling the soldiers for a new attack. Meanwhile, the Tibetans were trapped in the monastery, besieged by the PLA troops.

On March 24, Tibetan cadres sent by the Garzê prefectural party committee entered the monastery and began meeting with rebel leaders to communicate the government's conditions. Chinese sources provide no information on this point, and Tibetan sources differ. One version states that the Chinese side merely asked the Tibetans to lay down their weapons, with the PLA promising that land reform would not be carried out for three years and that it would withdraw from Lithang. Another version is that the PLA took a tough line and demanded that those within the monastery surrender within one day. The cadres secretly told the leaders that surrendering their weapons would definitely have negative consequences, and that breaking through the PLA encirclement also had no chance of success, but that if they didn't hand in their guns, the monastery might be destroyed and many would die. They would have to make the decision themselves. The leaders replied that they couldn't make the decision on their own and would have to discuss it with their people.

The result of the discussion was that the majority of those inside were unwilling to surrender, and decided to break through the encirclement.[24]

On March 23 and 24, under cover of artillery fire, PLA soldiers used small-group demolition to attack and occupy the structures outside the monastery one by one, and tightened the encirclement. The closest units were beneath the boundary wall, and the farthest ones were about 100 meters away.[25]

On the evenings of March 25 and 26, several Tibetan groups made separate attempts to break through the encirclement. Some managed to escape, while others were forced back into the monastery. Determined to "resolutely wipe out any enemies breaking through the encirclement," the PLA reinforced and built bunkers at the spots where Tibetans were most likely to break through the siege.

On March 25, the Chengdu Military Command ordered the Kangding garrison to establish two command posts, i.e., the north route and south route command posts. Under the command of the frontline command post, these two posts were responsible for military operations in northern and southern Kham. The first task of the Southern Kham Command Post was to control Lithang and then unify command of the battles in the southern Kham region.[26] For this reason, the CCP had to capture Lithang at any cost.

From March 27 to 29, the PLA continued its "political offensive" while at the same time preparing its units for battle. The command post mustered seven cannons, 500 kilos of explosives and five companies and one artillery company for the final attack.[27] The battle plan was also decided:

> . . . find the right sally point to execute the attack from north to south. Two companies from the 65th Regiment and two companies from the

> 68th Regiment would be assigned to the main attack. Four 57 mm recoilless guns and three 82 mm mortars would be used as fire cover. As the first step, two companies from the 65th Regiment would attack and seize the main assembly hall. After that, dividing the monastery into two halves along the north-south line, the 65th Regiment would take the right (west) wing and the 68th Regiment the left (east) wing, fighting at the same time house by house. With one 57 mm recoilless gun and one 80 mm mortar as fire cover, one company was to seize the dozen or so detached houses located on the hill along the southern boundary wall, so that more than 300 buildings situated in the hollow and flat area of the monastery would be under our control, in order to ensure that the units from the north would successfully break in from the two wings.[28]

Both sides left behind many legends of the battle. One version circulating within the Lithang garrison claims that after the unsuccessful assault, the Sichuan Military District sent an urgent cable to the Central Military Commission (CMC), and that the defense minister and CMC vice-chairman Peng Dehuai was so enraged by the news that he yelled, "Send aircraft to bomb it for me!"[29]

For the purposes of its blitzkrieg strategy, and to shock the rebelling Tibetans into submission, the PLA requested that the CMC deploy the air force. At that time, the Chinese Air Force's sole long-range heavy-duty bomber unit was its Fourth Independent Regiment, directly commanded by the CMC.

The CMC thereupon deployed its top-secret weapon.

3

On the morning of March 29, two Tupolev Tu-4 bombers took off from Shaanxi's military airport.

The Tupolev Tu-4, nicknamed "the Bull," came from the Soviet Union, a gift from Stalin to Mao. In January 1953, ten Tupolev Tu-4s flew from the Soviet Union to the Shijiazhuang airport in Hebei Province, near Beijing, for a formal handover to China. On March 15, the air force's long-range heavy-duty bomber Fourth Independent Regiment was established in

Shijiazhuang. Airmen were trained by experts sent from the Soviet Union, and two were selected to undertake further study in the USSR.[30]

The first battle fought by the Fourth Independent Regiment was the Battle of Lithang in 1956. As the sun rose to its median over the plateau, gleaming on the golden roof canopy of Jamchen Choekhor Ling's main assembly hall, two bombers appeared in the sky and "strafed and bombed the enemy."[31] Chinese sources do not specify whether any bombs hit the monastery; Tibetan sources mention that most of the bombs missed the target.[32] However, the bombing had a strong psychological effect on the Tibetans trapped inside the monastery:

> On the same night (of the bombing), rebels inside the monastery launched another desperate attempt to break through the siege. More than 500 managed to get out from the southeast side of the monastery. After more than five hours of fierce fighting, a small number of Tibetans were able to fight their way out and fled, but the majority were pushed back.[33]

March 30, at 4 a.m., PLA troops launched the final assault. Shielded by artillery bombardment at a 50-meter range, the PLA troops used explosives to blow open the back door of the main assembly hall, and commando units surged in and climbed onto the roof, where they captured the commanding point and secured the building.[34] Meanwhile, the units on the south captured the houses along the southern wall. After that, "each unit moved toward designated directions, attacking and searching, and completely annihilated the enemies."[35]

At this point, the Bumyak chieftain Sonam Wangyal had broken through the encirclement and led his men around to the back of the monastery hill. They were resting when several horsemen approached hurriedly with the news that the monastery had been breached.[36]

Upon hearing this news, Sonam Wangyal insisted on returning to the monastery, though others tried to dissuade him. Unwilling to abandon him, his companions decided to accompany him and live or die together.

That morning, all of them died in battle except for Yorupon Sonam Wangyal himself and one companion. Amid the cannon roar, the two of them ran into a temple and prayed before a statue of the Buddha. They then took off their protective talismans and placed them before the Buddha. By then, the monastery's northern gate and debate hall had already been breached by the PLA, and those unable to escape were still fighting. Sonam Wangyal and his companion left the temple and proceeded on a raid from which they would never return.

In the collective memory of the Tibetan people, the death of Yorupon has become legend. He fought to the last, his companions dying one after the other, the remaining companion who prayed with him already mortally wounded. The PLA commanding officer ordered gasoline sprinkled in front of the main assembly hall and threatened to set it on fire. At that moment, Sonam Wangyal declared his surrender. But he refused to capitulate to rank-and-file soldiers and demanded that the "highest officer" come forward to accept his surrender. It is said that the officer who came forward was a regimental commander:

> Yorupon was carrying three guns: one rifle and two handguns. He first handed over the rifle, and then pulled out one of the handguns from his breast to hand it over. The commander ordered someone to take him away. At that moment, Yorupon suddenly bent down, pulled his second handgun from inside his boot and opened fire on the commander.[37]

The PLA soldiers present all opened fire, and the Bumyak chieftain was struck by countless bullets, falling in front of the main assembly hall.

The Ganzi Prefecture Gazetteer includes a terse record of this battle: "March 30, a PLA regiment surrounded and annihilated an armed rebellion entrenched at the Litang lamaist temple, shooting dead the Maoya chieftain Sonam Wangyal, and the siege of Litang county seat was lifted."[38]

The Lithang Rebellion had lasted nearly three weeks before being crushed. The Battle of Lithang lasted nine days, and was probably the most intense battle in Kham. Official sources give varying figures regarding the number of Tibetan casualties. On April 9, 1959, the CCP Central Committee issued an internal document to all provinces providing only a figure of "more than 1,300 enemies captured."[39] An internal report published by the Ganzi military in 1999 stated that the PLA "annihilated

2,004 under the traitor Maoya chieftain (311 dead, 80 wounded, 1,613 taken prisoner)."[40] The *Litang Gazetteer* gives the figure as "more than 1,000 (including 12 Chinese counterrevolutionaries) arrested, more than 430 guns, three light machine guns, and one 60 mm mortar captured." It does not mention that the mortar had been captured from the PLA. However, those figures covered only the PLA's final offensive against the monastery, not the full number of casualties in the entire Battle of Lithang.

The *Ganzi Military Gazetteer* provides a list of all of the PLA soldiers killed, from the Red Army era to those who died in action in Garzê Prefecture in the 1970s—except for those killed in Lithang in March 1956. All that is recorded are 83 names, without any details. This makes it impossible to confirm that these officers and men were killed in the Battle of Lithang, nor is there any way to ascertain the deaths of any commanders at the battalion level or above.[41] Only one source reveals that the casualties in the regiment that stormed the fortification included "137 at the level of company commander and below, and 122 wounded at the rank of platoon leader and below,"[42] but these are only the casualty figures for the 65th Regiment, not for all of the participating units. Apart from regular army troops, there were also militia sent from Dartsedo County, and there don't seem to be any figures at all pertaining to their casualties.

This battle being the PLA's first major military operation in the Tibetan region, its shock wave was felt by both the Chinese and the Tibetans. Tibetans were shocked by the "iron bird," a powerful modern weapon they had never before seen or heard of, while the Chinese commanders were surprised by the willpower of the Tibetan resistance. In the following years, Tibetan willpower and Chinese modern weaponry would clash over and over again.

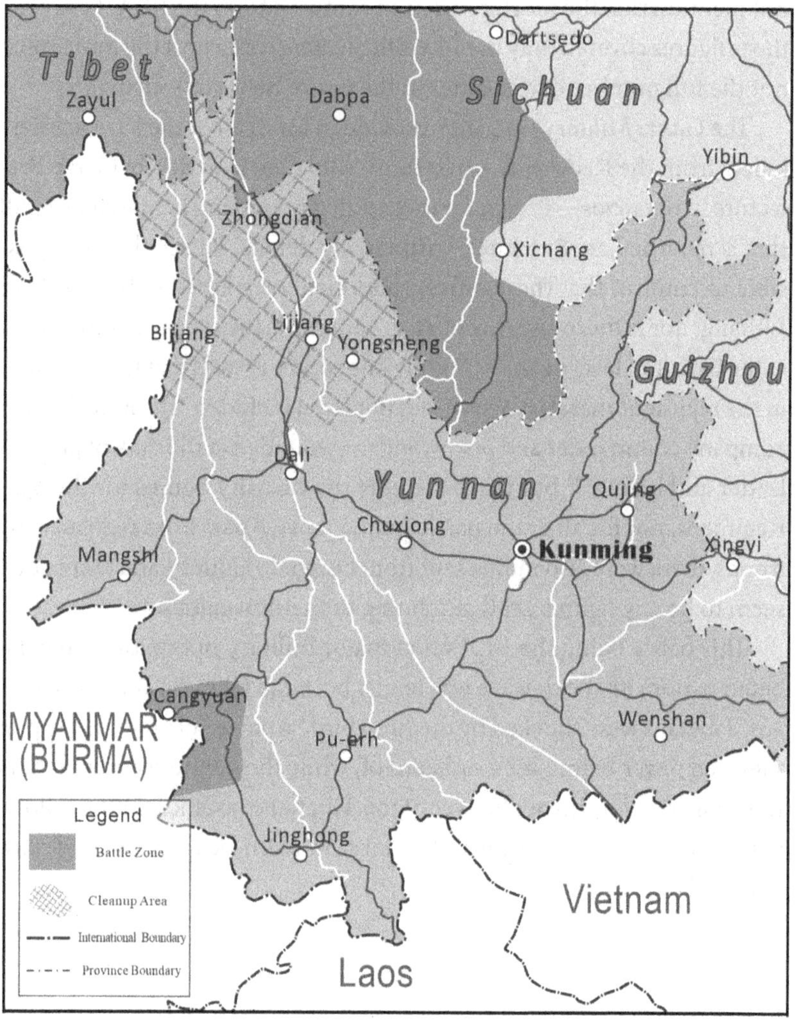

MAP 3. PLA Yunnan Military Command battle regions, 1956–1960. Source: Marvin Cao.

Chapter 4
CHATRENG
The Broken Mala

1

At the time when the Tibetans in Lithang rose up in revolt, Chatreng County was in a precarious situation.

Chatreng was located to the southwest of Lithang, and bordered on the south by Yunnan Province. The Shokchu (Shuoqu) River, more than 270 kilometers long, originates in central Lithang and flows south into the Drichu River, crossing the entire county. The valleys of its middle reaches are rich and fertile, with swathes of terraced fields dotted with villages. Viewed from high up, the river is thought to resemble a cord strung with stockaded villages like the beads of a *mala,* the Buddhist rosary. The county is called Xiangcheng in Chinese,[1] but its devoutly Buddhist residents call their home Chatreng, which means "*mala in hand.*" The county consists of the upper, middle, and lower reaches, hence its other Chinese name of "Sanxiang," meaning "three towns."

Even among the Khampas, renowned for their valor, the Chatrengpas stood out. Chatreng had been invaded several times in its history, which, along with the frequent internal disputes between its headmen, had engendered a bold fighting spirit among them. A 1941 survey described the Chatrengpas as "heavily-armed, whether rich or poor. According to surveys in recent years, there are 5,000 privately-owned firearms in Sanxiang."[2]

The Chatrengpas continually revolted against external political power, and a closer look suggests that the behavior of these external powers was an important factor. The government's imposition of burdensome taxes was a major impetus for revolt. Even the suppressors of the Chatreng uprising in 1911 acknowledged, "In Chatreng alone, grain tax increased by several multiples, and the tribals found it hard to bear, resulting in this disturbance."[3] Due to the hostility of the Chatrengpas, the Xiangcheng County government established by Xikang Province existed largely in name only, and when the CCP took over in 1951, it consisted of "one low building of about 100 square meters, several tables and chairs, 10,000 liters of barley, 5,300 liters of wheat, and 150 liters of buckwheat."[4]

To the Chatrengpas, the CCP's arrival was just a change of Chinese officials. In the early years of the Communist regime, these new arrivals made cautious approaches to the local populace. They opened several stores and built a hospital, distributed food relief, provided free medical treatment, and spent copious amounts of silver dollars to buy and hoard grain, as well as bringing in weapons. The Chatrengpas couldn't tell if these people were soldiers or officials, but although they never quite trusted them, they gradually became accustomed to their presence.[5]

The situation quickly deteriorated, however. At that time, many places in the Kham region still used Tibetan currency, but the CCP cadres and staff were paid in silver dollars. During the Nationalist era, the county government of only a dozen or so officials hadn't greatly burdened the local populace, but as an increasing number of CCP functionaries of all types entered Chatreng from 1951 onward, the accompanying influx of silver dollars resulted in a devaluation of the Tibetan currency and an increase in the price of foodstuffs.[6] Even so, apart from a couple of tribal skirmishes during the years 1952 to 1955, the Chatrengpas had yet to engage in any conflict with the CCP. Influential monks and members of Chatreng's upper strata were given official positions, while the people had no contact with the regime, still referring to the county government as the *yamen*, as in imperial times (the *yamen* was the government administrative office in imperial China).[7]

In February 1956, the CCP Xiangcheng County Work Committee and county government called in 300 "activists" from the five districts under their jurisdiction to attend a training class in the county seat, where they were taught to "vent their grievances, calculate exploitation, and enhance class consciousness."[8] On this foundation, the CCP cadres established a land reform work team headed by Ren Zhigao, the secretary of the Xiangcheng Work Committee, with three vice-chairmen, including one Tibetan cadre. The work team had five sub-teams under it, and the plan was for each district to send a sub-team out to launch land reform.[9]

Around mid-February, Chatreng's two main monasteries received a document from the work team. As Tibetans recall it, the document included seven points:

> 1) Lamas and monks have to be eliminated; 2) monasteries and their contents have to be eliminated; 3) worship and ritual are prohibited; 4) the wealthy and eminent members of the community have to be eliminated; 5) all land will be appropriated by the state; 6) all property will be appropriated by the state; 7) everyone has to obey the Liberation Army and serve them. If you do not agree to this, we will bomb you from the air and send troops on the ground and wipe you out.[10]

This document was probably the "land reform regulations" issued by the Xiangcheng land reform work team.[11] It has never been published, so there is no way to ascertain whether its contents are consistent with Tibetans' recollections, but the above narrative shows the Tibetans' clear understanding of what "democratic reform" involved.

The Tibetan leaders of Chatreng secretly held a meeting to discuss the document and then sent a messenger to deliver a strongly worded reply:

> You officers, district heads, and soldiers are here in our land without the slightest justification, and have no business imposing these seven

points, which are completely unacceptable. You had better leave immediately, otherwise we have also made our war preparations, and there is no doubt that we will fight.[12]

Chinese sources reveal that in mid-February, Ren Zhigao went four times to Sampeling Monastery for talks, but do not divulge the content. Clearly the talks accomplished little, as both sides began to prepare for war.[13]

Chinese sources attribute the Chatreng uprising to the Dalai Lama's tutor, Trijang Rinpoché,[14] accusing him of "plotting an armed insurrection" and of sending people to liaise with monasteries in Gyalthang (Zhongdian),[15] Dabpa, Bathang, Derong, and other counties.[16] No other sources have surfaced to date that support this allegation. Tibetan sources state that when the Tibetans of Lithang decided to revolt, they sent people to liaise with neighboring counties, Chatreng included,[17] but survivors of the Chatreng revolt recall that local residents had already learned about what had happened during land reform in other localities, and as soon as they heard that land reform was going to be carried out in their homeland, they immediately and spontaneously rose up to protect the monastery.[18]

At the time, government officials were concentrated in three strongholds: the county government office building, the commerce bureau, and the hospital. From mid-February onward, all of them began overhauling their fortifications, storing up grain and water, and mobilizing combatants.

On March 16, more than 2,000 Tibetans from all districts congregated at Sampeling, and the monks began performing religious rites.

On March 20, Tibetans swarmed down on the three government fortifications, with both sides opening fire. Six Tibetans were killed, and on the government side, a Tibetan cadre was injured. That night, Tibetans lit bonfires and pitched tents on the hillsides surrounding the monastery. The Xiangcheng Work Committee ordered those inside the hospital to withdraw to the county government office building. Hospital staff buried 70,000 silver dollars underground, set the building on fire, and then evacuated the hospital, following a drainage ditch to the county government building. Snipers fired at them along the way, and a Tibetan cadre was struck and killed.

Chinese sources refer to the incident as "the battle to defend the Xiangcheng County government." Sources from both sides stated that the battle mainly involved Tibetans surrounding the county government and cutting off its water supply in an attempt to force the government officials to withdraw from Chatreng. There was occasional sniper fire, but this "defense battle" involved none of the intense fighting seen in Lithang. More than 200 people took refuge inside the county government building, which was three stories tall and surrounded by a wall. The county government had a malfunctioning machine gun that could only fire a single shot at a time, and 40-odd rifles, with about 80 bullets each. Intent on saving ammunition, the government side was cautious about opening fire, and lacking heavy weapons, the Tibetans were likewise unable to storm the fortification. Consequently, the confrontation dragged on for more than ten days.

The main reason for the sustained confrontation was that the county government's radio was broken, preventing it from contacting the prefectural government for more than a week. Once communications were finally restored and the county government had requested reinforcements, the reply was that the prefecture's limited military force had been exhausted and the Chatreng cadres would have to figure out their own way to break the siege.[19] The county party committee then held an enlarged meeting to discuss the situation. Aware that their arms were insufficient, their manpower limited, and a breakthrough of the encirclement unlikely to succeed, they decided to appeal directly to Beijing for help.

2

Late March nights in Chatreng, more than 2,800 meters above sea level, are bitterly cold. Kargyal Dondrup sat near the campfire wrapped in a fur cloak, hovering near sleep.

Suddenly, the sound of singing ripped through the silence. Behind the enclosure walls of the county government building, a Chatrengpa woman was singing a folk tune familiar to Kargyal Dondrup, and her high, clear voice sent the sweet melody floating through the crisis-filled night:

If you don't burn smoke offerings[20] today,
It will be on every mountaintop tomorrow.

The song sounded tense and urgent, like a warning.

"It will be on every mountaintop tomorrow"? Kargyal Dondrup was puzzled and felt uneasy. He had a vague feeling that the woman behind the wall was trying to convey some kind of message.[21]

The singing stopped abruptly. Huddled around their campfire as the night wore on, the Chatrengpa never imagined the disaster heading their way.

At that moment, at Shaanxi's Wugong County Airport, the CCP's secret weapon—the Tupolev Tu-4 long-range bomber—was already being prepared for battle under orders from the Central Military Commission.

Several days earlier, while the men of Chatreng were on the hillside facing off with the Chinese officials, a cable had been delivered to State Council Premier Zhou Enlai.

It was the request for help from the Xiangcheng county party committee, transmitted by the Sichuan provincial party committee with an explanation appended: "More than a hundred comrades in Xiangcheng have been under siege for more than half a month. They now lack ammunition, water, and grain but are still holding out. The provincial party committee has no troops to dispatch and asks the Central Committee to immediately find a way to rescue the Xiangcheng cadres."[22]

Zhou Enlai wrote a single line on the report and then gave it to his secretary for immediate handling. The cable was passed along to Defense Minister Peng Dehuai.

A few days later, the Xiangcheng county party committee received a reply cable from the CCP Central Committee, transmitted through the Sichuan provincial party committee. Zhou Enlai had written the following memo on the report: "Send paratroopers to rescue the Xiangcheng cadres."[23] The Xiangcheng Work Committee immediately sent a cable back explaining that the terrain of Xiangcheng was complex and unsuitable for paratroopers, and suggested that ground forces be sent from Yunnan instead, along with aircraft to blow up the "command post of the rebel bandits," i.e., the Sampeling Monastery.

The next day, the Xiangcheng cadres received a reply cable stating that Zhou Enlai had ordered the Kunming Military Command to rush troops to Xiangcheng within four days.[24] The Kunming Military Command subsequently sent a cable notifying the Xiangcheng Work Committee that the troops had been dispatched.

It was on that night that the unknown woman sang her disguised warning.

3

April 1, 1956. As noon approached, two aircraft swept across the mountain peaks and circled over the valley.

Inside the government office building behind the enclosing wall, the radio officer nervously adjusted the radio frequency, but was unable to establish contact. The aircraft dropped a pile of red-and-green leaflets with a message written in both Chinese and Tibetan: "We know that most of you are innocent people who have been deceived, so we cannot bear to drop bombs on your heads. If you persist in heeding the words of evildoers, and refuse to end the encirclement and continue to oppose the government, bombs will soon be dropped on your heads. By then regret will be too late."[25]

An aircraft dropped a bomb on the hillside across from Sampeling,[26] then banked away and flew off.

Around 9:00 AM on April 2, four Tupolev Tu-4 bombers came roaring in, their gun turrets spitting tongues of flame as 23mm rapid-fire cannons strafed people on the mountain slopes and near the enclosing wall. With no place to hide, people fled toward the monastery. In the afternoon, once everyone had been chased into the monastery, the Tupolev Tu-4s began dropping their bombs: "At 4:00 PM, the aircraft dropped bombs on the rebel bandit command center. At that time, everyone observed the thunderous sound followed by clouds of dust and flames lighting the sky, and pieces of wood hurling into the air with the smoke."[27]

This explosion was more than a "thunderous sound." Dozens of bombs landed on the monastery, inflicting catastrophic destruction: 3 temples and around 40 dormitories were blown up, and more than 200 monks and laypersons were killed. After the bombing ended, the surviving Tibetans poured out of the monastery, some of them surrendering on the spot but most of them fleeing into the hills.

On April 3, the Kunming Military Command's 126th Regiment sent an advance battalion into Chatreng. The thirteen-day "battle to defend the Xiangcheng County government" ended with three dead on the Chinese side. According to Tibetan sources, the bombing had lasted ten days.[28] Many dwellings and temples in the stockaded villages on either side of the Shokchu were destroyed, and countless monks and laypeople were killed. In order to evade capture, all of the young, hardy men fled into the hills, leaving only children, women, and the elderly behind.

From March to April 1956, the PLA Air Force's long-range heavy-duty bomber 4th Independent Regiment chalked up its first victory by bombing three targets: Lithang's Jamchen Choekhor Ling Monastery, Chatreng's Sampeling Monastery, and Bathang's Ganden Pendéling Monastery. In nearly a month of combats, the Fourth Independent Regiment carried out 29 airdrops and 21 bombings in three combat missions,[29] unloading around 300 bombs.

Chatreng, the "mala in hand," was broken into pieces. The total number of Tibetans killed and wounded in this operation has never been revealed to this day.

Chapter 5
NYARONG
The Wrath of the Dragoness

1

In June 1956, the Dhunkhug headman Aten finished his studies at the Southwest Minorities Institute in Chengdu and returned home, in the company of several classmates. Apparently, he had no idea about the series of events happening in Garzê. When the group reached Dartsedo, the headquarters of Garzê Prefecture, the Tibetan CCP leader Shana[1] called them in for a talk. After being told to study some documents and discuss the "policy on pacifying rebellion," Aten realized that his homeland had gone to war.[2]

While the Tibetan regions were engulfed in the flames of war, the main Tibetan leaders continued to be held in Dartsedo for meetings. Aten sought out the most prominent leaders from Nyarong, his homeland, to gain a better grasp of what was going on, but he was watched wherever he went, and it was impossible to engage in any in-depth discussion.[3]

After spending a few days in Dartsedo, Aten mounted his horse and rode toward his home with a heavy heart.

Near Aten's hometown, the county seat of Nyarong, there was an ancient fortress. Legend had it that King Gesar's[4] favorite consort, Drukmo, had once lived there, so it was called Drukmo Khar, or "Castle of the Dragoness." Nyarong had been riven by war and unrest for more than a century, and a hard life of endless battles had bred a fierce fortitude in the Nyarongpa. Located in the middle of Kham, Nyarong was like the region's heart, a land as solid and powerful as its men and women. Nyarong's most famous rebel was in fact a young woman from the Gyari clan.

The Gyari clan of Ralang (Raolu)[5] was highly influential as one of Nyarong's four *qianhu*, a Chinese term meaning "chieftain of a thousand households." As soon as the CCP entered Nyarong, Gyari Nyima, the *qianhu* at the time, was appointed county head. He had two wives who were sisters, seven years apart in age. The elder, around 30 years old at the time, was named Norzin Lhamo; the younger, in her early twenties, was named Dorjé Yudon.

In mid-January, 1956, Gyari Nyima was summoned to Dartsedo for the conference. Meanwhile, a land reform work team of more than 130 cadres arrived in the county. It was soon expanded into a team of 257, including 185 Tibetan activists, and was divided into four sub-teams, one for each district, to launch land reform simultaneously in Nyarong.

They started the reform by registering information about every family, including details on each family member, as well as the land, livestock, houses, and other assets owned by the household, in preparation for dividing the populace into classes.[6] At this stage, Gyari Nyima managed to come back home and discussed with his wives how to deal with the situation. They made the choice that had always been made over the course of more than a century whenever the Nyarongpa encountered oppression from outside: revolt.[7]

On February 10, Gyari Nyima's elder wife, Norzin Lhamo, together with other influential headmen, was called to the county seat to study the land reform policy, leaving the younger wife, Dorjé Yudon, to look after the family's home.

Soon activists began going door-to-door with Chinese soldiers and cadres to confiscate firearms and bullets. On February 24, the leader of the Ralang sub-team, a Chinese cadre, went with two other cadres to the home of Gyaltse Aru, the headman of Gyaltse Village in Ralang township, to take weapons. After taking one gun from the headman's home, the cadre demanded to "borrow" the British-made handgun that the headman carried on his person. Instead of handing in his handgun, Gyaltse

Aru pulled it out and pointed it at the Chinese cadre, slowly backed out of the room and escaped. That night, dozens of people from the village surrounded the sub-team. The siege lasted 12 days and ended with the work team returning to the county seat on March 6, and a Chinese cadre wounded and a Tibetan activist dead. This incident was referred to as "the first shot of the Nyarong rebellion."[8]

On March 7, the local sub-team leader brought people to search the home of Gyarashi's[9] *qianhu* ("chieftain of a thousand households"), Gyurmé. Gyurmé had been appointed vice-chairman of Xinlong County's Political Consultative Conference and was in Dartsedo at that time, leaving only his mother, wife, and elderly housekeeper at home. The result of the search stunned all of Nyarong: Everyone in Gyurmé's family, young and old, was shot and killed.[10]

Two days after this incident, more than thirty men arrived at the county seat on horseback from Peltsa (Picha) Village and demanded the release of their headman, Ador.[11] A brief exchange of gunfire followed, with two casualties on each side. This incident was subsequently referred to as "the Picha rebel bandits besieging the county seat."[12]

On March 13, the land reform sub-teams in lower Nyarong and in Norkhog (Luogu) Township were attacked simultaneously, and one sub-team leader and twelve team members were killed.

The situation became so tense that Dorjé Yudon knew she couldn't wait for her husband and elder sister to come home, nor could she wait for the date Lithang had set to revolt, so she immediately sent messengers to the other Nyarong leaders. Around this time, a courier that Dorjé Yudon had sent to Drango County was intercepted, and the plan for the rebellion was exposed, so Dorjé Yudon decided to launch the operation even earlier.

By March 14, insurrections broke out in 78% of Nyarong County's rural townships. Some 2,787 households took part, representing 70.16% of all households in the county's rural area, and the number of participants composed 16.7% of the county's total population.[13] At that time, the county had 61 headmen and 73 senior monks, which shows that the vast majority of those who took part in the uprising were what CCP propaganda termed the "liberated masses."

The conflict intensified at the end of March, and the county party committee cadres retreated inside the Drukmo Khar. Dorjé Yudon led a group to besiege the fort and cut off its water supply. The Tibetans had no heavy weapons, so they couldn't fight their way into the fort, but the county cadres were likewise helpless to break through the encirclement, so a deadlock ensued.

In mid-April, a PLA regiment from the Chengdu Military Command moved in on Nyarong.

2

By the time the Dhunkhug village headman Aten reached home, at the end of June, his homeland had changed beyond recognition. Nyarong's resistance had been suppressed by the mighty regular army, and nearly all of the able-bodied men had fled into the hills.

When Aten entered his home, his wives were shocked, hardly daring to believe he'd actually returned. Weeping, they told him that land reform had been launched during his absence, and that his household had been classified as "serf owners." The democratic reform sub-team had brought people to ransack their home, and their family's land and livestock had been confiscated, along with other household items. Even several sacks of grain borrowed from friends had been carried off. Neighbors came over to visit and told Aten many stories about the "democratic reforms": the confiscation of assets, the denunciation of headmen and lamas . . .

After spending several days at home, Aten went back to report for duty. He questioned his direct supervisor about why someone like him, who was by no means wealthy, had been classified as a "serf owner." The answer he received was that the party's policy was to classify as "serf owner" anyone with leadership ability and who was trusted by the ordinary people. Such people had to be vilified as members of the ruling class in order to undermine the masses' trust in them. Of course, not all of these people were wealthy, but that was the strategy. In any case, all of them were reactionary feudal elements who would become serf owners if given the opportunity. Aten was considered one of these, even though the party was grooming him as an activist.

In the months that followed, Aten and another student at the Southwest National Minorities Institute, along with two monks, were sent to eastern Nyarong with the PLA's "rebellion pacification troops" to assist the army in carrying out "political struggle." During one military operation, Aten learned to his shock and fury that troops had been ordered to kill all "rebel bandits" on sight, whether male or female, elderly or children.[14]

In his memoirs, Aten records his attendance at a mass rally. Everyone was called to a public meeting, where military cadres told them that they had come to carry out "democratic reform," and that this was the only way for the masses to be thoroughly liberated. "We're here to help you. We're going to allocate land to everyone who has no land." One cadre after another gave speeches saying this kind of thing.

The people were silent, and finally an elderly man in shabby clothes stood up. "My name is Shanam Ma," he said:

> I am a poor man and an old one, as you all can see. There are a few things that have to be said here today and it is best that I say them. Since I am poor, I have nothing to lose; since I am old, death will come soon anyway. I have this to say to you Chinese. Ever since you entered our land, we have barely been able to tolerate your behavior. Now you try to force some strange new "democratic reforms" on us that we all think are ridiculous and nothing but a mule load of conceit. What do you mean you will give us land, when all the land you can see around you has been ours since the beginning of time? Our ancestors gave it to us, and you cannot give it to us again. Who has given you the right to force your way into our country and push your irrational ideas onto us? We are Tibetans and you are Chinese. Go back to your homes and to your people. We do not need you here.[15]

Another man stood and said something similar, and the others present cheered loudly. Infuriated, the military cadres ordered the two men arrested.

A few days later, the local people were called together for another rally to denounce these two men, who were declared "supporters of the armed rebellion." During the denunciation meeting, the two men were badly beaten, and by the time the meeting ended, they were half dead.[16]

On November 13, a goodwill troupe sent by the CCP Central Committee arrived in Dartsedo. The troop had two missions: to pacify the local people by distributing relief items such as grain and clothing, and to find out the cause of the rebellion. The troupe stayed in the area for about two weeks, convened forums for people at all levels of society, and visited 31 monasteries, presenting gifts and alms to the monks.[17] On November 24, the goodwill troupe split into five groups to carry out propaganda in each county.

The goodwill troupe's fourth group went to Nyarong County, where it held a rally to distribute food and fabric and to present silk and various other gifts to members of upper-level society. The goodwill troupe publicly criticized the local officials and told people that the "errors" in the reforms were due to local cadres misunderstanding the spirit of the Central Committee's "peaceful reforms" and violating upper-level directives. All reform-related activities ceased during the month the goodwill troupe remained in Garzê. However, as soon as the troupe left, reform resumed, and everything returned to the old ways.

All these experiences gradually changed Aten's views. Less than two years later, he gave up the benefits he stood to gain by working for the CCP, and with his wives and daughter he left his homeland and set off on the road of exile.

Chapter 6

THE FIRST BEND IN THE YELLOW RIVER

1

The Yellow River flows east from Yulshul (Yushu) and Golok, then suddenly turns northwest at the juncture of Qinghai, Gansu, and Sichuan provinces, looping back into Qinghai in a nearly 180-degree arc that is known as the "first bend in the nine-bend Yellow River." Here vast grasslands stretch hundreds of kilometers over the counties of Machu (Maqu),[1] Sungchu (Songpan), Kakhog (Hongyuan), Ngawa, and Dzorgé (Ruo'ergai). The Chinese gave the name Songpan to the grassland within the borders of Ngawa Prefecture,[2] which for centuries had been primarily inhabited by Tibetans.

Ngawa Prefecture has a varied topography, from the soaring mountains and deep gorges of Gyalrong in the southeast, to the grassland plateau populated by herders, more than 3,000 meters above sea level, in the northwest. Farming predominated in southern regions such as Trochu (Heishui) and Barkham (Ma'erkang), while herding was the principal way of life on the plateau.

In 1953, the CCP established the Sichuan Province Tibetan Autonomous Region (TAR). When Xikang Province was eliminated in 1955, most of Kham became part of Sichuan as the Garzê Tibetan Autonomous Prefecture (TAP), and the Sichuan Province TAR became the Ngawa

TAP. Consequently, the Songpan grassland and its 65 predominantly nomadic herding tribes, under more than 20 major and minor headmen, came under the jurisdiction of Sichuan Province in 1956.[3]

The southernmost portion of the prefecture was occupied by a mixture of Chinese, Tibetan, and Qiang ethnic groups. In 1954, the CCP carried out a cooperative pilot project in Maowun (Maoxian) County and began establishing state-owned farms. On October 4, 1954, the Sichuan provincial party committee decided to launch land reform from winter 1954 to spring 1955 in the mostly Chinese-inhabited areas of Lunggu (Wenchuan), Maowun, Sungchu, and Namphel (Nanping)[4] counties, as well as in the areas inhabited by a mixture of ethnic groups. This early-stage land reform in Ngawa, referred to as "reduction of rent and interest" and "adjustment of debt," proceeded a step ahead of Garzê Prefecture and had achieved some results: "Land rent in the mixed agricultural and pastoral townships was reduced by more than 80%. Corvée was basically eliminated."[5] For this reason, when the Sichuan provincial party committee decided to launch land reform in the Tibetan areas at the end of 1955, they believed that conditions were ripe in Ngawa.

At the beginning of January 1956, the first peasant congress was held in Barkham to establish the land reform committee. Two months later, on March 17, uprisings began in the county's Zongbur (Ribu) Township. Resistance had begun in many places in Garzê by then, but there is insufficient information from currently available sources to determine whether the rebellions in Barkham were connected to those in Lithang, Chatreng, and Nyarong.

The uprisings spread rapidly from Barkham to other areas in Ngawa Prefecture.

In April, an insurrection occurred among the herders of Dzorgé (Ruo'ergai) on the first bend of the Yellow River, involving more than 3,500 people from 15 tribes.[6]

Another insurrection on May 14 in a village under the jurisdiction of Trochu (Heishui) County resulted in the death of the cadre heading the land reform work group there.[7] In a domino effect, the rebellions spread to 11 other Trochu County villages, involving a total of 4,786 people and "more than 2,000 firearms of various kinds."[8]

By mid-May, insurrections had occurred in seven of Ngawa Prefecture's 13 counties, with some 15,000 people taking part.[9]

Why did the Tibetans of Ngawa Prefecture rebel in 1956? Official sources blame secret collusion between a "minority of landlords" and "individual upper-level political and religious figures, and a tiny minority of bandit remnants who slipped through the net."[10] However, according to official figures, participants in the county's uprisings included eight "Kuomintang (Nationalist party) remnant bandits," 39 "bandit chieftains and assassins" and 117 "minor bandit chieftains," while the rest were "hoodwinked masses."[11]

Land reform in Trochu began on January 4, 1956, and proceeded in stages, as in other regions. This process lasted three months, ending on April 1 with the establishment of cooperatives. The Tibetan uprising in Trochu County occurred after land reform was completed, in 13 of the 14 cooperatives established in Trochu at the time, and several cadres stationed at the cooperatives were killed.[12] Official sources acknowledged "certain policy errors committed by a minority of cadres in the execution of their democratic reform work," but did not specify what these "errors" were.

2

After the uprising broke out in Ngawa, the CCP immediately sent troops in to suppress it.[13] On May 6, the CCP's Mao County Military District and Gansu Xiahe Military Sub-region formed an "alliance command post" that sent four regiments and one battalion into Dzorgé to suppress the herders. After more than twenty days of fighting, 3,020 Tibetans in the area were "annihilated."[14]

On May 30, two PLA regiments and one company entered Trochu and engaged in "43 large and small battles, annihilated 5,571 enemies, and seized a total of 2,367 firearms of various types." In other words, less than half of the 5,000-plus "enemies" possessed firearms.[15]

During the process of repressing such rebellions, a tragedy occurred that would have major repercussions. PLA troops indiscriminately killed

Tibetans even where no insurrection had occurred, in what was referred to as the "Mewa (Mowa) problem."

In June 1956, the situation was so tense in Ngawa that the party committees of the TAP and the Chengdu Military Command front-line command post ordered the work team stationed in Mewa *shokka* to withdraw. The work team evacuated, with the garrison troops and cadres, that same night, but more than 40 armed individuals from the *shokka* tailed them along the way. The PLA troops opened fire, killing several Tibetans, with one person injured on their own side. After the work team left, goods valued at tens of thousands of *yuan* remained behind in the trading company, along with more than 30,000 *yuan* in the bank. The Mewa people distributed the goods in the shop to the poor, but left the money in the bank.

The next day, PLA troops searching the hills saw "a group of Tibetan cavalrymen sitting on the ground boiling tea, and they killed several with machine guns, realizing only afterwards that these were Mewa elders."[16] This classified report states, "The Tangke garrison reported that 13 elders of the Tangke tribes had assembled to plot an armed rebellion. When our troops discovered them and went forward to question them, the elders drew their swords and slashed at the squad leader and also mounted their horses, preparing to shoot, so the troops used submachine guns to shoot them dead."[17] The shooting of 13 tribal elders by the PLA troops created a furor, and the Xinhua News Agency *Internal Reference* report acknowledges that this incident made the situation in Mewa "even more strained and complicated."[18]

The murdered elders were members of the Thangkor (Tangke)[19] *shokka*, which had not yet staged a rebellion, but had its grievances against the government. In 1955, the government had mobilized a group of Chinese youths from Chongqing and Chengdu to form a "youth wasteland cultivation team" to establish farms and attempt to grow wheat and barley in the pasturelands of Sichuan's northwestern plateau.[20] In March 1956, the "Thangkor farm" began cultivating large swaths of pastureland owned by pastoral communities such as the Thangkor and Mewa. The cultivation not only spoiled the pastureland, but also squeezed the herders out of their living space, and the government forced the herders to graze their herds together and seized their firearms. As subsequent negotiations between a Central Committee "goodwill troupe"[21] and local headmen made clear, the wasteland reclamation at Thangkor was a major contributor to local tensions.[22]

From March to June 1956, all of Ngawa was in a state of war. The PLA dispatched a mighty army that "annihilated" more than 11,500 Tibetan herders in Trokyab, Barkham, Dzorgé, Trochu, and Sungchu.[23] In six counties where uprisings had not yet occurred, more than 13,000 civilian workers and militia were drafted to carry out logistical support for the PLA frontline forces.[24]

3

The military suppression in Sichuan's Garzê and Ngawa prefectures came to an end in August 1956. Although scattered fighting continued in some areas, the situation in most of the region had been forcibly stabilized.

In Beijing, on July 22, Mao, Zhou Enlai and Deng Xiaoping received Tianbao (Sanggyé Yeshe), Li Weihan, and the third deputy secretary of the Sichuan provincial party committee and vice-chairman of the provincial people's political consultative conference, Liao Zhigao, among others, at Zhongnanhai to hear their reports regarding the Sichuan situation. The talks went on for more than four hours. In the content of the conversations that has been published, Mao stated that "democratic reform is essential, and determination toward reform is correct," and designated the battles that had occurred in Garzê as "basically class struggle rather than ethnic struggle." Mao nevertheless acknowledged that "this battle had mass character," and in order to capture the "ethnic and religious banner," Mao directed the United Front Department and Sichuan provincial party committee to make some concessions, including reducing the proportion of people classified as landlords and rich peasants in order to "isolate landlords and neutralize rich peasants," to call truces and engage in negotiations in the battle zones, to "temporarily leave the temples alone," to recruit ethnic minority party members, and so on.[25]

The gist of this conversation was subsequently referred to as the "Central Committee July Directive."

In December, the CCP central committee goodwill troupe came to Ngawa and immediately took part in resolving the "Mewa problem," persuading the Ngawa leader Palgon Trinlé[26] to personally arrange for negotiations with the Mewa headmen, which lasted from December 9 to 11. The negotiations finally reached an agreement under which the government would compensate the families of the men who had been killed by PLA troops with 1,500 kilos of barley and 1,400 *yuan* in cash, and compensation of 250 *yuan* for each horse killed. Furthermore, the firearms and horses seized in the battle would be returned. Since the goods left behind at the trading company in Mewa had already been distributed to the masses, they would be treated as government aid, while the headmen for their part would return the money left in the bank to the government.

The negotiations between the goodwill troupe and the Thangkor headmen went less smoothly. The Thangkor headmen were unhappy with the Sichuan provincial government's policies and demanded to be allowed to move to Gansu (where land reform had not yet begun). They subsequently proposed eleven more conditions, including a demand that the government not interfere with the migration of the Thangkor, that the Thangkor pasturelands no longer be reclaimed, that the people not be required to return the items they'd looted, and that practical and feasible stipulations be made regarding the protection of religion.[27] Ultimately, the goodwill troupe and the headmen reached an agreement under which the tribal militia surrendered, and the "Mewa problem" was temporarily resolved.

By this time, armed rebellions had occurred in many spots in Kham and Amdo. In early 1956, a rebellion broke out among herders of the Dartsan (Dacan) *tsowa* in the Yulgen (Henan) Mongol Autonomous County close to Gansu's Malho TAP, and there was an exchange of gunfire between the herders and the local garrison and work team. Soon after that, the Shigtsang (Xicang) and Larigul (Larenguan)[28] tribes of Luchu (Luqu) County in the Kanlho TAP in Gansu also joined the insurrection.

On June 11, more than 1,000 PLA troops, including infantry, cavalry, and mortar and heavy machine-gun units, set off for Kanlho to suppress the rebellion. Military sources state that 1,024 Tibetans were killed, wounded, or taken captive.[29]

By the end of 1956, many of these clashes had been put down by heavy military actions by the PLA. However, the flame of Tibetan resistance was not extinguished. It soon spread out to all three districts of traditional Tibet.

Chapter 7

TIBET

Occupation and "Reform"

1

The news of reforms launched in the Tibetan regions of Yunnan and Sichuan inevitably influenced the Tibet Work Committee. Cadres at all levels became impatient with repetitive "united front" work and were "all champing at the bit to carry out reforms in Tibet."[1]

Although Tibet had been handled differently from the other regions, social reconstruction was one of Mao's fundamental policies for Tibet. Mao's general policy on Tibet included two keywords: occupation and reform. While in Moscow on January 2, 1950, Mao sent a cable to the CCP Central Committee and Peng Dehuai,[2] stating, "Although the population of Tibet is not large, its international status is crucial. We must **occupy** Tibet and **reform** it into a people's democracy."[3] Events in Tibet from 1950 onward followed these two fundamental guidelines.

Preparation for the first stage, i.e., the occupation of Tibet, started on January 10, 1950, when Mao directed the Central Committee to "establish a party-led organ to manage Tibet."[4] Two weeks later, the Central Committee authorized the 18th Army's report on establishing the Tibet Work Committee (TWC) and its choice of personnel to serve on it. On January 28, the 18th Army TWC was formally established in Sichuan and took responsibility for all operations involved in occupying Tibet.[5]

To the outside world, however, the TWC continued to be known by its military designation, and members of the TWC by their military identities.[6]

The Chamdo Work Committee was established on September 11, 1950, three weeks before the "Battle of Chamdo"[7] broke out. On September 25, 85 personnel sent to work on the Chamdo Work Committee gathered in Garzê, at what was referred to externally as the "18th Army Front Line Command Post."[8] The Chamdo Work Committee, headed by Wang Qimei, set off from Garzê on October 6, the day that the CCP fired the first round in the Battle of Chamdo, and arrived in Chamdo on October 24, the day that the battle ended.[9]

In 1951, the main task of the 18th Army was to "complete the occupation of Lhasa and even all of Tibet."[10] On February 8 of that year, the 18th Army called a meeting during which it divided Tibet into the military sub-regions of Chamdo, Tengchen (Dingqing), Shigatsé (Rikaze), Gyantsé (Jiangzi), and Lhasa City, and then established the CCP Lhasa Work Committee.[11] The 18th Army's rear headquarters began entering and establishing a garrison in Garzê in March. On April 17, the TWC decided to establish six regional work committees and a municipal committee.[12] On May 23, the Tibetan delegation signed the "Seventeen-Point Agreement" in Beijing before obtaining authorization from the Dalai Lama and the Tibetan government.[13] In fact, even before the agreement was signed, the CCP "had set its policy and timeline for entering Tibet and wasn't prepared to waver on it, regardless of whether or not the negotiations achieved results."[14] Furthermore, by then the 18th Army had already completed its preparations for occupying Tibet.[15]

Two days after the "Seventeen-Point Agreement" was signed, Mao issued an order for the PLA to march into Tibet. Starting on July 1, troops moved in on Tibet from four directions.[16] Since the "Seventeen-Point Agreement" didn't stipulate that the CCP would enter Lhasa to establish a party organization and only stated that the PLA would enter Tibet to "strengthen national defense," the CCP entered Tibet under the guise of the army.

On September 9, 1951, a PLA 18th Army "advance detachment" of more than 400 personnel under the command of General Wang Qimei entered Lhasa. However, most of its members were not soldiers but rather cadres, including propaganda, united front, public security, and foreign affairs personnel, escorted by a company of PLA soldiers. Lin Liang, head of the advance detachment's political department, had been appointed secretary of the Lhasa municipal party committee prior to this.[17] Soon after the "advance detachment" arrived in Lhasa, the municipal party committee was formally established and began operations, but it was referred to externally as the "Political Department of the Advance Detachment in Tibet."[18]

On October 26 of that year, Zhang Guohua and Tan Guansan led another 1,900 personnel from the 18th Army apparatus and its directly subordinate departments into Lhasa.[19] This included 584 people from the Southwest Bureau's Tibet Work Committee. The 154th Regiment entered Lhasa at the same time, bringing the total number of personnel to more than 5,100.[20] On December 1, Fan Ming led troops into Lhasa from the northwest under the name of the 18th Army Independent Detachment, and 700 cadres from the Central Committee Northwest Bureau's Tibet Work Committee arrived at the same time.[21] After entering Lhasa, the two TWCs merged into the CCP Tibet Work Committee.[22] In total, more than 6,000 party and military personnel entered Lhasa within the space of just four months.[23] By January 1952, the TWC apparatus had grown to 2,082 personnel and had established three area work committees.[24] Under the guise of the Independent Detachment, the TWC secretly established area work committees, formed party branches, and recruited party members throughout Tibet.[25]

At the same time, other PLA detachments entered Dzayul (Chayu),[26] Ngari, Taizhao,[27] Lhuntsé (Longzi),[28] Nagchu, and other strategic towns and districts.

The Tibet Military Command (TMC) was formally established on February 10, 1952. By August, the TMC had established six garrison commands and the Ngari cavalry unit.[29] At this point the CCP had more than 10,000 troops stationed in Tibet's main cities and other key locations, basically completing its comprehensive military occupation of Tibet and importing a complete CCP party apparatus. Because the party's main leaders were also military leaders, Tibet was effectively under military control.

But the military occupation was only the first step.

2

When the CCP party organization and military first entered Tibet, in accordance with Mao's directive, its main policy was not to "mobilize the masses" or reorganize the Tibetan army, but rather to implement an "anti-imperialist patriotic united front." Meanwhile, the TWC worked against time to resolve issues of transportation as well as production for their own needs so they could establish a footing in Tibet as quickly as possible.

In order to establish this rapid footing, the PLA began cultivating virgin land and planting crops as soon as it arrived.[30] There was only one planting season on the Tibetan plateau, however, and that was not enough to meet the PLA's food needs, while the cost of importing foodstuffs from inland was prohibitive.[31] In 1952, the CCP used diplomatic channels to allocate and transport 2,500 tons of rice from Guangdong Province to India and then bring it into Tibet through Dromo (Yadong). The first shipment arrived at Dromo in July. By April 1953, all of the rice had arrived, basically solving the food supply problem for the PLA and allowing it to establish a preliminary footing in Tibet.[32]

In July 1954, as described in chapter 1, the Dalai Lama and Panchen Lama went to Beijing to attend the National People's Congress. By then, the Qinghai-Tibet and Sichuan-Tibet highways were about to be open to traffic,[33] and the TWC had gained definite results in its united front work, improving relations with upper-level monks and lay leaders.[34] The TWC felt the situation was stable enough to begin preparing for social reform, and on November 22 it requested instructions from the CCP Central Committee on the question of "how to characterize all of the current reforms being undertaken in Tibet (including future land reform)."[35]

The answer came more than a half year later, on September 4, 1955: "Any reforms carried out among the Tibetan people must be part of the main task of the country's transition period."[36] According to CCP theory, "socialist transformation" was a top-down revolution led by the CCP, and its mission was to "completely eliminate the components of urban and rural capitalism" and establish a socialist society.[37]

The fact that Beijing replied to the TWC's question in September 1955, just when the Xikang and Sichuan provincial party committees were discussing land reform in the Tibetan and Yi minority areas, shows that the CCP had already fixed the specific objectives of social transformation in Tibet. For the TWC, this was the equivalent of the Central Committee issuing a directive: All objectives realized in the mainland would also be carried out in Tibet, and the transformation of Tibet was no exception.

Beginning in the second half of 1955, the TWC began moving from cautious united front work toward creating conditions for socialist transformation.[38]

When Mao received the leaders of a Tibetan tour group and Tibetan youth tour group on October 23, 1955, he told them, "After reforms, the nobility and the lamas will live the same as they did before. Whether or not to carry out reforms is up to you. You can discuss it."[39] A month later, Mao sent separate letters to the Dalai Lama and Panchen Lama that didn't even mention the word "reform."[40] Yet it was around this same time that Zhang Guohua sent Mao's secret directive to Fan Ming on preparing for reform in Tibet, which stated that "it was necessary to prepare for fighting."[41]

February 12, 1956, was New Year's Day in both the Chinese and Tibetan calendars. On that day, Tibetan officials[42] in Beijing went to Zhongnanhai to pay their New Year's respects to Mao and other national leaders. During their conversation, Mao gave two promises: After reform, "the nobility's lives will not change and will be the same as before or even better"; and "religious beliefs will also be exactly the same as before; people can believe whatever they believed before."[43] As to the specific timing of the reforms, Mao promised that it would be up to the Tibetans to decide.[44]

Although Mao emphasized that he didn't want Tibet to immediately embark on "democratic reform," he provided a clear timetable for the Preparatory Committee to begin researching the issue once it was established. Mao told the officials at the meeting to "go back and mull it over" and report to the Dalai Lama and Panchen Lama: "If it's feasible, then go for it."[45]

In January 1956, the Dalai Lama and the Panchen Lama each sent Mao telegrams with their New Year's greetings, and Mao again made no mention of reform in his reply cables.[46] And yet, by that point the CCP's social transformation of Tibet was well beyond the "mulling" stage and was in fact about to be implemented. The Tibet Autonomous Region (TAR) Party Congress held in Lhasa from January 16 to February 3, 1956, discussed a report by First Deputy Party Secretary Zhang Guohua.[47] Drafted by TWC deputy secretary Fan Ming, this report proposed twelve items for 1956, the most central of which was carrying out "preparation work for democratic reform."[48] Two weeks later, Chamdo held its second party congress to transmit the spirit of the TAR Party Congress and discuss "preparation work for democratic reform."[49]

As in the other Tibetan regions, all of this was first discussed and decided within the CCP.

3

One of the objectives of land reform in Sichuan's Tibetan areas was to serve as a model for the subsequent transformation of Tibet. The director of the Central Committee United Front Department, Li Weihan, made this clear in a speech at the fifth National United Front Work Conference on February 28, 1956.[50] However, very much against the expectations of the CCP's policy-makers, the land reform in Sichuan's Tibetan areas that was meant to serve as a model immediately encountered intense resistance from Tibetans.

As news of torture, taxation of monasteries, forcible confiscation of firearms, seizure of assets, and public denunciation of headmen and lamas reached Lhasa, the Tibetan leadership and public became alarmed. It was against this background that Vice-Premier Chen Yi came to Lhasa for the celebration of establishing the Preparatory Committee for the Autonomous Region of Tibet (PCART).

At the same time that the Khampas were engaged in intense resistance against the CCP's coercive land reform, the TWC was internally discussing preparations for reforms while also preparing and publicizing the establishment of PCART.[51] Before the Central Committee delegation arrived, the first group of Tibetan children joined the CCP's mass children's organization, the Young Pioneers, and soon after that, the TMC staged a ceremony to award rankings to the Tibetan army and Panchen Honor Guard Battalion.[52]

The Central Committee delegation led by Vice-Premier Chen Yi arrived in Lhasa on April 17, 1956.[53] Before Chen Yi set off, Mao had entrusted him with several matters, the first of which was to prepare for "reforms."[54] He was also instructed to find out the reason for the revolt in Kham.

The aforementioned process shows Mao's implementation of the second part of his plan for Tibet. The first step was to establish PCART, an organ of political power, to "gradually replace the traditional Tibetan government and feudal social organizations,"[55] and now the second step was to launch social reconstruction using the experience in Sichuan and other provinces as a model. Meanwhile, Mao continued to pacify the Dalai Lama, Panchen Lama, and other high-ranking Tibetans in order to keep the situation stable and allow time for preparation work to be carried out behind the scenes.

At a grand gathering of 1,083 people held in Lhasa on April 22, 1956, the Dalai Lama gave an opening speech that declared the formal establishment of the PCART. The Tupolev Tu-4 long-range bombers that just one month earlier had bombarded the Lithang, Chatreng Sampeling, and Bathang Ganden Pendéling monasteries[56] flew over Lhasa at ten o'clock that morning, dropping more than 300 kilos of multicolored leaflets over the Potala palace[57] and inspiring awe in people who had never seen "iron birds" before. Little did they know that three years later, these same airplanes would drop bombs on their homeland.

At the ceremony establishing the PCART, Chen Yi and Zhang Guohua both talked about "reforms." Chen Yi reiterated Mao's two promises to the assembled religious and lay leaders: that reform would be carried out "in accordance with the will of the Tibetan people," and "absolutely cannot be carried out by proxy by another ethnic group."[58] Zhang Guohua's speech followed the party line that the reforms "should not be undertaken in haste."[59]

However, the TWC was already planning to begin "reforms" as soon as the PCART was established. It had begun drafting the reform plan and had decided to launch the pilot project in Chamdo.[60] Once Chen Yi reached Tibet, the reform timetable became even clearer: "Insist on reforms, carry out the reform pilot project, and complete the reforms in three years."[61]

Chen Yi held a series of united front activities in Lhasa, hosting banquets for local officials and religious leaders, visiting the three major monasteries and distributing alms, and repeatedly holding forums with Tibetans of all ranks and social levels to understand their thinking and the reasons behind the uprisings in Kham.[62] After the delegation reported the situation to the Central Committee, Mao wrote a memo on the report on May 8, 1956, and required the Sichuan provincial party committee and Kangding prefectural party committee to analyze the delegation's report "according to the actual situation."[63]

On May 31, a Central Committee sub-delegation passed through Garzê on its way back to Beijing and "at key points along the Sichuan-Tibet highway made visits, gave alms, and presented gifts at temples and among leaders at the level of deputy county head and above," as well as holding seminars for cadres, upper-level religious and lay figures, and peasants in order to hear the views of all sides.[64] This shows that the highest levels of the CCP could not have been ignorant of the reasons for the Tibetan resistance in Kham.

Even so, the TWC's reform plan was not suspended. The TWC intensified its propaganda on reform. *Tibet Daily* published essays to launch the propaganda offensive, and the TWC recruited cadres and officials from the local population even as thousands of cadres from China's inland regions began arriving in Tibet.

On June 30, the TWC presented the Central Committee with its work plan for the next five years, and proposed "this winter and next spring implementing democratic reform focal pilot projects in Changdu and Rikaze."[65] As part of its plan to complete "democratic reform" within five years, it proposed quotas such as recruiting 4,000 to 6,000 public security policemen and adding 2,400 economic police,[66] recruiting 23,000 Tibetans into the party and 30,000 to 50,000 into the Communist Youth League, as well as training 50,000 to 70,000 Tibetan workers.[67] From then on, the preparatory work underwent a major expansion.

In Mao Zedong's talk with Sichuan provincial leaders known as "the July Directive," a number of concessions were made to ameliorate the effect of Tibentan rebellions on Lhasa. During the talks, Mao said, "future reforms in the Tibetan regions west of the Jinsha River must avoid major battles; by exhausting all efforts, it is possible to avoid war." But right after that, he added a "supplementary clause: be prepared to fight in a minority of areas where battles are impossible to avoid. There are 365 days in a year, and even a single day of fighting requires preparation. But we have to strive not to fight."[68]

These words suggest that although Mao acknowledged that reform might involve fighting, he had not yet decided to use warfare to carry out social transformation in Tibet. Even so, in 1956, the TMC's 308th Artillery Regiment was shifted from Zhamog (Zhamu)[69] to Lhasa, where it built artillery barracks on Lhasa's southern riverbank, across from the southeast end of the Dalai Lama's summer palace, Norbulingka. This installation, which the Tibetans called the "new army camp," may have been related to that "supplementary clause" in the talks.

On July 24, 1956, Zhou Enlai called together upper-level representatives of various ethnic groups in Beijing to transmit the "July Directive."[70] Zhou Enlai blamed the armed insurrections among Sichuan's Tibetan and Yi ethnic groups on "some people who once stood on the heads of the masses and cannot bear to give up their current personal benefits." He never mentioned the real reasons why members of the Tibetan and Yi ethnicities had rebelled, nor the harsh military repression that the CCP had inflicted on those regions. In the aftermath of the Kham suppression, Zhou Enlai made suggestions ("five opinions") that offered a certain degree of compromise.[71]

Even so, "compromise" was only a strategy for furthering the CCP's agenda, and there was no possibility that resistance among the masses would change the party's imperative of launching reform on the principle of "eliminating private ownership" in minority regions.

After learning of the situation in Kham during the CCP-imposed reforms, the Dalai Lama decided to initiate reform on his own in accordance with the "Seventeen-Point Agreement." In August 1956, he summoned all the senior government officials and told them to examine progress on the reform items announced in 1954. The government consequently held a meeting to discuss the relevant arrangements. Differing views were expressed during the meeting, but ultimately the government made the following resolutions:

1. Eliminate corvée labor, but before executing this, request subsidies from the Central Committee, and execute this measure after the Central Committee authorizes these subsidies.
2. A reform pilot scheme should be carried out under the unified leadership of the PCART. Reform pilot projects in the areas under the Panchen Lama's Administrative Council and in Chamdo would also be led by PCART.
3. A primary school should be established in each *dzong*.
4. At the suggestion of Lha'utara Tubten Tendar (*zhongyi qinmo*, i.e., senior secretary), it was decided that local leading cadres who were members of the PCART (at the level of department head and above) should regularly hold meetings, report on their work, and request instructions on related problems, with the *tsedrung* (accounts secretary) entrusted with draft organizational plans for the meetings.[72]

It is significant that the Tibetan government proposed carrying out reform pilot projects under the leadership of the PCART rather than under the TWC, because the relatively large number of Tibetan officials on the PCART allowed for greater Tibetan participation, while having the TWC lead the "reform pilot projects" would have implied excluding Tibetans from the process.

However, there are no indications that the TWC accepted this plan or the demand to have the "reform pilot scheme carried out under the leadership of the PCART." For the CCP, the entity leading the reforms was a paramount question of political power. When and how reforms would begin, and whether policies should be adjusted according to circumstances, all had to be decided by the party. This point was demonstrated with crystal clarity as the process subsequently developed in Tibet, starting with Chamdo, where the CCP's pilot reform program began in 1956 under the leadership of the Chamdo Party Committee.

Chapter 8

THE CHAMDO PILOT PROJECT AND "SIX YEARS WITHOUT CHANGE"

1

As the Dalai Lama left Beijing in mid-March 1955 and headed back for Lhasa, he began to understand what was actually involved in the CCP's "democratic reforms." His misgivings deepened as he traveled westward, and the hope and excitement that his trip to the inland had brought began to dissipate.[1]

During the Monlam Chenmo prayer festival in February 1956,[2] leaflets began to appear in Lhasa demanding that the People's Liberation Army withdraw from Tibet. The Chinese government responded by putting pressure on the Tibetan government to imprison three of the instigators.[3] After the PCART was established in April, the Central Committee delegation's sub-groups went to Shigatsé, Gyantsé, and other places to placate Tibetans in all sectors of society. Rumors were rampant in the markets and backstreets, some saying that "the establishment of the PCART brought ease and comfort to the nobility and the PLA but was nothing but bad news for ordinary people," and others that "the Dalai Lama's elder brother, Gyalo Dondrup, has already gone to the United States and will soon bring US and British troops to chase out the PLA." Yet others feared that the frequent flights in and out of Damshung (Dangxiong) airport were an ominous indication of impending war.[4]

Even as the reforms in Kham and Amdo sparked armed conflicts, the prospect of similar social reform in Tibet was not enough to bring the Tibetan government and the Panchen Lama's Administrative Council together to discuss how to deal with the situation that might emerge. The divergence in the attitudes of the two religious leaders showed that long-term ill will between Lhasa and Shigatsé played a role in the crisis that was about to emerge.[5] At the same time, some officials in Lhasa were disgruntled with their lack of personal advancement.[6]

With no improvement in the situation in Sichuan's Tibetan regions, tens of thousands of refugees from Kham and Amdo poured into Lhasa seeking the Dalai Lama's protection. The repeated battles in Kham and Amdo and the suffering of the people distressed the Dalai Lama. Once the PCART was established, however, the Tibetan government existed in name only, so all the Dalai Lama could do was register protests with Zhang Jingwu and Zhang Guohua, after which he sent two letters to Mao through the TWC.[7] At that point, the Dalai Lama still believed in the promises that Mao had made to him, and that everything happening in Kham and Amdo was the result of rash and reckless action by local cadres in contravention of Mao's directives.[8]

2

Mao wrote a letter to the Dalai Lama on August 18. By then, Mao had received Chen Yi's report and knew how all levels of Tibetan society felt about the CCP's social reform. In his letter, Mao acknowledged that "there have been disturbances in Sichuan," but that while "our work has also had its shortcomings," the main reason was "incitement by imperialist elements and Kuomintang remnant elements." The letter also said that "this is not yet the time for reforms" in Tibet, and that it was necessary to talk further, and complete mental preparation and make proper arrangements for everyone before implementation began. He also "hoped that the Tibet side would avoid disturbances as much as possible."[9]

At the time that Mao wrote this letter, however, "disturbances" were already occurring: "The intention to carry out reforms in Tibet has already given rise to an intense reaction in Changdu (mainly in the area east of Changdu and west of the Jinsha river). There has been social unrest here recently. The people are anxious, and there has been a string of looting incidents as well as rampant rumors."[10]

Chamdo, west of the Drichu River, was the area where the CCP had first established political power. The working motto of the Chamdo Liberation Committee over the previous few years had been to "execute the Seventeen-Point Agreement but not be bound by the Seventeen-Point Agreement. Do more, even to the extent of carrying out democratic reform."[11]

Before the PCART was established, the Chamdo area had been internally designated a test location for gaining experience with reform before implementing it throughout Tibet.[12] By then, fighting had already broken out in areas east of the Drichu, the Tupolev Tu-4s had already bombed the Lithang, Bathang, and Chatreng monasteries in Sichuan Province, and land reform had begun in Dechen (Deqin) County, Yunnan Province. Refugees were fleeing to Tibet from Sichuan and Yunnan, with some 1,000 households arriving in Chamdo alone, and they included "the wealthy as well as the poor."[13] They arrived with stories of public denunciations of lamas, forcible confiscations of weapons, and the seizure of private assets during the reforms.[14]

On April 30, 1956, Chen Yi met with officials of the third rank and above from the *Kashag*,[15] from the Panchen Lama's Administrative Council, and from the Chamdo Liberation Committee, and once again emphasized that "reform had to be carried out" but that "reform would be good, not bad."[16] After that, the Chamdo Liberation Committee held its fourth congress on May 21–23, with more than 300 monks and laypeople attending. This immediately caused unrest in Chamdo and created an extremely tense situation even before the trial implementation of land reform could begin.

Meanwhile, a large number of cadres were transferred to Chamdo from the inland to prepare for the launch of "reform," and large numbers of young people from the agricultural and pastoral areas were recruited for training as Tibetan cadres.[17]

On July 1, the TWC submitted to Beijing a work plan for 1956 to 1960 that included a proposal to launch reform pilot projects and a massive propaganda campaign in Chamdo and Shigatsé for the coming winter and following spring.

Beginning in June, the Chamdo party committee convened congresses to discuss the reforms. The congress held in Jomda[18] in the latter half of July declared the launch of reforms consisting largely of land reform, and that through "consultation,"[19] "the people's congress . . . pledges to resolutely execute the resolution passed by the PCART regarding reforms."[20] Yet internal documents acknowledged that "the upper, middle, and lower levels were coerced into passing the reforms at the (fourth) Chamdo Prefecture People's Congress and various *dzong* congresses; these people expressed superficial agreement at the meetings because they were under pressure, but in fact in their hearts they opposed it."[21]

In early August, the Jomda headman and chair of the *dzong* liberation committee, Chimé Gonpo, fled to the hills with the son of Dergé Gyalpo and occupied and blockaded a stretch of mountains, swearing never to accept the CCP's land reform. The Chamdo Liberation Committee sent its vice-chairman to talk them around, but Chimé Gonpo said he couldn't accept the kind of reforms that had been carried out east of the river.[22] He didn't believe in the CCP's policy of "peaceful consultation" and refused to return. As rumors spread of impending war, people fled into the mountains, leaving ripened crops unharvested in the fields. More than thirty maintenance crews working on the Kamtok (Gangtuo)-to-Chamdo segment[23] of the Sichuan-Tibet highway were raided; several of their outposts were burned down, and workers were injured.[24]

Even with resistance throughout Chamdo society, the TWC still sent its secretary general, Ya Hanzhang, to Chamdo to inspect "preparation work for reform."[25] When Ya arrived in Chamdo, he found it impossible to carry out preparation work, and on August 7, he reported to the TWC that two work teams had already been attacked and that "public anxiety was rife" in Chamdo.[26]

On August 10, the TWC secretary Zhang Guohua directed Chamdo to postpone the original plan and shift the main task to "do everything possible in united front work to mitigate the present tensions."[27] One week later, the regional work committee submitted an investigation report to the TWC acknowledging that "[during the congresses] we didn't carry out adequate consultation and discussion, and forced passage of the resolution. At the meetings, upper-strata elements unanimously expressed opposition to carrying out reforms."[28]

In early September, the PCART sent a high-level delegation[29] to Chamdo to smooth things over. Ngapo Ngawang Jigmé held several talks with members of the upper strata to communicate the content of documents relating to the reforms and to answer questions. The various local community representatives put forward three views:

1. They demanded that the PCART report to the Central Committee all of the errors that had been committed in implementing the reforms east of the river, and to promptly resolve the armed rebellions taking place there. People who had fled to Chamdo should be settled or sent back to their places of origin and return to their normal employment.
2. Were monasteries and lamas included in the consultation and voluntary implementation of reforms in the Tibetan regions? Did undertaking reform without fighting include unarmed fighting? Did the promise not to affect the income of monasteries include offerings and the giving of alms? It was hoped that the reforms and other matters would be carried out under the united leadership of the Dalai Lama and Panchen Lama and the PCART, in which case the community representatives would still be willing to accept reform even if mistakes occurred during the process.
3. It was hoped that the reforms would not affect religion.[30]

These views highlighted the fact that members of the upper strata were most concerned not about their personal assets, but rather about the future of religion and the safety of the monasteries. The fact that they would rather accept reforms led by the Dalai Lama and the Panchen Lama also showed their lack of trust in the Chinese government.

August and September 1956 brought multiple surprise attacks on work teams and convoys in Chamdo Prefecture, resulting in more than twenty casualties on the Chinese side. Soviet experts assisting the surveying and mapping were also imperiled and only escaped because PLA troops risked their lives to protect them. Transportation was impeded on the Sichuan-Tibet highway, with convoys frequently ambushed on this main supply line to Tibet. Most drivers had no battle experience and didn't even know how to fire a gun, so they worked in a state of terror. It was all that PLA troops and officers could do to keep from retaliating.[31]

By this time, there had been battles of varying scale in Dechen County in Yunnan, Garzê and Ngawa in Sichuan, Kanlho in Gansu, and Chamdo in Tibet. It was clear that people at all levels of society in all of the Tibetan regions opposed the CCP's reforms: There was resistance from the Dalai Lama, the Tibetan government, the three major monasteries, and right down to the local headmen and ordinary people, and in many eastern regions, local militia were prepared for a struggle to the death. Facing this situation, the Chinese government was forced to adjust its policies.

On September 4, 1956, the CCP Central committee sent a cable to the TWC rejecting the "five-year work plan" that it had submitted for 1956 to 1960 and ordered that the reforms be delayed, due to the fact that "the conditions are not yet ripe for implementing reforms in Tibet, and it is out of the question that our preparation work can be carried out in one or two years," as demonstrated by events in Chamdo. The Chinese government also acknowledged that "the Tibetan people up to now do not greatly trust the Han or the Central Committee" and "our party's extremely vital task is still to adopt all necessary and appropriate measures to dispel this mentality of distrust among the Tibetan people." To this end, Tibet's social reforms "are definitely not something for the first five-year plan, and perhaps also not for the second five-year plan, and perhaps must be delayed until the third five-year plan." During this time, the focus of the TWC's work was to "strive hard to produce results in order to facilitate preparations for reform."[32] In addition, the document proposed that in handling the problem of China's ethnic minorities, "it is necessary to consider the effect on various nationalities in the Asian region, especially the question of handling the Tibetan people."[33]

This directive of the CCP Central Committee to its subordinate organs was an internal party document. Although the document instructed the

TWC to explain its content to the Dalai Lama, Panchen Lama, and other upper-strata individuals, there is no evidence that the TWC did in fact give any account of it to the Tibetan leadership.[34]

3

While Chamdo was in upheaval, there was a sudden change in the plan for the Dalai Lama to go to India. Around June 1956, the Crown Prince of Sikkim, Dondrup Namgyal,[35] made a special trip to Lhasa to convey a letter from India's Mahabodhi Society inviting the Dalai Lama for activities commemorating the 2,500th anniversary of the death of the Buddha.

The Dalai Lama was ecstatic. Making a pilgrimage to India was not only his dream as a Buddhist, but even more importantly, at a time when Tibet was isolated and helpless, he wanted to meet Prime Minister Jawaharlal Nehru and seek guidance from this seasoned statesman. He immediately told Fan Ming, who at that time was in Lhasa managing the work of the TWC, and expressed his willingness to accept the invitation.[36]

Fan Ming's first response was to oppose it, but the matter was of such importance that he didn't dare act on his own initiative, so he immediately reported it to the Central Committee. On July 12, Zhou Enlai wrote a letter to the Dalai Lama regarding the visit, clearly stating his misgivings, and also mentioned the Dalai Lama's family members overseas. In a veiled threat, he reminded the Dalai Lama that the Chinese government was aware of the activities of his second-oldest brother, Gyalo Dondrup, in India.[37] In fact, Gyalo Dondrup and other Tibetan exiles were actively seeking international, and particularly American, support.

Soon after the Chinese government entered Tibet, the TWC and TMC each established their own intelligence apparatuses. The TWC's was headed by TWC deputy secretary Fan Ming, while the TMC's was headed by chief of staff Li Jue. Both submitted their own reports to higher-level departments. In 1956, Fan Ming sent intelligence to Beijing that he had obtained from India: "After the Dalai Lama leaves, he will not come back. He wants to seek the support of the American imperialists and international reactionary forces to declare independence for Tibet."[38]

Fan Ming had actually managed to obtain information about the Dalai Lama's visit to India, but the reality was not entirely as he presented it.

In 1955, India began preparing for Buddha Jayanti celebrations, to be held in Bodh Gaya in the fall of 1956, and intended to invite the Dalai Lama to attend. India placed considerable importance on this celebration and was inviting senior monks of all schools of Buddhism and Buddhist organizations from every country to attend. This was a purely religious activity, but Tibetan elites exiled in India, including Tsipon Shakabpa and the Dalai Lama's brother, Gyalo Dondrup, hoped to take this opportunity to persuade the Dalai Lama to seek political asylum in India. This would put him in a better position to gain support and help from India and the United States to change the situation in Tibet.[39]

Fan Ming's intelligence report may have been the reason that Beijing didn't approve the Dalai Lama's request after he had received the invitation through the Crown Prince of Sikkim in June of 1956. On October 1, then, Nehru formally issued an invitation to China for the Dalai Lama and Panchen Lama to attend the celebration in India.

Before the Chinese government could decide on its next move, the Hungarian uprising raised an outcry around the world, as Soviet tanks rolled through the streets of Budapest. The Dalai Lama was the foremost representative of Buddhism's Vajrayana tradition,[40] and his absence from a major religious celebration in India was certain to cause the rest of the world to draw undesirable conclusions at that time.

At a speech to the second plenum of the Eighth Central Committee on November 15, Mao Zedong mentioned the "Dalai Lama problem" in a resentful tone:

> The Buddha has been dead for 2,500 years and now Dalai wants to make a pilgrimage to India. Should we let him go or not? The Central Committee believes it's better to let him go and that it's not good not to let him go. He'll need to set off in a few days. We advised him to fly, but he insists on going by car and passing through Kalimpong, and Kalimpong has spies from every country, including Kuomintang secret agents.[41]

Mao directed the TWC and TMC to make full preparations: "Build the fortress and make sure there's plenty of food and water." As for the Dalai Lama, he said, "Let ten of them run off. It won't bother me."[42]

On November 17, 1956, the CCP Central Committee sent a cable to the TWC instructing it to do its utmost to provide tight security all the way to the Indian border, and also to make the best assessment possible of what was likely to happen when the Dalai Lama and Panchen Lama left Tibet. It ordered the TWC to "maintain a state of high alert and make ample preparations to deal with deteriorating circumstances."[43]

Chapter 9
DIPLOMATIC CLASHES
Zhou Enlai, Nehru, and the Dalai Lama

1

Mao's hesitation regarding the Dalai Lama's Indian visit involved a sensitive spot in the historical relationship between China, India, and Tibet. Due to geographical, economic, and cultural connections, Tibet had closer ties with India than with China, historically. Many Tibetan elites did business in India, and some of their children were educated there at private schools such as St. Joseph's College, a Jesuit college in Darjeeling.

During the Cold War era, India became a country over which both the United States and the Soviet Union tried to gain influence. Beijing believed that the Dalai Lama's Indian trip might expose him to potential foreign influence, especially from the United States, through his brother Gyalo Dondrup.

Prior to 1949, the US government had only limited knowledge of the situation in Tibet and no explicit "Tibet policy." It was not until April 1949, as the CCP was about to seize political power over all of China, that the US government noticed the "ideological and strategic importance" of Tibet and, for a time, considered recognizing Tibet as an independent nation. Various considerations led the US government to conclude that acknowledging Tibet's independent status would only accelerate the CCP's occupation of Tibet, while also infuriating the moribund Nationalist government. After weighing the situation, the US government decided that it would maintain friendly relations with the Tibetan government as long as this didn't give the Nationalist government the impression of "any alteration in our position toward Chinese authority over Tibet."[1]

In December 1950, the Tibetan government asked the Dalai Lama, newly installed in Tibet's paramount political and religious position, to go to Dromo, near the Indian border. He stayed in a monastery there and waited for the situation to develop, prepared to flee to India at any moment in case the CCP took Tibet by military force. At that time, both the CCP and the US government were vying for influence over the Dalai Lama. The CCP hoped the Dalai Lama would return to Lhasa as soon as possible,[2] while the US government hoped he would go into exile.[3] Finally, the Dalai Lama decided to return to Lhasa.

After the CCP occupied Tibet, much of the US government's understanding of Tibet's internal situation came from the Crown Prince of Sikkim. The royal family of Sikkim had intermarried with Tibetan nobility for generations and also had extensive contacts among India's upper crust and in foreign diplomatic circles. The Dalai Lama's second-oldest brother, Gyalo Dondrup, was another source of information about conditions in Tibet.[4]

After the insurrection in Kham in 1956, Gyalo Dondrup sent a letter to the US embassies and consulates in the United Kingdom, New Delhi, Calcutta, Hong Kong, and Taipei, as well as to India's main newspaper, *The Statesman*. The letter was not made public in England, the United States, or India, but was passed along to the United States State Department, the United States Central Intelligence Agency (CIA), and the armed forces.[5]

Although the CIA was interested in the Tibetans' resistance against Communist China, it didn't understand enough about the scale and extent of the resistance or its actual needs. The US government also needed the Dalai Lama or the *Kashag* government to come forward to ask for help before it could unequivocally justify assisting the Tibetans.[6]

On June 28, 1956, the Crown Prince of Sikkim returned to India from Tibet and went to the US consulate general in Calcutta, at which point the Americans became aware of the possibility of the Dalai Lama going to India. The Crown Prince told the consul general of the intense battles taking place in eastern Tibet and suggested that the Americans provide the Tibetans with arms and training, and he said that the Dalai Lama "clearly intended to leave his country."[7] American officials were very interested in this news.

The Dalai Lama's delegation to India left Lhasa for Shigatsé on November 20 of that year, and from there they were joined by the Panchen Lama's delegation on to Dromo.

2

In the hill town of Kalimpong, near Darjeeling, in the Indian state of West Bengal, an established Tibetan population ran shops, businesses, and guest houses catering to the caravan trade. After the CCP occupied Tibet, some Tibetan officials migrated to Kalimpong, or to the regional capital, Darjeeling.

In 1952, Gyalo Dondrup bought a house between Kalimpong and Darjeeling and lived there with his family. He spoke fluent Chinese "and in his appearance and bearing was indistinguishable from a Chinese," which led some *Kashag* officials to regard him as "pro-China." At the same time, his close relations with Kuomintang leaders led the CCP to regard him as "very possibly a Kuomintang agent and international spy."[8] Both sides worried about his influence over the Dalai Lama. Yet the Dalai Lama believed that his second-oldest brother's true loyalty was to Tibet.[9]

Kalimpong and Darjeeling, at 1,800 meters above sea level, were famous resort areas in India. When the Bengal plains languished in the stifling summer heat, members of the Indian and foreign elites flocked to these towns, with their crisp air below snow-capped mountains. Their winding streets teemed with Tibetan monks in deep-red robes, Indian yogis in saffron robes, Westerners of obscure identity, Taiwanese secret agents, Chinese Communist spies, and destitute exiled Khampas. Kalimpong had a Tibetan-language newspaper, the *Tibet Mirror*, that published news that made its way to India from the three Tibetan regions, such as pictures drawn by Tibetan witnesses of the 1956 bombings of monasteries in Kham.

After leaving Tibet, Gyalo Dondrup casually ran a business and took his family around Darjeeling's polite society during his leisure hours. He was a member of the tennis club, and one day in November 1956, he found himself playing doubles with an unknown American about the same age as him. After the game, the American guided him to a spot where they could chat in private and introduced himself as the CIA officer John Hoskins, stationed in Kalimpong.[10]

Several days later, Gyalo Dondrup went to Sikkim with Taktser Rinpoché (the Dalai Lama's and Gyalo Dondrup's oldest brother), who had hurried over from the United States. On the Sikkim side of the Nathu La pass that connects Sikkim with Dromo in Tibet, they met the Dalai Lama and his traveling party, which included his two other brothers. It was the first time that all five brothers had ever been all together at the same time (they were so far apart in age that they had not all grown up together).

On November 25, the Dalai Lama and Panchen Lama flew separately to New Delhi, where they were met by Indian VIPs and many Tibetans living in India, including former monks from the Lithang Monastery, Kelsang Gyadotsang and Athar Norbu. Athar Norbu's friend Lotse also poked his head above the crowd and watched from a distance.[11]

3

On the day he reached New Delhi, the Dalai Lama immediately launched into a string of high-profile diplomatic activities that served as a cover for a tense alternative itinerary.

Nehru received the Dalai Lama on November 26. The Dalai Lama described the situation in Kham and said that he wanted to stay in India until "we could win back our freedom by peaceful means."[12]

Nehru told him that India was "not in the position to give any effective help to Tibet, nor were other countries in a position to do so." He advised the Dalai Lama to return to Tibet and "work peacefully to try to carry out the Seventeen-Point Agreement."[13]

Two days later, the Chinese premier, Zhou Enla, arrived in New Delhi for a state visit.[14] But he had an additional mission: He was under Mao's orders to convince the Dalai Lama to return to Tibet.

Currently available materials provide no evidence that the Chinese government had learned of the Dalai Lama's asylum request. However, when he gave his speech at the ceremony commemorating the Buddha's *nirvana,* the Dalai Lama ignored the script that Ngapo Ngawang Jigmé (who had been given the PLA rank of lieutenant general in 1955 and appointed the first deputy commander of the TMC) had prepared for him in Lhasa; instead, he delivered a speech expressing what he himself wished to say. To the Chinese government, this was enough to prove that "the separatists had had an effect on him."[15]

Although Mao had commented internally that he didn't care if the Dalai Lama remained in India, that was not in fact the truth. For Mao, the Dalai Lama obtaining political asylum in India would implicitly destroy the CCP's myth of its "peaceful liberation of Tibet." Consequently, while the Dalai Lama was visiting India, Zhou Enlai put in his best efforts to ensure his return to Tibet.

Zhou Enlai had his first talk with the Dalai Lama on November 29, his second day in New Delhi.[16] Regarding land reform in Kham, Zhou acknowledged that "there were operational errors, and some things weren't done well," but he put the blame on local cadres: "Sichuan Province didn't consider things carefully enough when formulating policies, and when errors occurred they didn't correct them quickly enough, so they're to blame."[17] Of course, he didn't mention that Sichuan's land reform plan had originated with the Central Committee and had been approved by the highest levels of government, or that the Tupolev Tu-4s had bombed the Lithang, Chatreng, and Bathang monasteries under orders from the CMC.

During this conversation, Zhou Enlai promised the Dalai Lama: "All reforms in Tibet, including Changdu, Anterior Tibet (Qianzang), and Posterior Tibet (Houzang),[18] have to be agreed on by you. Chairman Mao wanted me to pass this message to you this time. As Chairman Mao sees it, this is definitely not the time to talk of reform, and it won't be done until everyone is settled."[19] He also mentioned that if the Dalai Lama's two older brothers found themselves short of money overseas, "We can instruct our embassy in India to send some foreign exchange for you to give to them."[20]

On the night of November 30, after Zhou Enlai attended a cocktail party at the Chinese embassy, he invited the Dalai Lama and his mother, older sister, two older brothers, and two tutors to dinner at the embassy.[21] During the banquet, the Dalai Lama's brothers frankly expressed their discontent to Zhou Enlai regarding the dispute over the status of the Dalai Lama and the Panchen Lama.[22] Zhou Enlai "remained as polite and suave as ever" in reacting to these pointed comments and made a number of promises, before making a request to the Dalai Lama's brothers: convince the Dalai Lama to return to Tibet.[23]

On December 7, Zhou Enlai reported to Mao that he felt that the visit of the Dalai Lama and Panchen Lama to India was going well, but that there was still a question of whether "the Americans would use Dalai's older brother to convince him to go to America."[24]

4

On December 12, 1956, the TWC sent a cable informing Beijing of possible rebellions in Lhasa and other places. The Central Committee's United Front Department drafted a reply on December 15. While vetting the draft cable the next day, Mao added a paragraph repeating the directive to delay the reforms that the Central Committee had already given the TWC on September 4, explicitly stating for the first time that "there would be no reforms for six years."[25] This was subsequently referred to as the "concessionary policy" of "no reforms for six years," but Mao attached a condition to this "concession": "If counterrevolutionary elements under foreign direction do not engage in consultation and insist on breaking the Seventeen-Point Agreement through rebellion and war and undermine the situation in Tibet, this may arouse the working people to rise up and topple the feudal system and establish a people's democracy in Tibet."[26]

In this draft cable, Mao directed the TWC to "widely communicate the policy of no reforms for six years within the party and among the Tibetan upper strata" and to "arrange for an informal discussion with the main officials of the PCART and *Kashag*." In other words, what this means is that before the Dalai Lama visited India, Beijing's order to delay the reforms was still being discussed at the highest levels, and even the Communist Party's middle and lower-ranking cadres in Tibet hadn't been notified. While vetting the draft cable, Mao also added the words: "Also send it to the embassy in Burma to pass on to Premier Zhou, and send it to the embassy in India for their information." It is clear that the Dalai Lama's return to Lhasa was quite important to Mao. He not only had the directive of "no reforms for six years" passed on to Zhou Enlai, but also telephoned Zhou that same day to inform him of the situation in Tibet.[27]

On December 27, while the Dalai Lama was still in Bodh Gaya, where he had gone for the Buddha Jayanti celebrations, he received an urgent summons to return to New Delhi immediately. Zhou Enlai was returning to New Delhi for his second stop in India after his three-day visit to Pakistan on his six-nation tour. The first time had been an official state visit, but this second time he was just "passing through" India on his way back to China. The Dalai Lama hurried back to New Delhi as requested, where Zhou Enlai had a second conversation with him. Zhou talked about five issues, one of which was reforms in Tibet. Zhou told the Dalai Lama, "Chairman Mao wants to tell you it is certain that there will be no talk of reforms during the second five-year plan. After six years, if it looks like reforms are possible, it will still be up to you to decide, based on the circumstances and conditions."[28]

This conversation came a month after Zhou's first conversation with the Dalai Lama, and it was during that month that Mao made the final decision not to carry out reforms for six years. Mao's concession was a response to the possibility that the Dalai Lama might remain in India. During this conversation, Zhou Enlai also told the Dalai Lama that he had talked with Prime Minister Nehru and that the Dalai Lama could not expect help from Nehru.[29]

Finally, Zhou Enlai told the Dalai Lama, "Overall, the best thing is for you to return soon, because some people want to use your absence as an opportunity to create unrest and put you in a difficult situation that will be hard for you to manage after you go back. Chairman Mao hopes you'll return soon and not go to Kalimpong. It wouldn't be good for you to go there."[30]

The day after this conversation, Zhang Jingwu sent the Dalai Lama a cable through the Chinese Embassy in India, notifying him of the decision not to carry out reforms for six years. At the same time, he informed the Dalai Lama that "reactionaries within the *Kashag* are plotting to carry out an armed rebellion in Lhasa," and he, too, urged the Dalai Lama and Panchen Lama to return to Tibet as soon as possible.[31]

5

Kelsang Gyadotsang, the former monk from Lithang Monastery, and his twenty-odd companions followed the Dalai Lama around India in the guise of volunteer security guards. Gyalo Dondrup had arranged for the group of Khampas to pay their respects to the Dalai Lama in the hope of gaining his support for an open revolt, but the Dalai Lama advised them to be patient and to use nonviolent methods to fight for their freedom. Consequently, Kelsang and the others used secret channels to attempt to "create incidents" in Lhasa. The Khampas reckoned that if something happened in Lhasa, the Dalai Lama would be compelled to remain in India. News of the plot leaked out, however, and it did not succeed.[32]

Meanwhile, Gyalo Dondrup and his new tennis partner discussed the possibility of help from the US government. They decided to first select a group of reliable youths to be trained by the CIA in basic intelligence skills and then send them back to Tibet to gather intelligence that would help the CIA confirm recipients and means of assistance. In Bodh Gaya, the Dalai Lama's oldest brother, Taktser Rinpoché, took photos of the Khampas who had accompanied the Dalai Lama there and also spoke with them individually. These photographs were secretly sent to the CIA.[33] A few weeks later, six of them were selected to be the first group of CIA trainees and were sent to Saipan.

Zhou Enlai had a third conversation with the Dalai Lama on New Year's Day, 1957. Before this conversation, Zhou Enlai had had a long, confidential talk with Nehru during which he raised the Tibet issue and spoke of the McMahon Line (the boundary between India and Tibet originally negotiated by the British and the Tibetan government in 1914), suggesting that "after the Dalai Lama returns to Lhasa" a decision could be made on "recognizing this line."[34] Nehru took the hint and said: "Our policy has been to deal with the Chinese government about Tibet and the treaty on Tibet was also signed with the Chinese government. We are naturally interested in what happens in Tibet as one of our near neighbours but we don't want to interfere."[35] Zhou Enlai hadn't mentioned the longstanding border issue during his formal state visit, and it was only when he was passing through India on his return that he took the initiative to raise this issue with Nehru and make a subtle promise, clearly because he was asking something of Nehru. Nehru also understood that.

Zhou Enlai had a well-thought-out strategy for dealing with the young Dalai Lama. He had already reached a tacit agreement with Nehru on the possibility of the Dalai Lama seeking political asylum in India, and he told the Dalai Lama explicitly that if "turmoil occurred" in Kalimpong, Nehru would "take action to stop it."[36]

Now Zhou Enlai once again promised the Dalai Lama that there would be "no reforms for six years," and that "whether or not to have reforms after six years, and what kind of reforms, will be up to you to decide."[37]

As to the battle in Kham, Zhou Enlai made light of it, saying that it was only "some people who don't understand the situation who have been causing trouble, encircling one of our armies and preventing cadres and soldiers from getting anything to eat for a few days. In order to protect these troops, we sent in the air force to deliver grain, and a military conflict broke out as a result." He said he "hoped that Lhasa would send someone to make an inspection and assist in dealing with the aftermath."

Next, Zhou Enlai had a talk with the senior *Kashag* officials accompanying the Dalai Lama to India and told them, "Someone wants to keep the Dalai Lama in India and declare Tibet independent, and that will not be allowed to happen."[38]

After this round of talks, Zhou Enlai sent a cable to the Central Committee about the Dalai Lama returning to Tibet. "Dalai insists on going to Kalimpong and refuses to fly back to Tibet. I've already informed Dalai and his five officials of the advantages and disadvantages and have left it to him to decide, hoping he will return to Tibet soon. If he absolutely insists on going to Kalimpong, I'm not going to forcibly dissuade him. If unrest breaks out and he is unable to return to Tibet, the responsibility will be borne by Dalai and the Indian government."[39]

That night, Nehru talked with the Dalai Lama and explicitly told him that India would not support Tibet.[40]

Up to this point, it could be said that Mao had spared no effort in ensuring that the Dalai Lama returned to Tibet.

6

On January 22, 1957, the 21-year-old Dalai Lama and his retinue left Calcutta for Kalimpong. There he met the former Tibetan prime minister, Lukhangwa, who had just come from Lhasa on a pilgrimage and who asked the Dalai Lama to remain in India. In accordance with traditional etiquette, the *Kashag* government dispatched a delegation, led by Kalon Yutok, a cabinet minister in the Tibetan government,[41] to beseech the Dalai Lama to return to Tibet, but in private, Yutok told him that the situation in Lhasa was unfavorable and advised him not to go back.[42] The Dalai Lama's older brothers Gyalo Dondrup and Taktser Rinpoché held the same opinion; without going into detail, they told the Dalai Lama and his officials that the US government would support the Tibetan people's resistance.[43]

Ngapo Ngawang Jigmé, however, felt that American support was unreliable, not to mention that the Tibetans didn't have a concrete plan, and that under those circumstances, the Dalai Lama should return to Lhasa.[44] On January 31, Ngapo returned to Tibet before the others because his wife was about to give birth. He clearly understood that this implied throwing in his lot with the Chinese government. After returning to Lhasa, he immediately went to see Tan Guansan, who at that time was the Military Command political commissar in charge of operations in Tibet, and asked to join the party. He also requested that he and his entire family be allowed to accompany the PLA if it withdrew from Tibet.[45]

Once again, the Dalai Lama confronted a hard decision. He knew that he'd been forsaken by India, his only possible ally. Even if the distant US government provided some limited aid to Tibet, it wouldn't be "because they cared about Tibetan independence, but as part of their global strategy to oppose communist countries,"[46] and that kind of support was unreliable. On the other hand, he had doubts about Mao's promise not to carry out reforms for six years. As he hesitated, the Dalai Lama resorted to the tradition of requesting instructions from the state oracle, and the oracle told him to go back. In early February, therefore, the Dalai Lama and his retinue left Kalimpong for Sikkim.

Chapter 10

OBSCURE EVENTS IN 1957

1

The Dalai Lama's return to Lhasa in February 1957 was obstructed by a major snowstorm. After waiting in Sikkim for nearly a month, he finally arrived in Dromo on February 25. On the way back to Lhasa, he convened public meetings in Dromo, Gyantsé, and Shigatsé, trying to put people's minds at rest by telling them of Zhou Enlai's promise of "no reforms for six years."

Meanwhile, the CCP was making a major decision.

Mao publicly informed the party of his policy of "no reforms for six years"[1] in Tibet at the Supreme State Conference on February 27, 1957—but what about the other Tibetan regions?

At the end of February, Liao Zhigao, now the third Sichuan provincial party secretary (following the dissolution of Xikang Province in 1955), made a special trip to Dartsedo and called a meeting of prefectural party committee members and county party secretaries to solicit grassroots views on whether or not to continue with land reform. Land reform in Garzê was by then a foregone conclusion, and the county party secretaries were quite unwilling to abandon the task half-finished, arguing that "even if the democratic reforms were halted, the situation in Ganzi Prefecture would not necessarily stabilize, and the armed rebellions wouldn't end, so it would not serve to stabilize the situation in Tibet."[2] Therefore, the Sichuan provincial party committee sent a report to the Central Committee on March 5, giving reasons why the "reforms" should continue.[3]

On the same day, in Beijing, the secretary of the Central Committee Secretariat, Deng Xiaoping, presided over a Tibet work meeting that heard a report from Zhang Jingwu. The meeting, attended by the heads of relevant Central Committee departments and the leaders of the TWC, Zhang Guohua, Fan Ming, Zhou Renshan, Wang Qimei, and others, formed a resolution to undertake a "major retrenchment in Tibet work, the sooner the better," and to "resolutely and swiftly withdraw personnel."[4]

On March 9, while the Dalai Lama was still on his way back to Lhasa, the Central Committee Secretariat held another meeting, this time to discuss the problems in Garzê. Deng Xiaoping presided over the meeting and delivered the summing-up speech. The meeting decided to "resolutely carry out reforms east of the river," meaning that the reforms in Sichuan's Tibetan regions would continue. As for war: "When fighting is necessary, fight ruthlessly and be prepared to fight hard. . . . We're in a state of war, and not fighting yesterday doesn't mean we can't fight today. We should concentrate our forces on one place at a time and pacify one area at a time. We can never let up on political win-over and military attacks, but we have to fight some good battles before we can win them over."[5] Two days later, Mao wrote a memo approving the report of the Sichuan provincial party committee.[6]

Less than two weeks after the issuing of this document, known as the "Central Committee March Directive," the Garzê prefectural party committee revised its land reform policy. After a brief easing in 1956, then, land reform measures in Sichuan's Tibetan regions toughened up once again.

Meanwhile, the TWC was busy arranging for personnel to be withdrawn to the inland regions. At that time, the TWC and PCART apparatus had 406 organs of various kinds and more than 45,000 cadres, students, and workers. These were to be reduced to 3,700 personnel, while the 50,000-strong army would shrink to 13,000–18,000. But when it came time to implement the reductions, although the numbers of personnel were indeed reduced, the strongholds were not removed according to plan, and the area work committees were not withdrawn.[7] The 3,000 minority cadres who had already been recruited were sent for training as a reserve for future land reform.

The two meetings of the Central Committee Secretariat thus adopted completely different policies for Garzê and for Tibet regarding land reform. In Tibet, the policy was to "resolutely withdraw," while in Kham it was to "resolutely continue."

On April 2, 1957, the Central Committee Secretariat sent Su Yu[8] to Sichuan as a representative to inspect the pacification of Tibetan rebellions and the implementation of reforms, and at the same time "to make appropriate military arrangements to safeguard the democratic reforms in areas east of the Jinsha river."[9] In a speech to leaders of the Chengdu Military Command and Sichuan provincial party committee on April 8, Su Yu told them that the significance of "reforming and strengthening this region [western Sichuan]" was to "create the conditions for reforming Tibet," and that crushing the Tibetan people's resistance with military power was "a demonstration to the Tibetan ruling class. It influences the Tibetan masses and enhances their consciousness, while at the same time influencing Tibet's upper strata and making them aware of the overall trend."[10]

The Chinese government's willingness to impose land reform in Kham and Amdo through armed force also involved economic and strategic factors. Su Yu explained this point in a speech at a Chengdu Military Command Military Joint Conference on May 6: "The ethnic minority areas of Sichuan's Kang Prefecture, northern Yunnan, southern Gansu, and southern Qinghai have very rich underground mineral resources: gold, silver, iron, copper, tin, tungsten—all kinds of things. . . . Of course we should exploit these rich resources."[11] Su Yu went on to say that because the southeastern coastal provinces were China's industrial center, and the coast was also "the direction from which our enemies can most easily attack . . . in terms of national defense, it is very important for us to build iron and steel bases and industrial bases in the rear area."[12] Sichuan in particular, with its large population, had more optimal conditions than the northwest to serve as a rear area.

2

The Dalai Lama reached Lhasa on April 1, 1957.

Among the crowd gathered to welcome him stood a young Amdo woman, Drolkar Gye, wearing a splendid gown and a costly coral necklace. She watched the Dalai Lama's entourage arrive, her heart heavy with foreboding.[13] Drolkar Gye was from the Khetse *tsowa,*[14] a pastoral area, in the Labrang (Labuleng) region.[15] Over the previous few years, great changes had come to her homeland, and her husband had become an "armed rebel" and fled to Lhasa. Drolkar Gye had followed her husband into exile. As he was often away, she ran a small shop to eke out a living. It could be considered a peaceful existence, but now even in Lhasa the situation was becoming increasingly tense. Unable to return home and with nowhere else to go, Drokar Gye struggled on, believing that better things were yet to come. Now that the Dalai Lama had returned from India, she allowed herself to hope that life would soon return to normal.

After only a few months' absence, the Dalai Lama discovered that the atmosphere in Lhasa had become quite abnormal indeed. The number of tents in the open area outside the city had increased significantly—they made up a disorderly refugee camp set up by Tibetan families who had fled from Kham and Amdo. The Chinese government office buildings around the Jokhang temple, meanwhile, had installed defense fortifications in their windows and on their roofs.[16]

How critical was the situation? A violent incident on January 10 of that year had left three Tibetans (one of them a member of Lhasa's small Muslim population) dead and three injured.[17] This was the first instance of armed conflict since the PLA had entered Lhasa in 1951. The incident had reportedly been triggered by "bad elements" who "provoked Tibetan cadres," and although there were casualties, it went no further.

Another conflict between the PLA and Tibetans, however, which occurred in late March and was referred to as the "incident of Kunsang the cart driver," nearly triggered an exchange of gunfire between the PLA and the Tibetan Army. In accordance with tradition, the *Kashag* government had been building a new residence for the current Dalai Lama in the Norbulingka compound, where several previous Dalai Lamas had had their summer palaces. The construction project required rocks to be hauled on horse-drawn carts from the banks of the Lhasa River. One day, a horse cart loaded with rocks was obstructed by PLA soldiers guarding the bridge, and an argument broke out. The cart driver, named Kunsang, raised his whip, and a soldier shot him dead. A Tibetan army battalion then encircled the PLA guard unit's barracks, after which the PLA unit stationed in Lhasa sent reinforcements to encircle the Tibetan troops. The TMC ordered a regiment stationed in Zhamog to hurry to Lhasa within seven days.[18] Eventually, Zhang Guohua went to the Norbulingka compound to apologize to the Dalai Lama over the matter.[19] The incident was resolved, but it caused great anger among the residents of Lhasa.[20]

It was in the midst of these tensions that the Dalai Lama returned to Lhasa. The crowd welcoming him home included a group of Khampas, some of them traders who lived in Lhasa and others refugees who had fled CCP's reforms in Kham.

As the Dalai Lama's guard of honor entered the Potala palace, the crowd dispersed.

3

At this time, all three Tibetan regions were experiencing greater disintegration than ever before in history. Rulers and leaders who had enjoyed established positions of power had now become the Chinese government's "united front targets," drawing hefty official salaries, and people at the bottom rungs of society were succumbing to the CCP's propaganda offensive. The result was a massive reorganization of political power. At society's lowest levels, some joined the resistance, while others joined the new power circles.

A Lithang wool trader named Gonpo Tashi found himself in the eye of the storm. His encounters with the Chinese government had begun early on. Once in 1949, when his caravan was carrying 110 loads of wool and tobacco to Dartsedo, Chinese cadres had confiscated his goods as "smuggled foreign merchandise" and locked up the caravan drivers. After repeated negotiations, his employees were released, but not his goods. After the Chinese government entered Lithang, he became a united front target and was selected to join a tour of the inland regions, but he found an excuse to refuse and sent a servant in his place.

Given his frequent trips to Lhasa, Gonpo Tashi kept a home there and was active among the Lithang businessmen in the city. In 1956, news of an emergency situation in Gonpo Tashi's homeland reached Lhasa. He knew that the piecemeal resistance of the local militia was no match for the powerful Communist army, and that it would be necessary to unify forces. In early 1957, therefore, he began considering how to organize the armed forces of the three regions into a popular military organization. He knew very well that the Tibetans' weapons were outdated and the men lacked training, and that outside support was needed.

Gonpo Tashi went to the Tibetan government for help, only to meet with polite refusal, so he turned his attention outside the borders. He had three nephews, the Gyadotsang brothers Wangdu, Burgang, and Kelsang. The brothers had lost their mother at an early age and Gonpo Tashi had raised them. At that time, all of them were in Kalimpong; when the Dalai Lama visited India, the three brothers were among the twenty or so young Khampas who had volunteered to serve as his bodyguards. While in India, they provided Gonpo Tashi with essential assistance by buying weapons and radios and passing information to him. He himself seems to have had no direct contact with CIA personnel in India from 1955 to 1959, but his nephew Kelsang had some brief contact with the American embassy.[21]

Everyone knew that the Chinese government had eyes and ears throughout Lhasa, and given Gonpo Tashi's prominence in the local Khampa business community, it would have been very difficult for him to call a meeting to discuss united resistance against Communist rule without attracting attention. But after the Dalai Lama returned to

Lhasa, Gonpo Tashi came up with the idea of presenting him with a gold throne. He had two objectives in mind: to use the throne project as an opportunity to bring various leaders together to discuss a united resistance, and at the same time to galvanize the Tibetan people's loyalty to the Dalai Lama in a way that united the various social strata. He relayed the idea of the gold throne to the Dalai Lama through the lord chamberlain, Phala Tubten Woeden,[22] and after securing agreement, he contacted a wide range of people in order to find a workspace and hire artisans. Using the project as cover, he then set about preparing a popular armed force. After more than a month, the casting of a magnificent gold throne had been completed, and a guerrilla force called Chushi Gangdruk—"Four Rivers and Six Ranges"—had begun to take shape.

The gold throne was presented to the Dalai Lama during a grand religious ceremony at Norbulingka on July 4, 1957. It was accompanied by a letter in which representatives of various localities asked the Dalai Lama to assume leadership of all three Tibetan regions and ensure that land reform was not carried out for six years in any of them.[23]

However, the CCP Central Committee's directive to the TWC on May 14 had already explicitly stated that the Dalai Lama had no say in other Tibetan regions.[24] In other words, the Dalai Lama was in no position to comment on events in Kham and Amdo.

4

From April to May 1957, while Gonpo Tashi and his friends were secretly plotting a united popular resistance, battles were still ongoing in Yunnan and Sichuan, and the Chinese government was beginning a series of military arrangements in Chengdu.

From May 2 to 6 of that year, the PLA general chief of staff, Su Yu, called a joint military conference of the leaders of the Sichuan, Gansu, Qinghai, and Yunnan military sub-regions, as well as the secretary of the Chamdo Work Committee, to exchange experiences and lessons and to resolve the issue of mutual cooperation in battle operations. Su Yu passed along the Central Committee's intentions: "The better we fight and the more enemies we annihilate, the better we can facilitate negotiations and the more easily we can mobilize the masses." He also stated that "under our absolute advantage," they would use the method of "catching the ringleader in order to catch the bandits," and the battle strategy of "destroying the main instigators so the others will be too afraid to fight, prompting internal vacillation and affecting the overall situation."[25] Su Yu had devised a pithy and easy-to-understand formula with which the Military Command representatives could refer to this military tactic.

In that same month, the CCP Central Committee directed Yunnan as follows: "In the Tibetan agricultural areas it is necessary to mobilize the masses, mainly through political contention but backed by military force, in order to pacify the armed rebellion and prepare for reforms."[26] Yunnan's Lijiang military sub-district followed up by organizing a "frontline command post" that prepared to push through land reform with the backing of military force. A new round of military actions was about to begin.

At this time, far away on Saipan Island, the six Khampas were finishing their training and the CIA was preparing to send them back to India. Gonpo Tashi's nephew Kelsang Gyadotsang was responsible for buying the Tibetan robes, bowls, boots, and other items they needed for their return to Tibet.[27]

And while these various forces were wrestling or preparing to wrestle with each other, the Nyarong leader Dorjé Yudon and her family were hiding from pursuing PLA troops in the hills along the Nyagchu; the Dhunkhug village headman Aten, who had been recruited as a grassroots cadre, was already having a change of heart; and along the Nyichu between Garzê and Sertar counties, the young monk Yetan was hiding in the mountains with his parents and sisters after their home had been burned down in battle.

Chamdo was in a state of war. Its people steadfastly rejected the Chinese government's reforms, and armed farmers and herders in the mountains engaged in repeated confrontations with the PLA and its advanced weaponry.

In Qinghai's Golok Prefecture, on the lush pasturelands at the headwaters of the Yellow River, a new term began circulating that herders found hard to understand: collectivization. The herder Ngolo and her family were tense and uneasy, uncertain what to do. Members of the Khangsar tribe in Chikdril (Jiuzhi) County were also anxious, as all kinds of rumors spread.

Several months later, the verdant grasslands of Qinghai would be engulfed in a surging red tide.

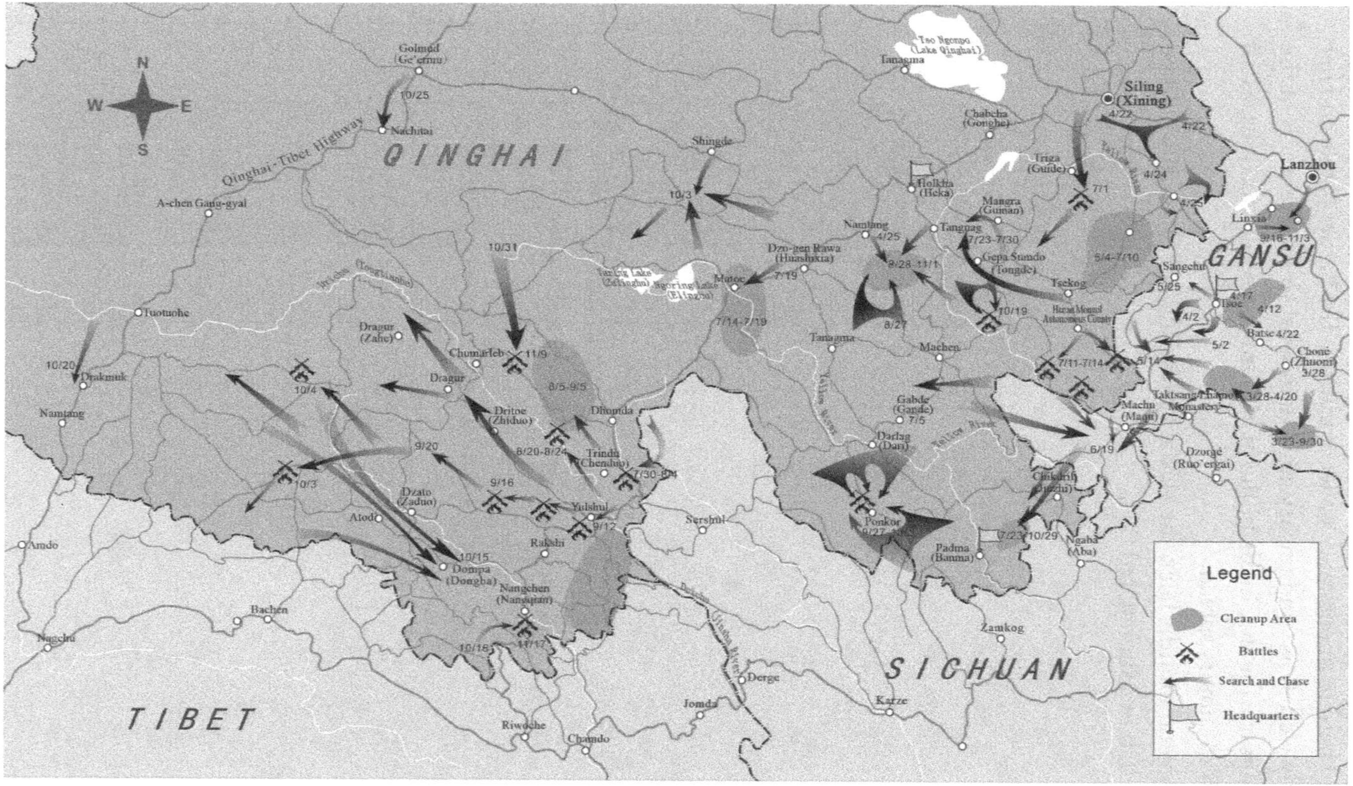

MAP 4. Major PLA military campaign areas and dates in Qinghai, 1958. Source: Marvin Cao.

Chapter 11

GUNSHOTS IN THE GOLOK GRASSLANDS

1

On May 15, 1958, multicolored flags fluttered over the Drugchen Sumdo grasslands in eastern Chikdril County in Golok Prefecture, Qinghai Province. A temporary rostrum had been built near a large tent, and gongs, drums, and a phonograph were on hand for the groundbreaking ceremony for the county's first state-private partnership (SPP) pasture. This pasture was under the jurisdiction of the Khangsar chieftain[1] Panchen Norbu Sonam,[2] and the meeting place was next to the chieftain's tent. Panchen Norbu Sonam was receiving medical treatment in Chengdu at the time, and local affairs were being handled by his eldest son, Kelsang Tseten, who was deputy county head.[3]

The groundbreaking ceremony had been scheduled for ten o'clock, but when township and county-level officials arrived on horseback, they found the meeting place deserted. Upon inquiring, the cadres learned that most of the herders invited to the meeting had gathered a kilometer away. When the district leaders invited them over, several of the headmen[4] responded that they didn't agree to the establishment of the SPP pasture. The situation was immediately reported to the county party secretary, who asked Kelsang Tseten to call the headmen to his tent and talk them around. He also sent seven cadres to accompany the headmen into the tent, while the herders were kept at a distance outside. Several armed police officers soon stationed themselves at a commanding vantage point with a machine gun, and the atmosphere became tense.

Panchen Norbu Sonam was the fifth-generation *qianhu* of the Khangsartsang clan. He had multiple ties with upper-strata families in Golok and Kanlho: Wangchen Lhagyal, the headman of the Khanggen, another major clan in central Golok, was his cousin, and each had married a sister of the fifth Jamyang Zhepa.[5] Panchen Norbu Sonam had won public support when he united Golok's tribes to resist the invasion of the warlord Ma Bufang, and he maintained close cooperation with the CCP after it came to power. In 1952, he had led more than 250 of the tribe's finest fighters to assist the CCP in fighting Kuomintang remnants in Kanlho, for which he had been presented with a commendation by the CCP Northwest Military and Political Committee. In that same year, a CCP work team peacefully entered Golok without encountering any resistance, and Golok's main tribal leaders had welcomed them and provided them with considerable assistance. When the Golok work team sent a regional work committee team to the Khangsar in 1953, Panchen Norbu Sonam designated the Drugchen Sumdo grasslands as the place where the work team would be stationed, and the government had established the Chikdril county seat there.

The Chinese government's organization of cooperatives in the pasturelands took two basic forms: the first was to use collectivization to change the herders' individual private ownership into collective ownership; the second was to change the herd-owner economy into an SPP system, then take the further step of changing it into public ownership. As Zhu Xiafu, then deputy secretary of the Qinghai provincial party committee, explained on March 8, 1958: "The process of socialist transformation completes the task of democratic reform."[6] The Khangsar clan was relatively well off, which is why the Chinese government started implementing an SPP there.[7]

The atmosphere inside the big tent was solemn. Kelsang Tseten explained to the headmen that establishing the SPP pastureland had been Panchen Norbu Sonam's decision, but no one believed him. Suspecting the government of holding Panchen Norbu Sonam under duress, they demanded to see him. They emphasized that they didn't oppose the CCP or socialist transformation, but they demanded a delay while a team of county cadres and local representatives went to Chengdu to request instructions from Panchen Norbu Sonam. They would then accept whatever decision he said. Kelsang Tsetan reminded them that he himself was in a position to make the decision, but a headman refuted him, saying, "You're the chieftain's eldest son, but you're still not the chieftain. We want to wait for the chieftain to come back and hear his decision. Right now we don't agree with having all of our livestock confiscated."[8]

Kelsang Tsetan relayed these demands to the county leaders, but the county party secretary rejected them outright. The chieftains of two of Chikdril County's other major clans, the Khanggen and Drasar, were also present, and were asked to persuade the Khangsar headsmen, but to no avail, and the groundbreaking rally was canceled. That wasn't the end of the matter, however.

After returning to the county seat, the cadres immediately organized four ten-member combat groups, each equipped with a machine gun, and by 4:30 p.m they had occupied command points on the periphery of the county seat to prevent an armed attack by the Khangsar, even though the Khangsar had had no intention of attacking. As the news spread, the Khangsar hastily called in dozens of armed herdsmen to stand guard on the hill beside the herders' encampment, to ward off an attack. The two sides began exchanging gunfire at nightfall. Due to the distance between them, no one was hurt.

Early the next morning, sentries discovered one of the county combat groups scaling a hilltop near the herders' encampment. A gunfight ensued, during which three government troops and one tribesman were killed and the combat group's machine gun was seized. Later that morning, tribesmen looted a caravan transporting goods from Ngawa to Chikdril. Seeing how the situation had deteriorated, the headmen called an urgent meeting and decided to flee.[9]

The Khangsar's boycott of the SPP pasture, along with the armed conflict that followed, sparked a military conflict in Chikdril that led the Chinese government to launch a massive military suppression of herders in this region.[10]

2

The "Khangsar incident" in Golok occurred against the backdrop of the Great Leap Forward that was sweeping across China.

On December 8, 1955, the deputy director of the Central Committee's United Front Department, Wang Feng, went to Qinghai to "investigate and research" the "socialist transformation" of animal husbandry. This wasn't a field investigation, but rather the provincial party committee calling together fourteen people, including prefectural, county, and district party secretaries from various prefectures, along with four Tibetan cadres, for an eleven-day symposium in the provincial capital followed by a discussion among municipal-level ethnic minority representatives. Wang returned to Beijing and submitted his report to the United Front Department[11] and proposed reforms in animal husbandry similar to the land reform in other Tibetan regions.[12]

The Central Committee established a pastoral work group and gave it a week to study the matter, then called a national conference to discuss the issue of socialist transformation in the pastoral areas.

It was at this time that revolts broke out in Sichuan's Tibetan regions. The Qinghai provincial party committee decided to slow down the organizing of cooperatives in the pastoral areas in an effort to prevent people there from rising up in revolt.

From February to May 1957, the second party secretary and governor of Qinghai Province, Sun Zuobin, and the vice-governor, Tashi Wangchuk, brought an ethnic minority song-and-dance troupe to Tsolho, Yulshul, Golok, and other places for "inspection and appreciation." They held meetings with upper-strata monks and laymen and placated them by reiterating the policy of "no denunciations, no class divisions, both hired herders and herd-owners benefit." As they came to understand that the upper strata of society still had considerable misgivings about "socialist transformation," Sun Zuobin and Tashi Wangchuk assured them that socialist transformation would not happen at the present.[13] The report they submitted to the Qinghai provincial party committee held that "as long as we work hard and well under the present conditions, there is very little, if any, possibility of a substantial armed rebellion." They reported pledges from upper-strata figures in the region that "as long as the policy doesn't change, we definitely will not change."[14]

However, on February 2, 1958, a *People's Daily* editorial proposed the slogan of "a nationwide leap forward" in the national economy, and as a result, the Qinghai provincial party committee stepped up the pace of organizing cooperatives. Sun Zuobin and Tashi Wangchuk were purged at an enlarged meeting of the Qinghai provincial party committee held from January 3 to March 8, 1958.[15]

Mao delivered six speeches at a Politburo meeting in Chengdu in March that approved the drafting of a series of "great leap" plans.[16] By the time the Eighth Party Congress held its second session in Beijing on May 5, the Qinghai provincial party committee had called a meeting of prefectural and county party secretaries, during which it was decided to accelerate the socialist transformation of animal husbandry according to a specific timetable. For Golok Prefecture, where the "operational fundamentals are relatively poor," it was recommended to "adopt the method of more pilot schemes, going fast whenever possible, striving to have at least 20% of all herder households join animal husbandry cooperatives and joint state-private-owned pastures this year."[17] The plan was to establish an SPP pasture in the Khangsar area on May 15, less than two weeks after the session ended.

3

By this time, the Tibetan areas of Sichuan, Gansu, and Yunnan were already in a state of war. At the beginning of 1958, insurrections had broken out in parts of Qinghai's Malho Prefecture, involving 19 townships and more than 11,000 people.[18] In Gansu's Kanlho Prefecture, three Communist cadres were killed during a rebellion by the Ngulra (Oula) clan in Machu County on February 28, and another rebellion occurred in Choné (Zhuoni) County on March 18. By mid-May, more than 30,000 Tibetans had staged insurrections all over Kanlho Prefecture.[19]

In March, the director of the Central Committee United Front Department, Li Weihan, the deputy director, Wang Feng, and the vice-chairman of the Central Ethnic Affairs Commission, Yang Jingren, set off for the northwest to discuss the situation in Gansu with the provincial party committee. On April 3, they submitted a report on the situation, suggesting that superior military forces be used to resolutely and ruthlessly attack the rebels.[20] The report explicitly stated: "The past policy of 'giving precedence to political struggle' is no longer appropriate for the actual situation in Gannan at present," and changed it to "military suppression combined with political struggle, flexibly utilized." The report also found that the Tibetans in this region had gained three kinds of experience through long-term conflict with external forces: "First is to have firearms, second is to raise big livestock, and third is to protect the headmen. Because the headmen are the organizers and commanders." The report therefore recommended "using all appropriate means to put headmen, especially the more influential ones, under our control as quickly as possible, and put those who might rebel under house arrest." Furthermore, "several principal instigators should be killed with great fanfare."[21]

On April 12, the CCP Central Committee distributed this report to the Gansu, Sichuan, and Qinghai provincial party committees, endorsing its opinions with the caveat that "the question of killing . . . should be handled after the armed rebellion is pacified and after further research."

On that same day, the Qinghai Military Command Political Department issued its "Policy Provisions Regarding Pacifying Armed Rebellion in the Pastoral Areas."[22] Meanwhile, it rapidly employed various pretexts for placing influential ethnic and religious leaders under control. This helped ignite the local people's rebellion.

On April 17, Tibetans in the pastoral area of Xunhua (Yadzi) County began a revolt against collectivization, known at the time as "the Xunhua incident."[23] This was the first large-scale military suppression in Qinghai. On the same day, the "Qinghai Rebellion Suppression Command Post" was established under the deputy commander of the Qinghai Military District. After military arrangements were completed, the Qinghai provincial party committee on April 30 handed down its "Directive Regarding Pacifying the Armed Rebellion."

The directive held that "this rebellion [referring to the armed resistance by the Tibetans of Malho Prefecture and the Xunhua incident] is not a localized issue, but rather a problem throughout the entire Tibetan ethnic region." It was therefore "necessary to use all means to energetically carry out mass work and United Front work, expose rumors, and seize counterrevolutionary elements from outside, in an effort to prevent and delay armed rebellion."[24] This was subsequently referred to as the "rebellion prevention" policy.

The Khangsar herders had no way of knowing that when they boycotted the establishment of the SPP pastureland on May 15, the situation in Golok was reported to the highest levels of the Communist Party on that same day.[25] This frigid land far removed from any political center was about to be dragged into a bloody war of more than three years' duration.

4

On May 18, chaos reigned among the Khangsar. Men stood watching with their guns on the hill next to the encampment, while others, old and young, rounded up horses and yaks, gathered their goods and took down their tents, then shouldered leather rafts and hurried to the Yellow River. Hearing that war was looming, 11-year-old Damcho Pelsang ran around with the other children, both nervous and excited. His mother called to him and told him to round up the yaks as she rushed to pack up their things, saying, "Those Chinese want to start eating us up now." It was impossible to take all 40 of the family's yaks, so Damcho Pelsang and his older sister chased down a few of them and left the rest at the encampment. The family then hurried to join the others already gathered on the riverbank.[26]

Damcho Pelsang and his mother and sister rode the raft across the river behind several horses. The boy didn't know what war was, but the sudden move, the serious expressions on the faces of the adults, the strained atmosphere—all of it was highly unusual. Damcho Pelsang remembered stories that the old people told about the arrival of "outsiders," and he began to feel afraid.

The men herded the yaks and horses into the river while the elderly, women, and children crossed on rafts. In less than two hours, the hundreds of Khangsar households had crossed the Yellow River, and each family then chased down its own horses and yaks and herded them to a pasture that belonged to the Walbentsang (Awancang) clan.[27] The Khangsar chieftain Panchen Norbu Sonam and the Walbentsang chieftain Wangye were related by marriage; Wangye's wife was Panchen Norbu Sonam's older sister, giving the two clans a special relationship.

At that point, the county government's combat groups were not yet out fighting after their setback at the Drugchen Sumdo grasslands. The Khangsar chieftain Panchen Norbu Sonam had not yet returned from Chengdu, and his son Kelsang Tseten had been placed under government "protection" and was out of contact.[28] It therefore took two days for the county government to learn that the entire clan had escaped to Machu. The county work committee recalled the work teams that were dispersed through the townships and began preparing defense fortifications, digging ditches around government office buildings, building blockhouses, and stocking up on food and water. The fact was, however, that although the Khangsar had crossed the river, the other tribes were grazing their livestock in their own pastures as usual. There were no incidents of local forces "besieging the county seat" within the borders of Golok Prefecture, as claimed in official Chinese sources. This claim was used as a justification for the military suppression shortly after this incident.[29]

Herders in all localities had vigorously resisted the animal husbandry cooperative movement, and even the cooperatives that had been established were unable to operate because they lacked accountants or financial management systems, and their cadres didn't understand the Tibetan language. Even so, the Qinghai provincial party committee had no intention of postponing implementation. On June 2, 1958, the provincial party committee submitted a report to the Central Committee with a plan for "basically achieving the organization of cooperatives" in Tsolho, Malho, and Yulshul prefectures between June and August of that year, and in Golok before June 1959.[30]

On June 18, 1958, the provincial party committee submitted to the Central Committee its "Directives to the Entire Province on the Problem of Suppressing the Armed Rebellion," which reported that "counterrevolutionary armed rebellions" in Qinghai had already "spread into a pervasive problem." It was "a separatist movement plotted by imperialists and Lhasa reactionaries and a reflection of socialist transformation and opposition to transformation; it is an intense fight-to-the-death class struggle."[31]

The military policy of the Qinghai provincial party committee was: "When there's a war to fight, take the opportunity to annihilate the enemy; when there's no war to fight, coordinate with local party and government organs to deeply mobilize the masses; track down, exterminate, and arrest counterrevolutionaries; confiscate firearms; transform political power; and organize animal husbandry into cooperatives."[32]

Mao's official reply to this document on June 24 affirmed that "the Qinghai provincial party committee's guiding principles are completely correct,"[33] and he circulated the document to the Central Military Commission and to all the provincial party committees. This effectively authorized Qinghai to carry out its slaughter. On June 29, the Qinghai provincial party committee forwarded the report, along with Mao's memo, to all of its counties and prefectures.

In July, the Central Committee handed down a directive stating: "The problem in the Tibetan regions is a problem of strategy and revolution. Problems of revolution must use revolutionary methods, and the revolutionary methods adopted must be swift and thorough. . . . Qinghai talked too much about peace at the outset, and it is correct to adopt revolutionary methods now." This implied the Central Committee's endorsement of Qinghai's actions. Not only that, but the Central Committee promoted the "Qinghai method" to other localities as well: "Places that have undergone transformation need supplementary action from now on, and places that haven't undergone transformation need to adopt the Qinghai method, the revolutionary method. . . . Apart from the prohibition against executing headmen, other prohibitions against surveillance, detention, control, and removal are lifted."[34]

Within just a few years, more than 48,000 men, women, and children from every stratum of society would die under deplorable circumstances.[35]

5

On the night of July 22, the Lanzhou Military Command's First Cavalry Division moved in on Chikdril County.

The herders of Chikdril were no strangers to the First Cavalry. In 1952, more than 200 Khangsar warriors had spent half a year fighting with them against remnants of Ma Bufang's army. Now, six years later, the First Cavalry was once again moving into Golok, but this time to exterminate their former comrades-in-arms.

On the afternoon of the next day, dark clouds gathered and produced a torrential rain. Braving the rain, a company from the cavalry division sped off to battle at a place called Jigdur Sumdo (Jiudaisongduo) in the middle of the county. Rivers flowing through the valleys between gentle mountain slopes converged to form a lush pastureland where the Khanggen clan grazed its herds.[36] In 1958, the Khanggen had 14 settlements, with some 1,176 households. In the summer of 1958, thousands of herders from Kanlho and other places had ended up in Jigdur Sumdo and nearby areas.

Reaching its destination as dawn broke, the 1st Cavalry's 3rd Company immediately launched its attack. At the sudden outbreak of gunfire, herdsman standing guard leapt onto their horses and headed into the hills, disappearing in the mist and rain while troops fired into the tents, killing women and children who didn't have time to flee.[37] That afternoon, the main force divided into two teams, one heading southeast toward the Palyul Monastery to encircle the Khanggen and the other heading northeast for a raid on Jomdha (Jianmuda), north of Sogruma (Suohurima).

By July 25, the Khanggen tribe had dispersed; chieftain Wangchen Lhagyal and his younger brother, the incarnate lama of Palyul Monastery and head of Chikdril County, led a group of 30 fleeing toward Pema (Banma).[38] The Ngaro (Arao) *tsowa* under the Khanggen organized a fierce resistance at Jomdha, a triangular plain surrounded by grassy mountains, with a monastery located between two small rivers. The Ngaro were a small group with a dozen or so men of varying ages, but they put up a resistance to the death under the headman Trulchen, facing down a mass of battle-hardened PLA cavalrymen with only their antiquated rifles and a handful of bullets. The shallow trenches they'd dug on the spur of the moment offered no protection from the charging warhorses or hail of bullets, and one by one, they fell.

6

Sitting in the grass with his family and neighbors, Damcho Pelsang grasped his rosary and chanted prayers while his mother spun a *mani* prayer wheel and wiped tears from her face. The elderly, women, children, and monks chanted prayers to protect the men in battle as gunfire rumbled in the distance. Hearing what sounded like peals of thunder, Damcho Pelsang trembled and raised his eyes, but saw not even a wisp of cloud in the sun-dazzled sky. But when he turned, he saw peculiar clouds rising ominously between the blue sky and green grass.[39]

Early that morning, a great clamor had sent Damcho Pelsang rushing out of his tent, where he saw his cousin, the son of his maternal uncle, leading his horse with his gun slung across his back. Dozens of men were setting off with their firelocks and hunting rifles, led by field commander Hor Thor Sher, a sturdy man of medium height, his long hair braided and coiled around his head. A man beside him led two spare horses in case the horse Hor Thor Sher was riding was killed while he was directing the battle.

Damcho Pelsang's uncle was a headman, and when the tribe went to war, the headman's adult sons had to lead the men in battle; this was ancient tradition. The field commander Hor Thor Sher leapt onto his horse and gave a shrill whistle, which the other men on horseback echoed with a chorus of battle yells. Damcho Pelsang saw his cousin flash him a smile and then speed off with the others toward the river. A strange feeling surged in Damcho Pelsang's heart, and he gripped his mother's hand as he watched the horsemen disappear behind the grassy hills.

Hidden in the hills not far from the ferry pier, about one hundred Khangsar and Walbentsang fighters led by Hor Thor Sher looked down on a grassland and then further out at the gleaming Machu River—known downstream as the Yellow River—that gave Machu County its name. Here, where a 180-degree turn formed the first of the "nine bends," its gentle currents produced a lush pastureland that nurtured livestock breeds renowned far and wide.[40]

Someone shouted, "The Chinese soldiers are coming!" Leaping to his feet, Hor Thor Sher saw a long line of men on horseback crossing the grassland from the direction of the ferry pier. The Khangsar fighters had no heavy artillery or machine guns, only single-loaders. As the situation had become tense in recent years, some had sold off family property to buy firearms, but bullets were scarce and expensive. Hor Thor Sher told everyone to stay calm and wait for the soldiers to draw near. The mounted column grew into one several times the size of the clan militia. Suddenly, Hor Thor Sher gave a yell and flew onto his horse, brandishing his sword as he charged down the hillside. Dozens of fighters followed close on his heels, charging onto the plain to disperse the soldiers. Gunfire erupted, and as bullets flew like rain, the herdsmen retreated. A little later, Hor Thor Sher led another charge down the hill.

Suddenly, there was a thunderous noise as a cannonball landed among them. Shrapnel flew in all directions, and the men scattered in chaos as more cannonballs followed.

Amid the explosions rang the whinnying of horses and the cries of men. Scanning the battlefield through the smoke, the field commander saw felled horses and men, the headman's son lying prone on the dark green grass.

Hor Thor Sher wheeled his horse around and gave the order to retreat. At that moment, a machine gun sent a hail of bullets through the air. Hor Thor Sher's mount collapsed before he could leap clear. Pulling his leg from under his dead horse, the field commander lay down behind the corpse and rested his rifle on its belly to steady his aim as he carefully fired his remaining shots.

As the soldiers surged forward, Hor Thor Sher suddenly stopped firing; he had run out of bullets. Tossing aside his gun, the field commander rose to his feet as the soldiers charged at him. Shots rang out. Hor Thor Sher's arms flew into the air as if he were praying. Another shot sent the Khangsar field commander tumbling to the ground, his arms spread wide in a final embrace of the soil that had nourished him and his ancestors.[41]

In the evening, as the sun set like fire against the sky, survivors carried his cousin's body back. Eleven-year-old Damcho Pelsang stared at the bloodstained chest, bidding farewell to his cousin and to his childhood.

7

In mid-August, the families under the Khangsar tribe rounded up their livestock and set off for the Yellow River. Each household pushed its leather raft onto the river and floated to the opposite shore.

By then, resistance among the Qinghai Tibetans had spread to 5 autonomous prefectures, 24 counties, 240 tribes, and 307 monasteries, involving more than 90,000 people.[42] The Chinese government sent in 5 army divisions and 30 regiments of various kinds, plus 25 companies of armed police and local militia, for a total armed force of more than 50,000, including air force,[43] artillery, infantry, cavalry, armored troops, and others, in a massive military suppression of herders who were resisting the organizing of their pastures into cooperatives. Golok was part of the first wave of suppression planned by the Qinghai Military District.[44]

The Khanggen had already dispersed, and the Drasar had surrendered;[45] the "three Goloks" were engulfed in the flames of war. With their chieftain away and their field commander dead, the Khangsar families had little choice but to return.

After fording the river, the women led their young and elderly, driving their livestock, while the men, armed and on horseback, protected them from the rear.

Damcho Pelsang silently followed his mother and older sister on the journey home. Suddenly, the sound of intense gunfire came from behind them. Damcho Pelsang turned and saw black clouds forming between the sky and grass.

The PLA had surrounded the remaining fighters on a low hill, and blood spilled again in fierce fighting. As the soldiers charged toward them, the Khangsar leader gave a long cry and then issued an order: "Surrender!"

Facing countless red stars and row upon row of gun muzzles, the Khangsar warriors, who had once risked their lives in battle against the Ma army, laid down their antiquated firearms one by one.

A few weeks later, on September 7, the Second Regiment of the PLA's First Cavalry Division noticed wisps of smoke coming from a mountain ravine. Four companies of soldiers immediately split up, with two companies climbing the mountain slopes on either side while the other two held the mouth of the ravine. Then a battalion of soldiers launched an attack on Wangchen Lhagyal, chieftain of the Khanggen clan, and another 30 or so men as they sat boiling their tea. An hour later, Wangchen Lhagyal, his younger brother, and 10 others lay dead, and the rest were taken prisoner.[46]

That same month, the Qinghai provincial party committee ordered arrests in every county, and the PLA and local cadres began mass raids on the Golok grasslands. Heavily armed soldiers and local militiamen searched tents and arrested nearly every adult male. In Damcho Pelsang's *tsowa*, only five males aged 16 or above were left behind among 30 households. In Chikdril County, 802 people were arrested in 1958.[47]

As snow arrived on the plateau that year, Damcho Pelsang stood along the road leading to the county seat and watched a procession of herders approaching from deep in the grasslands. His kinsmen, monks and laymen alike, were strung together in groups of five to ten, with their arms bound behind them, trudging toward the county seat in Drugchen Sumdo under military escort. Behind them, clan elders drove yaks loaded with *tsampa* and some basic implements. The majority of them would never return, including the man Damcho Pelsang's older sister had married just a week before he was arrested.

After being incarcerated for several months, the men were split into groups and sent to labor reform farms in Golmud (Ge'ermu) and other places. In Chikdril County, 1,050 people, nearly 10% of its total population, were arrested within three years. More than half of these captives died in prison over the next five years,[48] and some were in jail until the early 1980s. Of the hundreds of herdsmen arrested from the Khangsar clan, only about 20 of them ever made it home again.[49]

According to official figures, at least 9,262 people were arrested in Golok Prefecture,[50] the vast majority of them males in the prime of life, and a severe gender imbalance resulted. "In many places, the proportion of young men to young women was one to seven, and in some places it was one to ten."[51]

On October 10, 1958, Chikdril County announced the establishment of people's communes. The three clans in central Golok were regrouped into the "Red Star," "Red Flag," "Glorious," "Vanguard," and "Advance" people's communes. The communes confiscated all of the herders' belongings, allowing each household only one yak-hair tent, one pot, one ladle, one teapot, one *tsampa* box, one yak-skin bellows, and for each person in the family one bowl.[52] Darje's account confirms what the tenth Panchen Lama wrote in his *70,000 Character Petition:* that "in the communes, every person has only three personal belongings: a set of clothes, a set of bedclothes, and a bowl and pair of chopsticks."[53] In fact, in the "socialist paradise" that the Chinese government constructed, many families did not even have a bowl and chopsticks, and were obliged to "use spittoons as pots, yak horns as ladles, and empty cans as bowls."[54]

During the Red Tempest of 1958, the herders of the Golok grasslands were bombed by PLA artillery and aircraft, swept up by cavalrymen, and attacked from all sides by infantrymen. Hardly a family was left intact, and the "three tribes of Golok" were reduced to tribes of widows.[55]

8

Decades later, in a coffee shop in Dharamsala next to the Tsuklakhang temple, Lama Tenkyong told me the story of his family. Soon after the Khangsar field commander Hor Thor Sher died in battle in summer 1958, the commander's younger brother, a lama, and his brother-in-law, Tengkyong's grandfather, were arrested and imprisoned. Tengkyong's father, 15 years old at the time, was also taken away, but was released after a few days. The other men never came home, and the family never learned where or when they died.

"Grandmother always said that Hor Thor Sher was lucky to be killed in battle," Tenkyong told me. "Later, the headmen and lamas were taken to a denunciation rally and badly beaten. Our chieftain's wife, the younger sister of Huang Zhengqing . . ."

"You mean the younger sister of the fifth Jamyang Zhepa?" I interrupted.

Tankyong nodded. "She died during a denunciation rally that lasted all day. Grandmother said that if Hor Thor Sher hadn't died on the battlefield, he'd have been beaten to death at the rally, one punch and kick at a time, and that would have been even worse."

In the summer of 1990, Tenkyong, who had become a monk not long before, visited his Walbentsang homeland. The pasture is now known as "the place where the young lions of the Khangsars play," and in the decades since that violent episode, the Walbentsang herders have refrained from grazing their livestock there. Small piles of stones dotted the grassland, and a veteran of the war told Tenkyong that these marked where each horse and man died that day.

The young monk took a prayer flag from the fold of his robe, walked up the hillside and hung it from a bush. Then he stood at the top of the hill with his palms pressed together and prayed for the Tibetans who had died in battle that day, and for the soldiers from afar who had died in a foreign land.

I put down my pen, not knowing what to say. The sun beaming through the doorway lit the wall across from me in a dazzling tangerine glow. From outside the door came the sound of drums and bugles as monks began evening rituals in the temple.

Chapter 12

THE YELLOW RIVER MASSACRE

1

As we noted in chapter 6, the Yellow River[1] leaves Qinghai through Chikdril County in Golok, flows into Gansu through Machu County, and then enters Sichuan through Dzorgé County before turning northwest back into Qinghai, forming an elliptical right turn known as "the first bend in the Yellow River." The spot where the river returns to Qinghai marks the trijunction with Gansu and Qinghai provinces. The area north of the river is the Yulgen Mongol Autonomous County in the Malho TAP of Qinghai, and the area south of the river is Machu County in Gansu. Plains of lush grassland line the river on its gently winding route between the two provinces.

In the early hours of June 1, 1958, silence reigned over thousands of tents, steeped in the predawn darkness at Khosin Tuglothang (Keshengtuoluotan),[2] north of the Yellow River. Tribesmen stood guard with firearms in the low hills surrounding the grasslands, while starlight glimmered faintly on the river's silent flow.

In the depths of night, no one knew or perhaps even imagined that just east of them, on the Ngulra[3] grasslands, the darkness concealed a mass of soldiers preparing a tense predawn operation. Seasoned war-horses were herded into the river, towing a string of rubber dinghies chained together.

A group of soldiers then swiftly placed wooden planks on the dinghies, forming a temporary military pontoon bridge, over which soldiers from the PLA's First Cavalry Division crossed the river. Gathered on the opposite shore, the soldiers leapt onto their horses on their commanding officer's barked orders and sped off for Khosin Tuglothang.[4]

2

According to official Chinese sources, on May 3, 1958, "counterrevolutionary armed insurrections" occurred in some parts of Yulgen County.[5]

Yulgen was a pastoral area mainly occupied by ethnic Mongols, and was thus also known as the Henan Mongolian Banners.[6] At the time that the People's Republic was established, the Henan Mongols, led by Princess Tashi Tsering,[7] included three banners and six large *tsowa*, among them the Tibetan Tsang Arik.[8] And although they were known as the Henan Mongolian Banners, they had become assimilated to Tibetan culture. They followed Tibetan Buddhism, Tibetan was their main spoken and written language, and their living habits were also highly influenced by Tibetan culture. Princess Tashi Tsering's husband was the son of Lobsang Tsewang,[9] the oldest brother of the Fifth Jamyang Zhepa of Labrang Monastery. After the CCP came to power, it vigorously courted Tashi Tsering, and she was made head of the Yulgen Mongol Autonomous County. There are no documents showing that she ever expressed opposition to the Chinese government's imposition of "socialist transformation of animal husbandry," nor indicating whether she was placed under the CCP's control.

According to official records, this is what happened in 1958: "Beginning on May 3, 1958, after the Dacan (Dartsan), Sirouqunwa (Sirik Chungwa), Keshengshu (Khasum Tsohor), Waisi (Besi), and other tribes of Henan County engaged in open rebellion, the traitorous masses and their families packed up their tents and belongings and drove their livestock to a gathering place at Keshengtuoluotan, intending to cross the Yellow River and join up with the rebel bandits of Gannan."[10]

The fleeing herders were comprised of nearly 1,600 households, totaling 7,487 people. In 1958, Yulgen County had 2,218 households, totaling

10,500 people, but that included soldiers and cadres; the "animal husbandry population" was 9,927. This means that 72% of the herder households and 75% of the total herder population were involved. In other words, the government's cooperative movement met with widespread resentment and people simply escaped. They gathered at Khosin Tuglothang with the intention of crossing the Yellow River and escaping to the Ngulra grasslands in Machu County.

At daybreak on June 1, the First Cavalry Division charged into Khosin Tuglothang and occupied the commanding points around it. As dawn broke, signal flares rose in the air, after which intense gunfire shattered the morning stillness.

The "Keshengtuoluotan Battle of Annihilation" had begun.

3

This battle was one of the major military actions in Qinghai in 1958, but until now, few details about it have come out.

The main Tibetan source concerning this incident is Alak Tsayu Tenzin Pelbar's *The Tragedy of My Homeland*. The author (writing as Zhayi Rinpoché) provides a brief narrative of the course of this battle, citing two (unnamed) people who served as PLA translators at the time. According to Alak Tsayu's account, those gathered at Khosin Tuglothang were "more than 3,000 households of more than 10,000 herders and tens of thousands of livestock."[11] The First Cavalry Division of the PLA's Lanzhou Military Command crossed the river at night and surrounded the herders gathered there. "Bullets and cannon shells rained down on the place where the herders were staying, and flames lit the sky, shrouding the hills in smoke."[12] Alak Tsayu provides no information on how many herders were killed or wounded.

To date, only three official Chinese sources refer to this battle. The first was published in 1996 and provides a figure of 7,487 for "the number of people taking part in the rebellion," as well as "1,732 rebel bandits with 1,357 guns and 2,535 mounts."[13] This account makes it appear that the people gathered along the Yellow River were not all of the "7,487 coerced herder masses," but rather 1,732 armed men. That is to say, six or seven tribes were camping along the river that night, and all the men, armed or not, had removed themselves and gathered on a hilltop, where they were "surrounded and annihilated" by the PLA. This account implies that in this battle, the PLA only attacked male fighters and did not harm women, children, or the elderly.

The second source is the prefecture gazetteer published in 1999, which provides an alternative version: "On May 31, *7,487 people were amassed* at that spot, including 1,732 rebel bandits prepared for battle with 1,357 guns and 2,335 *war-horses*."[14]

In both accounts, the number of men possessing arms and the number of horses are basically the same, but what is not clear is exactly how many herders had gathered at Khosin Tuglothang. The 1999 publication states that 7,487 people had gathered there. In the early 1950s, a community of 200-plus households from Golok Prefecture had moved into Kanlho, so it is possible, as Alak Tsayu states, that the thousands of people gathered there included about one thousand from Golok. From these sources, it can be concluded that the herders who had "amassed" on the Keshengtuoluo benchland included at least 7,487 people from three of the four major banners of Yulgen County, and of them, 23% were "ready for battle," i.e., the able-bodied men, and only 18% possessed firearms.

As for the so-called Gannan rebel bandits, i.e., the Ngulra *shokka* of Machu County: the Henan Mongolian Banners had a long-standing relationship with the Labrang Monastery, and the Ngulra was one of the nomad communities under the monastery's direct jurisdiction, separated from Yulgen only by the river. The herders gathered on the river bank were trying to seek refuge in Machu.

The 1996 source devotes just a single sentence to the course of the "Battle of annihilation": "On June 1, the armed rebel bandits had all amassed on the northern shore of the bend in the Yellow River and on Kesituoluohu hill at Keshengmanitan, and were surrounded and annihilated by our rebellion pacification troops." The impression this sentence gives is that fewer than 2,000 "armed rebel bandits" on a small hill were "surrounded and annihilated" by an unspecified PLA unit.

The Tibetan and official Chinese accounts both specify the location of the battle in the area of what is now Khosin (Kesheng) Township in the southeast of Yulgen County, 66 kilometers from the county seat. Satellite maps show that the river makes two turns between Khosin Township on the north shore and Ngulra Township on the southern shore, with the bends in the river forming one large and one small grassy plain. A ferry runs between a pier near the Shingza (Xiangzha) Monastery, located near the present Khosin Township government offices, and another in Ngulra Township. The PLA's "1958 rebellion pacification sketch-map" indicates that on June 1, the First Cavalry crossed the river from the east, after which the soldiers split into two routes, approaching Khosin Tuglothang from the north and south in a pincer formation. The satellite map shows that the east-west running Yellow River makes two north-south U-turns near Ngulra Township, and that the surprise attack on Khosin Tuglothang occurred at a segment where the river turns in a south-north direction.

No source indicates that these herders ever attacked the PLA or Chinese government work teams. They were fleeing from forced cooperatization, and any males capable of bearing arms were protecting their families rather than taking up arms for war. It doesn't make sense that all of these men would have gathered on a hilltop and left their people exposed to danger. The area was not a vast grassland; it was surrounded by hills on three sides. With nearly 10,000 people gathered in hundreds of tents, along with a large number of livestock, the grassland must have been packed with people and animals.

The 1999 gazetteer provides slightly more detail:

> At that time, more than 400 rebel bandits amassed in the Oula area crossed the river in heavy fog on the morning of June 1 to lend support. The PLA's First Cavalry Division adopted the long-distance raid military tactic, surrounding the rebel bandits at dawn and then launching an attack. The battle ended at 18:00 that day. Weapons seized included 1,404 firearms of various types, 10,976 rounds of ammunition, and 865 knives and spears.[15]

This passage specifies that the First Cavalry launched its attack at dawn, and that it was only after the PLA began attacking the herders at Khosin Tuglothang that the Ngulra militia crossed the river to lend its aid. This account also makes clear that the battle lasted at least ten hours, ending at six o'clock in the evening.

The third source is Qinghai's military gazetteer published in 2001. It would seem reasonable to assume that the military would provide more details about a battle, but this book has only once sentence: "On June 1, the First Cavalry Division in coordination with allied neighboring troops annihilated more than 1,200 armed rebel forces at Keshengtuoluotan, Henan County."[16] Yet the PLA's "1958 rebellion pacification sketch-map" in the same book (Figure 5-3-09) shows that the number of people "annihilated" in the "Keshengtuoluotan Battle of Annihilation" was 1,600. *The* military gazetteer, which is the most recently published source, provides the least information as well as the lowest number of people "annihilated," and the figures provided in two different parts of the same book contradict each other.

Which army unit made up the "allied neighboring troops"? None of the three official Chinese sources make this clear. Decades later, a man who had fought as a soldier at Machu near the Yellow River bend recalled the battle he had participated in. The location was referred to as "Laohuzui [Tiger's Mouth]," where "a large number of bandits" were encircled. From the hills, he saw "a dazzling white band of bandit tents, and on the grassland, there were also thousands of yaks, sheep, and horses that the bandits had plundered." The new recruit witnessed two fighter planes flying over, and the soldiers "were all very excited" to see that "the fighter planes flew down very slowly for their attack, but then they flew back up very quickly." After the battle, the solders "didn't even bother to clean up the battlefield before going off on our next mission."[17]

The veteran recalled that the "Tiger's Mouth" was the place where his unit crossed the Yellow River on the pontoon bridge, the terrain conforming to the general configuration of Khosin Tuglothang. The area they surrounded was full of tents and livestock, which is also consistent with the Tibetan memoir and the officially disclosed information.

The recollections of this soldier show that the terminology used with the PLA soldiers led them to regard the herders as "rebel bandits" and their livestock as plundered booty. The implication is that PLA soldiers would have shown no mercy once they opened fire on the herders.

What the aircraft bombed may have been the Ngulra people from Machu, who had moved to the ferry crossing on the southern shore of the river, not far from Khosin Tuglothang, in the latter half of May. According to the *Maqu County Gazetteer*, the group moved into the county's Lengku area[18] on May 30 and was bombed by a "scouting mission." The next day, PLA troops entered Machu and "began pacifying a rebellion at the first bend of the Yellow River on June 1." By the end of August, the area was cleared. However, the source admits that "due to the influence of the 'leftist' guiding ideology at that time, the policy of 'combining military attack with political striving and mobilization of the masses' was not resolutely implemented and executed, resulting in a serious error of magnification."[19]

What did the First Cavalry and its "allied neighboring troops" actually do on the grassland on the northern shore of the Yellow River at the Qinghai-Gansu border on June 1, 1958? One of the official sources admits that at the battle site there was "a mixture of bandits and masses." The source claims that during the battle "bandit leaders . . . drove the masses who had been coerced into rebelling into a forward position," because "not enough was done to divide and demoralize, with the result that some of the masses were accidentally injured."[20]

It defies logic and common sense to suggest that the men who were fighting to protect their people would push their own families to the front line during battle. The unspecified figures on collateral damage among the "masses" and the "error of magnification" are clearly the real reason why the military sources avoid mention of this massacre and why all the published sources conceal the facts as much as possible.

4

On June 1, 1958, the men, women, children, and elderly people living in thousands of tents on the grassland on the northern shore of the Yellow River between Qinghai and Gansu provinces were startled awake by the sound of intense gun and cannon fire. The misty morning air was rent with the cries of humans and horses as shrapnel ripped through the encampment. Hundreds of armed fighters from Ngulra crossed the river from the southern bank to rescue the others, fighting to the death. During the battle, Mongol warriors seized several machine guns from the PLA and held a mountain pass, but they were hopelessly outnumbered and killed to the last man. The pincer attack of the two army groups blocked the escape route to the highlands, leaving the people in the encampment with only two choices: to sit and wait to be killed by bullets or cannon fire, or to flee across the Yellow River. This was the route to survival, but also the route to death. Mothers clutching young children and tottering elderly people dodged bullets and cannonballs to plunge into the river one by one.[21]

It is impossible for us now to capture the horror of the battle along the river shore that morning. Official histories provide no details of how the PLA mowed down the herders, so we can only resort to the reminiscences of the PLA soldiers. There is no way to verify whether the following extract refers to the "Battle of Keshengtuoluotan," but there are enough reasons to believe that the scene was very similar to the one described here:

> The bandits and masses were in fact all mixed together, and it was impossible to distinguish between them. All we saw were people with guns slung across their backs, people waving prayer flags and prayer beads, people herding cattle and sheep, and horses loaded with children, all mixed together in the turbid waters of the Yellow River as they raced toward the shore and climbed the banks to save their lives. But what faced them were the army's machine guns, and each gunshot was followed by a body floating on the surface of the river, and blood flowing into the river's current . . .[22]

One of the official sources records the military accomplishments of the First Cavalry that day:

> 265 shot dead (including 2 bandit chieftains and 38 mainstays [i.e. die-hard rebels]), 143 wounded (including 5 bandit chieftains and 11 mainstays), 584 captured (including 13 bandit chieftains and 40 mainstays

> from other localities), 476 surrendered (including 7 bandit chieftains and 59 mainstays), 115 drowned while attempting to escape, 12 dead from other causes; total annihilated 1,595, composing 92.09% of the amassed rebel bandits; captured 1,404 firearms of various types (including 1,272 rifles, 115 homemade firearms, 3 light machine guns, and 14 handguns), 10,976 rounds of ammunition, 865 knives and swords of various kinds, 5 hand grenades, 5 pairs of binoculars, more than 10,000 *yuan* in silver coins, 1,500 RMB and various other goods; dispersed 137 rebel bandits (including 8 bandit chieftains and 12 mainstays), who carried off approximately 100 firearms.[23]

What about the 6,130 unarmed people on the river bank: the elders, women, monks, and children? How many of them were "mistakenly injured" or killed? Who were the people "drowned while attempting to escape"? Were the "dead from other causes" executed prisoners? The three Chinese sources currently accessible to the public are silent on all of these questions, nor do these sources provide figures on PLA casualties.[24]

The official source also provides a different group of statistics:

> In the four years from 1958 to 1961, a total of 1,513 people in the county were arrested, sent to labor reform, detained, or sent to training camps, composing 14.44% of the county's population in 1961. Among them, 967, or 9.23% of the total population, were arrested and sentenced. Reexamination of cases back then found that 705 people had been wrongfully arrested or punished, composing 46.60% of the people arrested.[25]

These figures do not include the people, old and young, male and female, who fell at Khosin Tuglothang or leapt into the Yellow River on June 1, 1958.

Three days later, in Yulshul, another pastoral region, a fierce battle broke out between a coalition of Ponru Méma and other tribes and a convoy of Chinese cadres and soldiers. This time, the Chinese government suffered a serious loss.

Chapter 13
YULSHUL IN FLAMES

1

On June 4, 1958, a convoy of 40 trucks crossed the Bayan Har mountains and headed southwest. The convoy came from Xining, the capital of Qinghai Province, and was transporting more than 400 people assigned to work in Yulshul Prefecture, including nursing school graduates, cadres, and a group of students from the Xining Public Security Cadre School,[1] as well as a large quantity of military supplies. Escorted by a platoon of soldiers, the convoy was heading for Jyekundo (Jiegu), where the prefectural government offices were located. After crossing the mountains, the convoy entered Yulshul's Trindu (Chengduo) County and followed a river that flowed from Ngoring Lake in the county's northeastern quadrant. In Trindu, the river converged with the Dzachu (Zhaqu) River[2] in Dhomda (Qingshuihe) Township, a major transport depot on the way in and out of Yulshul, where a district government and a PLA base were established.

Early that day, government officials in Dhomda had received a cable notifying them that the convoy would be passing through. Dhomda was more than 80 kilometers from the Trindu county seat, and 200 kilometers from Jyekundo. Barring the unexpected, the convoy would make it most of the way to Jyekundo that day. Although a major snowfall in Dhomda the day before had affected traffic conditions, it wasn't expected to obstruct the route from Dhomda to the Trindu county seat. The cable told staff in Dhomda to prepare to receive the convoy when it stopped to rest.

Perhaps because of road conditions, the convoy didn't approach Dhomda until the afternoon. Unbeknownst to the people in the trucks, they were entering the pastureland of the Ponru Méma nomads, who were famed for their ferocity and martial prowess. Even less did they know that hundreds of armed men from the Ponru Méma, Trindu, and Wangpo (Wangbo)[3] were waiting for them at a strategic spot.

Around three o'clock in the afternoon, the convoy turned into a narrow valley called Pangtu (Pangzhi) Gulch, around 15 kilometers from Dhomda. The highway followed the hilly terrain along the S-curve of the Dzachu River, and as the trucks slowed into the curving road, the front and rear of the convoy drew closer together. Suddenly there was the sound of intense gunfire, and bullets rained down.

Chaos descended as trucks burst into flames, and the convoy halted. The convoy included only one platoon of regular army soldiers; the students from the public security cadre school were still in training and had no battle experience. Available sources don't indicate whether anyone apart from the PLA soldiers was armed. Having just arrived in Qinghai from the inland provinces, the people in the convoy were probably still adjusting to the altitude and were completely unprepared for this sudden attack.

The soldiers escorting the convoy immediately returned fire; after a half-hour-long gun battle, the armed men charged onto the highway and began hand-to-hand combat using knives, swords, and hatchets. Several brutal hours later, the three tribes emerged victorious; all of the escorting soldiers were dead, while the attackers had suffered a dozen or so casualties and had looted all the goods.[4] This became known as the "Pangzhi Gulch incident."

Published Chinese sources are vague about the casualties on the Chinese side. Official publications provide two different sets of figures, one of them (the *Yushu Tibetan Autonomous Prefecture Gazetteer*) stating that "more than 40 party and administrative cadres and people's armed police were killed, 8 vehicles were destroyed, and a large quantity of goods was looted,"[5] the other saying "43 people were killed, 57 wounded, and 9 out of 38 vehicles were destroyed."[6] Tibetan accounts say that more than 600 people were killed.[7] However, the first set of Chinese figures refers specifically to more than 40 "party and administrative cadres and people's armed police," apparently not including the convoy's drivers, escorting soldiers, public security cadre school students, and others. Fang Yangda, deputy commander and chief of staff of the Yushu Rebellion Pacification Command Post in 1958,[8] recalls that when he received orders to take part in the "pacification of rebellion" in Gansu and Qinghai, the chief of staff of the Lanzhou Military Command sent someone to brief him on the situation: "Several dozen vehicles carrying supplies to Qinghai were attacked by armed rebels near Qingshuihe. The goods on the vehicles were looted, the vehicles were burned, and everyone in the vehicles was killed."[9] Given that there were more than 400 people in the convoy, the figures provided in the *Yushu Tibetan Autonomous Prefecture Gazetteer* are therefore dubious.

The "Pangzhi Gulch incident" was a serious setback for the Chinese government in the Tibetan regions, and that may be why official sources provide scant information on it. Even today, secrecy shrouds the number of people who were buried in an alien land in that event.

2

Why did the Ponru Méma and other tribes attack the convoy? Official Chinese sources provide no specific reason that might have triggered a popular revolt. Tibetan sources, however, indicate that the resistance by the Yulshul nomads was related to the Chinese government forcing them to "take the socialist road."[10]

In late January 1956, Yulshul Prefecture held a conference for all of the county heads and passed a resolution calling for the entire prefecture to embark on socialism, establish mutual aid groups, and run cooperative pilot schemes. In March, Yulshul's Bathang (Batang) airport, which would subsequently play an important role in the battles in the Tibetan regions, was opened to air traffic. At the same time, the prefecture sent out seven work teams to start propaganda and began making preliminary preparations for establishing mutual aid groups and cooperative pilot projects.[11] However, the "Sertar incident" in Garzê in February 1956 threw these measures into confusion.[12]

Although Yulshul was under the jurisdiction of Qinghai Province, it was part of the traditional Tibetan region of Kham. Geographically, Yulshul bordered Sershul (Shiqu), under Sichuan's jurisdiction, and its *qianhus* had close ties with headmen in Garzê and Ngawa. The Qinghai authorities were very concerned about the impact the "Sertar incident" might have on Yulshul, and the Chinese government also worried about the situation getting out of hand if Tibetan regions united in rebellion. With all this in mind, the Qinghai provincial party committee sent a work group on an urgent mission to Yulshul in April to assess the situation and to placate the middle and upper strata. By that time, land reform in Garzê had triggered an all-out Tibetan rebellion, and many refugees had fled from Garzê and Ngawa to Yulshul. Monks and laypeople from all social strata in Yulshul were anxious, but there had not yet been any armed revolts. Since 1956, the Qinghai provincial party committee had followed the directives of the Central Committee's Nationalities Affairs Commission in carrying out "socialist education," "eradication of the four pests"[13] and a "mass debate between theism and atheism." These campaigns, especially the eradication of pests and discussions of atheism in the monasteries, had caused considerable unease and discontent among the middle- and upper-strata monks and laypeople, but had not yet affected the overall situation.

From February 28 to March 17, 1957, Qinghai's vice party secretary and governor, Sun Zuobin, and vice-governor, Tashi Wangchuk, were in Yulshul for an inspection tour, the first visit by provincial-level officials since the founding of the PRC. They held a seminar for ethnic and religious representatives at the rank of district head and above on March 9. After returning to Xining, Sun Zuobin and Tashi Wangchuk submitted two reports to the provincial party committee. The first report, dated March 22, 1957, brought up many specific problems that they'd discovered in Yulshul and summed up 15 opinions and demands by Yulshul's upper strata to the government. The first one stated that people of all levels "endorse socialism, but are suspicious of socialist transformation . . . and hope to proceed more slowly." People also asked the government to preserve the sacred mountains, not to levy taxes on monasteries or people for livestock they slaughtered for their own consumption, etc.[14]

Among the issues raised in this report, high taxes were one problem that greatly affected people at all levels of society. As early as October 1952, the Yulshul prefectural party secretary, Ji Chunguang, had raised this issue with the Qinghai provincial party committee, acknowledging that "during the Ma bandit era,[15] the commercial tax was 4%, but now it's typically more than 4%, and in particular in Changdu and Xikang, it's lower than in Yushu. This has given rise to discontent among most traders, and the masses also object to the trade tax on foodstuffs and the slaughter tax."[16] The report by Sun Zuobin and Tashi Wangchuk indicated that the situation had only become worse in the five years since: a tanning tax of eight *yuan* was imposed on a yak hide worth nine *yuan*. The last Nanchen king, Tashi Tsewang Dorjé, at that time governor of Yulshul Prefecture, grumbled that tax was imposed on incense burned during religious rituals and ceremonies, that the *jintan*[17] and paper that monasteries purchased at the trade cooperatives for monks to use was also taxed, that the otter skins his wife had brought back from Tibet had been taxed more than it had cost to engage the draft animals to carry them, and that tax was even imposed on ordinary people for slaughtering livestock and tanning pelts for their own use.[18]

Apart from taxes, the work tasks that the province handed down were also incompatible with conditions on the ground: "For example, Yulshul had five salt lakes that produced about 2.5 million kilos of salt per year, but the salt bureau had been assigned to collect 3.5 million kilos. The province had called for 200,000 kilos of wool in the first quarter of 1956, when the prefecture was only able to produce 75,000 kilos. And in 1956, the provincial education bureau had stipulated that 470 students should be recruited, but in the end a few more than 200 were actually recruited—and even if 470 students had actually been recruited, there weren't enough classrooms and teachers for them."[19]

The newly established mutual aid groups were mainly composed of the most impoverished herders. With the encouragement and support of the work teams, these people often engaged in behavior that offended and troubled others. At the seminar, someone reported that members of one cooperative were engaged in a sideline of dismantling sacred *mani* cairns[20] to burn lime, "causing discontent among most representatives and the masses."[21]

While in Yulshul, Sun Zuobin and Tashi Wangchuk visited several herder households near the Jyeku Monastery, and "what impressed us most deeply was that they were in such poverty, and that their circumstances were much harsher than we'd imagined."[22] However, the report then cited the figures provided by the Yulshul prefectural party committee claiming that the prefecture "now has 3.2 million head of livestock, nearly twice as many as at the time of Liberation in 1949."[23] Apparently, the herders had not benefited from the increase.

In the second report that Sun Zuobin and Tashi Wangchuk submitted, on April 15, 1957, the 15 problems and other suggestions had been dropped, and the only problem mentioned was that "according to reports, more than 50% of Han cadres in Yushu Prefecture do not feel at ease in their work." But it recommended that no more cooperative pilot projects be launched that year, and proposed caution in the propaganda campaign related to "socialist transformation" of the animal husbandry industry.[24]

The Qinghai provincial party committee circulated the second report to all prefectural party committees and submitted it to the Central Committee, but there is no indication that the first report, which raised so many problems, was ever circulated or submitted upwards, and the Qinghai provincial party committee's United Front Department didn't include it in its collection of documents published in 1959. It is likely that the provincial party committee suppressed that first report.

One year later, Sun Zuobin was labeled an anti-party element because he "opposed the party's class line in the pastoral regions"[25] and Tashi Wangchuk was labeled a "local nationalist." Both men were purged.[26]

In April 1958, the Qinghai provincial party committee sounded the "leap forward bugle horn." Just one month later, 399 agricultural and animal husbandry cooperatives were established in Yulshul, along with 20 SPP pastures, and 6,751 herder households, or 22.5% of the total, joined those cooperatives and pastures.[27]

On May 18, the Trindu County party secretary, Xiang Qian, led a work team to a village to promote "socialist transformation," but was killed while presiding over a village meeting.[28] Less than two weeks later, Yulshul Prefecture convened its first people's congress. All of the delegates were headmen and influential monks, and the meeting lasted nearly three months, from May 29 to August 21. The meeting focused on "activities such as baring one's heart to the party."[29] In the CCP's terminology, this implied running study courses to make people take a public stand, and denunciations and other such activities may also have occurred. This congress served the practical purpose of isolating the upper strata from the local people, depriving people of their leaders so that they were unable to organize any resistance.[30]

The Ponru Méma leader Drakpa Wangyel had been tipped off, however, and didn't attend the congress. He immediately called a meeting of the community's most influential people, and they unanimously opposed establishing a cooperative. They knew from past experience that their opposition to the government would certainly be suppressed.[31]

The Ponru Méma had a tradition of resistance. One of the oldest *shokka* in the Trindu area, they were ethnic Mongols who had early on assimilated to Tibetan culture. In 1937, the Ponru Méma and Shuma (Xiuma) had battled Ma Bufang's troops to protest taxation, and after thrashing Ma's army, they had retreated to the area of Changthang (Qiangtang) bordering Nagchu in Tibet. In 1942, Ma Bufang sent his cavalry commander with 1,000 troops toward Nagchu to retaliate against the two groups. They rallied to meet the enemy head-on, but were ultimately outnumbered and all but obliterated. By the time the PRC was founded, all that remained of the Ponru Méma were 180 households, of around 1,000 people total, half the population of the early Republican era.[32] By 1958, the community had grown to 450 households, of 2,203 people total, and their leader Drakpa Wangyel had been appointed deputy head of Trindu County.

The Trindu *shokka* was mainly farmers, and they also opposed the organizing of cooperatives. When the Trindu and Wangpo chieftains learned that the county party committee was rounding up headmen under the pretext of a conference, they fled and hid in a monastery. Each of them then appealed to their people to come together, rallying more than 130 fighters. Once the three groups (the Ponru Méma, Wangpo, and Trindu tribes) joined forces, they stationed their men at a strategic point in Ponru Méma territory near Dhomda.[33] This happened to be the place where the Ponru Méma had faced off with Ma Bufang's troops 21 years earlier.

3

Behind the Pangtu Gulch incident described in section 1 of this chapter, there was a strategic policy change. In 1958, the Chinese government's battles in the Tibetan regions shifted from Sichuan and Yunnan to Qinghai and Gansu.

In April 1958, the CMC ordered the 54th Army in North Korea to send its 134th Division back to China, where the division would set off for Gansu under the temporary command of the Lanzhou Military Command. On April 29, the deputy commander of the 134th Division's reconnaissance unit, Wang Tingsheng, and head of the communications section, Wang Xu, led a 150-man advance force from North Korea to Lanzhou under "top secret" conditions.[34]

The 134th Division headed for Gansu in May and was stationed in Lanzhou, Wuwei, and in Minhe[35] and Xiangtang[36] on the Gansu-Qinghai border. Here the soldiers supplemented their equipment and underwent training to adapt to the plateau environment as final preparation for heading off to battle in Yulshul.[37]

While the Yulshul prefectural party committee was holding the regional leaders in Jyekundo to "bare their hearts to the party," the "Yushu Rebellion Pacification Command Post" was established.[38]

After receiving orders, the Lanzhou Military Command briefed the 134th Division's commanding officers on the situation: "armed rebellions" had occurred in all six Qinghai prefectures mainly occupied by Tibetans, and a dozen or so counties had been stormed and captured by "rebel troops and local lamas." Working personnel had been besieged in some places, and transportation had been cut off. Special mention was made of the attack on the supply convoy in the Pangtu Gulch incident. All of this was naturally attributed to the plotting of "die-hard elements" and "imperialism."[39]

In June, the deputy commander of the 134th Division and of the Yushu Command Post, Fang Yangda, set off from Lanzhou with his troops, heading for Xiangtang in Minhe County. On the eastern edge of Qinghai Province, Minhe was a transition zone between the loess plateau and the Tibetan plateau. Here the troops underwent acclimatization training.

At the same time, the air force's 25th Division was transferred from the military airport in Wugong County, Shaanxi Province, to the Xining airport.[40]

On June 24, Mao wrote a memo on the Qinghai provincial party committee's report in which he explicitly stated, "The armed rebellion by Qinghai reactionaries is excellent," and "the greater the disturbance, the better," because this created an opportunity to strike at them with no holds barred, and "the working people there can achieve liberation earlier."[41] This memo effectively gave the army permission to use its full power to crush Tibetan resistance.

Mao delegated this matter to President Liu Shaoqi, the party's General Secretary and State Council Vice-Premier Deng Xiaoping, Vice-Premier and Defense Minister Peng Dehuai, and CMC Secretary General and Defense Vice-Minister Huang Kecheng, directing that Deng and Huang should handle it.[42]

On June 29, the engineer corps that accompanied the army arrived in Xiangtang. The army engineers had already undergone more than a month of bridge-building training on the Yellow River's Lanzhou segment. All of the military forces gathered at Xiangtang to receive special outfitting and supplies for high-altitude operations. The battle troops assembled for a mass pledge rally and took a solemn oath: "In order to safeguard the victorious completion of socialist revolution and socialist construction in the Great Northwest, exterminate the exploitative feudalist serf system, deliver our suffering Tibetan compatriots, and completely, thoroughly, and cleanly eliminate the counterrevolutionary armed rebellion, we will never retreat until victorious."[43]

July 1, 1958, marked the 31st anniversary of the founding of the CCP. That morning, a convoy of 186 military vehicles filled with PLA soldiers set off from Xiangtang in a formidable array. It arrived at Xining that same night, and the Qinghai provincial party committee organized more than 30,000 residents for a grand welcome to lift their spirits.[44]

On July 2, the army set off from Xining, passed through Gormo, and entered Dzo-gen Rawa (Huashixia).[45] The main force amassed here for several days to make unified battle arrangements and assign battle tasks. Then the army split into three groups to form an encirclement as it moved in on Yulshul.

4

The "Pangtu Gulch incident" had come as a great shock to all levels of the Chinese government, but it had involved only the three Trindu nomad groups, and Yulshul had yet to experience the outbreak of all-out rebellion. After the Yulshul prefectural party committee convened its "first people's congress plenum," the situation went into a precipitous decline.

In accordance with the suggestions transmitted by Li Weihan and others in the Central Committee, the Qinghai provincial party committee required all prefectures and counties to "use meetings, study sessions, and other methods to round up ethnic and religious upper-strata individuals and put them under control in order to prevent an armed insurrection."[46] This preventative measure had exactly the opposite effect.

In traditional Tibetan society, the relationship between the headmen and the ordinary people was nothing like the relationship of class oppression presented in the Chinese government's subsequent propaganda, but rather resembled the traditional patriarchal clan system in mainland China. Research shows that before the Chinese government used land reform to transform the villages and "establish rural base areas" in order to seize power by "surrounding the cities from the countryside," the power relations in the villages were not purely those of class and class struggle.[47]

With various localities in turmoil and public sentiment tense and uneasy, the Chinese government rounded up local headmen, in particular revered senior monks, and placed them under control. The Chinese government may have seen this as "preventing possible trouble," but to the people, it looked like all of their leaders being locked up. This incident became a catalyst for popular revolt[48] and the detonator for the subsequent "Lhasa incident" on March 10, 1959.

Not long after the leaders were placed under control, the local Yulshul government carried out a mass arrest of "unstable elements" in Jyekundo Township and at the Thrangu Monastery[49] about five kilometers away during a religious ceremony, arresting hundreds of people. This incident sparked a rebellion at the Jyeku Monastery, just outside of Jyekundo near the prefectural government offices.[50]

While the delegates to the first "people's congress" in Jyekundo were under close surveillance by "security guards," a few of the leaders were able to escape incognito, while others, pretending to be activists, were allowed to return to their people to "convince them to surrender their firearms." Once reunited with their people, these leaders immediately rallied their militia, and their resistance was joined by other groups whose headmen still remained in detention. The Yulshul government in Jyekundo found itself under siege by the armed forces of the VIPs detained there. The tribesmen charged into the city, but were repelled.[51]

By the time that the Yushu Command Post's main forces marched westward, rebellion had spread throughout Yulshul. In the summer, nearly 10,000 PLA troops moved in, and Yulshul became the site of some of the most violent battles that the PLA fought in the Tibetan regions in those six years. By the time the smoke of war had cleared, more than 69,400 Yulshul herders had died in battle or in the famine that followed it. That was more than one-third of the total population of Yulshul at the time.[52]

5

The deputy commander and chief of staff of the Yushu Command Post, Fang Yangda, recalls that when the army moved in on Yulshul, "According to briefings from the upper levels and on-the-ground reconnaissance by our scouts, Yushu Prefecture had nine rebel bandit groups totaling more than 16,000 people entrenched near Yushu's Batang airport."[53]

What kind of "on-the-ground reconnaissance" had the scouting team carried out? The deputy commander of the reconnaissance unit, Wang Tingsheng, subsequently recalled, "After we reached Yushu, because rebellions were already ongoing in all the counties, the best we could do was gain an understanding of the situation from the autonomous prefecture government in Jiegu. We went to the Jiegu Monastery to pay our respects to the Living Buddha and to tour the temple, and inspected the Zhimenda ferry pier on the Tongtian river."[54] That was how the PLA learned about the "enemy situation."

The "nine rebel bandit groups" Fang Yangda referred to were inhabitants of what is now southeastern Yulshul County and southern Trindu County. They hadn't "entrenched" themselves there after "armed rebellions"; rather, this was their homeland, where they had grazed their herds for generations. Fang Yangda didn't explain whether the figure of 16,000 that he used was referring to adult males or the total population.

After community leaders were called to Jyekundo to "bare their hearts to the party," and hundreds of people were detained in the Thrangu Monastery and in the town of Jyekundo, groups that had never intended to resist felt compelled to do so. Tribal militia were mainly active within their own territories and had not yet formed an effective alliance or unified command, but they happened to be active on both sides of the Tongtian River, not far from the Bathang airport, and in the area of the main trunk of the Xining-Jyekundo highway. In order to ensure the free flow of transport routes and the safety of the airport, PLA troops entering Yulshul staged their first battle in the area north of the Tongtian River.

On July 28, the 134th Division's 400th Regiment, army engineers, artillery and scouts, and the 13th and 14th Cavalry Regiments of the Inner Mongolia Military Command arrived at Dhomda. They received an air force reconnaissance report of "more than 100 tents and hundreds of people amassed" on the grasslands at a place called Khanathang (Kanatan).[55] "Most of the people are mounted and have guns slung across their backs and are actively moving about, and there is a monastery nearby."[56] Khanathang therefore became a prime target of the Yushu Command Post.

Khanathang, the pastureland of the Khana tribe, covered both sides of the Dzachu River, which flowed from the southwest into Trindu and then turned south at Dhomda and east near the Drugyu (Zhujie) Monastery in Dinchen (Zhenqin) Township. The "nearby monastery" may have been the Khana Monastery, one of two monasteries of the Khana people. Tibetan sources state that the Khana and several other tribes had settled on a plain across from the monastery, and that the air force bombed them, but that the swampy land limited the impact of the bombs.[57]

The next day at noon, the two cavalry regiments set off from Dhomda and sped toward Khanathang. Several hours later, the 400th Infantry Regiment and an artillery battalion also set off from Dhomda over the highway, capturing the area around the Drugyu Monastery and forming an encirclement around the tribal fighters.

On July 30, PLA troops launched separate attacks. Decades later, Fang Yangda, the deputy commander of the Yushu Command Post, recalled that the tribal fighters had "minimal combat effectiveness," but that they often ambushed the PLA troops in the darkness, causing "quite a few losses."[58]

However, one Chinese soldier who participated in the battle at Khanathang told a different story. The battle started at nightfall, and "fierce fighting continued until dawn. Gunfire was ceaseless, cannons thundered, and signal flares and other flares rose into the sky one after another. The great plain glowed with light that changed night into day. Reflections of photoelectric light displayed layers of mountain peaks in their majestic array, presenting a marvelously magnificent vista."[59]

Tibetan sources state that at that time, most of the Khana men had gone elsewhere, and there were very few armed fighters in the tents that were surrounded at Khanathang.[60] How many "enemies" were actually at Khanathang? Memoirs by PLA soldiers mention only "100 or so enemies killed" and "around 100 bandits taken prisoner. We captured some firearms, knives and spears, along with horses and other goods, and rescued a group of masses who had been coerced into participating. We also captured the Shuma headman alive."[61]

At the Drugyu Monastery, more than 300 encircled tribal fighters engaged PLA troops in intense battle for more than three hours, until hand-to-hand fighting crushed resistance in one building after another.[62] At that time, the Drugyu Monastery had 240 monks, but it is not clear from the Chinese sources whether they were among the "more than 300 rebel bandits annihilated."

The army pressed on toward Zhe'u (Xiewu).[63] Fang Yangda says, "Before attacking Chengduo, our scouts learned that there were also rebel bandits in the area of Xiewu, but by the time we got there, all had fled." The recollections of a frontline soldier are completely different. According to the soldier, when the artillery company advanced into Xiewu, "We saw people going in and out of monasteries on the mountains on both sides. Artillerymen fired more than 20 howitzer shells at the monastery on the mountain to the left. Immediately buildings collapsed and smoke billowed upward, while terrified people ran helter-skelter, having no choice but to come down from the mountain and surrender." After the bombardment, the survivors surrendered. Ironically, the same soldier claimed that "the PLA liberated Xiewu and the monastery without firing a single shot."[64]

The soldier doesn't explain why the PLA fired on the monastery on the left but not the one on the right, nor does he say what kinds of people were going in and out. Firing on a monastery as soon as troops arrived was clearly indiscriminate killing as a show of force.

During the "battle to relieve the encirclement of Trindu," a soldier in a machine-gun unit recalls encountering "especially numerous and powerful enemies" and that the soldiers "were unable to ward them off on our own, so the company commander told me to contact the commander of the Fifth Squad." He escaped being killed by rolling behind a large boulder.[65]

Moving from Trindu to Jyekundo required crossing the Tongtian River. A soldier who took part in the battle recalled, "The scouting company moved light and fast, and after an hour of intense fighting, they captured the commanding points on both sides of the crossing. The pontoon bridge unit followed close behind, and in just three or four hours constructed a wide, stable pontoon bridge across the river."[66] What he didn't know was that the company had been surrounded in the village near the crossing, and that his commander Fang Yangda and cadres with the pontoon bridge unit had been ambushed while checking out the terrain near the Tongtian River. When the scouting unit learned of the ambush over the radio, they broke through the encirclement and, covered by machine guns, rescued Fang by ferry.[67]

After the main force of the PLA crossed the Tongtian over the pontoon bridge, they pushed on toward Jyekundo, the prefecture capital. Upon arriving, the advance force "used several pieces of heavy artillery to bombard the monastery. . . . The points of impact exploded with a sound like thunder; rubble and stone flew through the air, smoke billowed up, and the stubborn enemy met a violent end, with bodies scattered everywhere. Portions of the mountain collapsed and the ground split open, and bandit rats scurried around in panic. Not long after that, dozens of compounds and hundreds of buildings on the mountain were destroyed, and those who escaped death were all taken prisoner, with not one slipping through. We captured a number of firearms and other goods."[68]

The Battle of Trindu County lasted five days, all but wiping out the resistance of the Ponru Méma, Shuma, Khana, Trindu, and Wangpo tribes. The Yongshar (Yongxia) tribe fled to the source of the Yellow River under close pursuit by two reinforced companies of the 13th Cavalry Regiment from Khanathang. Provisions were airdropped to the pursuing PLA troops, allowing them to travel light and fast. The Yongshar finally surrendered at Chumarleb (Qumalai) on August 11.

In this battle, 1,228 Tibetans were killed, 139 wounded, and 2,094 taken prisoner. The PLA seized 2,797 firearms, 33,019 rounds of ammunition, and 8,290 knives and swords. The number of "liberated masses" is not disclosed, nor is the number of PLA casualties.[69]

The PLA engaged in large and small battles in Trindu for 38 days, using an infantry regiment, two cavalry regiments, and one battalion each of army engineers, artillerymen, and scouts, "annihilating and disintegrating 7,618 enemies."[70]

6

At seven o'clock in the morning on August 20, 1958, a cavalry company set off from Jyekundo and sped north. Their destination was Drongda (Zhongda), about 50 kilometers away.[71]

The chief of staff of the Yushu military sub-district, Deng Shaochi, was leading this cavalry company on a scouting expedition to the Ranyak (Rangniang) Monastery. Another three cavalry companies and one reinforced platoon led by military sub-district commander Zhu Tingyun set off for Ranyak from Jyekundo at 4:30 in the afternoon.[72]

Deng's cavalry unit charged into a valley where streams gurgled from the mountains and flowed into a small river. The Ranyak Monastery, one of Yulshul's largest and oldest, was nestled at the base of the mountain slope where the streams converged,[73] with a small village facing it. By the time the cavalry company arrived, more than 1,000 people were defending the monastery, including hundreds of fighters who had rushed from the village to join hundreds of monks.[74] Local fighters holding the hills around the monastery exchanged fire with the cavalry reconnaissance unit, taking the advantage of sniping from above. Finding it impossible to charge up the mountain, the cavalry company retreated after suffering substantial casualties.[75]

Zhu Tingyun arrived with his troops at seven o'clock that evening and immediately launched an attack on the mountain south of the monastery. Unable to withstand the assault, the Tibetan fighters retreated inside. Deng Shaochi and Zhu Tingyun drew up a plan overnight, ordering two companies to deliver the main attack from the east and west simultaneously, while one platoon occupied the township government building to obstruct the arrival of possible Tibetan reinforcements. Two platoons occupied the village, and one company occupied the mountains to its north and south, effectively encircling the monastery. All the military units were in place by four o'clock in the morning on August 21, and at 6:15, the PLA launched its attack.

Monasteries, especially the more established ones, are usually the sturdiest structures in Tibetan regions, with high, thick walls that make them easy to hold and hard to attack. In his memoirs, the deputy commander of the Yushu Command Post, Fang Yangda, recalls his experience. "Those monasteries had existed for centuries and were very solid. Capturing them involved heavy casualties on our side, and sometimes we were forced to disengage. . . . The Tibetan people had been Buddhists for centuries, and the monasteries were their spiritual homes, so they were built very sturdily; there was no way to approach or enter them, so we had to bombard them with shells and use explosives to blow them open, otherwise we could never get in."[76]

Ranyak Monastery was one of these. Conventional weapons could not breach its massive outer walls. After Zhu Tingyun and Deng Shaoqi directed four companies of soldiers to attack it for two days without success, they sought aid from headquarters.[77]

At dusk on August 22, the Yushu Command Post ordered a battalion to proceed without delay to the Ranyak Monastery. The battalion set off immediately on its 60-kilometer march, its advance force reaching there at 11 o'clock that night. By daybreak on the 23rd, all of the reinforcements had arrived, and all of the PLA units joined in a general offensive against the monastery at 6:30 that morning.[78]

As dawn broke, the monks and laymen inside the monastery discovered that all of the mountains surrounding the monastery had been occupied by PLA troops, and that they were thoroughly surrounded. Soon after that, soldiers surged down from the mountaintops, quickly surrounding several dormitories outside the monastery walls. This was immediately followed by an eruption of gunfire and the explosion of hand grenades. The village below the monastery was quickly captured, and a red banner waved on a rooftop, above several machine guns.

As the sun rose over the plateau, the main gate of the monastery was blasted open and several holes were blown into the outer wall. Under cover of machine-gun and cannon fire, infantrymen swarmed from the village east of the monastery as cavalry troops pressed in from the east, west, and north, hundreds of soldiers pouring in through the main gate and breaches in the wall. The defenders fired on the soldiers at close range from the roofs of the assembly halls, creating a tight barrage that beat back the troops, and a company of soldiers attempting to occupy the main hall was forced to retreat. Under fire cover, PLA soldiers launched another assault, which was likewise beaten back by monks and laymen inside the monastery. This was repeated several times.[79]

Unable to capture the monastery, the commanding officer ordered it blown up. The first target was the main assembly hall.

A platoon of soldiers carried explosives into the monastery and charged toward the main assembly hall, but was held back by Tibetan fire. The troops then organized powerful fire cover, and bullets rained on the assembly hall from the village directly opposite. Finally, a platoon of soldiers reached the door and swiftly packed explosives beneath the front walls. Near dusk, several earthshaking explosions rang out, and the building collapsed with a deafening roar.[80]

As PLA soldiers surged into the monastery, the monks and laymen inside continued to resist. Dozens of sword-wielding monks and laymen carried out a suicide attack, all of them shot dead beside the great stupa. Terrified villagers hiding inside the monks' quarters fled in all directions, only to be felled by bullets.[81]

That night, the moon rode high, illuminating the scene as the demolition platoon continued its work, blasting away each section of the wall and destroying each assembly hall and all of the monks' quarters. Bodies piled up in the ruins, and blood flowed in rivers. Dozens of survivors took advantage of the darkness to break through the encirclement, charging out the back gate of the monastery and fleeing into the mountains. Behind them, the flames of the burning monastery lit the night.[82]

By the middle of the night, all of the temple halls had been captured. Fang Yangda recalls, "The entire battle went quite smoothly, and not a single soldier was killed. It was only during the search for the remaining bandits that several soldiers were shot by bandit snipers."[83] That's because the vast majority of the nearly 1,000 monks and laymen inside the monastery had been killed in action.

The battle ended at 10:40 on the morning of the 24th.

These were the accomplishments of the "storming of the heavily fortified Ranyak Monastery": "224 rebel bandits annihilated, 11 prisoners taken and 517 firearms captured, including 41 rifles, one submachine gun, 475 homemade weapons, 507 rounds of ammunition, 335 side swords, and 3 pairs of binoculars. Among the army officers and men, 36 sacrificed their lives and 47 were wounded."[84] These figures suggest that nearly two regiments of cavalry and infantry fought for four days to capture a monastery defended by 235 people armed with only 41 rifles, which does not make sense.

How many monks and lay civilians actually died in the "storming of the Ranyak Monastery" will not be known until the relevant documents are declassified. What is certain is that the more than 700-year-old monastery was completely destroyed by the PLA in August 1958.[85]

By the time the 134th Division withdrew, in January 1959, after more than five months in Yulshul, it had racked up the following "military accomplishments": "Engaged in 148 battles, annihilated 9,557 of the enemy, and captured 2 light machine guns and 2,387 firearms."[86] That suggests that less than a quarter of the "annihilated" Tibetans had been armed with guns.

Chapter 14

BLOODBATH AT DRONGTHIL GULCH

1

"The location of the battle was Drongthil [Zhongtie] Township," the elderly monk Tubten Nyima told me at Gomang Dratsang,[1] in the Drepung (Zhebang) Monastery in exile. It was September 2010, and I had made a special trip to the Mundgod Tibetan Refugee Settlement in the southern Indian state of Karnataka, where the Ganden (Gandan) and Drepung Monasteries had been rebuilt. I had hoped to find some first-generation refugees from Tsikorthang (Xinghai), to gain a better understanding of the battle that had taken place more than 50 years earlier in that county in Qinghai's Tsolho Prefecture, in the northeast of Golok.

Taped on the wall behind the elderly monk was a color picture on glossy paper showing blue sky over grasslands and a Tibetan-style temple nestled beneath craggy mountains. Tubten Nyima told me this was the Drakar Drelzong (Saizong) Monastery, where he had become a monk as a young boy. The monastery was destroyed in 1958 and then again during the Cultural Revolution, and the monastery in the picture had been rebuilt on the site of the old one.

"Drongthil used to be very inaccessible. Further in were remote, heavily forested mountains that motor vehicles couldn't penetrate. Refugees from all over gathered in Drongthil, and later they were accused of being armed rebels and suppressed. Three years after the suppression, the water flowing down from the mountains was still undrinkable; it tasted rank because too many people and livestock had been killed in the mountains. For three years, no one drank the water there."

"Too many people were killed in battle, so for years no one drank the water there." That description had become familiar to me after Tibetans from various localities had used the same words to describe the horrific battles they'd survived. One implication of this description was that after the battles, no one cleared away the corpses, which were left exposed to the elements.

"It wasn't only people from Tsikorthang who came to Drongthil; there were also people from Triga [Guide] and other places.[2] Everyone fled on their own; there was no real organization, and people just ran over—monks and laypeople alike gathered there. During the [PLA] suppression, they killed people on sight, just killing everyone. It was like that back then—killing on sight."[3]

The situation Tubten Nyima described to me was a battle that occurred in the area of Drongthil Gulch in Tsikorthang County. It was one of the major campaigns of Qinghai's 1958–59 suppression of the Tibetan resistance and fleeing Tibetans. Official Chinese publications refer to it as the "Battle of encirclement and annihilation in southeastern Xinghai."[4]

2

On June 11, 1958, China's first provincial-level Tibetan newspaper, the bilingual Chinese-Tibetan *Qinghai Zangwen bao* (*Qinghai Tibetan Daily*), run by *Qinghai Daily*, published a report on its second page stating, "The Hainan Tibetan Autonomous Prefecture has basically carried out the organization of animal husbandry cooperatives." The report stated that as of May 28, "Throughout the prefecture, 678 animal husbandry cooperatives have been established (including 26 old cooperatives). There are 113 SPP pastures, and a total of 10,424 herder households have joined the cooperatives or pastures, composing 78.68% of the prefecture's 13,272 herder households."[5]

Another report stated that as of the end of May 1958, "1,311 animal husbandry cooperatives have been established in the whole of Qinghai Province, along with 221 SPP pastures, with a total of 23,278 herder households joining the cooperatives and pastures. They compose 34.9% of all herder households in the province."[6]

In the same edition, the newspaper published a congratulatory cable that the Qinghai provincial party committee had sent to the Hainan TAP on June 2: "Following the basic implementation of cooperatives in the Haixi and Haibei autonomous prefectures in early May, the Hainan Autonomous Prefecture has also scored a decisive victory in the socialist transformation of livestock husbandry. The autonomous prefectures of Hainan, Yushu, and Guoluo and the Henan Mongol Autonomous County are also stepping up the pace of their march toward organizing cooperatives. Based on the current enthusiastic demands of the vast herder masses to establish cooperatives and collective pastures, the pastoral regions of our province should be able to completely carry out basic organization of cooperatives before August this year."[7] That is to say, according to the plans of the Qinghai provincial party committee, the county's herding households would all be channeled into "animal husbandry cooperatives" and SPP pastures by the end of August 1958.

What the June 11 edition of *Qinghai Tibetan Daily* didn't report was that by the end of May 1958, intense resistance had emerged as the Malho, Yulshul, and Golok TAPs "stepped up the pace of their march toward organizing cooperatives." Seven days after this report was published, the Qinghai provincial party committee issued its "Directive on a Province-wide Suppression of Armed Rebellion,"[8] which acknowledged that "counterrevolutionary armed rebellions have spread and become a pervasive problem throughout the Qinghai region. Major and minor armed rebellions have occurred in all six autonomous prefectures in the province's pastoral regions."[9] The Qinghai provincial party committee attributed herder resistance to "imperialism and the conspiratorial separatist activities of Lhasa's reactionary faction, and a reflection of socialist transformation and opposition to socialist transformation; it is an intensely acute fight-to-the-death class struggle."[10] For that reason, it had to be suppressed by armed force.

Given the scale of resistance, the Qinghai provincial party committee requested reinforcements from the CMC, citing the gulag-style "labor reform farms" established in Hainan, Haibei, Haixi, and Chaidamu (Tsaidam). For fear that "the moment a mishap occurs, the danger [would] be extremely great," they requested motorized military capacity from the CMC and Lanzhou Military Command to allow "for flexible coordination of the overall battle situation."[11]

On June 24, Mao circulated this document with his comments:

> I ask Comrade [Huang] Kecheng[12] to print this document and distribute it to all comrades at the Military Commission meeting. At the same time, I ask Comrade [Deng] Xiaoping to print and distribute it to each provincial, municipal, and autonomous region party committee, distributing it first to Sichuan, Yunnan, Guizhou, and Tibet. Let everyone know of this matter. The reactionary armed rebellion in Qinghai is excellent, and an opportunity to liberate the laboring people is at hand. The guiding principles of the Qinghai provincial party committee are completely correct. Tibet must prepare to deal with the possibility of a full-scale armed rebellion. The greater the disturbance, the better. If Tibet's reactionary faction dares to launch a full-scale armed rebellion, the laboring people there can obtain liberation earlier, without a doubt.[13]

By early June 1958—following the outbreak of the "Xunhua incident" on April 17—10 counties and 39 townships under the Malho and Tsolho TAPs "experienced armed rebellions, with the most serious in Xinghai County."[14]

Both Tibetan and Chinese sources indicate that half a year after the counties of Gepa Sumdo (Tongde) and Mangra (Guinan) had actively established animal husbandry cooperatives and SPP pastures, intense armed conflicts broke out between Tibetans and local cadres and armed police. In Gepa Sumdo, an alliance of local militia besieged the county government, killed the county party secretary, and burned down the government office building.[15]

Even so, no currently available documents from either side indicate armed conflicts between the herders of Tsikorthang County and the county's government or work teams.

As in other regions, "socialist transformation" in Tsikorthang County began with propaganda. In 1956, cadres began convening mass meetings through local headmen or lamas, and then used Tibetan interpreters to describe the benefits of socialism.

This propaganda was too far removed from herders' daily life experience, and they couldn't make head or tail of it: "They said that 'socialism' meant putting all the cattle and sheep together, and there would be many benefits. All the wool would be gathered together, and all the butter would be churned together. Nobody liked the idea," Tubten Nyima told me.

The organization of cooperatives allowed the state to control finances through "credit cooperatives," so the cadres pushed the herders to deposit money in the cooperatives: "If you have one *yuan*, you must put it in the bank and not keep it at home. If you leave it at home, it will turn into a tiger that will eventually eat you up."

And what was "class struggle"? The cadres explained to the herders, "If the crops farmers planted are eaten up by bugs, and the herders' sheep are eaten up by wolves, shouldn't the wolves and bugs be killed?" Everyone answered together, "Of course wolves and bugs must be killed!" But these people didn't know that in this case "wolves and bugs" was supposed to refer to lamas, monks, and headmen.

"That was talking with poems and songs,"[16] Tubten Nyima told me with a laugh.

Though they were bewildered by the concept of socialism, the herders were not allowed to challenge or ask questions about it; nevertheless, basic common sense was enough to understand the essence of cooperatives. It was only natural that no one, apart from a small number of deeply impoverished farmers and herders, was willing to hand over their land and livestock to cooperatives.

One year previously, on April 5, 1957, Qinghai's provincial second secretary and governor, Sun Zuobin, had given a speech at an enlarged meeting of the Hainan prefectural people's political consultative conference, during which he made a promise to upper-strata monks and laypeople that "taking the socialist road in the future will involve peaceful consultation; if you agree with it, we'll do it, and if you don't agree, we'll postpone it."[17]

However, Sun Zuobin was subjected to group denunciation as an "ultra-rightist" in January 1958, and soon after that he was expelled from the party.[18] This naturally nullified the promises that Sun Zuobin had made to Tsolho's upper strata in his capacity as provincial governor.[19]

In April 1958, a large-scale "socialist transformation" movement began in Tsikorthang. When it reached the stage of practical operations, the county cadres didn't even bother with the carrot-and-stick approach that had been used in Garzê to force the upper strata to agree to "democratic reform," but just went straight to attacking ethnic and religious leaders: "The entire county engaged in the venting of grievances and struggle, holding more than 130 grievance-venting rallies with more than 60,000 attendances and more than 20,000 ventings of grievances. All herd owners, headmen, and upper-strata religious figures were denounced, and 217 religious figures were rounded up for group training."[20] At that time, the county's total population was less than 20,000, so one can only imagine the social reverberations of holding denunciation rallies on that scale within a month.

Soon after this, the PLA's killing of monks in the "Drakar Drelzong incident" pushed local people over the brink.

3

One day in May 1958, monks at the Drakar Drelzong Monastery were beginning their day as usual when a large number of PLA soldiers armed for an emergency burst into the monastery, occupying assembly halls and searching the living quarters. All of the monks were herded into the main assembly hall, and shortly after that the soldiers set up machine guns at the windows and doors. A cadre using an interpreter demanded that the monks surrender their firearms, threatening to shoot them dead if they refused.

"There were no weapons in the monastery, so what were we supposed to surrender? It was a lie!" Tubten Nyima, who was a monk at the monastery then, told me as we talked decades later. "Furthermore, the monks didn't resist at all."

According to Zhayi Rinpoché, the PLA massacred 18 monks at the Drakar Drelzong Monastery that day.[21] The Chinese government subsequently acknowledged the "Drakar Drelzong incident" as one of three major cases of "mistaken judgment in the enlargement of rebellion pacification in 1958."[22] However, the details of these three major cases have never been made public to date. How many monks did the PLA actually kill at Drakar Drelzong? How many monks were arrested that day? What happened to the rest of the monks? More than half a century later, all of that remains top secret.

The Drakar Drelzong Monastery, the largest in Tsikorthang, was located on one of the four sacred mountains of Tibetan Buddhism, in Amdo. In 1958, the monastery had 18 temples and stupas of various sizes, 15 *nangchen* compounds,[23] more than 150 dormitories with a total of 1,086 cells for monks, and 609 monks. It was also Tsikorthang's wealthiest monastery, possessing a horse ranch, a cattle ranch, a camel ranch, three sheep ranches, and thousands of *mu* of land. Prior to 1958, the monastery had invested 400,000 *yuan* in local industry.[24]

The monastery's abbot, Ngarotsang Rinpoché, enjoyed great fame and veneration among the people of the Tso-ngon (Qinghai) and Kanlho (Gansu) region. In 1950, he was selected for the Qinghai provincial people's political consultative conference, and in 1954 he became its vice-chairman and a delegate to the provincial people's congress. He became executive member of the Chinese Buddhist Association in 1957. Yet Ngarotsang Rinpoché went from "fellow traveler" to prisoner overnight.[25]

Soon after the Qinghai provincial party committee's congratulatory cable to Tsolho TAP in June 1958, herders began rebelling in Mangra, Gepa Sumdo, and Tsikorthang counties.

According to official figures, in Tsikorthang in June 1958, "2,340 households of 9,820 people, and 10 monasteries with 1,020 monks, for a total of 10,840 people" were involved in "opposing the leadership of the Chinese Communist Party, opposing the socialist system and opposing the cooperative movement."[26] The total population of Tsikorthang County at that time was 16,572, of which 10,028 were herders, and the county had 13 monasteries, with a total of 1,430 clerics.[27] That means that the number of herders taking part in the "armed rebellion" composed 97.9% of the county's herder population, and the participating monks composed 71.3% of all of the county's clerics.

In official Chinese sources, the "bandit chieftain" in the Tsikorthang "rebellion" is named Kunsang (Gengzang in Chinese). Kunsang was the manager of Drakar Drelzong and a powerful man in Tsikorthang, which made him a key United Front target for the county party committee. The government was always calling him to meetings, the content of which he would relay to the monastery's monks, and mass rallies of local residents or monks had to be arranged through him. After the Drakar Drelzong incident, Kunsang fled into the hills with monks and laypeople.

The July 26, 1958, issue of the Xinhua News Agency's *Internal Reference* reports that Tsikorthang herders "mounted a surprise attack and besieged" three township governments, destroying buildings and looting goods, and that they "actively searched out our armed working detachments and people's armed police to battle with them."[28] However, a county source says nothing about herders attacking the government, and only states that in those three townships, "a minority of reactionary headmen and upper-strata religious personages incited the masses to resist the confiscation of their firearms and launch an armed revolt."[29]

Official sources indicate that in the last half of July 1958, some upper-strata personages who had been appointed to party postings in Tsikorthang County, along with more than 10,000 monks and laymen and "more than 2,000 traitorous masses who had fled to Xinghai from neighboring areas, armed with more than 900 firearms, ganged together and divided into several groups to forcibly occupy the area east of the Ehesha (A-sang) Monastery and south of Zhongtiegou (Drongthil Gulch), with the intention of mounting a stubborn, long-term resistance in the area extending east to the Yellow River, north to the Qushen'an (Chu-ngon) River[30] and west to Maji (Amnye Machen) Mountain."[31]

Drongthil Gulch lay southeast of Tsikorthang, about 70 kilometers from the county seat, near Gepa Sumdo County and Machen (Maqin)

County in Golok. That region was part of the Amnye Machen range, and its towering mountains and deep valleys crisscrossed with ravines made it easy to hold and hard to attack. A rather wide ravine ran in front of Drongthil Gulch, the slopes on both sides covered with dense virgin forests. There were no roads at that time, so it was inaccessible to motor vehicles, and the herders felt quite safe there. No sources verify the claim that the people who fled to Drongthil Gulch intended to mount a "long-term stubborn resistance."

"That was the situation in our area; those who could flee, the young people and children, all ran off with cattle and sheep, and those who couldn't run, the old people, were left behind. It's not known whether they eventually starved to death or were killed; in any event, there was no way for them to survive. There was no resistance back then—everyone just ran into the hills. While they were being pursued there would have been some scattered resistance, but apart from that, there was no resistance," the former Drakar Drelzong monk Tubten Nyima told me. "The herders in our homeland had weapons, but most of them were flintlocks. When Ma Bufang ran off, some people bought weapons he left behind, that was all. Our home had a flintlock gun. Was it possible to rebel with such weapons? At that time, some men from our village carried guns in case of disputes over pastures, but they were incapable of resisting an army. What [weapons] did you have to rebel?"

In 1958, the herders of Tsikorthang mounted a mass exodus, and Tubten Nyima's tribe, living in a remote area close to Golok, also joined the flight. "The so-called 'rebellion' was what the Chinese called it afterwards, but there wasn't really any 'rebellion'—everyone just ran into the hills, and in order to forbid people from running away, they called it rebellion," Tubten Nyima said.

Describing the herder exodus as a rebellion also provided a rationale for deploying troops to massacre people.

In August 1958, the "Hainan Rebellion Pacification Command Post" was established, headed by the 134th Infantry Division commander Bai Bin, and commanded two cavalry regiments, three infantry regiments, and one infantry brigade.

On August 8, the Command Post moved in on Tahoba (Daheba) Township, where the Tsikorthang county government was located.

4

On June 30, 1958, just one week after Mao transmitted the Qinghai provincial party committee's "Directive on a Province-wide Suppression of Armed Rebellion" with his comments, Central Committee Vice-Chairman Zhu De left Beijing for an inspection visit to Shaanxi, Gansu, Qinghai, and Inner Mongolia.

On the evening of July 8, Zhu De wrote a letter to Peng Dehuai, Mao, and the Central Committee reporting on the situation in Gansu, Qinghai and Sichuan:

> Counterrevolutionary armed rebellions in the pastoral regions of Gansu, Qinghai, and Sichuan have been occurring since March 18, and after more than three months of encirclement and suppression, more than 26,000 [rebels] have been knocked off. At present around 15,000 or so remain at large, mainly in southern Gansu's Xiahe, Qinghai's Guoluo and Yushu, and northern Sichuan's Tangkun and other places.[32]

Arriving in Qinghai's capital, Xining, on July 10, Zhu De received military officers at the rank of garrison commander and above to hear their reports and issue instructions.

Before going into battle, the Hainan Rebellion Pacification Command Post, "due to a tight schedule and limited scouting resources, had very little firsthand intelligence on the enemy. . . . It mainly relied on the 'situation summary' obtained by the Xinghai County government, which said that the enemy had forcibly occupied the area surrounding the Ehesha Monastery."[33] On August 28, the Hainan Rebellion Pacification Command Post assembled its six regiments and sent them out along separate routes toward the southeastern portion of Tsikorthang County.

On September 2, the 402nd Regiment's advance force crossed the Chu-ngon (Qushen'an) River and engaged in a shootout with one of the nomad groups.

On September 3, the regiment's remaining troops arrived at their designated locations and managed to surround Drongthil Gulch, but failed to discover any "large force of the enemy" either north or south of the A-sang Monastery. On that day, the deputy commander of the reconnaissance unit of the 134th Division, Wang Tingsheng, using high-power binoculars, discovered "more than 1,000 rebel bandits" on the southeastern ridge of Amnye Machen Mountain, and more than 2,000 "coerced masses" in a ravine at the foot of the mountain. Wang drew a relief map and proposed a battle plan.[34]

On the morning of September 4, "iron birds" flew over Amnye Machen and Drongthil Gulch. The herders on the mountain pointed with wonder at the sky, hardly aware that these great iron birds were modern military weapons with massive destructive power. They may not have even suspected that the two aircraft were carrying out "aerial reconnaissance." What followed would surpass their imagination: a massive slaughter by six regular army regiments utilizing modern weapons, including bomber planes.

In the recollections of Tibetans, the "Battle to Surround and Annihilate Southeast Xinghai" began like this:

> In the early hours of the morning, multicolored signal flares went up from the nearby mountaintop, after which Chinese troops began opening fire on the mountaintop where the Tibetans were camped. Bomber planes flying at low altitude used machine guns to wildly strafe the mountaintop while dropping countless bombs, and the combined sound of the guns and bombs shook the earth like thunder.[35]

An official source published in 1997 describes this battle as follows: "The troops taking part in the battle began moving in on August 28, achieved encirclement on September 3, and launched an attack **in close coordination with the air force**. After two days of battle, a portion was annihilated."[36]

Another source, published in 2000, glosses over the PLA's military strength, participating units, and battle process, describing this major battle in just two sentences: "In order to liberate numerous impoverished herders, the Chinese People's Liberation Army and numerous militia and cadres carried out a fight to pacify rebellion. The main force of rebellion pacification troops entered the Xinghai region in August 1958."[37]

A military source published in 2001 reduces what the PLA referred to as a major campaign, the "Battle of Encirclement and Annihilation in Xinghai's Southeast Region," to this: "The various troops began moving in on August 28 and formed an encirclement around the enemy on September 3. **Under close coordination among the units**, after two days of fighting, more than 2,500 of the enemy were annihilated."[38]

A source published in 2003 records this battle in PRC military history with a single sentence: "(1958) July 31, **an assembled main force of six regiments** employed the battle tactic of divided advance along multiple routes and encirclement to annihilate more than 7,000 armed rebels amassed in Xinghai's southeastern portion."[39]

As shown in the above sources, the air force, which played such an enormous role in this battle, mysteriously disappears in materials published from 2000 onward. But an Air Force 25th Division airman who took part in the bombing subsequently wrote the following description of the battle:

> One time, a buildup of thousands of rebel bandits was surrounded by our troops on the top of Maqin [Amnye Machen] Mountain. At first the army launched a powerful attack on the mountain from four directions, but because the enemy occupied a commanding position and the mountain slopes were precipitous, the attack was not successful, and our troops suffered substantial casualties. The Rebellion Pacification Command Post ordered an immediate deployment of bomber planes to bomb the rebel bandits on Maqin mountain.
>
> After careful searching, Zhou Tingyan's unit located the rebel bandits amassed on the peak of Maqin Mountain. The rebel bandits seem to have never experienced the iron fist of the People's Air Force, and they fired on the aircraft with guns. Zhou Tingyan's unit[40] accurately dropped all of its bombshells, and more than 300 of the rebel bandits were killed or wounded on the spot. At the same time, the army troops took advantage of the situation to stage an attack and

charged fiercely up the hill. In one stroke, we annihilated this band of stubbornly resisting rebel bandits.[41]

Guan Shengzhi, at that time political commissar for the Lanzhou Military Command Air Force, recalls that Zhou Tingyan's unit dropped nine 100-kilo bombs on Amnye Machen Mountain, and that all of them hit their target.[42]

The director of the 134th Division's scouting unit, Wang Tingsheng, who personally carried out reconnaissance and formed the battle plan, summed up this battle in these few words: "On the morning of the 4th, under fire cover from our air force and artillery, the first cavalry and third regiment from the south, and the first and third battalions of the 402nd Regiment from the north, launched an attack on the enemy holding fast to the eastern ridge of Galang Mountain[43] and in one stroke annihilated the enemy," "liberating" more than 2,000 "coerced masses."[44]

The bombing of Amnye Machen was only part of the first stage of this campaign. This stage lasted more than two months, with the PLA fighting more than a hundred battles large and small, "annihilating" a total of 7,755, people and capturing "1,153 firearms of various kinds and 1,317 knives and spears. The Chinese People's Liberation Army lost 149 officers and men in battle, with another 196 wounded."[45]

The above "military accomplishments" indicate that there were only 2,470 weapons, including "knives and spears," among the 7,700 Tibetans who were killed, wounded, or taken prisoner. In other words, at least two thirds of the "rebel bandits" attacked by six regiments of regular army troops and bomber planes were completely unarmed.

Among the currently published sources, only one provides relatively detailed figures: as of the end of 1958, when the first phase of the battle ended, the PLA had "annihilated 6,898 rebel bandits, liberated 6,630 of the masses, and a few hundred others remained at large."[46] That means that the PLA "encircled and annihilated" nearly 14,000 people.

In his book, Alak Tsayu Tenzin Pelbar uses a formulation that by now has become sadly familiar: "In this tragic incident, at least 6,000 Tibetans and their livestock were killed in a mass slaughter by Chinese troops.... Because no one collected the corpses after this massacre by the Chinese troops, a stench filled the air for kilometers around. For three or four years afterwards, the streams that flowed from this area were tainted by decaying corpses, and even beasts refused to drink it."[47]

On October 9, 1958, Tsikorthang County's implementation of "people's communes" experienced a "meteoric rise," with six communes established along with "implementation of a supply system that included food, clothing, housing, medical treatment, culture, education, child and elder care, haircuts and bathing, weddings and burials, and items of daily use."[48] The "liberated" herders became "commune members," and all of their belongings became "public property," while the "supply system" described on paper never materialized in real life.

On December 12, 1958, the elderly and revered lama Ngarotsang Rinpoché died in Xining's Nantan prison, less than a year after his arrest.[49]

5

Having scored a smashing victory in its "Battle of Encirclement and Annihilation in Xinghai's Southeast Region," the main force of the PLA withdrew from Tsikorthang that winter and returned to its base area to rest and regroup.

After the army withdrew, the herders embarked on another exodus: "More than 1,900 people fled Wulong and Namthang [Wenquan] alone from December 1958 to May 1959, combined with rebel bandits who slipped through the net and refugees from other areas totaling 2,700."[50]

These herders fled to the vast mountain area covering what is now Tsikorthang County's Lungsang (Longcang) and Drongthil Townships and Machen County's Gangri (Xueshan) Township. The topography of this region is remote and inaccessible, with mountains soaring nearly 5,000 meters above sea level. Furthermore, Drongthil Gulch and the area of Gangri Township was where the first stage of the PLA's campaign had taken place. Why did herders flee there again?

It was because of severe food shortages in the pastoral areas, caused by extortionate requisition quotas and meager food rations under the state monopoly for purchasing and marketing.

The state monopoly for purchasing and marketing began operating in December 1953. It is usually believed that the state only stipulated monthly food rations for urban residents, but in fact it was not that simple. Strictly speaking, what the state stipulated was a monthly food ration for the "non-farming population." Herders qualified as part of the "non-farming population," as a result of which their food was also subject to a monthly ration. Each province added a "local supplement" to the state's purchases and also took a cut from the food distributed through the marketing monopoly, which meant higher requisition quotas and decreased rations.

Tsikorthang County began implementing the state purchasing and marketing monopoly in 1957. The grain ration for herders was set at 65 kilos per person per year, an average of 5.4 kilos per month, with an extra 15% provided to monks. In 1958, the grain ration was reduced to 5 kilos per month for everyone aged seven or older, and 3 kilos for those under seven. In 1957, Tsikorthang's herding population was provided with 2,727,400 kilos of grain, but in 1958 the supply was cut by nearly half, to only 1,433,500 kilos.[51]

The government was imposing extortionate requisition quotas at the same time. In 1957, Tsikorthang County's grain output was 1.05 million kilos, and the government's requisition quota was 601,300 kilos, or 57.26% of production. Based on the population at the time, prior to requisition each person would be allocated 62 kilos, but after requisition the allocation dropped to 26.4 kilos. In 1958, the total population of Tsikorthang was 16,572, and the total grain output was 1.59 million kilos. Government requisition was 571,500 kilos, or 35.94% of the total, leaving an average of 61.5 kilos per person. That was the average yearly grain ration for people in Tsikorthang County. In theory, herders mainly consumed meat and dairy products, but after the state purchasing and marketing monopoly began, butter was also subject to government procurement. In 1957, the government's requisition quota for butter was 88.6% of the amount produced, and in 1958 it was 83.5%. This deprived the herders of almost all of the butter that had been a staple of their food consumption. After the "animal husbandry cooperatives" were established, all of the livestock became collective property, and herders no longer had any ownership rights over them. Under these circumstances, famine became inevitable.

On May 24, 1959, the Hainan Rebellion Pacification Command Post submitted a report to Beijing describing problems that had developed and making some suggestions to the local government. The report mentioned in particular the situation in Tsikorthang County's Namthang Township:

> Food is scarce in the pastoral areas at present, added to which management has been suboptimal. . . . For instance, because food supplies are inadequate in Xinghai County's Wenquan Township, the masses have been eating cattle and sheep that died last winter and are stinking with rot, and disease and death are rampant. . . . From last November [1958] until now, 319 people have died of illness, composing 24.7% of the township's total population. The masses report that all of them starved to death (in fact there are multiple causes) and are very discontent with us. Between last December and May 10 this year, 165 have fled elsewhere to become bandits. The food supply problem has become pervasive and is affecting the struggle against the enemy. It is reported that the provincial party committee originally set a grain ration for the pastoral regions of 300 grams per person per day, but in some places economy has been imposed by reducing the ration to 250 grams. With poor management added in, and failure to actively seek food substitutes, food shortages have resulted.[52]

According to this source, Namthang Township began experiencing severe food shortages in November 1958, and large numbers of herders died. At a point when herders were eating long-dead animals to allay their hunger, the Qinghai provincial party secretary, Gao Feng, delivered a report at the tenth plenum of the second provincial party committee on January 9, 1959, in which he claimed that the year 1958 had "marked an all-out great leap forward in every construction undertaking, and it was also the year when the socialist revolution in the pastoral areas scored a decisive victory." Gao boasted that in the previous year "total grain output reached 1.32 billion kilos, an increase of 71.96% over 1957, and in absolute terms nearly double the five-year production increases during the First Five-Year Plan (322.8 million kilos). . . . Based on the current population, this amounts to an average grain ration of 600 kilos per person."[53]

The actual situation was that in 1958, the cultivated area for grain crops in Tsikorthang County totaled 11,089 *mu*, and total grain production was 1.59 million kilos, for an average yield of 143.39 kilos per *mu*. That came to less than 100 kilos of grain per person per year—and that was before the state's grain procurement.

That year, Tsikorthang County settled 6,000 migrants from inland China to open up grassland for argiculture. The livestock that were scattered and lost after the first wave of suppression were not returned to the herders, but were "collected" by the PLA, to establish three military pastures.

There was yet another reason why the herders were forced into the mountains: the random killing of those who were persuaded to surrender. The report of the Hainan Rebellion Pacification Command Post states:

> Looking again at the situation in Xinghai, from the time that the troops withdrew from there last year [1958] to February this year, 235 people were persuaded to return, but due to a failure to correctly implement policy, there were arbitrary arrests and killings that had a serious effect on our work. For example, in Wenquan Township, ten surrendering elements were arrested and sentenced to prison, four were mistakenly arrested, and five were wrongfully killed. . . . Because exposure has been inadequate up to now, there is no way to thoroughly investigate exactly how many people have been wrongfully arrested or killed in the entire county. In some cases, the killer has been found, but not the person who issued the order. Although this happened half a year ago, some of the masses personally witnessed the killing, and the corpses of some of those killed have been dug up by the masses, so the effect has been extremely bad. The rebel bandits say, "You can't believe what the Communist Party says," and they refuse to surrender. . . . As a result, since February it has been impossible to convince even one person to return; instead, as many as 1,000 of the masses have fled to become bandits.[54]

Random killings and detentions weren't limited to local governments. On March 15, 1959, the CCP Central Committee decided to use the "Lhasa incident" that broke out on March 10 as a pretext to carry out a "decisive battle" in Tibet and to launch battles throughout the Tibetan regions. In order to "utilize the political offensive to divide and eliminate the rebel bandits," to reduce manpower and material and financial resources, and to prevent Qinghai's Tibetan regions from becoming the "rear area" for Tibet, the Qinghai provincial party committee issued a directive requiring all units to carry out a policy of "less arrests, less killings, and mainly transformation," and required the party in the relevant prefectures and counties to "immediately take action to achieve obvious results in April and May."[55] The PLA launched its suppression of Qinghai in 1958, but it was not until May 1959 that the independent second cavalry regiment prohibited physically or verbally abusing or executing prisoners, and corrected the "erroneous mentality" among some commanders and soldiers of "killing more and capturing fewer alive."[56]

From the end of 1958 until the summer of 1959, herders that were escorted into the "socialist paradise" by the barrel of a gun descended into a hell on earth: The cooperatives brought them a level of famine they'd never experienced before, and herders forced to become commune members were reduced to utter destitution, facing a hopeless situation of "either being killed or starving to death."[57] Thousands of herders felt compelled to drive off the livestock that had once been theirs and flee their homeland once again, seeking refuge in the highlands of Tsikorthang's southeast region. It was the only recourse left to them.

In June 1959, having completed their rest and regrouping, the PLA's 2nd and 3rd Cavalry Regiments, its 163rd and 164th Infantry Regiments, and the Hainan People's Armed Police brigade and four local militia companies, with a total armed force of more than 5,100, once again set off for Tsikorthang to surround more than 2,700 herders who had fled to the hills. Thus began the second round of battles.

6

In the summer of 1959, two PLA cavalry regiments, two infantry regiments, and militia units under their command divided up into eleven groups and set off for the southeastern highlands of Tsikorthang County from the south, north, and west. The Yellow River lay to the east of the battle area, and the main ferry landing on the river's east bank had already been captured, cutting off access for herders who might try to flee across the river. The army troops formed several encirclements of various sizes to cast a tight net around the foot of the sacred Mount Amnye Machen.

The encirclement began closing in on June 6, and by June 10, six rings had separated and surrounded groups of herders hiding in different spots. When the second phase of the "Battle of Encirclement and Annihilation in Xinghai's Southeast Region" ended in October, more than 2,500 herders had been "annihilated" and more than 1,000 "liberated." During the battles of this second phase, the Drakar Drelzong manager, Kunsang, was accused of being a "rebel bandit ringleader." The party committee of the Hainan Rebellion Pacification Command Post gave the troops the slogan, "Perform meritorious service and catch Kunsang alive." "Immediately an awe-inspiring energy surged throughout the army units as everyone thought of ways to capture Kunsang. Even while dreaming, soldiers cried out, 'Pursue and annihilate Kunsang!'"[58] Kunsang died in action during this phase of the campaign.

According to the Qinghai Military Sub-region's statistics, as of the end of December 1958, the army had "engaged in battle 623 times and annihilated 60,864 rebel bandits (10,415 shot dead, 2,648 wounded, 21,958 taken prisoner, and 25,843 surrendered). They seized 48,793 firearms of various kinds, 482,901 rounds of ammunition, and 57,356 knives and spears."[59] However, the Xinhua New Agency's *Internal Reference*, circulated to China's top leaders, provided a different set of figures: "Rebel bandits launched a large-scale armed rebellion last year [1958] and came under our heavy attack. According to figures up to the end of last year, more than 80,000 rebel bandits were exterminated, and more than 50,000 firearms were seized."[60]

In Yulshul alone, the PLA engaged in battle 243 times, "annihilated 29,024 rebel bandits and seized 18,903 firearms," of which 12,878, or 68%, were crude, homemade weapons.[61]

Furthermore, that year Qinghai "punished" more than 42,000 herd owners, landlords, counterrevolutionaries, bad elements, and rightists.[62]

During this time, the troops deployed by the Chinese government included 28 infantry and cavalry regiments, 29 militia companies, 2 engineer corps, 3 transportation regiments, and various other "special forces and security platoons,"[63] including army depots, field hospitals, veterinary hospitals, and an anti-chemical unit of unknown purpose.[64] As of the end of 1958, the air force had deployed 12 aircraft in a total of 486 sorties; apart from reconnaissance, transport, and air drops, these aircraft also carried out "bombing and strafing as necessary."[65]

In 1990, Tubten Nyima, the former Drakar Drelzong monk who had fled to India and joined the Drepung Monastery there, visited his family that had been left behind.

"When I returned to my homeland," he told me, "it seemed that everyone was new. Apart from my relatives, all the rest were strangers to me." None of his former friends and companions remained, and the community seemed to have no elderly people, and only a handful of people his age. One of his brothers had been killed while trying to flee, and another had gone insane after being imprisoned in the monastery. Four uncles had starved to death during the famine in 1958.

"Another monk in the monastery who was my age and had been my classmate, he was a son of the headman, and another, named Lotse, were both killed during the struggle rallies." Tubten Nyima added, "They were both just ordinary monks and had committed no crimes. Like me, they had spent all their time at the monastery and hadn't done anything. I simply can't understand how something like that could happen."

I looked at Tubten Nyima, and at the picture of the Drakar Drelzong Monastery taped to the wall behind him, and could think of nothing to say. In 1958, the abbot of the monastery, Ngarotsang Rinpoché, had died in prison; in 1959, the monastery's manager, Kunsang, had died on the battlefield. Some of the monastery's monks died during the denunciation rallies, some were driven insane, some returned to secular life, and some ran off. Most of the monastery's halls and dormitories fell into ruin, and the surviving structures became livestock pens for the commune.[66]

Chapter 15

THE CROSSED-SWORD BANNER AT DRIGU LAKE

1

Lhasa, April 18, 1958.

A group of guests arrived at the home of the Lithang merchant Gonpo Tashi.[1] Prominent in Lhasa's Khampa business circles, Gonpo Tashi was constantly hosting guests of all kinds, who regularly gathered at his home. Probably no one guessed that this particular gathering would go down in history.[2]

On that day, there were 42 people present,[3] representing 23 different regions, mainly Khampas from places such as Lithang, Bathang, Chamdo, Gyelthang (Jietang),[4] Chatreng, and Nyarong. There were also a few people from Gyalrong and Amdo, and two *gyapons*[5] from the Tibetan army.

One of the men from Chamdo read out a pledge to fight in the resistance against the Chinese government to the end; to fight to safeguard the political and religious order of Tibetan society; to be willing to give their lives to this end; to strictly comply with the orders of the commanders of the Tibetan voluntary resistance force, the Chushi Gangdruk; to supply their own weapons and horses; and to ensure that plans for the resistance were not disclosed to anyone.[6]

No one expressed any objection. All those present signed the pledge, along with their fingerprints, and then entered the shrine room of Gonpo Tashi's home in turn.

"I knelt down before the Buddha statue and swore my oath, and then I prostrated three times." Fifty-four years later, Gyalrong Tenzin told me this at the Dondrupling Tibetan Refugee Settlement in Dehradun, India.[7]

I sat on a small couch under the window, across from Tenzin's shrine. Dusk was approaching, and pale golden rays of sun seeping through the window played on the brass Buddha statue. A black-and-white photo of Tenzin in his youth was propped on a cabinet next to the shrine. At the time that Tenzin placed his fingerprint on the document, he was 27; now he was a gray-haired old man of 79.

"How did you feel about the Tibetan government at that time?" I asked.

"We were very dissatisfied with some things the government was doing," he replied. "Lhasa had weapons, but when we asked, they wouldn't give us any."

By then, the Tibetan government had no substantial military power. The Seventeen-Point Agreement stipulated that the Tibetan army would be merged into the People's Liberation Army forces stationed in Tibet. When the PLA first awarded ranks in 1955, it also awarded ranks to officers of the Tibetan army. Although its flag hadn't changed, the Tibetan army had effectively been reorganized as part of the PLA. It's hard to imagine the government handing over weapons from the Lhasa arsenal to Khampa resistance fighters under those circumstances.[8]

From 1950 onward, Tibet was sliced up into the Chamdo Liberation Committee, the Tibetan government, and the Panchen Lama's Administrative Council, three relatively independent political bodies. These three organizations became part of the Preparatory Committee for the Autonomous Region of Tibet (PCART) when it was established in April 1956, and accepted its centralized leadership. At this point, the Tibetan government and the Dalai Lama were basically figureheads. In this way, the Chinese government had managed to take away the political power of the Tibetan government without turning a hair. Divisions had also emerged, with some officials cooperating with the Chinese government, some passively resisting, some maintaining neutrality, and some appointed to both the Work committee and the Tibetan government.

As a result, no one within the Tibetan government trusted anyone else, and no one felt comfortable speaking their minds at meetings.[9] Although Kham and Amdo were already engulfed in the flames of war, the Tibetan government, lacking any genuine political power, could only strive to maintain the status quo.

"So we had to establish our own army," Tenzin continued. "We would do it ourselves!"[10]

That is how the Chushi Gangdruk Defenders of the Faith came to be.[11]

2

After the Khampa revolts began in 1956, Gonpo Tashi had thought of integrating the resistance forces of all of the Tibetan territories to establish a volunteer resistance army, and on the pretext of creating a golden throne for the Dalai Lama, he had secretly called together regional leaders from all over the Tibetan territories to discuss this plan.[12] Afterwards, these Tibetan leaders had actively established ties and sought a common way forward.

A year of secret contact resulted in the formation of a core group, as well as attracting interest from several hundred people.[13] At the same time, Gonpo Tashi sought aid from all quarters. He bought weapons and radios through his three nephews in India, and he used his own funds and donations from wealthy merchants to purchase arms and transport them secretly to Tibet.[14]

Meanwhile, the Dalai Lama's second-oldest brother, Gyalo Dondrup, was also seeking support from the United States through CIA agents stationed in India. As a result of his arrangements, the first group of six Khampa youths finished their training with the CIA in the tenth month of the Tibetan calendar (November–December) in 1957, and the Lithang natives Athar and Lotse were the first to be airdropped to the area of the Samye (Sangna) Monastery, around 60 kilometers from Lhasa. Reaching Lhasa a few days later, they met with Gonpo Tashi, who introduced them to the Dalai Lama's lord chamberlain, Phala.[15]

Since the early 1950s, several underground organizations had been secretly active in Lhasa. The People's Assembly, banned in 1952, had gone underground long before. There was another organization, known as the Tibetan Anti-Imperialist Party,[16] of which little is known even today, and yet another, called the "Tibetan People's Religious Enterprises Union,"[17] whose activities seem to have been limited to handing out leaflets, writing slogans, and so on.[18] Currently available materials indicate that Chushi Gangdruk was the only military organization.

According to Tibetan sources, Lord Chamberlain Phala maintained contact with Gonpo Tashi[19] and knew about the Khampas' secret activities, but remained ambivalent about them. He didn't want the Dalai Lama or the Tibetan government to become embroiled in this matter, but neither did he firmly oppose what Gonpo Tashi and the others were doing.[20]

By this time, the Chinese government had an intelligence network in Lhasa, but the TWC seems to have been unaware of the secret meetings Gonpo Tashi was convening. The TWC was nevertheless clearly uncomfortable with the number of horse-riding, gun-toting Khampas in Lhasa.[21]

Besides people from Kham and Amdo who had fled to Tibet, there were also Han and Hui Chinese seeking refuge from land reform in the inland regions. Historically, there had always been quite a few Chinese in Kham and Amdo who did business with Tibetans, and when the provincial party secretary Li Jingquan launched land reform and the campaign to suppress counterrevolutionaries in Sichuan, some Chinese hid in Tibetan towns. On April 1, 1958, the TWC decided to "clear out" those people. Less than a month later, 456 of them were arrested in Lhasa, Shigatsé, Gyantsé, Dromo, and other towns and repatriated to the mainland.[22] In the latter half of April,[23] the TWC announced a screening and registration of refugees from Kham and Amdo, requiring them to apply for identity cards in order to remain in Lhasa. This caused a massive panic. The refugees saw it as an indication that the TWC would soon target them for mass arrests. For a time, Lhasa was in a state of high anxiety, and many refugees fled to the region south of the Tsangpo (Yalu Zangbu) River, which was not yet under the full control of the Chinese government.[24]

It was clear that Lhasa couldn't be held much longer against the Chinese government. What was the next step? In accordance with longstanding tradition, Gonpo Tashi, Athar, and Lotse went to the monastery for divination. The message they received was that they must leave Lhasa before the twentieth day of the fourth month of the Tibetan calendar, and must proceed to Driguthang (Zhegu) in Lhoka (Shannan) to establish the base camp for Chushi Gangdruk.[25] Driguthang, 4,650 meters above sea level, is the open and sparsely inhabited plain around the Drigu Lake between the Yarlung valley and the Himalayan border region. At that time, the TMC's troops were scattered among several strongholds on the northern fringe of Lhoka, and one of them, the prefectural government seat at Tsethang (Zedang), was about 80 kilometers from Driguthang.

In May, Gonpo Tashi and his core group left Lhasa separately and headed for Lhoka.

Chinese-language sources make no mention of Gonpo Tashi's actions. However, the *Chronology of Peng Dehuai* notes that on May 17, 1958, Tan Guansan sent a cable to the CCP Central Committee and CMC suggesting that the TWC's leading organs be merged with the Military Command's organs to facilitate leadership and allow a reduction of 3,000 personnel in Tibet. "In addition, the corresponding reduction of 5,000 transport, army base, and construction personnel means a total staff reduction of around 8,000, and will also facilitate dealing with any armed rebellions that might occur." Peng Dehuai wrote a memo agreeing to this suggestion and passed it on to Deng Xiaoping.[26] On June 24, Mao Zedong also instructed the TWC to "prepare to deal with the possibility of a full-scale armed rebellion there."[27] This shows that the Chinese government, despite lacking a thorough understanding of the situation in Tibet, was already preparing for a military suppression.

At the same time that this was happening, Khampas, Amdowas,[28] and a small number of Tibetan soldiers began leaving Lhasa in small groups and heading for Lhoka. Among them was a PLA officer who had defected, Jiang Huating, renamed Lobsang Tashi.[29]

Gyalrong Tenzin was notified that he should leave Lhasa for Lhoka. He mounted his horse and left immediately, having no time to dispose of the belongings he had left with a monk at the Sera (Sela) Monastery for safekeeping. It would be more than 30 years before he returned.

3

While Gonpo Tashi and his trusted friends were taking their vows to formally establish the Chushi Gangdruk Volunteer Army, the TWC and the Military Command were preoccupied with their own "rectification and anti-rightist movement."

On April 4, 1958, the TWC convened a conference of cadres at the county level or above to begin a "rectification and anti-rightist struggle." This meeting lasted more than seven months, finally adjourning on November 10. Around the same time, the TMC held an unusual party congress, attended by a work team headed by the deputy director of the cadre department of the PLA's General Political Department. The targets of "rectification" at the Military Command Party Congress were the deputy commander of the TMC, Li Jue; the deputy chief of staff, Chen Zizhi, and the deputy political commissar, Hong Liu, mainly because of a letter they had written in February 1957 and that they had asked the Military Command party committee to forward to the CMC and all military headquarters, to pass on to "our esteemed and beloved Chairman Mao." This document, subsequently referred to as "the petition by the five main departments,"[30] was denounced by the General Political Department as "reflecting a right-deviating escapist tendency."

Jiang Huating states that on November 20, 1956, Li Jue and the others jointly petitioned Mao regarding policy problems relating to national security and reform. The petition Jiang mentions contained eight main points, including "It is undesirable to impose reforms too hastily" and "The neighboring country [i.e., India] has no expansionist military strategy and poses no threat to Tibet; it is unnecessary to station massive military forces in Tibet, which is a waste of national resources and has a detrimental effect on Sino-Indian diplomatic relations."[31] It is reasonable to expect that a petition with suggestions relating to national policy would be submitted to Mao, and it does not seem that any great secrecy was attached to this incident at the time.[32] However, it is difficult to determine from currently available sources whether the petition Jiang Huating refers to was part of the "petition by the five main departments," or if these were two separate documents.

When the "petition by the five main departments" was attacked as "right-deviating escapism," Tan Guansan, in charge of the TMC at that time, was implicated as its backstage supporter. By that time, Li Jue had already been transferred to the PRC's Second Ministry of Machine-Building as head of the "Ninth Bureau," which was responsible for nuclear research and development. He was recalled to Tibet for criticism, but escaped punishment. The TMC's rectification movement ended with a caution administered to the deputy political commissar Hong Liu.[33]

The rectification in Tibet's administrative apparatus was launched on April 4, 1958. Zhang Jingwu and Zhang Guohua were away at the time, so Fan Ming was in charge of the cadre conference. By then, the TWC and the Military Command were effectively "one shop with two signs," so Li Jue was still the focus of criticism. When Zhang Jingwu and Zhang Guohua returned to Lhasa in early May, the wind shifted direction, and Fan Ming suddenly became the target of the rectification process he was directing.

On the surface, Zhang and Fan were engaged in a "struggle between north and south"—that is, an internal struggle between core members of the Southwest and Northwest bureaus—but the seeds of this conflict had been planted back when the Chinese government first occupied Tibet. On November 23, 1949, Mao cabled a directive to the First Secretary of the Northwest Bureau, Peng Dehuai, entrusting the chief responsibility for "resolving the Tibet problem" to that bureau, while the Southwest bureau assumed "secondary responsibility."[34] The Northwest Bureau reported back to Mao on December 30, estimating that proceeding from Qinghai to Tibet would require two years. Mao then sent a reply cable to Peng Dehuai, Deng Xiaoping, and others on January 2, 1950, relaying the decision that the Southwest Bureau would "manage" Tibet.[35] In accordance with the Central Committee's instructions, the Southwest Bureau established the Tibet Work Committee in Leshan, Sichuan Province, on January 24. In September and October of that year, the Central Committee instructed the Northwest Bureau to establish its own Tibet Work Committee. This meant that the Southwest Bureau and Northwest Bureau each had their own TWC.

After Fan Ming arrived in Lhasa with cadres from the Northwest Bureau and troops on December 1, 1951, the (Northwest) TWC stopped functioning, but two sets of officials, from the Southwest Bureau and Northwest Bureau, were still operating in Tibet. Right from the start, Zhang and Fan didn't get along, and each accused the other of factionalism.[36] The mid-level cadres below them also competed with each other.[37] In October 1953, the United Front department head, Li Weihan, and deputy director, Liu Chun, convened a "Tibet Work Discussion Meeting" in Beijing in an attempt to resolve internal conflicts in the TWC. The two sides fought for the upper hand for a full three months in what Deng Xiaoping referred to as the Panmunjom conference.[38]

There were of course practical reasons for this situation at the time, but the complications may also have been intentional on Mao's part. Given Tibet's remote frontier location, pitting one force against the other ensured that all officials in Tibet were restrained and monitored by others. Prior to 1958, Zhang Jingwu, Zhang Guohua, and Fan Ming each reported separately on Tibet to Beijing, giving Mao multiple means of understanding the situation.[39] Even decades later, researchers can still use the memoirs left behind by core members of both sides to understand a fuller picture than either of the parties concerned was willing to disclose.

The anti-rightist movement of the 1950s not only "rectified" intellectuals and members of the democratic parties but also served as a purge of the Communist Party and the military ranks. By 1958, the PLA had identified 5,400 rightists,[40] and this provided an opportunity to purge Fan Ming as the head of an "anti-party clique." Fan was subjected to public denunciations for five months, dismissed from his positions in the party and military, and then sent back to the mainland for sentencing. Many others were implicated in this case, "especially cadres who had gone to Tibet from the northwest—hardly any of them escaped. Some were expelled from the party, some were dismissed from their official positions, some were sent to prison, some were internally disciplined, some were transferred out of key departments, and some were put under controlled employment."[41] In other words, the core members of the Northwest Bureau were totally annihilated in this battle.[42]

Even so, the factional struggle in the TWC was only "internal struggle" within the Communist Party, and no matter which side won, it wouldn't change Tibet's fate.

4

On June 16, 1958, in Driguthang in Lhoka, hundreds of men, some shouldering rifles and firelocks and others empty-handed, proceeded in a continuous stream across the grassland. At the front of the long line, several men carried a throne bearing a photo of the Dalai Lama, and an incense burner sent thick plumes of smoke into the air. One group on horseback escorted the throne into a tent, completing this simple but solemn religious ceremony.[43]

The men arranged themselves in columns according to their clans or places of origin. The various units of the Chushi Gangdruk Volunteer Army were arranged, in columns of varying lengths, according to the Tibetan alphabet, with some regions represented by many men and some by only a few. Several men thrust a flagpole into the center of a pile of rocks and raised the colors of Chushi Gangdruk. On the yellow flag were embroidered two crossed jeweled swords.

The Chushi Gangdruk veteran Gyalrong Tenzin described the scene to me 54 years later: The Lithang merchant Gonpo Tashi stood beneath the crossed-sword banner and declared the formal establishment of the Chushi Gangdruk Volunteer Army to the hundreds of men standing before him. "Starting from today, we will be like brothers from the same father and mother," he said. "Even if we fight until only ten of us are left, as long as there's a place we can go, there will be a way out. We must all do our best!"[44] Behind him, representatives of various places also spoke encouraging words.

"That's all he said?" I asked Tenzin.

"That's all. He was a man of few words," Tenzin replied.

"Who designed the flag for Chushi Gangdruk?"

"I don't know," said Tenzin.

It appears, in fact, that no one knows for sure who designed this flag.[45]

More than half a century later, at the Dondrupling settlement in

Dehradun, an Amdowa named Lhaba described how he had joined the Chushi Gangdruk Volunteer Army.

As Lhaba set off from Lhasa on horseback with his gun slung across his back, he believed that he was joining a powerful, well-trained army. But when he reached Driguthang, all he found were a few old tents on a stretch of empty land.

"At the time, my heart felt a little sour [disappointed]," he said to me, smiling.

He went to one of the tents and told a Khampa that he wanted to "join up." The Khampa asked him, "Can anyone vouch for you?"

"No," Lhaba replied.

"No one to vouch for you?" The Khampa tilted his head. "Look over there. Like those two!"

When Lhaba looked "over there," he saw two men bound with ropes sitting next to a tent. Overcome with anger, he said, "I've ridden here on my own horse, carrying my own gun. Why do I need someone to vouch for me?!"

The Khampa said, "Sorry, those are the rules."

Lhaba suddenly thought of home, and asked the Khampa, "Where's the Amdo contingent?"

With directions from the Khampa, Lhaba found where the Amdo troops were stationed. The sight of nearly a hundred of his kinsmen brought a new wave of sourness to Laba's heart: "How could an army like this fight in a war? Some of them only had flintlocks, and some not even that—only swords and spears!"

Sitting on the porch of his home more than 50 years later, Lhaba couldn't help laughing as he recalled how he had joined the army. But at the time, this was Commander Gonpo Tashi's biggest worry and most urgent task. They had plenty of volunteers but too few guns and no heavy weapons, and the Tibetan government was unwilling to provide any, so they would have to resort to stealing. Gonpo Tashi learned through his connections that apart from the Tibetan army's arsenal in Lhasa, there were some pretty good British-style weapons stored in Namling *dzong* (Nanmulin), north of the river.[46]

On August 15,[47] Chushi Gangdruk split into two groups, and Gonpo Tashi led his main force, a cavalry more than 600 strong, northwest toward Namling.

Namling *dzong* is the site of the Shang Ganden Choekhor Monastery,[48] which was home to more than 1,000 monks at that time. In 1954, the government stored some of its weapons in the basement of the assembly hall. Three years later, the arms and ammunition were divided into three portions and stored in the monastery's three *khamtsen*, which were responsible for taking care of them.[49] With no outside support for Chushi Gangdruk, these weapons were Gonpo Tashi's last hope.

The volunteer army skirted Yamdrok (Yangzhuoyong) Lake,[50] crossed the Gampa pass[51] at an altitude of more than 4,900 meters, and west of Chushur (Qushui)[52] crossed the Tsangpo River, continuing west from there. On August 26, the main force of Chushi Gangdruk arrived in Nyemo (Nimu),[53] about 150 kilometers west of Lhasa. A 50-man scout team got lost on the way and ended up in Yangpachen (Yangbajing), 90 kilometers northwest of Lhasa.[54]

Preoccupied as they were with their internal purges, were the TMC and TWC even aware of the movements of the volunteer army? According to Chinese sources, on July 21, a lumber transport motorcade of the 8th Company of the 16th Motor Vehicle Regiment suffered a surprise attack by "armed rebel troops." This incident was "the beginning of the armed rebellions within the jurisdiction of the Tibetan government."[55] The incident occurred at Medro Gongkar (Mozhugongka), east of Lhasa and far from Driguthang.

Tibetan sources record no military operations in the month or so after Chushi Gangdruk was formally established. The main event at this stage was that under pressure from the TWC, the government sent messengers to Driguthang on eight occasions with letters demanding that Gonpo Tashi disband the volunteer army. In mid-August, the Tibetan government sent a group of officials to have a face-to-face talk with Gonpo Tashi, but Gonpo Tashi avoided the meeting and sent a representative instead. Not only was the delegation unsuccessful, but two fourth-rank officials stayed behind and joined the resistance army. At that time, Gonpo Tashi was busy establishing the internal system for the resistance army. He formulated and issued 27 rules for military discipline and discussed a plan for the next stage of operations.[56]

Beijing authorized the TMC to launch its first military operation in August. Troops from the 155th and 159th Regiments attacked "armed rebels from Sichuan and Qinghai" on the Lhasa- Nyingtri (Linzhi) segment of the Sichuan-Tibet highway for two weeks, ending on August 17.[57] At that time, the volunteer army had left Driguthang, and Fan Ming was still being denounced in the TWC.

On August 18, Deng Xiaoping commended the TMC's "limited military operation" in Beijing and directed commander Zhang Guohua and deputy commander Deng Shaodong: "Consolidate your position and safeguard transportation. If there's a threat to transportation or to yourselves, fight if you can handle it, but don't fight if you can't; let them cause more trouble; the greater the trouble, the more thorough the reforms. The PLA shouldn't go to battle without good reason, nor should troops be deployed without good reason. Now is the time to concentrate our forces. Strengthen the small strongholds."[58] This suggests that the TWC and CCP Central Committee were aware of the existence of the volunteer army, but were maintaining a defense strategy and were not taking them very seriously.

After the Chinese government reduced its military and government presence in Tibet, the only military bases in Lhoka were at Tsethang and Gongkar, and only a few troops were stationed in the army bases along the main highway that followed the Tsangpo River. This allowed the volunteer army to easily make its way from its Driguthang headquarters and cross the river at Chushur.

Several former PLA officers had joined Chushi Gangdruk by that time. Among them was a former storehouse security platoon leader named Chen Zhuneng, who gained Gonpo Tashi's trust and became head of his security team. After the volunteer army crossed the Tsangpo, Chen Zhuneng deserted. Arrested while attempting to enter Lhasa, he revealed Gonpo Tashi's whereabouts and plans. The Military Command was convening a three-level cadre conference to pass along Deng Xiaoping's instructions, but once the volunteer army's plans were known, the conference was immediately adjourned.

On August 24, two PLA regiments were dispatched under starlight to form a pincer attack on Gonpo Tashi and his volunteer army. One regiment reached Chushur four days later and then split into three groups, following Chushi Gangdruk along the north bank of the Tsangpo toward Nyemo. The other regiment rushed to Yangpachen by motorized transport, cutting off Gonpo Tashi's escape route.[59] The plan was to surround and thoroughly annihilate Gonpo Tashi and his volunteer army.

On an autumn day 54 years later, in the Dondrupling Refugee Settlement, I sat on Markham Lobsang Sherap's porch as he described his battle experience.

Around May 1958, Lobsang abandoned his business and ran off to Lhasa with his Khampa friends. Upon reaching Lhasa, they heard that Gonpo Tashi had already decided to go to Lhoka. Lobsang and his friends hurriedly bought guns and horses and set off for Lhoka.

"Even my wife didn't know that I went," he told me. "Later she escaped to India, and I did too. I found her, but she didn't want me anymore!" The elderly Lobsang laughed out loud, his snowy moustache shaking.

Lobsang Sherap was 35 years old when he joined the volunteer army. He had made some money in business and had a good gun and a good horse, and for that reason he was selected for the raid on the Shang Ganden Choekhor Monastery.

"We were attacked on the way and fought a battle," he said. "We changed direction and took another route." Lobsang sat cross-legged on a mat next to the wall, a cloth-bound scripture placed on top of an Adidas shoebox on a small table in front of him. With one hand he grasped a two-foot-tall *mani* prayer wheel, and in the other he rubbed his prayer beads, smiling as he recalled the past. He offered me only those few sentences regarding the battle he'd fought 54 years ago.

The battle at Nyemo was the first fought by the volunteer army. There were casualties on both sides; the PLA lost a heavy-machine-gun squad, while more than 30 resistance fighters were killed or wounded. A regiment of PLA soldiers arrived at dusk, and the two sides engaged in intense battle until nightfall. That night, under cover of darkness, the volunteer army took a major detour to break through the encirclement and make its way to Yangpachen. There, they came under sniper file, and another intense battle ensued.

The PLA encirclement ultimately failed, and the troops returned to Lhasa in September to rest and regroup. Victorious in his first battle, Gonpo Tashi proceeded to the Ganden Choekhor Monastery as planned and came away with a large number of weapons.[60]

"We were ambushed again on the way back," Lobsang Sherap continued. "In that battle I was injured." He put down his beads and pointed to his leg: "The bullet went in this side and came out that side."

Unable to continue on with the volunteer army, Lobsang remained where he was, hiding in the mountains with several other Chushi Gangdruk soldiers whose wounds were not too serious. Fortunately, they were never discovered.

The volunteer army continued north from Yangpachen, bypassing Damshung and crossing the Qinghai-Tibet highway into the northern steppes. In the latter half of October, Gonpo Tashi led his volunteer army into the Tengchen (Dingqing)–Pelbar (Bianba) area, where this phase of the war ended. It is unclear how many casualties both sides had suffered. A Chinese source published in 1995 states that "a total of 955 rebel bandits were annihilated (including 217 taken prisoner)";[61] figures published in 2008 reduce that number by nearly half, stating the total killed, wounded, and taken prisoner as 500, and PLA casualties as 134 dead and 111 wounded.[62] The TMC didn't achieve the anticipated results, and the volunteer army was able to rest and regroup in the Tengchen–Pelbar region, while local militia in Pelbar also began organizing resistance.

Lobsang and the other wounded soldiers hid in the mountains for 18 days, then returned to the base camp at Driguthang.

"How would we have any medical facilities at that time? The headquarters allowed us to go on leave at the hot springs. After soaking in the springs, our wounds were healed." Lobsang once again laughed out loud, recalling the time he had escaped death decades before.

5

Having received intelligence that Khampas had "established a military camp at Shannan," the TWC sent cables to the Central Committee on June 13 and 18, 1958, reporting "the possibility of armed rebellions occurring in the Tibetan territories."[63] The Central Committee sent a reply cable on July 14 telling the TWC to "take a hard line with the *kalon*s [ministers]" and repeating what Zhou Enlai had said to the Dalai Lama in India in 1956: "If reactionary elements insist on armed rebellion, the Central Committee will assuredly pacify the rebellion by armed force."[64] In other words, the Chinese government was not going to change its mind about transforming Tibet according to the Chinese model, even if military force was required. Four days later, Zhang Jingwu and Zhang Guohua went to Norbulingka palace to inform the Dalai Lama of Beijing's stance.

The Dalai Lama was in a predicament. On the one hand, he "greatly admired the guerrilla fighters"; on the other hand, he knew "what the Chinese could do so easily all over Tibet if we fought them." He therefore decided to try to persuade Tibetans not to take up arms.[65]

The Dalai Lama had the Tibetan government send representatives to Lhoka to communicate his views. While the Chinese army was imposing massive suppression on Tibetans in Gansu, Qinghai, Sichuan, and Yunnan in July and August 1958, the government's messengers were running back and forth between Lhasa and Lhoka demanding that Gonpo Tashi lay down his arms, but his resolve was unshakeable. Meanwhile, some of the Lhasa nobility had begun transferring their assets to India, and people close to the Dalai Lama were advising him to go into exile.[66]

On September 10, Beijing directed the TWC: "On the question of using the PLA to eliminate the armed rebels, this needs to be handled with discretion. We should act only when rebel forces directly threaten our army or major transport lines, and only when we're confident of success, because it's better not to fight than to fight badly. Please take note of this."[67]

On October 11, Beijing again directed the TWC: "Under no circumstances adopt the method of 'pacifying rebellion wherever it occurs' without inquiring into the circumstances, conditions, and chances of success, and likewise do not adopt the method of 'carrying out reform wherever there is rebellion.'" This didn't mean that the Chinese government was taking a lenient attitude toward resistance in Tibet; it was merely a strategy. The Chinese government felt that "a piecemeal approach was not going to solve the problem"[68] and might even be detrimental to the overall situation. "The counterrevolutionary toxins in Tibet's Changdu have to be released. Taking a hands-off approach and allowing things to develop and be revealed will facilitate a thorough resolution."[69] This document shows that although the flames of war were already spreading from Kham and Amdo to Tibet, the Chinese government felt it was still a "localized problem" that didn't yet require a "thorough resolution." The government therefore had no intention of immediately sending military reinforcements.

There may have been another reason for not dispatching a large contingent of troops at that time. In 1958, when Mao Zedong decided to launch the Great Leap Forward movement, there was a serious shortfall in capital. The defense minister, Peng Dehuai, was asked to reduce the budget. He had to work it out with the general logistics department, but was able to accomplish the task.[70]

Tan Guansan's May 1958 cable to Peng Dehuai suggesting that the TWC and TMC be merged in order to cut more than 8,000 staff was clearly also related to the need to reduce military expenditure. Deploying troops to Tibet was extremely costly,[71] and under the circumstances, the Chinese government was naturally reluctant to do it without good reason.

Another reason was that the battle between the volunteer resistance forces and troops from the TMC came just at the time that the "bombardment of Quemoy" was being planned and carried out. A coup in Lebanon in May 1958, and another in Iraq on July 14, increased volatility in the Middle East.

Closely monitoring the situation, Mao decided to take advantage of the immersion of the United States and Britain in the Middle East crisis. On the evening of July 18, Mao Zedong convened a meeting of CMC, air force, and navy leaders. The decision was made to "attack Jinmen [Quemoy] and Mazu [Matsu] to curb American imperialism."[72] This was the same day that Zhang Jingwu and Zhang Guohua went to the Norbulingka to communicate the Central Committee's instructions.

On the afternoon of August 23, what official histories refer to as "the third Taiwan Strait crisis" or the "8–23 artillery engagement" began. It continued for more than a month, but gradually began abating on October 5. Meanwhile, the Tibetan volunteer resistance army had its first round of battles with the PLA in August and September, within that same time period. The Chinese government had effectively opened two battle fronts at the same time, one in the southeast and one in the northwest, both drawing on crack troops and both deploying the air force.

"Concentrate military strength to fight wars of annihilation" was one of the Chinese government's fundamental principles of military engagement. It was not yet prepared, militarily or politically, to undertake an all-out military suppression in Tibet in 1958. Tibet's highway network was not yet complete, limiting the capacity for motor transport. The Lanzhou air force and Inner Mongolian cavalry were mainly suppressing revolts by Tibetans and Hui in Gansu and Qinghai, and if they had to send reinforcements to Tibet, they would need to deploy more troops for what was effectively the opening of a third battle front. It can be inferred that the Chinese government considered it far more important and urgent to deal with the southeast battle front than with the situation emerging in Tibet in 1958.

Mao wanted the CMC to "prepare to deal with war,"[73] which required keeping the situation stable in the strategic rear areas of the southwest and northwest. It was therefore more critical to use troops in Gansu, Qinghai, Sichuan, and Yunnan than in Tibet. In 1958, Zhu De and Peng Dehuai made separate inspection visits to the northwest and issued specific directives on military matters in Gansu and Qinghai. Preoccupied with the "third Taiwan Strait crisis" and stabilizing the strategic rear area, the Chinese government could not deal with a military action in Tibet for the time being. This is why the Central Committee repeatedly instructed the TWC not to engage in battle without good reason.

FIGURE 3. Chushi Gangdruk soldiers.
Source: Office of Tibet, Washington, D.C. Used with permission.

FIGURE 4. Gonpo Tashi.
Source: Office of Tibet, Washington, D.C. Used with permission.

FIGURE 5. Young Chushi Gangdruk soldier.
Source: Office of Tibet, Washington, D.C. Used with permission.

FIGURE 6. Gyalrong Tenzin.
Source: Jianglin Li.

FIGURE 7. Lobsang Sherap.
Source: Jianglin Li.

Chapter 16

THE 1958 "RELIGIOUS REFORM MOVEMENT"

1

In the early autumn of 2010, I flew from Chengdu to Qinghai, and on the rainy day after my arrival, I visited the Yarnang Choedra (Yanangquzha) temple at Kumbum [Ta'er] Monastery.

The Kumbum Monastery, the birthplace of Jé Tsongkhapa, is in Rusar (Lusha'er) Township, Rusar (Huangzhong) County, Qinghai Province. Built in 1560, it is one of the six great monasteries of the Gelugpa school.[1]

I was alone in the temple. The newly reopened monastery's Yarnang Choedra temple was not a must-see tourist attraction, and therefore not a key renovation target. In the drizzling rain, the compound looked very old, the stone tiles of the courtyard reflecting the gloomy daylight. Large watermarks stained the faded red walls of the temple's winding corridor as rain dripped from the eaves, the multicolored capitals of the wooden pillars were mottled, and their feet mildewed.

It was here, in 1958, that the arrest and denunciation rally took place.

Able to hold nearly a thousand monks, this compound was once where the monastery held its great assemblies and *cham* dances (masked dances performed during religious ceremonies and festivals), and monks had gathered at the temple on countless occasions to chant. The last gathering, more than half a century ago, occurred at the point of machine guns, and the monastery has never returned to its condition from before that time.

I stood alongside the long, covered corridor, gazing on the deserted courtyard where Arjia Rinpoché[2] experienced the most terrifying day of his life, more than half a century earlier.

Early in the morning on October 15, 1958, 8-year-old Arjia Rinpoché got out of bed and ate breakfast, just like any other day. But he noticed something strange in the atmosphere, and his teacher looked at the young boy and spoke "in a strange voice: 'It is impossible to predict what will happen today. Don't believe everything you hear; don't go against your conscience; don't do anything you know is wrong. If you get into trouble, pray to the Three Jewels and the Protectors.'"[3]

After breakfast, Arjia Rinpoché went with the others to the Yarnang Choedra and was immediately struck dumb by the scene before him.

All of the monks had gathered in the courtyard under the guard of dozens of fully armed PLA soldiers, and machine guns on the roof had their muzzles trained on the monks. On the high platform where religious assemblies were held sat an impressive array of work team members clad in blue "cadre suits," while young "activist" monks carrying coarse ropes and whips strode about with fierce looks on their faces. An oppressive silence reigned, and the air was stifling.

Then, Arjia Rinpoché witnessed the most horrifying scene in the more than 500-year history of the monastery:

> A Chinese official broke the silence with a loud shout: "Reveal your suffering! If you have suffered, speak out; if you are oppressed, overthrow those who oppose revolution; uncover the lid of feudalism!" Every monk present was forced to echo these words.
>
> Then the "activists," who had been given directions in advance, walked in among the group and roughly yanked out Ratu Rinpoché and pulled him to the stage, where they bound him and then began punching and kicking him:
>
> At that moment, as if they had simultaneously lost their senses, positivist monks, militiamen, and cadres began seizing hundreds of people in the courtyard. Panic broke out. Some tried to hide, but to

> no avail. One monk pretended to be one of the tormentors and began seizing others, but he was dragged out as well.[4]

During this first round, Arjia Rinpoché's teacher, housekeeper, and others he knew were arrested: "The seized monks were tied until their tormentors ran out of rope; then the monks' cloth belts were ripped from their robes and used as restraints. They were then forced to stand in front of the long bank of stairs that led to the platform, humiliated for all to see."[5]

At that time, Kumbum had 1,615 monks, of whom "219, or 13.52%, were upper-ranking power holders (among them 34 *tulkus*,[6] 86 managers, 1 *changdzo*,[7] 7 *genpa*,[8] 66 *gekoe*,[9] 23 *rabjampas*,[10] and 2 *umdzé*[11])."[12] During the denunciation rally that day, almost all the monk officials were arrested, except for young tulkus like Arjia Rinpoché.

2

What happened that day was not an isolated action by the local government but, rather, part of a political movement targeting Tibetan Buddhism. Official publications seldom mention this campaign. Most local gazetteers refer to it as the "four antis campaign," i.e., "anti-rebellion, anti-crime, anti-privilege, and anti-exploitation," or as an "anti-feudalism campaign,"[13] and in some localities it was referred to as "supplementary lessons in democratic reform." In internal documents, this campaign is referred to as "religious reform" or "religious systemic reform."[14] There have been many political campaigns since the founding of the PRC, but little is known of this one; it was a secret campaign in the history of the People's Republic of China.[15]

What was the reason for this secret campaign? It involved the CCP's policies and guiding ideology on religion. When the CCP was first established, its guiding principles explicitly stated "recognizing the dictatorship of the proletariat," "eliminating capitalist private property," "confiscating machinery, land, factories, semi-finished products, and other means of production,"[16] etc., but never mentioned religion. Yet, while the CCP claimed to represent workers and peasants, its early founders were all intellectuals with varying anti-religious tendencies. Chen Duxiu[17] believed that "all religion is an idol to deceive people," and "all of the gods and spirits respected and worshiped by the religious are useless idols to deceive people, and all should be destroyed."[18] Mao Zedong praised actions during the peasant movement to "prohibit superstition and attack Buddha," but felt that caution was needed for strategic purposes: "If too much of an effort is made, arbitrarily and prematurely, to abolish these things, the local tyrants and evil gentry will seize the pretext to put about such counterrevolutionary propaganda"[19] and sabotage the peasant movement.

When the Red Army passed through Ngawa during its Long March in 1935, the CCP leadership's attitude was clear: "Doing no work, lamas are social parasites. Lamaist temples usually function as organs of ruling power, owning large amounts of property and land. Lamaism is used by imperialists, Chinese warlords, and the native ruling class to maintain their rule."[20]

The party constitution that the CCP's Seventh Party Congress adopted on June 11, 1945, defined the party as established on the theoretical foundation of "Marxism's dialectical materialism and historical materialism."[21] As a political party that opposed any form of idealism, the CCP adopted the Marxist view holding that religion originated from humanity's erroneous understanding of the world and would naturally disappear with the progress of science and culture, but that it would continue to exist during a set historical period. During this phase, the CCP should limit the development of religion and use various means to expedite its extinction. This was the fundamental principle of the CCP's religious policies.[22]

During the "democratic revolution" phase, the CCP's chief objective was to seize political power, and to this end, the CCP was willing to form a "united front" with various social forces to isolate and attack its chief opponent, the Nationalist Party and government. After it seized power, the CCP needed to consolidate its power and avoid making enemies by initially establishing a "3–3 coalition government" in parts of the southwest and northwest occupied by ethnic minorities. This meant that at every level of the government apparatus, one third of the positions were held by Communist Party members, another third by progressives outside of the party, and one third by ethnic and religious figures. This method drew the support of religious and ethnic elites and helped the CCP gain a foothold in the minority regions. In 1951, the Qinghai provincial party committee issued a special directive for all localities to "conscientiously protect the monasteries":

> The monastery is a venue allowing the greatest access to the masses, and consequently is a significant target and focal point for launching operations in the nomadic regions. Maximum effort should be expended on lamas at all levels, especially junior lamas (junior lamas are in fact part of the laboring masses, and their lives are very difficult). Due to their traditional status, they can move freely and without obstruction throughout the pastoral regions, and it will be easiest to disseminate our party's influence and policies through them.[23]

After gaining a footing in these regions, the CCP gradually began to use its ideology to transform society, but this inevitably led to conflicts with the religious beliefs of non-Chinese peoples and the customs, habits, and ways of life centered on religion.[24] These conflicts intensified when the CCP launched land reform in Sichuan's Tibetan regions in 1956, and that's when the CCP began considering a move against religion. In July of that year, while listening to a report from Li Weihan and Liao Zhigao regarding problems with reforms in Garzê and Liangshan, which touched on dealing with monasteries, Mao explicitly said, "Leaving them alone for now doesn't mean leaving them alone forever."[25] On March 9, 1957, the CCP Central Committee Secretariat directed the Sichuan provincial party committee: "The temple issue requires discretion; the provincial party committee needs to study it well and propose methods. Be lenient, and don't cause things to collapse too quickly. It is a mistake to distribute large donations as in Ganzi; that actually helps them grow. [The temples] must decline. Don't help them develop: First, don't help them develop, and second, don't make them collapse too quickly."[26]

In May 1958, the Central Committee work report that Liu Shaoqi delivered at the second session of the Eighth Party Congress mentioned the rectification of work styles and anti-rightist struggle in the ethnic minority regions, and criticized problems such as local nationalism and surmounting Han chauvinist tendencies. The vice-chairman of the Nationalities Affairs Commission, Yang Jingren, stated that two contradictions existed among the Hui minority: One was "the contradiction between the socialist system and the religious system," and the other was "the contradiction between atheism and theism." Yang proposed resolving these two contradictions from the approaches of "education, management, and reform." "Education" meant "strengthening the dissemination of scientific knowledge to the masses, and strengthening education of the religious community to be patriotic and law-abiding," and at the same time "disseminating the materialist world view and criticizing the religious world view." "Management" meant "managing the religious leadership" and strengthening their transformation: "Resolutely struggle against rightists, reactionaries, and bad elements among the religious leaders and strip them of their capacity to dupe the masses. This will greatly facilitate eroding religion's fetters on the people." "Reform" meant "reforming the religious system."[27]

At a "Seminar on the Problem of Hui Islamism" that the Central Committee United Front Department convened in Qingdao from May 27 to June 7, the department's director, Li Weihan, elaborated on the theories behind the CCP's religious policies: "Religion is a historical category that follows the inexorable laws of occurrence, development, and demise.... Our social development requires that we not only look at religion as long-term and protect religious freedom, but also that we regard it as something that will gradually decline and perish, and accelerate this process from various angles to weaken it a little faster."[28]

As to why "religious systemic reform" hadn't been carried out in previous years, Li Weihan said:

> The guiding principle adopted toward religion over the past few years was to basically leave it alone and to only engage in political struggle with them... engage in political struggle and not involve religion. Was this principle correct? I feel it was, because at that time political reforms

> were not yet being carried out, so why move on religion? If we weren't going to move on counterrevolutionaries, why on religion? There was work to be done on building the party and Youth League and among the masses, so why move on religion instead of on those?[29]

By the time of the Qingdao Conference, the CCP had already carried out two rounds of military suppression in Garzê and Ngawa, most privately held arms had been seized, and land reform was largely completed. Military operations in Qinghai, Garzê, and Yunnan were in progress. Given the immense disparity in the power of the two sides, no one within the Chinese government doubted the outcome of the suppression. Tibetans no longer had the strength to resist "religious systemic reform," so the time was ripe to "move on religion."

On August 19, 1958, the Xinhua News Agency's *Internal Reference* reported that the Qinghai provincial party committee had convened a meeting of prefectural and county party secretaries in the pastoral regions in the latter half of July: "In accordance with the spirit of the Qingdao Conference of the Central Committee United Front Department, [the conference] discussed and passed a 'resolution regarding reforming the religious system,' deciding to thoroughly reform the religious system and abolish the oppressive exploitative system and spiritual bondage inflicted on ethnic minorities by religion." The resolution included four measures:

1. "Resolutely reform the religious system," abolish "land rent, livestock rent, and usurious loans by monasteries" as well as their mountain forests, grasslands, and various religious laws, and "gradually abolish the system of 'reincarnation of Living Buddhas.'"
2. "Thoroughly reform religious personnel and cause the majority of religious monasteries to disband. All counterrevolutionaries among the religious elite are to be arrested and dealt with in accordance with law; suspected counterrevolutionaries are to be put under collective control and education and stringently investigated, dealing with them in accordance with the law or placing them under control as appropriate. All rightists are to be thoroughly denounced and discredited and dealt with according to the gravity of their crimes.

Counterrevolutionaries, bad elements, and rightists are to have their crimes declared in public, and the masses are to be mobilized to report, expose, and struggle against them, stripping them of their political capital."

3. "While engaging in extensive mobilization of the masses to lift the lid off of feudalism, thoroughly discredit religion until it collapses."
4. "Strengthen education of party members and cadres regarding the current situation; cause them to recognize the reactionary nature of religion; thoroughly correct the right-deviating thinking that regards religion as a tiger's rump that cannot be touched; constantly eradicate superstition, liberate thinking, and boldly battle against religion."[30]

These four items show that the objective of "religious systemic reform" was not merely adapting certain religious laws and systems to social development, as stated in openly published documents, but was rather a wholesale political and economic suppression of religion, the ultimate aim of which was to "cause the majority of religious monasteries to disband."[31]

3

Why did the CCP choose to "move on religion" in 1958? Apart from fundamental ideological conflicts, there were even more practical reasons. Islam and Buddhism had many adherents in the minority regions, with organizational methods and tightly knit systems passed down over the centuries. Religious belief exercised a powerful social cohesive force among Tibetan and Hui believers in Buddhism and Islam, and in these regions, party cadres who shared neither the ethnicity nor the religion of the people were "outsiders" in a dual sense. This made it very hard for them to establish political power. Mao realized early on that strengthening local political power and firmly controlling those regions required relying on locals.[32]

However, in grooming party and Youth League members in those regions, religious beliefs immediately arose as an issue. When the CCP first came to power, its policies in these regions were different from those in the mainland. In October 1954, the CCP Central Committee explicitly directed all ethnic minority regions to allow "enlightened elements and revolutionary intellectuals" among the ethnic minorities to join the party after a set trial period, and "not to make renunciation of religious beliefs a condition for joining the party," otherwise, "it will be virtually impossible for us to build party work in many ethnic minority regions."[33]

Conflicts always existed, however, as Li Weihan made clear in a speech:

> Citizens have freedom of religious belief, but there is no freedom of religion in the party. That is unambiguous, because the world view of Marxists and Communists only allows for atheism and materialism and not theism and idealism. So in principle, there is no freedom of religion within the party. . . . In principle, theism and atheism cannot coexist within the party, but in actuality, many Hui party members hold religious beliefs. This is a contradiction.[34]

This contradiction might not be apparent most of the time, but when the Chinese government began forcing social reforms on ethnic minority regions and directly targeting monasteries, many party members faced the difficult choice of whether to submit to party discipline or to their religious beliefs. The situation in Yadzi (Xunhua) suggests that many party and Youth League members chose their religion: 68.4% of local party members and 69.5% of local Youth League members participated in the uprising; not only that, but 40.4% (156) of party members and 45.09% (262) of Youth League members "directly took part in attacking the county seat."[35]

Documents reveal that among the party and Youth League members who took part in the rebellion in Xunhua, 78% were considered to have extremely vague conceptions regarding the question of handling religion, and fairly strong religious faith. There was a strong tendency toward "protecting religion," manifested as "willingness to give up the party rather than the faith," and "willingness to give up one's life rather than the faith," and putting religion above the party. There were also quite a few party members who swore that they would "never betray religion and would steadfastly overthrow the enemy of religion—the Communist Party."[36]

Facing this situation, the CCP decided to channel these regions into the Chinese government's political, economic, and ideological system in the "democratic reform" movement.

Economic factors provided further reason for the Chinese government to "move on religion" at this time. Wang Feng, the deputy director of the United Front Department and vice-chairman of the Nationalities Affairs Commission, said in a speech that among the Mongols, Tibetans, Qiang, Tu, Yugu, and other ethnic groups that followed Tibetan Buddhism, there were "more than 5,000 monasteries of various sizes, and 450,000 religious personnel, among which there are more than 3,000 lamaist temples and 250,000 lamas in Tibet; 20,000 lamas in Mongolia and Xinjiang; and a total of 2,000–3,000 lama temples and more than 170,000 lamas in Gansu, Qinghai, Sichuan, Yunnan, and other provinces."[37] Over the centuries, monasteries had accumulated not only land, mountain forests, pastures, livestock, commercial capital, grain storehouses, etc., but also immense quantities of buildings, images and religious vessels made of gold, silver, and copper, and incalculable amounts of other treasures such as gemstones. According to the estimates of local governments, before 1958, in Garzê Prefecture, monastery holdings composed 18% of the land and 72% of the private commercial capital;[38] in Yunnan's Dechen Prefecture, monasteries owned 34% of all land in the prefecture. The Kumbum Monastery in Qinghai possessed more than 100,000 *mu* of land.[39] The personal assets of religious elites were also quite considerable.

When the Chinese government launched the Great Leap Forward in 1958, capital was so inadequate that military spending had to be reduced. The enormous wealth of the monasteries was naturally considered fair game, especially given the amount of human and material resources "wasted" on religious activities.[40]

The independence that the monasteries accrued through their abundant economic resources was intolerable to the Chinese government. In his speech, Wang Feng stated: "Abolish the monasteries' ownership of the means of production, usurious lending, corvée labor, and other such exploiting systems, and ban illegal commerce (commerce in the temples is all illegal, and halting their businesses activities will eliminate their economic base)."[41]

4

Even so, "religious systemic reform" aimed at "causing the majority of religious monasteries to disband" was in logical conflict with "freedom of religious belief." This touched on the essence of the Chinese government's religious policies. In 1958, the United Front Department director Li Weihan interpreted the constitutional provision on "religious freedom" in this way:

> The slogan of "religious freedom" originated in the period when capitalism was developing upward, and the bourgeoisie proposed it to oppose the feudal system. Consequently, under certain historical circumstances, it is a revolutionary slogan. We've employed this slogan while at the same time enriching and developing its revolutionary content, not only using it to oppose feudalism and the coerced beliefs of the exploiting class, but also striving, through the thorough realization of this slogan, for people to gradually progress from belief to non-belief.[42]

It might seem paradoxical to "thoroughly realize" freedom of religious belief in order to eliminate religion, but the subtlety lay in what the Chinese government referred to as the two aspects of "freedom of religious belief": "freedom of belief" and "freedom of unbelief." Li Weihan explained:

> Citizens have freedom of religious belief, which also includes the freedom not to believe and to change one's beliefs. We've always explained it this way. The complete formulation is: Every citizen has the freedom to hold religious beliefs and also the freedom not to have religious beliefs; has the freedom to believe in this religion, or in that religion . . . and furthermore has the freedom to go from not believing to believing, and the freedom to go from believing to not believing. Our explanation is the most comprehensive, and facilitates people changing their religious beliefs and even shedding their religious beliefs.[43]

As a result, the Chinese government used various means to encourage the "freedom not to believe." Destroying the economic base of the monasteries to threaten their survival, using "anti-rightist struggle" and campaigns against "local nationalism" to purge upper and mid-level religious figures and abolish the "reincarnation of Living Buddhas," prohibiting children under 18 from becoming monks or nuns, engaging in widespread propaganda to "eliminate superstition," arresting and imprisoning large numbers of prominent monks, encouraging believers to denounce and beat high lamas—all of these administrative measures and violent methods promoted the "freedom of unbelief" and limited the "freedom of belief."

As for the policy of "freedom of religious belief" enshrined in the Constitution, Li Weihan explained:

> Our party has two kinds of policies: One kind is fundamental policies such as freedom of religious belief, equality among the ethnic groups, the united front, etc., which are completely correct and unchanging in the long term. Another kind is specific policies, which are strategic political tactics used to execute the party's line and fundamental policies. These change according to changes in the objective circumstances. . . . As for religious belief, in the past we had a policy of protecting the freedom of religious belief, and that policy will continue. We have always thought that religious belief needs to be weakened until it is wiped out, therefore we have never said that religion would have a long, long life, and nor have we ever said that the religious system cannot be reformed.[44]

This indicates that in the Communist system, "policy" and "strategy" are related but not equal. A "policy" is a program within a certain time frame, and a "strategy" is the execution of a policy. A "long-term policy" is put into practice through a specific "strategy" formulated according to the circumstances at that time. The frequent contradiction between "strategy" and "policy" shows that "policy" is one thing and "strategy" is another. Many times, "policy" is used for external propaganda and "strategy" is for internal use, and when strategy goes off course and is challenged on the outside, "policy" is used to cover it up. Wang Feng made this even more explicit during a meeting of the United Front Department that he called on October 7, 1958:

> Why mention protecting the freedom of religious belief? This cannot be dropped; it is stipulated in China's Constitution, and having it prevents counterrevolutionaries from saying that we're eliminating religion. That gives us an advantage.[45]

In 1959, the director of the Qinghai Provincial United Front Department, Ji Chunguang, gave a similar explanation for the policy of "freedom of religious belief" at the twelfth enlarged meeting of the provincial party committee. He emphasized the need to "further strengthen the education of cadres in policy and ideology and enhance their proficiency in policy and ideology":

> Make every comrade explicitly recognize that our repeated emphasis on comprehensively implementing the policy of freedom of religious belief and our emphasis on strengthening religious work is only a means of winning over the religious masses and of gradually restricting and ultimately eliminating religion. In no sense does it imply sustaining or developing religion.[46]

This shows that there was a unanimous consensus within the Chinese government on the policy of "freedom of religious belief," but that the policy was explained differently depending on whether the audience was internal or external. Li Weihan's remarks were circulated at every level of the party in 1958, but were not openly published until 1981.[47] Wang Feng's remarks remain unavailable to the public to the present day.

Since the essence of "religious reform" was to completely destroy religion, it had to be called something else when implemented. In his speech, Wang Feng directed:

> Using the slogans of attacking counterrevolutionaries, opposing bad people and bad deeds, opposing religious privilege and exploitation, etc. (it is not necessary to raise the slogan of reforming the religious system), mobilize the masses outside of the monasteries and the impoverished lamas inside the monasteries to create a powerful pincer-style

> mass movement to reform the religious system. At the same time, counterrevolutionaries and reactionary elites who have aroused massive public indignation should be arrested or sent to training camps as appropriate, and must be resolutely exposed.[48]

The Qinghai provincial party committee stated:

> Reforming the religious system has a class struggle character of the poor opposing the rich, the people opposing the nobility, and lower-class people opposing the upper classes. Without resolutely carrying out reform of the religious system, it will be impossible to thoroughly eliminate the herd-owning class and strike a victory for socialist revolution.[49]

However, in terms of strategy:

> In order for slogans to be distinct, forceful, and easy for the masses to accept, do not openly refer to reform of the religious system outside of the party, but rather talk of thoroughly eliminating counterrevolutionaries inside the monasteries, and abolishing feudal exploitation and privilege in religion and the monasteries. This is strategic and achieves the objective of reforming the religious system and accelerating socialist revolution.[50]

That is the reason why the "religious reform movement" of 1958 was referred to as the "four antis campaign" or the "anti feudalist movement."

5

In terms of timing, the Central Committee's United Front Department held its "Seminar on the Islam Issue" from the end of May to the beginning of June, 1958, and then a "Seminar on the Lamaist Religion Issue" from September 22 to October 6, perhaps planning to resolve the issues in two steps.

Yet Gansu had already completed preparations for the campaign before the seminars. In April 1958, the PLA surrounded Labrang, Gansu's largest monastery. Troops constructed multiple fortifications on the mountains in front of and behind the monastery and erected a cannon on the mountaintop, with its muzzle aimed at the main assembly hall. On

May 22, a monk renowned in Gansu and Qinghai, the sixth Gungthang Rinpoché, was arrested for "counterrevolutionary" crimes and all of his assets were confiscated.[51] In the latter half of June, a work team from the Gansu provincial party committee occupied the Labrang monastery and formally began "religious reform" there. The roads to the monastery were blocked, cutting off its communications and its monks from the outside world. The monastery's approximately 4,000 monks, high lamas, and officials were divided into nine large groups and locked up in different places. After that, the senior monks, including all of the Rinpochés, *khenpos*,[52] *changdzos*, managers, and the more than 80 attendants of Jamyang Zhepa were all arrested.[53]

Nineteen-year-old Alak Tsayu Tenzin Pelbar was also arrested that day. Years later, he wrote in his memoir:

> The monks and high lamas arrested at the monastery that day were divided up into 20 "Liberation brand" trucks (40 in each truck). Because there were not enough handcuffs, two people were cuffed together when arrested. They were taken to Dashaping prison[54] in Lanzhou, China. At least 800 people were locked up that day. The second group to be arrested at Labrang arrived in Lanzhou on August 1. In that way, more than 1,600 people from Labrang Monastery alone were held in Lanzhou, Anxi,[55] Mazongshan,[56] and Pingliang,[57] as well as in prisons and labor reform camps that the Chinese government had established in the Tsoe [Hezuo] and Labrang monasteries and other places.[58]

Some of the arrested monks and monk officials were executed;[59] some were sentenced to imprisonment, including life sentences, and many starved to death in prison.

In July, a work team from Choné County in southern Gansu was stationed in the Tingdzin Dargyé Ling (Chanding) Monastery to "mobilize the religious elites and the masses of monks to vent their grievances and inform on others." On October 20, "apart from the Labuleng, Chanding, Hezuo (Tsoe) and Langmu (Taktsang Lhamo) monasteries, which were retained, 192 monasteries were destroyed and their monks were repatriated to their places of origin to resume secular life."[60]

"Religious reform" began at the Kumbum Monastery on August 7. At that time, the monastery had 1,615 monks. After undergoing "struggle by the masses," 440 were arrested and put into forced political training,[61] and 383 monks from Inner Mongolia were repatriated. The remaining monks were divided into three large groups and nine small groups, and a mass debate between theism and atheism was launched "on the basis of attacking bad elements." After that, "the mental attitude of the lamas at the monastery underwent an enormous change; the vast majority shed their robes and put on laymen's clothes, and applications to return to secular life became common practice."[62]

On September 17, 1958, more than a month after "religious reform" began, the Qinghai Province United Front Department submitted a report to the provincial party committee:

> According to statistics, 223 monasteries in the pastoral areas have been disbanded, 51.98% of the total, and 17,685 religious personnel have returned to secular life, composing 36.56% of the total. Among these, 97.5% of the monasteries in Huangnan Prefecture have been disbanded, and 55.1% of religious personnel have returned to secular life; adding in those arrested or sent to group training brings it to around 95% of the total. In Hainan Prefecture, 91.8% of the monasteries have been disbanded, and 87.9% of religious personnel have returned to secular life. In Haibei and Haixi prefectures, more than 80% of the monasteries have been disbanded, and more than 70% of the religious personnel have returned to secular life. The emergence of these new scenarios shows that religion is on the brink of total collapse.[63]

In a speech at the eleventh National Conference on United Front Work, held in Beijing on December 29, Du Hua'an, representing the Qinghai Province United Front Department, reported: "From August to November this year, 731 of the province's 859 lamaist temples were disbanded; 24,613 out of the 54,287 religious personnel are taking part in production, and religion's influence over the people's thinking has been seriously crippled."[64]

In just three months of "religious reform," 85% of Qinghai's Buddhist monasteries were "disbanded" and 45% of their clerics returned to secular life. How were these monasteries "disbanded," and how did the monks return to secular life? Local gazetteers published in recent years have provided many related accounts. In Tsekhok County, Malho Prefecture, Qinghai Province:

> 1958 religious systemic reform . . . 129 settled individuals[65] were arrested. Throughout the province, ten Tibetan Buddhist monasteries (seven of the Yellow Sect [Gelug] and three of the Red Sect [Nyingma]) were completely banned, and 42 out of 51 Living Buddhas were forcibly secularized, while 564 of 774 monks were forced to return to their places of origin for production work.[66]

In Darlag (Dari) County, Golok TAP:

> Before religious systemic reform, Dari County had five fixed monasteries and eight tent monasteries with 1,840 monks, including 76 Living Buddhas, 30 monk officials, and 31 managers, and religious personnel made up 13.7% of the population. In the latter half of 1958, in areas where there were no uprisings, Dari County integrated socialist transformation into animal husbandry, carried out religious systemic reform, confiscated livestock and pastures owned by the monasteries, and abolished lending and corvée labor by the monasteries. But under the influence of "leftist" thinking, the mobilized masses demolished four fixed monasteries and four tent monasteries, and monks were compelled to return to secular life, while Buddhist images were smashed and scrolls were burned.[67]

In Gansu's Pari (Tianzhu) Tibetan Autonomous County:

> (1958) September, a struggle against feudalism was launched, and apart from the Jile [Tawan] Monastery, all of the county's Tibetan Buddhist monasteries and five mosques were sealed off or destroyed. Among 869 religious personnel (including 28 Living Buddhas, 786 lamas, 4 imams, and 51 mullahs), apart from 132 who fled, committed suicide, or were dealt with according to law, the rest were forced to resume secular life and undergo labor reform.[68]

The people arrested in Kanlho Prefecture included "192 Living Buddhas (86.8% of the Living Buddhas in the prefecture), 667 monk officials,

384 monastery managers, and 2,812 monks (19.5% of all monks in the prefecture)."[69] Of the 7,572 monks in Kanlho Prefecture, 4,055 were arrested and punished; 249 who were elderly, ill, or disabled were left behind to look after the monasteries; and the rest were forced back to secular life.[70] Nearly 70% of the ethnic religious elite in Qinghai Province were arrested and punished or sent to group training or reeducation through labor.[71]

The Garzê and Ngawa TAPs in Sichuan formally launched religious reform later than Qinghai. Palyul County was the first to start its "four antis" campaign, which began in June 1958, while other counties started in October through December. The last was Sertar County, which held its campaign from February to September 1960.

In the latter half of July 1958, the Garzê prefectural party committee decided that the farming regions of the prefecture's northern and eastern counties would "launch a mass anti-rebellion, anti-crime movement at all the lamaist temples in this winter and next spring, and the spearhead of mass struggle will be directed at reactionaries in the temples," who would be "thoroughly discredited politically and thoroughly ruined financially."[72]

To this end, Garzê decided to transfer 250 cadres from prefecture-level organs, and that 200 cadres would be taken from each county, along with cadres and soldiers from the military sub-region, to create a contingent of more than 5,000 personnel who would be sent to each county. According to the plan, the campaign would employ the following methods:

> Boldly mobilize the masses to create a formidable mass movement.... Prior to the struggle, put upper-ranking lamas in group training, and first arrest a group whose crimes are most heinous, uncover their misdeeds, support the masses, and unfold the mass movement. In the process of struggle, in accordance with the development of the movement and the demands of the masses, arrest another group, kill a few more, put a group under supervision, and control (arrest quotas, report to the provincial party committee for instructions) and resolutely rout the feudal class politically. In tandem with political attacks, on the economic front adopt the methods of abolishing, confiscating, fining, etc. to make them completely collapse.[73]

As in Gansu and Qinghai provinces, Garzê Prefecture's "four antis campaign" included both political and economic aspects to deal with individuals regarded as counterrevolutionaries and bad elements in religious circles:

> Before, during, and after the struggle, according to varying circumstances, arrest a group, imprison some as appropriate, place others under supervision or in group training, and confiscate their property (including animal husbandry and commercial capital), or else fine them, or in some cases both confiscate and fine. They should be not only thoroughly ruined and discredited politically, but also destroyed economically.[74]

Monasteries were to lose all their privileges, and their land was to be confiscated along with "assets hidden in the villages and pastoral areas; prohibit temples from engaging in illegal business."[75]

In November 1958, the prefectural party committee convened a meeting of more than 800 "agriculture battlefront advanced representatives" in Dartsedo. One of the main topics of the meeting was the "four antis campaign," preparing "backbone resources" for a full-scale launch of the campaign at the grassroots level:

> Through the venting of grievances, exposure, and group discussion at the meeting, [participants] unanimously understood that all temples were in fact a component of the feudal ruling class and were tools at the service of the landlord class. The so-called grand lamas and Living Buddhas who controlled the temples looked sanctimonious on the surface, always chanting benevolence, but in fact were a bunch of counterrevolutionaries harboring dark designs and capable of every kind of evil, and were assassins. From this they realized that "all crows are black, and there are no good people in the landlord class," and "the larger the temple, the greater the crimes of its reactionary lamas."[76]

After these "backbone resources" returned to their localities, the "four antis" campaign was launched in a unified fashion throughout the prefecture. In order to ensure smooth progress, "one regiment or one battalion was stationed in almost every county to serve as backup."[77] This shows that the four antis campaign in Garzê was conducted at gunpoint, so to speak, and was a well-planned, top-down movement.

During the campaign, each county, in accordance with the prefectural party committee's plan, "vented grievances, dug out the roots of poverty, calculated the accounts of exploitation, displayed evidence, engaged in free airing of views and contentions, and could also put up big-character posters," and convened mass rallies where thousands of people could vent their grievances in order to "lift the cover off and destroy the prestige of the feudal ruling class." Those denounced were arrested on the spot and sometimes even executed at the rallies. On December 20, 1958, the Drango County court held a public trial, attended by more than 2,000 people, and one person was executed on the spot.[78] On the 31st, the Drango County seat held a public trial, attended by 3,000 people, during which a monk from the Hor Drango (Shouling) Monastery was executed as an "armed rebel bandit leader."[79]

Simultaneous with the "four antis" campaign, the Chinese government also carried out an "anti-rightist movement" in religious circles. In August 1958, the Qinghai Province United Front Department summoned all upper- and mid-level Buddhist religious personnel for a meeting and carried out "socialist mass debate," which department director Ji Chunguang referred to as an "experimental field" for mass debates in religious work throughout the province. In fact, it was an anti-rightist movement in religious circles, divided into four stages including "speaking out freely, airing views fully, topical debate, anti-rightist struggle, and baring hearts to the party."[80] Encouragement and mobilization led participants to offer "2,801 opinions, put up 3,158 big-character posters, and basically reveal their true thinking."[81] Once the "snakes were lured from their dens," they were subjected to "anti-rightist struggle." After this experiment:

> Every prefecture and county could also launch focused anti-rightist struggle, trying with one or two rightists. Since among the more than 2000 mid-level religious personnel in the entire province, rightists made up at least 20%, each locality targeted only one or two in its

> denunciation rallies, so that the proportion would not be too great. They were to be politically discredited and disposed of as necessary by their organizations, and their vacated places were offered to promote and settle leftists, so as not to be restrained by the old representation. This facilitated planting the Red Banner in all of the religious temples, placing temples and religious personnel under the leadership and control of the party, and occupying the religious battlefield.[82]

In the "Report Regarding the Situation of Religious Work and Opinions Going Forward," the Qinghai United Front Department repeatedly emphasized:

> After a large number of religious monasteries have been destroyed and a large number of religious personnel have returned to secular life, all localities must rapidly launch religious systemic reform work in the monasteries that have been purposely retained. . . . The monasteries that remain must be controlled by progressive elements and must be completely controlled under the party's leadership.[83]

The reason that some monasteries were "purposely retained" was detailed in recommendations that Ulanhu and Wang Feng made to the Central Committee in November 1958 in the name of the Central Committee Nationalities Affairs Commission leading party group:

> In order to look after the religious beliefs of the masses, block rumors and provocations by counterrevolutionaries inside and outside of China, and facilitate the centralized management of lamas who have not returned to secular life, preserving some temples is essential. As to the appropriate number to retain, this should be according to the influence of the temple and the views of the masses. Rank the temples; in principle it is undesirable to retain too few. . . . In terms of retaining temples, it is advantageous at present to retain more rather than less.[84]

Figures vary on the number of monasteries in the Tibetan regions before the "religious systemic reform" movement. The Nationalities Affairs Commission stated that there were more than 5,000 monasteries among the Mongolian, Tibetan, Tu, and Yugu followers of Tibetan Buddhism.[85]

Various other materials state that Sichuan's Tibetan regions had a total of 727 monasteries, Gansu had 369,[86] Yunnan's Dechen TAP had 24,[87] Qinghai had 859 (according to the provincial United Front Department),[88] and Tibet had 2,676 monasteries of various sizes.[89] This set of figures would indicate that the three Tibetan regions had a total of 4,655 monasteries of various sizes before the "four antis campaign."[90]

During the movement, all but four of Kanlho TAP's 196 Buddhist monasteries (98%) were destroyed.[91] Of Luchu County's 11 monasteries, 10 were destroyed in a single day, and 1,117 out of 1,550 monks were forced to return to secular life.[92]

Before "democratic reform," Ngawa Prefecture had more than 320 monasteries, among which "7 Tibetan Buddhist temples were listed as nationally protected important historical monuments"[93] and were therefore probably preserved.

What can be determined for certain is that in the Tibetan regions of Gansu, Qinghai, Sichuan, and Yunnan provinces, i.e., the traditional Tibetan regions of Amdo and Kham, the vast majority of monasteries were closed down, occupied, or dismantled by the beginning of 1959, and some were destroyed in battles.

6

How much in assets did the Chinese government plunder from monasteries in the Tibetan regions during the "four antis campaign" in 1958? To date there are no precise figures, but scattered records in local gazetteers and other materials provide a glimpse.

At the Kumbum Monastery in 1958, the Chinese authorities "arrested and tried 427 monks and Living Buddhas, confiscated and disposed of gold, silver, cash, jewels, jade, top-quality clothing, and 20-odd other articles of daily use with a total value of 1.598 million *yuan* (in 1959, 535,000 *yuan* worth of wrongfully confiscated assets were returned)."[94] These figures only apply to the value of the personal property confiscated from monks and do not include the jewels, commercial capital, gold and silver statuary and implements, and other items, belonging to the monastery itself.

Sichuan's Garzê Prefecture confiscated 212,000 head of livestock from the monasteries, along with 5.12 million kilos of grain, 247,000 farming implements, more than 34,000 buildings, 150,000 *mu* of land, and other property, with a total value of 10.27 million *yuan*.[95] This figure does not include cash, gold, or silver.

Garzê's Qianning County[96] confiscated 27,240 *yuan* in cash, 132 taels of gold,[97] 15,156 silver dollars, and 28,940 Tibetan rupees.[98] Sertar County confiscated property including "23 taels of gold, 10 taels of gold dust, 33,354 silver dollars, 167 silver sycees, 833 silver implements, 11,460 *yuan* Renminbi, 50 catties and 9,162 jewels, 6,240 *yuan* in foreign currency, 6,756 Tibetan rupees, and 4 wristwatches."[99]

Before the "four antis campaign," Dergé County's famous Palpung (Babang) Monastery's valuable religious artifacts included "7 large-scale gilded Buddha statues, 9,835 copper and brass Buddha statues of various kinds, 10,150 relatively precious Thangkas, more than 32,400 scriptures of various kinds, 129,845 printing plates, and more than 3,000 other Buddhist implements."[100] The important cultural artefacts at Dergé's Gonchen (Gengqing) Monastery included "more than 1,000 gilded Buddha statues of various sizes, more than 1,350 Thangkas of various kinds and more than 19,860 scriptures."[101]

What happened to all those artifacts? What happened to the countless metal statues and religious implements confiscated from thousands of monasteries? Were they melted down during the "great iron and steel-making campaign," or were they auctioned off on international markets? Available sources provide no answers. We only know one thing for sure: that of the property confiscated from the monasteries, "gold, silver, and jewels were handed over to the state treasury as required."[102]

By the beginning of 1959, "democratic reform" in the Tibetan regions of Gansu, Qinghai, Sichuan, and Yunnan was basically completed. In this process, the Chinese government first used the method of "land reform" to confiscate the personal property of the middle and upper strata, then used the method of "religious reform" to confiscate the assets of thousands of monasteries, and finally used the organizing of cooperatives to confiscate the personal property of the general Tibetan populace, wiping out the wealth that Tibetans had accumulated over hundreds of years.

Yet the destruction of monasteries and dispersal of monks did not mean the extinction of religious faith. After the religious persecution disguised as the "four antis campaign" swept through the Tibetan regions of Gansu, Qinghai, Sichuan, and Yunnan, religious belief went underground. In a country that enshrined "freedom of religious belief" in its constitution, hundreds and thousands of Tibetan Buddhists became underground believers in the late 1950s and early 1960s.

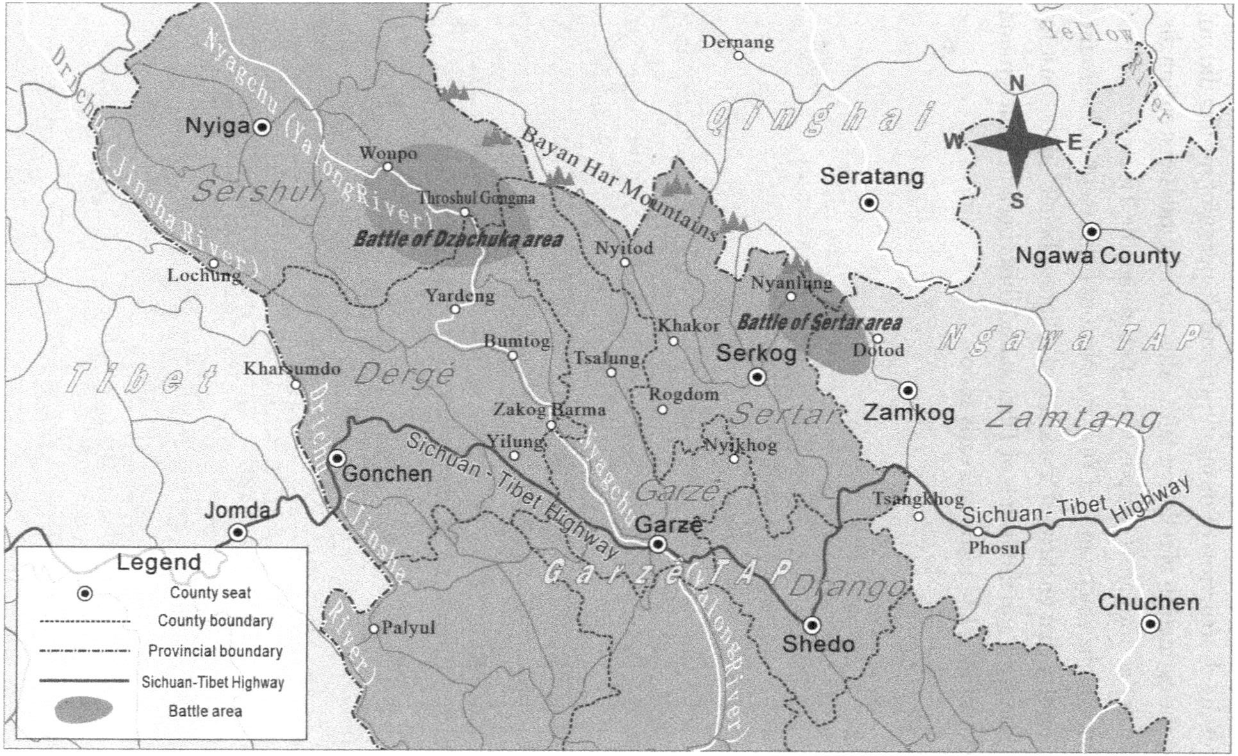

MAP 5. PLA Battles in the Sertar and Dzachuka areas, Sichuan Province, 1959. Source: Marvin Cao.

Chapter 17

LHASA, THE LAST HOPE

1

In the summer of 1958, the Red Tempest finally struck the banks of lakes Gyaring and Ngoring.

Nomadic communities throughout the Yellow River source region were called in for meetings where officials from the county government announced that households would have to combine all their livestock into a "cooperative."

Tradition required that all members had to discuss any major matters affecting the survival of the group. Facing this unexpected development, Ngolo's small group of less than 30 households gathered beneath their shrine, at their wits' end. No one wanted to hand over their livestock, but what would happen if they didn't? How could they resist, with just a few dozen men and a dozen or so firelocks designed to kill wolves? Even with more men and weapons, how could they equal the army camp across the river?[1]

The elders prayed, the men were silent, and the women wept. After a while, someone said, "Let's run!"

There seemed to be no alternative. They would find a place with water and grass and no Chinese where they could graze their cattle.

The cooperative movement was still in the propaganda stage, so these nomadic herders, men, women, and children, packed up their tents and ran for their lives, driving their cattle and sheep before them. Ngolo was married by then, with a baby not yet one year old. Her entire family took their livestock and belongings and fled with the rest of the group.

They were able to escape temporarily by hiding in the mountains. It never occurred to them that by the summer of 1958, it would be impossible to find a place with water and grass but no PLA in any of the pastoral areas of Gansu, Qinghai, and Sichuan.

One sunny day, when the air was fresh and cool, and Ngolo, with her baby on her back, was bustling about in the tent not far from where the animals were grazing, she suddenly heard a cry of alarm: "The Chinese soldiers are coming!"

A band of cavalry had appeared out of the blue and completely surrounded the mountain where they were hiding. Ngolo clutched her baby to her breast and ran out of the tent. What followed was like a nightmare: the sound of gunfire, the roar of cannons, horses galloping wildly, and people running in every direction.

A thunderous blast sent Ngolo reeling, and she tumbled to the ground, instinctively shielding her sobbing baby with her body.

Suddenly, Ngolo felt a hand grab her and pull her upright. Through bleary eyes she recognized the young herdsman beside her as her husband. Holding a crude gun in one hand and gripping her arm with the other, he plunged with them in among the panicked livestock. Ngolo lurched along, not knowing how long or how far, until finally the air no longer smelled of gunpowder and the grasslands were silent once more. Then they stopped running.

It was then that Ngolo noticed other people around her. She was cheered by the sight of her older brother and sister-in-law, but where were her father and mother? Where were her younger brother and sister and two nephews? Out of their whole family, only five had managed to break through the layers of encirclement. Only two families in the group had escaped.

They had no *tsampa,* no dried meat, no livestock, not even a bowl to dip water from the river. Two depleted families with nothing to their names—what could they do now? The men discussed the situation in low voices.

"We'll go to Lhasa," someone said. "Gyalwa Rinpoché[2] will protect us . . ."

2

At the time that the herder woman Ngolo left her homeland in Golok, Aten, the headman of Dhunkhug Village in Nyarong, received permission from his superior to leave the place where he was stationed, in order to visit his family.

Since finishing his studies in Chengdu in 1956 and returning to his homeland, Aten had been working as a grassroots ethnic party cadre. He and the other Tibetan cadres were not trusted, however, and found themselves under constant surveillance. The things he saw and heard were becoming increasingly intolerable to him, and he had begun secretly plotting his escape.

The construction of the highway from Dartsedo to Bathang at the beginning of the year had given the PLA an advantage in waging war in southern Kham. By then, land reform and the organizing of cooperatives had been largely completed in the farming areas of the Garzê and Ngawa TAPs. The Sichuan provincial party committee had then begun organizing cooperatives in the pastoral areas, and herders in the counties of northern Kham had begun armed resistance, giving rise to a second wave of rebellions in Sichuan's Tibetan areas and a second round of suppression.

In mid-March 1958, a war council in the Ganzi military sub-district decided to assemble seven regiments for a second military suppression of Tibetans who continued to revolt in Kham. The western front of this suppression involved three infantry regiments and one cavalry regiment in the region west of Garzê, and blockading the Jinsha River to cut off the escape route to central Tibet. The eastern front involved seven regiments and one cavalry company around Bathang, surrounding groups of rebelling Tibetans and annihilating them one by one.[3]

Nyarong County's Tibetan resistance forces had dispersed under the PLA's powerful military suppression in the first half of 1958. The largest guerrilla force, led by the Nyarong chieftain Gyari Nyima and his wife Dorjé Yudon, divided into two (one group led by Gyari Nyima and the other by his uncle and brother) and set off along separate routes for Lhasa. They were never reunited.[4]

The military and political operations in the name of "democratic reform" destroyed traditional Tibetan social structure, requiring a new power structure to be built from scratch. In this process, many of the Tibetan cadres and militiamen being groomed by the Chinese government found the "reforms" impossible to accept, and were only waiting for an opportunity to break away from their teams. Some ran off with weapons to join the guerrilla forces.[5]

As the only man in his family, Aten now faced this life-and-death choice, as well as whether to take his two wives and daughter with him. If he left them behind, would the work team punish them? After pondering this question, Aten decided it would be better for his family to stay together. He secretly contacted friends and relatives, and several families totaling 16 people of all ages, including 10 men, agreed to escape together. They had only 4 firearms among them.

One night in September, Aten and his companions mounted their horses and silently led several pack mules away from the village, loaded with provisions. They pushed on through the night to avoid PLA patrols, reaching the pastoral region of western Nyarong by daybreak. The rugged topography there made access difficult, so the PLA had never fully controlled the area, and small guerrilla forces continued to roam these mountains following the withdrawal of the main resistance forces to Lhasa. Aten had no set objective or destination; he only knew that in this region, there were people who continued to fight.

The refugees encountered the PLA at noon several days later. The men immediately opened fire while the women and children fled for the hills. Their ammunition was insufficient for a sustained battle, so after firing a few shots, the men also fled. Fortunately, the PLA soldiers were unable to catch up with them on the precipitous and rocky slopes, but while the refugees managed to escape, their mules and horses had run off in a panic with most of the provisions they had brought. Aten also lost track of his brother during the shootout, and never saw him again.

Continuing on for a few days, the remaining group encountered a guerrilla force—in fact, just 30 men and their families, who were refugees like themselves. They were short on food and ammunition, and the long, cold winter was approaching. The men found a safe place for their wives, elders, and children, with a few men to protect them, and those with guns teamed up to creep into the army camp while the PLA was out on patrol and steal their grazing cattle and horses. Several such encounters resulted in mixed success, with casualties on both sides.

After roaming around for nearly two months, the refugees noticed a significantly stronger PLA presence. By then, the battles in southern Kham had largely ended. Although the American CIA had airdropped two groups of trained guerrillas into Lithang to help local resistance forces, there is no indication that any weapons were airdropped into Lithang in 1958.[6] The tribal alliance was woefully inadequate to resist the crushing wave of PLA soldiers. Under attack from seven regiments, the resistance in southern Kham gradually collapsed. In autumn, the PLA shifted the focus of battle to northern Kham, with two regiments deployed near Dergé and Nyarong to thoroughly annihilate the remaining pockets of resistance, including Aten and his group.[7]

It having become impossible to stay in his homeland any longer, Aten decided to take his family across the Nyagchu River and flee to Lhasa.

3

In 1958, the Chinese government carried out a new wave of large-scale military suppression on Kham and Amdo. With access to Tibet blocked off at the Jinsha River,[8] large numbers of refugees were forced to flee to the northern pastoral region. They were scattered across the boundless grasslands in groups of all sizes. Referred to as "rebel bandits," they became targets of the PLA's military campaigns, chased down and killed by cavalry, encircled and suppressed by infantry, and bombed by the air force. Indiscriminate killing became routine, with no one held responsible for "collateral damage" or "mistaken bombings." Anyone who could be labeled a bandit was fair game, so the refugees were inevitably "bandits" if they were killed, or "liberated masses" if they were captured,[9] at which point they would be loaded into trucks and repatriated to their places of origin. Adult men were picked out and sent to prison or group training, and most were never heard from again.

While in flight, different groups and individual strangers helped each other to survive. Ngolo and her companions, empty-handed, encountered some nomad refugees from Yulshul herding a large number of yak and sheep, who gave them a few of their livestock in view of their desperate situation. Ngolo and her group continued along with them, and others from Golok joined later, swelling the group to more than 100 people.

By this time, the PLA was using the air force in combination with ground troops to do battle in the pastoral areas of Gansu and Qinghai. Infantry and cavalry unfamiliar with the terrain often relied on aerial scouting, which would report the whereabouts of "rebel bandits," enabling the ground troops to surround and attack them. Air force planes would often simply drop bombs on the people below, not only shooting those who fled but also killing their livestock, making it even harder for the refugees to get away or to survive on the plateau.

Lhasa was a long way from the Yellow River headlands, but not impossible to reach. For centuries, pilgrimages had been made every summer when the snow and ice melted, crossing the Tongtian River and passing through Nangchen and Sog Dzong (Suozong) on their way to Lhasa. Under normal conditions, this trip took several months, but with the flames of war raging through Golok and Yulshul, the route had become perilous. One Golok man suggested going west and then south, traversing the Changthang and then crossing the Thanglha (Tangula) mountain range to Namtso (Namucuo) Lake, and then continuing on to Lhasa. This route was much longer than that used by traditional pilgrims, but most of it was sparsely inhabited alpine steppe, too hard for Chinese soldiers to negotiate.

Along with other herders driven from their homeland by the Red Tempest, Ngolo embarked on the life-or-death road to Lhasa.[10]

Around this same time, in Nyarong, Aten was leading his family and companions north. The traditional trading route ran west from Bathang, across the Jinsha River to Markham, and through Chamdo,

Pelbar, Kongpo Gyamda, and Medro Gongkar, but the PLA had blocked off access to the river and was closing in from the east and west, forcing scattered resistance forces and large groups of refugees to go north instead.

One night, Aten and his companions crossed the Nyagchu River in Dergé County and entered Dzachuka (Zhaxika).[11] There they learned that many refugees and resistance fighters from all over had gathered in an area east of the river. Located south of the Bayan Har mountain range, Dzachuka was a high-altitude grassland more than 4,000 meters above sea level. Traversed by ravines, it was sparsely populated and had never been fully controlled by the PLA. Aten and his family stopped here for the time being.

By then it was almost the winter of 1958, and nearly 10,000 Tibetans had gathered there after fleeing from other regions.[12] They planned to pass the winter in the ravines and then move west when the weather turned warm again.

But as the spring of 1959 approached, the Chinese government made a major military deployment.

4

On January 14, 1959, the TMC headquarters cabled a report to the PLA's general staff headquarters regarding the situation in Chamdo, Lhoka, and other parts of Tibet. One week later, Mao wrote a memo on the cable: "This kind of war is very beneficial. It can mobilize the masses and temper the troops. It's best to fight regularly, and to fight for five or six years, or seven or eight years to annihilate the enemy. Then the conditions will be right to carry out reforms."[13]

On January 22, Mao cabled the TWC and again raised the idea of tempering soldiers through war: "The rulers of Tibet originally had very weak military strength, but now they have a large armed rebel force with strong fighting spirit, and they are serious enemies to us. But that's not a bad thing and in fact rather a good thing, because it may be possible to finally solve the problem through war. But, 1) it is essential to basically win over the masses within a few years and isolate the reactionary faction;

2) temper our troops into good fighters. Both can be accomplished when our troops fight armed rebels."[14]

In mid-February, the general staff headquarters gave Mao a report on the situation in Sichuan, Gansu, Qinghai, Yunnan, and Tibet. In a memo on the report, dated February 19, Mao mentioned "tempering the troops" a third time: "This kind of armed rebellion has enormous benefits—the benefits of tempering the troops, tempering the people, and providing ample reason for full-scale pacification of rebellion and thorough reforms."[15]

Given Mao's belief in the benefits of war, the CMC was naturally not going to pass up the opportunity. Although the main battles in Gansu, Qinghai, Sichuan, and Yunnan had largely ended in 1958, and most of the weapons in private hands had been confiscated, the Chinese government had no intention of halting or reducing its military operations.

Thus, in mid-February 1959, the CMC convened a "Rebellion pacification on-the-spot meeting" in Lanzhou, during which deputy chief of staff Yang Chengwu assigned tasks to each military command. He directed the Chengdu Military Command to "use 17 regiments and 7 battalions of troops, and plan to focus the main military strength on pacifying armed rebel forces in Shiqu, Seda, and Litang."[16] The CMC approved this report on March 20, the first day of the "Battle of Lhasa."

The Chengdu Military Command accordingly came up with its 1959 battle plan, planning to "basically pacify several groups of armed rebel forces, and then mop up and disperse the bandit remnants, first pacifying the rebellion in Shiqu, and then mounting a pincer attack from the east and west to round up and annihilate the rebel bandits in Seda." In the same month, the Chengdu Military Command's deputy commander, Huang Xinting, presided over a battle conference arranging military deployment for the Kangding military sub-region.[17]

From April 6 to July 21, 1959, the PLA launched the main battle of its second wave of suppression in Kham, the "Battle of Shiqu and Seda." This battle drew on 14 regiments and 7 battalions, including 4 cavalry regiments, from the Chengdu, Tibet, and Lanzhou Military Commands.[18]

This battle was divided into two stages. The first was the Battle of Sershul. According to plan, the PLA divided two regiments into three lines, north, south, and west, in northern Garzê to surround Sershul and Sertar.

The northern line, more than 250 kilometers long, reached from northwestern Sertar to northeastern Sershul along the Bayan Har mountains.[19] Most of this was pastoral areas at least 4,000 meters above sea level, so the Ganzi military sub-region transferred the Tibetan Regiment, made up mainly of Tibetans,[20] to seal off that region.

The commander of the Tibetan Regiment was Dramdul, a member of the "Spark Association," an early Communist group organized by Puntsok Wangyal, founder of the Tibetan Communist Party. Dramdul became head of Bathang County (at that time known as Ba'an) in 1950, and actively participated in the logistical preparation for the Battle of Chamdo.

The Tibetan Regiment was originally an infantry regiment, but for the purposes of doing battle in the plateau pasturelands, the Chengdu Military Command reinforced it with a cavalry battalion in 1957.[21] The objective of the northern line was to prevent Tibetan fighters and refugees from escaping to Golok and Yulshul.

The western line, 150 kilometers long, ran from Kharsumdo (Kasongdu)[22] in Dergé County to Ador[23] on the upper reaches of the Jinsha River. This line was on the border of Jomda County in Chamdo. The PLA used one battalion to block access to the main crossing at Denkhog, to prevent Tibetans from fleeing into Central Tibet.

The southern line, a section of the Sichuan-Tibet highway around 40 kilometers long, ran through the grasslands from Rongpatsa (Rongbacha)[24] to Yilhung (Yulong)[25] in Dergé County. The PLA used one infantry battalion, one armored vehicle company, and one motorized company to cut off the southern escape route for Tibetans.

The northern and western lines surrounded southern Sershul and northern Sertar from northern Sershul and western Dergé, and the mechanized units on the southern line were like a dagger between the western and northern lines[26] that formed a large ring of encirclement around Sershul.

This happened to be where Aten's family and the others were at the time.

On April 6, 1959, the Chengdu Military Command's Tibetan Regiment, using its cavalry battalion as a vanguard, set off from the Dralak (Zhala) Monastery[27] in central Garzê County and raced toward its destination, reaching the Manglung (Menglong) Monastery[28] in northwestern Sertar on April 13. The regiment left one battalion behind to intercept and attack at that segment, while the rest continued north, reaching their destination around April 19 and forming a line along the Bayan Har mountains to prevent refugees from escaping into Golok. By then, the other troops had also completed their deployment.[29] The plan was for 5 PLA infantry regiments to launch an attack on April 20 on Tibetans gathered in the area of Wonpo (Wenbo) and Zechen Gongma (Changxu Gongma)[30] in southern Sershul.

Aten and his companions knew nothing of the PLA troops setting off for their target areas and arranging their encirclement. However, sometime around early April, they discovered an increasing number of PLA troops around their encampment and sensed they were being surrounded. They decided it would better to try to break through the encirclement than to sit and wait to die.

One night, all of the resistance forces and refugees in the area united to break through the encirclement. A small team led by Aten and including his family broke through the PLA line and fled toward Sertar. Encountering other refugees en route, Aten and the others took some of them along. By the time they reached northern Sertar, their numbers had swelled to more than 2,000.

With so many people, they decided to break into smaller groups. On April 18,[31] Aten and others who had fled from Nyarong and Sershul left Sertar. The Washul chieftain Rigzin Dondrup was supposed to leave soon after that, with tribe members from Sertar and its vicinity.[32] Yet, two days later, the five PLA regiments launched a joint attack on the place where Rigzin Dondrup and the others were gathered, so this second group had no chance to escape and could only split into smaller groups, each attempting to flee on its own.

There were more than 200 families in Aten's group, as well as several hundred monks, totaling more than 2,000 people. This temporary amalgamation of refugee groups included the elderly, women, and children, with mules and horses bearing their belongings, so they moved slowly. It was only by luck that they had departed from what would become the battlefield, just two days before the PLA attack, but they had not yet broken through the encirclement. All along the way they were pursued, intercepted, and obstructed, and often as they prepared to stop and rest, a sudden cry of alarm from a sentry would send the encampment into chaos as the men formed a defense and the women, children, and monks rushed to pack up their belongings and lead the mules and horses away in a hurry. Although ammunition was scarce, the men with guns were good shots, and they were able to put off the PLA troops long enough to give the others time to escape. They should have headed southwest, but with the army in pursuit, the refugees were forced to head northwest, taking them even further from Lhasa.

In August 1958, the CMC ordered the PLA to begin an "aerial attack." Airmen had a very simple way of identifying "rebel bandits": "From the air the first things we discovered were herds of sheep; from far off we could always see hundreds of white sheep eating grass in a carefree way. As we neared the sheep herds, we'd discover yaks alongside them, as well as scattered tents, and then we could basically conclude that they were rebel bandits."[33]

This allowed the air force to display its skills to the fullest. Aten and his mounted companions scattered in all directions as an airplane came screaming toward them. Driving their herds slowly, the nomads became easy targets for aerial attacks; the airplanes dropped several bombs and then circled a few times at low altitude, killing defenseless people and animals in a hail of bullets.

There was no other source of food in the alpine grasslands, and the killing of their livestock drove the refugees to desperation. People were killed and injured in every battle, and some went missing in flight. As they headed north, people continued to drop out or go missing, and the group of refugees gradually dwindled.

They pressed on, day and night, not even knowing how many days they'd traveled. Suddenly, one day, Aten saw a motor road stretching before them. It was the highway from Xining to Jyekundo. He realized that they had reached northwest Golok, impossibly far from Lhasa. The refugees crossed the highway and continued onward. Several days later, as night was falling, they reached the edge of a murky green canyon. Aten reined in his horse and gazed into the distance. In the golden evening mist, he could see a pair of large lakes. He had led his wives and daughter from central Garzê to northern Golok, near the Gyaring and Ngoring lakes.

That night, the refugees set up camp in a ravine and finally enjoyed a good night's sleep along the twin lakes so far from their homeland. Aten and his family curled up in their tent, covered with an oilskin, and fell into a deep sleep. In the early hours of the next morning, Aten felt a cold draft, and half asleep, he cracked open his eyes and lifted a corner of his tent flap to look outside. In the darkness, snowflakes danced silently, covering the ground with white. He pulled his fur-lined gown closer and closed his eyes.[34]

6

The first stage of the Battle of Sershul and Sertar ended in late June 1959, with the PLA "annihilating a total of 5,550 people," including more than 4,500 who surrendered.[35]

On July 19, six PLA infantry regiments and one cavalry regiment, accompanied by the 1st Cavalry Division, split into several groups and embarked on the second stage, "the battle to surround and annihilate Sertar." The main battlefield was in eastern Sertar, on the border between Dzamthang (Rangtang) and Drango.

By that time, the young monk Yetan from the Zhichen Monastery had fled to Sertar with his father.

In September 2010, in a small room in the senior monks' home at Drepung Monastery in exile, Lama Yetan, now nearly blind, described this battle to me.

It was the spring of 1959, and thousands of Tibetans of three major *shokka* from Sertar, Drango, and other places[36] were hiding in northeastern Sertar. The number of PLA soldiers had steadily increased since the end of winter, and one day in mid-April, PLA troops appeared near their encampment and a small-scale battle broke out. After this, the people fled, remaining hidden in the mountain forests for the next few months.[37]

A major battle finally broke out in the summer.

Half a century later, Yetan still remembered how on that dark, rainy night, the inky sky was suddenly lit with red, green, and yellow "lamps." Yetan saw the "lamps" fly through the sky, emit a dazzling light, and then slowly drop to the ground. He didn't know that these were signal flares, and that their flight meant that troops were ready to launch an attack.

The chieftains knew that the whole area was already surrounded by the PLA, and that the situation was critical. After discussing among themselves, the chieftains decided that each would lead his own people in breaking through the encirclement to escape. The Tsongtoe acted as the vanguard, with the Sertar bringing up the rear, risking their lives to break through.

Yetan didn't know how long it was before a sudden flash of light burst out in the night sky, its deathly white glow followed by the sound of gunfire, and bullets began raining down. Instantly horses whinnied in terror, pack yaks tumbled to the ground, and people ran in all directions. This was a purposeful blocking action intended to scatter the people who were trying to break through the encirclement. The Tsongtoe chieftain continued leading people through the encirclement, not knowing where they were going. Yetan's father led the Washul chieftain Rigzin Dondrup and others on a detour away from the battlefield.

As dawn broke, the group reached flat, open grassland. Exhausted after running all night, they stopped to prepare some tea and rest. Just then, someone spotted a stretch of tents out in the distance, and cavalry speeding toward them; they were surrounded by troops.

The terror-stricken tribesmen grabbed their horses and prepared to flee, as the chieftains urgently discussed among themselves and decided to break into smaller groups and fight their way through. More than 20 armed men were assigned to protect the monks, who were urged to run into the hills as fast as they could. Fifteen-year-old Yetan didn't want to leave his father, but looking around in the morning light, the unarmed young monk could see trenches dug by PLA soldiers like death traps, further away on the grassland.

That was on July 23, 1959.[38]

People scattered in all directions amidst the sound of gunshots and the thundering hooves of war horses. Yetan saw some drop wounded from their mounts, and others thrown off when their horses were shot. In the chaos, Yetan heard his father shout, "Run! Run fast! Don't stop!" He began running wildly as bullets whizzed by and struck the ground near his feet. Suddenly, Yetan heard a movement behind him, as if he were being chased, and turning, he saw a riderless horse. He reached up and grabbed the horse's reins, and with a few hops leaped to its back. At that point he saw a relative and another monk near him. The three of them raced up into the hills with soldiers in hot pursuit. Suddenly, there appeared on the mountaintop a group of black-clad men who seemed like Buddha's emissaries, who began firing at the soldiers. Several soldiers fell, and the others turned their horses and retreated. Yetan had escaped with his life.

The chieftain of the Washul, Rigzin Dondrup, died in this battle, and Yetan's father was taken captive. Among the hundreds of them, only Yetan and two others had escaped. According to official sources, "more than 400 people were killed or wounded, and eleven were taken prisoner."[39]

The battle to encircle and annihilate Sertar ended on October 24. Eight regiments of soldiers "annihilated and seized more than 3,000 people, captured more than 1,900 guns, and caused more than 4,000 of the masses to return to their homeland."[40] The figures indicate that of those "annihilated," only 27% had been armed.

The Battle of Sertar was the last major battle in Garzê. The large-scale rebellions by Garzê Tibetans began and ended in Sertar.[41]

Yetan and his companions had broken through the encirclement, but they didn't dare linger or look back. They just kept riding, fleeing toward Lhasa, where the Dalai Lama could protect them. It was their only hope.

7

The herder woman Ngolo followed the fleeing people with her infant daughter on her back, proceeding step-by-step through the wilderness that lay between the source waters of the Machu and Drichu rivers.

They kept heading west, using the sun and stars for direction. Ngolo didn't know where they were or what places they passed. On the way they encountered a tribe from "a different nation" who wore clothing that was neither Tibetan nor Chinese, and they couldn't understand each other, so Ngolo doesn't know what ethnic group they belonged to. Perhaps they had encountered nomadic Kazakhs. They crossed one hill after another and one river after another. Summer passed into autumn, and the grass gradually yellowed. In days without war, this would have been the transitional season. Ngolo thought of family members who hadn't escaped, and wondered if her parents were still alive.

The frigid winter arrived, and while wind and snow made the journey harder, it also brought more safety to the refugees. Herders who had spent generations in the plateau regions were inured to the cold, but the Chinese soldiers found it impossible to do battle in the winter, and they withdrew to the lower altitudes to rest and reorganize. Except on the coldest days, Ngolo's band of refugees continued their way west, narrowing the gap step by step between the source waters of the Yellow River and Lhasa. Ngolo could think of nothing but Lhasa—Lhasa, where they would finally receive divine protection.

Winter passed and the pasturelands began to turn green. As summer approached, the refugees reached central Changthang.[42] By then, their group had dwindled to fewer than 100; of the 20-odd Golok families they had met on the way, only 5 were left.

They turned south, and despite the desolation of the wilderness, Ngolo finally began to feel a thread of hope as each step brought her closer to Lhasa. After they passed sacred Namtso Lake and crossed the Nyenchen Thanglha pass to Damshung, Lhasa was no longer a distant dream.

A few days later, they encountered a group of refugees from Lhasa who gave them some news: a few months earlier, Chinese soldiers had fought a major battle in the holy city of Lhasa, and Gyalwa Rinpoché had fled to India. Lhasa was no more!

FIGURE 8. Ama Drolkar, shortly after she escaped to India.
Source: Provided by Drolkar Gye.

FIGURE 9. Struggle meeting against monk officials in Sera Monastery.

"At a meeting in the courtyard of Sera Monastery, a group of us were branded criminals by the Chinese soldiers and taken away (sign above the stage reads 'Sera Monastery Military Committee')." (From a book titled *A clear mirror giving an impression of the inhuman atrocities committed by the Chinese Communists in Tibet*. Source: Office of Tibet, Washington, D.C. Used with permission. English translation: Matthew Akester.)

FIGURE 10. **Struggle meeting against Tibetan government official in Lhasa.**
"Rasa Gyagen, a former government official, was brought before a public meeting in East Lhasa 1959 with his hands tied behind his back, accused of supporting the reactionary rebellion. He was made to stand bent over for the duration of the meeting, but as he was elderly he could not remain standing, and fell over, whereupon he was stomped on and kicked and beaten so badly that he lost sight in one eye, until eventually he was taken to the hospital bleeding and unconscious. As soon as he recovered a little, they took him back for a third struggle session that left him incapacitated, and this treatment has been inflicted on most Tibetans." (From a book titled *A clear mirror giving an impression of the inhuman atrocities committed by the Chinese Communists in Tibet.* Source: Office of Tibet, Washington, D.C. Used with permission. English translation: Matthew Akester.)

Chapter 18

"LHASA IS NO MORE!"

1

In early 1959, neither the secretary of the Tibet Work Committee, Zhang Jingwu, nor the TWC's first deputy secretary and commander of the TMC, Zhang Guohua, was in Lhasa. Zhang Jingwu had become head of Mao Zedong's office in Zhongnanhai in 1955, and had spent every winter since then working in Beijing. Zhang Guohua was in Guangzhou being treated for heart disease. The former TWC deputy secretary Fan Ming had been purged by then, so the daily work was being handled by the second deputy secretary and Military Command political commissar, Tan Guansan.

By then, the flames of war had spread from Kham and Amdo to regions not far from Lhasa. In June 1958, the Chushi Gangdruk had been established, and as that news spread, refugees from Kham and Amdo in Lhasa started heading for Lhoka; even some Tibetan soldiers joined up, taking their guns with them.[1] Not long afterward, PLA troops stationed in Tibet engaged in armed clashes with Chushi Gangdruk, and morale in the volunteer army was boosted substantially when the PLA's "encirclement and annihilation" failed, and Chushi Gangdruk obtained a batch of new weapons.[2] On December 18, 1958, a PLA battalion commander and two companies of troops were escorting cadres from the Shannan Work

Sub-group and a convoy of vehicles loaded with supplies to Tsethang. The convoy was ambushed in Gongkar County, less than 100 kilometers from Lhasa, and the next day, reinforcements were ambushed on their way to render aid. A PLA deputy regimental commander, a battalion commander, and more than 90 others were killed in these two battles, and 35 people were injured, while nine vehicles were burned, another six were damaged, and two heavy machine guns, four light machine guns, and a quantity of handguns and rifles were captured.[3]

On January 4, 1959, the Chushi Gangdruk Volunteer Army led by Gonpo Tashi formed an alliance with resistance forces in Chamdo, and more than 800 Tibetan volunteers surrounded the county government compound in Zhamog.[4] On January 24, battles broke out simultaneously in Tengchen and Jomda, and the Shannan Work Sub-group was besieged the next day.[5]

The series of setbacks suffered by PLA troops in Tibet caused high anxiety within the TWC and Military Command, and cables flew back and forth between Beijing and Lhasa. Since July 1958, China's top leaders, including Mao and Deng Xiaoping, had repeatedly handed down directives to the TWC and Military Command telling them to prepare for war, and troops and cadres in Lhasa had been actively making these preparations. In early November 1958, Lhasa established militias within government organs, distributing weapons to cadres and staff and giving them military training, and each official organ began openly constructing defense fortifications.[6] A bunker was built on the roof of a Chinese government office building across from the Tsuklakhang (Dazhaosi) temple, and sandbags were piled in front of windows,[7] allowing only enough of a gap for one person to shoot through. All of this greatly heightened the tension in Lhasa, and both Chinese and Tibetans felt on the brink of peril.

During this time, the CCP Central Committee was preparing for the Second National People's Congress in 1959, and the Dalai Lama, as a standing committee vice-chairman, had been invited to fly to Beijing for the meeting.[8] Everyone in Lhasa was ill at ease, sensing that trouble could break out at any moment.

The Chinese cadres were also on edge, and didn't dare to go out for fear that "coming back might be a problem"; some even prepared for the worst, with wills and funeral arrangements. Everything was kept secret from the outside, even in family letters and cables.[9]

It was under these circumstances that the holy city of Lhasa welcomed in the Earth Pig year, in February 1959.

The new year brought a pleasant surprise for the Amdo woman Drolkar Gye: her husband came home.[10]

Drolkar Gye was born to Labrang's Khotse tribe,[11] subjects (*lhadé*)[12] of the Labrang Monastery. As such, they came under the direct management of the monastery, which appointed a headman every three years. Soon after taking power in China, the CCP had engaged in propaganda along the lines of "suppressing bandits and opposing local despots" in this region. Apa Alo (also known as Huang Zhengqing, or Lobsang Tsewang), the older brother of the fifth Jamyang Zhepa, was one of the most powerful men in Kanlho at that time. During the Nationalist era, he was appointed public safety commander for the Labrang region, and after the CCP took power, he was appointed to the Northwest Military and Political Committee and as a committee member of the Gansu Provincial Government, among other postings. Through him, the CCP developed its united front network among the elite of Gansu and Qinghai's Tibetan regions and mediated their conflicts with the Chinese government.[13] Apa Alo played a key role when the Chinese government set up its first local government in Kanlho. Even so, the propaganda of locally posted Chinese cadres made many disparaging references to him and to other Tibetan leaders.[14]

Drolkar Gye's husband was an upright and outspoken former monk, and he deeply resented the disrespect that CCP cadres showed toward his people's leaders. In a fit of rage, he had grabbed his gun and headed into the hills. Although he was eventually persuaded to return home, there were rumors that he might be arrested at any time. Unsafe in his homeland, he had no choice but to flee to Lhasa. Upon learning of her husband's whearabouts, Drolkar Gye had bid her parents farewell and joined a trade caravan on a journey of several months to be reunited with her husband. She was never to see her mother again.

The couple rented a small house near the Tsuklakhang and made a living as small traders. Not long afterwards, Drolkar Gye's father also arrived in Lhasa. Living with her father and husband, Drolkar Gye felt safe, and the three of them lived a few peaceful years. But the good times didn't last long; war broke out in Kham and Amdo, and the news from back home became increasingly dire, as tensions also increased in Lhasa. Drolkar Gye's husband lost interest in trading and set off for Shigatsé with dozens of friends, intending to escort the Panchen Lama out of his residence, but the Panchen Lama remained under close surveillance by the PLA, and no one could get anywhere near him.[15] Drolkar Gye heard from others that her husband and his friends had gone on to Lhoka. Now, just days before the Tibetan New Year, he had finally come home again.

Lhasa was filled with a holiday mood in spite of the tensions. Every home prepared what was needed for the festival, and the monasteries and wealthy residents were busily creating butter sculptures. This year during the holiday period, the Dalai Lama was going to take part in the Geshe Lharampa examination at the Tsuklakhang.[16] This event, which occurred only once every several decades, attracted large numbers of monks and pilgrims, along with the establishment of the three great monasteries who had come to Lhasa for the Great Prayer festival, so the population of the city was larger than normal.[17] Crowds bustled with excitement outside the temple, while those inside prostrated themselves before the statue of Jowo Rinpoché.[18] People ceaselessly added *sang*, a mixture of dried fragrant plants, to the incense burner outside the monastery, permeating the air with fragrant smoke throughout the day.

On the 29th day of the 12th month of the Earth Dog year in the Tibetan calendar, the day before New Year's Eve (February 7, 1959), was the *Gutor*, or "exorcism festival," and a traditional *cham* dance was performed as usual at the Potala palace. Since the Chinese had entered Tibet, the government would invite leaders from the TWC to the palace every year for the *Gutor* festival, and the Dalai Lama himself would watch the *cham* dance with them. This year, in the absence of Zhang Jingwu and Zhang Guohua, the deputy commander of the TMC, Deng Shaodong, went to the Potala with TWC secretary general Guo Xilan. Only a few *kalons* at the palace knew that, while watching the *cham* dance that day, the Dalai Lama accepted General Deng's invitation to view a cultural performance at the Military Command headquarters.[19]

When the long horns sounded from the palace's Deyangshar courtyard, Drolkar Gye was busy sweeping the courtyard of her home, cleaning the shrine, and preparing dinner, unaware that events at the Potala that day would change her life.

2

On the morning of February 14, the Dalai Lama proceeded to the Tsuklakhang to preside over the Great Prayer festival. Whenever the Dalai Lama went out, he was accompanied by a procession, and ceremonial arrival at the temple involved the grandest procession of all. Lhasa residents and others who had come for the Great Prayer festival lined the streets to pay their respects.

Around nine o'clock that morning, two watchmen for the Lhasa office of the Tibet-Qinqhai Highway Management Bureau also came out to watch. The watchmen, Zhao Xiaolin and Zhang Zhizhong, were also militiamen, and Zhao shouldered a submachine gun while Zhang carried two hand grenades as they stood at the entrance to the lane near their office, waiting for the procession. They may not have realized how suspicious they looked, carrying weapons along the road where the Dalai Lama would pass, and when two patrolling Tibetan soldiers spotted Zhao Xiaolin with his gun slung on his back, they arrested him and took him to the "police *depon*," i.e., the Sixth Depon barracks, responsible for public safety in Lhasa. Zhang Zhizhong tailed them to the entrance of the barracks, where he was also arrested.

In response, the Qinghai-Tibet Highway Management Bureau registered a complaint with the TMC, PCART, Public Order Joint Committee, and Tibetan government, demanding that the Tibetans release the two men and make a formal apology. With the situation already tense, this incident no doubt exacerbated distrust on both sides. The Chinese side saw it as "the Tibetan army and Tibetan armed rebels planning to provoke our party and army." Meanwhile, various rumors circulated among the Tibetan populace, some saying that two men had been "sent by the Panchen Lama to assassinate the Dalai Lama," or that they were "assassins sent by the Central Committee."[20]

The arrest of the two workers was most likely a misunderstanding. Although tensions were high in Lhasa at the time, and Mao had already directed the TWC to prepare for a "decisive battle," the Chinese government had not yet given up its United Front overtures to the Dalai Lama and the Tibetan government, and the military deployment had not yet begun; there was no need for the Chinese government to send assassins. Likewise, with fierce fighting already occurring on its periphery and a feeling of imminent danger in Lhasa, the Tibetan government was not going to look for trouble during the festival. The fact that two workers were carrying weapons while standing outside their workplace to watch the excitement nevertheless indicated that Chinese personnel felt uneasy; and the fact that Tibetan soldiers were alarmed at the sight of armed Chinese where the Dalai Lama was about to pass also showed the apprehensions among Tibetans. In the decades after this incident, publicly and internally published Chinese materials treated the "arrest of two innocent Han workers" as "the Tibetan government intentionally creating an incident," but none of these references presented the actual conditions under which the two workers were arrested.[21]

By the time this news reached the Dalai Lama, the two men had become "two Tsangpa[22] or Khampa disguised as Chinese," one of whom had "loaded a bullet into his gun barrel and so on" as the Dalai Lama approached. The Dalai Lama sent his brother-in-law, the Kusung Depon[23] Puntsok Tashi, to find out what had actually happened. Kusung Depon's inquiries established who the two men actually were, and verified the information with onlookers who were there at the time. The Dalai Lama worried that the matter would "create an incident dreadful to contemplate,"[24] and after he twice issued an order, the two workers were released the next day.[25] This incident gave rise to rumors, but had no further consequences. The matter nevertheless seemed like an ill portent that the upcoming new year's celebrations would not go smoothly.

The CCP Central Committee General Office submitted its *Situation Bulletin No. 16* to Mao on February 18. This bulletin included a Xinhua news dispatch reporting that "rebellion in the Tibetan regions has developed into a full-scale armed rebellion." Mao wrote a memo on the bulletin and passed it to Liu Shaoqi, Zhou Enlai, Chen Yi, Deng Xiaoping, and Peng Dehuai, stating that disorder in Tibet was welcome, as it would provide ample reason to carry out reform.[26]

The next day, Mao wrote a memo with edits to the "General Staff Department War Department Situational Report Regarding Pacifying Rebellion," and secretly sent the document to the TWC and to Military Command officers down to the regiment level, explicitly stating, "On the military side, we have no fear of armed rebellion and even welcome it, but it requires being prepared at any moment and promptly pacifying the rebellion."[27]

February 23 was the day of the full moon, and according to tradition, the Dalai Lama would expound on the Buddhist sutras at Sungchoera Square[28] outside the temple, and accompanied by the *kalon*s and nobility, would view the butter sculptures that lined Barkor (Bakuo) Street in the evening. But the Sungchoera was right across from the Tibet General Trading Company, and a rooftop fortification directly faced the podium where the Dalai Lama would speak.[29] Kusung Depon asked to have Tibetan soldiers stand sentry on the roof, but the Chinese side refused the demand as unreasonable.[30] Concerned for the Dalai Lama's safety, the Tibetan government and Kusung Depon canceled the day's program, giving rise to widespread speculation.[31]

The Chinese treated this as one of "a chain of episodes created by the Tibetan government to provoke an incident" and sent the TWC's propaganda department head, Chen Jingbo, to see the Dalai Lama. The Dalai Lama tried to smooth things over by explaining the arrest of the two workers and the cancelation of the activities, but the TWC's report to the Central Committee on February 27 didn't tell the full story. Instead, in accordance with its habitual thinking regarding conflicts of this kind, the TWC attributed the friction to: "1) Tibetan upper strata purposefully planning to create this incident, and involving some people in the Dalai office and Tibetan government in order to drag them into it; 2) Dalai and Tibetan government are clear on many things, and discussed them in advance or afterwards, proving premeditation."[32]

Although the new year's celebrations had run into some difficulties, the holiday passed peacefully overall. After the Great Prayer festival, the Dalai Lama moved back to the Norbulingka palace.

By this time, Mao's memos regarding "welcoming armed rebellion" and being prepared at any moment to "pacify armed rebellion" had already been transmitted to the army at the regimental level and above in Tibet.

From the highest levels down to the TWC, the CCP was prepared for a "decisive battle." All Mao needed was a trigger point for propaganda purposes.

3

After the new year, Lhasa gradually regained its calm, with the departure of the monks and others who had come to take part in the festival. Drolkar Gye's life returned to normal.

On the morning of March 10, she was making one of her usual visits to the temple, and had just entered Barkor Street when she saw peddlers panickingly gathering up their mats and wares, shop owners hurriedly closing their doors, and groups of people along the street anxiously conversing amongst themselves. Young people sped through the crowd on bicycles, startling and irritating people by ringing their bells. A man reined in his horse and yelled for people to make way, and Drolkar Gye stepped aside just in time to watch the horse and rider disappear, followed by a crowd of men and women, old and young, running down the street in confusion, their faces panic-stricken, as if something catastrophic had just occurred. Noticing that everyone was running in the same direction, Drolkar Gye approached a group of conversing women and asked what was going on.[33]

"The Chinese have invited Gyalwa Rinpoché to their military headquarters today!" one woman told her.

"Why would he go to the military camp?" Drolkar Gye asked with surprise.

"They say they want Gyalwa Rinpoché to watch a performance," another woman said. "Going to the Chinese military headquarters can't be good—maybe he'll never return! They'll take Gyalwa Rinpoché to Beijing . . ."

Drolkar Gye was horrified. Everyone in Lhasa knew of headmen and senior lamas in Kham and Amdo who had disappeared in just this way; the Chinese cadres would invite them to a meeting or a banquet, and they'd never be seen again.

"Those people are going to Norbulingka to stop the Chinese from taking Gyalwa Rinpoché away," one of the women told her.

While they were talking, several young people in the street shouted, "Hurry to Norbulingka—don't let Gyalwa Rinpoché be taken to the military camp!" Amid the chaos, she saw a group of men, some shouldering guns and others carrying clubs, run off in the direction of the Norbulingka palace.

Drolkar Gye felt as if she'd been struck by lightning, but after a moment she collected herself, turned around, and ran home. Her husband and father were gone, and she guessed they must have gone to Norbulingka too. Putting down her *mani* prayer wheel, Drolkar Gye opened the cupboard under her altar, took out a small bag of *sang*, walked over to the incense burner in the corner of the courtyard, and lit it up. A curl of smoke emerged from the chimney, carrying her prayers upward with it.

Drolkar Gye later learned that on that day, tens of thousands of people had surrounded Norbulingka and prevented the Dalai Lama from going to the military headquarters. Kalon Sampo, the Tibetan cabinet minister who had been appointed the deputy commander of the TMC in 1958, was beaten outside the gate of Norbulingka, and Chamdo Khenchung Sonam Gyatso[34] was killed by a mob. What happened that day went down in history as the "March 10, 1959 incident" or "The Lhasa Uprising."

This Amdo woman who had taken refuge in Lhasa had no idea what was happening at Norbulingka and Shuktri Lingka,[35] and even less could she have imagined the series of actions being launched in faraway Beijing by powerful people who held the fate of hundreds of millions in their hands.

In the days that followed, Drolkar Gye heard all kinds of news circulating in the city streets as she waited uneasily for her father and husband to return.

4

On the afternoon of March 10, 1959, the TWC reported the events in Lhasa in a cable to the Central Committee. Later that day, Tan Guansan wrote a letter to the Dalai Lama and had it delivered through a Tibetan monk. This was the first of three letters that Tan Guansan was to send to the Dalai Lama over the course of a week. These letters, together with the Dalai Lama's replies, were later published as propaganda.[36]

The next day, Chinese President Liu Shaoqi called in Zhou Enlai, Peng Zhen, Peng Dehuai, Chen Yi, Yang Shangkun, Xu Bing,[37] and others for a meeting to discuss the situation in Tibet.[38] Late that night, the Central Committee sent a cable ordering Ding Sheng, commander of the 54th Army, to organize a small command post, known as the Ding Headquarters, to enter Tibet and command the 134th and 11th Infantry Divisions. At the same time, the Chengdu Military Command's deputy commander, Huang Xinting, was ordered to organize a command post to take charge of battle operations in Chamdo for the 130th Infantry Division, the Kunming Military Command 42nd Division Frontline Command Post, and the Changdu Military Command.[39]

Simultaneously, the Central Committee sent a cable to the TWC notifying them that the CMC was "actively carrying out military preparations" and making specific military, political, and propaganda directives.[40]

On March 12, around the time that the Dalai Lama replied to Tan Guansan's first letter, defense minister Peng Dehuai presided over the 167th CMC meeting in Beijing and decided on military preparations for war in Tibet.[41]

All of this shows that after the outbreak of the "Lhasa incident," the highest levels of the Chinese government had no intention of avoiding bloodshed with a "political solution." In the next two weeks, the Politburo and Central Committee Secretariat held meetings nearly every day to discuss the Tibetan situation, usually with Liu Shaoqi or Deng Xiaoping presiding.

In the Takten Mingyur palace in the Norbulingka compound,[42] Tenzin Gyatso, the 14th Dalai Lama, tried his best to control the situation. He reassured Tibetans that he wouldn't go to the PLA headquarters, while at the same time trying to stall for time in his reply to General Tan Guansan's letter, and urging people to disperse so the crisis could be resolved peacefully.[43]

On March 13, the Dalai Lama called in the *kalons* and explained his reasons for going to the military camp to watch the performance, while issuing instructions regarding the current situation:

> On December 29 of the previous year,[44] according to custom, central government officials were invited to the *cham* dance, during which deputy commander Deng[45] said, "The Military Command's song-and-dance ensemble has learned some new dances; would the Dalai Lama like to see a performance?" I expressed my willingness to go, but the timing should wait until the ceremony [i.e., the Great Prayer festival] was finished, and any place would do. After I returned to Norbulingka on the 20th of the first month,[46] on the 22nd two cadres came from the United Front Department asking how to best arrange the timing of the performance. I said that it would have to wait for a few days after the ceremony, that it could be settled early in the second month, and it wasn't necessary to make excessive preparations. They replied, "This type of performance is usually in the evening, but this time it can be performed during the day for the Dalai Lama. Please go at 2:30 on the first day of the second month." The matter was settled in this way. I had planned to go, but on the morning of the 1st [i.e., the first day of the second Tibetan month, or March 10], monks and lay officials, *khenpos* representing the three major monasteries and many monks and commoners had misgivings, and wept and pleaded for me not to go and watch the performance. For that reason, although the arrangements had been made, I couldn't keep the appointment and felt deeply

ashamed. On that day, Kalon Sampo was struck with a rock and seriously injured, and Chamdo Khenchung was killed outside the palace gate, violating secular and religious laws. At that time, it was impossible to go out, so I could only stay, and having no other choice, I felt deeply distressed. If it were possible to satisfy the people's demands, it could end here, but as the saying goes, "When you have a place to sleep, you also want a place to stretch out," and a meeting was held at the ceremonial hall during which there was talk of so-called Tibetan independence. I gave orders not to hold this type of evil meetings inside the palace. After moving from the palace, on the 3rd, yesterday, a meeting was held at the Shol printing house, drawing up a list of names of representatives for the meeting and asking for them to be appointed. This kind of meeting could only give rise to disputes; everyone knew that there was nothing beneficial about them, so in the past, the order had been handed down that this kind of meeting wasn't permitted. Likewise, regarding the list of names for this meeting, I would never give approval. If they had been people who were clear about the short-term and long-term interests and advantages and disadvantages, they would have heeded my words and would have enthusiastically taken responsibility for the tasks suited to them, and would have lived obediently and law-abidingly. If they were unwilling to take heed of the advantages and disadvantages I pointed out all along, and acted arbitrarily, there was not a thing I could do about it. Believing me to be the incarnation of the Bodhisattva Avalokitesvara holding a white lotus, since my youth the Tibetan people have wished and resolutely obliged me to take on political and religious responsibilities. Although I lacked the natural gifts, acquired knowledge, and courage to take on this responsibility, because the Tibetan people so resolutely and ardently wished this of me, I had no heart to refuse and was obliged to take it on. On the one hand, I studied with my tutor and gave teachings to clerics and laymen, thus establishing a master-disciple relationship [with the people], while on the other hand I took on political responsibilities, which I've now been carrying out for about ten years. There have been rich developments in both politics and religion, but arbitrarily and excessively creating a disturbance this time without considering the advantages and disadvantages, no one can take responsibility for the results. No one will ever be allowed to provoke trouble like this again. Etc., etc., delivering the above directives.[47]

This document, which was seized from Norbulingka after the battle, has never been formally declassified or cited in any official Chinese publications relating to Tibet's modern history. It very clearly shows the Dalai Lama's attitude and views toward this incident, and that the Dalai Lama had no prior knowledge of what was going to occur on March 10. It can be said that the incident on that day was the culmination of a series of major incidents in Kham and Amdo over the previous few years, as well as an outburst of public indignation. Clearly, the people crying out for "Tibetan independence" on the streets of Lhasa were not those whom the Chinese government referred to as members of the "Dalai Clique," but rather the "liberated serfs" of Chinese propaganda.

Even so, the Dalai Lama's attitude toward the "March 10 incident" could not change the direction in which the matter unfolded.

On March 14, CCP General Secretary Deng Xiaoping presided over a meeting of the Central Committee Secretariat to discuss the Tibet problem. That afternoon, Zhang Jingwu and Zhang Guohua rushed back to Beijing from Guangzhou to report on the situation.[48] In the evening, President Liu Shaoqi called in Zhou Enlai, Deng Xiaoping, and other top government and military leaders to discuss the issue.[49] Deng Xiaoping also personally drafted a third letter to the Dalai Lama. Mao wrote a memo on the letter on March 15, instructing Deng to prepare another letter and to have both letters ready to "publish in the future."[50] Only a very few people knew that the three letters the Dalai Lama had written to Tan Guansan were being urgently delivered to Beijing by the air force.[51]

After the letter drafted by Deng Xiaoping was cabled to the TWC, it was delivered to the Dalai Lama on the 16th in Tan Guansan's name,[52] with a letter from Ngapo Ngawang Jigmé enclosed, hinting that the military might bomb Norbulingka.[53]

On March 15, the CMC issued an order to the Chengdu, Lanzhou, and Kunming Military Commands to prepare to enter Tibet, and planned to transfer three infantry divisions and two infantry regiments to Tibet along with an air force bomber regiment to prepare for battle. The CMC ordered the 134th Infantry Division to assemble at Golmud, Qinghai Province on March 26 and to enter Tibet before April 15, while the 11th infantry division was to follow after assembling at Dunhuang, Gansu Province.[54]

On that day, the TMC held a memorial for Sonam Gyatso, who had been killed by the protesters outside Norbulingka on March 10. Tan Guansan presided over the ceremony in the Military Command's main auditorium, but only around 100 people attended. Combat troops and TMC officials stayed away in case of an armed conflict. Those who attended entered and exited through the back door, with instructions on how to disperse if shooting started. The memorial was finished in haste, lasting only a few minutes.[55]

By March 16, one week after the "Lhasa incident," the Chinese military had nearly completed its deployment, and the first troops had already set out for Lhasa from Lintao, Gansu Province. Meanwhile, in Lhasa, the Dalai Lama's lord chamberlain, Phala, had nearly finished arranging a secret escape plan with the *kalons*.[56] That was the day that the PLA chief of general staff Huang Kecheng flew to Wuhan with Zhang Jingwu and Zhang Guohua to report to Mao on the events in Tibet.[57]

March 17 was an epochal date in the history of Tibet. That afternoon, two meetings were held almost simultaneously in Beijing and Lhasa.

At around 2:00 in the afternoon in Lhasa,[58] the Dalai Lama held a meeting with the *kalons* in Norbulingka to discuss how to reply to the letters from Tan Guansan and Ngapo Ngawang Jigmé.

Meanwhile, at 3:00 in Beijing, Liu Shaoqi presided over a Politburo meeting during which Huang Kecheng, who had just returned from Wuhan, communicated Mao's instructions regarding the situation in Tibet. This important official text has never been published, but one of the participants, Yang Shangkun, summarized its main points in his journal:

> 1) Agree with the Central Committee's direction, carry on, a good situation, at last the political initiative had come up; 2) do everything possible to prevent the Dalai Lama from fleeing, releasing him later is easy enough, in any case have him in our hands, but if by any chance he escapes, it

> doesn't matter; 3) troops entering Tibet surround Lhasa, surrounding it is advantageous, can cause divisions, "encircle without attacking," try to arrive before April 10, if Lhasa isn't attacked, first send a regiment to Shannan [Lhoka], control the key strong points and block retreat; 4) focus the pacification on Lhasa and Shannan, other areas can come later; 5) talk of pacification without mentioning reform, reform under pacification, extend differential treatment: reform first where pacified first, and later where pacified later, and no reform where there is no pacification; 6) agree to the CMC's arrangements regarding troops entering Tibet; 7) on diplomatic handling, agree to the designated locality method; 8) don't report in the newspapers; internal briefings, troops entering Tibet must openly issue announcement; 9) immigration shouldn't be too hasty; 10) what is Panchen's attitude? Why is there no news from him yet?[59]

This brief record reveals Mao's strategy of using the Lhasa incident to forcibly resolve the "Tibet Problem," as well as his policies for dealing with the aftermath. It shows that by March 16, Mao had completed all arrangements for the "decisive engagement."

Mao's directive also made clear that the Chinese government's series of major moves in Tibet were not to be made public, and that's why people inside China never knew any details about this major event at the time when it was unfolding.

At the meeting, CCP General Secretary Deng Xiaoping pointed out, "At present, the first thing is to prepare to resolutely pacify rebellion, reorganize the local Tibetan government and Tibetan army, carry out a separation of religion and state, and then carry out comprehensive democratic reform."[60]

While these two meetings were being held in Beijing and Lhasa, a dramatic incident suddenly occurred: A transport station militiaman on the Qinghai-Tibet highway, Zeng Huishan, fired two artillery shells at Norbulingka.[61]

The situation took an immediate turn.

The Dalai Lama quickly requested instructions from the state oracle, who told him to leave that night. Taking all factors into consideration, the Dalai Lama made the decision to leave.

Splits within the Tibetan government had become overt from March 10 onward; acting Kalon Sampo was being treated for injuries at the military hospital, and Kalon Ngapo Ngawang Jigmé had accepted protection from the PLA Military Command, so only Chief Kalon Surkhang and acting Kalons Liushar and Shasur remained at Norbulingka. The three *kalons*; the lord chamberlain, Phala; and the head of the security regiment, Puntsok Tashi split up and began making preparations for the Dalai Lama's escape.

At 10:00 Lhasa time that night (March 17), around midnight Beijing time, the Dalai Lama left Norbulingka incognito and crossed the Tsangpo River into Lhoka.[62]

On the 18th, Peng Dehuai presided over the 168th meeting of the CMC and heard a report from Deputy Chief of General Staff Yang Chengwu regarding the "Lanzhou rebellion pacification on-the-spot meeting." After that, Peng issued the following directive: "Disarming rebel forces doesn't mean the ethnic problem is solved. The resolution of ethnic issues is long-term work, and requires political and economic arrangements and restitution. At present, it's mainly military attacks."[63]

On March 19, top Chinese officials held a daylong meeting. In the morning, the Politburo met to discuss the Tibet issue, and in the afternoon, the Central Committee Secretariat held a meeting to discuss supplies for troops entering Tibet, along with policy issues. One of the participants in those meetings, Yang Shangkun, wrote in his journal: "According to the TWC's report, the Dalai Lama fled south on the 16th or 17th."[64] This shows that although the TWC had verified on the 19th that the Dalai Lama had fled, it hadn't yet ascertained whether he'd left on the 16th or the 17th, which indicates that the claim that "Mao Zedong let the Dalai Lama go" is not historically factual. Even so, political exigency has kept that claim circulating to the present day.[65]

A few hours later, the "Battle of Lhasa" broke out.[66]

5

Around 2 a.m. Lhasa time on March 20, Drolkar Gye was awakened by the sound of intense gunfire. Over the previous days, she had occasionally heard scattered shots in Lhasa, but now the gunfire was much more intense than usual. Sitting up in bed, she detected that the shots were coming from the direction of Norbulingka.

Her husband and father had still not come home, and someone had told her the night before that they were in Norbulingka . . . Drolkar Gye's heart pounded.

Then came a distant roaring sound, massive as a peal of thunder. She could hear women screaming, children crying, men shouting inside and outside of buildings, and doors opening and closing all around her. After a while, the thundering sound abated and the gunfire gradually became more scattered. Drolkar Gye grabbed her robe and wrapped it tightly around her, opened the door of her room, and went into the shrine room. The tiny glow of the butter lamp before the statue of the Buddha illuminated the terrified faces of the women of the house, most of whom were Khampas and Amdowas who had fled there with their husbands. All of their menfolk had gone to Norbulingka to protect the Dalai Lama, leaving their panic-stricken women burning with anxiety and not knowing what to do. Drolkar Gye walked over to the altar, lit a small butter lamp, and knelt to pray. All the children and women in the house knelt before the Buddha, tears streaming down their faces as they murmured their prayers.

A grayish-white ray of light filtered into the altar room through the window as dawn began to break.

Suddenly several loud sounds came from the direction of the Potala palace.

This was the first fight in the Battle of Lhasa, the assault on Chakpori Hill, right next to the palace.

At 5 a.m. Beijing time on March 20, the TMC Headquarters convened a meeting to discuss military arrangements for engaging in battle in Lhasa. At 10:00 that morning, political commissar Tan Guansan ordered the bombardment of Chakpori to capture the strategic command point inside the city and facilitate the next step, which was to bombard the Tibetan gathering point at Norbulingka. Five minutes later, three signal flares rose into the air, and an artillery group of 42 cannons belonging to the 308th Artillery Regiment stationed at Drip, on the south bank of the river, opened fire simultaneously. At least seven artillery shells flew toward Chakpori every minute on average, thoroughly destroying the monastery on the mountaintop.[67] That monastery, built in 1697, had been a school of Tibetan medicine founded by the 5th Dalai Lama, and it faced the Potala palace, a short distance away.[68]

Time stood still as the roaring of guns and cannons continued. It seemed as if the entire world were being destroyed in a massive explosion. Drolkar Gye felt that her building and every other one in Lhasa must be crumbling. Prostrating herself before the Buddha, she prayed for her father and husband, barely hoping that they might return alive.

The owner of the house was a middle-aged woman who had grown up in Lhasa and had seen everything. Stepping before the image of the Buddha, she picked up offerings of *tsampa* and some sacred items that had been blessed by an eminent monk[69] and distributed them among the women in the prayer room, saying, "It's possible that we'll all die today. Eat this for a good reincarnation in the next life."

The women swallowed the offerings and blessed items and then sat before the Buddha statue and prayed in expectation of death. After fleeing to Lhasa from Kham and Amdo, they had reached the end of their run.

The roar of guns and cannon continued all day and night, and then gradually dissipated. On the night of the 21st, the gunshots, cannonfire, and yelling were concentrated in the area of the nearby Jokhang temple.

"Three Jewels,[70] how can we survive this!" Drolkar Gye thought in despair. The nobility had early on sold their property to the Chinese, and many of the buildings around the temple were occupied by Chinese agencies. Chinese soldiers could just sit on the rooftops and aim their guns straight at the temple.[71]

As dawn broke, Drolkar Gye heard someone outside shout, "Don't fire on the Jokhang temple! It's our seat of Dharma!" This was immediately followed by another shout: "Everyone surrender for the sake of the Jokhang temple!"

Inside the house, the women discussed among themselves for a while and felt they had no choice but to surrender to the Chinese soldiers and beg them not to destroy the temple. Drolkar Gye and several other women climbed onto the rooftop with a ladder, holding a wooden pole with a white *khata* tied to it as a flag of surrender. On the roof they found a line of Chinese soldiers lying flat on their stomachs, and both sides were startled at the sight of the other. The women summoned their courage and said, "Don't fire on the Jokhang. We'll surrender!"

The Chinese soldiers jumped up, aimed their guns, and yelled as they advanced on the women, who turned and ran back in the direction they'd come from. Drolkar Gye felt she'd been shot in the back and hurried down the ladder, amazed that she hadn't fallen. At the bottom of the ladder, she patted her back and found there was no blood; the soldier had merely struck her on the back with his gun.

That day, the Tibetans who had gathered in the Jokhang surrendered, and soon after that, the Tibetans defending the Potala also laid down their arms. The Battle of Lhasa had ended.

Drolkar Gye and the other women waited eagerly, but not one of their men came home.

Once all the shooting was over, the women agreed to go out all together. They carried sacks[72] and rope to Norbulingka and the banks of the river, seeking the bodies of their husbands, brothers, and other loved ones. Not one of them expected to find their menfolk alive.

More than 50 years later, Drolkar Gye told me, "At that time, we women reluctantly went looking for their corpses, but what if we found them? One of the women found her husband's corpse, and all she could do was stand next to it and cry out, 'Mother! Mother! Mother!' over and over again. None of us dared to move. Although we'd brought sacks and rope, we didn't dare to do anything."

The battleground had obviously been roughly cleared, and while ornaments and other belongings dropped by Khampas were scattered along the riverbank, most of the corpses had been moved away.[73] Drolkar Gye recognized an older man she knew, still gripping his gun where he'd fallen on the riverbank, and next to him were several Khampas. A herder, and others she recognized, had fallen on the bank.

Drolkar Gye didn't find her husband or father that day. Over the next few days, the women moved together from one battlefield to another, seeking their men. Drolkar Gye looked everywhere but couldn't find her husband or father among the living or the dead.

One day, a Nepali with whom Drolkar Gye was friendly called her over to a street corner and whispered to her, "The Dalai Lama has fled!" Drolkar Gye felt as if a knife were twisting in her heart. The monastery on the top of Chakpori had disappeared, Norbulingka had been damaged beyond recognition, the Ramoché temple on the edge of the old town was full of bullet holes, and blood stained the ground in front of the Jokhang. She had no idea where her husband or father was, and the Dalai Lama was gone. Was this still the Lhasa she had known, or had that Lhasa disappeared as well? Drolkar Gye felt her heart crumble into dust.

6

While Drolkar Gye and other Lhasa women were roaming through the city in search of their loved ones, the CCP Central Committee was starting to arrange its next operation.

On March 25, Mao called an enlarged Politburo Standing Committee meeting that went down in history as the "Shanghai Conference." Tibet was one of the topics of discussion, and Deng Xiaoping communicated several opinions of the Standing Committee regarding Tibet and Sino-Indian relations. Apart from a plan to immediately launch social transformation in Tibet, a propaganda strategy was also formulated: "We have to condemn the Tibetan elite's rebellion clique, but give some leeway to the Dalai Lama by continuing to use the formulation that 'the rebellion clique kidnapped Dalai.'" At the same time, the Panchen Lama was proclaimed "acting chairman of the Tibet Autonomous Region Preparatory Committee." Deng also gave Xinhua News Agency director and *People's Daily* chief editor Wu Lengxi the assignment of drafting Xinhua's bulletin on the Lhasa incident.[74]

Deng presided over a meeting of the Politburo Standing Committee to discuss the Xinhua bulletin from 11 a.m. to 2 p.m. on March 27, and Mao personally made revisions. The news agency issued its bulletin the next day. At the same time, State Council Premier Zhou Enlai issued an order to abolish the Tibetan government and have PCART take full responsibility for government. By then, General Ding Sheng and the political commissar Xie Jiaxiang had arrived in Lhasa with advance personnel for the "Ding Headquarters" on March 24.

On March 26, the Dalai Lama reached Lhuntsé Dzong,[75] near the Indian border, and made a proclamation formally repudiating the Seventeen-Point Agreement and announcing the establishment of a provisional government.

On March 31, the Dalai Lama and his 80-person retinue crossed the McMahon Line and sought political asylum in India.[76]

Back in China's inland regions, the powerful state propaganda apparatus went into high gear with a massive propaganda campaign.

On the day that the Dalai Lama entered India, *People's Daily* published an editorial entitled "Thoroughly Pacify the Armed Rebellion in Tibet," and in accordance with Mao's directive two weeks earlier, it published the six letters between the Dalai Lama and Tan Guansan as proof that the Dalai Lama had been "kidnapped" and taken to India. On April 1, all of China's major newspapers and local newspapers published headline news regarding "comprehensive pacification of the armed rebellion in Tibet." At the same time, each locality immediately organized study and discussions for cadres, "democratic personages,"[77] and ordinary people, and their reactions and comments were quickly collected and reported to the authorities.[78]

On April 25, *People's Daily* published an editorial hailing the PLA's major victory in Shannan, while page 7 of the same issue was devoted entirely to an article written by the secretary of the TWC's propaganda department, Shan Chao.[79] Written in the form of a journal recording his personal experiences, the article related many details regarding the events in Lhasa. A month after the article was published, the TWC propaganda department wrote a letter to the Xinhua News Agency. This letter, which has never been made public, pointed out many inaccuracies in Shan Chao's article.[80]

For example, Shan Chao's "journal" for March 15 stated:

> The bandits have shown their true colors, going around the city breaking the law and committing crimes. It's just like when the Imperialist invaders attacked China.
>
> I hear that terrible things have been done at the nun's temple in front of the Jokhang temple, and that all of the dozens of young nuns have been raped. The doors of many shops have been destroyed by

> rebel bandits, and all of the good items have been plundered. The reactionary nobility and officials are passing by the TWC's gate in broad daylight, moving their homes to Norbulingka.[81]

The TWC's propaganda department pointed out:

> This is utterly inconsistent with fact. First of all, there is no nun's temple in front of the Jokhang temple, and before the battle there were no rebel bandits raping dozens of young nuns in Lhasa. At that time the militia regiment (command post for the Lhasa government offices) was gathering situation reports every minute, and the leading comrades of the militia regiment never heard of such a thing. Furthermore, before the fight, the enemy was taking care to "strive for the masses," and while there may have been individual instances of looting, it is not true that "the doors of many shops have been destroyed by rebel bandits, and all of the good items have been plundered."[82]

In his "journal" for March 18, Shan Chao wrote that the citizens of Lhasa had been coming to the TWC to vent their grievances, and he described in detail an old woman tearfully complaining that her son had been taken away to serve in the "volunteer army" by "a large band of reactionaries," and that her daughter had been raped.[83] The propaganda department pointed out that "none of this was true," and that the facts were just the opposite: "There were rumors of petitions to the TWC and Military Command, but not a single person came to the TWC to complain."[84]

On March 20, the Battle of Lhasa broke out. Shan Chao wrote:

> It was already after midnight and the weather was rather cold. I threw on my overcoat and went into the courtyard to get some air before going back in to continue selecting articles.
>
> Just as I reached the courtyard, I suddenly saw flames shooting up from Norbulingka, Mount Yuewang [Chakpori], and the Potala palace, and the entire city rang with the sound of gunfire and cannon. I looked at my watch and saw it was 3:40.[85]

The propaganda department letter said:

> The part about Shan Chao getting some air in the courtyard and seeing flames shooting from Norbulingka, Mount Yuewang, and the Potala palace . . . is completely fabricated. In reality, Norbulingka, Mount Yuewang, and the Potala palace did not simultaneously fire on us, nor were there "flames shooting up all over," or "the entire scene [note: it should be "entire city"] ringing with the sound of gunfire and cannon." Furthermore, Comrade Shan Chao wouldn't have been able to see Norbulingka from the United Front Department.[86]

Was the Battle of Lhasa supported by the people of Lhasa? Chen Bing, a military officer who took part in the battle, writes in his memoir essay: "After the combat ended, the masses lifted up *khata* and congratulated each other, celebrating their new life."[87] The *History of the Liberation of Tibet*, published in 2008, describes the situation after the battle in even greater detail:

> As soon as the fighting ended, the citizens of Lhasa ignored sporadic gunfire and stray bullets and ran out of their homes, burning incense and prostrating themselves, overjoyed and welcoming their new life. They complained to party and government cadres and army officers of the crimes of the armed rebels, helped collect weapons abandoned or hidden by the rebel bandits, and enthusiastically helped the troops sweep up the remaining rebel elements.[88]

It's hard to imagine that Chen Bing and the editors of *History of the Liberation of Tibet* didn't know what actually happened after the battle:

> After the battle, the enemy's past deception and reactionary propaganda led ordinary people to say, "The Chinese won and the Tibetans lost." They were afraid we would kill them, and when they went out on the streets they carried rods with *khata* hanging from them to express surrender (there were also some old women who took *khata*s to the TWC to surrender), and they did not celebrate the victorious pacification of the rebellion.[89]

The TWC propaganda department's letter was published in the Xinhua News Agency's *Internal Reference*, which was only circulated among high-level cadres and to this day has not been formally declassified, while Shan Chao's *People's Daily* article, although packed with lies and fabrications, was made available to the public.

The "kidnapping version"[90] that Mao suggested and that the Politburo Standing Committee decided on was formally published by Xinhua in March 1959: "They [the rebels] had the effrontery to carry off the Dalai Lama by force from Lhasa on March 17."[91] In the decades since, the CCP has never corrected this account.

Although the TWC's propaganda department formally sent a letter to *People's Daily* in May pointing out the inaccuracies in Shan Chao's article, several months later, another *People's Daily* publication published yet another article by Shan Chao in which he quoted a PLA soldier's story. It said that on the morning of March 22, a PLA reconnaissance team burst into the Potala palace and confronted the rebels: "They swept in like an arrow through the enemy's hail of flying bullets." After returning, one of the soldiers told Shan Chao:

> We burst into the enemy's command post at the highest spot. It was extremely dark, but we could hear the di-da-di-da sound of a telegraph inside. We went in and saw a woman sitting in front of a transmitter, absorbed in sending a message, and a revolver was inserted in her waistband. As soon as she saw me rush in, she grabbed for her gun. I darted over to her, and she was just raising her hand to shoot at me when my foot whizzed up and kicked the gun from her hand. Then with one shot I sent her home.[92]

This story has never reappeared in the decades since, and neither Tibetan nor Chinese materials mention a PLA reconnaissance team entering Potala palace and encountering a mysterious female telegraph operator.

In the summer of 1959, Zhou Enlai specially arranged a tour of Lhasa for Anna Louise Strong[93] and a dozen reporters from the Soviet bloc. Several months later, Strong published *When Serfs Stood Up in Tibet,* which defended the Chinese government's actions there.[94]

On April 25, the day Shan Chao's first *People's Daily* article was published, Yang Shangkun went to view the famous Tibetan "serf system" exhibition, an exhibition hastily set up in Beijing after the Dalai Lama's escape and the Lhasa incident to justify the suppression of the Tibetan rebellion. He recorded his impression: "I simply couldn't bear to look at it—so backward, degenerate, barbarous, licentious—it was unimaginable! If this kind of system isn't reformed, the Tibetan race will become extinct!"[95]

Mao was a master of propaganda, so he was not as gullible as Yang Shangkun. On April 7, Mao wrote a letter to Wang Feng, then deputy director of the United Front Department and vice-chairman of the State Ethnic Affairs Commission, and asked him 13 questions, including: "Someone says that rebelling lamas were skinned and hamstrung. Did such things happen?" and "Someone says that several human skins were found. Has that been verified?"[96]

In April and May 1959, the Xinhua News Agency's *Internal Reference* published several reports describing the basic situation in the Tibetan regions of Sichuan, Tibet, and Gansu,[97] possibly in response to Mao's letter. The April 19 and 21 editions of *Internal Reference* described the situation in Sichuan's Tibetan regions and in Tibet, and both mentioned finding human skins inside monasteries, but neither cited the source of the information. The edition on the 21st acknowledged that "it has not been ascertained whether [the skins] came from living persons."[98] Yet the April 27 edition of *People's Daily* published photographs showing a human skin, instruments of torture, and a man and woman with their eyes gouged out, saying that these were the "criminal acts of Khampa rebels." The May 16 edition of *People's Pictorial* displayed a photo of torture instruments and said, "According to statistics from some townships in Xinlong County in the Ganzi Tibetan Autonomous Prefecture, at least 138 people have had their eyes gouged out, their noses cut off, or been hamstrung by armed rebels."[99] However, the *Xinlong County Gazetteer* published in 1992 contains no such record.

This propaganda bombardment led even those who had planned it to fall for it. General Huang Kecheng, who was involved in the entire process of planning the Battle of Lhasa and knew exactly where the "Dalai Lama kidnapping" story came from, still used that version of events in his report to the National Defense Council on May 5, 1959.[100]

On May 10, 1959, *PLA Daily* published a Xinhua report that starting that day, a documentary film entitled *Pacifying the Armed Rebellion in Tibet* was being simultaneously shown in 12 cinemas. This documentary, produced by the Central News Documentary Film Studio, was soon showing in every province and city in the country. In September 2011, Li Zhenyu, a cameraman who had taken part in the filming of the documentary, recalled the production process: "After the initially edited rush was completed, the leader of the film studio watched it and felt it still lacked material, so I hurried back to Lhasa to shoot supplementary footage around the clock, then returned to Beijing to help with the later-stage work on the edited documentary 'Pacifying the Armed Rebellion in Tibet.'"[101] He didn't say what footage was "supplemented."

Less than a year later, the Chinese government published a great deal of popular literature regarding Tibet. The main themes of these books came in two types: One was "accusatory"[102] and the other was "laudatory."[103] A large number of photographs published in *People's Daily* and *People's Pictorial* elaborated on these two themes.

7

According to officially published figures, during the Battle of Lhasa, 545 Tibetans were killed or wounded and 4,815 were taken prisoner,[104] including Drolkar Gye's father.

PLA reinforcements from Gansu and Qinghai reached Lhasa from March 28 to 30, and the TMC immediately sent two artillery battalions for coordinated operations to surround the Drepung, Sera, and Ganden monasteries, as well as sending work teams into the monasteries to "thoroughly destroy the armed rebel bases":[105]

> Through political striving, more than 3,100 rebelling masses surrendered, handing over 1,200-plus guns and 39 [rifles]. . . . Around 3,000-odd rebel elements fled to the Pengbo [Penpo] valley, and air force scouts discovered this target. On March 30 and 31, two infantry battalions carried out a surrounding attack, taking 39 prisoners under the Tibetan army's Puma Khenchung[106] and Luozhu Gesang [Lodro Kalsang] and capturing 122 guns.
>
> In order to ascertain the whereabouts of fugitive rebel bandits and carry out the relevant airborne attacks, from March 21 to April 5, four Tupelov Tu-4 bombers were sent out on 15 sorties and executed 11 scouting missions, including 4 bombing and strafing operations, playing a key role in coordinated battle with ground forces.[107]

At the same time that this was happening, massive raids and investigations began in Lhasa. Adult men were locked up, interrogated, and individually categorized, and women were rounded up and questioned one by one. Sometime after March 22, the organizers of and active participants in the Lhasa Women's Assembly were arrested, and large numbers of people who had fled to Lhasa from Kham and Amdo were escorted back to their places of origin.[108]

Drolkar Gye found herself alone, with no one to turn to and nowhere to go. She knew she couldn't stay in Lhasa, but she also knew what fate awaited her if she returned to her homeland. She felt she had only one choice: to go to India.

Drolkar Gye packed up everything of value, took off the coral necklace she wore around her neck, lifted her wooden carrier rack onto her back,[109] and left Lhasa. She didn't know where India was or how long it would take to get there. She just asked along the way, eating when she could and sleeping in the open as she headed step by step toward the southern side of the Himalaya mountains.

More than 50 years later, in the Dondrupling Tibetan Refugee Settlement in Dehradun, northern India, 81-year-old Drolkar Gye wept as she described her long, lonely, arduous flight:

> I just kept walking, walking, walking until my feet were blistered. I sat on a rock along the road to rest, and I thought to myself, Am I dead or alive? In the past, I had been so timid that I hadn't even dared to go to the outhouse after dark. How was it that I was now in this desolate place all by myself? I thought I must be dead and that my soul was passing through this place. I stood up and saw my shadow. I scratched my foot along the ground and saw that it left a track. So I knew I was not dead. I could only keep walking, walking, walking.[110]

Step by step, Drolkar Gye's homeland receded ever further behind her. She crossed the snowy passes of the Himalaya and entered India.

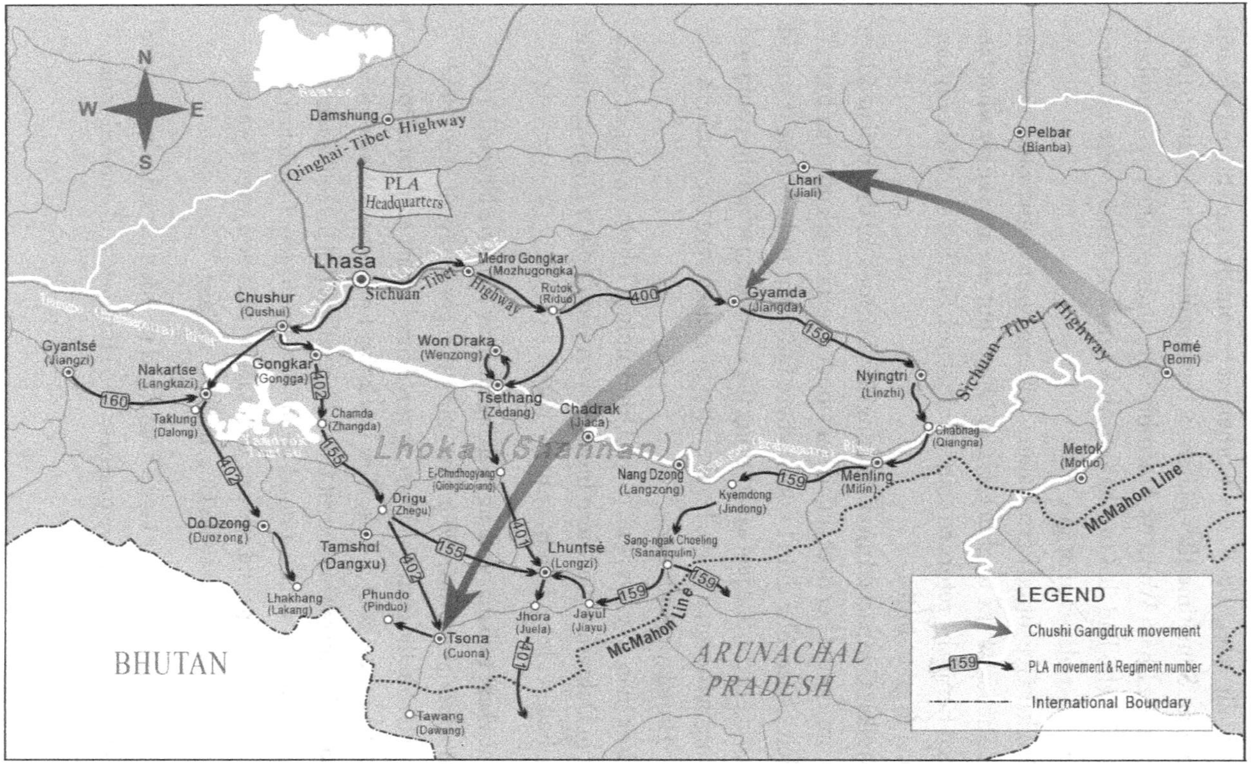

MAP 6. **PLA Lhoka campaign and Chushi Gandruk Movement, April 1959.**

Source: Marvin Cao.

Chapter 19

THE BATTLE OF LHOKA

1

On March 10, 1959, the commander of the 134th Division of the PLA's 54th Army, Bai Bin, who was suppressing Tibetan and Muslim revolts in Gansu and Qinghai, received an urgent order to immediately withdraw his troops and prepare to enter Tibet.[1]

On March 14, the commander of the 54th Army, General Ding Sheng, who was in Beijing for a military deployment meeting, ordered the 134th Division to head out three days later.[2]

On March 15, the 134th Division's 401st Regiment, artillery regiment, and other units stationed in Lintao, Gansu Province, proceeded by train to Xiadong, the furthest place open to railroad travel, and then by truck to Tibet via Golmud.

On March 17, the 134th Division's 400th and 402nd Regiments set off from the proximity of Xining, Qinghai Province, and division commander Bai Bin and political commissar Lan Yinong followed with the division's headquarters and subordinate troops. More than 200 trucks carried troops on the Qinghai-Tibet highway into Tibet. They were under orders to reach Damshung by March 24, and the entire division was to arrive in Lhasa by March 30.

On March 19, the Lanzhou Military Command's 11th Infantry Division set off in trucks from the area of Linxia and Lintao in southwestern Gansu. The division's advance force, the 31st Regiment, reached Golmud on the 25th. By then, the Battle of Lhasa had ended, so the division's 32nd Regiment was ordered to take up battles in Nagchu, while the rest of the troops were to undergo drills and await orders in Golmud and other places.[3]

On March 24, the 54th Army commander Ding Sheng and the political commissar Xie Jiaxiang flew to Lhasa with the "Ding Headquarters" and established a new command post in the mansion of Tibet's aristocratic Tsarong family.[4]

The troops of the 134th Division arrived in Lhasa from March 28 to 30; the 400th Regiment was garrisoned in the Ganden Monastery, the 402nd Regiment in the Sera Monastery, and the 401st Regiment and other units in Lhasa and in the Drepung Monastery.[5] This meant that Tibet's three most important Buddhist academies were occupied by PLA troops. The next day, the TWC and TMC joined to form a military control group that entered the three great monasteries and began "mobilizing the masses and organizing temple management committees with impoverished lamas as their backbone."[6] At this time, the Dalai Lama was still at the Tibetan-Indian border, waiting for the Indian government to grant him political asylum.

The 54th Army was an elite unit known as the "invincible army" and occupied a key position in the CCP's military history. The first army unit to come under the CCP's direct command, it had been repeatedly reorganized and had taken part in major battles through which the party had seized political power. In October 1950, the 54th Army had been sent to fight American troops in the Battle of the Kumsong River (also known as the Jincheng Campaign), the last large-scale battle in the Korean War.[7] Mao, Zhu De, Zhou Enlai, Peng Dehuai, and Lin Biao had all served in the 54th Army, and the current commander, Major General Ding Sheng, had become known as the "invincible general" for his valorous service from the Jiangxi Soviet Area to Korea.

After the reinforcements had entered Tibet, the TMC settled on Lhoka for its first battle. That area had yet to be brought under the

Chinese government's full control and had become a haven for Tibetan resistance forces, including the Chushi Gangdruk. The Chinese government considered Lhoka a "bandit rebel lair" that must be "cleaned up," so as soon as he arrived in Lhasa, Ding Sheng began planning the Battle of Lhoka.

Situated 3,700 meters above sea level, Lhoka adjoins Bhutan and India and had more than 20 cross-border routes. When the Dalai Lama set off from Norbulingka at midnight on March 17, 1959, he took the route from Lhasa to Lhoka, to Lhuntsé, then through Tsona (Cuona) and across the border to Tawang (Dawang). His entourage made the entire trip on foot and horseback in just two weeks.

The PLA had only been able to establish strongholds in a few *dzong* along the Tsangpo River, such as Gongkar and Tsethang.[8] The establishment of Chushi Gangdruk in Driguthang in June 1956 had made Lhoka the heart of the Tibetan resistance. According to Chinese sources, there were around 10,000 "armed rebel elements" in Lhoka in early April 1959, along with more than 6,000 Tibetan soldiers, lamas, nobility, and "coerced masses" who had fled there after the Battle of Lhasa.[9]

The figure of "10,000 armed rebel elements" is rather misleading. According to Tibetan sources, there were fewer than 2,000 members of Chushi Gangdruk in Lhoka at that time,[10] the rest being scattered throughout Nagchu, Chamdo, and other places. And many of the Khampas and Amdowas who had fled to Lhoka at that time were not members of Chushi Gangdruk or "rebel bandit elements" of any other kind, but were merely refugees.

On March 29, the TMC held a war council to arrange deployment for the "Battle of Shannan." In accordance with Mao's directive, the objective of this battle was to "stamp out so-called base areas" using the strategy of "closing the door and beating the dog," i.e., closing off the border areas to trap Chushi Gangdruk and annihilate them once and for all. The conference decided to utilize a massive armed force to "advance separately and attack jointly," coming in from the east and west to envelop the Lhuntsé-Jhora (Juela)-Tsona area on the Indian border, cut off Chushi Gangdruk's escape routes to the south, and then send in troops from the north to block Chushi Gangdruk from escaping northward. At the same time, two regiments of troops would be sent in between the eastern and western lines to exterminate Chushi Gangdruk in the middle of Lhoka, i.e., the area between Lhuntsé, Lhagyari (Lajiali),[11] and Driguthang, but the troops were not allowed to cross the McMahon Line.[12]

In order to accomplish this objective, the TMC and Ding Headquarters formulated a detailed battle plan: as the eastern line, the Tibet Military Command's 159th Regiment would cross the Tsangpo River at Chabnag (Qiangna),[13] about 400 km east of Lhasa, and would move southwest, reaching Sang-ngak Choeling (Sananqulin)[14] on April 16 and "shutting the door" on the southeastern side.[15]

The western line, consisting of two battalions of the 134th Division's 402nd Regiment and one brigade of the 160th Regiment, would advance from Chushur and Gyantsé toward Taklung Dzong (Dalong),[16] Do Dzong, and Lhakhang (Lakang) Dzong,[17] while at the same time a battalion would be transferred from the Lanzhou Military Command's 11th Infantry Division to coordinate with them in "closing the door" on the west side.

Two lines would then cut in between the east and west lines: the first, consisting of two battalions from the TMC's 155th Regiment and one battalion from the 402nd Regiment, would cross the river at Chushur, southwest of Lhasa, wind around the eastern side of Yamdrok Yumtso Lake by way of Gongkar, Chamda,[18] and Driguthang, and then split into two groups, with the main force of two battalions heading straight into Lhuntsé and Jayul (Jiayu),[19] and one battalion heading toward Tsona[20] and Jhora[21] near the McMahon Line. They were to reach their locations on April 16 and "close the door" on the southern side. The other line, consisting of the 134th Division's 401st Regiment, would take the Sichuan-Tibet highway to Rutok (Riduo),[22] cross the pass on foot to Won Draka (Wenzong),[23] then cross the Tsangpo in two groups. They would break up the Chushi Gangdruk's encirclement of Tsethang, coordinating with a battalion garrisoned at Tsethang to attack Tsethang and Trandruk (Changzhu).[24] These troops would then split into two groups and attack Lhuntsé from the east and west.

The north line consisted of the 134th Division's 400th Regiment, which would hold the 200-kilometer stretch from Lhasa to Taizhao[25] and prevent Chushi Gangdruk fighters from fleeing north to Nagchu, thereby "closing the door" on the north side.

This was an enormous "pouch battle." Once the "pouch" was formed, it would be gradually drawn tighter through movements and battles to squeeze Chushi Gangdruk into the center of Lhoka, where the volunteer army could then be wiped out in one stroke.

After the CMC approved the battle plan, the participating PLA units set off in five groups, starting with the east line, followed by the central and finally the west line.

On April 2, the two battalions of the 159th Regiment set off in trucks for Tselagang Dzong,[26] on the north bank of the Tsangpo River.

On April 4, the 401st Regiment, responsible for battles in the center, set off in trucks for Rutok.

On April 7, the 402nd Regiment crossed the river at Chushur in three groups at dawn and headed straight for Gongkar, and the two battalions of the 160th Regiment stationed at Gyantsé also set off.

With the "pouch battle" arranged in this way, Zhang Guohua and Ding Sheng were confident that their absolute superiority, along with superior weapons that included air force bombers, made success a certainty.

As it turned out, however, Zhang Guohua and Ding Sheng must have received erroneous intelligence or made errors of judgment, because when the "pouch battle" was laid out, Gonpo Tashi and the main force of Chushi Gangdruk that he commanded were actually located outside of the "pouch." Zhang and Ding believed that the group that was surrounding the TWC's Tsethang branch was the 2,000-odd fighters[27] led by Gonpo Tashi and Jama Sampel Dondrup,[28] but in fact it was a force of 440 fighters[29] led by another Chushi Gangdruk founder, Ratuk Ngawang, with perhaps a few nearby civilians mixed in. Jama Sampel Dondrup had led the fighters who attacked the PLA convoy heading for Tsethang in 1958, but wasn't part of the current encirclement. A cadre in the TWC's Tsethang branch who took part in the entire "battle to defend Tsethang" never mentioned the size of the enemy force in his autobiographical essay.[30] At that time, Tsethang was also the location of the Tibetan government's Tsethang Dzong, and there were plenty of monasteries and villages nearby. It could be that the TWC's Tsethang branch counted all those people among the "rebel bandits" it reported to the upper levels, thereby turning 400-odd fighters into more than 2,000.

When Zhang Guohua and Ding Sheng planned their "pouch battle," Gonpo Tashi and the main force of his volunteer army were in the Pelbar area of Chamdo, Jama Sampel Dondrup was in Lhagyari,[31] and the Chushi Gangdruk headquarters had moved from Driguthang. All of this shows that the TMC had little understanding of Chushi Gangdruk's movements,[32] and that it overestimated its numbers.

2

The first battle fought by the Chushi Gangdruk Defenders of the Faith had been in mid-August 1958, when Gonpo Tashi set out from Driguthang with more than 600 fighters to raid the government armory at the Shang Ganden Choekhor monastery.[33]

After that, Gonpo Tashi led the main force of his volunteer army north, passing along the south side of Namtso Lake, bypassing Damshung, crossing the Qinghai-Tibet highway, and heading east into Nagchu. The PLA continued to encircle, pursue, obstruct, and intercept them along the way, resulting in several intense battles. Finally, the PLA ambushed the exhausted Chushi Gangdruk fighters on the border of Kongpo Gyamda and Medro Gongkar counties, and they beat a hasty retreat under intense artillery fire that left Gonpo Tashi wounded.

At the end of October 1958, Gonpo Tashi led his troops to the area of Tengchen, Lho Dzong (Luozong),[34] and Pelbar, where they replenished their provisions and reorganized and supplemented their manpower with local resistance forces. On January 4, 1959, Gonpo Tashi led a combined force of 800 Chushi Gangdruk and local resistance fighters in besieging Zhamog, but their lack of heavy artillery and explosives prevented them from overcoming the enemy forces. After ten days, they learned that PLA reinforcements were about to arrive, so Gonpo Tashi led a retreat towards Pelbar. Gonpo Tashi's memoirs indicate that from the time he left Driguthang in August 1958 until the end of March 1959, he was mainly active in the region north of the Tsangpo River.[35]

During the 1959 Tibetan New Year, Gonpo Tashi was in Lho Dzong,[36] and then led part of the volunteer army to Shopamdo (Shuobanduo),[37] where he mobilized local civilians to join the resistance. After that, Gonpo Tashi decided to lead his troops back to Lhoka. In the meantime, the Lhasa incident broke out, and although Chushi Gangdruk's headquarters were now in Lhagyari, Gonpo Tashi was far off in southwestern Chamdo and heard nothing of the battle. On March 22, Gonpo Tashi led his troops to Bankar (Baiga),[38] where he learned from a news broadcast on All India Radio that the Dalaï Lama had fled Lhasa.[39] That day, the Battle of Lhasa ended, and the Dalai Lama and his entourage reached the Riwo Dechen (Riwudeqin) Monastery in Chongyé (Qiongjie), while PLA reinforcements from Gansu and Qinghai were still rushing toward Lhasa.

On April 2, the deputy commander of the PLA's 159th Regiment, Wu Chen, led two battalions to Tselagang[40] and prepared to cross the river, only to encounter a blocking attack by Tibetans at Chabnag, on the opposite shore. After they drove the Tibetan snipers off with mortars and began crossing the river, Wu Chen discovered that the preparations had been inadequate: They'd only brought four dinghies, and the river was hundreds of meters wide, so it took more than ten hours for the two battalions to cross. After crossing the river, Wu Chen led his troops straight for Lhuntsé on the longest stretch of the "pouch formation." They had been ordered to arrive by April 8, which gave them six days to cover a distance on foot that would normally take four days on horseback.[41]

On that day, Gonpo Tashi learned of the Dalai Lama's arrival in India. By then, Gonpo Tashi had left Bankar and was traveling southwest, nearing Lharigo (Lariguo).[42]

He reached Kongpo Gyamda on April 4. At that point, Wu Chen and his east line troops were still in the Menling (Milin)[43] area; Gonpo Tashi and Wu Chen were therefore as close to each other as two ships passing in the night. From then on, both moved rapidly southwest, heading for the same destination; unbeknownst to Wu Chen, the Chushi Gangdruk fighters that he'd been ordered to annihilate were traveling almost parallel with him.

After the 159th Regiment crossed the river, it forced its way through multiple blocking maneuvers by Tibetan resistance forces and finally reached the glacial mountain area. Wu Chen's troops crossed the mountains through two-foot-deep snow, proceeding with immense difficulty to the precipitous area north of Dronpa (Zhunba).[44] There, a razor-sharp precipice forced them to sidle one by one along a narrow plank walkway, leaving their horses and heavy artillery behind with troops assigned to guard them. Making their way cautiously along the face of the cliff greatly slowed their progress.

In the meantime, the route that Gonpo Tashi was taking had been completely overlooked by the pouch formation, so he encountered no blocking or interception. Wu Chen had chosen a difficult route in order to prevent the Tibetan fighters from leaving the country through Metok (Motuo)[45] and Tsona, but Gonpo Tashi had never had such a plan.

Chushi Gangdruk was a resistance force made up of volunteers from dozens of localities, and although the organization had a clear-cut hierarchy and military discipline, it had no modern communications equipment. Gonpo Tashi was the foremost leader, but he was a trader with no military experience. Soon after its establishment, Chushi Gangdruk had split into two groups, one of which followed Gonpo Tashi, fighting one battle after another in northern and eastern Tibet, the other remaining at the Driguthang headquarters, which soon afterward moved to Lhagyari. By early 1959, Chushi Gangdruk had broken into multiple pieces, with small squads defending crossings on the Tsangpo River, 400-odd troops led by Ratuk Ngawang and others surrounding Tsethang, and other units defending other localities. These groups could only communicate with each other by messenger. Under pressure from a powerful army, Chushi Gangdruk was vastly outnumbered and inadequately armed, and could not easily organize an effective resistance.

Gonpo Tashi and other leaders of the volunteer army may have known nothing about the PLA troops that Ding Sheng and Huang Xinting had brought to Tibet for their "decisive engagement," but word had reached them of reinforcements greatly bolstering the PLA's ranks and of the air force being brought into play. Now that the Dalai Lama had escaped to India, the situation in Tibet had changed, and Chushi Gangdruk's leaders needed to quickly decide their next step. A true "hawk," Gonpo Tashi had no intention of crossing the border as he approached Lhuntsé from Kongpo Gyamda, so it had been an error of judgment to send Wu Chen along that route to block Chushi Gangdruk.

The result was that Chushi Gangdruk's main force, led by Gonpo Tashi, reached its destination before the PLA troops who had intended to intercept them.

3

On April 4, two days after the east line troops set off to form their encirclement, the 401st Regiment of the 134th Division of the 54th Army set out for Lhoka. This regiment was the main attack force for the Lhoka campaign and was one of the "daggers" that was to be plunged into the larger encirclement. The 401st Regiment was under orders to break up the Tibetan encirclement of Tsethang and to coordinate with air force and ground troops to wipe out Chushi Gangdruk there[46] and to attack the Tibetan resistance forces in the Won Draka area on the way. Tsethang, about 200 kilometers by road from Lhasa, was on the south bank of the Tsangpo, while Won Draka was on the north side, about 10–12 kilometers northeast of Tsethang.

On April 5, the regiment set off for Won Draka, but before crossing the river, its advance force encountered a blocking attack.[47] According to Ding Sheng's brief recollection, the regiment learned of 1,000 Tibetan volunteers amassed near Won Draka and therefore shifted its main force, which delayed it in joining the encirclement.[48] But according to another narrative, after the advance force's scouting unit was blocked, the company's deputy commander and deputy political instructor "panicked at the sight of a pincer attack by the enemy and crawled on the ground, not daring to move," staying in place for a full two hours. The company "didn't take measures to eliminate or expel the enemy, but just fired randomly to show they were fighting, and this delayed the attack." The 401st

Regiment's 9th Company resisted orders to charge at the enemy until the battalion commander arrived with the main force and ordered them into battle. One platoon leader even "made the excuse of foot pain to avoid battle and dropped back."[49] These missteps slowed the regiment down, and it didn't cross the river until two days later.

The 401st Regiment was supposed to join a battalion of locally stationed troops to "break the siege at Tsethang" on April 8. Perhaps because of its late arrival, the PLA troops stationed at Tsethang launched their attack earlier than planned, on the night of April 7.

The military strategist behind the siege of Tsethang was Lobsang Tashi, the former deputy commander of the PLA's 155th Regiment and artillery commander formerly known as Jiang Huating. He had accompanied Gonpo Tashi to Namling to seize weapons, and on the way back to Lhoka had been separated from the others during a PLA attack. After that, he had returned to Lhasa for a time and then tried to find a way back to the Chushi Gangdruk headquarters. As it happened, he had once commanded the PLA unit garrisoned at Tsethang, so he was very familiar with it. At that time, the TWC's Tsethang branch and one battalion of troops were stationed in Tsethang and Nedong (Naidong), and Chushi Gangdruk had encircled both. Lacking heavy artillery, the Tibetans had no way to capture the solid fortifications, so they simply encircled them, while the local PLA unit had to focus on defense rather than attack.

Chushi Gangdruk spent the night of April 7 fighting the PLA troops garrisoned in Tsethang. At that time, the 401st Regiment was still crossing the river. Learning that PLA reinforcements would soon arrive and leave them hopelessly outnumbered, Ratuk Ngawang and the other leaders decided to pull out that night. More than 300 fighters retreated to nearby Mount Gongpori (Gongbori), and Ratuk Ngawang sent a messenger to notify the fighters encircling Nedong that they should also pull out. The fighters then withdrew from Gongbori to Trandruk, roughly six kilometers from Tsethang, where they had a logistics and provisions depot. By then, the Tibetan volunteers who had encircled Tsethang and Nedong had lost their will to fight, and many went south with civilians and monks from the three great monasteries fleeing from Lhasa. By dawn, Ratuk Ngawang had only 50-odd fighters left.[50]

But it wasn't only Chushi Gangdruk that had lost its fighting spirit; morale was poor among the PLA soldiers as well.

The 401st Regiment decided that before proceeding to Tsethang, its first action after crossing the river would be to cut off Chushi Gangdruk's escape route. The regiment therefore set off in two groups after crossing the river in the early hours of April 7, intending to encircle Trandruk by 7 a.m. the next day. A company of advance troops soon encountered a blocking attack, however; they then "panicked, and while returning fire on the rebel bandits, they shot blindly and randomly. The company's commanders did not calmly organize a prompt counterattack but moved very slowly, and the face-off lasted for more than an hour before the rebel bandits were expelled."[51] The unit then proceeded to take the wrong route, along the way encountering "scattered rifle fire from a few rebel bandits" and "shootings from recoilless cannons," and the company's political instructor and a soldier were wounded.[52]

By then, the Tibetan volunteers who had been surrounding Tsethang and Nedong had scattered in all directions, each regionally organized unit fighting or fleeing at will. The Chushi Gangdruk fighters who fired on the PLA had only encountered them by chance, and after firing a few rifle shots and two shells, they went down the mountain and sped toward Potrang,[53] south of Trandruk. The shells had been enough to halt the PLA's advance, however; the unit falsely reported that it was under "intense attack" from three sides and was then ordered back to its base to repair the fortifications. On the way, the troops saw "70-odd rebel bandits attempting to flee south," but didn't attack them.[54]

The other group from the 401st Regiment lost its way as soon as it crossed the river. When the troops finally reestablished contact after several hours, they discovered that they were not in their designated locations, and they were therefore unable to complete the encirclement. Most of the Chushi Gangdruk fighters led by Ratuk Ngawang escaped from Trandruk during that interval. At noon, the air force bombers arrived over Trandruk according to plan, but Ratuk Ngawang's main force was long gone, and the air force's bombing and strafing ended up killing a large number of fleeing monks and civilians instead.[55]

At 1:00 in the afternoon on April 8, two PLA companies coming from two different directions stormed and captured the peak of Mount Gongbori, near Tsethang. There are different versions of how many Tibetan fighters were on the mountain at the time. Tibetan sources say there were only 10 or so Gyalrong tribesmen there, who had refused to flee,[56] but Ding Sheng's memoir claims that "454 of the enemy were annihilated."[57]

At daybreak on April 7, the 402nd Regiment, which was meant to carry out a "direct attack," set off from Lhasa and sped toward Chushur. Under cover of night, the soldiers split into groups in Chushur, crossed the river, and headed straight for Gongkar. The plan was that two battalions should reach their designated locations at 6 p.m. and launch an attack on Tibetan resistance forces in that area. However, one battalion failed to arrive in time to complete the encirclement, so the other battalion launched the attack on its own. The Tibetan resistance forces immediately fled toward Paldi (Baidi),[58] Nakartsé,[59] and Lhodrak,[60] with the 402nd Regiment in pursuit.[61]

On that same day, the battalion of the TMC's 160th Regiment that had been stationed in Gyantsé set out to close off the line from Taklung to Do Dzong from west to east, thereby cutting off Chushi Gangdruk's escape route to Bhutan.

April 8 was the day on which all of the PLA units were to have reached their designated locations for the encirclement. Yet the location of the east line troops was unknown; the west line troops had just reached the Tsangpo in the early hours of that morning and didn't capture Mount Gongbori until noon that day; and the central line troops were still on the march.

The pouch formation had come to nothing so far. Furthermore, the air force, cavalry, and artillery had already been dispatched, the troops that had set off earliest had already been on the move for a week, and commanding officer General Ding Sheng had no idea where the enemy's main force was.

The Ding Headquarters was forced to change its plan.

4

On April 11, the 401st Regiment, still in Trandruk, was ordered to ascertain whether Chushi Gangdruk's main force was in Driguthang, so the regiment split into two routes and set off for that area. In the afternoon, the regiment's advance scouting unit had just reached Potrang[62] when it was met with a blocking attack by 40-odd Tibetans. The scouting unit quickly rebuffed the attack, but after forcing its opponents to retreat, it advanced only a little further before encountering an ambush. This time the enemy had machine guns and cannons, and the two PLA companies "immediately halted their advance and remained in place for more than two hours without attacking the rebel bandits," while falsely reporting that the enemy numbered more than 1,000.[63] This led the 401st Regiment's commanding officers to believe that they had encountered the "main force of the rebel bandits" and immediately change their plan to one of pursuit and attack. This made the small pouch at Driguthang impossible to complete, but also delayed the insertion from Driguthang to Tsona and the drawing in of the large pouch. Although the 155th Regiment arrived at Tamshol (Dangxu) on time at dawn on the 12th, one unit got lost, so the small pouch assigned to that regiment was not completed either.

The Lhoka operation was a series of pouch battles of varying sizes. There was a "large pouch" formed by the east, west, and north lines, as well as "small pouches," referring to rings of encirclement used to take out Chushi Gangdruk bit by bit. This was a common military tactic for the PLA, and the basic one used to suppress Tibetans. The large and small pouches in the Lhoka Campaign were almost complete failures, however. A key reason was that the commanding officers at different levels did not understand the actual situation of Chushi Gangdruk, and their conventional military thinking led them to exaggerate the number of rebel fighters. As a result, whenever they were ambushed, they imagined that it was by "units covering the flight of the main force" and therefore launched into blind pursuit, believing they could overtake and attack Chushi Gangdruk's main force. But the fact was that the ambushes were carried out by small splinter detachments, or by Tibetan Army remnants fleeing from Lhasa, or by small groups of Ratuk Ngawang's troops who had temporarily teamed up in flight. They ambushed the PLA troops whenever the opportunity arose and, given the PLA's greater firepower, then immediately withdrew and continued their flight. This guerrilla spontaneity, with absolutely no pattern, managed to stymie Ding Sheng's troops at every turn. This delayed and ultimately prevented the formation of the large pouch Ding had planned, while the small pouches assigned to the various units basically came to nothing.

By that time, Chushi Gangdruk's main force, in any real sense, consisted of the 1,000 or so fighters led by Gonpo Tashi. That unit, returning to Lhoka from the Chamdo area, slipped into the large pouch that Ding Sheng had arranged, but the PLA's two flanks were spread too far apart to close the pouch, while the other troops pursued Ratuk Ngawang's scattered men willy-nilly within the large pouch. As a result, a PLA force of nearly 10,000, searching throughout Lhoka for the main force of Chushi Gangdruk, merely brushed shoulders with them. Added to this problem was Ding Sheng's anxiousness to score a victory. After troops were rushed over from Gansu and Qinghai, the soldiers assigned to the main attack were sent to the plateau before they had had a chance to rest or become adapted to the environment. Exhausted and struggling to maintain morale, they constantly supplied inaccurate information to the upper levels, dropped out of the fighting, disobeyed orders to advance, or launched only perfunctory attacks.

Feedback from the various units led Ding Sheng to conclude that the main force of Chushi Gangdruk was fleeing toward Lhuntsé, and although this conclusion wasn't completely accurate, it wasn't far off. In fact, the main force led by Gonpo Tashi had already reached Lhuntsé by April 13.[64]

On the basis of Ding Sheng's conclusions, a new pouch formation was planned, and Ding ordered his units to divide into five routes to surround Lhuntsé by dawn on April 18. Several days later, he learned that the main force of Chushi Gangdruk was moving toward the Indian border, and immediately decided to move the encirclement forward to April 17.[65]

On April 16, the 402nd Regiment, responsible for a frontal attack, deployed two battalions in a surprise attack on Do Dzong in Lhodrak, near the Bhutan border. At that time, an ad hoc contingent of around 240 Tibetans was in Do Dzong, composed of nearly 100 Tibetan army soldiers as well as Chushi Gangdruk fighters, armed monks, and a few Amdo refugees. These people were garrisoned in the former government building and adjacent Donyiling Monastery, and had constructed fortifications in the surrounding area. The mountaintop building occupied a commanding position, and nearly half of the fighters were trained Tibetan army personnel, including dozens of soldiers from the security team that had returned after escorting the Dalai Lama to the border. These fighters had weapons and ammunition, including both light and heavy machine guns airdropped by the CIA in mid-February. As a result, this battle turned into the most intense one in the Lhoka campaign.

The Chinese side of the battle was led by the commander of the 402nd Regiment and the Tibetan side by Rupon[66] Sonam Tashi, a commander under the first *depon* of the Tibetan army. The 402nd Regiment had just arrived in Do Dzong and had not yet had time to organize its ranks when the Tibetans took the initiative to attack, and a bloody battle ensued. Ding Sheng's memoirs briefly summarize the battle as follows: "The main force of the 402nd Infantry Regiment carried out a long-range raid on Do Dzong at dawn on April 16 and surrounded the enemy. The enemy of 240-plus men put up a stubborn resistance and was not thoroughly annihilated. The regiment pushed on to Lakang on April 21."[67]

PLA and Tibetan sources record the battle from different perspectives, however. Materials from both sides indicate that the battle at Do Dzong lasted three days, with more than 40 hours of actual fighting. The commander of the 402nd Regiment organized three attacks, only to be rebuffed by the firmly entrenched Tibetan forces. The Tibetans, clearly short on ammunition, "used large rocks, large chunks of wood, and burning cotton rags" to "inflict major casualties"[68] on the attacking PLA troops. On the morning of the 18th, the air force dispatched two Ilyushin Il-28 bombers to Do Dzong, but because of the "false war situation reports," the alleged casualties couldn't be withdrawn from the battlefield, and the bombers had to return with their loads intact.[69] On the afternoon of the 19th, "the 402nd Regiment launched a live-fire attack on the *dzong* government building, along with fierce artillery fire," and the Tibetan army was finally overwhelmed and retreated. Both sides suffered heavy casualties in this battle. Chinese sources state that 141 Tibetans were killed,[70] wounded, or taken prisoner, while 48 PLA soldiers died in action and 64 were wounded.[71]

April 17 was the date of the second encirclement in the Battle of Lhoka. By then, the 401st and 144th Regiments had made it to their designated locations, and Tsona had been occupied by the PLA, but the east line's 159th Regiment was still more than 100 kilometers from Lhuntsé,[72] and the 402nd Regiment was stuck in Do Dzong. This left a gaping hole in the pouch formation, which once again failed.

But in fact, even if the pouch had been formed as planned, it would have been too late. On April 14, 1959, Chushi Gangdruk had held its last war council within the borders of Tibet. The leaders of Chushi Gangdruk and remnants of the Tibetan army were joined by lamas from the three great monasteries who had pulled out with them. Views were divided at this meeting: Gonpo Tashi forcefully pushed for continuing to fight and seizing back Tsona, but the army remnants advocated retreating across the border and preserving their strength. On the second day of the council, Gonpo Tashi received a verbal message from the Dalai Lama urging him to abandon the war and withdraw from Tibet.[73]

Gonpo Tashi decided to lead the main force of Chushi Gangdruk across the border. Abandoning their heavy loads, the fighters crossed the snowy mountains and then split into two groups, each of which left a contingent behind to serve as a rear guard to shield the main force and then retreat to the Indian border along with the fleeing civilians. One of the rear-guard contingents was led by Jiang Huating.

Jiang Huating stood on the snow-capped mountain for a long time watching the PLA soldiers, his former comrades-in-arms, plod through the snow, their cannon shells landing soundlessly in the vast snow drifts around him. Then he turned and followed the Chushi Gangdruk Defenders of the Faith, with whom he'd braved untold dangers, across the McMahon Line.[74] From then on, the "Chinese Lobsang Tashi" became a legend in the history of the Tibetan people.

On April 20, Gonpo Tashi's troops arrived at the Indian border near Tawang and awaited permission to cross. On that same day, the 402nd Regiment, having suffered heavy casualties in the Battle of Do Dzong, rested and reorganized where they were. The 159th Regiment had not yet arrived at the battlefield, and the other troops were still exchanging telegrams with the TMC, trying to understand the order for pursuit and attack.

At this point, the Lhoka campaign was basically over. By April 26, the PLA controlled the main thoroughfares from Lhoka to India and Bhutan. On April 29, two PLA companies crossed the McMahon Line in pursuit of fleeing Tibetans.[75] That same day, the Chushi Gangdruk commander-in-chief, Gonpo Tashi, reached Tezpur, on the plains of Assam.

The main force of Chushi Gangdruk largely withdrew to India. In the following years, the core of the volunteer army metamorphosed into the Mustang guerrilla force and then, later, into Establishment 22. The Mustang guerrilla force was supported by the American CIA, while Establishment 22 was a regular Indian Army Special Frontier Force composed primarily of Tibetans. The withdrawal and reorganization of Chushi Gangdruk allowed the Tibetan armed resistance to continue into the 1970s.[76]

5

On April 25, 1959, *People's Daily* published an editorial entitled "Hailing the Mighty Victory in Suppressing the Bandit Revolt in Shannan, Tibet." The editorial proclaimed to the entire country:

> Troops from the PLA's Tibet Military Command, acting under orders on a punitive expedition against the Tibetan traitorous clique, thoroughly suppressed an armed rebellion in the Lhasa region and then marched south and quelled a bandit rebel lair in the Shannan region led by Andrugtsang Gongbao Zaxi [Gonpo Tashi], scoring a major new victory.[77]

Yet, at a secret National Defense Council meeting ten days later, the deputy defense minister Huang Kecheng reported on the "Battle of

Shannan" in this way: "The majority of armed rebel forces in this region (including those who fled from Lhasa), apart from one unit that was annihilated by us, and a portion that dispersed and went into hiding in Tibet, escaped across the border."[78]

How many members of Chushi Gangdruk, then, actually "escaped across the border"? Chinese sources provide various figures. Ji Youquan states that it was more than 2,000.[79] Jiang Huating's memoirs state that when the various rebel forces converged at the Tibet-India border, they totaled around 3,000, including Chushi Gangdruk fighters, Tibetan army soldiers, and others,[80] which is in the same ballpark as Ji Youquan's figure. However, Ding Sheng's memoir gives the number as more than 5,000,[81] and a figure published in 2008 is larger yet, at more than 8,000.[82]

Chinese sources also give varying statistics for the number of Tibetans killed, wounded, or taken prisoner in this campaign. Ji Youquan and the authors of *Jiefang Xizang shi* (*History of the Liberation of Tibet*) both give the same figure, namely 2,393,[83] but both the 54th Army Military History Office's "Record of the 134th Division's Participation in Pacifying Rebellion in Tibet" and the deputy commander of the 134th Division's scouting unit, Wang Tingsheng, give the figure as 1,577.[84] Chinese sources reveal that before the Battle of Lhoka, that region had "more than 10,000 armed rebels led by Andrugtsang Gonpo Tashi and others."[85] Stating that more than 8,000 escaped and 2,393 were "annihilated," the *History of the Liberation of Tibet* "balanced the accounts," making Zhang Guohua and Ding Sheng's miscalculations disappear from sight.[86]

One official publication also provides another set of figures. In Lhoka, the PLA "captured mortars and three recoilless guns, 536 rifles of various kinds, and 833 homemade firearms."[87] This set of figures reveals what the "invincible army" was fighting in this "decisive engagement": Among the people "annihilated" in the battle, 41% were unarmed, and even of those who were armed, 62% possessed only crude firearms.

So who were these unarmed Tibetans? Tibetan sources include this record:

> On [Tsona hill], corpses were scattered on the ground as far as the eye could see; the bodies of dozens of monks and laymen were everywhere, and blood and vestments reddened a vast stretch of ground.
>
> When we reached the shore of Yamdrok Yumtso, we saw hundreds of Tibetan corpses along the lake and on the nearby grassland. Most of the dead were monks, and the enemy had already disappeared by then. The lake was tinted red by the fresh blood of the victims.[88]

No matter how their victory was hailed outside, the "invincible" Ding Sheng was furious that his troops, enjoying the overwhelming advantage of numbers and superior weapons, had faced Chushi Gangdruk, armed mainly with crude firearms, and still allowed them to slip through the net, failing to achieve his objective in this campaign. For that reason, the Lhoka campaign was in fact a defeat for the PLA.

Decades later, essays by the 54th Army's Military History Office contains only a vague mention of the army "accomplishing its mission of preventing the enemy from fleeing north," with not a word mentioning how the entire main force of Chushi Gangdruk escaped their encirclement and retreated to India;[89] nor is there any mention of PLA troops slaughtering Tibetan monks and laypeople.

6

The military operations in Tibet included two stages. The first stage was known as "attacking rebels" and was mainly a military operation. The second stage, after the main battles were over, was called "cleaning up the rebels" and involved hunting down fugitives while also carrying out political activities among the local people, with military backup, coupled with preliminary grassroots political work and propaganda. It was also a process of grassroots government-building. Unlike in the Chinese inland, in Tibet this process was implemented directly by the PLA.

After the first phase of the Lhoka campaign ended, the 134th Infantry Division, under orders from the CMC, "divided up tasks" and launched the second phase: 193 cadres and veteran soldiers were transferred to form work teams, and at the same time more than 400 people were organized into work groups to accompany the army to each locality for "in-depth arousing of the masses." During the cleanup of bandits, a total of 2,606 mass rallies were held, with a total attendance of 102,434; as well as 771 seminars, with a total attendance of 22,929; 4,646 visits to the poor; and finally, 5 exhibitions of various kinds, with a total attendance of 2,599.[90]

In order to root out the Tibetan resistance, the army confiscated privately held firearms and seized all horses. Over a period of six months, the 134th Division confiscated "865 long and short firearms" in the Lhoka region, as well as "4,443 homemade firearms and 525 horses."[91] After this formidable military suppression and seizing of weapons and horses, the division "universally established impoverished farmer and herder groups, peasant and herder associations, and grassroots people's governments, and brought about preliminary democratic reform, successfully completing the tasks entrusted to them by the upper levels."[92]

However, the task that Mao had assigned to the TWC, the Military Command, and Ding Headquarters was not merely to suppress resistance among Tibetan farmers and herders and to establish grassroots government. In his series of memos at the beginning of 1959, Mao clearly directed that the further objective of warfare in Tibet was to train troops through battles.

The Lhoka campaign was the first large-scale military action that the TMC conducted on the central Tibetan plateau. This campaign did not achieve the anticipated military objective, and it exposed the PLA's weakness in fighting on this terrain. This meant that General Ding Sheng needed more practice.

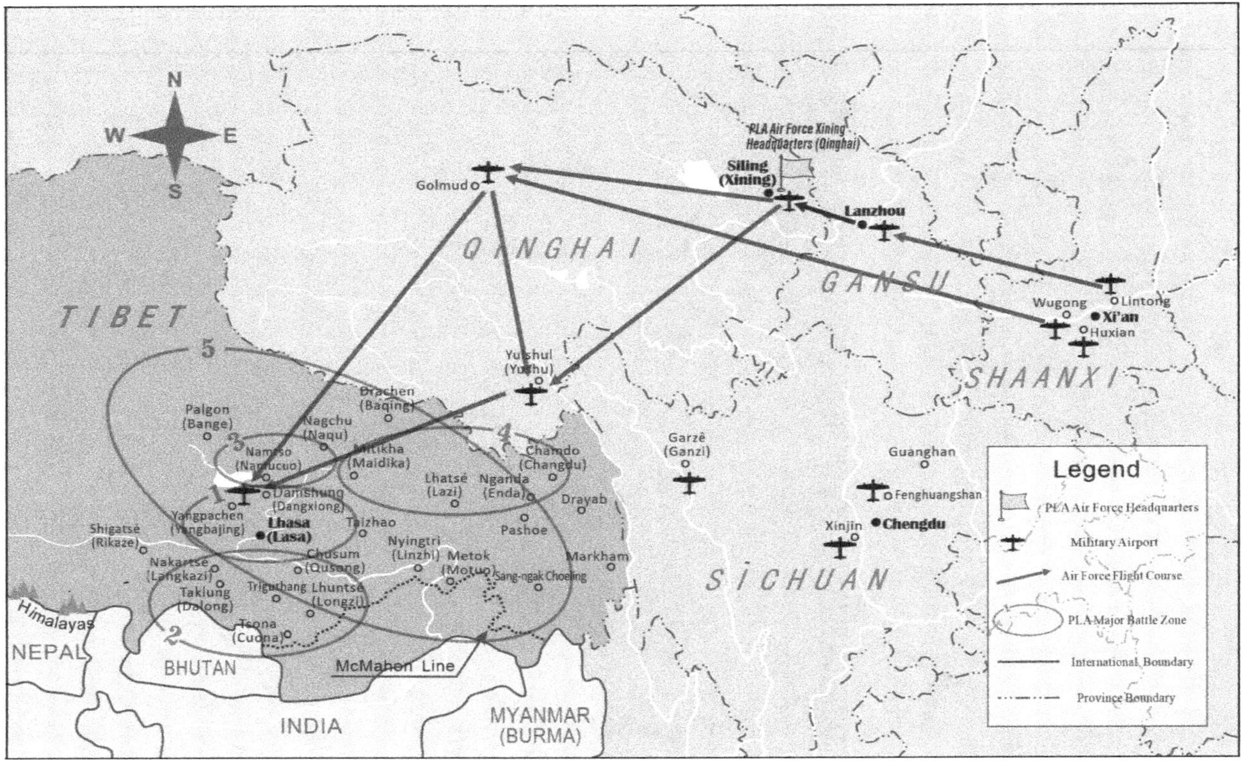

MAP 7. PLA Air Force combat missions in Tibet, 1959–1960:
1.Battle of Lhasa (Bombings in Penpo Valley) | 2.The Lhoka Campaign | 3.The Namtso Campaign | 4.The Mitikha and Chamdo Campaigns | 5.Mop-up Battles | Source: Marvin Cao.

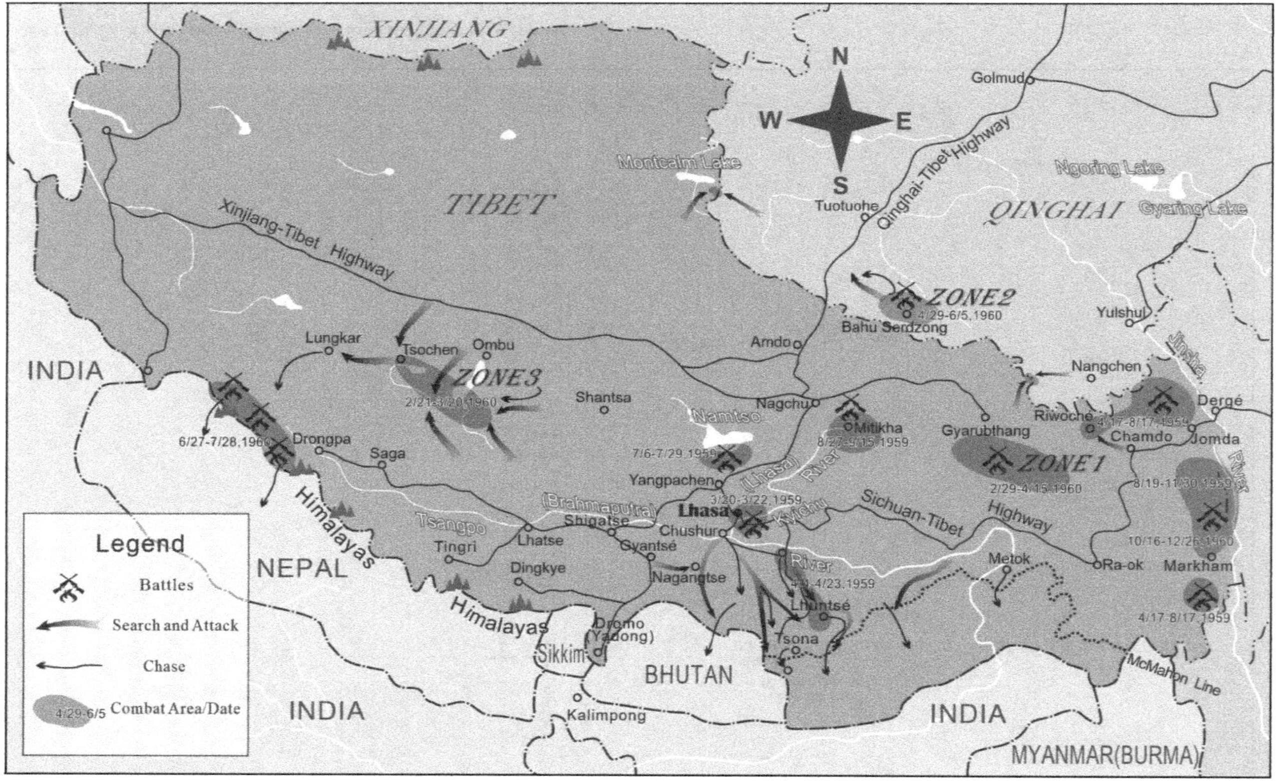

MAP 8. Major PLA Campaigns in Central Tibet, 1959–1960.
Source: Marvin Cao.

Chapter 20

FROM NAMTSO TO MITIKHA

1

In the summer of 1959, the herder woman Ngolo and her husband, together with refugees from other places whom they met along the way, took a roundabout route from the source of the Yellow River across Changthang. When they had nearly reached their destination, they heard the news of a battle in Lhasa, and of the Dalai Lama fleeing to India.

The refugees' last hope died with that news, and only one route was left to them: the road to India. But they were already exhausted from their long journey, and they and their livestock needed to rest before they could take up another long trip. The area around Namtso offered vast stretches of grassland and no Chinese soldiers, so the refugees pitched their tents in a grassy, well-watered valley to regain their strength.

With its open, hilly topography and frigid temperatures, Changthang was inhabited only by nomads. In the past, herders from Golok and Yulshul had driven their herds to this place in times of crisis, and from 1958 onward, Tibet's northern plateau once again became their refuge. As spring turned to summer in 1959, more than 100 different groups gathered there, most of them from Amdo and Kham, with a few local herders mixed in as well as people like Ngolo, who were just passing through. Most had arrived before the Battle of Lhasa and had gathered in the region mainly because there were no PLA stationed there; but following the Battle of Lhasa, the PLA launched the Battle of Lhoka, which prevented the refugees from continuing south and forced them to turn west toward Ngari. Driving their herds and with their monks in tow, the nomads moved slowly, and some had just arrived in the Namtso region.

It was at this time that a PLA unit headed straight toward them down the Qinghai-Tibet highway.

Chinese-language sources contain no record of these refugees attacking road maintenance teams or passing military convoys. The only reason that they became military targets was that the place where they took shelter was near the highway. The southern shore of Namtso Lake lies on the northern slope of the sacred Nyenchen Thanglha mountain (Nianqingtanggula), separated from the Nagchu-Yangpachen section of the Qinghai-Tibet highway by just one mountain pass. The Damshung airport, an important transit station for military supplies, was nearby. The TWC therefore regarded the refugee herders as a serious threat to their transportation routes.

On March 19, 1959, the CMC ordered the Lanzhou Military Command's 11th Infantry Division to proceed to Tibet. The division's 31st Regiment served as the advance force by rushing to Lhasa as reinforcements for troops stationed there. The 11th Division, an independent national defense division, was made up of the Military Command's toughest battle troops, and the majority of its mid-ranking officers had been trained at military academies. This division had fought in Kanlho twice, in both 1956 and 1958, and was one of the main military units used to suppress the Tibetan and Hui resistance. The division's soldiers were stepping up their military drills as Ngolo, her husband, and baby were progressing toward Namtso.[1]

On May 10, the division command post sent its scouting company, medical battalion, and 32nd Regiment into Tibet. Beginning on May 22, Ding Sheng commanded this unit in fighting on both sides of the highway from Nagchu to Ngari. The well-drilled 32nd Regiment carried out a "fishing net tactic," and within 50 days it had "annihilated 113 enemies, effected the surrender of 119 bandits, liberated 345 women and children, and captured 129 firearms and more than 10,000 head of livestock."[2] This source doesn't state where these people came from.

One day, Ngolo was watching the cattle and sheep in the pasture when she suddenly saw a bright light on the horizon, like a glittering star. The "star" moved at high speed and in an instant became a huge bird, accompanied by a piercing roar as it swept over her head. Before she could react, there were several loud booms, and black smoke billowed from the pasture, as cattle and sheep were thrown to the ground and blood splattered the green grass. Terrified livestock ran helter-skelter, along with panicked human beings. The "iron bird" circled overhead a few times, then transformed back into an unknown star and disappeared without a trace.[3]

Ngolo had never dreamed that she and her infant daughter and the other refugees temporarily gathered there would become targets of the Battle of Namtso, Ding Sheng's second campaign in Tibet.

2

The Battle of Namtso spanned the area west of the 90-kilometer Nagchu-Yangpachen segment of the Qinghai-Tibet highway, east of Shentsa Dzong (Shenzhazong)[4] and south of Palgon Dzong (Bangezong).[5] In the summer of 1959, nine nomad groups from Nagchu and Damshung, along with several who had fled from Qinghai, were scattered throughout this region, settling in different valleys and having no unified organization or activities. They joined to elect several leaders and agreed to provide mutual help and protection to each other; if one group spotted PLA troops, they'd quickly notify the others.[6] According to Tibetan sources, some of these groups ambushed small PLA units, but Chinese-language sources make no mention of substantial military conflicts in this area in 1958 or early 1959.

Chinese-language sources refer to these scattered refugee tribes as "armed rebels," and the tribesmen responsible for protecting the women, children, and monks are referred to as the "bandit rebel main force," their families the "coerced masses," their chieftains the "rebel leaders," and their horses "war-horses," thus turning the herders into a "military force."

In mid-June of 1959, a PLA company on a scouting mission around Chinglung Dzong (Qinglongzong)[7] encountered a "rebel force" of around 1,500 people. They belonged to the nine nomad groups mentioned above as well as a monastery from Damshung, and about 500 of them were "combat-ready," with 300 or so firearms.[8] That is to say, this "rebel force" consisted of all the men, women, elderly, and children of those nine communities and their tent monastery, of whom one-third were able-bodied men. Since the 500-odd "combat-ready rebels" had only 300-odd firearms among them, the rest were probably monks.

After brief contact of only ten minutes or so between the two sides, the tribes fled south toward Namtso Lake. The PLA company followed them and discovered a major "enemy situation" in an area around the shore of the lake: a gathering of 16 nomad groups, totaling nearly 4,000 people.[9]

When Zhang Guohua and Ding Sheng—who just a month earlier had allowed Chushi Gangdruk to slip through their hands in spite of overwhelmingly superior military strength—received the report, they immediately decided to organize a major battle. This battle was commanded by the deputy commander of the 54th Army, Wei Tongtai, with its command post in Yangpachen, not far from Damshung. According to the battle plan, three infantry regiments and one artillery battalion from the Ding Headquarters would split into three groups to surround and wipe out the nomads gathering between the southern shore of Namtso Lake and the Nyenchen Thanglha mountain.

On July 4, 1959, the participating PLA battle units set off.

One infantry battalion traveled by motor vehicle from Nagchu to Damshung and the next day headed across the pass to the southern shore of Namtso Lake.

Another infantry battalion moved from west to east toward the southern shore of the lake.

An infantry regiment crossed the snow-covered range from Damshung and headed north for a flanking attack.

An artillery battalion was posted on the highway between Yangpachen and Damshung to close the escape route to the south.

All units arrived at their designated locations before dawn on July 6.

On that day, more than 3,000 PLA soldiers armed with modern weapons launched a three-pronged attack on a dozen nomad groups:

> On July 6, the bandits split into three echelons in an attempt to follow the lake northeast and escape.
>
> The first echelon was 100-plus rebel bandit households from nine Qinghai and Yushu tribes. Around 16:00 that day, after going to the southeast of Namu lake, they continued fleeing northeast. The fourth company of the 32nd Regiment launched an attack from Sangshung Sasung (Sanxiongshasong)[10] and wiped out the enemy's main force of 60-odd mounted men on the shore of the lake.
>
> The second echelon of 200-odd rebel bandits was gathered northeast of Mount 7050.[11] The third echelon of 500 rebels bandits (including more than 200 on horseback) was on the north side of Mount 7050 . . . After the ninth company (of the 32nd Regiment's 3rd Battalion), in coordination with the 7th and 8th Companies, annihilated the main force of the third echelon, it turned around, and with one platoon of soldiers covering the entire company, it attacked the second echelon of bandits.[12]

Even from this military language, it's not hard to see that these three "echelons" were in fact herders attempting to save their lives by breaking through the encirclement. The description of the "first echelon" as consisting of "more than 100 households" clearly means that not all were armed men, while the "main force of 60-odd men on horseback" was clearly the menfolk of these households who were attempting to break through the PLA encirclement to provide a way out for their families. The 11th Infantry Division officers and men had fought in Kanlho's pastoral region before, and they had to have known that when the nomads fled their homeland, they took along their women, children, elders, and monks. Knowing perfectly well that some of the people among those "100-odd households" were unarmed women and children, they opened fire on them nonetheless.

The fleeing nomads were pinned down in an open expanse between the mountains and the lake without cover, surrounded on three sides with the vast lake at their back. A 16-year-old monk named Nyima who experienced the attack described it in this way:

> Early that morning, someone ran over and told us the Chinese were here. We had an agreement with Tibetans on the east and west sides of the lake to give notice if enemy forces were discovered. At this news, we immediately packed up our things and gathered the young men together to prepare for war. In a little while, enemy soldiers in the mountains blew a bugle call and then poured down on us from every mountain pass, launching the battle. The fighting was extremely violent, and many men and women along the lake jumped in and drowned themselves out of despair. Dead bodies floated all along the lakeshore—it was terrifying. Some men, after running out of bullets, drew out their swords to attack. . . . The enemy was in front of and behind us, and with no means of escape, the women, children, and elders were told to climb the mountain and hide among the rocks, while the rest fought the enemy soldiers before them.[13]

On July 7, the full force of a regiment from the 11th Division joined with allied forces and the air force to launch a general offensive. Three jets bombed and strafed people hiding out on the mountaintop. The monk Nyima remembers how he barely survived the bombing:

> When the bombs exploded on the mountain, shards of rock flew in all directions, and smoke hid the sky. My ears seemed to lose their function amidst the thunderous roar. Most of the people on the mountain were women, children, and elderly people, and the bombing by the airplanes sent blood and flesh flying everywhere, and severed limbs lay all about. When the airplanes left the sky above us, I heard the wailing and weeping of women and the wounded. The airplanes circled around again and dropped more bombs and strafed the mountain. I don't know how I managed to survive—I couldn't think and had no sense of direction, I just kept running. At least 60 people were blown to bits near me, and the others were bloodied by rock fragments. Two people next to me were blown in half.[14]

After two days of slaughter, almost all the Tibetans had either been killed, been taken prisoner, or had surrendered after running out of ammunition. By the afternoon of July 8, "the majority of the armed rebels" had been "annihilated" by the PLA.

On July 9, some of the PLA troops headed south and another group headed north to launch a "fishnet search" through every valley and cave. Some of the nomads who had escaped were hiding in the valleys east of the lake. The PLA air force opened the hatch of a transport plane, tied a heavy machine gun to the floor, and flew between the mountains shooting at any "bandits" it found.[15]

On July 12, the deputy commander of the 54th Army, Wei Tongtai, held a war council and ordered the troops to go out in platoons and squads and rigorously search every valley and mountain pass. "As soon as you discover bandits, you must chase them down and resolutely exterminate them."[16]

The Battle of Namtso ended on July 26 with the complete annihilation of the 4,000-plus "armed rebels." The Lanzhou Military Command 11th Infantry Division that was part of the main force in the battle claimed the following accomplishments:

> In 24 days of battle, annihilated 2,188 bandits (332 dead, 47 wounded, 1,107 taken prisoner, 702 surrendered), liberated 13,132 [sic] women and children, and captured 639 firearms of various kinds, 5,165 rounds of ammunition, 752 knives and spears, 317 horses, 9 pairs of binoculars, and 32,360 head of cattle and sheep. More than 100 horses were killed or wounded.[17]

According to Ding Sheng's memoirs, the Battle of Namtso "annihilated 2,035 enemies, liberated 1,151 coerced masses, and seized 531 firearms of various kinds and 4,223 rounds of ammunition."[18] Ding referred to this campaign as "the first successful battle of annihilation in the pacification of the rebellions in the TAR's pastoral regions." What the general didn't mention was that the targets of this campaign were a dozen or so nomad tribes, and that 74% of the Tibetans that the army annihilated had been unarmed.

An official publication from 2008 includes an account of this battle but doesn't provide details or mention the PLA's "military success." However, it describes how the 11th Infantry Division "gathered in" and protected "lost and scattered livestock" along Namtso Lake, and how it took care of more than 2,200 "masses without food, clothing, or shelter" around the lake after the battle.[19]

3

After the Namtso campaign, the PLA troops that had participated in it spent three weeks resting and reorganizing, after which the TMC and Ding Headquarters launched the Mitikha (Maidika) campaign on August 26.[20]

Mitikha is the source area of the Miti Tsangpo (Maidi Zangbu) River,[21] east of the Nagchu-Damshung stretch of the Qinghai-Tibet highway and south of the vital communication line from Nagchu to Chamdo. The PLA launched a large-scale preemptive military operation against herders gathered in this area in order to safeguard transportation routes.

Mitikha is a major watershed on the Nyenchen Thanglha range, a wetland with a surface area of nearly 900 square kilometers, at an average of nearly 4,800 meters above sea level. Its rich water sources, vast stretches of grassland, and swamp made it a purely pastoral area. The Chinese government hadn't established direct contact with herders in this area before 1959, and the nearest PLA garrison was in Nagchu. Nomads fleeing from Qinghai had settled there since the latter half of 1958, and survivors of the Battle of Lhasa had also fled to this area. By the summer of 1959, the area hosted 20 refugee groups along with local herding communities, for a total of 80 communities[22] with a population of more than 13,000, of which around 5,000 were "combat-ready."[23] Most were distributed around Pu Tso (Pengcuo) Lake, with a few scattered around Sangchen Sumdo (Sanqingsongduo)[24] and other areas.

The newcomers pastured their animals alongside the locals. They weren't prepared for battle, and therefore had no unified command or operations. According to Chinese sources, a conflict broke out between local nomads and Chinese government organs in Sog Dzong (Suozong) on August 12,[25] which Tibetan sources relate in greater detail.[26] Perhaps because of this, the TMC decided to launch the Battle of Mitikha in August 1959 instead of 1960 as originally planned. The operations of the TMC and reinforcements from outside were unified under an allied command post led by the deputy commander of the 54th Army, Wei Tongtai.

Unlike the hastily organized Battle of Lhoka, the successful Battle of Namtso had provided Zhang Guohua, Ding Sheng, and the others with experience in synthesized warfare on the Tibetan plateau, which in turn allowed them to prepare detailed planning for the Mitikha campaign. It was divided into three phases:

PHASE 1: At 5 p.m. on August 27, PLA units would complete their encirclement, and from August 28 to September 6 they would launch attacks on the pastoralists of Mitikha.

PHASE 2: From September 7 to September 16, PLA units would "clean up" the survivors in the area.

PHASE 3: From mid-September to early December, one regiment would stay behind to continue searching for "bandit remnants" while the rest of the units withdrew.

The main engagement was in the area of Pu Tso Lake, with the ring of encirclement expanded to include Sangchen Sumdo, southwestern Nagchu County, Driru (Biru), and other adjoining areas. Pu Tso lies in a basin at the upper eastern limit of the Mitikha wetland, bordering Driru. The area around the lake is ringed by mountain ranges and crisscrossed by ravines. By sending troops to hold the ravines, the PLA could cut off the escape routes around the lake.

The TMC deployed four regiments, including two artillery battalions, one cavalry regiment, and motorized and armored units, to attack Mitikha from four directions, centered on Pu Tso. The troops coming from each of the four directions divided into 3 groups each, making a total of 12 groups, to form a two-layered ring around Mitikha, the inner ring enclosing the lake and the outer ring catching those who attempted to flee. This battle plan required tightly controlling the major passes of the

Mitikha region to prevent anyone getting through, after which the main force of the troops would insert into the center from four directions. In the process, they would wipe out the scattered nomads while tightening the encirclement, pushing the "armed rebels" toward the lake to annihilate them completely.

The encirclement was set for August 27. The PLA units began preparing on August 10, and cadres at the level of squad leader and above were all trained to deal with the terrain. In order to ensure ready access to supplies throughout the battle, the logistics department organized civilian workers to quickly construct a 50-kilometer highway[27] and established five supply depots near the battle area, where 847 tons of goods were transported, while also organizing a transport team of 6,179 yaks.[28]

4

In the first half of 1959, Khyungpo Tengchen was another place that saw heavy military confrontation.

Historically, Tengchen was part of the 39 Hor *tsowa*,[29] a region of western Kham with a distinct ethnic, political, and religious identity, in what are now the Nagchu and Chamdo prefectures of the TAR. The Hor rulers had a long history of animosity toward the Lhasa government, which had reasserted its rather tenuous control of the region after 1912.

The TWC's Hortso 39 branch was established in July 1951, before Zhang Jingwu, the director of the TWC, entered Lhasa, and was one of the first three branches founded in addition to the Lhasa City branch.[30] In 1958, the Tengchen CCP subcommittee and government office had about 60 cadres based in the former *dzong* building, guarded by a company of PLA soldiers stationed across the river.

In the middle of 1958, the Karu Pon, a Tengchen chieftain and chairman of the Tengchen Liberation Committee, mobilized some 2,000 tribal militia and wrote a letter to the Chamdo Liberation Committee listing a number of Chinese misdeeds and demanding that the PLA troops and offices leave the area.[31] The Chamdo Liberation Committee denied the allegations in the letter and ordered the cadres and soldiers to prepare for rebellion. On January 4th, 1959, the Chinese cadres were organized into armed militia.

In January, Karu Pon and his men made a plan to attack the *dzong*, hoping to drive the Chinese out. On January 23, dozens of Tibetans hid in the houses close by. The next morning, when the soldiers opened the main gate to post a sentry, dozens of Tibetans poured in and launched a sudden attack. Both Tibetan and Chinese sources state that the attack was not successful. Most of the attackers were killed in the battle; the rest retreated. Sources differ on the Chinese casualties: the Tibetan source claims that more than 10 PLA soldiers were killed; the Chinese source states that 1 soldier was wounded and 2 killed, including the deputy commander.[32] After the attack, the occupants of the *dzong* fled for the greater safety of the army camp.

A couple of days later, hundreds of Chushi Gangdruk fighters arrived at Tengchen. They brought cannon and shelled the camp. They surrounded it, but their weapons were insufficient to take it, and the stalemate lasted for about three months. Shortly after the siege started, however, the air force bombed Tengchen for ten days and killed a large number of local residents.[33]

According to the Tibetan source, the Tibetan fighters then decided to withdraw in order to lessen the ongoing civilian casualties, and the Chushi Gangdruk force headed for Lhoka.[34] Chinese sources give no clear account: one source claims that the siege was not completely lifted until the middle of July.[35]

Many of those fighters retreated into Sog Dzong and joined forces with the local fighters. They became part of the targets for the Battle of Mitikha.

While the PLA commanders were busy making battle preparations, resistance groups in the Hor region of eastern Nagchu laid siege to the garrison occupying Sog Dzong. Sog Dzong was the site of Tsenden Monastery, a famous monastery and the largest in the area, and the Lhasa government had established a *dzong* administration there in 1916. In May 1959, a Sog County (Souxian) administration was created under the Nagchu prefecture.[36] Two months later, the county party committee was established and stationed in the Tsenden Monastery.[37]

The siege of Sog started in the 6th lunar month (August–September 1959).[38] An alliance of local militia, numbering some 3,000 according to Tibetan sources, encircled the Tsenden Monastery from three sides, with the Sokchu River on the remaining side. The monastery had been built on an isolated hilltop, with a village below. The Chinese had the advantage of shooting down from the roof of the main assembly hall. Poorly armed and lacking heavy weapons, the Tibetans were not able to dislodge them. The siege went on for about a month.

One Chinese source states that on August 12, the rebels "suddenly launched a large-scale attack."[39] That day, about 80 Tibetan fighters stormed into the monastery and captured the main assembly hall. However, they were not able to fight their way up to the roof, and the Chinese cadres and soldiers managed to escape by night.[40]

News of the attack was cabled to General Wei Tongtai, PLA field commander of the Battle of Mitikha.[41] Wei decided to adjust the battle plan, ordering two battalions to seal roads and mountain passes to the east of Sog and Driru, then send bombers to break the siege. Wei's plan was to use the bombing to create a false impression that the PLA's main target was Sog and Driru, rather than Mitikha, to drive those fleeing Sog into the Pu Tso area, as the other escape routes would be blocked. Wei's troops would then be able to wipe out the local resistance forces all at once.

Three days later, on August 15th, the bombing of Sog started.[42] Of the 16 bombs dropped that day, 7 "hit the bull's eye,"[43] and more than 200 Tibetans were killed or wounded.[44] Chinese sources do not specify how many days the bombing lasted; Tibetan sources say it lasted several days.[45] On August 18th, one battalion of PLA reinforcements arrived at Sog. By this time, most Tibetan survivors had left. Some of them headed southeast toward Pelbar while others went north to Nyenrong (Nierong),[46] to join the resistance forces already gathering there. They would become the targets of the Zone 1 and Zone 2 campaigns the following year.

5

On August 19 and 20, one PLA regiment split into three groups and proceeded north from Manshung (Mila),[47] Kongpo Gyamda (Gongbu Jiangda), and Drugla (Zhula)[48] to Lhari, and by the 27th had gained control of all of the mountain passes in southeast Mitikha.

On August 21, another regiment set off, also in three groups, with one battalion traveling by motor vehicle from Lhasa north to Koluk (Gulu)[49] on the Qinghai-Tibet highway and then marching east into Mitikha. This unit gained control of the passes in southwestern Mitikha by the 25th. The other two battalions reached their designated locations on that same day and took control of the mountain passes on the northern side.

One artillery regiment set off on August 22nd and crossed the Miti Tsangpo River, closing off the west side of Mitikha. This line was close to the Qinghai-Tibet highway, and heavy weapons were deployed here in order to prevent the tribes from joining together to charge across the highway. The TMC's armored unit arrived in the Nagchu to Shachukha (Xiaqiuka)[50] road area at dawn on August 26 and then patrolled Damshung, Nagchu, and Shachukha as the second blockade line west of Mitikha.

On the 24th, a regiment of the 11th Infantry Division set off to insert itself into the south side of Mitikha and close off all the mountain passes there.

On the same day, another three companies from the division rushed up the Qinghai-Tibet highway from the Namtso area to Driru, and the next day they dispersed among the mountain passes east, south, and north of Mitikha as an outer block line.

Also on the same day, three 120-mm light-mortar companies from the TMC's 308th Artillery Regiment set off from Lhasa, reaching the southwest side of Mitikha on the 26th and sealing off the mountain passes on the south side. And finally, four companies under the TMC had left Lhasa and reached their designated locations that same night, blocking off the mountain passes northeast of Mitikha.

All of the military units had settled into their designated locations by 5 p.m. on August 27.

The Battle of Mitikha began, and as it developed, the 12 army units split again into 36 groups, forming multiple layers as they pressed toward Pu Tso Lake.

Chinese sources indicate that the most intense fight in this campaign was the Battle of Mount Techen.[51] On one side was a PLA infantry battalion and on the other, about 300 "rebel bandits" and "a few hundred ordinary people,"[52] possibly three tribes from Yulshul. After the nomads realized that the PLA had surrounded them, they moved east to look for a breakthrough point, encountering a PLA battalion in the process. During this extremely violent battle, the battalion used cavalry to head off 70 mounted tribesmen attempting to force their way through. The PLA fired light and heavy machine guns to repel them, forcing them up to the crest of the mountain range, where another company attacked them. The nomads, men and women, old and young, cried out as they threw rocks down on the soldiers, and more than 100 men tied themselves together with a leather rope and carried out a suicide attack. Both sides fought until they ran out of ammunition, after which the Tibetans stabbed at the PLA soldiers with their swords in desperate hand-to-hand fighting. Finally, three companies of PLA reinforcements arrived, and their numerical superiority quickly brought the battle to a close. During the two-hour battle, 119 Tibetan herders were killed, 61 wounded, and 129 taken prisoner,[53] while 15 PLA soldiers were killed and 5 were wounded.[54] In Ding Sheng's memoir, this was the greatest "military success" of the Mitikha campaign.[55]

The campaign ended on September 20 with the PLA claiming the following accomplishments: "More than 40 large and small battles, 5,563 enemies annihilated, including 2,869 persuaded to surrender, 2,438 firearms of various kinds captured, and 7,517 coerced masses liberated."[56] These figures indicate that the number "annihilated" composed 42% of the total of 13,080 people, while the number of weapons seized corresponded to only 18.6% of the targeted Tibetans.

Before the Mitikha campaign, the TMC had scouted out the area and gained an understanding of the local situation through "internal connections." When the Chinese government entered Tibet, it established an office in Nagchu in 1951 and a TWC branch in 1953, followed by the establishment of several *dzong* party committees from 1956 onward. The TWC was therefore not entirely ignorant of the situation in the pastoral region. They knew very well that the "10,000-odd people" in Mitikha were mainly refugees and local herders with rustic weapons and limited combat capacity. What, then, was the point of such a massive campaign, drawing on four regiments of airmen, cavalry, infantry, artillery, and armored units and arranging a dual-layered encirclement, not to mention bringing in immense amounts of supplies while the inland was suffering from the Great Famine?

Decades later, General Ding Sheng revealed in his memoir: "In this battle . . . [our troops] accumulated experience with large army units encircling and fighting and implementing and executing policy in the pastoral area, achieving the anticipated battle objective."[57]

That is to say, one of the anticipated objectives of the Mitikha campaign was to practise the military tactic of "large army units encircling the enemy." It was combat training using the lives of Tibetan nomads. This was the directive that Mao Zedong repeatedly gave to the CMC and the TMC in his memos.[58]

The 11th Infantry Division's post-battle summary referred to the "encirclement tactic" as "the most basic and most effective military tactic for annihilating large numbers of rebel bandits."[59] From then on, this tactic was employed in other battles in Tibet and became the fundamental military tactic of the TWC and the Ding and Huang command posts.

Miraculously, Ngolo managed to escape the PLA's large and small encirclements. She, her baby daughter, and her husband, along with other refugees, proceeded northwest from the Namtso area, reduced to a massacre site by the PLA, into Changthang, which was still safe for now.

Chapter 21

ENCIRCLING THE PLATEAU IN THE DEPTHS OF WINTER

1

At the end of 1959, Chinese military operations had been ongoing for four years in Sichuan, nearly two years in Qinghai, and nearly one year in central Tibet. PLA troops had occupied cities, towns, and pastoral regions on the Tibetan plateau, pressing Tibetan resistance forces into remote, mountainous regions. By the beginning of 1960, some 30,000 Tibetans were reported to have "openly engaged in armed rebellion" in Tibet.[1]

On January 16, 1960, the TMC held a war council and proposed a Great Leap Forward-type slogan: "In the War of 1960, clear out the bandit gangs in autumn, clear out the remnants at the end of the year, and basically complete democratic reform."[2]

The war council divided future military operations into four battle zones with numerical designations. The western portion, governed by the Chamdo Liberation Committee, was Zone 1; the border area between Qinghai and Tibet was Zone 2; the area around Dingri and Saga[3] southwest of Shigatsé (Rikaze) was Zone 3; and the area southwest of Chamdo was Zone 4. Zones 1 and 2 were designated the focal battle zones. The Ding Command Post would be responsible for Zones 1 and 2, the 11th Infantry Division would be responsible for Zone 3 and the Ngari (Ali) Garrison, and troops under the Huang Command Post[4] and

Chamdo Garrison would be responsible for Zone 4.[5] To achieve the goal, the TMC went against convention by advancing in winter[6] and bringing the battle schedule forward to late February and early March, a time of frigid temperatures, when snow blanketed the plateau's mountain passes.[7]

To ensure the success of battles in Zone 1, the first battle in 1960 was fought in Zone 3.

From February 21 to March 20, the TMC deployed ten battalions of infantry and cavalry[8] in a "big encirclement" tactic for the Battle of Zone 3. This battle zone extended east to Shentsa (Shenzha);[9] west to Saga; north to the area of Lake De'u Yangtso (Tanyanghu), Lake Dangra Yutso (Dangreyongcuo), and Lake Trari Namtso (Zharinanmucuo);[10] and south to Dingri, covering parts of Ngari, Nagchu, and Shigatsé regions.

This battle aimed at annihilating "seven bandit rebel gangs" that had gathered there. The "bandit rebels" numbered more than 3,700,[11] of whom around 2,800 were "battle-ready"; the entire group was said to have "1,450 rifles, more than 700 musketeers, and more than 1,800 horses."[12] Reportedly, these "rebel bandits" were led by Powo Amgön, a prominent local headman, and Arak-tsang, a "well-known lama from Qinghai,"[13] but Chinese sources make no mention of these herders engaging in any military actions in that area. A military source says that these rebels were "running rampant, plundering the people's cattle and sheep, and forcing the masses to take part in the rebellion."[14] The sketchy narrative suggests that this group of people consisted of seven nomad groups and their livestock, some of them having fled Qinghai with a well-known lama.

These herders hadn't engaged in hostilities against the PLA, so why were they targeted for the first attack of 1960? It was because this scarcely populated pastoral area more than 4,000 meters above sea level abutted Nepal and Bhutan to the south, providing a potential escape route to fleeing Tibetans. Following Mao Zedong's instructions that the basic principle and strategy in the "pacification of rebellion" was to "close the doors to beat the dog," by choosing this area for its first battle in 1960s, the TMC aimed at preventing Tibetans from escaping across the border into Nepal and Bhutan. The fact that the herders grouped close together during the winter made it easy for the army to "round up and wipe out the whole gang."[15]

In February 1960, the 11th Infantry Division moved its command post from Da Qaidam,[16] Qinghai province, to Shigatsé, under TMC's unified command. The 33rd Regiment advanced into Tibet together with the division's command post. The division's artillery and antiaircraft gun regiments had been moved to Gansu from Qinghai for training while waiting for orders to be deployed into Tibet.

The Battle of Zone 3 was also divided into the "attacking phase" and the "cleanup phase." The plan was to deploy a PLA force of ten battalions strong to round up and wipe out the herders in the area covering Lake De'u Yangtso, Lake Dangra Yutso, and the Mendong Monastery.[17]

On February 21, 1960, the battle was formally launched. In the following couple of weeks, PLA troops pressed from different directions toward the battle area. However, the herders led by Arak-tsang had left the area and escaped westward before the PLA military operations started. Local herders led by Powo Amgön also escaped toward the Mendong Monastery. The PLA troops brought in reinforcements and planned to lay out an enormous encirclement in the area surrounding the monastery. About a week later, one infantry regiment and one cavalry detachment managed to reach the Mendong Monastery, only to find that Powo Amgön and his men had escaped again, this time toward Ngari. Due to the intense cold, a large number of PLA soldiers suffered frostbite, and many lagged behind, slowing down the entire troop. Because of this, other troops never made it to their designated locations to form the encirclement ring. To make things worse, the troops that did make it to Mendong then ran out of provisions and had to pull back to Nagchu.[18]

As in other battles, the PLA troops were chasing an imagined "rebel main force," but in reality, the herders were not organized as a formal army. Large groups would break up into small ones during fighting and escape, fleeing in different directions. After several weeks of chasing, encircling, and fighting, the PLA commanders found themselves unable to find and engage any "rebel main force" in Zone 3, and also failed to catch Powo Amgön. As a result, Powo Amgön led his men out of the net.

It took another year and 60 more battles before he finally surrendered, in March 1961.

The first stage of the Battle of Zone 3 ended on March 12, 1960. During this stage, the PLA troops "fought 25 battles, annihilated 409 enemies, and seized 232 firearms of various kinds."[19]

After resting and reorganizing, the PLA launched the second stage, aimed at "cleaning up the bandit rebels" and establishing local government. This phase lasted from March 26 to May 10. In this stage, the PLA troops broke down into small units to search for herders hiding in the mountains. Also in this stage, the PLA troops fought 13 battles in which 1,379 "bandits" were "annihilated" and 1,245 firearms were seized.[20] This gave the TWC control over the area west of Shentsa, south of the Nagchu-Ngari highway, and north of the Yarlung Tsangpo (Yalu Zangbu) River.

In accordance with the CMC's principle of "pacifying one area, consolidating one area, and then shifting to another area," the combat troops fought while at the same time "establishing 42 rebellion pacification and security preservation committees and 73 subgroups among some 11,560 people in 60 tribes and 19 monasteries, and completing the 'three antis and three calculations'[21] in the 8 monasteries with a larger number of monks and nuns." All of this was to "lay a solid foundation for the government to establish grassroots political power and carry out democratic reform."[22]

In the Battle of Zone 3, 453 Tibetans were killed, 448 were taken prisoner, and 887 surrendered, while the PLA seized 197 rifles, 1,280 crude firearms, 3,649 rounds of ammunition, 687 knives and spears, and 432 horses.[23]

The 11th Infantry Division summarized the significance of this battle:

> This battle further enriched the experience of the troops in fighting in the plateau region; gave troops the most realistic tempering in a harsh environment; mastered methods of working on the Tibetan masses in the pastoral areas, testing cadres and enhancing combat effectiveness; while mobilizing the masses in intense social reform, providing the mass of officers and men with a profound class education.[24]

Nevertheless, the Battle of Zone 3 was considered a failure, because the troops failed to wipe out the rebels' main force; one of the regiment commanders was disciplined for this.[25]

2

After a brief rest and regroup, the Ding Command Post launched the Battle of Zone 1, "in order to quickly make up for the failure to annihilate the main rebel force in Zone 3."[26]

Zone 1 included 15 *dzongs*,[27] with Pelbar at the center, in the border area administered by today's Chamdo, Nyingtri, and Nagchu cities. The war zone extended 300 kilometers east to west and 200 kilometers north to south, in a region at an average height of 4,000 meters above sea level. In 1958, Gonpo Tashi had led part of the main force of the Chushi Gangdruk Defenders of the Faith to this area and rallied the support of local residents. According to Chinese sources, of the 15 *dzongs* in Zone 1, "bandit rebels completely controlled Bianba [Pelbar], Shading [Sateng], and Shuodu [Shopamdo], while the other *dzongs* were occupied in full or in part by bandits."[28] The TMC believed that there were "more than 14,000 bandit rebels" in this region, including more than 5,000 "core members" possessing "more than 5,000 steel guns and more than 100 light and heavy machine guns."[29] The term "core members" in official Chinese sources usually refers to people who are capable of fighting, which would be men in the prime of life.

After Gonpo Tashi led the main force of Chushi Gangdruk out of Tibet, Pelbar and the nearby area became one of the hubs of the Tibetan resistance. A Tibetan source also shows that by this time, refugees from other regions, former Tibetan army officers and soldiers, and militia from Pomé had gathered in the Pelbar area. Together with the local tribal militia led by Pelbar Rinpoché and the Tibetan government official Dudul Choying, they formed a semiformal military force with a few thousand men.[30] However, they did not form a unified organization nor an overall battle plan. In September 1959, 19 Tibetans trained by the CIA were airdropped into this area. The CIA also made 7 airdrops of weapons from October 1959 to January 1960.[31] Even so, the 14,000 people in the area possessed only 5,000 "steel weapons" (rifles), meaning that only 36% of them were properly armed. According to PLA sources, the unarmed people in these 15 *dzongs* were "coerced local masses,"[32] i.e., women, children, the elderly, and an unknown number of monks.

The commander of the 54th Army, Ding Sheng, treated the Battle of Zone 1 as a mission to be accomplished to its fullest extent. The TMC transferred 9 regiments, with a total fighting force of 18,000, to "assemble a superior military force for a battle of annihilation" in coordination with the air force.[33] Sending 18,000 PLA[34] troops to fight 5,000 Tibetans armed with 1 rifle each and a total of 100 machine guns was of course unlikely to result in any surprises.

On January 6, 1960, the Ding Command Post received a report that a PLA intelligence post in Lholung (Luolong) was under attack by some 1,000 Tibetans, and that the division had deployed about seven companies to encircle the enemies. The headquarters dispatched two battalions as reinforcement, with orders to wipe out all the rebels at any cost. This was the first military engagement in the Battle of Zone 1.[35] The next day, the Ding Command Post held a special war council in Lhasa to formulate its battle tactics. The war council decided to start out by forming a large encirclement with small skirmishes to surround and annihilate the enemy, using the method of "layers of encirclement and peeling the skin one layer at a time" to eliminate the resisting Tibetans in Pelbar and Shopamdo.[36] The council also required the troops taking part in the battle to maintain strictly unified operations: "Strike hard in hot pursuit, don't hesitate to grab one or one thousand, make small victories accumulate into big victories, and don't let a single bandit slip through the net."[37] The Ding Command Post was well prepared for this battle. In November 1959, it had sent ten companies of troops to establish intelligence posts in the area, while also carrying out pre-battle drills, replenishing equipment, sending civilian workers to quickly build highways, and organizing some 10,000 yaks to transport supplies.[38]

The PLA deployed an infantry regiment and two armored vehicle companies on the highways from Nagchu to Amdo Méma (Anduo Maima)[39] and from Nagchu to Sog (Suo County), blocking off roads and mountain passes on the west side of the war zone that fleeing Tibetans might take to the Qinghai and Changthang plateaus. Three infantry regiments proceeded from Zhamog to Tengchen for blockading and encirclement, cutting off the escape routes on the east side of the war zone. At the same time, three regiments pierced the encirclement, two from north to south and one from south to north, while the rest of the troops were responsible for attacking and cleaning up the enemy.[40]

On February 8, the Ding Command Post held another war council at Zhamog, with the objective of "unifying the guiding concepts for battle"[41] and ensuring that all commanding officers understood the objective of the battle.

By February 25, the PLA battle units had amassed along the edges and created a circle around the battle zone.

By February 28, all of the PLA battle units had completed their preparations.

On February 29, the Battle of Zone 1 was officially launched.

This battle was split into three phases. The first phase, from March 8 to March 15, aimed at "sweeping the perimeter": the *dzongs* encircling Pelbar, including Bankar, Sateng, Yi-ong (Yigong), Lholung, and Tengchen. The objective of the "sweep" was to eliminate small resistance forces and at the same time drive larger resistance groups toward the main battlefield. On March 11 and 12, two PLA air force Ilyushin Il-28 bombers made a total of 12 sorties to Pelbar and Lhatsé (Lazi)[42] for bombing and strafing.[43]

The second phase, from March 16 to April 15, aimed at "advancing to attack the heart," i.e., surrounding and annihilating the "main force of bandit rebels" on the battlefield.

The third phase, beginning on April 16, aimed at "searching and cleaning up." After 47 days of fighting, the PLA had racked up the following accomplishments:

> Annihilated 12,200 of the enemy, including 1,140 killed, 4,820 taken prisoner, 1,049 surrendered, and 5,150 won over politically (46.3% of the total annihilated). Seized seven recoilless guns, 6,910 firearms of various kinds, more than 387,000 rounds of ammunition, 5,733 knives and

spears, 2,061 mules and horses, 6 radio transceivers, and 268 parachutes and other items.[44]

On April 16, the Battle of Zone 1 switched to the third and final phase, i.e., the "cleanup" phase. In the following weeks, PLA soldiers and local CCP committees launched a "widespread and powerful political assault" on the remnants of Tibetan resistance. Soldiers went from door to door to pressure local residents to bring back their male family members. More than 3,000 rebels surrendered and returned home, bringing back 2,700 guns of various kinds. During this phase, sporadic battles took place in many places, and more than 300 rebels who refused to surrender were captured and killed.

The Battle of Zone 1 was one of the bloodiest battles fought in Tibet. Nine PLA regiments, aided by the air force, pursued and attacked "bandit rebels," including more than 10,000 local residents. After the battle, the participating PLA units were publicly commended in a CMC bulletin.

Decades later, Zhang Xiangming, director of the TWC General Office in 1959, wrote in his memoir (restricted to internal circulation):

> At the time of the 1959 armed rebellion, rebel elements were running rampant in the Bianba [Pelbar] and Shading [Sateng][45] area. When the rebellion was at its worst in Changdu, it also started in the Bianba area. Local armed rebels active in the area of Bianba and Shuobanduo [Shopamdo] exterminated a company of our soldiers. So when our troops pacified the rebellion in this area, they also killed a lot of people. It's hard to work in the Bianba area even today, because nearly every family lost someone.[46]

In the late 1970s, Sichuan, Qinghai, Kanlho (Gannan), and other areas made a gesture to redress the "enlargement of the pacification of rebellion" of the 1950s by providing small amounts of compensation to the victims. In March 1979, the TAR "applied leniency" to more than 6,000 of the "rebellion participants" of 1959 who were still in custody or under surveillance,[47] [48] but it didn't reexamine all of the cases from 1959 to 1961, and in fact wasn't even willing to acknowledge the "enlargement of the pacification of rebellion," mainly because the "military firmly disagreed":

> It's impossible to speak of an enlargement of the pacification of rebellion. Who among them [the military] knew if they were attacking rebels or the masses? . . . So the military firmly refused to mention an enlargement of the pacification of rebellion [in reports to the Central Committee]. . . . If even the 1959 pacification required renewed implementation of policy, what would become of Tibet?[49]

This indicates that PLA commanders and soldiers knew full well what kind of people they were attacking and killing in battle.

3

On April 20, 1960, while the cleanup phase of the Battle of Zone 1 was still going on, the Ding Command Post launched the Battle of Zone 2.

Zone 2 was the alpine pastoral region along the Qinghai-Tibet border, covering Mugshung (Moyun),[50] Drachen (Baqing),[51] Nyenrong, Nagchu, and Amdo (Anduo).[52] The main focus was the area of Changthang across the Thanglha range from Nyenrong and Sog. There are many streams and lakes in this area, with an average elevation of 4,000 meters above sea level; the largest lake is Nira Tso-gen (Yirancuogai),[53] at 35.1 square kilometers. The Damchu (Dangqu) River, one of the three main sources of the Yangtze, also flows through the area. Traditionally, it was a pastureland inhabited by several nomad groups.

It is likely that refugees from Qinghai and Sichuan had gathered in this area since 1958, and after the series of major battles in Tibet after March 1959, survivors fled there as well. By the middle of 1959, around 5,000 people had gathered around the Nira Tso-gen Lake. Added to the local population of over 4,000, that made more than 10,000 people in the area. They formed a loosely organized resistance army, divided into seven groups according to their origins,[54] with Nangchen Loba Lama and the Sogde chieftain Norbu Tsering as general commanders.[55]

In September 1959, the CIA's Team 6 of trainees discovered this group. They reported the news to the CIA and requested weapons assistance. From December 13, 1959 to January 15, 1960, the CIA sent eight planes to this area, in three trips, and dropped a large quantity of guns, explosives, medical supplies, etc.[56] Chinese sources claim that the group had about 3,000 rifles, 200 light machine guns, 10 antiaircraft machine guns, 10 cannon, and 6 to 7 transmitters,[57] but Tibetan sources indicate that they had much more.[58]

On January 15, 1960, the CIA inserted the 16-member Team 7 in the Nira Tso-gen area to assist the group. They organized the resistance army, separating fighters from their families[59] and training them in guerrilla warfare tactics. Their aim was to disrupt traffic on the Qinghai-Tibet highway, the PLA's main supply line, and although available sources do not show active engagement prior to the battle, they were considered to have "a certain degree of combat capability"[60] and were thus a serious threat. Afraid that the area might become the next Tibetan resistance base, the PLA determined to destroy this group completely.

In March 1960, Luo Ruiqing, then a standing member of the CCP's CMC, the Deputy Defense Minister, and Chief of General Staff, chaired an "on-the-spot meeting for 'pacification of rebellion and border protection.'" In addition to related regional military commands, participants in this meeting included representatives from the General Staff, General Politics, and General Logistics departments. In the meeting, a decision was made that the Battle of Zone 2 was to be operated by "coordination between military commands."[61]

To achieve this goal, the Ding Command Post deployed eight regiments totaling more than 12,000 men from the Tibet, Qinghai, and Lanzhou Military Commands,[62] including artillery, cavalry, infantry, armored vehicle, and motorcycle units. In addition to combat troops, 1,707 civilian workers, 1,380 horses, and 8,518 yaks were drafted to provide logistical support.[63]

Ding Sheng used the same "encirclement strategy" for this battle. From April 27 to May 2, the participating PLA units split into 24 groups that converged simultaneously from the west, south, and southeast to form an enormous ring of encirclement 370 kilometers in circumference.[64] The plan was to launch the general attack on May 7, but air scouts discovered that Tibetans in the Nira Tso-gen area were slowly moving northwest. Believing that they were trying to escape into the areas west of the Qinghai-Tibet highway, Ding Sheng dispatched a powerful force, forming the west line of the encirclement, to seal that off, and launched the assault two days earlier.

By 6 a.m. on May 5, all units had arrived at their designated positions. Around 11:00 a.m, the PLA Xining Air Force Command Post joined the battle. In two days, 16 bombers carried out 32 rounds of bombings and strafings in the area where the Tibetan resistance fighters were concentrated.[65] Meanwhile, cavalry and infantry troops on the ground pressed in from all directions toward the Nira Tso-gen area, occupying strategic points and cutting the Tibetan forces into small groups. Outnumbered and inexperienced with such fierce battle, the Tibetans were not able to organize effective resistance, and even escape did not seem to be an option. Both Tibetan and Chinese sources state that PLA bombers chased the fleeing Tibetans and showered them with bombs and bullets.[66]

However, the Tibetan forces did not merely "scurry off in all directions," as the Chinese source describes it.[67] Directed by the CIA trainees, the Tibetan forces in fact scattered to fight separately against some of the PLA units. Both Chinese and Tibetan sources record some fierce battles after the Nira Tso-gen bombing.

At dawn on May 6, a PLA cavalry unit reached a place called Tayangdo.[68] The area was guarded by about 1,000 fighters from the local Sogde tribe, positioned on the surrounding hills. The cavalry unit immediately reported to the command post asking for reinforcement and launched an attack on the southern hill, which was reportedly guarded by about 200 Sogde fighters. Tibetans occupied the commanding heights, and the PLA charges were repeatedly beaten back. It took the cavalry unit six assaults to finally capture the hill by 2 p.m. Around 4 p.m., PLA reinforcements in the form of two cavalry regiments and one infantry battalion arrived. The battle lasted for almost four more hours, but by 7:45 p.m., all the hills were captured. The majority of the Tibetan fighters fought to the end; a small number of survivors broke through the surrounding lines, but were then forced to run east toward the center of the encirclement.[69]

Meanwhile, at another location, an infantry unit discovered a caravan of more than 300 yaks and about 40 people. The unit believed that it was a "rebel transportation team" and attacked it from two directions, "pressed it into a gully, and wiped it out."[70] The Chinese source does not give any evidence that the yak caravan was indeed a "rebel transportation team," and apparently the "team" did not resist while being attacked. It could just have been a passing caravan caught in the battle. When the PLA soldiers entered the gully, however, they were ambushed by Tibetan fighters from surrounding hills. This battle lasted for a couple of days. In the end, the Tibetan fighters were overwhelmed by the PLA reinforcements, while the unit that had "wiped out" the caravan suffered heavy losses, with "85% wounded and two dozen killed."[71]

Similar battles took place in many locations. By May 14, the major battles along the Thanglha range were completed. In this stage, "more than 4,000 rebel bandits were annihilated."[72] After this, PLA units pushed into the Behu Seldzong region, shrinking the encirclement ring from 370 down to 180 kilometers in circumference, and deployed half of the troops to tighten the encirclement ring. The rest of the units started to "clean up" scattered survivors. One cavalry unit "followed two families of Qinghai rebels," another "annihilated three families of Qinghai rebels." In order to "get rid of the burden of prisoners and large number of captured cattle," the unit left some soldiers behind to guard the captives, while the rest continued its "cleanup" by "annihilating two families of Sichuan rebels" in one location and "wiping out nine families of Qinghai and Sichuan rebels" in another.[73]

The Battle of Zone 2 ended on June 5, 1960.[74] The Ding Command Post, using 6 army branches with a force of more than 12,000 and 133 air force missions, including 37 bombings,[75] achieved the "annihilation of 5,084 people (including 7 airdropped enemy agents) under the commander-in-chief and Sogde chief Norbu Tsering; seized 2,249 long and short firearms, 180 light machine guns, 6 anti-aircraft machine guns, 7 recoilless cannon, and 6 radio transceivers"; and also "gathered up" 21,226 head of cattle and sheep.[76] Norbu Tsering was captured during the battle after he was heavily wounded, but there is no information about his fate or that of Nangchen Loba Lama.

This was the first battle that the PLA had fought on the plateau with "land and air coordinated battle operations and cooperation between military commands."[77] In other words, General Ding Sheng carried out a massive training exercise through actual battle in the name of "pacifying rebellion." In this battle, the air force dispatched various kinds of aircraft on 133 sorties, including 37 rounds of bombing and strafing.[78]

4

Two weeks after the Battle of Zone 2 was completed, the TMC deployed a force of around 5 regiments from the 11th Infantry Division and the 4th Division of the Xinjiang Military Command to launch the Battle of Ngari.

This battle zone was along the western Nepal border, between Lektse (Laze)[79] and the Kunggyu Tso (Gongzhu) Lake, covering an area of about 50 kilometers from north to south and 170 kilometers from east to west in Drongpa (Zhongba) County,[80] a sparsely populated pastoral area 4500 to 6000 meters above sea level.

The targets of the attack were Tibetans who had escaped from Lhasa, Lhoka, Namtso, and the Battle of Zone 3, as well as some 10,000 local nomads, of whom about 3,000 were "battle-ready," with about 1200 guns.[81] Beginning in May 1960, PLA troops had been moving into locations on the east, west, and north sides of the battle zone. Aware of the army buildup, refugees in the area began to escape into Nepal. By the middle of June, about 1,000 refugees had crossed the border.[82]

On June 20, troops moved into the battle area. The plan was to deploy four battalions plus one company to block major mountain passes on the northern (Tibetan) side of the Tibet-Nepal border, preventing rebels and refugees from escaping into Nepal. The next day, troops arrived at designated locations and began to "clean up" the rebels.

Before the battle started, the TWC's Ngari branch organized an armed work team of about 40 members to coordinate the combat troops. Eighty percent of the work team members were Tibetans, and all of them wore Tibetan-style clothes instead of army uniforms. However, their first, and probably most important, engagement, involved "friendly fire" with a PLA unit.

On the misty morning of June 24, the armed work team was resting in a valley after a whole night of marching when the sentry noticed a few armed horsemen appear on a nearby hilltop. Believing them to be escaping rebels, the team head ordered his men to climb a hill and take them by surprise. The horsemen soon discovered the approaching Tibetans, however, and opened fire. The team head ordered his men to get 6 machine guns together, and they showered the horsemen with bullets, taking down a few. After about three hours and a dozen casualties on each side, when the sun had dispersed the mist, the work team recognized that their "enemies" were in fact PLA soldiers. They stopped shooting, shouting out their identity, and took off their Tibetan robes to reveal army uniforms underneath. Altogether, 16 were killed and 11 wounded in this "friendly fire."

Four days after this incident, PLA soldiers opened fire on a group of Nepalis, the only engagement in the entire counterinsurgency that drew international attention.

At dawn on June 28, the sentry reported to the commander of the PLA company guarding the Kora La, a mountain pass leading to Nepal's Mustang area, that a dozen rebels on horseback were approaching the border. The soldiers quietly got into position and waited for them to come closer. As soon as the men entered their range, the soldiers opened fire. A couple of people in the party were gunned down; the rest dismounted and took cover. Sources differ after this point: available Chinese sources claim that at daybreak, the PLA unit discovered that the group were Nepali merchants. Soldiers brought the whole party back to their camp, including the body of the one dead merchant (who was in fact a Nepali police officer disguised as a merchant to find out what was happening on the Tibetan side of the border area), escorted them into a tent, treated the one wounded man, and reported the incident upwards through the chain of command.[83] According to sources in Nepal, however, six of the party managed to escape and brought the news to the outside world.[84] In July, after a series of diplomatic exchanges, the Chinese premier Zhou Enlai apologized to the government of Nepal and paid 50,000 rupees in compensation.[85]

Both incidents indicate that PLA units routinely opened fire on anyone of Tibetan appearance, armed or not.

The Battle of Ngari ended on July 28. Over the course of 32 days, the PLA claimed the following accomplishments:

> 49 large and small combat operations, 4,318 bandits annihilated (80 killed, 1,895 taken prisoner, 174 surrendered, 2,169 won over politically). Seized 1,192 steel firearms of various kinds, 1,611 crude firearms, 1,198 knives and spears, 4,095 rounds of ammunition, 878 horses, 17 binoculars, and liberated 6,223 women and children.[86]

The Battle of Ngari was commended as a major victory by the CMC General Staff Headquarters and General Political Department in their reports.[87] Of the 10,541 Tibetans directly involved in that battle, 6,223 (59%) were "liberated" women and children.[88]

FIGURE 11A AND 11B. Tibetan trainees at Camp Hale, Colorado.
Source: Office of Tibet, Washington, D.C. Used with permission.

FIGURE 12. Camp Hale memorial.
Source: Jianglin Li.

Chapter 22

THE MEN WHO FELL FROM THE SKY

1

One autumn day in 1958, the new head of the CIA's Far Eastern Division, Desmond Fitzgerald, notified the Tibet Task Force that the "5412 Special Group"[1] had approved continuing covert operations in Tibet.[2]

The CIA's covert operations against communist countries were a product of the Cold War, aimed at weakening communism's grip on other countries. Where conditions allowed, these operations developed underground resistance organizations and facilitated covert operations and guerrilla activities in countries ruled or threatened by communist regimes.[3] After news of hostilities in Kham reached India through Kalimpong in the spring of 1956, the CIA was interested: Resistance activities were occurring in China, a communist country and the Soviet Union's ally; the information was authentic and contact was reliable. Since a rudimentary resistance movement had already formed, it could be pushed forward with only a limited amount of assistance.[4]

All of this conformed to the CIA's stipulations for covert operations per NSC Document No. 5412. Therefore, in the summer of 1956, a new branch of the China section of the CIA's Far East Division was established: the Tibet Task Force, code-named ST CIRCUS.[5] The mission of this group was to train Tibetan intelligence operatives, who would teach guerrilla tactics to the rebel forces and provide necessary weapons and other supplies, while at the same time gathering intelligence for the CIA. The airdrop portion of this project was code-named ST BARNUM.[6]

By the fall of 1958, the first crew of CIA agents trained on Saipan Island had returned to Tibet and established contact with the CIA,[7] and the Chushi Gangdruk Defenders of the Faith had been established. In July of that year, the first ST BARNUM C-118 transport plane had successfully airdropped the first batch of weapons within Tibet's borders. Everything was going smoothly at that point.

ST CIRCUS immediately began preparing to train a second crew of operatives. Tibetans had a hard time acclimatizing to Saipan, so the task force decided to find a more suitable location in the United States. The highest elevation in the United States is in the Colorado Rocky Mountains, where a small town called Leadville is situated at 3,094 meters above sea level, the highest altitude of any town in the United States. Silver mines had been discovered in this area at the end of the nineteenth century, triggering a "silver rush" that caused the town's population to burgeon to the point where it became the second-largest city in Colorado. The silver rush quickly ended, however, and the occupants of Leadville vanished with it. As of 1958, the town had a population of just over 3,000. The nearby town of Redcliff had declined even further, from a silver town to a virtual ghost town, and the CIA considered it a perfect location: This was a land that few people knew about and the world had forgotten. Hidden in a valley near Leadville was an abandoned military base called Camp Hale, nicknamed the Ranch.

Camp Hale was built in 1942, not long after the United States entered World War II. At that time, it was the base for the US Army's 10th Mountain Division, providing soldiers with training in military tactics and survival skills in mountainous and snowy environments. At its peak, the base provided training for 14,000 soldiers and held 400 prisoners of war from Nazi Germany's Africa Corps. After the base was shut down in 1945, these prisoners were tasked with dismantling the structures. When ST CIRCUS sent people to inspect the site in autumn 1958, all that remained were a dozen or so empty buildings, with no electrical supply or running water. The army was more than happy to lend this base to the CIA, but by then the weather was cold and the ground frozen, and the base couldn't be handed over until spring, when electrical lines and water pipes could be laid.

Fortunately, the CIA had its own training base, Camp Peary, nicknamed the Farm, near Williamsburg, Virginia. ST CIRCUS established a temporary training base there, and in November 1958, the eight Khampas from Lithang arrived for half a year of intensive training. They attended classes seven days a week, learning map-reading, radio transmission, the handling of explosives, rock-climbing, parachuting, and other skills and guerrilla tactics.[8] The Dalai Lama's third-oldest brother, Lobsang Samten, sometimes went to Camp Peary for a few days at a time to serve as an interpreter. The second training period ended in March 1959, at which point ST BARNUM started off by sending the young Khampas back to Tibet with weapons and supplies.

It was just then that the situation in Tibet took a drastic turn.

The Lhasa uprising erupted on March 10, 1959 and the Dalai Lama, his family, and key government officials fled the city.[9] On March 22, Athar and Lotse, the radio operators for the CIA's first crew of trainees, rushed to Chongyé in Lhoka and met the Dalai Lama at the Riwo Dechen Monastery. From then on, Athar sent daily cables to CIA headquarters that were handed to President Eisenhower after being translated by the elderly monk Ngawang Wangyal.[10] On March 31, Athar sent his last cable from within Tibet's borders, notifying headquarters that the Dalai Lama had arrived safely in India, and requesting weapons for 30,000 people.[11] This request greatly exceeded what the CIA had in mind: from the outset, the objective of ST CIRCUS was "harassment" rather than war, and a plan of such scope was far beyond its purview.

For the CIA, the direct result of the Lhasa events was the loss of contacts within Tibet's borders. After receiving Athar's cable, ST CIRCUS and ST BARNUM immediately went into operation. This was while the PLA was still engaged in Lhoka. The main force of Chushi Gangdruk led by Gonpo Tashi may have already reached Lhuntsé, and would cross the McMahon Line a few days later, and Athar and Lotse were also about to withdraw from Tibet. A C-118 transport plane carrying weapons and supplies landed at Pakistan's Kurmitola Airport in mid-April, ready to lift off at a moment's notice, but without knowing where these weapons were to be dropped. The plan for the second group of trainees to return to Tibet also had to be shelved for the time being.[12]

That didn't mean the end of ST CIRCUS, however. After the Battle of Lhasa, the large number of refugees pouring into India made recruitment easy, and by then Camp Hale was ready as well. After a few setbacks, 15 Khampas and 3 Amdowas arrived in Colorado with 3 interpreters in mid-May 1959 to join the second crew of trainees, who by then had transferred from Virginia's Farm to Colorado's Ranch.

At Camp Hale, more than 3,000 meters above sea level and surrounded by mountains, the Tibetans felt at home. This was a top secret operation; even the trainees themselves were not informed of their location. The camp was surrounded by sentries to prevent intrusion by outsiders, and before field training, every detail was meticulously planned to prevent attracting notice. The CIA also issued a string of false information through the army to make local residents believe that this long-abandoned training base was doing national-security-related research. Local residents never even know there was a secret group of Asians living nearby.[13]

2

In March 2011, I sat at a long table in the archive room of the Hoover Institution at Stanford University, opened a folder, and carefully removed a pile of thin, yellowed sheets of paper covered in typewriting that had been copied using carbon paper. After 50 years, the type was fading. It was the record of a conversation in 1959 between the leader of ST CIRCUS, Roger E. McCarthy, and the commander of Chushi Gangdruk, Gonpo Tashi. The document was undated, but according to other sources, McCarthy spoke with Gonpo Tashi for three days in June 1959 in a secret location in Darjeeling, with Lhamo Tsering, Gyalo Dondrup's assistant, serving as interpreter.[14] ST CIRCUS personnel referred to this 50-odd-page document as the "blue paper." During this three-day conversation, Gonpo Tashi told McCarthy about his personal experience, the reasons for the Tibetan people's resistance, the establishment of Chushi Gangdruk, and the main battles they'd fought.[15]

Roger McCarthy had traveled to Darjeeling to see Gonpo Tashi not only to understand the situation and prospects of the Tibetan resistance, but for an even more pressing reason: The second training session at Camp Hale had finished, and sessions for the third crew had begun. The BARNUM aircraft was ready to take off at any time, but ST CIRCUS didn't know where it should airdrop its trainees. McCarthy hoped to obtain some information or suggestions from Gonpo Tashi. When the Chushi Gangdruk fighters entered India, they'd had to surrender all their weapons at the border and had become refugees. Survival was their first priority. Under these circumstances, could Chushi Gangdruk play any further role in the resistance movement? The contents of the "blue paper" show that Gonpo Tashi was unable to give McCarthy any clear answer to his question at that point.

Even so, tens of thousands of Tibetan refugees from various places had gathered in northern India in the summer of 1959, and they brought lots of information with them. After analyzing all the leads, ST CIRCUS felt relatively confident in reports that the Namtso Lake area still had active resistance groups. Maps showed that this area was relatively close to a highway and not too far from Lhasa, and several thousand people were said to have gathered there. Sending operatives there might make it possible to help the Tibetan resistance forces. Although there was no way to verify the intelligence, ST CIRCUS couldn't come up with any better ideas.[16]

One night in mid-September, a large bus quietly set out from Camp Hale. Arriving at Peterson Air Force Base near Colorado Springs in the dead of night, it made its way toward a C-130 Hercules military transport aircraft parked on the tarmac. As soon as the bus's occupants had boarded and taken their seats, the aircraft took off. The shades were securely fastened on the aircraft's windows in order to prevent anyone outside from looking in and to prevent those inside from looking out. After landing for refueling at McClelland Air Force Base near California's capital, Sacramento, the Hercules flew to Hawaii, where it refueled again at Hickam Air Force Base on Oahu.

In what seemed like an ill omen for the Namtso mission, an engine failed soon after takeoff, forcing the Hercules to return to Hickam. The occupants were then switched to another Hercules aircraft that flew straight to Okinawa, Japan, and then touched down at the Takhli Royal Thai Air Force Base on September 18. Late that night, the Hercules flew north with the second crew of operatives, a batch of weapons and supplies, two Khampas who had previously been left in Okinawa because they had contracted tuberculosis, and "kickers" who were responsible for tossing supplies out of the aircraft.

This would be BARNUM's third airdrop of personnel. The previous two both took place in September 1957, when BARNUM sent in two groups of six Lithang natives each, trained on Saipan Island. The first group had touched down near the Samye Monastery, and the second near Lithang. With the help of the first group, BARNUM had made two successful airdrops of weapons at Driguthang in Lhoka.

Now the Hercules flew over Burma and into Tibet, and the pilot soon saw a large lake glimmering in the moonlight below. Based on outdated maps, the pilot concluded that this was Namtso, where the third group was meant to land. The nine Khampas jumped out one by one. In case they were taken prisoner, they carried poisonous "L capsules" that would kill them in less than a minute.

The kickers tossed down a radio, weapons, medical supplies, and other items, and the Hercules flew back to Thailand.[17]

The leader of the third group, Ngawang Phuljung, who had taken the English name Nathan, had been assigned with transmitting a message by radio as soon as possible after hitting the ground to notify headquarters of their safe arrival. The members of ST CIRCUS waited anxiously in Thailand, but never received any news. Finally, several months later, Ngawang Phuljung reached Darjeeling by the overland route and contacted the CIA. Only then did ST CIRCUS learn that the information they'd received from the refugees was outdated: The PLA had already "cleared" that area, and the Battle of Namtso had ended more than a month before the third group landed. Even worse, the nine-member group had been dropped onto the wrong spot, an entire day's march from Namtso and near a PLA military camp.

After landing, the members of the group realized the danger they were in and that they might easily be discovered by the soldiers garrisoned nearby. The only thing they could do was to leave the drop-off point as quickly as possible. With no time to locate the supplies, they had no radio to contact headquarters. During their journey, they found the situation much different from when they'd left Tibet. PLA soldiers were scouring the area, and people didn't dare have any contact with them; some even suspected them of being Chinese cadres disguised as Tibetans and treated them with hostility. It was clear that they could serve no useful purpose, so they finally returned to Darjeeling through Nepal.[18]

Knowing nothing of this at the time, ST CIRCUS was hurriedly arranging to send another crew of operatives back to Tibet. This crew was divided into the fourth, fifth, and sixth groups, each with six members. ST CIRCUS planned to airdrop two of the groups into Pelbar and the other somewhere into Amdo.

Pelbar was chosen as a result of McCarthy's conversation with Gonpo Tashi. Although Gonpo Tashi was of course unable to predict the future of the resistance movement, he had mentioned that he had once led the main force of Chushi Gangdruk from Namling through northern Tibet to the Pelbar area, and had found people there intensely opposed to the Chinese communist regime. Chushi Gangdruk had helped them organize a resistance army that had expelled all the Chinese cadres, and Tibetans now completely controlled the area. ST CIRCUS took note of the location, and after some research, they felt resistance forces could be further developed there.

Another reason for choosing this location was that most of the members of these three latest groups of operatives came from Kham and Amdo and were familiar with the environment and local dialect, so their return would not attract undue notice.

The "Pelbar group" prepared and then set off from Camp Hale in mid-November 1959,[19] making its way to the Takhli base in the same way as the Namtso group had done.

3

Donyo Jagotsang, the son of Jagö Topden (the well-known and powerful minister of Dergé Gyalpo), sat in the cabin of the Hercules and adjusted the L capsule bound to his arm as he prepared to jump. After his companions had lined up and jumped one by one from the plane, Donyo took a deep breath as his instructor had taught him and took his turn. Twenty-two years old, he was the leader and radio operator of Group 4.[20]

The three groups had decided on airdrops at different locations, but at the last minute, ST CIRCUS changed the plan and had them all drop into Pelbar, ordering Group 6, the Amdowa group, to proceed from Pelbar to Yulshul.

The snowy mountains glowed pale blue in the light of the full moon, and a winding river glimmered below. In a valley, a monastery's golden roof emitted a gentle radiance. This was the Pelbar Monastery.[21] As Donyo dropped, the soil of his homeland reached up to him like a mother's embrace. Landing in the grass next to a small stream, he was reunited with his companions on either side. Dropping 18 people at once with so little information on the local situation was undoubtedly risky; they could easily fall into a trap. Fortunately, all of them were safe.

Word quickly spread of "men dropping from the sky," and at daybreak, a large group of resistance fighters hurried over with knives and spears and surrounded the invaders at a safe distance. Someone who looked like the leader of the men who had dropped from the sky called out that he wanted to pay his respects to the Pelbar Rinpoché. At that time, the Pelbar Rinpoché, Ngawang Lobsang, and the Dzong secretary, Dudul Choying, were the commander and deputy commander of the rebel army in this area.[22] Upon hearing the man's Kham accent, the resistance fighters became less wary and slowly closed in. Seeing that the newcomers displayed no hostility, they took the leader to see the Pelbar Rinpoché. Local fighters were greatly encouraged when they learned that the Americans had sent these men and were willing to supply them with weapons.[23]

By the time the CIA trainees reached Pelbar, the resistance forces in this area had already become fragmented, and the surrounding areas were either occupied by or in a deadlock with the PLA. The TMC had already designated this area "Zone 1" and planned to attack it after finishing battles in the other regions.[24]

Several days later, CIA personnel in Thailand finally received a cable informing them that the personnel in all three groups had arrived at their designated location. They also received a request for arms. The Americans couldn't satisfy all of the demands, but were willing to provide some assistance.[25]

On October 16, a C-130 transport plane appeared in the sky over Pelbar and dropped a batch of weapons and supplies. After receiving these weapons, the Amdowa group left Pelbar for Qinghai according to plan. After crossing the Thanglha range, they encountered a concentration of refugees totaling around 5,000 people gathered near Nira Tso-gen Lake on the Qinghai-Tibet border in Changthang. They gave these people some rudimentary training and helped ST BARNUM airdrop three batches of weapons to the area.[26]

According to currently available sources, from September 1957 to January 1961 the Tibet Task Force airdropped six crews of trainees in ten groups, totaling around 50 people, to meet with and aid resistance forces within Tibet's borders. It is unclear how many additional people may have entered Tibet through India. From July 1958 to January 1960, ST CIRCUS made 17 flights and 9 airdrops, providing resistance forces in Tibet with weapons, medical supplies, tents, radios, and other supplies. This included 2 airdrops to Chushi Gangdruk in Lhoka, 4 airdrops to Pelbar, and 3 to Nira Tso-gen.[27] From the time covert operations in Tibet began in 1956, 238 Tibetans were trained in camps from Saipan Island to Camp Hale in Colorado.[28]

Among the first group of CIA trainees airdropped into Tibet, Athar and Lotse escorted the Dalai Lama to India, starting on March 20 and reporting to the CIA along the way. The second group of trainees established only temporary contact, which was soon cut off, with the CIA. The third group was unable to serve any purpose. Five members of the third group then joined the seventh group and were airdropped into Nira Tso-gen, in what the PLA called Zone 2, in January 1960. Most of them died in action there. One member of the third group, Yeshe Wangyel, later became a member of the tenth group and was airdropped a second time into the Markham area in January 1961. Groups 4 through 10 were able to play a definite role in their various locations. Most of their members died in action. All members of Group 10 swallowed their L capsules just before being overcome, and all but one died on the spot.[29]

How many weapons did the Tibet Task Force provide to Chushi Gangdruk and other resistance organizations before 1961? Based on available sources, the amount of weapons, ammunition, medical supplies, food, and other supplies that the United States provided to Tibetan resistance forces was very limited in comparison with the intensity of the battles they faced. According to figures provided in Lhamo Tsering's memoirs, weapons and ammunition were airdropped directly to Chushi Gangdruk on two occasions and included 403 rifles, 2 mortars, 210 shells, 120 semiautomatic rifles, 15 pistols, and 49,110 rounds of ammunition. This was nowhere near enough to arm all of Chushi Gangdruk's fighters.[30]

Pelbar received a larger number of weapons, with four airdrops from December 1959 to January 1960.[31] Detailed figures relating to two of the airdrops show they included around 1,000 rifles of various kinds, 30 hand grenades, 1 M-4 heavy machine gun, 4 M-M machine guns and 1,000 bullets, 20 pistols, and several cases of explosives.[32] Even if the other two airdrops were roughly the same, however, the supplies would have fallen far short of arming the resistance forces in the Pelbar, Pomé, and Tengchen area. The Nira Tso-gen area received airdrops of 7,760 rifles, 4,700 hand grenades, 7 heavy machine guns, 300-odd submachine guns, several light machine guns and pistols, and a large quantity of other supplies.[33]

Around the same time, from 1956 to 1963, China provided North Vietnam with military aid that included "270,000 guns of various kinds, 10,000 cannons, nearly 200 million rounds of ammunition, 2.02 million artillery shells, 15,000 telegraphs, 5,000 wireless radios, more than 1,000 motor vehicles, 15 aircraft, 28 boats, and 1.18 million military uniforms."[34] As a standard of comparison, this indicates how trivial the CIA's military supplies to the Tibetan resistance fighters were. Even at the height of the Cold War, the Americans had no intention of actually helping the Tibetans fight a war, unlike the Chinese government's objective in aiding the People's Army of Vietnam.

More important, it was impossible to form a fixed and reliable supply line of arms and assistance from ST CIRCUS, while PLA troops carried 100 rounds of ammunition for each rifle, 200 rounds for each submachine gun, 600 rounds for each machine gun, and around 30 artillery shells for each cannon. During battle, the logistics department set up a series of supply depots that were typically a five- to seven-day march from the center of their war zones. At the same time, it organized large numbers of livestock to carry ammunition and other supplies as the battle progressed.[35] For that reason, the PLA seldom ran out of ammunition while fighting.

However, the existence of the Tibet Task Force and the weapons, ammunition, and other supplies that dropped from the sky did significantly boost the morale of the Tibetan resistance fighters, who believed that the world's most powerful country was secretly helping them.

ST CIRCUS was quite successful at keeping its operations covert. Based on currently available Chinese sources, although the Chinese government knew of foreign aircraft making airdrops to Tibet as early as 1959, they were unable to obtain details. When reporting on the Tibet situation to the National Defense Council on May 5, 1959, Deputy Defense Minister Huang Kecheng said that the "rebel bandits in Shannan" (Lhoka) had received material assistance from "an aircraft from an unknown country."[36] The CMC at one point stipulated that if an enemy aircraft were discovered in Tibetan airspace and could be taken down within the borders, it could be shot down; otherwise, it could only be monitored and reported. But PLA airmen never saw these aircraft,[37] possibly because the US military aircraft only flew into Tibet at night, infrequently, and with no fixed pattern. Even the relatively more frequent airdrops to Pelbar were made only once a month for four months.[38]

Did Taiwan provide any military aid to Tibetan resistance forces during this time? Based on declassified files, Taiwan appears to have been "unable to do what it dearly wanted to do" on the military side. Taiwan's air force did at one point look into the feasibility of "directly airdropping material supplies, psychological warfare items, and commanders and liaison personnel." At that time, Taiwan had only C-54 transport planes, which could not make the flight from Taiwan to the Tibet-India border.

They would have had to fly from Thailand to Tsona, the same route taken by ST BARNUM, and this would have required permission from the United States.[39] No documents available to date indicate any instance of Taiwan airdropping weapons to resistance forces within Tibet's borders from 1959 to 1961. Taiwan did, however, airdrop intelligence personnel into Gansu, Qinghai, and Sichuan in 1960.[40]

In early October 2008, at the Tibetan refugee settlement on the outskirts of the town of Bir in Himachal Pradesh, Donyo Jagotsang, now 71 years old, told me that of the 18 men who landed in Pelbar with him, only 7 had survived. Out of Group 4, which he led, 4 died in action; everyone in Group 5 died; and so did 3 members of Group 6.

The conclusion that can be drawn, both from the memoirs of those who participated in the CIA's ST CIRCUS task force and from the personal recollections of Tibetan participants, is that the Tibetan resistance and armed conflicts that began in 1956 were not caused in any way by the CIA. For the Americans, the CIA's ST CIRCUS plan from 1956 to 1962 was just a covert operation for gathering intelligence and for harassment. The training in guerrilla warfare that the CIA provided to a small number of Tibetans was effective to a certain degree, but the airdropping of trainees and weapons had only a limited effect on the basic direction and ultimate outcome of the war. The CIA's role was more to boost the morale of the scattered Tibetan guerrilla forces and to give the Tibetans confidence in their resistance against the Chinese government.

From 1962 onward, some Chushi Gangdruk fighters went to Nepal and established a guerrilla base in Mustang, a remote district on the border with Tibet, almost entirely cut off from the outside world. From their base there, they occasionally crossed the border to harass PLA transport convoys. The CIA continued to provide monetary and material aid to Mustang until the 1970s. In 1974, the CIA ended its aid to Mustang, and the Tibetan guerrilla forces, responding to a personal appeal from the Dalai Lama, laid down their weapons and dispersed into refugee settlements in India and Nepal. With that, the curtain dropped on the Tibetans' armed resistance.

FIGURE 13. Tsering Dorjé.
Source: Jianglin Li.

Chapter 23
CHAMDO'S FIGHT TO THE DEATH

1

At 11 p.m. on March 11, 1959, less than 48 hours after the Lhasa incident broke out, the CCP Central Committee sent a cable ordering the commander of the 54th Army, Ding Sheng, to move his Ding Headquarters into Tibet for battle. At the same time, the Central Committee sent another cable ordering the deputy commander of the Chengdu Military Command, Lieutenant General Huang Xinting, to await orders for his frontline command post, known externally as "Unit 301," to move into Tibet. The Huang Headquarters would take command of the 54th Army's 130th Infantry Division, the Kunming Military Command's 42nd Infantry Division, and the troops under the Chamdo Garrison Command, for a total of 10 regiments and 16,000-plus soldiers.[1]

Huang Xinting was a veteran party member and high-ranking PLA officer who had served in various positions and fought in a number of major battles since 1935. In 1953, Huang participated in the Korean War as the commander of the 1st Army of the Chinese People's Volunteer Army. After returning to China, he had studied modern military theory at the military academy, making him a senior PLA officer who could claim both rich wartime experience and formal academic training.

On March 14, the CMC officially ordered the Huang Headquarters into Tibet to take charge of the battles in the Chamdo region.

On March 17, the 42nd Infantry Division under the Yunnan Military Command was ordered to proceed toward Chamdo via Tsakhalho. On March 24, that division's frontline command post set off from Yunnan with the 126th Infantry Regiment, one military engineer battalion, one scouting company, the 60th Field Hospital, and other units.

On March 20, the Battle of Lhasa broke out.[2]

On March 21, the commander of the 54th Army's 130th Division, Dong Zhanlin, who was studying in Beijing, received an urgent order to rejoin his unit immediately.

Dong Zhanlin flew back to Chengdu that same day and rushed to Ya'an, where the division was stationed. The 130th Division had returned to China from the Korean War only a short time before, and some of its soldiers and officers were preparing to demobilize and transfer to civilian work; two of its regiments were assisting the local government in building railways. After receiving orders, the demobilization was halted and all of the troops shifted to combat preparation.[3]

On March 25, Commander Dong Zhanlin and Political Commissar Geng Qing set off with their troops from Ya'an by motor transport. Ya'an is only about 600 meters above sea level, so the troops had to acclimate to the high-altitude environment in Tibet. The troops assembled at Garzê for acclimation training on March 29, and a convoy packed with fully armed troops entered Tibet one week later. With a machine gun mounted to the front of each vehicle, the convoy looked like a huge armored dragon weaving along the highway toward Chamdo.[4]

On March 26, Huang Xinting set off from Chengdu via the Sichuan-Tibet highway, with the staff of the Huang Headquarters, arriving in Chamdo on April 2. There the Huang Headquarters immediately established radio communications to facilitate battle coordination with the frontline command posts in Yulshul and Golok, Qinghai Province, and with the Dartsedo and Mao County military sub-districts. On April 3, the Huang Headquarters held a war council to discuss a battle plan.

By the time the 130th Division entered Tibet, the Chamdo people had been resisting for three years by burning highway maintenance depots along the Sichuan-Tibet highway, destroying army depots, and digging up roads, so military engineers had to act as an advance party, opening up roads and building bridges. The 130th Division's convoy moved slowly into Tibet, reaching Chamdo on April 14. By then, Chamdo was practically a ghost town, with most of its residents having fled into the mountains.[5]

The Chamdo region, on the west bank of the Drichu River, was part of Kham and was a political, economic, and cultural center, as well as a transportation hub that served as Tibet's "east gate." The Tibetan government had in 1918 established its Chamdo administration,[6] giving Chamdo jurisdiction over 26 *dzong*.[7] After Xikang Province was created, Chamdo was included under Xikang's domain, but China's Nationalist government never established any presence west of the Drichu, so Chamdo remained under the jurisdiction of the Tibetan government. In September 1950, the Communist government decided to establish a transitional government organization in Chamdo called the "Changdu Liberation Committee," under the direct leadership of Beijing. Restructured several times, it formed a "multiple leadership" that greatly complicated the situation in Chamdo.[8]

The Chinese government had initially divided Chamdo into three large parts, and established TWC sub-branches in Chamdo, Hordé Sogu, and Pomé. These sub-branches were underground party organizations that functioned under the name of "liberation committees."[9] In April 1955, these three sub-branches were merged into the TWC's Chamdo sub-branch. Tsakhalho and Dzayul were administered by Yunnan for a period of time, and were only handed over to Chamdo in 1954.[10]

After the PLA conquered Tibet, the troops stationed there were not as highly disciplined as propaganda subsequently depicted them, and repeated violations occurred. The March 7, 1953 edition of the Xinhua News Agency's *Internal Reference* reported some of the "bias and errors" of troops stationed in Tibet:

> Troops stationed in Rikaze damaged Panchen Lingka (Kunkyobling),[11] cutting down its trees and demolishing the bathhouse, which raised objections from the Panchen Clique. The impact on the masses was

> very bad, and as a result some of the masses became suspicious of our policy of protecting religion. Personnel in Bomi (Pomé) destroyed the masses' sacred *mani* cairns and prayer wheels, and openly argued with lamas, saying religion is superstition and that lamas are parasites. This had a very negative effect. . . . At the Jomo (Jiaomo) army depot near Taizhao (Jomda), due to urgent transport tasks, cadres put two bullets in an envelope to threaten local headmen to bring in yaks. Instances of binding and beating the masses have also occurred in other areas. Cadres in Hordé Sogu mobilized the masses to cut trees and build houses without paying them wages, causing the Tibetans to believe that we also support corvée labor. Some purchasing staff sent from Lhasa to Shannan haven't given the masses fair prices and have coerced them into selling vegetables, cattle, sheep, pigs, chickens, etc.[12]

Such incidents were not limited to those areas. The former secretary of Pelbar, Dudul Choying, was appointed deputy director of the Pelbar office of the Chamdo Liberation Committee in 1952. His autobiographical essay mentions his great displeasure over soldiers at the army depot beating his children.[13]

The Xinhua News Agency's *Internal Reference* report also mentioned how the private lives of soldiers and cadres in Tibet showed a lack of respect for Tibetan customs:

> Because the licentious and degenerate thinking of military and civilian cadres hasn't been thoroughly dealt with, improper male-female relationships occur everywhere. After a certain battalion advanced into Shuobanduo and was stationed there for six months, there were more than 100 instances of sexual misconduct, resulting in three people becoming disabled. Troops in Lhasa government offices have also been involved in prostitution, opium smoking, and other degenerate incidents. . . . There are also phenomena of felling trees on sacred mountains, accidentally setting hill fires, shooting eagles, killing dogs, catching sacred fish, slaughtering cattle and sheep without following Tibetan custom, rambling through temples, and other violations of policy and discipline.[14]

The places where this kind of untoward behavior occurred, including Shopamdo and Hordé Sogu, became the areas of the most intense Tibetan resistance.

While the Lhoka campaign south of Lhasa was still raging, the first battle of the Huang Headquarters began in Chamdo, east of Lhasa, in April 1959. Over the next three years, Chamdo became a slaughterhouse.

2

When the Huang Headquarters entered Chamdo, it received a report of "34 groups . . . of armed rebels totaling more than 16,000 people."[15] These "34 groups" were probably villages and nomad groups resisting CCP's "democratic reform." This figure was about the same as the number of troops commanded by Huang Xinting.

The Huang Headquarters' battle plan was to deploy four regiments to northeastern Chamdo and three regiments to Tsakhalho in the south, and use three regiments to repair roads, first rushing to repair the highway from Khargang (Kagong)[16] to Terton (Dedeng)[17] Monastery and protecting the highway from Kamtok (Gangtuo) to Chamdo. In this area, the leader of the Tibetan resistance was the former head of Jomda Dzong[18] and chairman of the Liberation Committee, Chimé Gonpo, who reportedly had more than 3,000 fighters. They were locked in as the target for the first phase of battle by the Huang Headquarters.[19]

On April 14, 1959, the 130th Division crossed the Drichu west of Dergé and then crossed the Ngé-la (Aila) pass. Ahead of them lay the Wara (Wala) Monastery, Jomda's largest, built in 1253. Upon receiving a report that the division's advance force was encountering "harassment" at the Wara Monastery, Division Commander Dong Zhanlin immediately ordered the troops to open fire.[20]

On April 16, the 130th Division arrived at the Tangpu-Jomda-Khargang-Chunyedo-Topa[21] line, and Dong Zhanlin ordered the troops to begin fighting. Late the next night, one PLA regiment split into east and west routes that headed north from Khargang and Chunyedo, past the Dzigar (Zijia) Monastery,[22] to attack the Terton Monastery. During the day, another regiment had advanced north from Topa and surrounded the Khampa (Kangba) Monastery,[23] and that afternoon, a PLA battalion "routed enemy troops defending the Dzigar Monastery"—in fact, probably monks trying to protect the monastery. The 130th Division command post occupied the monastery and turned it into a temporary barracks.[24]

Like his senior officer, General Ding Sheng, Division Commander Dong Zhanlin sent his troops out to attack the "rebel main force," but the population of the Jomda-Chamdo area had fled in droves, and entire villages were hiding in the mountains, so there was no "rebel main force" such as he imagined. It was hardly surprising, then, that Dong Zhanlin received a report several days later that the various regiments had little to show for their efforts.

The most significant conflict in the first stage of the Huang Headquarters' battles in Chamdo was in the Dutsa (Douzha) area,[25] where fugitive monks from Jomda's eight monasteries and about 2,000 refugees were staying. On May 9, a PLA transportation team came under attack and some supplies were taken. A few days later, two regiments and the engineering battalion of the 130th Division staged an attack on this area.[26]

On the night of May 18, the two PLA regiments formed a double encirclement around Dutsa, but the complex terrain prevented them from establishing the position of the "rebel bandit main force," so they asked the air force to send out a scouting plane. At noon the next day, an "iron bird" flew over Dutsa and discovered white tents and hundreds of cattle and horses in a valley. After the airmen called the air force command post in Xining and recommended strafing the area to "point the way" for the ground troops, a bomber flew over and shot at the tents and livestock on the ground. The surrounding troops immediately rushed to the location, after which fierce bombardment by the 130th Division alternated with the strafing by the air force bomber. With two regiments of soldiers plus a bomber fighting some 2,000 monks and refugees, the outcome was easy to predict. Nearly 100 managed to break through the first ring of encirclement, only to be blocked by a battalion of PLA troops in the second encirclement.

Surrounded and under fierce attack from above and on the ground, the Tibetans decided to die rather than surrender. Finally running out of ammunition, they smashed their empty guns. Eighty of them died on the spot, 14 were wounded, and 1 was taken prisoner.[27]

When the commander of the 130th Division, Dong Zhanlin, wrote his autobiography decades later, key details of this "successful battle of annihilation" disappeared, and it was simplified as follows:

> At 10 a.m. on May 19, airmen reported to division headquarters that they had discovered a group of enemies moving south from the Douzha area. Based on synthesized intelligence, it was decided that these were rebel bandits led by the Bajia Living Buddha.[28] Deputy Division Commander Lian Jieming immediately asked me, "Division Commander, should we commence bombing?" I immediately answered, "You can strafe them a little, but don't harm the coerced masses. The main thing is to intimidate the enemy!"[29]

Dong doesn't explain the source of the "synthesized intelligence" nor how the airmen identified the "coerced masses" from the air. He does not reveal how his troops massacred Tibetans there nor give any detail of the aerial bombing.

Dong Zhanlin's memoirs mention taking 127 prisoners and "liberating thousands of coerced masses."[30] Huang Xinting's biography mentions "annihilating 2,483 enemies and seizing 2,000-plus firearms of various kinds." It makes no mention of the total number of people involved, only saying that "70% of the hoodwinked masses returned home to engage in production,"[31] so there is no way of ascertaining whether these 70% were included among the 2,483 who were "annihilated."

The first stage of the Huang Headquarters' battle operations began on April 17 and ended on August 17, 1959. Two days later, the Huang Headquarters assembled around ten regiments of troops and began the second stage in southeastern Chamdo, i.e., the Gonjo (Gongjue)-Drayab (Chaya)-Markham (Ningjing) line.

The battle was launched at the end of summer, and the troops had to finish before winter arrived, so this stage of the battle was a mission with a deadline. The primary objective of this round of fighting was to "annihilate the enemy's effective strength," so the Huang Headquarters used four regiments to block access to the Drichu and Dzachu (upper Mekong) rivers, and six regiments split into north and south routes to attack the enemy in an "east-west block and intercept, north-south joint attack" tactic. After forming a double encirclement followed by a "combing-style cleanup," the operation ended on November 30. Sources give widely diverging numbers of Tibetans killed, wounded, captured, or surrendered in this round of operations. Dong Zhanlin's memoir gives no figures, while Huang Xinting's biography records a total of 10,800 annihilated and the seizing of 6,000 guns.[32] Ji Youquan puts the number annihilated at more than 26,100.[33] The total population of the area at that time was around 57,900.[34]

After this battle, the Huang Headquarters was disbanded and the troops returned to Sichuan. However, that was not the end of the battles in Chamdo. In 1960 and 1961, Chamdo was the battleground for the Battles of Zone 1[35] and Zone 4.

3

On the morning of December 4, 2010, in Dharamsala, India, in a small house overlooking Kangra Valley, I interviewed Tsering Dorjé, the second son of the Phupa Pon Tsering Gyaltsen, leader of the 18 Markham headmen.

Tsering Dorjé sat cross-legged on a small Tibetan-style couch below the window and told me of his experience. Half a century later, the 15-year-old youth had become a gray-haired elder. When he was young, Tsering Dorjé had learned Chinese, and he spoke several heavily accented Chinese phrases to me during the interview.

Before 1956, Tsering Dorjé had passed his days happily. His father earned 280 silver dollars a month as chairman of the Markham County Liberation Committee, and the government regularly sent people to his home with tea, sugar, butter, and other goods. After the Chinese government occupied Chamdo, they immediately established a Nationalities Primary School, where Tsering Dorjé enrolled to study. As the "chairman's kid," he was well-treated by the Chinese cadres and soldiers. Starting in 1954, the children of Tibetan headmen and officials were all sent to China to study, and Tsering Dorjé was selected to study at the Central Institute for Nationalities[36] in Beijing. Just as he was about to leave home, however, conflicts broke out in Bathang and Lithang, and his parents, afraid to have him travel so far away, decided to keep him at home.

In 1956, when Tsering Dorjé turned 15, a series of incidents occurred one after another in the Markham area, and he watched his homeland turn upside down.[37]

In November 1956, Tsering Dorjé's father, the Phupa Pon, and the other local headmen convened an "18-headman conference" and decided to mobilize a revolt against the Chinese government's "reforms."

"Everyone elected my father as the *magchi*, or commander, and Tsawa Lama of Lholung Monastery was deputy commander," Tsering Dorjé told me. Soon after that, Phupa Pon led an attack on the PLA platoon guarding the rope-pulley bridge over the Dzachu River. Apart from snatching weapons and other supplies, they killed 21 and wounded 3.[38] After this, the chairman of the Chamdo Liberation Committee, the wealthy Markham merchant Pangda Dorjé,[39] rushed over to mediate.

Meanwhile, Tsering Dorjé and his mother, younger brother, and two younger sisters stayed at home, where news of their father reached them through various channels. He heard others say that Pangda Dorjé had come to see his father with a letter from the Tibetan government demanding that he stop the resistance and release the PLA soldiers they had captured. Pangda Dorjé said that the Central Committee had already decided not to impose reforms for at least six years, and that the cadres who said "it's either peaceful reforms or reforms by armed force" were wrong and were ignorant of policy. Finally they got down to specifics, and Pangda Dorjé demanded that the rebels surrender the seized weapons and release the prisoners. Phupa Pon demanded that the PLA withdraw from his homeland. Tsering Dorjé heard that they were unable to reach an agreement. Finally, his father sent back the PLA captives, but refused to return the weapons. That allowed things to quiet down for a time.

After a while, Tsering Dorjé heard about his father "facing the enemy on his own." People said that a big official from Lhasa named Tan Guansan had wanted to see Phupa Pon and invited him to a feast. In order to show that he wouldn't seize him, the official ordered his subordinates to erect a tent on the grassland and invited Phupa Pon to meet him there. Tsering Dorjé heard that his father went with more than 20 fighters, and when they reached the door, Phupa Pon had his fighters stay outside while he went in to speak with the official alone. Of course, they were unable to reach an agreement. Tsering Dorjé heard that when his father walked out of the tent, a bugle suddenly sounded, and groups of armed PLA soldiers came rushing down from the hills on all sides. He and his men had been surrounded the whole time. Nevertheless, collecting himself, Phupa Pon jumped on his horse and galloped off.[40]

That was in 1957. The situation was strange: Tsering Dorjé stayed home while his father and older brother led their warriors into the mountains, and there were small flare-ups all over Chamdo as local militia staged attacks, snatching goods and attacking highway maintenance crews. Meanwhile, the county continued to send someone over with his father's wages.

"If it were only for the headmen's benefit, we would have had no need to oppose the reforms," Tsering Dorjé told me. "At that time, the headmen were committee members earning 150 silver dollars a month plus supplies of tea and sugar." Senior officials from Lhasa also came and promised that the reforms wouldn't change the lives of these headmen, and that if anything, they would live even better than before.

"That was still the time of the United Front. While the United Front was going well, they'd always give us things," Tsering Dorjé says with a smile.

By 1958, the situation had become tense, and increasing numbers of troops were stationed in Chamdo. It was no longer safe at home, so Tsering Dorjé's father took him and his brothers and sisters into the mountains. It was then that Tsering Dorjé found out that his father was in contact with the outside world, and that his older brother, Yeshe Wangyel, had already taken his family to India.

On March 31, 1959, the Yunnan Military Command's 42nd Infantry Division arrived in Dechen (Deqin) County. Three PLA regiments soon entered Markham, Tsakhalho, and other places, and a large-scale military operation began.

"Did you fight in any battles?" I ask Tsering Dorjé.

"At first I just followed my father," he said, "but eventually I began to fight."

Half a century later, Tsering Dorjé still remembered that battle. It was on a grassland with no mountains or water around. He was with Tsawa Lama. According to long-standing custom, when it came time for a battle, monks, the elderly, women, and children were all sent to a safe place.

Tsering Dorjé heard intense gunfire, and far in the distance he saw a group of huge war-horses galloping toward them. The men in his own group, mounted on horses with no battle training, charged at their attackers head-on, and they began fighting at close quarters. "It was dreadful," Tsering Dorjé said, and then he fell silent for a long time.

"Did you know that the Dalai Lama had escaped?" I asked him, breaking the silence.

"Yes," Tsering Dorjé replied. "There were papers all over that had been dropped from an airplane saying that bad people had kidnapped the Dalai Lama." At that time, an attempt was being made to sap the Tibetans' will to resist by sending PLA aircraft to Tibetan regions to drop leaflets spreading the news that the reactionaries had kidnapped the Dalai Lama and taken him to India. Mao had personally issued this directive to the TWC.[41]

They learned of the Dalai Lama's escape at the end of 1959 or early 1960. Before that, Tsering Dorjé had been with his father in the mountains, dealing with the pursuing troops of the PLA. They had no idea what had happened in Lhasa and had been trying to contact the Tibetan government, requesting instructions and support. They also sent messengers to India, trying to get weapons from the outside world, but nothing came their way.[42]

One battle followed another, and the iron birds roared through the sky overhead, dropping bombs on pastures, monasteries, and villages. In order to avoid senseless death, most of Phupa Pon's men, who lacked weapons or bullets, finally went down from the mountain and surrendered. All of those who surrendered were eventually imprisoned.

The remaining resisters dispersed. Tsering Dorjé accompanied his father and Tsawa Lama with more than 500 people going north to Drayab.

By then, the Ding and Huang command posts were both in Tibet. The commander of the 54th Army's 130th Division, Dong Zhanlin, commanded the troops in the first battle in Chamdo, in the Jomda area north of the Sichuan-Tibet highway, while troops from the Kunming Military Command attacked the Markham area.

"After the Dalai Lama left, did you ever think of an ultimate objective?" I ask. "Did you think of going to India?"

"No. We wanted to continue the guerrilla war in our homeland," Tsering Dorjé replied.

When the 18 headmen pledged to revolt, they were ready to die on their native soil. It wasn't that they didn't have a chance to escape. They sent someone to India with a letter asking for arms to be supplied to them as soon as possible, but the letter never arrived. Every village was controlled by work teams composed of PLA soldiers and Chinese cadres. The Tibetan fighters had little to eat in the mountains, and they were almost out of ammunition. The best they could do was to seize food and ammunition in skirmishes.

On January 25, 1960, Phupa Pon died in a fierce battle, together with 83 of his fighters.[43]

"How . . . did he die?" I asked Tsering Dorjé hesitantly.

"He was shot," Tsering Dorjé replied. "Our men put him on a horse, but he couldn't stay seated, and he fell off. They put him back on the horse again and he fell again . . . So he died. Afterwards, Chinese soldiers took his body to Chamdo and denounced it for four days."

I couldn't think of anything to say. The small room was deathly silent.

During a confrontation one day in March, Tsering Dorjé, 19 years old by now, was shot and seriously wounded; he found himself in a forest surrounded by a mass of PLA soldiers. More than 20 of his companions flatly refused to flee without him, and they placed him under a tree and kept fighting until every one of them was dead. Tsering Dorjé was taken prisoner.

"They call it the Battle of *sihao diqu* (Zone 4)," Tsering Dorjé told me. This campaign lasted about two months, from March to May, 1960. For this battle, Zhang Guohua drew on ten battalions of troops.[44]

The last phase of the PLA's major campaign in Tibet was the Battle of Markham and Sa-ngen, from October to December 1960. By the end of 1960, there were only about 2,000 Tibetan resistance fighters left in Tibet, scattered in different places.

In February 1961, the PLA Central Staff Department issued "four cleanup standards for the complete pacification of the Tibetan rebellion": "First, all the openly active rebels and hidden rebel leaders are completely wiped out; second, guns and counterrevolutionary documents in the hands of reactionary elements are completely or largely confiscated; third, the masses are fully mobilized, reactionary social foundations are completely destroyed, grassroots administration is consolidated, and political advantage is stabilized; and fourth, the recurrence of large-scale rebellion is rooted out."[45]

Following these instructions, the TMC handed down a Great Leap Forward-type directive ordering all military units to "clean up 80% of existing bandit gangs and 60% of existing scattered bandits" before the August 1 Army Day, and by the end of the year to "thoroughly eliminate bandit chiefs and scattered bandits to achieve the 'three alls' (all rebel bandits annihilated, all guns and reactionary documents confiscated)."[46]

On January 15, 1961, Phupa Pon's oldest son and Tsering Dorjé's older brother, Yeshe Wangyel, together with another 6 CIA trainees, was airdropped back into Tibet. This was his second airdrop, and his group was the last one that the CIA dropped into Tibet.[47]

After Yeshe Wangyel managed to return to his homeland, he learned from herders that his father had died in battle and his family had been taken prisoner. His group met the resistance fighters led by Tsawa Lama. By this time, the situation was getting more and more difficult for them. Yeshe Wangyel tried to cable the CIA requesting weapons, but was unable to establish contact.

On May 18, 1961, Yeshe Wangyel and the others in the tenth intelligence group were surrounded by a mass of PLA soldiers.[48] After running out of ammunition, they bit down on their L capsules. Six of them died on the spot, and the only survivor was no longer able to speak.[49]

Tsawa Lama, deputy commander of the Chamdo resistance force, was surrounded in another place. Facing the swarming soldiers, Tsawa Lama shot his last bullet, laid down his gun, and sat down cross-legged on the slope. By the time the soldiers approached to capture him, Tsawa Lama was already dead.[50]

The fires of resistance that had burned in Chamdo for five years were finally extinguished. Sporadic battles lasted for a few more months as PLA soldiers continued to "clean up" small groups of fighters hiding in mountains.

From April 1959 to April 1961, the Ding and Huang command posts and the subsequent Chamdo Command Post "fought more than 2000 battles, annihilated more than 40,000 enemies, and captured more than 12,000 rifles, 24,000 homemade muskets, and 11 cannons of various kinds."[51]

This number includes the PLA's battle results from Zone 1, but doesn't include people that the work teams seized in each village, nor the monks arrested in hundreds of monasteries.

4

Chamdo, the Tibetan region occupied by the Chinese after the Battle of Chamdo in October 1950, was under the direct jurisdiction of the State Council and was where "United Front work" had been done most effectively, yet it was also the Tibetan region where insurrections occurred the earliest and where the battles lasted the longest. Even after the Dalai Lama left for India and Chushi Gangdruk withdrew from Tibet, resistance in the Chamdo region lasted for nearly three more years.

On April 20, 1959, in view of the fact that "a region-wide armed rebellion has formed in the Chamdo region, and most of the members of the Chamdo Region Liberation Committee and the various *dzong* liberation committees are taking part in the armed rebellion, the two levels of liberation committees have lost their function, and there is no way to preserve social order and implement and execute the state's directives,"[52] the State Council declared the disbanding of the Chamdo Liberation Committee and immediately established the Chinese People's Liberation

Army Chamdo Military Control Commission. In the years that followed, Chamdo was effectively under military control.

On April 28, 1959, the TMC handed down a written directive for army units to organize local work teams and launch local work in all localities as the first step in building a grassroots government. In principle, every regiment was expected to organize 4 work teams with ten personnel in each.[53] To this end, in the Chamdo region, as in the other Tibetan regions, military operations and "democratic reform"—i.e., land reform, the suppression of counterrevolutionaries, "religious reform," the establishment of local government, and other such activities—were executed simultaneously. In October 1959, after the second stage of battle was mostly completed, the 130th Division deployed a total of 36 work teams in all localities.[54]

The first matter addressed by the work teams was "suppressing counterrevolutionaries," which meant seizing large numbers of people, sometimes taking people into custody while they were attending group training or meetings. At the same time, the monasteries in the Chamdo region were all closed down and the monks sent to farms or to prison. Of all of the Chamdo region's 572 monasteries, only the Chamdo Monastery remained open, and that was being used as a military camp and prison. Large numbers of the region's elite were locked up, leaving only a few notables such as Pagbalha Gelek Namgyal.[55]

The "four nos policy," i.e., no killing, no imprisonment, no sentencing, and no denunciation of those who surrendered, was only for external propaganda purposes. According to published sources, from July to September 1960, the Chamdo region subjected 4.7% of the population to arrest and group training; of those, 5% were wrongfully arrested, and 10–15% were arrested "without cause," to prevent them from rebelling.[56] Before the hostilities, the total population of Chamdo was around 260,000.[57] Based on that, without taking into account the number of people killed during the battles, at least 12,200 people must have been arrested. Before the hostilities, Chamdo had more than 35,000 monks and priests,[58] but after the monasteries were closed down, clerics who hadn't taken part in the resistance were sent to farms for what was essentially labor reform. These two instances alone involved tens of thousands of people. Among the people seized were "upper strata friends" and "laboring people"; even women with children were taken as prisoners of war.[59]

Battles, arrests, the destruction of religion, and "reform on horseback," i.e., coercive reforms that had to be completed within a few days, created a Red Terror and incited even more intense resistance. Chamdo was in an incessant state of war over a protracted period, and this attracted the notice of China's top officials.

In August 1960,[60] the CCP Central Committee sent General Zhang Aiping, the PLA deputy chief of general staff; Ding Sheng, the commander of the 54th Army, and Zhang Guohua, the second secretary of the TWC, to Chamdo to investigate and handle the problem. They managed to temporarily assuage the tensions by releasing some upper-strata individuals, opening some monasteries, bringing back some monks, relaxing food supplies, and other such "conciliatory policies." They also disciplined a Chamdo Military Sub-region deputy commander and a political department director.

In March 1962, the Chinese government announced victory in the "pacification of Tibetan rebellion."[61]

Two months later, the 10th Panchen Lama submitted his Seventy-Thousand-Character Petition to Zhou Enlai. In the following months, top CCP leaders held a series of meetings with him, trying to pacify the young leader, who was very concerned about the situation in Tibetan regions. Questioned by the Panchen Lama on June 25, 1962, Zhang Guohua acknowledged that "the problem was very serious" in Chamdo, and that it was related to the military. He admitted that Chamdo had a "prisoner policy problem" and a "rebellion suppression and reform problem," and that the military had "specific conduct problems," along with the problem of "educating cadres" and so on. Although the prison was moved out of the Chamdo Monastery by June 1962, troops were still stationed there, and some elite figures who had been released were arrested once again.[62] The records of these meetings were marked as top secret and were never officially declassified.

Chapter 24
THE LIFE-OR-DEATH JOURNEY

1

In the summer of 1959, Aten, the headman of Dhunkhug Village in Nyarong, traveling with his two wives and 9-year-old daughter and some 1,500 other refugees, reached Gyaring and Ngoring lakes at the source of the Yellow River. That night, the thoroughly exhausted refugees pitched their tents in a V-shaped ravine.[1]

Around midnight, Aten was awakened by the sound of gunfire, which seemed to come from everywhere at once. Their encampment was clearly under attack. Totally unprepared, the group had no time to organize any kind of resistance. Aten leaped to his feet, grabbed his gun, and told his wives to take his daughter and run west as quickly as possible. It was just before dawn, and the ravine was shrouded in thick mist. Guns fired nonstop as women shouted, frightened horses whinnied, the wounded cried out in pain, and children howled. The churning mist obscured the human forms dashing helter-skelter in the darkness. Aten couldn't see the troops who surrounded them, only flashing clusters of blood-red light.

Two horses came running alongside Aten, and he shouted for his wives to grab them. At that moment, Aten heard his younger wife scream and saw her fall to the snow-covered ground. Rushing over, he saw blood gushing from her shoulder. Then he heard his daughter cry out in pain.

He dashed over and raised her robe, and saw her intestines pushing through a ragged hole that a bullet had ripped in her abdomen. Grabbing the reins of a horse, he helped his two wives mount it and told them to flee. Then he picked up his mortally wounded daughter and ran for the hills.

One year earlier, Aten had taken his wives and daughter from Nyarong to Dzachuka (Shiqu), then to Sertar, and from Sertar to Golok, protecting them with his rifle along the way as they were ambushed, encircled, bombed, and pursued. All he wanted was to take his family to a safe place where his daughter could grow to adulthood. Not long after leaving Sertar, they had spotted a nomad encampment and ridden over, hoping to obtain some food. But when they reached it, they were shocked to find the tents in tatters and the bodies of men, women, and children lying everywhere amidst the stench of death. In times of hardship, there is no such thing as childhood; Aten's daughter seemed to have learned all about the world overnight. Looking at the scene of slaughter around them, she asked tearfully, "Father, why do our people have to suffer so much? We have given them our homes and all our possessions. Why do they still have to kill all these poor people?"[2]

Throughout their flight from the Nyagchu valley to the source of the Yellow River, Aten had always carried his daughter with him on his horse, clutching her small body close to his breast as if that would be enough to keep her safe from harm. Now, as he ran with her, mortally wounded, for the hills, he was in a panic. He needed to get her away from here, and if fate was kind, he might find a doctor . . . Pressed against him, his daughter was soaked with sweat and whimpered in pain; he knew that his running increased her suffering. Aten stopped and bent down and gently laid his daughter in grass lightly blanketed with snow. The child's breathing was faint, and Aten's mind went blank. The sturdy Khampa knelt on the grass and kissed his daughter, and his heart emptied as he watched the life drain from her.

Gunfire blasted all around him, and galloping hooves thundered. Aten ran up the hill, hoping to grab a mule, but saw that now his other wife was also wounded and had fallen to the ground. After helping the badly injured woman onto the mule, he gave it a slap that sent it bolting toward the hilltop.

Dawn's light spread, gradually dispersing the mist. In the first rays of the morning sun, Aten came across two of his companions just as a group of mounted soldiers came charging at them. The three of them fired at once, and the soldier in front fell from his horse, but the others continued to speed toward them, shooting. The three Khampas hid behind rocks as the band of horsemen swept past and disappeared into the mist.

Making his way to the hilltop, Aten found his wife on the ground, breathing her last. She took her coral necklace from around her neck and placed it in his hand, telling him to run for his life. Aten gripped her hand and watched her fade away. They were gone, all of them—the two wives and the young daughter who had accompanied him through so much peril.

As the intense gunfire continued, the sun gradually rose, its golden rays dispersing what remained of the mist. Aten stood on the hilltop and watched the battle going on in clusters in the valley below. His countrymen were still doing all they could to shield their women and children and the monks as they attempted to break through the encirclement. Not far from him, a group of cavalrymen searched the hills. Aten's companions had scattered, and the only one who remained with him was a youth from Dergé. They picked up their guns and rejoined the battle. Suddenly Aten felt a sharp pain in his shoulder, and then another bullet hit his right rib. Aten staggered back up the hill and grabbed a grazing horse, but just as he climbed onto its back, hundreds of soldiers charged at him, and a bullet pierced his leg and struck the horse's belly.

Hit with three bullets, Aten staged a last showdown with the cavalrymen. It was only then that he saw that his attackers were from the Hui minority, remnants of Ma Bufang's army[3] who had been recruited into the PLA. In this battle, the Chinese government was using the traditional tactic of emperors of old to "play one group of foreigners against another," and had sent Mongols and Hui to attack Tibetans. Mounted troops from Inner Mongolia were seasoned from fighting for the Communists in China's civil war; and, in addition to being crack marksmen and accomplished horsemen, they were used to the pastoral area. Their massive war-horses, known colloquially as Xining horses, gave them a considerable advantage when battling Tibetans.[4] In this battle, Aten could only rely on his marksmanship to protect himself. He shot at the troops pursing him and picked up the submachine gun their leader had dropped, then used what remained of his strength to climb onto a Xining horse and ride off alone into the boundless grassland.

At nightfall, Aten came across more than 70 of his companions, including his cousin Dowang and Dowang's son. Of the 16 people who had left their native place together, only 4 were still alive; of the 1,500 attacked in the battle that day, only around 200 escaped.

One night two weeks later, their encampment came under renewed attack by the PLA, and Aten was shot again. The group scattered again, and the only person who remained with Aten was his cousin Dowang. Using his best efforts, Dowang brought Aten up a mountain so high that it remained snow-covered all year round, and he settled him into a shallow cave.

In the days that followed, Aten's four bullet wounds became infected. He was burning with fever and his life hung by a thread as he fell in and out of consciousness. Dowang washed Aten's wounds with melted snow and sustained him with raw meat from wild animals and pieces of ice. Finally, Aten's tenacious life force conquered death. After regaining consciousness, Aten learned that Dowang had gone back to the encampment to look for his son, finding his dead body among a dozen or so corpses scattered there. That meant that Aten and Dowang were now the only 2 survivors from their native place.

Once Aten's wounds were healed, he and Dowang descended the mountain and continued their life-or-death journey. They had nothing left but their guns, and there was no path for them to follow through the vast grassland—only a general direction. Dowang supported the weakened Aten, both of them sustaining each other as they walked in the direction of the setting sun.

2

The 15-year-old monk Yetan and two others had escaped the last battle in Garzê, "the battle of encirclement and annihilation in Sertar." Two days later, they came upon a large group of tents in a ravine, and found that it was the Drango people, who had gotten away before them. Soon afterwards, they encountered members of a group from Dzachuka who had also been scattered, led by their headman, Paseng Ngaro; this group included a dozen or so armed men.

Now there were around 200 refugees, including an old man in his 70s and a baby less than one year old, as well as children who had become separated from their parents, and three monks. The Drango headman had been killed in an attempt to break through the encirclement at Sertar, and that tribe was now being led by his younger brother. The brother was a monk who could not lead men in battle, so Paseng Ngaro from Dzachuka became the leader.

Their destination was Lhasa. The Drichu River was cut off and the powerful Chinese army was pressing them toward the northeast. With his wealth of battle experience, Paseng Ngaro led the refugees in the direction of Yulshul.

The group kept heading north, driving their livestock and the yaks and horses carrying their tents and cooking utensils. Lacking barley flour, they could only slaughter their livestock or occasionally replenish their food supplies by looting cooperatives that they came across. Now and then they encountered other scattered refugees, but some were collaborators that the Chinese government had sent out to persuade refugees to return home, while others were activists gathering intelligence for the Chinese government.

The motley group kept going, sometimes fighting or fleeing PLA soldiers and other times ambushing small groups of soldiers. Although never formally trained, Paseng Ngaro had fought many battles. He divided the 200-odd people into small groups that could help and protect each other, and any food they found was shared equally. The makeshift tribe had very few complete families, so each small group became a temporary family, with the older members looking after youngsters like Yetan. When they encountered PLA soldiers, as soon as shots were fired the headman would immediately lead the able-bodied men to advantageous terrain while the elders, monks, women, and children quickly packed up the tents and belongings, loaded them onto their beasts, and fled. Among the refugees were several young monks around Yetan's age. According to tradition, they were not allowed to bear arms and fight, so the headman assigned them to look after the horses. As soon as fighting started, it was every boy for himself, and each would jump on a horse and ride away as quickly as possible. Wherever they pitched their tents, their horses were close by. Yetan always kept an eye on his horse so he could gallop off at a moment's notice.

The group had more than 400 horses, but the long journey had reduced them to a pitiful state, and they were becoming increasingly scrawny. The headman knew that whenever the PLA went to battle, horses were left at the rear with a few soldiers watching them. These war-horses were healthy and strong, and their saddlebags were loaded with grain and other items. Whenever an opportunity arose during battle, Paseng Ngaro would send a few dozen men to steal horses, and several successful raids had allowed them to replace their sickly horses with strong ones. At night, the headman personally arranged guards in two-hour shifts and taught those standing sentry how to conceal themselves. In this way, the refugees hiked and fought their way across the alpine steppe, completely ignorant of everything that was happening in Lhasa.

While they were on their way to Yulshul and Golok, the main battles in that area had ended and the large-scale military operations had come to a close. The PLA had entered its "cleanup" and government-building phases, and cadres, militia, and activists were preoccupied with the "four antis campaign."[5] By this time, the center of the conflict had moved to central Tibet, where the troops from Qinghai had shifted to suppressing rebelling Tibetans in the Battle of Mitikha, while the air force carried out bombing and strafing missions in Chamdo, Namtso, Mitikha, and other places. Perhaps because of this, Yetan and his group repeatedly encountered small groups of PLA scouts but never any large army units, nor did they experience any large-scale attacks. Knowing none of the reasons for this, Paseng Ngaro simply acted on instinct and experience and, guided by the sun and stars, led the group of refugees from the north toward the west and then south, following a huge arc toward Lhasa.

After crossing the Qinghai-Tibet highway, as they approached a V-shaped ravine near the Gyaring and Ngoring lakes, Yetan saw something he would never forget.

More than fifty years later, in the Gomang Dratsang old monks' home in the exile Drepung Monastery, Lama Yetan described the scene to me. "The ground was covered with the bodies of humans and horses and the robes and religious instruments of lamas and garments worn for the *cham* dance, and there were coins and coral and turquoise beads scattered all around. At that time, those things looked like nothing but stones, and no one went over to collect them. Everyone was thinking about when they, too, might die."[6]

What Yetan was seeing was Aten's former encampment. There were many such destroyed encampments on the plateau at that time. Countless men, women, elders, children, and monks had died in night raids, aerial bombardments, or battles of "encirclement and annihilation" and had become a part of the statistics of "rebel bandits killed." No one buried them, so they just decayed where they lay on grasslands and in mountain forests, becoming one with the alpine steppe.

"After seeing that, I couldn't sleep for days," Lama Yetan told me. "That horrible scene just kept floating before my eyes."

After that, the group of refugees turned toward the southwest, and many days later, they found themselves facing the mighty expanse of the Tongtian River, source of the Yangtze.

Around the same time, the wounded Aten and his cousin Dowang climbed down from the mountain. They had no horse or tent, no food or eating utensils, but fortunately they still had their guns. Dowang managed to bag an antelope, and the two men ate the raw meat to stave their hunger and drank melted snow to allay their thirst. Aten bore the pain of his wounds, and the two of them hiked west. Having both survived battle and lost their families, they knew the same sorrow and didn't need mutual sympathy. They prayed as they walked.

Several days later, they encountered 8 of their scattered companions. Out of their group of more than 1,500 refugees, all had been killed or captured but the 10 of them. Several days later, in the golden mist of sunset, they saw a vast river and near it an encampment. It was the group of refugees led by the Drango and Dzachuka headmen. Yetan was one of the youngest in this group.

3

More than 200 people, plus horses and other livestock, made a massive target. Perhaps due to sheer luck, the iron birds scouting from the skies above didn't discover them, but "search teams" of various sizes were scouring the plateau at that time, some of them made up of regular PLA troops and others of local armed militia.

On the banks of the Tongtian, the refugees spotted a dozen or so PLA soldiers floating down the river in a rubber boat. They laid an ambush along the river and killed all of the soldiers, in the process gaining weapons and other supplies, as well as a machine gun.

"The younger brother of the Drango headman was a monk," Lama Yetan told me. "When his older brother was killed, he asked one of us three lamas to go perform Buddhist rites. Afterwards, he asked that lama, 'Is it a sin to kill Chinese soldiers?' The lama felt this was a very difficult question to answer. He said, 'It should be a sin. After all, the soldiers are also human beings.' The headman's brother didn't believe it: 'It's a sin to kill soldiers? They're enemies of the dharma! How can it be a sin to kill them?'"

No matter how Buddhism might explain it, the process of being pursued and fleeing on this life-and-death journey made killing or being killed a fact of life. A distorted ideology had torn society into pieces, making enemies of people who had never had anything to do with each other.

After their ambush, the refugees began crossing the river. There was only one ox-hide boat for more than 200 people; only a few could cross at a time, and then the boat had to be dried over a fire before the next group could cross. It took an entire week for all of the people and horses to cross. After crossing, they turned southwest toward Changthang.

The headman Paseng Ngaro didn't know that they were falling into a trap by heading for Lhasa in the fall of 1959, and that each step brought them closer to danger. The refugees were traveling along the "eastern line," the area east of the Qinghai-Tibet highway, with its snow-capped mountains, marshes, and waterways. They traversed mountains and rivers, crossed the area known as Qinghai to the Chinese administration, and entered what the Chinese called Xizang (Tibet). Yetan didn't know anything about these administrative divisions; he only knew that they were in Changthang, and that ahead of them lay Sog Dzong, under the jurisdiction of the Tibetan government. They had no idea that the Tibetan government no longer existed, nor that Sog Dzong had been blown up and become a battlefield just over two months earlier.

It was sheer luck that by the time the group approached Sog Dzong, the Battle of Mitikha had ended and the PLA had withdrawn its four regiments from the area.

As dawn was about to break one morning, people busily packed up their tents and utensils while Yetan and two other youths guarded the horses. Yetan watched his companions playing, occasionally raising his head to keep an eye on his horse. As the sun rose over the mountains, he suddenly heard a strange noise coming from far away. Yetan and his friends stood up and saw several black dots moving in the distance.

"I thought it was wild yaks," Lama Yetan told me, laughing. "There were lots of wild yaks in that region. I fixed my eyes on those black objects . . . One black dot was in front, and two followed behind . . ."

Suddenly there was a flash of light reflecting off the window of a vehicle. Yetan and his companions yelled, "The Chinese soldiers are here!"

Paseng Ngaro grabbed his gun and jumped on his horse shouting, "This way! Today we have to resist! If we can't stop them, we'll be in great danger! We have to go after them today! If we let the vehicles come near us, we're finished! We have to go after them!" A group of armed men leaped onto their horses and followed him down the hill.

The encampment descended into chaos. Everyone ran to grab horses and load them with tents and other belongings, and fled. Quickly reaching a safe distance, they stopped and waited for the men who had gone to attack the convoy.

After a while, the men raced back. Yetan heard others say that Paseng Ngaro had instructed them to shoot out the tires of the vehicles. They hid on the mountain slope, and as the vehicles neared them, the headman gave the order, and they all started firing and burst all the tires. In the desolate mountains, the vehicles could not pursue them with flat tires, and it would take time for reinforcements to arrive, so the refugees were safe. They were probably near the highway from Nagchu to Gyarubthang (Jilutong), which was very close to Sog.

"In Sog Dzong, we grabbed someone at the cooperative," Lama Yetan told me. At that time, no genuine "cooperatives" had been established in Tibet, so "someone at the cooperative" probably referred to an "activist." That's when they learned that Lhasa had fallen and that the Dalai Lama had gone to India. There was no going forward, and if they wanted to survive, they would have to follow their Gyalwa Rinpoché, the Dalai Lama, to India.

Paseng Ngaro led his group on west, the Changthang plateau sprawling before them.

Very soon, the frigid weather and frozen ground of winter arrived. They were in dangerous terrain, but for Tibetans used to life on the plateau, the higher and colder the location, the safer they were. They couldn't stop to wait out the winter; if they were discovered, a larger group of soldiers would come after them. The group hid by day and came out at night, navigating by the stars to lead them west. In order to prevent foals from crying out in the night, Paseng Ngaro had them haltered and tied to the tails of the mares. People didn't talk and horses made no sound as the refugees hurried in silence through the bone-chilling wind and cold. The Changthang had numerous lakes, but most were saline, and the refugees often went for days at a time with only melted snow to drink.

Day after day they trudged along towards Ngari, from winter into spring. Before bidding their homeland farewell, they wanted to worship at the holy mountain, Gang Rinpoché,[7] but as they were drawing near to the mountain, they encountered a local man who said that the area was already occupied by PLA soldiers. They could only turn south toward the border between Tibet and Nepal.

After parting from his father, Yetan had spent more than a year traveling from Sertar to the Nepal border. On the way, he had seen three people die, over the course of 33 battles, and many more die of other causes.

A narrow path led the refugees up a tall, snow-covered mountain. Alone in the world, Aten, who had joined Yetan's group, stood on the mountain path and gave a last look at his homeland as icy wind blasted against his tear-streaked face and howled across the war-torn land.

This was in May 1960. Just a little more than one month later, that area became the site of the Battle of Ngari.

Chapter 25
WHEN THE IRON HORSE RACED ACROSS THE PLATEAU

1

In October 1962, the Qinghai Military Command completed its third phase of warfare, and that put an end to the battles to suppress the Tibetan resistance. This secret war, formally referred to as "the struggle to pacify rebellion," had lasted six and a half years, from February 1956 to October 1962.

The end of the war was marked by "three completes": "rebel bandits completely annihilated, firearms and reactionary documents completely confiscated," as well as the elimination of "small rebel bandit groups" of ten or more people in the battle region.[1] By this standard, the duration of the fighting differed in each region.

According to current administrative divisions, the fighting lasted longest in the Tibetan region of Sichuan Province, continuing for more than six years there, from February 1956 to December 1961.[2]

In Qinghai, the fighting lasted four-and-a-half years, beginning with the "Xunhua incident" in April 1958 and ending with the completion of "Phase Three" in October 1962.

In Tibet, the fighting lasted around five years, beginning in the Chamdo region in July 1956 and ending with the battles in Markham and Sa-ngen (Sanyan) in April 1961,[3] but if achieving the "three completes" is used as the criterion, the military actions lasted six years, until March 1962.[4]

The fighting in Yunnan lasted four years, from April 1956 to March 1960.

In Gansu, insurrections broke out in the Kanlho TAP in 1956 and 1958, but the battles in 1956 were limited to a small area. The insurrection that began in March 1958 covered the entire prefecture, but once the Lanzhou Military Command's 11th Infantry Division became involved, in November 1958, the main military operations basically ended.[5]

The scale of the warfare can be gauged from the number of battles, but the statistics, which can be found scattered among various sources, are incomplete. The main combat forces were under the Chengdu, Kunming, and Lanzhou Military Commands, and a particular military unit could fight at different times in different places. Furthermore, the method for calculating the number of battles differed among the various regions. The statistic for Sichuan is given as "more than 10,000 battles large and small,"[6] which clearly includes every military conflict. Twelve large-scale military campaigns were carried out in Tibet from 1959 to 1961,[7] each campaign involving multiple battles of varying scales and degrees. For example, in the "Huang Command Post Second Stage Battle Operation" from August to November 1959, PLA units engaged in 840 large and small combats.[8] There were 3,639 battles in Qinghai.[9] The 11th Infantry Division engaged in 996 battles in Kanlho,[10] and the Kunming Military Command's 42nd Division fought 308 battles in Garzê, Chamdo, and in Yunnan's Dechen Prefecture.[11] Based only on the aforementioned incomplete statistics, then, during more than six years of warfare in the Tibetan regions, the PLA engaged in at least 15,700 combats of various sizes.

Some regions also provide incomplete statistics on the number of Tibetans "annihilated" in the PLA's military operations. Qinghai records the number of "enemies annihilated" as more than 127,000.[12] Sichuan puts the number of Tibetans annihilated in six years at 145,000,[13] but deducting around 20,000 members of the Yi ethnic minority brings that number closer to 120,000. The number given for Tibet is around 93,000,[14] for the Kanlho TAP around 22,400,[15] and for Yunnan about 13,700.[16]

In 1956 and 1957, Sichuan's Tibetan region experienced a temporary policy reversal, and some Tibetans who had surrendered during those two years became part of the resistance again from 1958 onward. As a result, the statistics for Sichuan may have counted some people twice. However, many of those who experienced battles and fled the country, such as members of the main force of Chushi Gangdruk and their family members as well as some other fighters from various areas who managed to escape to India, Nepal, or Bhutan, are not included in this number. The above figures are the Chinese government's official statistics for so-called "annihilated rebel bandits," but the number of Tibetans affected by military conflicts was certainly higher.

On November 1, 1961, the CMC's General Political Department issued a directive to PLA units stationed in the various Tibetan regions regarding political work by the armed forces "following the basic pacification of rebellion." This directive mentioned some figures:

> In these years, the number of rebel bandits annihilated has totaled XX [sic] tens of thousands, along with the capture of 135 cannons of various kinds and around 310,000 firearms of various kinds, and only around XX [sic] scattered bandit remnants remain.[17] At the same time as the military operations to pacify rebellions, troops successfully carried out political work that caused major disintegration among the enemy (around 210,000 rebel bandits surrendered, 46% of the total number of enemies annihilated).[18]

This document was classified as "secret," so the figures for "rebel bandits annihilated" have been redacted. However, based on the number and percentage of surrendered people, it is possible to calculate that the total number of Tibetans "annihilated" was around 456,000. According to official sources, the total Tibetan population in 1957 was around 2.7 million,[19] so if this figure is more or less accurate, the number of Tibetans "annihilated" in battle constituted 17% of the Tibetan population. In other words, nearly one out of every five Tibetans was drawn into this war.

Furthermore, figures disclosed in some internal documents indicate the scale of battle in designated regions. To take the Tibetan region of

Qinghai as an example: according to figures from the Qinghai Military Command, in the 18 months from 1958 until the end of June 1959, the PLA "annihilated" 79,053 Tibetans, including 12,624 killed, 3,587 wounded, 29,764 captured, and 33,078 surrendered.[20] At the height of the PLA's suppression, from April to December 1958, "10,415 were shot dead, 2,648 wounded, 21,958 captured, and 25,843 surrendered."[21] Furthermore, Qinghai "liberated 76,258 women and children" over the course of 18 months.[22] Added to the 79,053 people "annihilated," that means that at least 155,311 Tibetans were directly affected by the war. In 1957, the Tibetan population of Qinghai numbered 513,415,[23] so that means that roughly one-third of all Tibetans in Qinghai were directly affected during the 18 months of suppression. During the entire four years of battles, the province racked up a total of "16,600 enemies killed, 4,876 woundings, 46,800 instances of captures, and 58,800 surrenders[24] (including around 20,000 people from neighboring areas and 31 secret agents airdropped by the Americans or Chiang forces)."[25]

The Tibetans numbered among the annihilated did not all have "fighting capacity." Apart from the Chushi Gangdruk Defenders of the Faith, which was a semi-regular army made up entirely of men, the resistance forces in all three Tibetan regions consisted mainly of traditional tribal militia, who were assembled for battle when necessary. In the course of battle, as we have seen, the PLA surrounded men, women, the elderly, children, and monks in one group, and when the air force bombed and strafed, and when the artillerymen shelled at their "targets," they did not, and in fact could not, distinguish between combatants and noncombatants. An analysis of the main battles in the various localities shows that a substantial portion of the people "annihilated" by PLA troops were unarmed, and the large number of "cutting tools" or "blades" seized after battle shows that even many of those who took part in active fighting did not carry firearms. Some of the "cutting tools" seized were probably the small knives that Tibetans used to cut their food. The TAR achieved the "three completes" in March 1962. From March 1959 to March 1962, a total of 93,093 Tibetans was killed, wounded, captured, or surrendered, and 35,523 firearms were seized,[26] representing 38% of the "annihilated."

It was common for prisoners of war or those who surrendered to be killed without cause. A 1961 report by the Qinghai provincial party committee acknowledged that the Qinghai provincial party secretary Gao Feng had emphasized that "'in the pastoral regions, eliminating feudal strongholds requires war,' and directed that more should be killed in battle, and that reactionary headmen should be 'executed when caught.' Some army units and local operatives randomly executed prisoners and criminals, in some cases under circumstances that were appalling and simply unforgivably evil."[27]

National Defense History, published in 2003, reveals that during the war, "In the Yushu Military Sub-command alone, commander Sun authorized the secret execution of 128 persons who had surrendered or captured,"[28] and that there was "unauthorized alteration of the policy of leniency to prisoners" resulting in "prisoners of war being bound, hung, killed, and beaten."[29] Qinghai's Xunhua County saw instances of "group execution of prisoners, and 65 deaths by indiscriminate killing or in training camps."[30]

Executions were carried out by one of two methods: the public execution of individuals captured on the battlefield, for the purpose of "educating the masses"; and "execution on the battlefield," in cases where "the educational value of arrest and public trial was not significant."[31] This involved killing designated individuals in battles. Memoirs by Tibetans tell of captives who were incapacitated by illness or wounds being executed.[32] *National Defense History* acknowledges that in Yulshul Prefecture, the PLA "indiscriminately killed the masses attempting to flee."[33] This bland statement covers up a horrifying incident of mass slaughter:

> Peng Jiguang, a battalion commander in the 183rd Regiment who took part in pacifying rebellion, questioned two prisoners of war in Chumelka[34] in July 1960, and when they didn't answer to his satisfaction, he executed them on the spot. In November of that year, that battalion liberated more than 20 of the masses in the Kunlun mountain region. Two of the women, who had three children with them, attempted to flee in a panic, and the company commander of the machine gun unit

chased them down and then killed them with a revolver and dagger. The battalion commander also ordered his subordinates to strip the victims bare and put them on display to intimidate the masses. A company of the 2nd Cavalry Regiment that took part in the pacification of rebellion killed more than 40 civilians who were attempting to flee on two instances in the Muta[35] area in 1960, giving the reason that the fugitives were armed rebels. A search of the battlefield found that the so-called weapons of the victims consisted of two hunting rifles and four side swords.[36]

A report that the Qinghai Provincial CCP Party Committee submitted to the Central Committee on March 23, 1981 mentions the rectification of a "major case of injustice" in which "86 innocent people were wrongfully killed" at Gomang (Guomaying) Commune in Mangra County. The Guinan County Gazetteer records:

> In the process of this pacification of rebellion, an error of "enlargement" occurred, and subsequently, after reexamination of the case, a mass rally was held in Guomaying on June 24, 1981, to publicly rehabilitate and restore the reputations of 86 innocent people who died, and to comfort the bereaved in accordance with regulations. Another 780 people who had been wrongfully arrested, convicted, or implicated also had their judgments corrected. The main persons responsible for the enlargement, Zhang Guoquan and others, were dealt with according to law.[37]

This simple narrative gives no indication that the 86 wrongful deaths occurred in this way:

> On June 19, 1958, in accordance with the normal methods for pacifying and preventing rebellion in the Qinghai pastoral region, 42 so-called problematic persons were assembled in the conference room of the Xiashituo (Gomang) Township[38] government offices in Guinan County on the pretext of study. In fact, this was an arrest in disguised form; the windows and doors of the conference room were shut tight, armed sentries kept close watch outside, and those taking part in the "study" had no freedom of movement. Early that morning, shots

> suddenly rang out near the village. . . . Zhang Guoquan was seething, believing that rebel bandits were about to attack the government office, and that those locked inside were sure to collaborate with them. He decided to kill everyone in that small, one-story building, whereupon a massacre occurred amidst intense gunfire mingled with people's screams in this conference room with a banner proclaiming "Serve the People" hanging on the wall. A subsequent investigation found that not one of those unarmed victims was a rebel bandit, and that many of them were young people attending the "study session" in place of their elders. One of them was a teacher at a state-run primary school.[39]

The following record was preserved in the 1959 notebook of the deputy party secretary of Hainan Prefecture, Zhang Zhenzhi:

> The rebel bandits had used methods such as evisceration and skinning alive to brutally murder the deputy head of Guinan County, Li Yindong, the deputy party secretary of Xiashiduo District, Wang Chengku, and three other cadres,[40] so the county's cavalry company took revenge by killing 43 prisoners of war under escort after a victorious battle to pacify rebellion. These prisoners had surrendered after a frontline propaganda campaign by our army. Among them, 14 women were executed on the decision of deputy county head Li Wenxuan and military service department director Feng Zaimin, who had led the cavalry company to the bank of the Yellow River. Apart from these 43 people, while searching a tent along the road, the cavalry company fatally shot an elderly Tibetan woman due to communication difficulties. In this way, the cavalry company killed 44 people in Guomaying, which along with the 42 people killed in the government office conference room made a total of 86 people wrongfully killed. These are the "86 innocent people" referred to in the *Guinan County Gazetteer*. Of these 86 people, 70 were male and 16 were female, including one who was eight months pregnant. Most tragically, 3 members of the same family were all killed together.[41]

According to this notebook, more than 86 people were killed in that township: "On June 27 of the same year, the head of the Guinan Farm, Zhang Guangxi, went with others to the Zhacang (Dratsang) Monastery in Xiashiduo and seized eight *akhas*,[42] killing one when they were halfway back and six more when they had almost reached Xinjie."[43] This record shows that even a farm director had the power to seize and kill at will.

The indiscriminate killing in Qinghai Province was not merely the reckless behavior of grassroots cadres, but rather was in accord with the directive of the provincial party secretary, Gao Feng. Yin Shusheng, who was then a cadre in the provincial public security bureau, recalled in his later years:

> At a meeting of the provincial party secretariat on April 28, 1958, to discuss measures to pacify rebellion, the provincial party secretary Gao Feng said, "Rebellion is good! It gives us an excuse to attack the enemy! Local officials and troops just need to figure out and keep in mind who the bad people are, and we can get rid of them in battles. Someone has to take charge of this. The struggle right now is tougher than in 1949, and the battle line is very extensive. The public security organs need to get Qinghai sorted out within three years." At a meeting at the provincial party secretariat on June 16, Gao Feng said, "This time I've decided to eliminate the feudalist strongholds lock, stock, and barrel and complete two revolutions at once. Regarding those stumbling blocks, kill those who can be killed on the battlefield whenever possible; eliminating feudalist strongholds in the pastoral region mainly requires battles. Seizing their chieftains finishes half of the task; shooting them means they're gone, so shooting them accomplishes the task in full."[44]

The Communist Party's top officials were not ignorant of these circumstances. In a June 2, 1959, memo on a report by the party committee of the Hainan Rebellion Pacification Headquarters, Mao wrote that the report was a "Marxist document with profound guiding significance" and ordered it transmitted in the name of the CMC to the Tibet, Chengdu, and Kunming military commands.[45] This document criticized instances in which the execution of policy by local governments constituted "deviation that brings undesirable results to our work of persuading rebels to surrender."[46] When circulating the report, the political department of the Lanzhou Military Command noted that the many important questions it raised "were worth serious attention and study," but clearly didn't take forceful measures to halt these "deviations."

The PLA troops fighting in Tibet "were only educated in patriotism, heroism, and opposing right-deviation, and seldom on ethnic minority policies and other aspects,"[47] and their commanders held that "Changdu Prefecture rebel elements are intransigent and ill-suited for the four nos policy . . . One company commander said, 'There are no good people west of the Jinsha river.'"[48] These examples are just the tip of the iceberg, but they indicate that random killing was not an aberration for the troops and local cadres.

This situation was in fact a direct result of the CCP Central Committee's guiding policy of "military attack, political striving, and mobilization of the masses." This policy put "military attack" first, and the guiding principle of battle was: "When the enemy defends, attack; when the enemy flees, give chase; when the enemy scatters, exterminate; the first battle must be victorious; suppress a locality, consolidate it, and then shift."[49] This gave PLA troops the green light for indiscriminate killing. Monks defending their monasteries, fleeing nomads, pilgrimage groups, traveling merchants, and others were all regarded as enemies to be attacked and exterminated.[50]

With the whole country engaged in the Great Leap Forward, the military's senior officers even launched "a great leap forward in warfare," requiring troops to complete military operations within a set time period. In September 1958, the pacification headquarters and County Work Committee of Zhongdian,[51] Yunnan Province, issued a joint notice requiring a "cleanup of rebel groups in Zhongdian" within that month. In early December, they again required "struggling hard for 50 days to clean up Zhongdian."[52] In June 1959, the party committee of Ngawa Prefecture's "frontline command post" even "called on all PLA officers and men to go all out, guard against arrogance and rashness, and advance on the crest of victory, treating June and July as breakthrough months to complete pacification work one month ahead of schedule as a gift for National Day."[53]

2

After a military operation ended, the main method of "consolidation" was to mass-arrest the local able-bodied men. The power to arrest was delegated down to the township level, and each level handed down arrest quotas to the next level, creating a large-scale fishing expedition. Arrest targets differed from place to place; in Tibet it was "not to exceed 2% of the total population."[54] The population of Tibet in 1959 is given variously as 1 million, 1.18 million, or 1.2 million.[55] Using the lowest number, 1 million, would have meant an arrest target of 20,000. The figures for the other Tibetan regions are incomplete, but available regional figures indicate a shocking number of arrests in each place. In parts of Kanlho, the arrest quota even exceeded the total adult population.[56]

Qinghai Province handed down a quota of 2,000 to 2,500 arrests for Yulshul Prefecture. The prefectural party committee's instructions stated, "Mistaken arrests are the prefecture's responsibility, missing arrests are the lower levels' responsibility."[57] Some places therefore ensured the filling of their quotas by simply rounding up all males 18 or older,[58] and a total of 22,780 people were arrested in the prefecture.[59] The Tibetan population of Yulshul Prefecture was 159,419 in 1957,[60] so even without accounting for people killed in battle or escaped, these arrests composed 14.3% of the population.

In Kanlho Prefecture and Pari (Tianzhu) County, 13,814 people were arrested.[61] Kanlho stipulated the arrest of 21 types of people,[62] and the number of people arrested from March 1958 to June 1961 composed 8.6% of the Tibetan population in 1958.[63]

In Sichuan's Ngawa and Garzê prefectures and Mili County, more than 14,600 people were arrested and dealt with from 1956 to 1958.[64] This number is calculated on the basis of the number of people "rehabilitated" in 1980, as recorded in some county gazetteers, rather than on the total number of arrests.[65]

On March 23, 1981, the Qinghai provincial party committee reported to the central committee that 52,922 people had been arrested in 1958 on the pretexts of "pacifying and preventing rebellion," composing 10% of the Tibetan and Mongol population in the pastoral area.[66] These were just the arrests in that one year. According to the "pacification of rebellion" figures in gazetteers for Qinghai's various TAPs, not counting the Haixi Mongol and Tibetan Autonomous Prefecture, 59,183 people were arrested. In Haixi Prefecture, 693 people were arrested and sentenced, and 11,282 locked up for "collective training" in 1958.[67] If this number is included, the total number of arrests in Qinghai rises to 71,158, about 13% of the total Tibetan and Mongol population in Qinghai's pastoral areas. Yulshul recorded the largest number of arrests, at 22,780, followed by 16,272 for Tsolho,[68] 9,262 for Golok,[69] 8,506 for Malho,[70] and 2,363 for Tsojang.[71]

According to internal documents from Qinghai Province, "The finalized figures in the provincial party committee's Document No. [1982] 55 states, 'In 1958, 85,285 people were disposed of in the entire province, including 64,347 in the pastoral areas, amounting to 8% of the total population. Erroneous killings numbered 899. People who died in jails or training camps totaled 17,277.'"[72] These figures don't include people killed on the battlefield.

According to incomplete figures in currently available sources, at least 125,000 people were arrested in all Tibetan regions on the pretext of pacifying or preventing rebellion. The main source of this figure is the rehabilitation figures for the various counties of Gansu, Qinghai, Sichuan, and Yunnan in the early 1980s. Some counties only recorded the number of people rehabilitated and not the total number of people arrested. This figure only includes the various Tibetan autonomous prefectures, without including ethnically diverse areas such as the counties of Qinghai's Tsoshar Prefecture.[73] The number of arrests in TAR was based on 2% of the total population. There is ample reason to believe that this figure is an underestimate.

Many of those arrested were imprisoned for years. During a period of "clemency" and "rectification" in Qinghai, Tibet, and the Ngawa, Garzê, and Kanlho prefectures in 1979, 1,147 people were released from custody.[74]

A large number of those people had been seized to "prevent rebellion," and some merely to fulfill an arrest quota. At a provincial public security work seminar on April 9, 1958, Qinghai's provincial party secretary, Gao Feng, gave the following instructions:

> Some people who are not currently engaged in destructive behavior may still be dangerous elements, and we can deal with them through the method of secret arrest. It has to be done artfully to avoid detection, using all kinds of methods like getting them into a fight, or having people inform on each other or turn each other in. Once all the dangerous elements are dealt with, there will be fewer problems in society. . . . Who told them to stir up trouble at this time [the Great Leap Forward]? Grab them all and don't let even one of them off, and let them die in prison.[75]

Kanlho Prefecture stipulated that "not a single captured prisoner of war can be released, and those who haven't been captured yet should be chased down by all means necessary rather than allowing them to remain at large."[76]

Consequently, a situation developed in the Tibetan regions in which any male in the prime of life could be arrested and punished indiscriminately. In Chentsa County of Qinghai's Malho Prefecture, only 2.9% of the population took part in rebellion, but 9.73% of the population was arrested.[77] In Golok Prefecture's Chikdril County, 1,249 people, or 13% of the population, were arrested or sent to training camps.[78] In Machen County, 1,844 people, or 18.47% of the nomadic population, were arrested in 1958.[79] The highest percentage of arrests occurred in Yulshul Prefecture's Chumarleb County, where no resistance took place, but 21% of the population was arrested.[80] Other sources state that 1,982 people in Chumarleb County were arrested, detained, or sent to training camps, which would be 29.3% of the total population.[81]

Indiscriminate killing and imprisonment resulted in extreme gender disparities among the Tibetan population. A Yulshul Prefecture census in 1964 found that the male-female ratio was 80.21:100, while in Golok and Malho prefectures it was 88.89:100, clearly lower than elsewhere.[82] Yulshul's Trindu County had a male-female ratio of 78.84:100, and the county's Serkhog (Saihe) Township had the most serious gender disparity, at 69.67:100.[83]

Tashi Wangchuk, the vice-governor of Qinghai Province who was purged in 1959,[84] recalls:

> Under the influence of the opportunistic erroneous line of "exterminating the rebellion beforehand" . . . some shocking cases of injustice occurred in the Tibetan regions, such as "ghost towns," "widow villages," and even so-called "leave a few seeds"—in Yulshul and other places, many young boys draped themselves in sheepskin and mixed in with the herds of sheep in order to avoid being killed.
>
> In Yulshul and Golok, countless men and women, old and young, among the Tibetan masses were bound and loaded into military vehicles and taken to Xining by the truckload. When they were unloaded at the prison gate, many of the prisoners had fallen into a coma and couldn't stand up, and in some cases they died in transit.[85]

In May 1962, the 10th Panchen Lama submitted a petition to the Central Committee stating that during his inspection visit to Qinghai, he discovered that "many people were arrested and imprisoned during and after the period of suppression of the rebellion, which caused large numbers of people to die abnormal deaths," to the point that "Tibetans paid no heed to multiple obstructions by local cadres and came to pay their respects, begging, 'Do not extinguish the people of our snowy land!'"[86]

This situation is verified by the Chinese government's classified documents. On February 2, 1962, the Xinhua News Agency's *Internal Reference,* restricted to senior party officials, published a report disclosing that "in many places in Guoluo and Yushu, the ratio of men to women in the prime of life is one to seven or more, and in some places there are more than ten women for each man. . . . An increasing number of young women want to marry but are unable to do so because there aren't enough men."[87]

3

How many troops did the PLA deploy to suppress the Tibetan resistance?

In a conversation with the 10th Panchen Lama, Ngapo Ngawang Jigmé, and others on May 7, 1959, Mao Zedong said, "Right now the PLA has added two and a half divisions in Tibet: one division is in Shannan, one is in Changdu, and half a division is protecting transportation on the Qinghai-Tibet highway."[88] At the time that Mao said this, the fighting had just begun in Tibet, and of the twelve campaigns, the Lhasa and Lhoka campaigns had just finished, the first phase of the Chamdo campaign was going on, and nine others had yet to be launched. These two-and-a-half divisions, combined with six regiments of troops stationed in the TMC, were only the armed forces that the Chinese government was using in Tibet at that specific time, and in fact only the ground forces; it didn't include the air force or troops that were in the other Tibetan regions.

"Military strength" has two connotations: one refers to the number of the army's organizational units or number of troops, and the other refers to the army's actual capacities, which includes but is not limited to the number of troops and equipment. Based on the currently available material, scarce and scattered as it is across various provincial and military gazetteers, it is impossible to come up with exact figures. By combining the material from these scattered sources, however, it is possible to gain a general understanding of the situation.

Counting the military organizational units taking part in battles in all of the Tibetan regions, the units under the Lanzhou, Kunming, Xinjiang, Inner Mongolian, Tibet, Chengdu, and Beijing military commands[89] totaled at least 8 infantry divisions,[90] 3 air force divisions, 2 independent air force regiments,[91] the equivalent of about 3 cavalry divisions,[92] and regiments and detachments of various specialist branches of service,[93] as well as the pontoon bridge units of the Shenyang and Jinan military commands. This does not include rear-service units such as transport or engineering corps, field hospitals, supply stations, or army depots.

Because rebellions broke out in the various Tibetan regions at different times, the army's tactical doctrine was to "pacify, consolidate, and transfer." For this reason, the same organizational unit would fight in different places at different times. The total number of troops doing battle in each war zone can serve as a reference for the scale of warfare.

From 1959 to 1961, apart from those stationed there and the air force and rear-service personnel, there were around 60,000 troops that directly participated in battles in Tibet.[94]

Starting in March 1956, the Chengdu and Kunming Military Commands mustered 40 regiments and 14 independent battalions, totaling more than 80,000 troops, to do battle in the border region between Sichuan and Yunnan. Of these, the Chengdu Military Command contributed more than 60,000 troops.[95]

From March to December 1958, Gansu deployed 2 infantry divisions, 2 independent infantry regiments, and 2 cavalry regiments from the Lanzhou Military Command, for a total of around 25,000 troops.[96]

From April 1958 to October 1962, Qinghai's battle deployment included 3 infantry divisions, 2 infantry regiments, and 8 cavalry regiments, along with all of the Qinghai Military Command's cavalry detachments, the 13th, 23rd, and 25th Airborne Divisions, and some fighter planes from the independent 5th Regiment,[97] along with rear-service personnel, for a total of more than 70,000 troops.

From these figures it can be seen that a cumulative PLA force of around 235,000 was deployed in the three Tibetan regions over the course of six and a half years.

Apart from regular army troops, each locality also organized large bands of armed militia to assist in the fighting. In Qinghai, 15 militia cavalry companies, 8 militia infantry companies, and 2 people's police companies took part in battle [98] and fought 828 times, or 23% of the total number of battle operations.[99] In Sichuan's Garzê and Ngawa prefectures and Mili County, more than 34,800 members of county production brigades, militias, and people's armed forces units fought in battles over several years.[100] Gansu organized 32 militia units released from production duties to assist the army in battle,[101] and Yunnan used more than 36,100 militiamen and 430 police officers.[102] These incomplete figures, which do not represent all of the manpower involved, already total around 71,000 personnel.

According to currently available public and semiclassified sources, during more than six years of fighting the PLA suffered 10,495 casualties, among whom it can be calculated that 4,448 were killed and 5,223 wounded.[103] These are incomplete figures, and include only casualties among regular army personnel; they do not include militiamen and local cadres killed or wounded in battle. The most senior PLA officers killed in action were Huo Ruhai, deputy commander of the Yushu Rebellion

Pacification Command Post, and Sun Shouzhen, deputy commander of the air force's 25th Airborne Division.[104]

As for the number of people wounded or suffering illness, according to public sources, in Tibet alone "twenty field hospitals were opened at the same time . . . and treated 32,200 ill and wounded."[105]

In accordance with Mao's instructions, one of the objectives of warfare from 1959 onward was "seasoning troops,"[106] i.e., training the PLA for high-altitude combat effectiveness. After the Korean War ended in 1953, the PLA, which had just begun its modernization process, had no opportunity for actual combat, and the General Staff Headquarters, General Political Department, General Logistics Department, and various military academies took advantage of the "pacification of rebellion" to send cadres and fellows "down to the companies to serve in the ranks" and to "study warfare in the midst of war."[107] The armed services taking part in the war included military engineers, anti-chemical warfare corps, transport, communication, and scouting units. The troops were drilled not only in combat effectiveness but also in logistical transport, supply, material allocation, and so on. This war also allowed the PLA to establish a logistical transport and supply network on the Tibetan plateau.

The PLA lacked air supremacy during the Korean War, but on the Tibetan plateau it could fully utilize and train its air force. Guan Shengzhi, former deputy political commissar of the air force under the Lanzhou Military Command, recalls that according to incomplete figures, the air force's participation in battle on the plateau included "34 fighter plane units and 30 fighter planes dispatched in major combat 224 times, clocking up nearly 700 hours of flight time, carrying out 33 bombings, 53 strafings, 33 scouting and photography missions, and 123 visual scouting missions."[108] The air force also took part in 5 campaigns in Tibet.[109] In the course of battle, it lost 2 airplanes. While carrying out bombings, a deputy brigade commander in the 25th Air Force Division, Zhou Tingyan, and his unit were all killed in action, and the deputy commander of the 25th Airborne Division, Sun Shouzhen, was killed when his airplane crashed.[110]

Apart from the battle units, the PLA deployed a large number of rear-service units, including motor regiments, army bases, ammunition supply depots, war-horse bases, veterinary hospitals, field hospitals, material transport stations, refueling stations, etc. In 1956, the Sichuan and Yunnan Military Commands built a total of 22 army bases, 8 logistics groups, a transport battalion using 300 horses, a war-horse base, 5 large and 11 small army stations, 2 transportation companies, 5 mule and horse brigades, 4 supply sub-zones, and 16 supply depots.[111] During the fighting in southern Kham, "every soldier taking part in battle required on average 2.6 rear-service personnel and 9.6 draft animals to meet the requirements of combat."[112] During the first wave of fighting in Kham in March 1956, the PLA's fighting force consisted of 5 regiments and 1 battalion, for a total of around 12,000 personnel, and deployed around 31,200 logistics personnel.[113]

From 1958 to 1961, Qinghai used 3,357 motor vehicles for transport alone, and deployed 1 regiment and 7 battalions of army engineers to build roads.[114] It also built 2 veterinary hospitals for war-horses, 35 military depots, and 55 supply and transport stations.[115]

While engaged in battle in Tibet, the PLA deployed 4 motor regiments and built 2 military depot headquarters, 25 military depots, 103 supply bases and transport stations, and 20 field hospitals.[116]

Furthermore, according to incomplete statistics, from March 1956 to March 1962, the military commands of Kunming, Chengdu, and Tibet mobilized a total of 130,000 civilian laborers,[117] while Qinghai mobilized a total of 7,299 civilian laborers, interpreters, and guides in 1958 and 1959, and Gansu deployed 5,980 civilian personnel in one year.[118] That makes at least 143,279 civilian workers mustered throughout the Tibetan regions during the fighting. More than 4,000 people were deployed only to herd yaks during battle operations in Qinghai.[119]

The above incomplete figures show that some 300,000 people directly participated in the war as regular army personnel, militiamen, or civilian personnel.

Because a highway network had not yet been completed, provisions were delivered by airdrop or by motorized transport. The PLA made 2,731 airdrops in Qinghai,[120] 356 in Sichuan in 1957,[121] and 961 in Tibet (today's TAR).[122] These incomplete statistics make a total of at least 4,048 airdrops of provisions to PLA combat troops.

After being transported on the existing highways or through airdrops, provisions then had to be delivered to the depots by civilian-owned animals. During the war years, Sichuan, Yunnan, and the TAR commandeered a total of 570,000 pack animals,[123] while Gansu mustered around 4,530.[124] In 1959, meanwhile, Qinghai alone deployed 460,000 yaks, 2,905 camels, and 3,500 horses.[125] That makes a total of more than 1.04 million livestock requisitioned. In 1958, 85% of the yaks in Golok's Chikdril County were sent to "support the front," many of them collapsing and dying along the way. In 1959, "there was nearly one yak for each human being and horse, but by 1961, there was only one yak for every eight people (or horses)."[126] The requisition and deaths of large numbers of yaks also made life much more difficult for the herders, of course, and could have been a contributing factor to the famine in Gansu and Qinghai's Tibetan regions.

The years 1958 to 1961 were the years of the Great Famine throughout China, and while tens of millions of people were starving to death, large amounts of stored grain were used during the war to suppress Tibetan resistance rather than to alleviate hunger. In Qinghai Province, frontline soldiers received at least 6.22 million kilos of grain and 8,082 kilos of non-staple foods. At the height of the Great Famine in 1960, the Qinghai Military Command held a stockpile of 35 million kilos of grain.[127] Yunnan Province was one of the areas hardest hit in the famine. In July 1958, the Yunnan provincial party committee reported to the Central Committee that 50 of its counties had been hit with edema, and that some 26,000 people had already died. By August 20, 18,900 people had died in some prefectures.[128] Yet from 1956 through the end of 1958, Yunnan Province transferred a total of 28.695 million kilos of "frontline support grain" and 353,500 kilos of cooking oil.[129] The railway department loaded 733 railway cars from March to June 1959, sending 2,000 tons of rice to Tibet on March 15–17 alone.[130]

During the campaigns in Chamdo, the logistics command post in Nagchu allocated 100,000 kilos of provisions and transported 544 kilos along with 37,800 daily field rations to the front line. The General Logistics Department only "allocated and transferred hundreds of thousands of daily rations and eight months of provisions,"[131] so the TWC was required to come up with a portion of the supplies. During the Battle of Lhoka, the 134th Division "utilized 210,000 catties [105,000 kilos] of military staple and non-staple foodstuffs captured in battle, purchased 140,000 catties, and requisitioned and borrowed 110,000 catties [55,000 kilos] to ensure what was required for battle."[132] Tibet's grain production was very limited, and when the military "captured," "requisitioned," or "borrowed" foodstuffs, it was effectively taking food from the mouths of the people. Furthermore, the army engaged in large-scale hunting of wild animals in Tibet; within one two-week period, the TMC's 155th Regiment hunted down enough animals to supply more than 15,000 kilos of meat.[133]

After 1958, the foodstuffs needed by battle units were mainly provided by local governments, which meant that at the height of the Great Famine, the Chinese government seized food directly from starving people to supply the army. There is no way of calculating how many starvation deaths were related to this war in Sichuan, Qinghai, and Gansu, which experienced the highest number of deaths in the Great Famine.

Apart from foodstuffs, the war effort also needed tents, bedding and clothing, guns and ammunition, petroleum products, livestock fodder, medicine, and other materials. According to the Logistics Department of the Chengdu Military Command, more than 157,000 tons of materials were transported to Tibet over the Qinghai-Tibet and the Sichuan-Tibet highways over a three-year period.[134] The air force airdropped a total of 560.8 tons of foodstuffs, weapons, ammunition, and equipment from March 1959 through the end of 1961.[135]

In these few years, Qinghai transported to the war zone a total of "31,400 (sets) of quilts and clothing, 9,985 firearms and cannons, 6.15 million rounds of ammunition, 2.07 million kilos of petroleum," as well as 4,779 tents and more than 500,000 candles.[136] From 1958 to 1963, the "frontline support outlay" of the various levels of the Qinghai government totaled 32.1 million *yuan*, an average of 6.42 million *yuan* per year.[137] The total cost of this war remains classified information to this day.

4

War, the suppression of rebellion, the anti-rightist campaign, “religious reform,” local government-building, and the Great Famine all occurred simultaneously in the Tibetan regions. Over the course of six years, Tibetan people suffered devastating attacks on their political, economic, cultural, and religious lives.

The Tibetan population decreased sharply from 1956 to 1964. Because the 1953 census figures for Tibet were estimates, an analysis of the more reliable figures for the Tibetan population in Gansu, Qinghai, Sichuan, and Yunnan may produce a more realistic reference. In 1957, the Tibetan population of Gansu Province was 255,947, but it had fallen to 188,050 by 1959 and then to 174,581 by 1961, meaning a loss of 81,366 people, or nearly a third of the population, in four years.[138]

The Tibetan population of Sichuan Province was 686,234 in 1958, but by 1964 it had dropped to 605,537, a loss of 80,697 people.[139] The Tibetan population of Qinghai was 513,415 in 1957, but had dropped to 422,662 by 1964, a loss of 90,753 people.[140] The Tibetan population of Yunnan’s Dechen Prefecture was 64,611 in 1953, but had dropped to 61,827 by 1964, a loss of 2,784 people.[141] Dechen Prefecture had no population figures for 1957 and Sichuan had no population figures for 1955. Even so, from these incomplete figures in publicly accessible sources, it can be seen that from 1956 to 1964, the Tibetan population in these four provinces decreased by at least 255,600. Since the prewar population figures are incomplete, the real number is likely to be higher.[142]

However, a detailed analysis of demographic figures for Qinghai’s Golok and Yulshul prefectures indicates that the population loss was even more severe than revealed by official population studies. From 1957 to 1963, the population of Yulshul dropped 41.3%, from 159,419 to 93,483.[143] The population didn’t return to its 1957 level until 1977.[144] In Golok, according to figures that were “adjusted” for the first time in 1985, the population in 1953 was 100,343, including around 700 members of the “Golok Work Regiment” and “Golok Cavalry Detachment” that entered Golok in 1952;[145] minus those outsiders, the Tibetan population of Golok in 1953 was 99,643. In 1964, it was 56,100,[146] showing a population loss of 43,543, or 43.7%.

Since figures are lacking for Tsolho Prefecture, there is no way to calculate the total reduction in the Tibetan population there, but in the "full rebel" Tsikorthang County, the herder population dropped from 14,050 in 1957 to 10,169 in 1960, a reduction of 3,881 people.

Thus, in the two prefectures of Golok and Yulshul and the one county of Tsikorthang alone, the population decreased by around 110,000, when the official number was 90,753 for the entire province of Qinghai.

The demographic figures for some prefectures and counties give an even clearer indication of population loss. For example, Yulshul Prefecture's Trindu County had a population of 14,476 in 1957, but by 1960 it had dropped to 10,226, a decrease of 29% in three years.[147]

In Sertar County, Garzê, where the "first shot" was fired in the Khampa rebellion, the county work committee on January 1956 declared that the county had "48 large and small tribes with a population of more than 25,600, 24 lamaist temples, and more than 5,000 monks," for a total of around 30,600 people. This was a small increase over the 29,543 recorded in 1953. In 1957, Sertar's "ethnic minority population" was 24,785, a reduction of 5,815 in one year. In 1962, the "ethnic minority population" of that county was 17,641,[148] but allowing for an increase of 939 people resulting from the redrawing of the county boundaries in 1961, the population of the original Sertar County was 16,702, a decrease of 13,898 people, or 45.4%, from 1956.

How much of this was the result of the refugee tide caused by war? In 1969, the Tibetan government in exile published a book in India entitled *Tibetans in Exile 1959–1969*, which recorded in detail the Tibetan refugee populations in India, Nepal, Sikkim, Bhutan, and other places. According to the records in this book, by the end of the 1960s the total population of Tibetan refugees was 85,000, which included all of the children born in the refugee communities in those ten years.[149] Documentary materials and field surveys show that among the first generation of refugees in the Tibetan exile community, most came from Sichuan's Tibetan regions and the current TAR, with very few coming from Qinghai, Gansu, or Yunnan.[150] Therefore, it is safe to say that refugees were not a major factor for the Tibetan population loss presented above.

Recent research on the Great Famine has resulted in the number of Tibetans who died in battle, as "prisoners of war," or as "potential rebel bandits" being swept into the total number of fatalities from the Great Famine. As a result, the secret war that occurred on the Tibetan plateau has not only disappeared from the narratives of official histories, but also in the fog of statistics.

5

The "democratic reforms" in the Tibetan regions had yet another clear objective, which was to "destroy the feudal economy" through fines and confiscation. There is insufficient data to calculate the total value of assets confiscated in the Tibetan regions during "democratic reform," but statistics from some areas can be used as a reference.

In December 1959, the assets confiscated by the Sertar County party committee included:

> 16,759 head of cattle, 929 horses, 6,877 sheep, 1,150 grams of gold, 500 grams of gold dust, 33,354 silver dollars, 167 silver sycees, 833 pieces of silverware, 1,156 RMB, more than 25 kilos of gemstones, 6,240 *yuan* in foreign currency, 6,756 Tibetan rupees, four wristwatches, 5,319 kilos of butter, 1,307 kilos of cheese curd, 13,365 kilos of tea, 30,993 kilos of grain, 7,307 animal hides, 19,824 clothing items, 25 tents, and 2,553 utensils and tools.[151]

In Sichuan's Mili County, upper-strata individuals "surrendered" and "returned unlawfully possessed" 216 kilos of gold and 941 kilos of silver.[152] Confiscated land, houses, livestock, material goods, and farming implements were not included in these figures. In Ngawa Prefecture's semi-pastoral areas alone, 480,000 *mu* of land (around 80,000 acres) was confiscated, along with 26,300 "surplus buildings."[153] In the six counties of southern Garzê, a total of 950,000 kilos of grain was confiscated, as well as 2,000 homes, some 40,000 household implements, and around 60,000 heads of livestock of various kinds.[154]

The assets confiscated from 9,433 households in Kanlho Prefecture included:

> 99,200 head of cattle, 27,000 horses, 427,000 sheep, 1,000 mules, 1,443,000 kilos of grain, 22.6 kilos of gold, 798,100 silver dollars, 3,349,400 RMB, 7,266 sycees, 128.8 kilos of silver, and 339,400 items of clothing, for a total value of 28,298,000 *yuan*.[155]

This was only the tip of the iceberg, given that there were more than 140 counties in the Tibetan regions.

What was done with the confiscated property? Sichuan's Dzorgé (Ruo'ergai) County provides a glimpse:

> On the economic front, a combination of indemnity payments, fines, and confiscation unearthed feudal real property valued at around 900,000 *yuan*, 819,280 *yuan* in cash (including gold and silver ornaments), 73,598 kilos of grain, and various items of feudal movable property valued at 3,332,467 *yuan*, basically destroying the feudal economy. At the same time, joint state-private ownership and joint communal-private ownership carried out socialist reform on feudal lords, herd owners, and the animal husbandry economy of wealthy herders, establishing six joint state-private ownership pastures with 13,698 cattle, 6,611 horses, and 78,767 sheep. In the entire county, 5,078 herder households, composing 72.55% of total households, were allocated 434,390 *yuan* in goods and materials for daily living, with each household receiving an average of 86.54 [sic] *yuan* in fruits of the victorious democratic reform, with a maximum allocation of 700 *yuan* per household.[156]

The total value of goods confiscated during "democratic reform" in Dzorgé County, then, not counting the grain, was 5,051,747 *yuan*, which would have averaged to 995 *yuan* for each herder household in the county, but in fact they were each given an average of only 85.54 *yuan's worth (note that the calculation in the text above is off by one yuan)*. That means that less than 10% of the "fruits of the victorious democratic reform" were given to the people.

In Trochu (Heishui) County, also in Ngawa Prefecture, the "fruits of the victorious democratic reform" were disposed of in this way:

> Compensation and fines totaled 762,509.92 *yuan*, allotted to the collective for the construction of 16 supply and marketing cooperatives and 14 credit groups, retaining 90,000 for business capital, 50,000 to sustain production, 60,000 used to build bridges, roads, and other capital construction, and 223,445.62 *yuan* distributed to 5,532 peasant households.[157]

As the figures indicate, households received an average of 40.39 *yuan* after the government took its cut. In Kanlho Prefecture, what was distributed to the people wasn't cash, but rather "materials for daily living," with an average value of 300 *yuan*.[158]

Ngawa Prefecture's 10,000-plus herder households received around 3,960,000 *yuan* in "fruits of victory," an average of 367 *yuan* per household.[159]

Confiscated or levied homes were mainly confiscated to become government property rather than being allocated to individual families. In Derong County, Garzê Prefecture:

> Confiscated and levied homes, apart from a portion allocated as living quarters to a small number of impoverished peasants and farm laborers, all became state property for the use of party and government institutions in the various districts and townships. The storehouses of agricultural cooperatives and the places where work groups were stationed in the villages around 1960 also used these state-owned buildings (as of 1970, apart from some civil construction in the county town used as offices, the building usage remained the same).[160]

The "fruits of victory" that each household received from "democratic reform" were clearly inadequate to improve their lives, and their symbolic meaning was far greater than their practical significance. The greatest beneficiary of this "democratic reform" in the name of the "laboring people" was, in fact, the CCP government.

The Tibetan regions of Gansu, Sichuan, Qinghai, and Yunnan provinces, although "attacking local tyrants" under the name of "democratic reform," didn't "distribute the farmland" in any genuine sense. The confiscation of assets and establishment of people's communes took place at the same time, and the confiscated land was directly incorporated into the communes.

The "democratic reform" implemented against the backdrop of war also allowed the Chinese government to establish grassroots government organs and party and youth league organizations in the Tibetan regions. During the "democratic reform" period, Ngawa Prefecture "established and strengthened" 162 township-level governments and recruited 914 party members and more than 2,750 youth league members.[161]

From 1951 to 1959, 16 general party branches and 236 regular party branches were established in Tibet. In 1960 alone, 123 party branches and 252 youth league branches were established. From 1951 to 1959, the Chinese government established a number of quasi-governmental offices in areas administered by the Tibetan government, and in 1960 283 district-level government bodies and 1,009 township-level government bodies were established.[162]

This suggests that if "liberation" meant the Communist Party taking total political power, Tibet was not "peacefully liberated." Rather, warfare was used to destroy the existing political structure, expel the existing senior leaders, and establish new government organizations—basically the same method of "liberation" used in the Chinese mainland.

From 1956 to 1962, the iron horse galloped wildly across the plateau. Wherever its iron heels trod, the flames of war were ignited, monasteries collapsed, scriptures were burned, people were killed, and leaders fled into exile. The political system, economy, military, culture, and society of the Tibetan people were completely destroyed.

6

On September 8, 2010, at the Gomang Dratsang Old-Age Home of the Drepung Monastery in southern India, Lama Yetan sat cross-legged on a mat and calmly told me about his life.[163]

As I silently gazed at the elderly man before me, the face of the boy who lost his father in the midst of battle appeared in my mind. Amidst rapid gunfire, his father yelled, "Run! Run fast! Run fast!"

"And your father . . . What happened to him?" I asked.

"He was executed," Lama Yetan said.

Lama Yetan's father, the headman of the Drangtsa clan along the Nyichu River in Garzê County, was taken prisoner and escorted by the PLA to the Tongkhor (Donggu) Monastery, where the rivers converged. All of the monks and villagers nearby were rounded up at that monastery. The soldiers ordered the monks not to wear their robes. Nearly a thousand monks and laymen sat crammed together in the monastery's debate yard, surrounded by soldiers, with their guns leveled, as a public trial began.

Soldiers dragged Lama Yetan's father, arms bound behind him, into the yard. Yetan's two younger sisters were with him.

"They wanted to execute our father in front of my sisters and all the monks and villagers," Lama Yetan said.

A PLA officer told the assembled lamas and villagers, "Look closely. This is what happens to people who oppose the Communist Party and the state!"

Looking at the black gun barrels surrounding them, the lamas and villagers reflexively began chanting mantras, and their droning voices infuriated the PLA soldiers. The officer shouted, "Stop chanting! It's not allowed! If you keep doing that, you're opposing the government and you'll be executed along with this man!"

The PLA soldiers aimed their guns at the chanting people.

The chanting died out, and silence fell over the debate yard. The officer waved his gun in the air and warned again, "Whoever chants or even moves his lips is a counterrevolutionary, and he'll be killed on the spot, no matter who it is!"

The soldiers who were carrying out the execution raised and aimed their guns threateningly, and the plaza became deathly silent.

"Your sisters were standing with your father?" I asked softly.

"Yes. My two sisters were both standing with him, one on his left and the other on his right."

Lama Yetan's face was solemn. His nearly blind eyes gazed off into the distance, as if he could see the blue sky, green grass, and rolling hills around Tongkhor Monastery in his homeland. His aged hands quivered slightly as he grasped his prayer beads. He then went on relate what relatives told him many years later:

A shot rang out, and blood gushed from the Drangtsa headman's head as he crumpled to the ground between his daughters.

At that instant, there was a sudden burst of exalted, rapid, and solemn chanting on the debate yard. The long, mournful wind of the plateau carried the voices of a thousand monks and laymen repeating the mantra, "Om mani padme hum, om mani padme hum . . ."

FIGURE 14. Lama Yetan.
Source: Jianglin Li.

FIGURE 15. His Holiness the Dalai Lama with Tibetan orphans, Dharamsala, 1960.
Source: Office of Tibet, Washington, D.C. Used with permission.

AFTERWORD

1

At the end of March 1959, the political and spiritual leader of Tibet, the 14th Dalai Lama; Tenzin Gyatso, crossed the McMahon Line and arrived in India under political asylum, beginning a life of exile that has now lasted more than half a century. Tens of thousands of Tibetans soon followed him.[1]

The 23-year-old Dalai Lama knew he had to assume the historic mission of saving the Tibetan people and culture from extinction. On March 26, 1959, in Lhoka's Lhuntsé Dzong, five days before he entered India, the Dalai Lama had announced the establishment of a provisional government, and he later established a government in exile in the northern Indian city of Mussoorie, where he was living at that time. At the end of August 1959, the first Tibetan Buddhist seminary in exile was established at the temporary refugee camp in Buxa, on the border between India and Bhutan.

During the period of British colonialism, Buxa had been a prison; Mahatma Gandhi and India's first prime minister, Jawaharlal Nehru, had both been imprisoned there. The exercise area for prisoners was converted into a debate yard. Many refugees had brought along scriptures and Buddhist images passed down from their ancestors, and these were collected for the use of the seminarians. At a time when countless monasteries were being destroyed in the Tibetan regions, more than 1,500 exiled monks and nuns studied under these straitened circumstances in Buxa as a means of ensuring the survival of their faith.

The first school for Tibetan refugee children was established at Mussoorie in April 1960. In that same month, the Dalai Lama and the *Kashag* government officials and their families moved to Dharamsala, in Himachal Pradesh. In less than one month, a Tibetan Refugee Nursery School was established for orphans who had lost their parents during flight or in refugee or road construction camps. The Dalai Lama's mother and older sister personally looked after the orphans, in what became the precursor of the present Tibetan Children's Village.[2]

In 1960, while the fires of war still raged in the Tibetan regions, the Bylakuppe Tibetan Refugee Settlement was established in India. One of Lhasa's three great monasteries, the Sera Monastery, was later reborn there.

On September 27, 1964, the founder and commander of the Chushi Gangdruk Defenders of the Faith, Gonpo Tashi, died in Darjeeling after a flare-up of old injuries. The former PLA officer who had accompanied him through northern and eastern Tibet, and who had changed his name from Jiang Huating to Lobsang Tashi, refused an opportunity to go to Taiwan, and he and his wife spent the remainder of their lives in the Bylakuppe Tibetan Refugee Settlement,[3] where he passed away on May 2, 1991. The memoirs of Gonpo Tashi and Lobsang Tashi have become valuable resources for understanding this period of history.

The young monk Yetan from Garzê County, having survived 33 battles, crossed into Nepal with Aten and others and made his way to India, where he joined the Buxa seminary. A few years later, the hot, crowded environment of the seminary and the deficient nutrition of the monks led to an outbreak of tuberculosis, and dozens of monks died. The rest of the monks were resettled in groups in settlement areas, and Yetan ended up in the Mundgod Tibetan Refugee Settlement. Under the southern Indian sky, the refugees chopped down trees, cleared fields, and rebuilt their lives, along with the Ganden and Drepung monasteries.

Tubten Nyima, the monk from Tsikorthang, fled Lhasa in the heat of battle in March 1959 and reached India through Lhoka. He took part in rebuilding Drepung Monastery and is now spending his twilight years with Lama Yetan at the monastery's Gomang Dratsang Old-Age Home.

Drolkar Gye, the Khotse woman from the Labrang area, reunited with her husband in India. The two of them joined a Tibetan theater troupe organized by refugees, which performed on tours around the Himalayan region. When the theater troupe dissolved a few years later, its members established a refugee settlement in Dehradun. After her husband died, Drolkar Gye formed a new family with her late husband's good friend, Jinpa; a Nepalese housekeeper named Borkha; and Borkha's son and daughter. Now more than 80 years old, Drolkar Gye still shows the charm of her younger years. The little courtyard where Ama Drolkar grows her chives remains etched in my memory.

The herder woman Ngolo, who lived along Golok's Gyaring and Ngoring lakes, escaped with her husband and baby daughter from the bombardment and pursuit of PLA soldiers in the Battle of Namtso. With more than a hundred other refugees, they detoured west and traversed the length of the Changthang plateau, finally reaching Ladakh after a three-year journey. A year later, they went to live in the Dekyiling Tibetan Refugee Settlement in Dehradun, where Ngolo raised her daughter and more children. By the time I entered her home with my camera in October 2010, Ngolo's eldest daughter, whom she had carried at her breast when fleeing their homeland, had gone to live in a Western country. The young herdsman who had pulled her from the battlefield all those years ago was suffering from late-stage throat cancer and was unable to tell me his story.

Damcho Pelsang, from the Khangsar clan in Golok, grew up in hardship. He escaped battle and survived famine but was unable to avoid the Cultural Revolution, when nineteen of his kinsmen were persecuted, some of them to death. In 1993, Damcho Pelsang fled his homeland and reached India, where he became a monk.

Gyari Nyima, the resistance leader from Nyarong, brought his two wives out of the double encirclement and continued west to India. They settled in New Delhi. Decades later, his son, Lodi Gyari, became a special envoy in negotiations between the Dalai Lama and the Chinese government.

The Khampa youth Aten from Nyarong arrived in Dharamsala in 1960.[4] There is no further information on what happened to him after that.

2

In 1981, Tashi Wangchuk, who was then deputy party secretary of Qinghai Province, petitioned Deng Xiaoping and asked him to resolve the "problem of the enlargement of the struggle to pacify rebellion" in Qinghai in 1958. On March 6, Deng Xiaoping sent a memo to the Central Committee Secretariat to handle this matter. After that, the relevant provinces and TAR began organizing special groups to open old archives and reinvestigate cases in order to "rehabilitate and correct" instances in which people had been wrongfully arrested and sentenced from 1956 to 1962.[5]

This included people who had been arrested, sentenced to prison, detained, or sent to "group training" or "reeducation through labor." "Correction" took the form of declaring people not guilty, amending the judgments against them, and reducing their sentences. Based on the statistics provided in local gazetteers, Garzê, Sichuan Province, had the lowest proportion of "rehabilitation and correction," at 35%,[6] while the highest proportions were in the Tsonub Mongol and Tibetan Autonomous Prefecture. In Tsonub Prefecture, "armed rebellion cases" manufactured by local cadres led to 11,974 people being persecuted in varying degrees. These were subsequently declared completely fictitious "unjust cases," and everyone involved was rehabilitated; in other words, the rehabilitation rate in Tsonub was 100%.[7]

In Qinghai's Yulshul, Golok, and Malho prefectures, where the suppression had been most severe, the rehabilitation rates were 98.52%, 83.6%, and 71.64%, respectively;[8] and in Tsojang Prefecture the rate was 76.72%.[9] The rehabilitation rate in the Kanlho TAP was 98.5%,[10] including "8,561 people who did not take part in rebellion but were designated and handled as participants in rebellion."[11] Currently available sources provide arrest figures only for Tsolho and Ngawa prefectures, and no figures on rehabilitation and correction. The relevant figures for the TAR have not yet been declassified. For this reason, it is impossible on the basis of currently available sources to calculate the overall rate of "rehabilitation and correction" in the Tibetan regions, nor is it possible to know how many Tibetans died in prison.

The fragmentary figures found up to now nevertheless indicate how serious the "enlargement of the pacification of rebellion" was. In Qinghai alone, 52,922 people were arrested and punished, of whom 44,556, or 84%, were "wrongly arrested and wrongly sentenced." Of those arrested, 23,260 died in prison and 3,300 in "group training classes," while another 173 people were "wrongfully killed,"[12] for a mortality rate of 52.6%.

Localized statistics are also revealing. For instance, in Tsojang Prefecture, "1,263 people died while in prison, in group training, or in reeducation through labor, constituting 53% of those arrested and punished."[13]

Qinghai Province applied to Beijing for relief or comfort for victims or their family members, an average of 376.60 *yuan* per person.[14] Furthermore, "while handling the aftermath of the enlargement of the pacification of rebellion, it is necessary to extensively publicize the party Central Committee's concern for people of all ethnicities in Qinghai."[15]

Kanlho Prefecture issued a bereavement allowance of 100 *yuan* for each person who died under the "five wrongs," and households whose assets had been wrongfully seized were given a relief payment of 100 *yuan*, while those who had been imprisoned were paid compensation of 50 to 100 *yuan*.[16]

3

One irony is that many of the worst actors in this war ultimately suffered even worse ends than some of their victims.

Defense Minister Peng Dehuai and Vice-Minister Huang Kecheng, who planned and commanded the Lhasa Campaign in March 1959, were purged at the Lushan Conference only three months later.[17] Fifteen years later, during the Cultural Revolution, Mao's final political campaign and purge, which lasted ten years, Peng Dehuai died alone and wretched after being denounced and beaten; he was not rehabilitated until four years after his death.[18]

President Liu Shaoqi, who presided over the Politburo meeting on March 11, 1959, at which it was decided to resort to military force against

Tibet, died a mere ten years later, also alone after suffering horrendous abuse.[19]

Sichuan's provincial party secretary, Li Jingquan, also suffered dreadfully during the Cultural Revolution; his wife died in prison, and one of his sons was beaten to death by Red Guards.[20] The secretary of the TWC, Zhang Jingwu, died during the Cultural Revolution after being beaten and imprisoned, and his remains were discarded anonymously.[21] Wang Qimei, who served as secretary of the Chamdo Work Committee and deputy political commissar of the TMC, as well as chairman of the Chamdo Military Control Commission and political commissar of the Chamdo Command Post during the war, was one of the people directly responsible for the military massacres and mass arrests in Chamdo. He was a loyal Communist Party member who had demonstrated his fealty in 1937 by handing down the order to "execute at will" his own younger brother, who was accused of "defecting to the enemy." In 1953, Wang wrote a letter to the Beijing Municipal Public Security Bureau requesting that the sentence against his brother be increased. Yet, during the Cultural Revolution, Wang was declared a traitor, persecuted, and died in confinement.[22]

Ding Sheng, the commander of the 54th Army who commanded battles in Gansu, Qinghai, and Tibet, subsequently served as deputy commander of the Guangzhou Military Command and then as commander of the Nanjing Military Command during the Cultural Revolution. Accused of "taking part in the conspiratorial armed rebellion activities of the Jiang Qing counterrevolutionary clique," he was dismissed from his party and military positions and was not rehabilitated during his lifetime; at his funeral, he was not even allowed to be referred to as "comrade," but only as "elder Ding Sheng."[23]

Dong Zhanlin, who commanded the 130th Division of the 54th Army during the military campaigns in Chamdo, was subsequently promoted to deputy commander of the 54th Army and then commander of the 11th Army. Implicated in Lin Biao's fatal attempt to flee China in 1972, Dong was put under isolation and investigation, and over the course of two years he was denounced more than 600 times.[24] The commander of the Huang Command Post, Huang Xinting, was persecuted during the Cultural Revolution and imprisoned for six years.[25]

After the 10th Panchen Lama submitted his "Seventy-Thousand-Character Petition," Zhou Enlai said during a conversation with him on July 24, 1962, "If the Dalai Lama doesn't turn around, can we allow his reincarnation?"[26] Less than 14 years later, Zhou Enlai died of cancer, and three years after that, the Dalai Lama made his first visit to the United States; since then, he has continued to travel all over the world. The Dalai Lama was awarded the Nobel Peace Prize in 1989 and has become a spiritual leader revered throughout the world.

4

In the Battle of Ngari, from June to the end of July 1960, some refugee herders fled to the Mustang region of Nepal, on the Tibetan border, where they formed the embryonic "Mustang Guerrilla Force." With the help of the CIA, hundreds of former Chushi Gangdruk members scattered among road construction camps tossed their picks and shovels aside and headed for Mustang to form the second army of the Tibetan resistance. Their main activity was to cross the border and ambush military vehicles on the Xinjiang-Tibet highway, resulting in a section of the highway becoming paralyzed for a time.[27]

The greatest success of the Mustang guerrilla force was not in their military operations but rather in their intelligence-gathering. In October 1961, a detachment of Mustang guerillas ambushed a PLA vehicle, and a deputy regimental commander died in the battle. His jeep contained a briefcase full of classified documents, which was delivered to the CIA. It was from these documents that American intelligence analysts first learned of the failure of China's Great Leap Forward and the famine that had struck the entire country, as well as the breakdown in Sino-Soviet relations.[28]

Fifty years later, I obtained a photocopy of one of the documents that had been in the briefcase. This was a 49-page pamphlet printed on inferior paper entitled *Basic Teaching Materials on the Situation and Tasks in Tibet (trial edition)*, printed by the political department of the TMC and clearly meant as material for the political education of officials and soldiers stationed in Tibet. Printed on October 1, 1960, it was produced after all of the 12 major campaigns fought within Tibet's borders had been completed. The second lesson in the materials contains a widely quoted figure: "From March of last year up to the present, around 87,000 people have been annihilated."[29]

These teaching materials also describe a blueprint for Tibet's future:

> Within eight years, Tibet's cultivated land will increase from the present 3 million *mu* to 10–12 million *mu*, and grain production will increase from the present 400 million catties to 4–5 billion catties; Tibet's population will also increase from the present 1.2 million to around 3 million (including migrants from the inland regions). . . . If food supply can be resolved, large factories from the inland areas can be moved in along with their manpower and machinery, and Tibet can be industrialized.[30]

Over the subsequent years, the Chinese government used all kinds of methods to implement this plan in Tibet, even directly transferring 2,000 people from the Xinjiang Production-Construction Corps to Tibet for the military reclamation of wasteland.[31] However, the Chinese government's battle against nature ended in failure. In 2011, the cultivated land in all of Tibet totaled 5,525,500 *mu*, with basic farmland totaling 4,657,000 *mu*,[32] less than half of the target projected for the late 1960s. This is probably as much land as will ever be cultivated in Tibet.

The process of "fighting while reforming" in Tibet, as in the other Tibetan regions, used the threat of war to push forward the cooperative movement. Within half a year starting in April 1961, "mutual aid groups in most regions were established with great popular support, and at least 90% of farming households joined the groups." Those mutual aid groups "had publicly owned means of production gathered together for unified use; this in fact was equivalent to the primary or top-grade agricultural cooperatives inland."[33]

This document also disclosed that the central task of the soldiers stationed in Tibet in the 8 years after the war was to "strive to construct a socialist new Tibet with preliminary modern-scale agriculture, manufacturing, and scientific culture by 1967," while the main task at that time was to "develop agricultural production, solve the problem of food supply, create the conditions for large numbers of migrants in the future, and prepare the basic foundation for Tibet to develop industry."[34]

However, 1967 turned out to be the second year of the "unprecedented Great Proletarian Cultural Revolution." The aforementioned blueprint was therefore not implemented, and indeed the situation turned out exactly the opposite. The Tibetan regions, still battered by war and famine, suffered a second wave of destruction under the Red Tempest of the Cultural Revolution, as the PLA suppressed "renewed rebellion" among Tibetans in Qinghai, Sichuan, and Tibet.[35] Furthermore, Tibet's communization process occurred later than in China's inland regions, which meant that Tibet was dealing with the Cultural Revolution at the same time that it was establishing people's communes, in the 1970s. In less than 15 years, the people's communes were eradicated[36] and the various communes in Tibet were likewise disbanded.

During the Cultural Revolution's campaign to "destroy the four olds," the remaining 529 monasteries in Tibet were almost all destroyed, apart from the Potala palace and a few others.[37] The Ganden Monastery, one of the three great monasteries of Lhasa, was reduced to ruins. On September 8, 1966, under the organization of the Gyalthang County government, crews of township and county cadres personally took part in destroying the famous Sumtsenling (Songzanlin) Monastery there. Within six days, Sumtsenling, the largest monastery in Yunnan's Tibetan region, built in 1679, was stripped of all its contents, leaving only a ruined shell.[38] The structures of the Labrang Monastery in Gansu Province were either destroyed or occupied, with only one-quarter of the original monastery remaining.[39]

5

Information on the activities of the Panchen Lama during the years of warfare in the Tibetan regions is scarce. While all the events were taking place in Lhasa, Shigatsé seems to have remained calm and tranquil. On March 19, Mao Zedong asked the Panchen Lama to "declare a stand."

The next day, the deputy secretary of the Shigatsé Work Sub-committee and director of the sub-committee's United Front Department went to see the Panchen Lama and reported to him what had happened in Lhasa, which was the first he had learned of the basic situation there. A highway had been built between Lhasa and Shigatsé early on, and the TWC and the Shigatsé Work Sub-committee were also in contact over the radio, so for the Panchen Lama to have been unaware of such a major event in Lhasa indicates that the work committees and his own office must have been withholding information from him.[40]

After the Dalai Lama fled, the Chinese government appointed the Panchen Lama acting chairman of the TAR Preparatory Committee, using him to stabilize the situation in Tibet. The Panchen Lama went to Beijing twice in 1959, and Zhou Enlai, Mao Zedong, and other top officials showed him the greatest courtesy and expressed their faith in him. The Panchen Lama cooperated with the TWC and took part in drafting a series of documents that gave legal status to the socialist transformation that had effectively been implemented through war.[41]

Even so, while the Panchen Lama and his officials cooperated with the Chinese government and supported "democratic reform," and were high-level United Front targets whom the Chinese government energetically strove to utilize, they were still unable to avoid persecution. While the Panchen Lama was in Beijing taking part in the celebration marking the tenth anniversary of the founding of the People's Republic of China, his parents in Shigatsé were denounced and their home was ransacked, and a work group took over the Tashi Lhunpo (Zhashilunbu) Monastery and denounced upper-ranking monks, driving one *khenpo* to starve himself to death.[42]

From 1960 to 1961, the Panchen Lama made inspection visits to the Tibetan regions of Qinghai, Sichuan, Gansu, and other places. At that time, the battles had not yet ended in some areas, and the socialist transformation known as "democratic reform" was still ongoing, so trauma was evident throughout the Tibetan regions. Wherever the Panchen Lama went, senior monks had been locked up, beaten to death, or had fled across the border. The reforms hadn't brought prosperity to the Tibetans but, rather, dragged them to the brink of death. Local cadres privately told him about the famine, and people wept and wailed as they implored him, "Don't let all living creatures suffer famine! Don't let Buddhism die out! Don't let the people of our snowy land become extinct!"[43]

The 24-year-old Panchen Lama was deeply shocked by what he learned. After returning home, he wrote his famous "Seventy-Thousand-Character Petition." Ignoring the tearful pleas of his tutor Ngulchu Rinpoché, he submitted his petition to the CCP Central Committee on May 18, 1962. Although the petition used the Chinese government's jargon to "soften" its criticism, a leader's searing pain for his people on the brink of life and death could be sensed between the lines.

After the Panchen Lama submitted his petition, Zhang Jingwu, Peng Zhen, Xi Zhongxun, Li Weihan, and other senior Chinese officials spoke with him in more than 20 meetings. Facing the Panchen Lama's challenges and questioning during these meetings, the officials either sidestepped major issues in favor of trivia or shirked their responsibility; Peng Zhen even gave the Panchen Lama a lesson on the history of the CCP, telling him to study *The Selected Works of Mao Zedong*, especially the "Investigation Report on the Hunan Peasant Movement."[44]

Zhou Enlai spoke with the Panchen Lama in Beijing on July 24, 1962. This was the last time a top Chinese official would discuss the "Seventy-Thousand-Character Petition" with the Panchen Lama. During the conversation, the Panchen Lama still insisted that "the problem of religion hadn't been handled well, and too many people had been imprisoned." He also said that at the ethnic minority conference convened not long before, no one from the Sichuan Tibetan regions had dared to speak, but that the problems there were serious: "Please show some concern for Sichuan's Tibetan regions." He told Zhou Enlai, "We feel that the worst Tibetan region is Qinghai, the second is Kanlho, Gansu Province, the third is Kham in Sichuan, the fourth is Ngawa, and the fifth is Tibet. Even the relatively better places require correction, not to mention Sichuan's Kham region."[45]

During a conversation with Li Weihan, the Panchen Lama pointedly said, "The situation in Qinghai and Gansu's Tibetan regions is serious; some of it is unspeakable. . . . Since 1956, the Tibetan region of Xikang has been rubbed raw. The rubbing has gone on for a long time and has caused bleeding for a long time. A lot of people have disappeared, and there's no one left to cry out." He passed along remarks by Tibetan leaders in that region that completely negated the "reforms": "People in the Xikang Tibetan region told me that nothing has been done right there. . . . Religious work hasn't been done right and has no achievement." He asked the Central Committee to "please show some concern, because they're also human beings."

Half a century later, reading the Panchen Lama's conversation with Li Weihan is still a moving experience: "On religious and ethnic issues. Please give some genuine help. The situation in these aspects is enough to make one weep. I myself have wept."[46]

At the Panchen Lama's insistence, meetings were held in Beijing for more than 20 days, and some of the suggestions in the "Seventy-Thousand-Character Petition" were accepted and drafted into four documents.[47] However, since the CCP Central Committee refused the Panchen Lama's request to personally oversee the implementation, the documents were never implemented, and this matter became one of the reasons that the Chinese government decided to "give up on" the Panchen Lama.[48]

The Panchen Lama paid a heavy price for his efforts to remedy the desperate situation of the Tibetan people. In 1964, the CCP Central Committee decided to use the "four clean-ups" movement to purge the Panchen Lama. He was denounced and humiliated in public and dismissed from all of his official positions. At the end of the year, the Panchen Lama was sent to Beijing and separated from his people.

When the TAR was formally established, on September 1, 1965, therefore, the Dalai Lama was in exile in India, and the Panchen Lama was confined in Beijing.

In August 1968, the Panchen Lama was sent to prison, where he spent nearly ten years in solitary confinement before being released in October 1977. In 1980, the Panchen Lama returned to Tibet after an absence of 16 years. After that, he made several inspection visits to the various Tibetan regions and spared no effort to save Tibetan culture, which by then was on the brink of extinction. In January 1989, the 10th Panchen

Lama, only 51 years old, passed away in Tashilhunpo Monastery. His death triggered the second "Lhasa incident." The rebellion was suppressed by military force, and Lhasa was placed under martial law for 14 months.

In the fall of 2008, I visited the Central School for Tibetans in Kalimpong, India. This is one of the boarding schools that the Indian government has established for the children of Tibetan exiles. The school was converted from a factory building donated by an Indian industrialist, and to this day it retains some of the factory's old, rusty machinery. The principal said he kept the old machinery there on purpose so that the children would know the history of the school. The children played ball on the playground, and their happy shouts could be heard constantly. Next to the basketball court was a Hindu temple.

After my interviews with teachers and students, the principal, who himself grew up in exile, took me to the school's prayer hall. He turned on a light, and I saw that before the Buddha statue, on the right and left sides, were placed two thrones of the same height. The one on the left held a color photo of the 14th Dalai Lama, and the one on the right held a color photo of the 10th Panchen Lama.

Looking at the photo of the Panchen Lama made me think of that conversation in the Fujian Hall of the Great Hall of the People on June 25, 1962. On that day, facing down Xi Zhongxun, Li Weihan, Zhang Jingwu, Zhang Guohua, and other senior CCP officials, the Panchen Lama, only 24 years old, insisted on behalf of his people:

> On some issues it's said that my viewpoints are incorrect. Today I'm not going to immediately admit that I'm wrong; I'm going to think about it, and if I'm wrong, I'll admit it, but if I'm right, I'll persist. My demands relate to ethnic problems, religious problems, problems of the people's livelihood, and the problem of releasing prisoners and elites.[49]

The principal told me, "I want the children to remember that both the Dalai Lama and the Panchen Lama are national heroes to our Tibetan people."

ACKNOWLEDGMENTS

Many people assisted me in the researching and writing of this book. I would first of all like to express my deepest gratitude to His Holiness the Dalai Lama for repeatedly accepting my interviews to clarify important questions.

I wish to thank my mother, who joined the People's Liberation Army at the age of 16, advanced south from her homeland in bordering Russia to Jiangxi Province with the 4th Field Army at the age of 17, and joined the Chinese Communist Party at 18. Given the generation gap between my mother and me, I know my mother's qualms, and I am grateful that after reading the Chinese edition of my book *Tibet in Agony: Lhasa 1959*, my mother believed in the value of what I was researching and writing. When I went to India for the fourth time to do field research in 2010, my mother took some of her retirement money and stuffed it in my travel bag, urging me to take care of myself in India. I deeply appreciate my mother for her understanding.

I must also thank my daughter, Selina. While I was conducting interviews in the refugee settlements, she arranged her own student exchange program, packed her bags, and went to Europe to study. She never resented my neglect, and in every email told me not to worry. I am filled with gratitude and regret. I thank my daughter for her support and for never doubting that her mother was doing something meaningful.

I thank Sanggye Khyab for repeatedly accompanying me to Tibetan refugee settlements in northern and southern India to carry out interviews, and for translating important interviews into Chinese. Jamyang Ngodup, a descendant of Phupa Pon, former member of the Chamdo Liberation Committee and a commander of the Chushi Gangdrup Defenders of the Faith, provided me with important leads and also served as my interpreter for several interviews. When I was collecting material in Taipei and Hong Kong, Lu Huijuan and Tsoi Wing-mui opened their homes to me, and I thank them for their trust. Kunchog Dropa, a monk from Tewo, Kanlho Prefecture, who was manager of the Kirti Monastery's guesthouse in Dharamsala, and another monk at the monastery, Darje, from Ngawa, Sichuan Province, gave me a great deal of help.

Matthew Akester, who is fluent in Tibetan, learned of my research a few days before I left Dharamsala and offered his assistance, translating the Tibetan materials quoted in this book into English. During the translation process, Matthew helped me a great deal in proofreading the entire manuscript and gave me many valuable suggestions. He also translated His Holiness the Dalai Lama's preface to this book into English. Lauran R. Hartley, Tibetan Studies librarian at Columbia University's C.V. Starr East Asian Library, solved many difficult problems for me by locating valuable historical documents and photographs among the library's holdings.

I thank Stacy Mosher for her painstaking translation of this book into English, which will allow more people to understand this largely unknown period of history. I appreciate Peter Bernstein for representing this book, and Marvin Cao for creating the maps published here. Marcela Maxfield, senior editor at Stanford University Press, provided me many valuable suggestions for condensing the book and making it easier to read for people who may not be familiar with Chinese and Tibetan history and culture. Marie Deer walked me through the editing process, and I deeply appreciate her patient and meticulous work.

I especially thank several friends in mainland China who experienced this history personally while working in the Qinghai region. After reading some of my essays about this part of history, they wrote to me, offering supporting evidence from their own experience and giving me invaluable pointers. Regrettably, I am unable to thank them here by name. When someday this book can be published in mainland China, I will thank each of them individually.

Over the past few years, I've had the good fortune to become acquainted with hundreds of kindhearted elderly people, sitting with them in foyers, parlors, Buddhist temples, and courtyards as they've told me of their personal experiences. The youngest of them was over 70 and the oldest was 94. In this book's bibliography, I've listed the names of more than 50 interviewees, but there are many other names that I am unable to acknowledge individually. I thank them sincerely for accepting my interviews and for setting down their testimony for history.

GLOSSARY

Place Names in the Tibetan Regions,Tibetan to Chinese (Based on Current Administrative Divisions)

TAR: Tibet Autonomous Region

Tibetan	Chinese
Amdo (County, TAR; region)	Anduo
Amdo Méma (Township, Qinghai)	Anduomaima
Amnye Machen (Mountain range)	Animaqing
A-sang (Monastery, Qinghai)	Ehesasi
Barkham (County, Sichuan)	Ma'erkang
Barkor (Street, Lhasa, TAR)	Bakuo
Bathang (County, Sichuan)	Batang
Bayan Har (Mountains)	Bayankala
Bankar (Country, TAR)	Baiga
Beri Méma (Tribe, Qinghai)	Bairi Maima
Bumyak (Pasture, Sichuan)	Maoya
Chabnag (Township, TAR)	Qiangna
Chakpori (Hill, Lhasa)	Jiabori
Chamda (Township, TAR)	Zhangda
Chamdo (City, TAR)	Changdu

Changthang (Region, TAR)	Qiangtang
Chatreng (County, Sichuan)	Xiangcheng
Chentsa (County, Qinghai)	Jianzha
Chikdril (County, Qinghai)	Jiuzhi
Chinglung Dzong (Township, TAR)	Qinglongzong
Choné (County, Gansu)	Zhuoni
Chongyé (Monastery, TAR)	Qiongjie
Chumarleb (County, Qinghai)	Qumalai
Chu-ngon (River, Qinghai)	Qushen'an
Chunyedo (Township, TAR)	Qingnidong
Chushur (County, TAR)	Qushui
Chusum (County, TAR)	Qusong
Dabpa (County, Sichuan)	Daocheng
Damshung (County, TAR)	Dangxiong
Dangra Yutso (Lake, TAR)	Dangreyongcuo
Darchen (Monastery, Sichuan)	Dajin
Darlag (County, Qinghai)	Dari
Dartsan (Tribe, Gansu)	Dacan
Dartsedo (County, Sichuan)	Kangding
Dechen (TAP, Yunnan)	Diqing
Dergé (County, Sichuan)	Dege
Derong (County, Sichuan)	Derong
De'u Yangtso (Lake, TAR)	Tanyanghu
Dhomda (Township, Qinghai)	Qingshuihe
Dhunkhug (Village, Sichuan)	Dunku
Dinchen (Township, Qinghai)	Zhenqin
Do Dzong (Part of Lhodrak County)	Duozong
Drachen (County, TAR)	Baqing
Drakar Drelzong (Monastery, Qinghai)	Saizong

Dralak (Monastery, Sichuan)	Zhala
Drango (County, Sichuan)	Luhuo
Drangtsa (Village, Sichuan)	Zhangzha
Drepung (Monastery, TAR)	Zhebeng
Drichu (River, Sichuan)	Jinsha
Driguthang (Lake, TAR)	Zhegu
Driru (County, TAR)	Biru
Dromo (County, TAR)	Yadong
Drongda (Township, Qinghai)	Zhongda
Drongpa (Township, TAR)	Zhongba
Drongthil (Township, Qinghai)	Zhongtie
Drugla (Township, TAR)	Zhula
Drugyu (Monastery, Qinghai)	Zhujie
Dutsa (In Jomda County, TAR)	Douzha
Dzachu (River, Qinghai)	Zhaqu (Mekong)
Dzachuka (County, Sichuan)	Shiqu
Dzamthang (County, Sichuan)	Rangtang
Dzato (County, Qinghai)	Zaduo
Dzayul (County, TAR)	Chayu
Dzigar (Monastery, TAR)	Zijia
Dzo-gen Rawa (Township, Qinghai)	Huashixia
Dzorgé (County, Sichuan)	Ruo'ergai
Gampa La (Mountain, TAR)	Gangbala
Ganden (Monastery, TAR)	Gandan
Ganden Pendéling (Monastery, Sichuan)	Kangning
Gangri (Township, Qinghai)	Xueshan
Garthar (Former County, Sichuan)	Qianning
Garzê (County; TAP)	Ganzi
Gepa Sumdo (County, Qinghai)	Tongde
Golmud (City, Qinghai)	Ge'ermu

Golok (TAP, Qinghai)	Guoluo
Gomang (Township, Qinghai)	Guomaying
Gonchen (Monastery, Sichuan)	Gengqing
Gongkar (County, TAR)	Gongga
Gongpori (Mount, TAR)	Gongbori
Gyalthang (County, Yunnan)	Zhongdian, Xianggelila
Gyantsé (City, TAR)	Jiangzi
Gyaring (Lake, Qinghai)	Zhalinghu
Gyarubthang (County, TAR)	Jilutong
Gyerba (Township, TAR)	Jieba
Gyesur (County, Sichuan)	Jiulong
Hor (Tribe, Sichuan)	Huo'er
Hordé Sogu (Area, TAR)	Sanshijiuzu
Hor Drango (Monastery, Sichuan)	Shouling
Jamchen Choekhor Ling (Monastery, Sichuan)	Changqing Chunke'ersi
Jayul (Estate, TAR)	Jiayu
Jhora (Estate, TAR)	Juela
Jokhang (Tsuklakhang temple, TAR)	Dazhaosi
Jomda (County, TAR)	Jiangda
Jomdha (Valley, Qinghai)	Jianmuda
Jyeku (Monastery, Qinghai)	Jiegusi
Jyekundo (City, Qinghai)	Jiegu
Kakhog (County, Sichuan)	Hongyuan
Kamalok (County, Qinghai)	Minhe
Kamtok (Village, TAR)	Gangtuo
Kanlho (TAP, Gansu)	Gannan
Khanathang (Pasture, Qinghai)	Kanatan
Khanggen (Tribe, Qinghai)	Kanggan
Khangsar (Tribe, Qinghai)	Kangsai
Khargang (Township, TAR)	Kagong

Kharsumdo (Township, Sichuan)	Kasongdu
Khosin Tuglothang (Riverbank, Qinghai)	Keshengtuoluotan
Kongpo Gyamda (County, TAR)	Gongbu Jiangda
Kumbum (Monastery, Qinghai)	Ta'ersi
Kyichu (River, TAR)	Lasa he
Labrang (Monastery, Gansu)	Labuleng
Lhagyari (Area, TAR)	Lajiali
Lhakhang Dzong (Area, TAR)	Lakangzong
Lhari (County, TAR)	Jiali
Lharigo (Area, TAR)	Lariguo
Lhatsé (County, TAR)	Lazi
Lhodrak (County, TAR)	Luozha
Lho Dzong (County, TAR)	Luozong
Lhoka (City, TAR)	Shannan
Lholung (County, TAR)	Luolong
Lhuntsé (County, TAR)	Longzi
Lieden (Former County, Sichuan)	Yidun
Lithang (County, Sichuan)	Litang
Luchu (County, Gansu)	Luqu
Lunggu (County, Sichuan)	Wenchuan
Lungsang (Township, Qinghai)	Longcang
Machen (County, Qinghai)	Maqin
Machu (County, Qinghai)	Maqu
Malho (TAP, Qinghai)	Huangnan
Mangra (County, Qinghai)	Guinan
Manshung (Area, TAR)	Mila
Maowun (County, Sichuan)	Maoxian
Markham (County, TAR)	Mangkang
Matoe (County, Qinghai)	Maduo
Medro Gongkar (County, TAR)	Mozhugongka

Mainling (County, TAR)	Milin
Metok (County, TAR)	Motuo
Mewa (Township, Sichuan)	Mowa
Mili (County, Sichuan)	Muli
Mitikha (Area, TAR)	Maidika
Miti Tsangpo (River, TAR)	Maidi Zangbu
Mugshung (Pature, Qinghai)	Moyun
Nagchu (City, TAR)	Naqu
Nakartsé (County, TAR)	Langkazi
Namling (County, TAR)	Nanmulin
Namthang (Township, Qinghai)	Wenquan
Namtso (Lake, TAR)	Namucuo
Nangchen (County, Qinghai)	Nangqian
Nathu La (Mountain Pass, TAR)	Naiduila
Nedong (County, TAR)	Naidong
Ngari (City, TAR)	Ali
Ngaro (Tribe, Qinghai)	Arao
Ngawa (Prefecture, Sichuan)	Aba
Ngé-la (Mount, TAR)	Aila
Ngoring (Lake, Qinghai)	Elinghu
Ngulra (Township, Gansu)	Oula
Nira Tso-gen (Lake, Qinghai)	Yirancuogai
Norkhog (Township, Sichuan)	Luogu
Nyagchu (River, Sichuan)	Yalongjiang
Nyarong (County, Sichuan)	Xinlong
Nyemo (County, TAR)	Nimu
Nyenchen Thanglha (Mountains, TAR)	Nianqingtanggula
Nyenpo Yutsé (Mountain, Qinghai)	Nianbaoyuze
Nyenrong (County, TAR)	Nierong
Nyichu (River, Sichuan)	Niqu

Nyingtri (City, TAR)	Linzhi
Paldi (County, TAR)	Baidi
Palgon (County, TAR)	Bange
Palpung (Monastery, Sichuan)	Babang
Palyul (County, Sichuan)	Baiyu
Pangtu (Valley, Qinghai)	Pangzhi
Pari (County, Gansu)	Tianzhu
Pelbar (County, TAR)	Bianba
Pema (County, Qinghai)	Banma
Peltsa (Township, Sichuan)	Picha
Pomé (County, TAR)	Bomi
Zhamog (Town, TAR)	Zhamu
Purang (County, TAR)	Pulan
Pu Tso (Lake, TAR)	Pengcuo
Ralang (Township, Sichuan)	Raolu
Ramoché (Temple, TAR)	Xiaozhaosi
Rangakhar (Township, Sichuan)	Xinduqiao
Ranyak (Monastery, Qinghai)	Rangniang
Rebkong (County, Qinghai)	Regong/Tongren
Riwo Dechen (Monastery, TAR)	Riwudeqin
Rongpatsa (Area, Sichuan)	Rongbacha
Rusar (Town, Qinghai)	Lusha'er
Rutok (Township, TAR)	Riduo
Sampeling (Monastery, Sichuan)	Sangpi
Samye (Monastery, TAR)	Sangye
Sangchen Sumdo (Area, TAR)	Sanqingsongduo
Sangchu (County, Gansu)	Xiahe
Sang-ngak Choeling (Township, TAR)	Sananqulin
Sera (Monastery, TAR)	Selasi
Serkhog (Township, Qinghai)	Saihe

Sershul (County, Sichuan)	Shiqu
Sertar (County, Sichuan)	Seda
Shachukha (Township, TAR)	Xiaqiuka
Shang Ganden Choekhor (Monastery, TAR)	Xianggadanqingke
Shentsa (County, TAR)	Shenzha
She'u (Town, Qinghai)	Xiewu
Shigatsé (City, TAR)	Rikaze
Shingza (Monastery, Qinghai)	Xiangzha
Shokchu (River, Sichuan)	Shuoqu
Shol (Village, TAR)	Xue
Shopamdo (Township, TAR)	Shuobanduo
Shuktri Lingka (Park, TAR)	Xiujilinka
Sog (County, TAR)	Suoxian
Sogruma (Pasture, Qinghai)	Suohurima
Sumtsenling (Monastery, Yunnan)	Songzanlin
Sungchu (County, Sichuan)	Songpan
Tahoba (Township, Qinghai)	Daheba
Taklung (Township, TAR)	Dalong
Taktsang Lhamo (Monastery, Gansu)	Langmu
Tamshol (County, TAR)	Dangxu
Tangpu (Township, TAR)	Tongpu
Tashi Lhunpo (Monastery, TAR)	Zhashilunbu
Tawan (Monastery, Gansu)	Jilesi
Tawu (County, Sochuan)	Daofu
Techen (Mount, TAR)	Dijin
Tengchen (County, Yunnan)	Dingqing
Terton (Monastery, TAR)	Dedeng
Tewo (Township, Sichuan)	Tiebu
Thanglha (Mountain)	Tangula
Thrangu (Monastery, Qinghai)	Changu

Tingdzin Dargyé Ling (Monastery, Gansu)	Chanding
Tongkhor (Monastery, Sichuan)	Donggu
Topa (Township, TAR)	Tuoba
Trandruk (Monastery, TAR)	Changzhu
Trari Namtso (Lake, TAR)	Zharinanmucuo
Triga (County, Qinghai)	Guide
Trindu (County, Qinghai)	Chengduo
Trochu (County, Sichuan)	Heishui
Trokyab (Former country, Sichuan)	Chuosijia
Tsaidam (City, Qinghai)	Chaidamu
Tsakhalho (Township, TAR)	Yanjing
Tsalung (Township, Sichuan)	Chalong
Tsekhok (County, Qinghai)	Zeku
Tselagang (Area, TAR)	Zela
Tsethang (County, TAR)	Zedang
Tsikorthang (County, Qinghai)	Xinghai
Tsoe (Monastery, Gansu)	Hezuo
Tsojang (Prefecture, Qinghai)	Haibei
Tsolho (Prefecture, Qinghai)	Hainan
Tsomé (County, TAR)	Cuomei
Tsona (County, TAR)	Cuona
Tsonub (Prefecture, Qinghai)	Haixi
Tsoshar (City, Qinghai)	Haidong
Ü-Tsang (Part of TAR)	Weizang
Walbentsang (Township, Qinghai)	Awancang
Wara (Monastery, TAR)	Wala
Washul Sertar (Tribe, Sichuan)	Axuseda
Woeser (Monastery, TAR)	Weise
Won Draka (Area, TAR)	Wenzong
Yadzi (County, Qinghai)	Xunhua

Yamdrok Yumtso (Lake, TAR)	Yangzhouyong
Yangpachen (Town, TAR)	Yangbajing
Yilhung (Township, Sichuan)	Yulong
Yulgen (Mongol Autonomous County, Qinghai)	Henan
Yulshul (County, Qinghai)	Yushu
Zechen Gongma (Township, Sichuan)	Changxu Gongma
Zhe'u (Township, Qinghai)	Xiewu
Zhichen (Monastery, Sichuan)	Xiqing
Zongbur (Township, Sichuan)	Ribu

NOTES

Preface to the English Edition

1. Translator's note: Also known as the Tibetan Uprising or Tibetan Rebellion, the Lhasa incident was a revolt that erupted in the Tibetan capital on March 10, 1959, against the People's Republic of China, which had taken control of Tibet under the Seventeen-Point Agreement in 1951. For details see Li Jianglin, *Tibet in Agony*.

2. That is, Ü-Tsang (Weizang), Kham (Kang), and Amdo (Anduo). The traditional three Tibetan regions are now part of Gansu, Qinghai, Yunnan, and Sichuan Provinces and the Tibet Autonomous Region (TAR), and are therefore now referred to as the "Four-province, one-region Tibetan area." The long evolutionary process from the Tibetan (*Tubo*) empire to the "four provinces and one region" is not within the scope of this book.

3. On February 11, 1955, the Chinese government reorganized the original six military commands, creating twelve military commands: Shenyang, Beijing, Jinan, Nanjing, Guangzhou, Wuhan, Chengdu, Kunming, Lanzhou, Xinjiang, Inner Mongolia, and Tibet. Seven of these military commands participated directly in battle, while two other regions provided logistical support such as military hospitals and pontoon bridge units.

4. "Zhongguo Renmin Jiefangjun zhongzhengzhibu guanyu panluan jiben pingxi hou zhu Zangzu diqu budui zhengzhi gongzuo de zhishi," *Gongzuo tongxun*, November 21, 1961, p. 28.

5. At that time, Deng Xiaoping (1904–1997) was secretary of the Secretariat of the Chinese Communist Party and a member of the CCP's politburo. Yang Shangkun

(1907–1998) was head of the Central Committee General Office and secretary general of the Central Military Commission (CMC); Peng Dehuai (1898–1974) was the minister of defense; Su Yu (1907–1984) was the PLA chief of staff from 1954 to 1958 and the vice-minister of defense from 1958 onward; and Zhang Aiping (1910–2003) was the PLA deputy chief of staff from 1954 to 1959 and from 1959 onward was the deputy director of the State Commission on Science for National Defense.

6. *Zhongguo renmin jeifangjun quanshi*, p. 234.

7. *Sichuan shengzhi: junshi zhi (Sichuan Province Gazetteer: Military Gazetteer)*, p. 297.

8. "Summary of the Northwest Region First Ethnic Minorities Work Conference," in *Jianguo yilai zhongyao wenxian xuanbian. 1961. Vol. 14*, pp. 819–44.

9. The former vice-governor of Qinghai Province, Tashi Wangchuk, was instrumental in pushing for this redress. For details, see Li Jianglin, *Tibet in Agony*, pp. 63–65.

10. The English edition was published in 2017. The Chinese edition was published in 2010 as *1959 Lasa! Dalai Lama ruhe chuzhou* (Lhasa 1959! How the Dalai Lama escaped), Taipei, Lianjing chuban gongsi.

11. Bell, *Tibet*, p. 5.

12. *Tuci* (literally "local official") is a Chinese term for traditional chieftains among non-Chinese peoples, granted office by the central government.

13. For a useful review of political and social divisions in 19th- and 20th-century Kham, see chapter 1 of Yudru Tsomu, *The Rise of Gönpo Namgyal.*

14. Today's Zuoni County, Gannan Tibetan Profecture, Gansu Province.

15. In today's Aba Tibetan Autonomous Prefecture, Sichuan Province.

16. In today's Aba County, Aba Tibetan Autonomous Prefecture, Sichuan Province.

17. Today's Ganzi Tibetan Autonomous Prefecture, Sichuan Province.

18. Jamyang Norbu, *Warriors of Tibet.*

Chapter 1

1. In today's Matoe (Maduo) County, Golok Tibetan Autonomous Prefecture, Qinghai Province.

2. Golok was geographically divided into three parts: "Upper, Middle, and Lower," known as "the three-part Golok" or "the three Goloks." Traditionally, Golok had been settled by three large tribes: Wangchenbum, Archungbum, and

Pemabum. Most of the territory of Archungbum is in the present-day Chikdril (Jiuzhi) County of the Golok Prefecture. In the first half of the 19th century, Archungbum was divided into five subgroups, including Khangsar, Khanggen, and Drasar.

3. This narrative is drawn from my interview with Ngolo on October 20, 2010. In the 1950s, ordinary Tibetan people had a different term for the Communist Party's work teams and the PLA than for the Kuomintang Army.

4. Located in present-day Chikdril County, its highest peak reaching 5,369 meters above sea level.

5. Today it is under the jurisdiction of Chikdril County. In 1956, the fifteen nomadic groups under the jurisdiction of the Khangsar totaled 749 households, while its agricultural areas included six stockades and twenty-seven villages. Most of these villages later came under the jurisdiction of Sichuan Province's Aba County. See *Jiuzhi xianzhi*, p. 110.

6. Yan Zhengde and Wang Yiwu, *Jinghai baike dacidian*, pp. 207–8.

7. This narrative is drawn from my interview with Damcho Pelsang on November 30, 2010.

8. In Tibetan, the syllable "pa" means "person," so Khampa means "people of Kham."

9. In today's Yulshul Prefecture, Qinghai Province.

10. The Tibetan term *gyalpo* means "king" and the four larger kingdoms were Chakla, Dergé, Bathang and Lithang. In Chinese, they are referred to as *tusi*, a name for the leader of an ethnic minority. "Tu" means "local" and "si" means official. After establishing political power, the CCP used a series of social reforms to eliminate this system.

11. Lai Zuozhong and Deng Junkang, "Dege tusi jiazu . . . ," p. 177.

12. Zhao Erfeng (1845–1911) was a Qing official who at one point held a senior position at the Sichuan-Yunnan border. In 1908, the Qing emperor appointed him minister (*amban*) stationed in Tibet, but he never took office.

13. In 1931, the Derong County government fell and the county head was killed. The government wasn't restored until 1937. From 1935 to 1936, the heads of Dabpa and Chatreng counties were expelled, and the heads of Dergé and Dengkhok counties were killed. *Ganzi Zangzu Zizhizhou minzu gaige shi*, pp. 12–14.

14. Zhao Xinyu and Qin Heping, *Kangqu Zangzu shehui lishi diaocha ziliao jiyao*, pp. 104–5. This book provides a detailed description of the situation in the various counties of the Kham region during the Republican era.

15. The story of Aten comes from Jamyang Norbu, *Warriors of Tibe.*

16. The rulers of the Hor states of northern Kham in present day Garzê, Drango, and Dawu counties under Garzê Tibetan Autonomous Prefecture (TAP) are believed to have descended from the intermarriage of Mongol or northern tribe (Huren) troops with local Tibetans during the wars of the 17th century.

17. The present-day Sertar County in Garzê TAP. Washul is the biggest tribe in the Sertar area, so the area is traditionally known as Washul Sertar (Axuseda).

18. "Telegram regarding recruiting and grooming a large number of ethnic minority cadres," in Mao Zedong, *Jianguo yilai Mao Zedong wengao,* vol. 1, pp. 138–39.

19. Mao Zedong, *Mao Zedong xuanji,* 5:35. The English translations of this and other lengthy passages from Mao's works come from *Selected Works of Mao Tse-tung,* vol. 5, published by Foreign Languages Press, Beijing, and available on the Marxist Internet Archive, www.marxists.org.

20. "Regarding Ethnic Minority Work in the Northwest Region," in Zhou Enlai, *Zhou Enlai tongyi zhanxian wenxuan,* p. 192.

21. The Land Reform Law of the People's Republic of China, Article 10.

22. Regarding the process of signing this agreement, see Goldstein, Sherap, and Siebenschuh, *A Tibetan Revolutionary,* pp. 140–53.

23. "It Is Worth Noting the View that Land Reform in the Tibetan Areas Must Avoid Hasty and Excessively High Demands," in Qin Heping, *Sichuan minzu diqu minzhu gaige ziliaoji,* p. 37.

24. "Direct transition" meant transitioning directly from the stage of "primitive society" to that of "socialist society" and establishing government and cooperatives without land reform.

25. In 1955, the Yunnan garrison transferred more than 690 personnel to compose 95 ethnic minority work groups, and in 1956 it transferred 1,227 personnel to organize into 163 work groups in ethnic minority regions. See *Yunnan bianjiang minzu diqu minzhu gaige,* p. 18.

26. *Ganzi Zangzu Zizhizhou minzu gaige shi,* p. 41. The Kangding prefectural party committee was established on March 18, 1950, and became the CCP Ganzi Prefecture Committee on January 1, 1957.

27. *Ibid.,* pp. 43–44. The Xikang Ethnic Minority Cadre School and the Tibetan Thirteenth regiment were both established in 1951.

28. *Ibid.,* pp. 41–42.

29. *Sichuan Zangzu renkou*, pp. 23–24; "Basic Conditions in Sichuan's Tibetan Areas," Xinhua News Agency *Neibu Cankao*, April 19, 1959. The figures in this report for monasteries, monks, and nuns are from "before democratic reform."

30. Mao Zedong, *Mao Zedong xuanji*, 5:197.

31. Xinhua News Agency *Neibu Cankao*, February 1, 1954.

32. The *khata* is a ceremonial scarf presented in greeting according to Tibetan tradition, with specific protocols concerning the ranks of the people involved. The stance of the Dalai Lama and Mao in this exchange indicates that the two met as equals, despite their age difference, and the Dalai Lama did not show submission to Mao.

33. Jampel Gyatso, *Mao Zedong yu Dalai Banchan*, p. 7.

34. *Ibid.*, p. 124.

35. At that time it was Taktser (Hongyan) village in Huangzhong County, Qinghai Province. In 1978, Hongyan was incorporated into Shihuiyao Hui Autonomous Township in Ping'an County, Haidong Prefecture.

36. Translator's note: One *mu* is equivalent to about 0.165 acre, or 666.67 square meters. 40 *mu* would be about 6.6 acres.

37. Xinhua News Agency *Neibu Cankao*, February 9, 1953, pp. 128–29; February 17, 1953, pp. 220–21.

38. Xinhua News Agency *Neibu Cankao*, January 31, 1953, p. 221.

39. Interview with the Dalai Lama, June 29, 2009.

40. Translator's note: The first large-scale meeting of Asian and African states, most of them newly independent, took place in Bandung, Indonesia, on April 18–24, 1955.

41. Jampel Gyatso, *Mao Zedong yu Dalai Banchan*, p. 129. In his autobiography, the Dalai Lama states that he had a "strange meeting" with Zhou Enlai in Chengdu, during which Zhou said some positive things about religion but didn't bring up anything else. See Dalai Lama, *Freedom in Exile*, p. 120.

42. Puntsok Wangyal (1922–2014) was a founder of the Tibetan Communist Party and was at one time a member of the CCP's Tibet Work Committee. For an assessment of Puntsok Wangyal's life, see Goldstein, Sherap, and Siebenschuh, *A Tibetan Revolutionary*.

43. *Ibid.*, pp. 201–2.

44. For the full text of the "Seventeen-Point Agreement, see https://en.wikipedia.org/wiki/Seventeen_Point_Agreement.

45. Dalai Lama, *My Land and My People*, p. 64.

46. For the entire text, see *Xizang wenshi ziliao xuanji*, vol. 9, pp. 137–41.

47. Translator's note: Corvée, known as *ula* in Tibetan, was a tax imposed in the form of forced labor.

48. The Tsé Lekung was the office on the top floor of the Potala palace, staffed mostly by monks, and the Shol Lekung was the office below the palace, staffed mostly by laymen.

49. *History of Democratic Reform in the Ganzi Tibetan Autonomous Prefecture*, p. 41.

50. Qin Heping, "Guanyu Sichuan Ganzi Zangqu yu Xizang diqu minzhu gaige de renshi," p. 412.

51. For the full text, see *Sichuan shengzhi: Fulu*, pp. 215–19.

52. It was passed by the sixth plenum of the Seventh Central Committee.

53. *Dangdai Zhongguo minzu gongzuo dashiji*, vol. 2, p. 74.

54. *Dangdai Yunnan Zangzu jianshi*, p. 44.

55. Fan Ming, *Xizang neibu zhi zheng*, p. 370.

56. *Ganzi Zangzu Zizhizhou minzu gaige shi*, p. 42.

Chapter 2

1. Translator's note: That is, recounting past suffering and victimization.

2. Qin Heping, *Sichuan minzu diqu minzhu gaige ziliaoji*, p. 180. Gyesur County was an ethnically mixed area made up mainly of Tibetans, Yi, and Chinese.

3. "Decision on the Division of Rural Classes," passed on August 4, 1950 and promulgated on August 20.

4. *Ganzi Zangzu Zizhizhou minzu gaige shi*, pp. 50–51.

5. Qin Heping and Ran Linwen, *Sichuan minzu diqu minzhu gaige dashiji*, p. 182.

6. This policy resulted from lessons learned during the CCP's reforms in the Inner Mongolian pastoral regions. For related documents and reports see *Neimenggu de tudi zhidu gaige*.

7. These were the counties of Bathang (Batang), Lithang (Litang), Chatreng (Xiangcheng), Derong (Derong), Dabpa (Daocheng) and Lieden. Lieden Country was dissolved in 1978.

8. Qin Heping and Ran Linwen, *Sichuan minzu diqu minzhu gaige dashiji*, pp. 26–27.

9. Qin Heping, *Sichuan minzu diqu minzhu gaige ziliaoji*, pp. 88–95.

10. *Ganzi Zangzu Zizhizhou minzu gaige shi*, p. 43: From January to March, 1956, 7,752 cadres and activists were involved in land reform in the Garzê TAP, including

2,580 Tibetan cadres, and in the villages they recruited 4,052 people temporarily released from production.

11. Xinhua News Agency *Neibu Cankao*, August 20, 1952. P. 262.

12. *Seda Xianzhi*, p. 5.

13. *Seda Xianzhi*, p. 7. Regarding the timing of the insurrection among Sertar County's Washul tribe, there are many conflicts among the Chinese materials. *Ganzi Zangzu Zizhizhou junshi zhi* records: "February 25 . . . The Seda area's great chieftain Rigzin Dondrup (who became head of Seda County after liberation) . . . planned and organized more than 2,000 from thirty-seven tribal settlements in the Seda area, along with more than 1,600 firearms, led by the headmen of each tribe under Rigzin Dondrup's unified command, to take part in an armed rebellion." However, *Seda Xianzhi* (the *Seda County Gazetteer)* contains no such record.

14. *Ganzi Zangzu Zizhizhou minzu gaige shi*, p. 56.

15. Ame Ade, *Jiyi de shengyin*, p. 87.

16. *Ganzi Zangzu Zizhizhou minzu gaige shi*, p. 58.

17. Barnett, *Resistance and Reform in Tibet.* pp. 192–93.

18. *Sichuan shengzhi: junshi zhi*, p. 295. In addition, according to data on the same page of this book, "This rebellion spread to forty-four out of fifty counties in the Liangshan and Xichang Yi regions and to the Ganzi and Aba Tibetan regions, an area of about 250,000 square kilometers and a population of 1.4 million. An estimated 150,000-plus people took part in the rebellion at various times (with more than 5,000 people fleeing the regions), and there were more than 130,000 guns." See also *Ganzi Zangzu Zizhizhou minzu gaige shi*, p. 101; and *Ganzi Zangzu Zizhizhou junshi zhi*, p. 185.

19. Zhang Dingyi, "1954 nian Dalai," pp. 50–51.

20. See chapter 1, section 4.

21. According to the preliminary plan on land reform in the Tibetan regions submitted to the Central Committee by the Xikang and Sichuan provincial party committees on September 22, 1955, there were some eighty thousand firearms in Garzê and Ngawa, of which 70% were held by ordinary people. See *Sichuan shengzhi: Fulu*, p. 216.

22. In 1953, the Chinese government began implementing planned grain requisition in the countryside along with a rationing policy in the cities, known as the state monopoly for purchasing and marketing. Once the policy was implemented, the government placed strict control on foodstuffs. Peasants could no longer take their excess grain to the markets to trade it freely but were obliged to sell their

grain to the government at set low prices, and the government imposed excessively high procurement quotas on the peasants. Likewise, urban residents couldn't buy foodstuffs at the market but had to obtain food at fixed prices at the grain shops established under the government's unified system. This policy continued until the 1980s. It effectively deprived the peasants of the freedom to deal with their excess produce and is considered one of the reasons for the destitution of China's peasants during this period. Although this system was imposed on Tibet and the Tibetan regions later than in the inland regions, at this time the government was already imposing high grain requisition quotas on the Tibetan regions in the form of agricultural taxes. This is described in greater detail below.

23. *Ganzi Zangzu Zizhizhou junshi zhi*, p. 184.

24. Goldstein, Sherap, and Siebenschuh, *A Tibetan Revolutionary*, pp. 196–97.

25. Zhang Xiangming, *Zhang Xiangming 55 nian Xizang gongzuo shilu*, p. 69.

26. Barnett, *Resistance and Reform in Tibet*, pp. 192–93; Dawa Tsering, *Xueji xueyu*, pp. 75–77.

27. Trokyab was dissolved in 1959 and absorbed into Barkham and Dzamthang (Rangtang) counties.

28. Qin Heping and Ran Linwen, *Sichuan minzu diqu minzhu gaige dashiji*, p. 138.

29. *Ganzi zhouzhi*, p. 1319.

30. Qin Heping and Ran Linwen, *Sichuan minzu diqu minzhu gaige dashiji*, p. 57.

31. In Chinese sources, the term used is *jianmie*. It is a frequently used military term meaning "to wipe out (an enemy unit)," to defeat completely. The term does not mean "completely kill," but it includes those killed, wounded, surrendered, and captured.

32. *Luhuo xianzhi*, p. 13.

33. According to the preliminary land reform plan that the Xikang and Sichuan provincial party committees submitted to the Central Committee on September 22, there were around a thousand people in the upper strata of Garzê Prefecture, including around six hundred headmen and around four hundred senior lamas, and more than five hundred of them had been given official positions. See *Sichuan shengzhi: Fulu*, p. 217.

34. Qin Heping and Ran Linwen, *Sichuan minzu diqu minzu gaige dashiji*, p. 137.

35. *Ganzi Zangzu Zizhizhou minzu gaige shi*, pp. 1–27.

36. *Tralpa* were taxpayer families that leased land from landowners and had to fulfill corvée obligations. For more information on the Tibetan land system, see

Carrasco, *Land and Polity in Tibet*; Goldstein, "Taxation and the Structure of a Tibetan Village"; Miller, "Last Rejoinder to Goldstein on Tibetan Social System."

37. *Gepa*, as hired hands, had a lower social status than *tralpa*.

38. *Sichuan shengzhi: Fulu*, pp. 8–9.

39. Zhang Zhengming, "Ganzi Zangqu shehui xingtai de chubu kaocha," p. 11.

40. Since the 1980s, there has been much research published on the history of the CCP's land reform and on land reform policies. For land reform methods and the violent land reform carried out in the Jin-Sui region under the leadership of Li Jingquan and He Long, see Gao Wangling and Liu Yang, "Tugai de jiduanhua"; Zhi Xiaomin, *Liu Shaoqi yu Jin-Sui tugai*.

41. *Ganzi Zangzu Zizhizhou minzu gaige shi*, pp. 55–57.

42. *Ibid.*, p. 140.

43. *Ganzi Zangzu Zizhizhou junshi zhi*, pp. 185–86.

44. *Ganzi Zangzu Zizhizhou minzu gaige shi*, p. 140.

45. Calculated from the list of military personnel killed in action during the four years of "pacifying the rebellion" in Ganzi Prefecture. See *Ganzi Zangzu Zizhizhou junshi zhi*, pp. 303–67.

46. *Ganzi Zangzu Zizhizhou junshi zhi*, p. 186.

47. In the 1950s, the PLA was organized into a Soviet-style "3–3 system": in each army there were three divisions, in each division there were three regiments, in each regiment there were three battalions, and so on down to the squad level. A squad was made up of ten soldiers, and a company had around a hundred soldiers.

48. On April 9, 1956, the CCP Central Committee's "Guanyu Sichuan sheng Yizu he Zangzu diqu fangeming panluan qingkuang de tongbao" (Notice Regarding the Situation of the Counterrevolutionary Rebellion in the Yi and Tibetan Ethnic Minority Areas of Sichuan Province) stated that there were "more than 13,000 rebels." See *Tongzhan zhengce wenjian huibian*, Vol. 3, pp. 1777–81. Another Chinese source, *Ganzi Zangzu Zizhizhou junshi zhi*, gives the number as 16,000.

49. *Ganzi Zangzu Zizhizhou junshi zhi*, p. 187.

Chapter 3

1. I.e., the counties of Lithang (Lihua), Dabpa (Daocheng), and Chatreng (Dingxiang, today's Xiangcheng).

2. *Litang xianzhi*, p. 255.

3. Miao Pi-yi, *Miao Pi-yi huiyilu*, p. 142.

4. Details of this meeting will be described in chapter 5, section 2.

5. Dawa Tsering, *Xueji xueyu*, pp. 90–92; interview with Ratuk Ngawang, December 3, 2009.

6. Deng Jiahua, "Yi Litang pingpan," p. 405.

7. *Ganzi Zangzu Zizhizhou Litangsi, Dajinsi, Ganzisi, Babangsi diaocha cailiao*, p. 10.

8. Interview with Ratuk Ngawang, December 3, 2009.

9. In Lithang's Bumyak (Maoya) township, for example, families possessing 10 or more head of livestock had a corvée obligation to the headman, and were divided into nine classes. Those with 140–299 head of livestock had to provide two good guns, and families with 300 or more head of livestock had to provide three guns. Families with 9 or fewer animals had no corvée obligation. For details, see *Ganzi Zangzu Zizhizhou Litangxian Maoya muqu shehui diaocha baogao*, pp. 235–36.

10. See *Sichuan shengzhi: Fulu*, p. 216.

11. Chinese-language materials state that the "head traitors," such as Tsewang Rigchen, were all monks at the Lithang Monastery. See Dorjé Tseten, "Kangnan Litang pingxi panluan he minzhu gaige qingkuang gaishu," p. 90.

12. The request was rejected. Interview with Ratuk Ngawang, December 3, 2009.

13. *Litang xianzhi*, p. 15.

14. *Ganzi Zangzu Zizhizhou Litangsi, Dajinsi, Ganzisi, Babangsi diaocha cailiao*, p. 1.

15. *Ibid.*, p. 20.

16. This is a township in Dartsedo County east of Lithang; Yidun (Lieden) County was southwest of Lithang.

17. Yidun County was dissolved in 1978 and divided between Lithang and Bathang counties.

18. Today's Minle village in Gaocheng (Kaotrin) township, Lithang County.

19. Bumyak's hot spring, about five kilometers west of today's Lithang County seat.

20. *Litang xianzhi*, p. 355.

21. This was likely a temporary military airport.

22. Information on the PLA's military deployment for the Battle of Lithang comes from *Litang xianzhi*, pp. 354–56.

23. *Ganzi Zangzu Zizhizhou junshi zhi*, p. 188.

24. Dawa Tsering, *Xueji xueyu*, pp. 95–96; Ratuk Ngawang, *mDo khams spo 'bor sgang gi Li thang*.

25. *Litang xianzhi*, p. 355.

26. *Ganzi Zangzu Zizhizhou junshi zhi*, pp. 187–88.

27. *Litang xianzhi*, p. 356.

28. *Ibid.*

29. Jian Jun, *Xueyuan gouhuo*.

30. Zhang Guoxiang and Sun Yong, "Zhongguo tu-4 chuanqi," p. 32.

31. *Litang xianzhi*, p. 356. See also *Ganzi Zangzu Zizhizhou junshi zhi*, p. 188.

32. Dawa Tsering, *Xueji xueyu*, p. pp. 93–94.

33. *Litang xianzhi*, p. 356. About the escaping, see Dawa Tsering, *Xueji xueyu*, p. 95. See also Goldstein, *A History of Modern Tibet*, vol. 3, ch. 8.

34. *Litang xianzhi*, p. 356.

35. *Ibid.*

36. Interview with Geshe Lobsang, November 21, 2009.

37. Interview with Ratuk Ngawang, December 3, 2009.

38. See *Ganzi zhouzhi*, p. 50; *Litang xiangzhi*, p. 15; *Ganzi Zangzu Zizhizhou junshi zhi*, p. 188.

39. "Zhongyang guanyu Sichuan sheng Yizu he Zangzu diqu fangeming panluan qingkuang de tongbao" (Central Committee notice regarding the situation of counterrevolutionary armed rebellion in the Yi and Tibetan ethnic minority areas of Sichuan Province), in *Tongzhan zhengce wenjian huibian*, p. 1778.

40. *Ganzi Zangzu Zizhizhou junshi zhi*, p. 188. Those taken prisoner probably included monks who were in the monastery at the time.

41. *Litang xiangzhi*, p. 353.

42. *Ibid.*, p. 356.

Chapter 4

1. When Zhao Erfeng abolished the gyalpos in 1908, he established the area as Dingxiang County. When the province of Xikang was established in 1939, Dingxiang County was put under its jurisdiction. After the CCP assumed power and occupied the area in 1951, it was renamed Xiangcheng County.

2. Zhang Chaojian, "Sanxiang yipie" (A brief survey of Sanxiang), in Zhao Xinyu, Qin Heping, and Wang Chuan, *Kangqu Zangzu shehui zhenxi ziliao jiyao*, pp. 411–18.

3. Sun Shaoqian, "Pingxiang jishi" (Record of putting down Dingxiang rebellion), in Zhao Xinyu, Qin Heping, and Wang Chuan, *Kangqu Zangzu shehui zhenxi ziliao jiyao*, pp. 258–71.

4. *Xiangcheng xianzhi*, p. 16.

5. Kargyal Dondrup, *Mdo khams cha phreng kyi lo rgyus gser gyi snye ma*. (Matthew Akester kindly translated some pages of this book for me.)

6. *Xiangcheng xianzhi*, p. 197.

7. Kargyal Dondrup, *Mdo khams cha phreng kyi lo rgyus gser gyi snye ma*, p. 160.

8. *Xiangcheng xianzhi*, p. 19.

9. *Ibid.*

10. Kargyal Dondrup, *Mdo khams cha phreng kyi lo rgyus gser gyi snye ma*, p. 160.

11. A group set up during land reform.

12. Kargyal Dondrup, *Mdo khams cha phreng kyi lo rgyus gser gyi snye ma*, p. 160.

13. *Xiangcheng xianzhi* (Xiangcheng County Gazetteer), p. 275.

14. The Third Trijang Rinpoché, Lobsang Yeshe Tenzin Gyatso (1901–1981), became junior tutor of the Fourteenth Dalai Lama in 1951. Sampeling was Trijiang Rinpoché's home monastery.

15. Today's Shangri-La City in Yunnan's Dechen Tibetan Autonomous Prefecture.

16. *Xiangcheng xianzhi*, p. 275.

17. Carole McGranahan, *Arrested Histories*, p. 76.

18. Dawa Tsering, *Xueji xueyu*, p. 97.

19. *Xiangcheng xianzhi*, p. 278.

20. In Tibetan Buddhism, believers burn dried juniper with *tsampa* (roasted barley flour) and other fragrant materials to show respect to deities, to pray for blessings, and to ward off evil.

21. Kargyal Dondrup, *Mdo khams cha phreng kyi lo rgyus gser gyi snye ma*, p. 160.

22. *Xiangcheng xianzhi*, p. 278.

23. *Ibid.*

24. Qin Heping and Ran Linwen, *Sichuan minzu diqu minzhu gaige dashiji*, p. 111.

25. For a facsimile of the leaflets, see Ji Jiansheng, "Niu Qian jiang shou hua 'gongniu.'" This text does not state that the leaflet was scattered over Chatreng, but the content is consistent with that of the leaflets recalled by Tibetans.

26. According to *Xiangcheng xianzhi*, p. 279, the aircraft "fired several rounds and scattered some leaflets" that day. According to the recollections of Tibetans, the aircraft dropped a bomb that day.

27. *Xiangcheng xianzhi*, p. 279.

28. Tibetan sources state that this battle lasted 19 days. See Kargyal Dondrup, *Mdo khams cha phreng kyi lo rgyus gser gyi snye ma*.

29. *Ganzi Zangzu Zizhizhou junshi zhi*, p. 188. The number of bombs dropped was calculated according to a biographical essay by Liu Hengxun, one of the Tupolev Tu-4 airmen who took part in the bombing of Bathang. See Liu Hengxun, "Chuanxi pingpan jishi."

Chapter 5

1. Shana (1918–1967) joined the Chinese Communist Party in 1937, and from 1955 onward served as head of the Ganzi Tibetan Autonomous Prefecture People's Government, deputy commander of the Kangding Military Command, and held other local and central-level positions. He was persecuted and died during the Cultural Revolution.

2. Jamyang Norbu, *Warriors of Tibet*, p. 107.

3. *Ibid.*, p. 108.

4. The legendary king of Ling, subject of the Tibetan *Epic of King Gesar*.

5. Today's Raolu Township, Xinlong County, Garzê TAP.

6. Luo Yinjun, "Huiyi Xinlong xian de minzhu gaige," pp. 227–54.

7. For details on the resistance of the Nyarong Tibetans and its suppression, see Jamyang Norbu, *Warriors of Tibet;* McGranahan, *Arrested Histories*, pp. 80–85: *Ganzi Zangzu Zizhizhou junshi zhi*, p. 198; *Sichuan shengzhi: junshi zhi*, p. 297; *Xinlong xianzhi*, pp. 13, 241; Xinlong County Literary and Historical Materials Editorial Committee, *Xinlong xian wenshi zhiliao diyiji*, pp. 45–67.

8. Luo Yinjun, "Huiyi Xinlong xian de minzhu gaige," pp. 230–31.

9. Today's Gyarashi Township, Xinlong County, Garzê TAP.

10. Jamyang Norbu, *Warriors of Tibet*, p. 105. Luo Yinjun, who took part in land reform in Xinlong County, recalls this incident in his memoir, but doesn't mention Gyurmé's family being killed. He only acknowledges that "under the particular historical conditions of that time, in various times and places, it was impossible for our comrades not to have some problems in their work methods, and they were upbraided." However, he does say that after the incident, Gyurmé's relatives wanted "to take revenge for Gyurmé's family." See Luo Yinjun, "Huiyi Xinlong xian de minzhu gaige," pp. 232–33.

11. In today's Peltsa township, Xinglong County. Ador was a *baihu*, i.e., headman of one hundred households.

12. Luo Yinjun, "Huiyi Xinlong xian de minzhu gaige," pp. 231–32.

13. Xinlong County Literary and Historical Materials Editorial Committee, *Xinlong xian wenshi zhiliao diyiji*, p. 54; Luo Yinjun, "Huiyi Xinlong xian de minzhu gaige," p. 245.

14. Jamyang Norbu, *Warriors of Tibet*, p. 112.

15. *Ibid.*, p. 113.

16. *Ibid.*, pp. 113–114.

17. *Ganzi Zangzu Zizhizhou minzu gaige shi*, pp. 66–67.

Chapter 6

1. Now part of Kanlho Tibetan Autonomous Prefecture.

2. The grassland is also referred to as the Ruo'ergai (Dzorgé) grassland or Ruo'ergai marsh.

3. In 1987 the prefecture was renamed Ngawa Tibetan and Qiang Autonomous Prefecture. Traditional Ngawa was approximately equivalent to the current Ngawa County, while the current Ngawa Prefecture includes the traditional Gyalrong and other places.

4. The county's name was changed to Jiuzhagou (Dzitsa Dégu) County in 1998.

5. *Aba Zangzu Zizhizhou gaikuang*, p. 139.

6. Part of today's Ruo'ergai County, Ngawa Tibetan and Qiang Autonomous Prefecture, Sichuan Province. See *Aba Zangzu Qiangzu Zizhizhou zhi* (Aba Tibetan Autonomous Prefecture Gazetteer), p. 768.

7. The village was the present-day E'en Village in Hongyan Township, Heishui County, Ngawa Tibetan and Qiang Autonomous Prefecture.

8. *Heishui xianzhi*, p. 38. At that time, the county had 13 townships.

9. Xinhua News Agency *Neibu Cankao*, January 4, 1957.

10. *Heishui xianzhi*, p. 38.

11. *Ibid.*

12. *Xinhua News Agency Neibu Cankao*, June 21, 1956, p. 559.

13. For details, see Xinhua News Agency *Neibu Cankao*, January 14, 1957, pp. 239–41.

14. *Aba Zangzu Qiangzu Zizhizhou zhi*, p. 768.

15. *Ibid.*, p. 769.

16. Xinhua News Agency *Neibu Cankao*, January 14, 1957, p. 239.

17. *Ibid.*, p. 241. This explanation contradicts the first portion of the report, which was that the troops only realized that the men were tribal elders after they had killed them.

18. *Ibid.*, p. 239.

19. Located in what is now Thangkor (Tangke) Township, Dzorgé (Ruo'ergai) County, Ngawa TAP.

20. *Sichuan shengzhi: Nongye zhi*, vol. 2, p. 168.

21. The Chinese government's "goodwill troupes" (*weiwentuan*) carried out inspections at the local level while at the same time pacifying local sentiment with dance performances, film screenings, and relief provisions of food and clothing.

22. *Xinhua News Agency Neibu Cankao*, January 14, 1957, pp. 241–42.

23. According to statistics relating to the "pacification of the rebellion" provided in *Aba Zangzu Qiangzu Zizhizhou zhi*, pp. 766–70.

24. Xinhua News Agency *Neibu Cankao*, June 21, 1956.

25. Qin Heping, *Sichuan minzu diqu minzhu gaige ziliaoji*, p. 42.

26. Palgon Trinlé (1915–1966) was the last chieftain of the Metsang, Ngawa's ruling family. After 1949 he served as vice-chairman of the Ngawa Provisional Military and Political Committee, vice-chairman of the Ngawa TAP People's Government, deputy head of the Ngawa TAP, vice-chairman of the second and third sessions of the Sichuan Province People's Political Consultative Conference, and delegate to the first through third sessions of the National People's Congress. He drowned himself during the Cultural Revolution, after his wife committed suicide.

27. Xinhua News Agency *Neibu Cankao*, January 14, 1957, pp. 241–44.

28. Located in today's Shigtsang and Larigul townships, Luchu County, Kanlho TAP.

29. This was the "Battle of Shaiyintan." For details, see *Zhongguo Renmin Jiefangjun bubing dishiyishi junzhanshi*, pp. 220–22. The Tibetan name for Shaiyintan is Sayéthang, in Gashul (Gaxiu) Village, Tso-nyin (Gahai) Township, Luchu County in the Kanlho TAP. This case was reexamined and redressed in 1984.

Chapter 7

1. Zhang Xiangming, *Zhang Xiangming 55 nian Xizang gongzuo shilu*, p. 67.

2. Peng Dehuai (1898–1974) was at that time First Secretary of the CCP Central Committee Northwest Bureau, as well as commander of the PLA's First Field Army and of the Northwest Military Command.

3. *Mao Zedong Xizang gongzuo wenxuan*, p. 6; emphasis added.

4. *Ibid.*, p. 9.

5. Zhang Guohua was the secretary and Tan Guansan the deputy secretary of the eight-member work committee.

6. On March 20, 1951, the CCP's Northwest Bureau established the Northwest Tibet Work Committee. After Fan Ming led troops from the northwest into Tibet as an escort for the Tenth Panchen Lama and arrived in Lhasa in December 1951,

the Northwest Tibet Work Committee merged with the TWC, with Zhang Jingwu serving as secretary and Zhang Guohua, Tan Guansan, and Fan Ming as deputy secretaries. See *Zhongguo Gongchandang Xizang Zizhiqu zuzhishi ziliao 1950–1987*, pp. 7–8; and Yang Yizhen, *Xizang jiyi*, vol. 1, p. 39.

7. In the early hours of October 6, 1950, more than 20,000 troops with the PLA's 18th Army as its main force launched a military offensive against the 8,000-strong Tibetan army (which included more than 3,000 militiamen). The Tibetan army was defeated, with most of its forces annihilated. For the PLA's military strength and battle deployment, see *Changdu zhanyi wenxian ziliao xuanbian*, pp. 67–68.

8. Yang Yizhen, *Xizang jiyi*, vol. 1, p. 169.

9. *Ibid.*, vol. 1, pp. 169–70.

10. *Ibid.*, vol. 2, p. 417.

11. *Zhongong Lasa dangshi dashiji 1951–1966*, pp. 1–2.

12. *Lasa zai qianjin*, p. 7.

13. The "Seventeen-Point Agreement for the Peaceful Liberation of Tibet" was signed in Beijing on May 23, 1951. The Dalai Lama learned the news over the radio. Regarding the negotiations over the agreement, see Goldstein, Sherap, and Siebenschuh, *A Tibetan Revolutionary*, pp. 140–53; see also Dalai Lama, *Freedom in Exile*, p. 63.

14. *Xizang gongzuo wenxian xuanbian (1949–2005)*, p. 40.

15. In January 1951, the 18th Army organized a cavalry unit of 830 horses and 826 men to enter Tibet. In February, the 7,437-strong 18th Army military vehicle and transportation units began moving into Garzê with food and materials needed by the troops in the Tibet advance detachment. On March 17, the 18th Army established 40 army bases on the route from Garzê to Lhasa and established and organized an enormous rear support unit. On April 11, work began on the Garzê airport, with some 20,000 soldiers and civilian workers brought in to push it ahead at top speed. See Yang Yizhen, *Xizang jiyi*, vol. 2., pp. 429–30. See also *Zhonggong Xizang dangshi dashiji 1949–1994*, p. 9.

16. The 18th Army was the main force entering Tibet, arriving from Garzê in Sichuan and Chamdo in Tibet. Other troops came from Qinghai, Yunnan, and Xinjiang to control various locations in Tibet. By this time, the 18th Army had more than 64,000 troops amassed in its front and rear headquarters and its construction and support units. See Yang Yizhen, *Xizang jiyi*, vol. 2, pp. 437–38.

17. *Jiefang Xizang shi*, p. 179; *Lasa zai qianjin*, p. 7.

18. *Zhongguo Gongchandang Xizang Zizhiqu zuzhishi ziliao 1950–1987*, p. 36.

19. The 18th Army Forward Unit that Zhang Guohua and Tan Guansan led as

the main force into Tibet totaled 10,700, troops divided into two echelons moving toward Lhasa, but some of these were stationed in other localities and didn't enter Lhasa. A portion of the troops that entered Lhasa subsequently continued on to Shigatsé and Gyantsé. See Yang Yizhen, *Xizang jiyi*, vol. 1, pp. 390–98.

20. Yang Yizhen, *Xizang jiyi*, vol. 2, p. 443.

21. A total of 1,110 personnel moved into Tibet from the northwest, including 300 PLA soldiers and 700 cadres, 400 of whom were party members. See Yang Yizhen, *Xizang jiyi*, vol. 1, p. 56.

22. This was the origin of the "southwest faction" and the "northwest faction" among Tibet's party leaders and cadres.

23. Among the 18th Army troops that entered Tibet, 3,000 were stationed in Lhasa, 2,600 in the vicinity of Lhasa, more than 600 in Shigatsé and more than 1,600 in Gyantsé and other places. More than 8,000 were stationed west of Jomda (Taizhao). See Wang Gui, "Huiyi zai Xizang zhanwen jiaogen de jianxin suiyue."

24. These were the Chamdo Liberation Committee, presented publicly as the Chamdo Area Work Committee, and the Pomé and Hordé Sogu Area Work Committees, which were referred to as "offices." See Yang Yizhen, *Xizang jiyi*, vol. 2, p. 431. Hordé Sogu was the general designation applied in the Qing dynasty to the 39 tribes of Tibet's eastern Nagchu and northwestern Chamdo regions.

25. In 1951, there wasn't a single CCP member in Tibet. By 1955, there were 1,491 party members, and 51 party branches had been established. See *Zhongguo Gongchandang Xizang Zizhiqu zuzhishi ziliao 1950–1987*, p. 67. By the time the TWC went public on July 1, 1955, two highways had been opened to traffic (in December 1954). See *ibid.*, p. 36.

26. Today a county under Nyingtri (Linzhi) City.

27. The Taizhao settlement was established by a Qing expeditionary force in 1910–11. It was located in today's Gyamda Township, Kongpo Gyamda County, Nyingtri City.

28. Now Lhuntsé (Longzi) County, Shannan City.

29. The Ngari cavalry unit was established in March 1952. The six garrison commands included Chamdo, Tengchen, Pomé, Gyantsé, Shigatsé, and Nagchu, all established in August 1952. See *Zhongguo Gongchandang Xizang Zizhiqu zuzhishi ziliao 1950–1987*, p. 468.

30. Seventy percent of the PLA troops that entered Lhasa were transferred in November 1951 to Lhasa's western suburbs to cultivate virgin land, clearing 342 acres in seventeen days. See Yang Yizhen, *Xizang jiyi*, vol. 2, p. 444.

31. In October 1953, on orders from the Central Committee, the Northwest Bureau organized a camel train of more than 18,000 camels to transport more than 150,000 kilos of grain to Tibet. The camel train set off in October 1953 and returned from Nagchu in March 1954. On the way, more than 9,000 camels died, as well as 103 transport personnel. See Qiao Cangyu, "Canjia jin Zang yunshu zongdui ji Qingzang zhulu gongcheng."

32. For details see Yang Yizhen, *Xizang jiyi*, vol. 2, pp. 443–55.

33. The "Qingzang Chuanzang Highway" was fully opened to traffic on December 25, 1954.

34. In the name of the "united front," the TWC's United Front Department engaged in a surreptitious survey of the political attitudes of Tibet's upper-level monks and laypeople, dividing them into "left, center, and right." See "*Who's Who in Tibet*" (*Xizang renwu jieshao*), published in November 1952 by the Central Military Commission Liaison Department Reference Room and marked "top secret," describing 419 upper-level individuals in Tibet. The material on 100 of these people came from investigations carried out in Tibet.

35. *Xizang gongzuo wenxian xuanbian (1949–2005)*, p. 141.

36. For the full text, see *ibid.*, pp. 141–43. "Transition period" refers to the period of time "from the establishment of the People's Republic of China to the completion of socialist transformation," as explained by Mao Zedong. See *Jianguo yilai zhongyao wenxian xuanbian*, vol. 4, pp. 700–701.

37. *Ibid.*

38. Fan Ming, *Xizang neibu zhi zheng*, pp. 329, 370.

39. *Mao Zedong Xizang gongzuo wenxuan*, pp. 124–31.

40. *Ibid.*, pp. 132–34.

41. Fan Ming, *Xizang neibu zhi zheng*, p. 370.

42. In attendance were an official from the Panchen Lama's office, Lhamon Yeshe Tsultrim; the former Chamdo governor and government minister Lhalu Tsewang Dorjé; one of the signatories of the Seventeen-Point Agreement, Sampo Tenzin Dondrup; the head of the Dalai Lama's Beijing office, Gyaltsen Drakpa; the head of the Panchen Lama's Beijing office, Sanggyé Palden; and Choekyi Gyatso Rinpoché from Sichuan's Mili (Muli) Tibetan Autonomous County.

43. *Mao Zedong Xizang gongzuo wenxuan*, p. 136.

44. *Ibid.*, pp. 136–37.

45. *Ibid.*, p. 137.

46. *Ibid.*, p. 135.

47. *Zhonggong Xizang dangshi dashiji 1949–1994*, pp. 60–61. The full text of Zhang Guohua's report remains classified.

48. Fan Ming, *Xizang neibu zhi zheng*, p. 329. Fan Ming's memoir doesn't reveal the content of the "twelve points."

49. Cheng Yue, *Zhongguo Gongchandang Changdu diqu lishi dashiji: 1949–2009*, p. 55.

50. Qin Heping, *Sichuan minzu diqu minzhu gaige ziliaoji*, p. 78.

51. *Xinhuashe xinwengao*, p. 15.

52. While in Lhasa, Chen Yi visited the Lhasa primary school and reviewed PLA troops and the PLA's Tibetan Honor Guard unit.

53. This delegation had more than 800 members and was divided into several branch delegations, including a Literature and Arts Work Team with more than 160 members, which brought in more than 90 Peking Opera, acrobatics, and song-and-dance performances and more than 70 movies. See Yongqingbamu, Wang Juong, and Zhang Hong, *Zang shi yaowen (1949–2011)*, p. 40.

54. Fan Ming, *Xizang neibu zhi zheng*, p. 331.

55. Goldstein, Sherap, and Siebenschuh, *A Tibetan Revolutionary*, p. 193.

56. For details, see chapters 4 and 5.

57. Zhang Guoxiang and Sun Yong, "Zhongguo tu-4 chuanqi," p. 33.

58. *Youguan Xizang wenti de wenjian he cailiao huibian (guonei bufen), 1949–1959*, p. 170.

59. *Ibid.*, p. 176.

60. Zhang Xiangming, *Zhang Xiangming 55 nian Xizang gongzuo shilu*, pp. 67–68.

61. Fan Ming, *Xizang neibu zhi zheng*, p. 332.

62. For Chen Yi's activities in Lhasa, see Yongqingbamu, Wang Juong, and Zhang Hong, *Zang shi yaowen (1949–2011)*, pp. 40–49.

63. *Mao Zedong Xizang gongzuo wenxuan*, p. 142. The Central Committee delegation's report has not yet been declassified.

64. Qin Heping and Ran Linwen, *Sichuan minzu diqu minzhu gaige dashiji*, p. 116.

65. *Xizang de minzhu gaige*, p. 8.

66. Translator's note: In China, economic police are civilian security forces that look after large factories, mines, and other major enterprises.

67. Zhang Xiangming, *Zhang Xiangming 55 nian Xizang gongzuo shilu*, p. 302.

68. *Ibid.*, p. 43.

69. Zhamog (Zhamu) is the county seat of today's Pomé (Bomi) County.

70. For the full text, see Bai Jingyuan, Ma Qicheng, and Li Zhuqing, *Zhou Enlai tongzhi dui minzu wenti yu minqu zhengce lunshu xuanbian*, pp. 39–44. This is an internally circulated edition that differs from the public version of Zhou's remarks. For the public version, see Zhou Enlai, *Zhou Enlai tongyi zhanxian wenxuan*, pp. 323–28.

71. The five opinions were: 1) Work hard for peaceful reforms; the relevant policies must be carried out in accordance with the will of the masses and after consulting upper-level personages and obtaining their agreement. 2) Movable property such as surplus draft animals, surplus farming implements, surplus foodstuffs, and surplus buildings of landlords should not be touched. 3) Take an even more cautious attitude toward temples in the Tibetan regions, and do not touch the cultivated land and other assets of temples for the time being. 4) The ethnic minority issue must be handled properly, and ethnic minority cadres must be groomed. 5) Cease hostilities and engage in peace talks with rebel forces that are still in the mountains. See Bai Jingyuan, Ma Qicheng, and Li Zhuqing, *Zhou Enlai tongzhi dui minzu wenti yu minzu zhengce lunshu xuanbian*, pp. 40–43.

72. Xinhua News Agency *Neibu Cankao*, September 8, 1956, p. 202.

Chapter 8

1. Interview with His Holiness the Dalai Lama, June 28, 2009.

2. The Great Prayer festival was begun by the founder of Tibetan Buddhism's Gelugpa school, Jé Tsongkhapa, in 1409. According to the conventions instituted by the Fifth Dalai Lama, Monlam Chenmo was celebrated on the third through twenty-first days of the first month of the Tibetan calendar, and it became the most important festival in Lhasa.

3. Dalai Lama, *Freedom in Exile*, p. 105; *Zhonggong Xizang dangshi dashiji 1949–1994*, p. 61.

4. Xinhua News Agency *Neibu Cankao*, June 22, 1956, p. 587.

5. *Ibid.*, p. 585.

6. *Ibid.*, p. 587.

7. Interview with His Holiness the Dalai Lama, June 30, 2009.

8. Dalai Lama, *Freedom in Exile*, p. 111.

9. *Xizang gongzuo wenxian xuanbian (1949–2005)*, p. 105.

10. Xinhua News Agency *Neibu Cankao*, September 7, 1956, p. 187.

11. Li Benxin, "Changdu diqu dashi tiyao," p. 53.

12. Zhang Xiangming, *Zhang Xiangming 55 nian Xizang gongzuo shilu*, pp. 67–68.

13. Xinhua News Agency *Neibu Cankao*, October 22, 1956, p. 1064.

14. See, for example, Pachen and Donnelley, *Sorrow Mountain*, pp. 105–7.

15. In Tibet's traditional government structure, officials were divided into seven ranks, with seventh being the lowest. The Dalai Lama was not included in this ranking system. See Shakabpa, *One Hundred Thousand Moons*, vol. 1, p. 85.

16. Cheng Yue (ed.), *op. cit.*, p. 56.

17. Li Benxin, "Changdu diqu dashi tiyao," p. 53.

18. In 1959, Jomda Dzong merged with Denkhok Nupma Dzong to form Jomda (Jiangda) County.

19. On how the "consultation" was conducted, see Dalai Lama, *Freedom in Exile*, p. 108.

20. Cheng Yue, *Zhongguo Gongchandang Changdu diqu lishi dashiji: 1949–2009*, p. 58.

21. Xinhua News Agency *Neibu Cankao*, September 7, 1956, p. 188.

22. I.e., east of the Drichu (Jinsha River).

23. Kamtok (Gangtuo) is the first village on the west bank after crossing the Drichu from Dergé. The stretch of highway from Kamtok to Chamdo is 260 kilometers long.

24. Cheng Yue, *Zhongguo Gongchandang Changdu diqu lishi dashiji: 1949–2009*, p. 58; Xinhua News Agency *Neibu Cankao*, September 7, 1956, pp. 187–88.

25. Li Benxin, "Changdu diqu dashi tiyao," p. 53.

26. Cheng Yue, *Zhongguo Gongchandang Changdu diqu lishi dashiji: 1949–2009*, p. 60.

27. Wang Ruilian, *Lishi de kuayue: Qingzu Changdu jiefang liushi zhounian zhuanji*, p. 42. These measures included continuing to pay wages to upper-level individuals who had fled to the mountains, mobilizing them to return, etc.

28. Cheng Yue, *Zhongguo Gongchandang Changdu diqu lishi dashiji: 1949–2009*, p. 61; interview with Tsering Dorjé, son of a Markham chieftain, December 4, 2010.

29. The group included the 16th Karmapa, Ngapo Ngawang Jigmé, and Pangda Dorjé. Pangda Dorjé (1905–1974) was a member of the Pandatsang family, who were among the wealthiest merchants in Markham. From 1950 onward, he served as chairman of the Chamdo Liberation Committee, deputy secretary general of the PCART, vice-chairman of the first and second sessions of the TAR People's Political Consultative Conference, delegate to the first three sessions of the National People's Congress, and member of the second session of the Chinese People's Political Consultative Conference.

30. Xinhua News Agency *Neibu Cankao*, October 22, 1956. This issue of *Neibu Cankao* says that Ngapo and the others went to Chamdo in early August, but *Zhonggong Xizang dangshi dashiji 1949–1966*; Li Benxin, "Changdu diqu dashi tiyao"; and the October 11, 1956 issue of *Neibu Cankao* all say that they went in September.

31. Xinhua News Agency *Neibu Cankao*, October 11, 1956, p. 913.

32. *Xizang gongzuo wenxian xuanbian (1949–2005)*, pp. 184, 185.

33. *Ibid.*, p. 184.

34. Neither of the Dalai Lama's two autobiographies mention TWC leaders transmitting the content of this document to him before he went to India.

35. The Crown Prince of Sikkim was at that time chairman of the Mahabodhi Society.

36. Dalai Lama, *My Land and My People*, pp. 139–40.

37. *Xizang gongzuo wenxian xuanbian (1949–2005)*, pp. 165–67.

38. Jampel Gyatso, *Mao Zedong yu Dalai Banchan*, p. 173. It's not clear when Fan Ming obtained this intelligence, but Fan Ming himself believed that what Mao said on November 15, 1956, about the Dalai Lama's trip to India was based on this intelligence. From that it can be inferred that Fan Ming reported this intelligence to Beijing before the Dalai Lama set off for India. For Mao's remarks on the Dalai Lama's trip to India, see *Mao Zedong Xizang gongzuo wenxuan*, pp. 152–53.

39. Gyalo Dondrup said that he and Shakabpa proposed two conditions to Nehru: 1) grant the Dalai Lama political asylum in India; and 2) promise to use his friendly relations with the Chinese government to convince the Chinese government to withdraw from Tibet, or at least to reduce the number of troops stationed there. After more than a year of secret talks, Nehru accepted these two conditions. See Gyalo Thondup and Thurston, *The Noodle Maker of Kalimpong*, pp. 157–58. In his memoir, the Dalai Lama mentioned that he decided to "explore the possibility of seeking political asylum" in India when he met Nehru. However, in the record of Nehru's conversations with the Dalai Lama on November 26 and 28, 1956, there is no indication that the Dalai Lama made a request for political asylum. See Nehru et al., *Selected Works of Jawaharlal Nehru*, pp. 522–23. See also Dalai Lama, *Freedom in Exile*, p. 117.

40. Vajrayana Buddhism, also known as Tantric Buddhism or Esoteric Buddhism, is one of the three schools of Buddhism; the other two are Mahayana and Hinayana (Theravada).

41. *Mao Zedong Xizang gongzuo wenxuan*, p. 152.

42. *Ibid.*

43. *Pingxi Xizang panluan*, p. 61.

Chapter 9

1. "Status of Tibet" on the FRUS website: *Foreign Relations of the United States, 1949, The Far East: China*, vol. 9, 1064–97, specifically p. 1069.

2. When Zhang Jingwu entered Tibet, he first hurried through India to Dromo with a personal letter from Mao urging the Dalai Lama to return to Lhasa as soon as possible. See Zhao Shenying, *Zhongyang zhuzang daibiao Zhang Jingwu*, pp. 10–11, 19–20.

3. Halper and Halper, *Tibet: An Unfinished Story*, p. 113.

4. Gyalo Thondup and Thurston, *The Noodle Maker of Kalimpong*, p. 167; see also Knaus, *Orphans of the Cold War*, p. 138.

5. Smith, *Tibetan Nation*, pp. 410–11. The author of this book quotes a primary source dated July 20, 1956, which is one month later than the Xinhua News Agency *Neibu Cankao* report, but based on the content quoted, it should be the same document.

6. Gyalo Thondup and Thurston, *The Noodle Maker of Kalimpong*, p. 170.

7. Conboy and Morrison, *The CIA's Secret War in Tibet*, p. 28.

8. *Xizang renwu jieshao*, pp. 8–9.

9. Dalai Lama, *Freedom in Exile*, p. 122.

10. Conboy and Morrison, *The CIA's Secret War in Tibet*, p. 33.

11. For the story of Athar Norbu and Lithang Lotse, see Li Jianglin, *Tibet in Agony*, pp. 136–46.

12. Dalai Lama, *My Land and My People*, p. 148.

13. *Ibid.* For brief notes on this talk, see Nehru et al., *Selected Works of Jawaharlal Nehru*, pp. 520–21.

14. Zhou Enlai left Beijing on November 17, 1956, and visited Vietnam, Kampuchea, India, Burma, West Pakistan, Nepal, and Afghanistan.

15. *Zhou Enlai yu Xizang*, p. 390.

16. Zhou Enlai also spoke with the Panchen Lama that day, but the content of their conversation is unknown. For a record of Zhou's first conversation with the Dalai Lama, see *Zhou Enlai yu Xizang*, pp. 142–48.

17. Zhou Enlai, "Tong Dalai Lama de tanhua" (Conversation with the Dalai Lama), in *Xizang gongzuo wenxian xuanbian (1949–2005)*, pp. 185–88.

18. Anterior Tibet referred to the Lhasa and Lhoka area, while Posterior Tibet referred to the area around Shigatsé.

19. *Zhou Enlai yu Xizang*, p. 146.

20. *Ibid.*, p. 470.

21. *Ibid.*, p. 390. I have not found a record of the conversation at this banquet, other than what I cite below from *My Land and My People*.

22. Dalai Lama, *My Land and My People*, p. 149. Regarding the issue of the status of the Dalai Lama and Panchen Lama, see Fan Ming, *Xizang neibu zhi zheng*. Traditionally, Dalai Lamas had temporal power, which the Panchen Lamas did not. Therefore, the Dalai Lama was the supreme leader in Tibet and the Panchen Lama was second to him. During this time, some CCP cadres were trying to elevate the Panchen Lama to the same status as the Dalai Lama, thereby touching on a highly sensitive issue for Tibetans.

23. Dalai Lama, *My Land and My People*, p. 149.

24. The source of this information is the *Tibet Daily* reporter Yun Rui, in his article collected in *Zhou Enlai yu Xizang*, p. 391.

25. There was only one year left of the first five-year plan (1953–1957), so if nothing was done during the second five-year plan, that would make six years. The situation during the third five-year plan (1966–1970) would determine whether or not to go ahead with reforms. (The second five-year plan was in 1958–1962. The third 5-year plan was delayed due to the failure of the Great Leap Forward and the subsequent famine, and therefore did not begin until 1966.)

26. Mao Zedong, *Jianguo yilai Mao Zedong wengao: Yijiuwujiunian yiyue—Yijiuwujiunian shi'eryue / di ba ce*, vol. 8, p. 265.

27. Li Ping and Ma Zhisun, *Zhou Enlai nianpu 1949–1976*, vol. 1, p. 647.

28. *Zhou Enlai yu Xizang*, p. 149.

29. *Ibid.*, p. 150.

30. Li Ping and Ma Zhisun, *Zhou Enlai nianpu 1949–1976*, vol. 1, pp. 650–51. For a record of the conversation, see *Zhou Enlai yu Xizang*, pp. 149–51.

31. *Zhou Enlai yu Xizang*, p. 394.

32. Interview with Kelsang Gyadotsang, May 10, 2009. Kelsang didn't give details of what kind of incidents they intended to create, only saying that the plan did not succeed. This was quite possibly the "rebellion" that the TWC referred to in its cable to Beijing on December 12, 1956.

33. Conboy and Morrison, *The CIA's Secret War in Tibet*, p. 36.

34. Nehru et al., *Selected Works of Jawaharlal Nehru*, vol. 36, pp. 600–601.

35. *Ibid.*, 601.

36. *Zhou Enlai yu Xizang*, p. 153.

37. *Ibid.*, p. 154.

38. Li Ping and Ma Zhisun, *Zhou Enlai nianpu 1949–1976*, vol. 2, p. 2.

39. *Zhonggong Xizang dangshi dashiji 1949–1966*, p. 68.

40. Dalai Lama, *Freedom in Exile*, p. 120.

41. Yutok Taashi Dongdrup (1906–1983) was from the 10th Dalai Lama's clan. He served in a number of positions in the Tibetan government. After 1956, he lived in India, then in Taiwan, eventually moving to Canada where he remained until his death.

42. Interview with His Holiness the Dalai Lama, June 30, 2009.

43. Dalai Lama, *Freedom in Exile*, p. 121.

44. *Ibid.*

45. Goldstein, Sherap, and Siebenschuh, *A Tibetan Revolutionary*, pp. 201–2.

46. Dalai Lama, *Freedom in Exile*, pp. 121–22.

Chapter 10

1. Mao Zedong's speech, "Guanyu zhengque chuli renmin neibu maodun" (On correctly handling contradictions among the people), published in *People's Daily*, June 19, 1957.

2. Qin Heping and Ran Linwen, *Sichuan minzu diqu minzhu gaige dashiji*, p. 176.

3. For the full text of the report, see *Tongzhan zhengce wenjian huibian* (Compilation of United Front Documents), vol. 3, pp. 1696–98.

4. *Zhonggong Xizang dangshi dashiji 1949–1966*, pp. 73–74.

5. Qin Heping, *Sichuan minzu diqu minzhu gaige ziliaoji*, pp. 27–29.

6. *Ibid.*, p. 44.

7. *Zhonggong Xizang dangshi dashiji 1949–1966*, p. 70; Yang Yizhen, *Xizang jiyi*, vol. 2, pp. 652–53.

8. Su Yu (1907–1984) was at that time chief of staff of the PLA. Traveling with him were the deputy director of the general logistics department, the director of the General Staff Headquarters war department, the director of the general logistics department health department and cadres from these various departments.

9. *Su Yu nianpu*, p. 388.

10. *Su Yu wenxuan (1949.10–1984.1)*, p. 245.

11. *Ibid.*, p. 255.

12. *Ibid.*, pp. 255–56.

13. This narrative is drawn from interviews with Drolkar Gye on October 20 and 24, 2010.

14. Today's Kecai Township in Sangchu (Xiahe County), Kanlho (Gannan) Tibetan Autonomous Prefecture.

15. Today's Sangchu County.

16. Interview with His Holiness the Dalai Lama, June 30, 2009.

17. Xinhua News Agency *Neibu Cankao*, January 14, 1957, p. 246.

18. Tsering Wangchuk, *Xinxiang ziyou*, pp. 11–12.

19. Luozhu Chodron, "Shisishi dalai xingong xiujian qingkuang," p. 33.

20. Khenchung Tara, personal secretary to the Dalai Lama, mentioned this incident in his memoir. He believes it was one of the reasons for the deteriorating relations between the Tibetans in Lhasa and the Communist Party personnel stationed there. See Tarawa Tenzin Choenyi, "Introducing Myself."

21. Interview with Kelsang Gyadotsang, May 10, 2009.

22. [Andrugtsang] Gompo Tashi, *Four Rivers, Six Ranges*, p. 51.

23. *Zhonggong Xizang dangshi dashiji 1949–1966*, p. 76.

24. *Xizang gongzuo wenxian xuanbian (1949–2005)*, p. 199.

25. *Su Yu wenxuan (1949.10–1984.1)*, p. 268.

26. *Diqing Zangzu zizhizhou Zizhizhou zhi*, p. 35.

27. Interview witth Kelsang Gyadotsang, May 10, 2009.

Chapter 11

1. The Tibetan term is *Ponpo*, pronounced as *Honpo* in Amdo. In Chinese it is transliterated as *hongbao*.

2. This is the area of the present-day Drugchen Sumdo Township in Golok's Chikdril County, and Rigchen was a *tsowa* under the Khangsar headman Panchen Norbu Sonam. The "Three Goloks" of "Central Golok" were three main clans, the Khangsar, Khanggen, and Drasar. At that time, the Khangsar had 4 large and 21 small *tsowa* under it, with a total of 749 households.

3. For details on the resistance of the Khangsar to the establishment of SPP pastures, see Darje, *Guoluo jianwen yu huiyi*, pp. 101–14. Further information is drawn from my interview with Lama Tenkyong, November 21, 2010, and my interview with Damcho Pelsang, November 30, 2010.

4. The Tibetan term is *lonpo*.

5. The fifth Jamyang Zhepa, Lobsang Jamyang Yeshe Tenpe Gyeltsen (1916–1947), was abbot of Labrang Monastery in Sangchu (Xiahe) County, Kanlho (Gannan).

6. Zhu Xiafu, "Zhongguo Gongchandang Qinghaisheng diyijie weiyuanhui diwuci quanti huiyi (kuoda) jongjie baogao" (Summary report of the (enlarged)

fifth plenum of the second Qinghai Province Communist Party committee," in *Minzu zongjiao gongzuo wenjian huiji 1949–1950*, pp. 259–80.

7. Before the reforms, Chikdril County had 1,998 households, totaling 7,090 people, and a total of 176,782 livestock of various kinds, an average of 25 per person. Yaks, horses, and goats were converted into headcounts of sheep according to the following formula: 1 yak = 3 sheep, 1 horse = 7 sheep, 2 goats = 1 sheep. See *Jiuzhi xianzhi*, pp. 76–77; Xing Haining, *Guoluo Zangzu shehui*, p. 76.

8. Darje, *Guoluo jianwen yu huiyi*, 106.

9. *Ibid.*, pp. 107–8.

10. The 2001 *Qinghai shengzhi: junshi zhi* uses the term "overt armed rebellion" to refer to the incident on May 15, 1958, in which the Khangsar resisted the establishment of the SPP. The 2005 *Jiuzhi xianzhi* describes the incident thus: "On May 15, under the plotting of individual herd-owners, some areas under the Khangsar tribe launched armed rebellions that subsequently spread to the Khanggen tribe." In his memoirs, the former head of Golok Prefecture, Darje, says that the county party committee's report of an "armed rebellion" was not true and was "pure fabrication." In an interview with the author, he confirmed that the Khanggen and Drasar carried out no "armed rebellion." Interview with Darje, August 22, 2012. See also *Qinghai shengzhi: junshi zhi*, p. 520; *Jiuzhi County Gazetteer*, p. 20; Darje, *Guoluo jianwen yu huiyi*, pp. 110–11.

11. For the text of this document, see *Tongzhan zhengce wenjian huibian*, vol. 3, pp. 1656–62.

12. *Ibid.*, p. 1657.

13. *Sun Zuobin*, p. 289.

14. *Ibid.*, p. 285.

15. *Zhongguo Gongchandang zuzhishi ziliao*, p. 807. Tashi Wangchuk, one of the people "denounced and dealt with" at this time, was denounced because he opposed reclaiming wasteland in the Qinghai pastoral areas. In 1959 he was dismissed from his position because he suggested that a problem of "magnification" had arisen in the "pacification of armed rebellion" in the Tibetan regions.

16. *Ibid.*

17. Xinhua News Agency *Neibu Cankao*, May 13, 1958. In May 1958, the Golok prefectural party committee assigned the counties under its jurisdiction a quota of 240 pilot schemes for animal husbandry productive cooperatives and 35 SPP pastures. Chikdril County's quota was 61 cooperatives and 10 SPP pastures. See Darje, *Guoluo jianwen yu huiyi*, *op. cit.*, p. 99.

18. *Huangnan Zangzu Zizhizhou zhi*, p. 1031.

19. *Gannan Zangzu Zizhizhou zhi*, vol. 2, pp. 1264–65.

20. *Tongzhan zhengce wenjian huibian*, vol. 3, p. 1793.

21. "Li Weihan, Wang Feng, Yang Jingren san tongzhi guanyu pingxi Gannan Zangqu panluan wenti de yijian" (Opinions of comrades Li Weihan, Wang Feng, and Yang Jingren regarding the problem of pacifying the armed rebellion in the Gannan Tibetan region), in *Tongzhan zhengce wenjian huibian*, vol. 3, pp. 1792–94.

22. For the full text, see *Minzu zongjiao gongzuo wenjian huiji 1949–1959*, vol. 2, pp. 1026–32.

23. The Xunhua Salar Autonomous County (known in Tibetan as Yadzi) was an ethnically diverse county inhabited by Salars, Tibetans, Mongolians, Chinese and a number of other ethnic groups. Tibetans there began a revolt against collectivization, and were joined by Salar rebels soon afterwards. By April 24, thousands of rebels of various ethnicities had besieged the county seat. For details on the Xunhua incident, See Li Jianglin, *Tibet in Agony*, chapter 3.

24. "Qinghai shengwei guanyu pingxi wuzhuang panluan de zhishi" (Qinghai provincial party committee's directive regarding pacifying the armed rebellion), in *Minzu zongjiao gongzuo wenjian huiji 1949–1959*, vol. 2, pp. 1054–58.

25. Xinhua News Agency *Neibu Cankao*, May 15, 1958. The memoirs of the former head of Golok Prefecture, Darje, include extracts from a document preserved in the Chikdril County archive. This document indicates that the chiefs and commoners of all of the clans were against the organization of cooperatives, but it doesn't show that the chiefs were "prepared for an armed rebellion." See Darje, *Guoluo jianwen yu huiyi*, pp. 100–101.

26. Damcho Pelsang's story comes from the author's interview with Damcho Pelsang, November 30, 2010.

27. From what is now Walbentsang (Awancang) Township in Machu County, Kanlho.

28. Darje, *Guoluo jianwen yu huiyi*, p. 108.

29. *Ibid.*, p. 112.

30. *Tongzhan zhengce wenjian huibian*, vol. 3, pp. 1699–701.

31. *Ibid.*, p. 1788.

32. *Ibid.*, p. 1789.

33. Mao Zedong, *Jianguo yilai Mao Zedong wengao*, vol. 7, p. 286.

34. *Ganzi Zangzu Zizhizhou minzu gaige shi*, p. 157.

35. Calculated according to officially published population statistics. See Li Jianglin, "Qinghai caoyuan shang xiaoshi de wangling."

36. The Khanggen tribe's traditional grazing areas were in Chikdril County's Palyul (Baiyu), Sogruma (Suohurima), and Wa'eryi townships.

37. The former governor of Golok Prefecture, Darje, writes in his memoirs that 72 herders were killed or wounded in this battle. In my interview with him, Darje said there were more than 90 casualties. He said 15 or 16 of these were people who were wounded and then abandoned on the battlefield, where they subsequently died. Interview with Darje, August 22, 2012.

38. Today's Padma (Banma) County, Golok TAP.

39. Interview with Damcho Pelsang, November 30, 2010.

40. Trokho horses, Ngulra sheep, and Walbentsang yaks were named for local nomad clans.

41. Interview with Tenkyong, November 21, 2010. Tenkyong's paternal grandmother was Hor Thor Sher's younger sister.

42. *Minzu zongjiao gongzuo wenjian huiji 1949–1959*, vol. 2, p. 1093.

43. The air force deployed 13 aircraft.

44. *Qinghai shengzhi: junshi zhi*, pp. 519–21.

45. Although the Drasar chieftain surrendered all his weapons to the PLA without fighting, he was still detained. Interview with Darje, August 22, 2012.

46. *Qinghai shengzhi: junshi zhi*, p. 527.

47. In accordance with the arrest quotas assigned by the upper levels, surrendering herders were all arrested and handed over to the county public security bureau. See Darje, *Guoluo jianwen yu huiyi*, p. 223.

48. *Ibid.*

49. Interview with Damcho Pelsang, November 30, 2010.

50. The figures published in the *Guoluo Prefecture Gazetteer* (*Guoluo Zangzu Zizhizhou zhi*) state that 8,735 people were arrested, but according to the statistics provided by the gazetteers of the six counties under Golok Prefecture, the arrests totaled 9,262. Among them, Darlag County stated only that 1,758 people were "wrongly handled," rather than providing the total number of people arrested. Matoe (Maduo) County only provided figures for 1958 and none after that. Therefore, the number of people arrested in the "pacification" and "rebellion prevention" in Golok Prefecture is probably higher than this number.

51. "Qinghai muqu funv de yaoqiu" (The needs of women in Qinghai's pastoral areas), Xinhua News Agency *Neibu Cankao*, February 2, 1962.

52. Darje, *Guoluo jianwen yu huiyi*, pp. 115–16.

53. Chos kyi dbang phyug, *A Poisoned Arrow*, p. 110.

54. "Qinghai muqu funv de yaoqiu," *Neibu Cankao*.

55. In his essay *Remembering Comrade Tashi Wangchuk*, Puntsok Wangyal writes, "Afterwards, leaders of the Central Committee Nationalities Affairs Commission who were in Labrang for an inspection visit proposed an even more leftist and extremely erroneous guiding principle of 'mainly military encirclement and suppression, supplemented by political striving.' . . . This created 'ghost towns' and 'widow villages' in some Tibetan regions, and shocking cases of injustice such as the so-called 'leaving a few seeds.' Many young boys in Yulshul and other places draped themselves in sheepskins and mixed in with the sheep in order to avoid being killed. This left behind serious social wounds that were very difficult to cure." In Puntsok Wangye (Puntsok Wangyal, *Pindeng tuanjie lu manman*, p. 355. In an interview with the author on August 22, 2012, the former governor of the Golok TAP, Darje, confirmed the mass arrest of males in Golok.

Chapter 12

1. Called Machu in Tibetan.

2. Khosin Tuglothang is in today's Kesheng Township in the Yulgen Mongol Autonomous County, and has a small hill known as Tolohai (a transliteration from the Mongolian), or Mount Doglo, which gives the place its name.

3. Ngulra is now Oula Township in Machu County.

4. Zhayi Rinpoché, *Wo guxiang de beican shi*, pp. 78–79.

5. *Henan Menguzu zizhixian zhi*, p. 31.

6. Banners were administrative divisions introduced during the Qing dynasty. The Manchurian emperors reorganized Mongolian tribes under their rule into a number of banners, with designated territories and princes.

7. Tashi Tsering (1920–1966) was the last ruler of the Hoshuud Mongols in today's Yulgen County. For more on her life and her death during the Cultural Revolution, see Yangdon Dondrup and Diemberger, "Tashi Tsering: The Last Mongol Queen of 'Sogpo' (Henan)."

8. Also known as Sogpo Arik, a branch of the Tibetan Arik clan living under Mongol rule in what is now Yulgen Mongol Autonomous County.

9. Lobsang Tsewang (1903–1997) was known in Chinese as Huang Zhengqing.

10. *Huangnan Zangzu Zizhizhou zhi*, p. 1032.

11. Zhayi Rinpoché, *Wo guxiang de beican shi*, p. 78.

12. *Ibid.*

13. *Henan Menguzu Zizhixian zhi*, p. 731.

14. *Huangnan Zangzu Zizhizhou zhi*, p. 1032. Emphasis added.

15. *Ibid.*

16. *Qinghai shengzhi: junshi zhi*, p. 519.

17. Li Lushan, "Zhandou zai Gannan he Xizang."

18. Location unclear.

19. *Maqu xianzhi*, pp. 676–77.

20. *Huangnan Zangzu Zizhizhou zhi*, p. 1032.

21. Zhayi Rinpoché, *Wo guxiang de beican shi*, p. 78.

22. Han Youren, *Yichang yanmo le de guonei zhanzheng*, p. 102.

23. *Henan Menguzu Zizhixian zhi*, p. 731.

24. The former governor of Golok Prefecture, Darje, told the author that 105 PLA soldiers were killed or wounded in the "Battle of Keshengtuoluotan." Interview with Darje, August 22, 2012.

25. After the CCP's Northwest Bureau convened a Northwest Ethnic Minorities Work Conference in October 1961, Yulgen County carried out a reexamination of the persons arrested, producing the numbers cited above. See *Henan Menguzu zizhixian zhi*, p. 701.

Chapter 13

1. To date there are no accurate figures regarding the number of people in the convoy. *Qinghai shengzhi: junshi zhi* and *Yushu Zangzu Zizhizhou zhi* mention this attack, but neither states the number of people in the convoy, only the fatalities. See *Yushu Zangzu Zizhizhou zhi*, pp. 30, 673. An autobiographical essay by Zhou Yihang, who was a land reform cadre in Dhomda at the time, states that there were more than 400 people in the convoy. For details, see *Jinri Pan'an*. Tibetan sources state that there were more than 600 people in the convoy. See Dawa Tsering, *Xueji xueyu*, pp. 145–202.

2. The upper reaches of the Lancang (Mekong) River.

3. The pasturelands of these three *shokka (Chi-shok)* were located in what is today Dinchen (Zhenqin) Township in Trindu County, Yulshul Prefecture.

4. For a Tibetan source, see Dawa Tsering, *Xueji xueyu*, pp. 152–54.

5. *Yushu Zangzu Zizhizhou zhi*, p. 30.

6. *Ibid.*, p. 673.

7. Dawa Tsering, *Xueji xueyu*, p. 153.

8. He was also deputy commander of the 134th Division, 54th Army.

9. Fang Yangda and Huang Yaming, "Jijizhongliu."

10. See Dawa Tsering, *Xueji xueyu*, pp. 148–54.

11. *Yushu Zangzu Zizhizhou zhi*, p. 27.

12. See chapter 2, section 2 of this book.

13. The "four pests" in the pastoral regions were marmots, field rats, caterpillars, and wolves.

14. Sun Zuobin and Tashi Wangchuk, "Zhengque chuli hao minzu guanxi" (Correctly handle ethnic relations), in *Sun Zuobin*, p. 260.

15. I.e., Ma Bufang, the Kuomindang-era warlord and one of the major figures of the Ma family that ruled Qinghai until 1949.

16. *Minzu zongjiao gongzuo wenjian huiji 1949–1959*, vol. 2, pp. 501–5.

17. *Jintan* is a Japanese herbal medicine popular in China.

18. Sun Zuobin and Tashi Wangchuk, "Zhengque chuli hao minzu guanxi", p. 259.

19. *Ibid.*, p. 262.

20. A cairn or wall of stones carved with Buddhist mantras or scriptures.

21. Sun Zuobin and Tashi Wangchuk, "Zhengque chuli hao minzu guanxi", p. 266.

22. *Ibid.*, p. 264.

23. *Ibid.*, p. 265.

24. *Ibid.*

25. *Minzu zongjiao gongzuo wenjian huiji 1949–1959*, vol. 1, p. 264.

26. Puntsok Wangye, *Pindeng tuanjie lu manman*, p. 348. Puntsok Wangyal (Wangye) himself was dismissed from his postings in the Chinese Communist Party but was allowed to retain his government postings.

27. *Yushu Zangzu Zizhizhou zhi*, p. 30.

28. *Ibid.* See also Dawa Tsering, *Xueji xueyu*, pp. 151–52.

29. *Yushu Zangzu Zizhizhou zhi*, p. 30. Tibetan sources state that after this drawn-out "people's congress" ended, the participating headmen were all sent straight to prison. In the 1980s, several of them were released and allowed to return home, but the rest died in prison. See Dawa Tsering, *Xueji xueyu*, p. 156.

30. This meeting was related to the suggestions of Li Weihan and others to the CCP Central Committee regarding "putting the relatively influential headmen under our control." See *Tongzhan zhengce wenjian huibian*, vol. 3, p. 1792.

31. Dawa Tsering, *Xueji xueyu*, pp. 149–50.

32. *Yushu Zangzu Zizhizhou zhi*, pp. 668–69; Chen Qingying, *Zhongguo Zangzu buluo*, pp. 42–43.

33. For details, see Dawa Tsering, *Xueji xueyu*, pp. 148–54.

34. Wang Tingsheng, *Wangshi huimou*, p. 133.

35. The Minhe Hui and Tu Autonomous County in today's Haidong City, Qinghai Province.

36. This is a village in Chuankou (Khongkhug) Township in the Minhe Hui and Tu Autonomous County.

37. Fang Yangda and Huang Yaming, "Jijizhongliu."

38. According to *Qinghai shengzhi: junshi zhi*, the Yushu Command Post was established on July 15, 1958, but by then the battles in Yulshul had already begun. The *Yushu Zangzu Zizhizhou zhi* says the command post was established on April 19, 1958. The commander of the Qinghai Province Military District, Sun Guang, was commander and political commissar of the command post, while the deputy commander of the Wumeng Sub-region of the Inner Mongolia Military Command, E'erdun, and the commander of the Yulshul Military Command, Zhu Tingyun, served as deputy commanders; the deputy commander of the 134th Division, Fang Yangda, served as deputy commander and chief of staff, and the deputy director of the political department of the Qinghai Military Command, Dai Jinying, served as deputy political commissar and director of the political department. The main force consisted of the 134th Division's 400th and 401st Regiments, two battalions of the division's artillery regiment, the independent corps of engineers battalion and reconnaissance battalion, and the 13th and 14th Cavalry Regiments of the Inner Mongolia Military Command. Other participating military units included the 13th, 23rd, and 25th Air Force Divisions, the pontoon bridge battalion, motor brigade, vehicle regiment, field hospital, etc. See *Qinghai shengzhi: junshi zhi*, p. 519; and *Yushu Zangzu Zizhizhou zhi*, p. 30. See also Fang Yangda and Huang Yaming, "Jijizhongliu."

39. Fang Yangda and Huang Yaming, "Jijizhongliu." See also Wang Tingsheng, *Wangshi huimou*, p. 134.

40. Hong Weiquan, "Xueyu jiaofei ji," p. 13.

41. Mao Zedong, *Jianguo yilai Mao Zedong wengao*, vol. 7. p. 286. For the full text of the report see *Minzu zongjiao gongzuo wenjian huiji 1949–1959*, vol. 2, pp. 989–92.

42. *Ibid.*

43. Peng Zhiyao, "Yige laobing de pingpan riji."

44. Fang Yangda and Huang Yaming, "Jijizhongliu."

45. This is now part of Matoe County in Golok Prefecture.

46. Darje, *Guoluo jianwen yu huiyi*, pp. 112–13.

47. There has been considerable research in recent years regarding China's rural social forms and the relations between classes prior to land reform. See for example Xie Youtian, *Xiangcun shehui de huimie*; and Huang, "Rural Class Struggle."

48. At a speech during a group discussion of the Tibetan delegation at the Sixth National People's Congress on the morning of March 28, 1987, the Tenth Panchen Lama said, "While in Qinghai in 1958, I heard there was an internal party document stating the need to instigate armed rebellions and induce armed rebellions, and to then resolve religious and ethnic issues once and for all in the process of pacifying rebellion." However, the relevant document has not been declassified. For details, see Panchen Lama, *Qiwanyanshu*, p. 112.

49. Known in Chinese as the Changu temple, five kilometers south of Jyekundo, the prefecture capital.

50. For details, see Dawa Tsering, *Xueji xueyu*, pp. 156–60.

51. *Ibid.*, pp. 159–60.

52. See population statistics in *Yushu Zangzu Zizhizhou zhi*, pp. 107–8.

53. Fang Yangda and Huang Yaming, "Jijizhongliu."

54. Wang Tingsheng, *Wangshi huimou*, p. 135. Tongtian River is the Chinese name for the upper reach of the Drichu (Jinsha River).

55. Located in today's Dinchen (Zhenqin) Township in Trindu County.

56. "Huiyi Yushu pingpan douzheng pianduan."

57. Dawa Tsering, *Xueji xueyu*, p. 162.

58. Fang Yangda and Huang Yaming, "Jijizhongliu."

59. "Huiyi Yushu pingpan douzheng pianduan."

60. Dawa Tsering, *Xueji xueyu*, p. 162.

61. "Huiyi Yushu pingpan douzheng pianduan."

62. Peng Zhiyao, "Yige laobing de pingpan riji."

63. This is now She'u (Xiewu) Township in Trindu County.

64. "Huiyi Yushu pingpan douzheng pianduan."

65. "Guxi laoren Zhang Chengzuo rudang 50 nian fengxian 50 nian yilu jianxin.".

66. "Huiyi Yushu pingpan douzheng pianduan."

67. Fang Yangda and Huang Yaming, "Jijizhongliu."

68. "Huiyi Yushu pingpan douzheng pianduan." The Jyeku Monastery, built in

1398, was Yulshul's largest monastery of the Sakya school. Prior to 1958, it had 5 assembly halls, more than 600 monks' quarters, and 850 monks. Two of the monastery's three Rinpochés (incarnate lamas) died in 1958. See Pu Wencheng, *Ganqing Zanchuan fojiao siyuan*, p. 298.

69. *Yushu Zangzu Zizhizhou zhi*, p. 674.

70. *Qinghai shengzhi: junshi zhi*, p. 528.

71. Today's Drongda (Zhongda) Township in Yulshul City.

72. *Qinghai shengzhi: junshi zhi*, p. 528.

73. The Ranyak Monastery, known as one of "Kham's three great monasteries," was built in 1295. In 1958, the monastery had 4 assembly halls, 435 monks' quarters, more than 450 monks, and nine Rinpochés. For further information on the monastery, see its website (in Chinese): http://rangniang.byethost11.com/tw/rangniang.html. New website Accessed June 12, 2021.

74. Fang Yangda's memoirs say there were "more than 600 rebel bandits," while *Qinghai shengzhi: junshizhi* says there were "more than 400 mainstays." Neither of these Chinese sources is likely to have included monks. The number stated here in the text comes from Tibetan sources. See Fang Yangda and Huang Yaming, "Jijizhongliu"; *Qinghai shengzhi: junshi zhi*, p. 528; Dawa Tsering, *Xueji xueyu*, p. 173.

75. Dawa Tsering, *Xueji xueyu*, pp. 173–74.

76. Fang Yangda and Huang Yaming, "Jijizhongliu."

77. *Ibid.*

78. *Qinghai shengzhi: junshi zhi*, pp. 528–29 states that a general offensive was launched against the Ranyak Monastery at 12:08 a.m. on August 23, 1958.

79. Dawa Tsering, *Xueji xueyu*, pp. 176–79.

80. *Ibid.*

81. Dawa Tsering, *Xueji xueyu*, p. 178.

82. *Ibid.*

83. Fang Yangda and Huang Yaming, "Jijizhongliu."

84. *Yushu Zangzu Zizhizhou zhi*, p. 674.

85. Reconstruction of the Ranyak Monastery began in 1985; at that point there was not a single intact building within the boundary wall. The rebuilt portions of the monastery cover less than one-tenth of the original compound. See the monastery's website at http://rangniang.byethost11.com/cn/rangniang.html#.

86. Wang Tingsheng, *Wangshi huimou*, pp. 135–36. PLA casualties totaled 169.

Chapter 14

1. The three Great Monastic Universities, i.e., Sera, Ganden, and Drepung, were rebuilt in exile, in the Indian state of Karnataka. A monastic university usually has a number of colleges, called *dratsang* in Tibetan. (Gomang Dratsang is also translated as Drepung Gomang Monastery. See the official website of the Drepung Gomang Monastery: http://drepunggomang.org/. Accessed September 28, 2011.

2. According to Chinese sources, people who had fled from Gepa Sumdo (Tongde) County also took refuge at Drongthil Gulch.

3. Interview with Tubten Nyima, September 6, 2010.

4. *Qinghai shengzhi: junshi zhi*, pp. 525–26.

5. *Qinghai Zangwen bao*, June 1, 1958, p. 2.

6. *Ibid.*

7. *Ibid.*

8. For the full text, see *Tongzhan zhengce wenjian huibian*, vol. 3, pp. 1787–91.

9. *Ibid.*, p. 1787.

10. *Ibid.*, p. 1788.

11. *Ibid.*, p. 1790.

12. Huang Kecheng (1902–1986) was appointed deputy chief of staff and commander of the general logistics department of the People's Liberation Army in 1952; in 1954 he was further appointed vice-minister of defense and secretary general of the CMC; in October 1959, he was appointed general chief of staff. He was purged, along with Defense Minister Peng Dehuai, during the Lushan Conference in 1959.

13. *Tongzhan zhengce wenjian huibian*, vol. 3, p. 1787.

14. *Qinghai shengzhi: junshi zhi*, p. 519.

15. The narratives provided in Chinese sources vary. According to *Tongde xianzhi*, on July 2, 1958, the party secretary of Tongde (Gepa Sumdo) County, accompanied by 58 engineering corps and militia personnel on horseback, encountered "rebel bandits," and the party secretary and four others were killed in the ensuing battle. According to *Qinghai shengzhi: junshi zhi*, "more than 3,000 armed rebel bandits" besieged the county party committee, and the county's "main leaders" and more than 50 others were killed while trying to break through the encirclement. See *Tongde xianzhi*, p. 16; *Qinghai shengzhi: junshi zhi*, p. 515; Zhayi Rinpoché, *Wo guxiang de beican shi*, p. 79.

16. Interview with Tubten Nyima, September 6, 2010. The former governor of Golok Prefecture, Darje, also notes in his memoirs that there were language barriers when "the Great Leap Forward" and other such concepts were publicized among the herders. See Darje, *Guoluo jianwen yu huiyi*, pp. 100–101.

17. *Sun Zuobin*, pp. 277–78.

18. *Ibid.*, p. 78.

19. From January 13 to March 18, 1958, the Qinghai provincial party committee convened an enlarged fifth plenum of its second provincial party committee, mainly to denounce Sun Zuobin, Tashi Wangchuk, and others.

20. *Xinghai xianzhi*, p. 24.

21. Zhayi Rinpoché, *Wo guxiang de beican shi*, p. 79. Tubten Nyima stated that two monks were accused of putting a curse on the Chinese during a Buddhist ceremony, and for that they were executed and all of the senior monks in the monastery taken into custody.

22. These three major cases involved Tsikorthang County's Amnye Machen, the Drakar Drelzong Monastery, and the Themchen (Wongtak) incident. In the early 1980s, Tsikorthang County reexamined these three cases and declared 679 of those involved not guilty. See *Xinghai xianzhi*, p. 288.

23. The local term for a *labrang*, or residence for reincarnated lamas.

24. *Xinghai xianzhi*, pp. 289, 444.

25. Ngarotsang Rinpoché was arrested in 1958 and died on December 12 of that year. He was declared innocent in 1981. See *Xinghai xianzhi*, pp. 471–72.

26. *Xinghai xianzhi*, p. 346.

27. *Ibid.*, p. 116.

28. Xinhua News Agency *Neibu cankao*, July 26, 1958.

29. *Xinghai xianzhi*, p. 24.

30. Located at what is now the border between Tsikorthang County and Gepa Sumdo County.

31. *Xinghai xianzhi*, p. 346. Amnye Machen was made part of Golok Prefecture's Machen County in 1958, and is now in Gangri Township.

32. *Qinghai shengzhi: junshi zhi*, pp. 1134–35. "Tangkun" may refer to the Tanggula mountain range in the border area between Sichuan and Qinghai.

33. Wang Tingsheng, *Wangshi huimou*, p. 138.

34. *Ibid.*

35. Zhayi Rinpoché, *Wo guxiang de beican shi*, p. 79.

36. *Hainan Zangzu Zizhizhou zhi*, p. 653. Emphasis added.

37. *Xinghai xianzhi*, p. 24.

38. *Qinghai shengzhi: junshi zhi*, p. 525. Emphasis added.

39. Wang Zhongxing and Liu Liqin, *Guofang lishi*, p. 129. Emphasis added.

40. Zhou Tingyan's unit was under the command of the 74th Regiment of the Lanzhou Military Command's Bomber 25th Division, and flew Tupolev Tu-2

bombers. In October 1958, when Zhou Tingyan's unit was dropping leaflets over Yulshul, his aircraft stalled and was forced to land, and Zhou died in a battle with Tibetan fighters on the ground. Tibetan sources say the aircraft was shot down while flying at a low altitude. See "Weiwu buqu" in *Weizhen changkong*, pp. 252–57; and Dawa Tsering, *Xueji xueyu*, p. 187.

41. Jiang Dasan, "Blog. 74 sui lao feixing renyuan de boke."

42. Guan Shengzhi, "Zhuiyi hongzha hangkongbing ershiwushi lishi pianduan."

43. The highest peak of Amnye Machen, called Machen Gangri by Tibetans.

44. Wang Tingsheng, *Wangshi huimou*, p. 140.

45. *Hainan Zangzu Zizhizhou zhi*, p. 654.

46. *Xinghai xianzhi*, p. 346.

47. Zhayi Rinpoché, *Wo guxiang de beican shi*, p. 80.

48. *Xinghai xianzhi*, p. 24.

49. The Tsolho prefectural party committee rehabilitated Ngarotsang Rinpoché in 1981. See *Xinghai xianzhi*, p. 472.

50. *Xinghai xianzhi*, p. 346.

51. *Xinghai xianzhi*, p. 227.

52. *Minzu zongjiao gongzuo wenjian huiji 1949–1950*, vol. 2, p. 1006.

53. Gao Feng, "Jixu kefu youqing baoshou, guzu ganzin wei jinnian gengda, genghao, gengquanmian de yuejin er fendou" (Continue to surmount right-deviation and conservatism, go all out in struggling for an even greater, better and more comprehensive leap forward this year), in *Minzu zongjiao gongzuo wenjian huiji 1949–1959*, vol. 1, pp. 309–26.

54. *Minzu zongjiao gongzuo wenjian huiji 1949–1959*, vol 2. pp. 1004–5.

55. *Ibid.*, p. 1060.

56. *Ibid.*, p. 1081.

57. *Ibid.*, p. 1006.

58. *Pingpan yinxiong zhuan*, p. 146.

59. *Minzu zongjiao gongzuo wenjian huiji 1949–1959*, vol 2. pp. 1093–1101.

60. Xinhua News Agency *Neibu Cankao*, March 6, 1959, p. 13.

61. *Yushu Zangzu Zizhizhou zhi*, p. 672. This figure is equivalent to 18% of Yulshul's total Tibetan population. For the Tibetan population of Yulshul TAP, see *Yushu Zangzu Zizhizhou zhi*, p. 107.

62. Xinhua News Agency *Neibu Cankao*, March 6, 1959, p. 13.

63. Wang Zhongxing and Liu Liqin, *Guofang lishi*, p. 128.

64. *Yushu Zangzu Zizhizhou zhi*, p. 663.

65. Wang Zhongxing and Liu Liqin, *Guofang lishi*, p. 129.

66. Interview with Tubten Nyima, September 6, 2010.

Chapter 15

1. Translator's note: Gonpo Tashi was introduced in chapter 10.

2. Most of the details regarding this meeting come from the author's interview with one of the participants, Gyalrong Tenzin, on October 23, 2010. Gyalrong is an area incorporated into today's Ngawa TAP. Gyalrong Tenzin means "Tenzin from Gyalrong." It is customary to add the name of a person's hometown to his actual name, probably to differentiate people with identical names.

3. The memoirs of Gonpo Tashi do not indicate when or where the meeting was held, but in the record of the CIA agent Roger McCarthy's interviews with Gonpo Tashi in July and August 1959, the date of the pledge taken there is given as April 7, 1958 (the 19th day of the second month of the Year of the Dog in the Tibetan calendar, i.e., 1958). See "Autobiography of Gonpo Tashi," Bruce Walker papers, Box 3, p. 15. *Zhonggong Xizang dangshi dashiji 1949–1994* states that the meeting was held on April 20, 1958. Regarding the number of people who attended the meeting, Gyalrong Tenzin told me that 30 people attended, while another participant, Ratuk Ngawang, states in his memoirs that 42 people attended. See McGranahan, *Arrested Histories*, pp. 96–97; and *Zhonggong Xizang dangshi dashiji 1949–1994*, p. 80. April 18 is the date Gyalrong Tenzin gave me.

4. Called Zhongdian in Chinese, in Dechen TAP, Yunnan Province, now Xianggelila (Shangrila) City.

5. A Tibetan Army ranking, denoting a command of 100 soldiers, equivalent to a company commander.

6. It is not clear what subsequently happened to this document, which the Chinese government referred to as the "Alliance Letter"; neither its full text nor the original document has been published in either Chinese or Tibetan.

7. Interview with Gyalrong Tenzin, October 23, 2010.

8. According to Tibetan sources, the key to the arsenal was held by the army commander, Sampo Tsewang Rigzin, who was also deputy commander of the TMC and a major general in the PLA. See Dawa Tsering, *Xueji xueyu*, p. 430.

9. Interview with His Holiness the Dalai Lama, June 30, 2009.

10. Interview with Gyalrong Tenzin, October 23, 2010.

11. Chushi Gangdruk (four rivers, six ranges), is the traditional name for the Kham region. The four rivers are the Drichu (Jinsha, upper reaches of the Yangtze),

Nyagchu (Yalong), Ngulchu (Salween), and Dzachu (Mekong); the six mountain ranges are the Tsawagang, Markhamgang, Zalmogang, Pomborgang, Mardzagang, and Minyak Rawagang.

12. [Andrugtsang] Gompo Tashi, *Four Rivers, Six Ranges*, p. 51. See also chapter 10, section 3.

13. Dawa Tsering, *Xueji xueyu*, pp. 204–5; interview with Gyalrong Tenzin, October 23, 2010.

14. Interview with Kelsang Gyadotsang (Gonpo Tashi's nephew), May 10, 2009.

15. Tubten Woeden (1911–1986) was a member of the Phala family, one of the aristocratic families of Tibet. About the first crew of resistance fighters trained by the CIA, see Li Jianglin, *Tibet in Agony*, pp. 136–49.

16. The April 28, 1959, issue of the Xinhua News Agency's *Neibu Cankao* reported that soldiers had discovered a "constitution of the Tibetan Anti-Imperialist Party" and its Chinese translation in Norbulingka palace. I have been unable to find any other information on the "Tibetan Anti-Imperialist Party" to date.

17. The October 25, 1958, edition of *Neibu Cankao* reported on an "affidavit" by this organization, but provided no specifics about the organization. See Xinhua News Agency *Neibu Cankao*, October 25, 1958, pp. 9–14.

18. The May 4, 1957, edition of *Neibu Cankao* reproduced an AFP report from Kathmandu regarding a "Mima Party element" ("*mima*" is a transliteration of the Tibetan term *mimang*. *Mimang Tsongdu* means People's Assembly) occupying and destroying a 500-kilometer segment of the Kham-Tibet highway within the borders of Xikang. For a time, battles in Sichuan's Tibetan regions led to the suspension of transportation on the highway, but there is no evidence that this had anything to do with the "People's Assembly." It may have been carried out, for instance, by the Markham rebels in 1956.

19. [Andrugtsang] Gompo Tashi, *Four Rivers, Six Ranges*, p. 51.

20. Dawa Tsering, *Xueji xueyu*, pp. 209–10.

21. According to the recollections of Fan Ming, who at that time was deputy secretary of the TWC, "more than 5,000 rebel elements from Sichuan, Qinghai, Gansu, Yunnan, and other Tibetan regions and the Changdu region came to Lhasa" in 1958. Fan Ming, *Xizang neibu zhi zheng*, p. 380. Xu Hongsen recalls that in a conversation with the *kalons* (ministers) on August 19, 1958, Zhang Jingwu mentioned groups of people arriving in Lhasa from Sichuan and Qinghai, bringing guns and horses and herding livestock. Zhang admitted that he was "not entirely

sure" what those people were doing, and asked the *kalons* to investigate and find out what their purpose was in coming to Tibet. See Xu Hongsen, "1958 qi-ba yue Zhang Jingwu tong galunmen de jici tanhua jianlu," pp. 204–5.

22. *Zhonggong Xizang dangshi dashiji 1949–1994*, p. 79. According to Gonpo Tashi's memoirs, around 1,500 people were repatriated. See "Autobiography of Gompo Tashi," Bruce Walker papers, Box 3, p. 16.

23. According to Gonpo Tashi's 1959 memoirs, the TWC publicly announced its screening of people from Kham and Amdo on May 25, 1959. See "Autobiography of Gompo Tashi," Bruce Walker papers, Box 3, p. 16.

24. [Andrugtsang] Gompo Tashi, *Four Rivers, Six Ranges*, pp. 58–59.

25. Athar Norbu, *bsTan srung dang blangs dpa' bo Li thang A thar nor bu'i mi tshe lo rgyus*; "Autobiography of Gompo Tashi," Bruce Walker papers, Box 3, p. 16. Driguthang is the plain of the Drigu Lake, within the borders of what is now Drigu (Zhegu) Township, Tsomé (Cuomei) County, Lhoka (Shannan) City, Tibet Autonomous Region.

26. Wang Yan, *Peng Dehuai nianpu*, p. 683.

27. *Tongzhan zhengce wenjian huibian*, p. 1787.

28. I.e. people of Amdo.

29. Jiang had been deputy commander of the 155th Regiment and artillery battalion commander, but left the PLA in 1958 to join the Chushi Gangdruk army.

30. In February 1957, the TMC headquarters, political department, logistics department, cadre department, and finance department gave a joint report to the Central Military Commission, also forwarded to Mao, which detailed some problems in the Military Command relating to army barracks, officer marriages and family life, wages, health, shortages of daily necessities, and lack of cultural life. For details, see Jampel Gyatso, *Li Jue zhuan*, pp. 184–98.

31. Tsering Wangchuk, *Xinxiang ziyou*, pp. 21–23. In addition, the PLA's Logistics Information Agency published an article in 1957 about deficiencies in living conditions, a lack of barracks, and other problems. The author worked in the PLA's general finance department and clearly stated that the conditions reflected in the article were problems "observed and heard about" during inspection work in the Tibetan regions. Zhang Peihui, "Yao guanxin gaoyuan bianfang budui de shenghuo."

32. In a conversation with the author, the Dalai Lama said that around this time, he heard that an army officer called "Director Li" had written a letter to Mao advising against too many troops being stationed in Lhasa. Interview with His Holiness the Dalai Lama, June 30, 2009.

33. According to Jiang Huating's recollections, more than 400 people in the Tibet military apparatus were implicated during the anti-rightist movement, and Tan Guansan had some military officers arrested on the spot. Jiang decided to leave the army just before being purged, and sought refuge with Chushi Gangdruk. For details, see Tsering Wangchuk, *Xinxiang ziyou*, pp. 23–29.

34. *Mao Zedong Xizang gongzuo wenxuan*, p. 4.

35. *Ibid.*, pp. 6–8.

36. When Fan Ming arrived in Lhasa with the 18th Army Independent Detachment on December 1, 1951, he wanted the cavalry to enter the city with great pomp, but Zhang Guohua opposed it. Fan Ming made a grand entrance anyway, but received a cold reception from both Zhang Jingwu and the Tibetan government, which enraged him. For details, see Goldstein, Sherap, and Siebenschuh, *A Tibetan Revolutionary*, pp. 157–58. See also Zhang Xiangming, *Zhang Xiangming 55 nian Xizang gongzuo shilu*, p. 43.

37. See Xu Mingde, *Wo zhe yibeizi*, pp. 293–97.

38. Zhang Xiangming, *Zhang Xiangming 55 nian Xizang gongzuo shilu*, p. 46; Fan Ming, *Xizang neibu zhi zheng*, p. 259; Zhao Shenying, *Zhang Guohua jiangjun zai Xizang*, pp. 91–95. Translator's note: Panmunjom was where North and South Korea hammered out their armistice.

39. For example, Fan Ming held out on Zhang Jingwu and Zhang Guohua about arranging for intelligence personnel to collect intelligence in Kalimpong, India, resulting in a diplomatic dispute between China and India for which Zhang Jingwu and Zhang Guohua were criticized by Zhou Enlai. Fan Ming believed that Mao believed what he reported. See Jampel Gyatso, *Mao Zedong yu Dalai Banchan*, pp. 172–73.

40. Wang Yan, *Peng Dehuai nianpu*, p. 682.

41. Fan Ming, *Xizang neibu zhi zheng*, p. 394.

42. Xu Mingde, *Wo zhe yibeizi*, pp. 300–301.

43. [Andrugtsang] Gompo Tashi, *Four Rivers, Six Ranges*, p. 62.

44. Interview with Gyalrong Tenzin, October 23, 2010.

45. In his memoirs, Jiang Huating says that he was the first to design the flag for Chushi Gangdruk, but there are discrepancies between the flag he describes and the photos taken at the time Chushi Gangdruk was established. See Tsering Wangchuk, *Xinxiang ziyou*, p. 39.

46. Today's Namling (Nanmulin) County under Shigatsé City, TAR.

47. In Tibetan sources, the exact date that the Volunteer Army set off for

Namling is unclear. Jiang Huating's memoirs state that it was June 26, 1958, but that was only ten days after the volunteer army was established, so it seems doubtful. The *Chronicle of Events in the History of the CCP in Tibet* says it was August 15.

48. Located next to the former Namling *dzong,* in the present Namling County, close to the county seat.

49. Jampa Jiangba, "Zai panfei qiangjie wuqi de beihou," pp. 93–94.

50. Also known as Yamdrok Yumtso, in today's Nakartsé (Langkazi) County, Lhoka City.

51. Gampa La, the border between today's Gongkar (Gongga) County and Nakartsé County.

52. Today's Chushur County, Lhasa City.

53. Today's Nyemo County, Lhasa City.

54. "Autobiography of Gompo Tashi," Bruce Walker papers, Box 3, p. 22.

55. *Jiefang Xizang shi,* p. 344.

56. [Andrugtsang] Gompo Tashi, *Four Rivers, Six Ranges,* pp. 69–72.

57. Ji Youquan, *Xizang pingpan jishi,* p. 45.

58. *Ibid.* Where *Zhonggong Xizang dangshi dashiji 1949–1994* quotes this directive, it edits out two sentences: "Let them cause more trouble; the greater the trouble, the more thorough the reforms," and "Strengthen the small strongholds."

59. Ji Youquan, *Xizang pingpan jishi,* p. 46.

60. Including 4 mortars, more than 390 artillery shells, 10 light machine guns, 18 assault rifles, 385 rifles, 378 bayonets, and 73,000 rounds of ammunition. See [Andrugtsang] Gompo Tashi, *Four Rivers, Six Ranges,* pp. 74–75.

61. *Zhonggong Xizang dangshi dashiji 1949–1994,* p. 82.

62. *Jiefang Xizang shi,* p. 347.

63. *Pingxi Xizang panluan,* pp. 64–65.

64. For the full text, see *ibid.*

65. Dalai Lama, *My Land and My People,* p. 160.

66. Interview with His Holiness the Dalai Lama, June 30, 2009.

67. *Pingxi Xizang panluan,* p. 67.

68. *Ibid.,* p. 69.

69. *Ibid.*

70. Wang Yan, *Peng Dehuai nianpu,* p. 671.

71. According to Jiang Huating's recollections, one regiment stationed in Tibet required expenditures equivalent to that of three divisions inland. See Tsering Wangchuk, *Xinxiang ziyou,* pp. 22–23.

72. Wang Yan, *Peng Dehuai nianpu*, p. 692.

73. *Ibid.*, p. 698.

Chapter 16

1. "Virtuous order," one of the four main schools of Tibetan Buddhism. Tsongkhapa Lobsang Drakpa was born in 1357.

2. The abbot of the Kumbum Monastery, Arjia Rinpoché, is considered a reincarnation of Tsongkhapa's father.

3. Arjia Rinpoché, *Surviving the Dragon*, p. 33.

4. *Ibid.*, p. 34.

5. *Ibid.*

6. A *tulku* is the reincarnation of a lama of a specific lineage. (In Chinese, they are called "living Buddhas.") There are different levels of *tulkus*, the Dalai Lama being the highest.

7. The *changdzo*, or treasurer, was in charge of the monastery's finances, resources, and other practical affairs.

8. *Genpa* refers to an elder monk or retired *gekoe*, who is influential within the monastery but does not hold any formal office.

9. *Gekoe* are monk disciplinarians.

10. *Rabjampa* is a respectful form of address for a monk scholar.

11. *Umdzé* means chant-master, usually one of the main officeholders in a Tibetan monastery.

12. "Fangeming de chaoxue," p. 10.

13. See, for example, *Ganzi Zangzu Zizhizhou minzu gaige shi*, pp. 86–88.

14. See, for example, a speech made by Wang Feng, then deputy director of the Central Committee United Front Department and vice-chairman of the Nationalities Affairs Commission, on October 7, 1958: *Minzu zongjiao gongzuo wenjian huiji 1949–1959*, vol. 2, p. 785. For an English translation of Wang Feng's speech, see "Destruction of Tibetan Buddhism" at Li and Akester, War on Tibet: Chinese and Tibetan documents on the history of the Communist occupation in English translation: http://historicaldocs.blogspot.com/2013/05/destruction-of-tibetan-buddhism-chinese.html.

15. *Zhonghua Renmin Gongheguo rishi 1958 nian*, published in 2003, makes only a brief mention of the hostilities in Qinghai in its "Overview" and makes no mention at all of the 1958 "religious reform" movement. See p. 4.

16. "Zhongguo Gongchandang gangling" (Guiding principles of the Chinese Communist Party), in *Zhonggong dangshi cankao ziliao*, vol. 2, pp. 197–99.

17. Chen Duxiu (1879–1942) was a founder and the first general secretary of the Chinese Communist Party. A leading intellectual in the May Fourth (New Cultural) Movement, he was expelled from the CCP in 1929.

18. Chen Duxiu, "Ouxiang pohuai lun," p. 89.

19. Mao Tsetung, *Selected Works of Mao Tsetung*, vol. 1, p. 46.

20. "Zhongguo Gongchandang Zhongyang Weiyuanhui gao Kang Zang Xifan minzhong shu" (CCP Central Committee's letter to the people of Kham, Tsang, and Xifan [Yi]), in *Minzu wenti wenxian huibian 1921.7–1949.9*, p. 289. For an English translation of the entire document, see "Eat the Buddha!" at Li and Akester, War on Tibet: Chinese and Tibetan documents on the history of the Communist occupation in English translation: http://historicaldocs.blogspot.com/2012/05/eat-buddha-part-iv-documents-issued-by.html.

21. *Zhonggong dangshi cankao ziliao*, vol. 9, p. 569.

22. *Minzu zongjiao gongzuo wenjian huiji 1949–1959*, vol. 2, pp. 755–56.

23. *Ibid.*, pp. 96–100.

24. As early as 1952, the Xinhua News Agency's *Neibu Cankao* reported on "contradictions between religion and production" in Yulshul Prefecture. See Xinhua News Agency *Neibu Cankao*, August 12, 1958, pp. 119–20.

25. Qin Heping, *Sichuan minzu diqu minzhu gaige ziliaoji*, p. 39.

26. *Ibid.*, pp. 27–29.

27. *Minzu zongjiao gongzuo wenjian huiji 1949–1959*, vol. 2, p. 766.

28. *Ibid.*, p. 738.

29. *Ibid.*, p. 748.

30. Xinhua News Agency *Neibu Cankao*, August 19, 1958, pp. 6–9.

31. *Ibid.*, p. 7.

32. In November 1949, Mao stated, "Thoroughly resolving ethnic problems and completely isolating the nationalist reactionary faction is impossible without a large contingent of communist cadres who come from ethnic minorities." See Mao Zedong, *Mao Zedong wenji*, vol. 6, p. 20.

33. *Minzu zongjiao gongzuo wenjian huiji 1949–1959*, vol. 2, pp. 1–33.

34. Li Weihan, *Tongyi zhanxian wenti yu minzu wenti*, pp. 503–19.

35. *Minzu zongjiao gongzuo wenjian huiji 1949–1959*, vol. 2, pp. 993–94.

36. *Ibid.*, p. 558.

37. *Ibid.*

38. *Ibid.*

39. Xinhua News Agency *Neibu Cankao*, March 10, 1959, p. 10.

40. *Minzu zongjiao gongzuo wenjian huiji 1949–1959*, vol. 2, p. 782.

41. *Ibid.*, p. 785.

42. Li Weihan, "Zai Huizu Yisilanjiao wenti zuotanhui shang de jianghua jilu," in *Minzu zongjiao gongzuo wenjian huiji 1949–1959*, p. 736.

43. *Ibid.*, pp. 736.

44. *Ibid.*, pp. 748–49.

45. Li Weihan, "Wang Feng tongzhi yijiu wuba nian shiyue qiri zai Lamajiao wenti zuotanhui shang de jianghua" (Comrade Wang Feng's speech at the seminar on the problem of Lamaism on October 7, 1958), in *Minzu zongjiao gongzuo wenjian huiji 1949–1959*, vol. 2, p. 784.

46. *Minzu zongjiao gongzuo wenjian huiji 1949–1959*, vol. 2, pp. 428–33.

47. For the published version of the text, see Li Weihan, *Tongyi zhanxian wenti yu minzu wenti*, pp. 503–19.

48. *Minzu zongjiao gongzuo wenjian huiji 1949–1959*, vol. 2, p. 785.

49. *Ibid.*, p. 1070.

50. *Ibid.*

51. Gungthang Rinpoché (1926–2000), one of Tibetan Buddhism's most popular leaders, was arrested in Chengdu on May 22, 1958, without being charged. He was released on April 13, 1979. For details on his arrest and life in prison, see Wang Yunfeng, *Huofo de shijie*, pp. 90–110.

52. A *khenpo* is a senior monk qualified to ordain other monks. *Khenpos* usually have the highest scholarly degree and hold high monastic positions, such as head of a monastic university (*dratsang*).

53. Zhayi Rinpoché, *Wo guxiang de beican shi*, p. 90.

54. Dashaping prison was established in 1949 as a high-security prison for prisoners who had committed serious crimes.

55. Today's Guazhou County, Jiuguan City, Gansu Province.

56. Located in the Subei Mongol Autonomous County, near the border with Mongolia.

57. A prefecture-level city in eastern Gansu Province.

58. Zhayi Rinpoché, *Wo guxiang de beican shi*, p. 91. The territory that Tibetans refer to as Labrang included a larger area than the present Xiahe County.

59. In *Wo guxiang de beican shi*, Zhayi Rinpoché states that more than 200

Tibetans arrested in Gansu in 1958 were executed (dates unspecified) in the Honghaozi prison in Gannan Prefecture and in Manke'er prison in Labrang (location uncertain) and lists the names of dozens of those who were executed. Zhayi Rinpoché, *Wo guxiang de beican shi,* p. 87.

60. *Gannan Zangzu Zizhizhou zhi,* vol. 1, p. 102.

61. People subjected to this collective training were considered not criminals but "bad elements." During the "training" period, they were isolated from society.

62. The arrested included 18 rinpochés, 68 *gekoes,* 14 *genpas,* 59 managers, 3 *changdzos,* 22 elders, and 111 ordinary monks. A total of 145 people were sent to group training, including 1 rinpoché, 23 managers, 7 elders, 6 *gekoes,* and 108 ordinary lamas. See "Fangeming de chaoxue," p. 13.

63. "Guanyu zongjiao gongzuo qingkuang he jinhou yijian de baogao" (Report on the situation of religious work and opinions going forward), in *Minzu zongjiao gongzuo wenjian huiji 1949–1959,* vol. 2, pp. 846–51.

64. "Guanyu Qinghai sheng minzu gongquo qingkuang he jinhou yijian de baogao" (Report on the situation of ethnic minority work in Qinghai Province and opinions going forward), in *Minzu zongjiao gongzuo wenjian huiji 1949–1959,* vol. 2, pp. 466–72.

65. At that time, upper-strata religious figures were all appointed to positions at various levels of the government, referred to as "settling." "Settled individuals" refers to these people.

66. *Zeku xianzhi,* p. 306.

67. *Dari xianzhi,* p. 241.

68. *Tianzhu xianzhi,* p. 25.

69. *Zhongguo Gongchandang Gannan lishi (1921.7–2003.7),* p. 234.

70. *Ibid.*

71. *Qinghai shengzhi: Fulu,* pp. 794–801.

72. *Ganzi Zangzu Zizhizhou minzu gaige shi,* p. 85.

73. *Ibid.,* p. 87.

74. *Ibid.,* p. 86.

75. *Ibid.*

76. Sha Na, "Zai Ganzi Zangzu Zizhizhou nongye xianjin danwei daibiaohui shand de zongjie baogao," p. 49.

77. *Ganzi Zangzu Zizhizhou minzu gaige shi,* p. 86.

78. *Luhuo xianzhi,* p. 300.

79. *Ibid.,* p. 293.

80. *Minzu zongjiao gongzuo wenjian huiji 1949–1959*, vol. 2, p. 916.

81. *Ibid.*, p. 917.

82. *Ibid.*, p. 921.

83. *Ibid.*, p. 850.

84. *Ibid.*, p. 730.

85. *Ibid.*, p. 781.

86. *Gansu shengzhi di 71 juan zongjiao zhi*, p. 116.

87. *Diqing Zangzu Zizhizhou zongjiao zhi*, p. 20.

88. *Minzu zongjiao gongzuo wenjian huiji 1949–1959*, vol. 2, p. 468.

89. *Xizang geming shi*, p. 164.

90. This figure includes Tibetan Buddhist monasteries in Gansu's Linxia Hui Autonomous Prefecture. The source does not define "monastery," but the term usually refers to a religious venue regularly inhabited by monks and does not include religious venues such as meditation caves and *mani* houses (simple huts fitted with large *prayer* wheels).

91. *Gannan Zangzu Zizhizhou zhi*, p. 102.

92. *Luqu xianzhi*, p. 25.

93. Zhang Lihe, "Chuanxibei gaoyuan de Zangchuan fojiao xianzhuang," pp. 44–45.

94. *Huangzhong xianzhi*, p. 238.

95. *Ganzi Zangzu Zizhizhou minzu gaige shi*, p. 89.

96. Qianning (Gartar) County, in northeastern Garzê TAP, was dissolved in July 1978 and merged with Tawu and Nyagchuka counties.

97. 1 *tael* = 37.5 grams.

98. *Daofu xianzhi*, p. 237.

99. *Seda xianzhi*, p. 11.

100. *Dege xianzhi*, p. 420.

101. *Ibid.*

102. *Daofu xianzhi*, p. 327.

Chapter 17

1. Ngolo's story in this chapter comes from my interview with her on October 20, 2010.

2. Tibetans' way of referring to the Dalai Lama.

3. *Ganzi Zangzu Zizhizhou junshi zhi*, pp. 193–95.

4. McGranahan, *Arrested Histories*, p. 84.

5. *Ganzi Zangzu Zizhizhou junshi zhi* (p. 193) states that from January to November 1958, "At least 40 rebellions occurred throughout the prefecture, involving 66 defecting cadres, 55 militiamen, and with more than 100 firearms taken."

6. The CIA's second airdrop of personnel occurred on September 3, 1957. The first airdrop of weapons to Chushi Gangdruk in July 1958 was within the TAR. There were three more airdrops of weapons near Pelbar, in September, November, and December 1959. See Dawa Norbu, *China's Tibet Policy*, pp. 269–71.

7. *Ganzi Zangzu Zizhizhou junshi zhi*, pp. 195–96.

8. *Ibid.*, p. 193.

9. In the Chinese government's official documents, the number of people "annihilated" after a battle usually included "annihilated rebel bandits" and "liberated coerced masses."

10. Interview with Ngolo, October 20, 2010.

11. Present Sershul (Shiqu) County covers the far north of Garzê TAP, but traditionally, Dzachuka refers to a larger territory at the borders of the present-day Qinghai, Sichuan, and TAR, covering 25,000 square kilometers. The place where Aten passed the winter seems to have been in northeastern Dergé County, near the Garzê border.

12. Xin Yuchang, *Ganzi shihua*, p. 71.

13. Mao Zedong, *Jianguo yilai Mao Zedong wengao*, vol. 8, p. 12.

14. *Mao Zedong Xizang gongzuo wenxuan*, p. 164.

15. Mao Zedong, *Jianguo yilai Mao Zedong wengao*, vol. 8, p. 47.

16. *Ganzi Zangzu Zizhizhou junshi zhi*, p. 196.

17. *Ibid.*

18. According to PLA sources, Yang Chengwu directed the Chengdu Military Command to deploy 17 regiments and 7 battalions, but only 14 regiments and 7 battalions actually took part in battle; the other 3 regiments may have been logistics units. See *Ganzi Zangzu Zizhizhou junshi zhi*, p. 196.

19. Two different sources give two different sets of information about this line. According to *Shiqu xianzhi* (Sershul County Gazetteer), the northern line runs 250 kilometers long, from Datangba in northern Garzê County to a place called "Cakenianya"; neither location can be identified on today's maps. See *Shiqu xianzhi*, p. 351.

20. The Tibetan Regiment was established in May 1951 under the numerical designation Chinese People's Liberation Army Southwest Military Command 6th Regiment, with Shana, a member of the Xikang TAR People's Government

Committee and head of its Economics Office, as commander. In 1952, the regiment's numerical designation was changed to the Southwest Military Command 10th Independent Regiment, and then changed again in 1956 to Chengdu Military Command Tibetan 1st Regiment, and in 1959 to Chengdu Military Command Infantry 13th Regiment. The regiment became inactive in 1986. See Li Mingzhong, Li Kunbi, and Bai Yuzhen, "Zeng Quezha zhuan."

21. Li Mingzhong, Li Kunbi, and Bai Yuzhen, "Zeng Quezha zhuan," p. 191.

22. Today's Kasongdu Township, Dege County, in Sichuan's Ganzi TAP.

23. Chinese: Aduo; the specific location is uncertain. It is likely in southern Sershul and includes Dengkhog (Dengke), as that is the main crossing point in that region.

24. Rongpatsa is a district in Garzê County The district covers an area of 1178 square kilometers, including 4 townships and 49 villages. The army is likely to have departed from Rongpatsa Fare, a town on the northern side of the Sichuan-Tibet highway.

25. Today's Yilhung Township, Dergé County.

26. *Ganzi Zangzu Zizhizhou junshi zhi*, pp. 196–97.

27. In today's Tsalung Township, Garzê County.

28. In today's Nyitoe Township, Sertar County.

29. Yixijunmin, "Bu pingfan de zuji," p. 264.

30. Wonpo is today's Wenbo Township in Sershul (Shiqu) County. Zechen Gongma is today's Changxu Gongma Township in Sershul County.

31. Aten mentions in his memoir that his group left two days before the PLA's main attack; this agrees with the Chinese source, but the date would be April 18, 1959. See *Ganzi Zangzu Zizhizhou junshi zhi*, p. 197. See also Jamyang Norbu, *Warriors of Tibet*, p. 138.

32. The account in *Ganzi Zangzu Zizhizhou junshi zhi* is roughly consistent with Aten's and Yetan's recollections. Both of them personally experienced this battle, and the dates of their narratives are basically identical, but diverge from the dates in the Chinese sources. *Ganzi Zangzu Zizhizhou junshi zhi* records the date of the "rebel bandit displacement" as April 18, and the army's attack as launched on April 20. Aten recalls leaving Sertar on the 18th day of the fifth month (June-July) of the Tibetan calendar.

33. Jiang Dasan, "Blog. 74 sui lao feixing renyuan de boke."

34. Jamyang Norbu, *Warriors of Tibet*, pp. 142–43.

35. Xin Yuchang, *Ganzi shihua*, p. 71.

36. These three large *shokka* included more than 30 *tsowa* from Sertar led by chieftain Rigzin Dondrup, the Tsangma from today's Drango County led by chieftain Tsewang Namgyel, and the Tsongtoe, led by Lama Tenzin, brother of the chieftain.

37. Interview with Lama Yetan, September 7 and 8, 2010.

38. *Ganzi Zangzu Zizhizhou junshi zhi*, p. 198, and *Seda xianzhi* record that the Washul chieftain Rigzin Dondrup died in battle on July 23. Yetan recalls that he escaped from the battle in which Rigzin Dondrup was killed.

39. *Seda xianzhi*, p. 358.

40. *Ibid.*

41. Sporadic battles continued in Sichuan's Tibetan regions right through to 1962.

42. Changthang, known as "northern Tibet" in Chinese (Zangbei), is the sparsely inhabited high plateau north of the Thanglha range, stretching 2000 kilometers from east to west, from northern Yulshul Prefecture all the way to Ladakh.

Chapter 18

1. *Zhonggong Xizang dangshi dashiji 1949–1994*, p. 83.

2. See chapter 15.

3. See Ji Youquan, *Xizang pingpan jishi*, pp. 64–69.

4. The present Pomé County government compound. There is a large discrepancy between sources on each side regarding the number of people who surrounded Zhamog. Jiang Huating's memoirs state that there were more than 800 Tibetans and more than 100 people from the county party committee and troops stationed there, while Chinese sources say there were more than 1,500 from Chushi Gangdruk surrounding 60 people in the county party committee. See Tsering Wangchuk, *Xinxiang ziyou*, p. 63; and *Zhonggong Xizang dangshi dashiji 1949–1994*, p. 86.

5. *Zhonggong Xizang dangshi dashiji 1949–1994*, p. 87.

6. The Lhasa Government Organ Militia Regiment was established in November 1958. See *Zhonggong Xizang dangshi dashiji 1949–1994*, p. 84.

7. Interview with the Dalai Lama, June 30, 2009.

8. On December 17, 1958, Tan Guansan, who was in charge of the TWC while both Zhang Jingwu and Zhang Guohua were absent, went to the Norbulingka palace to inform the Dalai Lama that the CCP Central Committee had invited him to attend the Second National People's Congress. The Dalai Lama agreed to attend,

but the exact timing of the Dalai Lama's departure for Beijing had not yet been decided. See *Zhonggong Xizang dangshi dashiji 1949–1994*, p. 85.

9. Jiao Donghai, "Lasa pingpan er san shi," p. 46.

10. Interview with Drolkar Gye, October 20 and 24, 2010.

11. Today's Kecai Township, Xiahe County, Gannan TAP.

12. *Lhadé* is a term used in Amdo for communities owing fealty, usually to the *labrang* of a high lama, and accepting its authority.

13. See Huang Zhengqing, *Huang Zhengqing yu wushi Jiamuyang*, pp. 77–79.

14. Interview with Drolkar Gye, October 20, 2010.

15. *Ibid.* This first husband of Drolkar Gye's is dead, but her current husband, Khotse Jinpa, told me in an interview that around 30 Amdowa, including himself, had gone to Shigatsé at the end of 1958 or early 1959 to protect the Panchen Lama. They were received by the Panchen Lama's parents, and stayed for a period of time in the Tashi Lhunpo monastery, but then they were driven out by the Chinese, so they went to Lhoka and joined Chushi Gangdruk. This incident later became one of the reasons why the Panchen Lama was purged. See Zhang Xiangming, *Zhang Xiangming 55 nian Xizang gongzuo shilu*, p. 320; interview with Khotse Jinpa, October 19, 2010.

16. Geshe Lharampa is the highest academic degree in Tibetan Buddhism.

17. Official publications subsequently referred to these people as "armed rebels." See *Pingxi Xizang panluan*, p. 17.

18. Tibetans use "Jowo Rinpoché" to respectfully refer to the life-sized statue of the 12-year-old Shakyamuni Buddha brought to Tibet by Princess Wencheng and later consecrated in the Tsuklakhang temple.

19. See Li Jianglin, *Tibet in Agony*, pp. 85–93.

20. Xinhua News Agency *Neibu Cankao*, February 26, 1959, p. 9.

21. See *Xizang geming shi*, p. 121; *Pingxi Xizang panluan*, p. 16; *Zhonggong Xizang dangshi dashiji 1949–1994*, p. 87.

22. I.e. from the Shigatsé area, which came under the jurisdiction of the Panchen Lama's Administrative Council from 1950 onward. Because of a rift between the 9th Panchen Lama and the 13th Dalai Lama, all kinds of conflicts existed between the Panchen Lama's Administrative Council and the Lhasa government. See Fan Ming, *Xizang neibu zhi zheng*.

23. The head of the Dalai Lama's security detachment, given the PLA rank of lieutenant colonel in 1955 and promoted to colonel in 1956.

24. *Pingxi Xizang panluan*, p. 72.

25. *Ibid.*

26. Mao Zedong, *Jianguo yilai Mao Zedong wengao*, vol. 8, p. 46.

27. *Ibid.*, p. 48.

28. Generations of Dalai Lamas had given public teachings in this public square on the south side of the temple for the high point of the Great Prayer festival.

29. The building occupied by the Tibet General Trading Company head office at that time had originally been the residence of the Sampo family. After the PLA entered Lhasa, the Sampo family sold its residence to the TWC.

30. *Pingxi Xizang panluan*, p. 71.

31. Puntsok Tashi, *A Life*, p. 252.

32. *Pingxi Xizang panluan*, p. 73.

33. Drolkar Gye's story in this chapter is derived from the author's interviews with Drolkar Gye on October 20 and 24, 2010.

34. Chamdo Khenchung Sonam Gyatso was the older brother of Phagpalha Gelek Namgyal, an important incarnate lama in Chamdo and the first vice-chairman of the Chamdo Liberation Committee from 1951 to 1956. At the time of the incident, Sonam Gyatso held a position in the PCART, and because of his close relationship with the Chinese government, Tibetans suspected that he was a spy for the CCP. *Khenchung* is the term for a fourth-rank monk official in the Tibetan government.

35. The ground in front of the Potala where the TWC compound was located.

36. For the contents of these letters, see Li Jianglin, *Tibet in Agony*, pp. 177–79, 183–84.

37. Xu Bing (1903–1972) was secretary general of the Chinese People's Political Consultative Conference during its second and third sessions (December 1954 to December 1964).

38. Liu Chongwen and Chen Shaochou, *Liu Shaoqi nianpu, 1898–1969*, vol. 2, p. 452.

39. Ding Sheng, "Dingzhi budui de Xizang pingpan zuozhan," p. 298.

40. *Pingxi Xizang panluan*, pp. 79–80. See also Li Jianglin, *Tibet in Agony*, pp. 162–65.

41. Wang Yan, *Peng Dehuai nianpu*, p. 723.

42. The residence of the 14th Dalai Lama at Norbulingka, built in 1956.

43. For details see Li Jianglin, *Tibet in Agony*, pp. 176–79.

44. The dates in this quote are all according to the Tibetan calendar, which is used in all records of the Dalai Lama's speeches. Explanatory notes were added by

the author. The reference here to "December 29th" means the penultimate day of the Earth Dog year, i.e., February 7, 1959.

45. Deputy Commander Deng refers to Deng Shaodong, who at that time was deputy commander of the TMC, at the military rank of major general.

46. I.e., February 28. There are differing accounts of which day the Dalai Lama returned to Norbulingka, but the date given in this record should be accurate.

47. The original text of this speech is in Tibetan; the Chinese translation was published in the May 26, 1959, edition of Xinhua News Agency's *Neibu Cankao*. The Chinese translator believed that the original text was recorded by Kalon Surkhang.

48. Yang Shangkun, *Yang Shangkun riji*, vol. 1, p. 365.

49. Those attending included the vice-chairman of the CPPCC and Beijing municipal party secretary Peng Zhen, defense minister Peng Dehuai, PLA chief of general staff Huang Kecheng, chairman of the Central Committee General Office Yang Shangkun, TWC secretary general Zhang Jingwu, PLA TMC commander Zhang Guohua, and vice-chairman of the State Ethnic Affairs Commission Yang Jingren. See Liu Chongwen and Chen Shaochou, *Liu Shaoqi nianpu, 1898–1969*, vol. 2, p. 452.

50. *Jiefang Xizang shi*, p. 364.

51. Hua Qiang, Xi Jirong, et al., *Zhongguo kongjun bainian shi*, p. 218.

52. *Deng Xiaoping junshi wenji di'er juan*, pp. 333–34.

53. Dalai Lama, *My Land and My People*, p. 190.

54. *Jiefang Xizang shi*, pp. 369–70; Li Jianglin, *Tibet in Agony*, pp. 172–73.

55. Jiao Donghai, "Lasa pingpan er san shi," p. 46.

56. For the arrangements made for the Dalai Lama to go into exile, see Li Jianglin, *Tibet in Agony*, pp. 174–75 and 180–83.

57. Yang Shangkun, *Yang Shangkun riji*, p. 365.

58. The Lhasa time zone is two hours behind Beijing. With the launch of Democratic Reform in April 1959, Lhasa was obliged to follow Beijing time.

59. Yang Shangkun, *Yang Shangkun riji*, p. 366.

60. *Deng Xiaoping nianpu 1904–1974*, vol. 2, p. 1496.

61. *Zhonggong Xizang dangshi dashiji 1949–1994*, p. 93; Ji Youquan, *Xizang pingpan jishi*, p. 92.

62. At the time that he set out, the Dalai Lama didn't plan to go straight to India. He planned to first go to Lhoka, and try to negotiate with the Chinese government from there. It was only after learning of the Battle of Lhasa that he

decided to go on to India. For the details on the Dalai Lama's flight into exile, see Li Jianglin, *Tibet in Agony,* chapters 14, 15, and 22.

63. Wang Yan, *Peng Dehuai nianpu,* p. 723.

64. Yang Shangkun, *Yang Shangkun riji,* vol. 1, p. 94. Wu Lengxi, who at that time was director of the Xinhua News Agency and chief editor of *People's Daily,* writes in his *Remembering Chairman Mao*: "Comrade Liu Shaoqi held a Politburo meeting on March 17. . . . Before the meeting was adjourned, the Central Committee learned that Dalai had left Lhasa, and immediately decided to send reinforcements into Tibet in preparation for dealing with a possible armed rebellion, but the policy was still to not fire the first shot" (*Yi Mao zhuxi,* p. 120). It appears that he may have remembered incorrectly. The *Chronicle of Events in the History of the CCP in Tibet 1949–1994 (Zhonggong Xizang dangshi dashiji),* the restricted publication *Suppressing the Armed Rebellion in Tibet (Pingxi Xizang panluan),* and the journal of Yang Shangkun, who participated in the meeting, all state that the TWC reported to the Central Committee about the Dalai Lama leaving Lhasa on March 19.

65. For example, in 2008, National Defense University professor and special technology major general Xu Yan repeated this claim: "On March 17, Dalai went south under cover of the Tibetan Army First Depon. After the PLA discovered him along the Lhasa River, in accordance with Mao's order issued five days earlier that 'our army is not to obstruct him,' they intentionally let him proceed." See Xu Yan, "Zangqu pingpan de wunian jianku suiyue."

66. For details on the Battle of Lhasa, see Li Jianglin, *Tibet in Agony,* chapters 17–20.

67. See Wang Guozhen, "Pili tianjiang cheng xiongwan"; Xu Yan, "Zangqu pingpan de wunian jianku suiyue."

68. For details on the bombardment of Chakpori Hill, see Li Jianglin, *Tibet in Agony, chapter* 17.

69. These items could include Tibetan herbal medicine or other offerings blessed by an eminent monk.

70. Referring to the Three Jewels of Buddhism: the Buddha, the Dharma, and the Sangha.

71. Tibetans regard the Jokhang or Tsuklakhang temple as their most sacred place of worship.

72. The sacks they used were each more than a foot wide and one to two yards long and could be packed with foodstuffs and other items and then loaded onto the back of a mule or horse.

73. According to the memoirs of Tubten Khetsun, a low-ranking government official who was arrested at Norbulingka, after the battle, many bodies were hastily buried in a trench at the west gate dug by Amdowas guarding the gate; more than a month later, they were dug out, doused in gasoline, and burned. See Tubten Khetsun, *Memories of Life in Lhasa*, p. 45.

74. Wu Lengxi, *Yi Mao zhuxi*, p. 121.

75. The present Longzi County, Lhoka (Shannan) City, TAR.

76. Hutheesing, *Tibet Fights for Freedom*, p. 70.

77. Referring to members of China's eight non-Communist political parties.

78. Xinhua News Agency *Neibu Cankao*, on March 31 and April 1, 1959, published "Inland Reactions to the Lhasa Incident."

79. Shan Chao, "Yuguo tianqing." Shan Chao had once served as leader of the 18th Army's performing arts troupe and was secretary of the propaganda department of the Lhasa and TAR party committees. He is now a member of the Chinese Writers' Association.

80. "Xizang gongwei xuanchuanbu dui Renmin Ribao fabiao 'Yuguo tianqin' yigao de yijian."

81. Shan Chao, "Yuguo tianqing."

82. "Xizang gongwei xuanchuanbu dui Renmin Ribao fabiao 'Yuguo tianqin' yigao de yijian," p. 21.

83. Shan Chao, "Yuguo tianqing."

84. "Xizang gongwei xuanchuanbu dui Renmin Ribao fabiao 'Yuguo tianqin' yigao de yijian," p. 21.

85. Shan Chao, "Yuguo tianqing."

86. "Xizang gongwei xuanchuanbu dui Renmin Ribao fabiao 'Yuguo tianqin' yigao de yijian," p. 22.

87. Chen Bing, "Panguo bi wang," p. 24.

88. *Jiefang Xizang shi*, p. 373.

89. *Xinhua News Agency Neibu Cankao*, May 31, 1959, p. 23.

90. *Pingxi Xizang panluan*, p. 89.

91. "Communique on Rebellion in Tibet issued by the Hsinhua (Xinhua) News Agency on March 28." In *Concerning the Question of Tibet*, p. 9.

92. Shan Chao, "Lasa pingpan jianwen," p. 9.

93. Anna Louise Strong (1885–1970), an American journalist and activist, was well-known for her reporting in support of the Communist movement in the USSR and China. She lived in Beijing from 1958 till her death in March, 1970.

94. Zhongguo Zangxue chubanshe (Chinese Tibetan Studies Publishing) published a Chinese edition of this book in 2009, after the third Lhasa incident in 2008.

95. Yang Shangkun, *Yang Shangkun riji*, p. 381.

96. *Mao Zedong Xizang gongzuo wenxuan*, p. 173.

97. See "Sichuan Zangqu jiben qingkuang" (The basic situation in Sichuan's Tibetan regions), April 19, 1959, pp. 2–4; "Xizang de jiben qingkuang" (The basic situation in Tibet), April 21, 1959, pp. 2–8; and "Gansu Zangqu jiben qingkuang" (The basic situation in Gansu's Tibetan regions), April 23, 1959, pp. 2–5; all in Xinhua News Agency *Neibu Cankao.*

98. Xinhua News Agency *Neibu Cankao*, April 21, 1959, p. 7.

99. *Renmin huabao*, May 16, 1959, p. 28.

100. Huang Kecheng, *Huang Kecheng junshi wenxuan*, p. 727.

101. Li Zhenyu, "Xizang wangshi."

102. For example, *Xizang nongnuzhu de xuexing zuixing* (The Gory Crimes of Tibetan Serf Owners), edited and published in December 1959 by Minzu chubanshe, which also published *Xizang nongnu de nuhou* (The Howls of Tibet's Serfs) and *Wan'e de Xizang nongnu zhidu* (The Nefarious Tibetan Serf System) in April 1960.

103. For example, *Xizang xinsheng qu* (Song of Tibet's New Life), published in September 1959 by Shanghai renmin chubanshe.

104. *Jiefang Xizang shi*, p. 373.

105. *Zhonggong Xizang dangshi dashiji 1949–1994*, p. 98.

106. This person's Tibetan name and position have not been identified.

107. Wang Zhongxing and Liu Liqin, *Guofang lishi*, p. 134.

108. Drolkar Gye told me that she, too, was questioned, and that she was able to get away by condemning the "rebels." Interview with Drolkar Gye, October 20, 2010.

109. Frames made of wooden rods and rattan were typically used by religious pilgrims, or anyone traveling on foot, to carry goods on their backs.

110. Interview with Drolkar Gye, October 20, 2010.

Chapter 19

1. Wang Tingsheng, *Wangshi huimou*, pp. 140–41.

2. Lu Shoubiao, *Cong shusheng dao hujiang*, p. 328.

3. *Zhongguo Renmin Jiefangjun bubing dishiyishi junzhanshi*, p. 232.

4. This was the home of Dasang Damdul Tsarong (1888–1959), former commander-in-chief of the Tibetan army and a cabinet minister.

5. Wang Tingsheng, *Wangshi huimou*, p. 142.

6. *Zhonggong Xizang dangshi dashiji 1949–1994*, p. 98.

7. Zhi Bin, Sun Xiao, and Jiang Zhentao, *Zhongguo "tiejun" chuanqi*, pp. 1–8.

8. Today's Tsethang (Zedang) Township, under Nedong (Naidong) County, Shannan City, TAR. This county was created through the merger of the former Nedong and Tsethang Dzongs.

9. Ding Sheng, "Dingzhi budui de Xizang pingpan zuozhan," p. 299.

10. [Andrugtsang] Gompo Tashi, *Four Rivers, Six Ranges*, pp. 90–91. The deputy commander of the 134th Division's scouting unit, Wang Tingsheng, admits in his memoirs that "our estimates of the strength of the Shannan rebel bandits were somewhat excessive." See Wang Tingsheng, *Wangshi huimou*, p. 147.

11. Today's Chusum (Qusong) County, Lhoka (Shannan) City.

12. For the military deployment in the Battle of Lhoka, see Wang Tingsheng, *Wangshi huimou*, pp. 144–55; Ji Youquan, *Xizang pingpan jishi*, pp. 123–24; and Lu Shoubiao, *Cong shusheng dao hujiang*, pp. 336–37.

13. Today's Chabnag (Qiangna) Township, Mainling (Milin) County, Nyingtri City, TAR.

14. Today's Sang-ngak Choeling (San'anqulin) Township, Lhuntsé County.

15. On the PLA's military deployments for the Battle of Lhoka, see Wang Tingsheng, *Wangshi huimou*, pp. 144–55; Ji Youquan, *A True Record*, pp. 123–24; and Lu Shoubiao, *Cong shusheng dao hujiang*, 336–37.

16. Today's Taklung (Dalong) Township, Nakartsé County, Lhoka, on the southwest shore of Yamdrok Yumtso (Yangzhouyong) lake.

17. In today's Lhodrak (Luozha) County, Lhoka. The county was formed in 1960 through the merger of Do Dzong (Duozong), Lhakhang Dzong (Lakangzong) and Sengge Dzong (Senggezong).

18. Today's Chamda (Zhangda) Township, Nakartsé (Langkazi) County.

19. Today's Jayul (Jiayu) Township, Lhuntsé County. This county was created through the merger of the former Lhuntsé Dzong, Jhora Shika (Juela Xika), and Jayul Shika (Jiayu Xika).

20. Today's Tsona (Cuona) County, Lhoka. When the Dalai Lama fled Tibet, he followed the westerly route from here to Tawang, in what was then the Indian North-East Frontier Agency territory.

21. Today's Jhora (Juela) Township, Tsona County, Lhoka.

22. Today's Riduo Township, Medro Gongkar (Mozhu kongka) County, Lhasa.

23. Today in Nedong (Naidong) County, under the direct jurisdiction of Lhoka Municipality.

24. Today's Trandruk (Changzhu) Township, Nedong (Naidong) County.

25. Today's Kongpo Gyamda (Gongbu Jiangda) County, Nyingtri (Linzhi) City, TAR.

26. Tselagang Dzong (Zelazong) was in what is today Nyingtri County, Nyingtri City, TAR.

27. *Zhonggong Xizang dangshi dashiji 1949–1994*, p. 87.

28. Jama Samphel Dondrup (1907–1974), a native of Lithang, was once deputy commander of Chushi Gangdruk. He crossed the border to India at the end of April 1959 and on September 18 of that year went to Taiwan, where he settled. He died on July 2, 1974.

29. Ratuk Ngawang, "Mdo khamsspon'borsgang gi sa'ichar'khodp'i Li thangdgon yul gnyis kyis btsan 'dzulpa la zhum med ngo rgol gyis rangsa srungskyob byas p'iskor," pp. 451–62. Furthermore, the 54th Regiment Military History Office's "134shi canjia Xizang pingpan jishi" (Record of the 134th Division's participation in the pacifying rebellion in Tibet) in *Zhongguo Renmin Jiefangjun bubing dishiyishi junzhanshi* (Military history of the Chinese People's Liberation Army Eleventh 11th Infantry Division) states that there were more than 500 Chushi Gangdruk fighters surrounding the TWC's Tsethang Branch, which is close to Ratuk Ngawang's recollections. See Shi Hongsheng, "Xizang pingpan zhong de houqin baozhang gongzuo," p. 171. However, an autobiographical essay in the same volme by the commander and political commissar of the 155th Regiment, Qiao Xueting, states that there were more than 1,600 fighters: *ibid.*, p. 107.

30. Zhao Junwen, "Bei baowei de qishisi tian."

31. [Andrugtsang] Gompo Tashi, *Four Rivers, Six Ranges*, p. 36; Tsering Wangchuk, *Xinxiang ziyou*, pp. 64–69.

32. Ji Youquan writes that up until April 12, the commander of the Shannan campaign, Ding Sheng, had no way of ascertaining the position of Chushi Gangdruk's main force. See Ji Youquan, *Xizang pingpan jishi*, p. 137.

33. For details see chapter 15, section 4 of this book.

34. Within the boundaries of today's Lholung (Luolong) County, Chamdo City, TAR.

35. [Andrugtsang] Gompo Tashi, *Four Rivers, Six Ranges*, pp. 87–93.

36. Within the boundaries of today's Lholung County, Chamdo. See Gonpo Tashi, p. 93.

37. Today's Shopamdo (Shuodu) Township in Lholung County. This county was formed from the merger of the former Lho Dzong and Shopamdo Dzong.

38. Today's Bankar Township in Driru (Biru) County, Nagchu.

39. See [Andrugtsang] Gompo Tashi, *Four Rivers, Six Ranges*, p. 96.

40. According to Ding Sheng's memoirs, the 159th Regiment set off on April 4th and crossed the river at Chabnag on the 7th and 8th. If Ding Sheng's recollection is accurate, it is not possible for Wu Chen's troops to reach Lhuntsé on April 8.

41. Ji Youquan, *Xizang pingpan jishi*, p. 125.

42. In today's Lhari (Jiali) County, Nagchu.

43. Today's Milin County, Nyingchi City.

44. Today's Dronpa (Zhunba) Township, Lhuntsé County.

45. Today's Metok County, Nyingtri City.

46. Chushi Gangdruk surrounded and attacked Tsethang three times. The first time was in July 1958, the second time in October 1958, and the third time from January 25 to April 8, 1959. See Chen Jinshui, "Zedang qixiangzhan baowei zhan de huiyi."

47. The location where that regiment was ambushed is in today's Gyerba (Jieba) Township, Nedong (Naidong) County, about 20 km from Tsethang. Gonpo Tashi states in his memoir that on April 5, the Chushi Gangdruk unit in charge of a supply convoy encountered "300 Chinese trucks with soldiers from Lhasa," and the two sides began fighting. Chushi Gangdruk fighters were overwhelmed and had to withdraw, leaving their supplies behind. See [Andrugtsang] Gompo Tashi, *Four Rivers, Six Ranges*, p. 102. Gonpo Tashi might have been just one day's distance from the PLA forces.

48. Ding Sheng, "Dingzhi budui de Xizang pingpan zuozhan," p. 300.

49. Ji Youquan, *Xizang pingpan jishi*, p. 128.

50. Dawa Tsering, *Xueji xueyu*, pp. 449–50.

51. Ji Youquan, *Xizang pingpan jishi*, pp. 133–34.

52. *Ibid.*, p. 134.

53. Today's Potrang (Pozhang) Township, Nedong (Naidong) County, Lhoka (Shannan) City.

54. Ji Youquan, *Xizang pingpan jishi*, p. 134.

55. Dawa Tsering, *Xueji xueyu*, pp. 452–53.

56. *Ibid.*

57. Ding Sheng, "Dingzhi budui de Xizang pingpan zuozhan," p. 299.

58. Today's Paldi (Baidi) Township, Nakartsé (Langkazi) County.

59. Today's Nakartsé County, the westernmost district of Lhoka, in the area of Yamdrok Yumtso Lake.

60. Today's Lhodrak (Luozha) County, Lhoka.

61. Ji Youquan, *Xizang pingpan jishi*, p. 129.

62. Potrang (Pozhang) Township is in Nedong County, about 20 km south of Tsethang.

63. Ji Youquan, *Xizang pingpan jishi*, p. 138.

64. See [Andrugtsang] Gompo Tashi, *Four Rivers, Six Ranges*, p. 103; Tsering Wangchuk, *Xinxiang ziyou*, p. 73; Dawa Tsering, *Xueji xueyu*, p. 455.

65. Ji Youquan, *Xizang pingpan jishi*, p. 140.

66. The Tibetan army was organized under commanding officers as follows: *depon* (regimental commander), *rupon* (battalion commander), *gyapon* (company commander), and *dingpon* (platoon leader). See Chen Bing, "Zangjun shilue" (Brief history of the Tibetan Army), in *Xizang wenshi ziliao xuanji*, vol. 4, pp. 85–99.

67. Ding Sheng, "Dingzhi budui de Xizang pingpan zuozhan," p. 301.

68. Lu Shoubiao, *Cong shusheng dao hujiang*, p. 343.

69. *Ibid.*

70. Ji Youquan, *Xizang pingpan jishi*, p. 131. The biography of Wei Tongtai states that in the Battle of Do Dzong, "115 bandits were killed, 31 taken prisoner, and 23 wounded." See Lu Shoubiao, *Cong shusheng dao hujiang*, p. 340.

71. Shi Hongsheng, "Xizang pingpan zhong de houqin baozhang gongzuo," p. 172.

72. The 159th Regiment arrived in Sang-ngak Choeling on April 18. Sang-ngak Choeling Township is in the northeast of Lhuntsé County, about 110 km from the county seat.

73. [Andrugtsang] Gompo Tashi, *Four Rivers, Six Ranges*, p. 104.

74. Tsering Wangchuk, *Xinxiang ziyou*, pp. 76–77.

75. According to military maps from that time, the PLA crossed the McMahon Line in several spots during the Battle of Lhoka. Jiang Huating's memoirs record Indian army patrol parties exchanging fire several times with PLA soldiers who crossed the border. See Tsering Wangchuk, *Xinxiang ziyou*, p. 72.

76. Establishment 22 still exists, but the Mustang guerrilla base ceased operations in 1974.

77. "Huanhu taoping Xizang Shannan panfei de zhongda shengli" (Hailing the mighty victory in suppressing the bandit revolt in Shannan, Tibet), in *Guanyu Xizang wenti*, p. 106.

78. Huang Kecheng, *Huang Kecheng junshi wenxuan*, p. 727.

79. Ji Youquan, *Xizang pingpan jishi*, p. 141.

80. Tsering Wangchuk, *Xinxiang ziyou*, p. 71.

81. Ding Sheng, "Dingzhi budui de Xizang pingpan zuozhan," p. 301.

82. *Jiefang Xizang shi*, p. 380.

83. Ji Youquan, *A True Record*, p. 142; *Jiefang Xizang shi*, p. 379.

84. Wang Tingsheng, *Wangshi huimou*, p. 146. *Shijie wuji fengyun lu*, vol. 3, p. 172.

85. *Zhonggong Xizang dangshi dashiji 1949–1994*, p. 99.

86. The deputy commander of the 134th Division's scouting unit at that time, Wang Tingsheng, recalls that before the battle, "Our estimates of the Shannan bandit rebel's strength was somewhat elevated; if there were originally 9,000 men, adding in 5,000-plus who fled from Lhasa in March made a total of more than 14,000 men." See Wang Tingsheng, *Wangshi huimou*, p. 147.

87. *Jiefang Xizang shi*, p. 379. In "Record of the 134th Division's participation in pacifying rebellion in Tibet," the numbers given are: "16 battles, 1,577 of the enemy annihilated, captured one cannon, 385 long and short guns, four machine guns and 706 homemade firearms." See Shi Hongsheng, "134shi canjia Xizang pingpan jishi", in *Shijie wuji fengyun lu*, vol. 3, p. 172; Wang Tingsheng's memoir contains similar figures, probably from the same source.

88. This quote comes from Dawa Tsering, *Xueji xueyu*, p. 453.

89. Shi Hongsheng, "134shi canjia Xizang pingpan jishi", in *Shijie wuji fengyun lu*, vol. 3, p. 172.

90. *Ibid.*, p. 173.

91. *Ibid.*

92. *Ibid.*

Chapter 20

1. *Zhongguo Renmin Jiefangjun bubing dishiyishi junzhanshi*, p. 233.

2. *Ibid.*, p. 234.

3. Interview with Ngolo, October 20, 2010.

4. Today's Shentsa (Shenzha) County in Nagchu (Naqu) City.

5. Today's Palgon (Bange) County in Nagchu.

6. Dawa Tsering, *Xueji xueyu*, p. 466.

7. Today's Chinglung (Qinglong) Township in Palgon County, Nagchu.

8. *Zhongguo Renmin Jiefangjun bubing dishiyishi junzhanshi*, p. 235.

9. Varying figures are given for the number of Tibetans attacked by the PLA in the Battle of Namtso, from between 3,000 and 3,500 to more than 4,000. See Ding Sheng, "Dingzhi budui de Xizang pingpan zuozhan," p. 302; *Zhongguo Renmin*

Jiefangjun bubing dishiyishi junzhanshi, p. 235; Ji Youquan, *Xizang pingpan jishi*, p. 154; and Lu Shoubiao, *Cong shusheng dao hujiang*, p. 346.

10. Today's Sangshung (Sanxiong) Township, Nagchu County, on the Damshung-Nagchu highway.

11. Mount 7050 is a military reference. The actual location of the hill is unknown.

12. *Zhongguo Renmin Jiefangjun bubing dishiyishi junzhanshi*, pp. 237–38.

13. Dawa Tsering, *Xueji xueyu*, p. 468.

14. *Ibid.*, p. 469.

15. Lu Shoubiao, *Cong shusheng dao hujiang*, p. 350.

16. *Ibid.*, p. 351.

17. *Zhongguo Renmin Jiefangjun bubing dishiyishi junzhanshi*, p. 238. The figure 13,132 appears to be a typographical error.

18. Ding Sheng, "Dingzhi budui de Xizang pingpan zuozhan," p. 303.

19. *Jiefang Xizang shi*, p. 383.

20. Many of the locations mentioned in Chinese sources regarding the Battle of Mitikha are mountains and ravines that are known only to local people, and different Chinese transliterations are used in different sources, so it's very difficult to verify specific locations. I have ascertained some current place names based on the memoirs and biographies of the battle's PLA commanders, Ding Sheng and Wei Tongtai, as well as TAR administrative plans and histories and some internal documents of the TMC. The main battle sites are within what is now the Mitikha Wetlands Nature Preserve. Based on current highway routes, it was about 70 to 100 km from Lhari to Mitikha.

21. The Miti Tsangpo river is the source of the Kyichu (Lhasa) river.

22. *Zhonggong Xizang dangshi dashiji 1949–1966*, p. 109, states that there were more than 800 tribes in Nagchu, Qinghai, and other areas, with "nearly 5,000 battle-ready fighters," while other sources state that there were 80-odd tribes with around 5,000 battle-ready fighters. See Ji Youquan, *Xizang pingpan jishi*, p. 163.

23. *Zhongguo Renmin Jiefangjun bubing dishiyishi junzhanshi*, p. 238, gives a figure of "more than 10,000 people," but other sources provide no figures. Based on the post-battle statistics of Tibetans killed, wounded, taken prisoner, and surrendered, as well as "liberated masses," the total was around 13,000 people.

24. In today's Lhari County, Nagchu.

25. Today's Sog (Suo) County in Nagchu.

26. See Dawa Tsering, *Xueji xueyu*, pp. 488–91.

27. In 1959, the TMC deployed military engineers and civilian laborers to rapidly construct a simple 745-km highway from Nagchu to Chamdo to serve as a military road for battle purposes in northern Tibet. This highway remains in use today. See Xu Zhengyu, *Xizang keji zhi*, p. 137.

28. Shi Hongsheng, "Xizang pingpan zhong de houqin baozhang gongzuo," p. 236; Lu Shoubiao, *Cong shusheng dao hujiang*, p. 358.

29. Referred to as the "39 Hor tribes" in Chinese documents.

30. The other two branches were Chamdo and Pomé.

31. Miao Pi-yi, *Miao Pi-yi huiyilu*, p. 263. The full letter has not been declassified.

32. See Dawa Tsering, *Xueji xueyu*, p. 484; Wang Zhengtin, "Dingqing baoweizhan" (Battle of protecting Dingqing), in *Shijie wuji fengyunlu*, p. 25.

33. Wang Zhengtin, then the deputy secretary of the Tengchen CCP Committee and political commissar, admits in his article that the air force bombed Tengchen for ten days, but gives no details. The Tibetan source gives more details about the bombing. See Wang Zhengtin, "Dingqing baoweizhan," p. 26; Dawa Tsering, *Xueji xueyu*, pp. 485–86.

34. Dawa Tsering, *Xueji xueyu*, pp. 486–88.

35. See Miao Pi-yi, *Miao Pi-yi huiyilu*, p. 265; Wang Zhengtin, "Dingqing baoweizhan," p. 27.

36. Nagchu Prefecture became Nagchu City in July 2017.

37. The Tsenden Monastery was built in 1667 and had about 700 monks before 1959. It was largely destroyed in the bombing. The current monastery was rebuilt in 1985 and now has 50 monks.

38. Dawa Tsering, *Xueji xueyu*, p. 488.

39. *Zhongguo Renmin Jiefangjun bubing dishiyishi junzhanshi*, p. 239.

40. Dawa Tsering, *Xueji xueyu*, p. 489.

41. Lu Shoubiao, *Cong shusheng dao hujiang*, p. 358.

42. Lu Shoubiao gives the date as August 26, 1959, but *Zhongguo kongjun bainian shi (The Hundred-year History of the Chinese Air Force), p. 217,* has it as August 15, which is more likely to be the correct date. See Lu Shoubiao, *Cong shusheng dao hujiang*, p. 359; Ding Sheng, "Dingzhi budui de Xizang pingpan zuozhan," p. 303.

43. Hua Qiang, Xi Jirong, et al., *Zhongguo kongjun bainian shi*, p. 217.

44. *Zhongguo Renmin Jiefangjun bubing dishiyishi junzhanshi*, p. 239.

45. Dawa Tsering, *Xueji xueyu*, p. 491.

46. Todays's Nyenrong (Nierong) County, Nagchu City.

47. Between present-day Kongpo Gyamda and Medro Gongkar counties.

48. Today's Drugla (Zhula) Township in Kongpo Gyamda County.

49. Today's Koluk (Gulu) Township in Nagchu County.

50. Today's Shachukha (Xiaqiuka) Township in Driru County.

51. Mount Techen is one of many hills in the Mitikha area. The description of the battle is based on Ji Youquan, *Xizang pingpan jishi,* but the specific location of Mount Techen is not clear. It is probably a mountain pass between today's Lhari Township and Mitikha. For an additional Chinese source on the Battle of Mount Techen, see *Zhongguo Renmin Jiefangjun bubing dishiyishi junzhanshi*, pp. 239–40.

52. Ji Youquan, *Xizang pingpan jishi*, p. 172.

53. *Ibid.*, pp. 172–76.

54. Lu Shoubiao, *Cong shusheng dao hujiang*, p. 363.

55. Ding Sheng, "Dingzhi budui de Xizang pingpan zuozhan," p. 305.

56. *Ibid.*, p. 305; Lu Shoubiao, *Cong shusheng dao hujiang*, p. 363. The 54th Army's Military History Office gives inconsistent figures: "A total of 41 large and small battles were fought by the various units, with 3,561 armed rebels annihilated and 2,476 firearms of various kinds seized. See Shi Hongsheng, "Xizang pingpan zhong de houqin baozhang gongzuo."

57. Ding Sheng, "Dingzhi budui de Xizang pingpan zuozhan," p. 305.

58. For Mao's directives regarding training soldiers through warfare in Tibet, see chapter 17, part 4 of this book.

59. *Zhongguo Renmin Jiefangjun bubing dishiyishi junzhanshi*, p. 256.

Chapter 21

1. Ji Youquan, *Xizang pingpan jishi*, p. 185. This figure does not include refugees from Kham and Amdo.

2. *Zhongguo Renmin Jiefangjun bubing dishiyishi junzhanshi*, p. 242.

3. Today's Saga County in Shigatsé City, TAR.

4. See chapter 18, part 4 of this book.

5. *Jiefang Xizang shi*, p. 388.

6. *Zhongguo Renmin Jiefangjun bubing dishiyishi junzhanshi*, p. 242.

7. *Ibid.*

8. Ji Youquan, *Xizang pingpan jishi*, p. 189: "The pacification of the rebellion in Zone 3 lasted 29 days, from February 21 to March 20. More than 10,000 bandit suppression troops annihilated only 500 enemies and then withdrew to Naqu."

9. Part of what is now Shentsa (Shenzha) County in Nagchu Prefecture, TAR.

10. All three lakes are located in today's Tsochen (Cuoqin) County, Ngari (Ali) Prefecture, TAR. Lake Trari Namtso is the third-largest lake in Tibet.

11. *Jiefang Xizang shi*, p. 393.

12. *Zhongguo Renmin Jiefangjun bubing dishiyishi junzhanshi*, p. 243.

13. Arak-tsang's name seems to appear in Chinese sources only and not in any Tibetan sources, and even in the Chinese sources there are no further identifying details.

14. *Zhongguo Renmin Jiefangjun bubing dishiyishi junzhanshi*, p. 243.

15. *Ibid.*

16. An administrative unit in Tsonub (Haixi) Mongol and Tibetan Autonomous Prefecture bordering Gansu province to the north.

17. The Mendong Monastery is near the seat of today's Tsochen County, Ngari Prefecture.

18. Ji Youquan, *Xizang pingpan jishi*, p. 189.

19. *Zhongguo Renmin Jiefangjun bubing dishiyishi junzhanshi*, p. 245.

20. *Ibid.*

21. *Ibid.* The "three antis and three calculations" were actions against rebellion, slavery, and feudal exploitation and the squaring of accounts with political oppression, class oppression, and economic exploitation. See *Jiefang Xizang shi*, p. 412.

22. *Zhongguo Renmin Jiefangjun bubing dishiyishi junzhanshi*, p. 246.

23. *Ibid.*, p. 245.

24. *Ibid.*, p. 246.

25. Ji Youquan, *Xizang pingpan jishi*, p. 190.

26. *Ibid.*

27. The 15 *dzongs* within Zone 1 were Tengchen, Kharnag, Sateng, Pelbar, Shopamdo, Lholung, Pashol, Nganda, Cho Dzong, Chumdo, Yi-ong, Lhari, Shokha, Driru, and Tridu. See Lu Shoubiao, *Cong shusheng dao hujiang*, p. 367; Ding Sheng, "Dingzhi budui de Xizang pingpan zuozhan," pp. 305–6.

28. Lu Shoubiao, *Cong shusheng dao hujiang*, p. 367.

29. *Ibid.* See also Dawa Tsering, *Xueji xueyu*, pp. 493–94.

30. Dawa Tsering, *Xueji xueyu*, p. 493.

31. Dawa Norbu, *China's Tibet Policy*, p. 270.

32. Shi Hongsheng, "Xizang pingpan zhong de houqin baozhang gongzuo," p. 177.

33. There are varying figures given for the number of PLA troops in Zone 1. *Jiefang Xizang shi* and Ding Sheng's memoirs state that there were 7 infantry regiments

and 1 artillery regiment carrying light weapons; Wei Tongtai's biography counts 9 regiments. Ji Youquan's *Xizang pingpan jishi* states that there were 7 infantry regiments and 1 infantry battalion, as well as the TMC's 308th Artillery Regiment and three cavalry detachments, which comes to a total of 9 regiments of various kinds. This doesn't include the air force scouts and bombers deployed later. See *Jiefang Xizang shi*, p. 389; Ding Sheng, "Dingzhi budui de Xizang pingpan zuozhan," p. 306; Lu Shoubiao, *Cong shusheng dao hujiang*, p. 367; and Ji Youquan, *Xizang pingpan jishi*, p. 191.

34. This figure comes from *Jiefang Xizang shi*, p. 389.

35. Lu Shoubiao, *Cong shusheng dao hujiang*, p. 374.

36. Lu Shoubiao, *Cong shusheng dao hujiang*, p. 368. See also *Jiefang Xizang shi*, p. 389.

37. Lu Shoubiao, *Cong shusheng dao hujiang*, p. 368.

38. Ding Sheng, "Dingzhi budui de Xizang pingpan zuozhan," p. 307.

39. Amdo Méma is within the borders of today's Amdo (Anduo) County, Nagchu Prefecture, and was the grazing land for Méma's tribes. The Amdo Méma army base was one of 14 army bases that the PLA established along the Qinghai-Tibet highway in 1956.

40. Lu Shoubiao, *Cong shusheng dao hujiang*, p. 370.

41. *Ibid.*

42. Today's Lhatsé (Lazi) Township, Chamdo City, TAR.

43. Lu Shoubiao, *Cong shusheng dao hujiang*, p. 370.

44. Ding Sheng, "Dingzhi budui de Xizang pingpan zuozhan," p. 307.

45. Sateng, in today's Pelbar County.

46. Zhang Xiangming, *Zhang Xiangming 55 nian Xizang gongzuo shilu*, p. 54.

47. These included 362 people still in prison, 1,413 who had continued to be subjected to reform under supervision after completing their sentences, and about 5,000 who had not been imprisoned but remained under surveillance. See *Zhonggong Xizang dangshi dashiji 1949–1994*, pp. 218–19.

48. On April 14, 1979, Garzê (Ganzi) and Ngawa (Aba), Sichuan Province, announced the release of 588 persons taken into custody before 1960 and the "lenient handling" of 363 people who continued to be subjected to reform under supervision after completing their sentences. Qinghai Province in June 1979 released 112 people from custody and allowed 277 people who had been held at labor reform farms after completing their sentences to return to their places of origin. Kanlho (Gannan) acknowledged internally that the "pacification of rebellion had been

enlarged," but didn't publicly release any of those in custody. Gansu Province's Kanlho TAP in 1979 released 59 "rebel participants" incarcerated in 1958 and "rehabilitated" 2,332 people (i.e. dropped charges against them and admitted they had been wrongly persecuted). See *Gannan Zangzu Zizhizhou zhi*, vol. 2, p. 1021; *Zhongguo jin xiandai minzu shi*, p. 840.

49. Zhang Xiangming, *Zhang Xiangming 55 nian Xizang gongzuo shilu*, p. 219. On the same page, Zhang mentions that around the mid-1980s, Beijing sent a joint investigation group composed of personnel from the Central Committee United Front Department, the Ministry of Public Security, and the PLA General Political Department to Nagchu and Lhoka to investigate the "enlargement of the pacification of rebellion," but the investigation left the issue unresolved.

50. Today's Mugshung (Moyun) Township in Dzato (Zaduo) County, Yulshul TAP, Qinghai Province.

51. Today's Drachen (Baqing) County in Nagchu Prefecture, TAR.

52. Today's Amdo (Anduo) County, Nagchu.

53. Transliterated in Chinese as "Niri'acuogai lake," it is in today's Dzato County, Yulshul TAP, Qinghai Province.

54. Dawa Tsering, *Xueji xueyu*, p. 533.

55. Sogde was one of the largest nomad groups in Nagchu.

56. Dawa Tsering, *Xueji xueyu*, p. 534.

57. Ding Sheng, "Dingzhi budui de Xizang pingpan zuozhan," p. 308.

58. According to Lhamo Tsering, the first CIA airdrop to Team 6, which arrived at Behu Seldzong on November 13, 1959, contained 1680 rifles and 368,800 bullets; the second drop, at Ratse Ken on January 10, contained 2 machine guns and 2080 rifles, although one plane turned back without dropping its cargo; the third drop, at Nira Tso-gen, five days later, contained 300 4-mm shells, 7 heavy machine guns, 4000 8-shooter and 5-shooter rifles, and 4700 hand grenades, as well as the 16 members of Team 7. See Tsongka Lhamo Tsering, *bTsan rgol rgyal skyob*, pp. 177, 183.

59. According to a Tibetan source, the goal of separating the fighters from their families was not completely achieved. See Dawa Tsering, *Xueji xueyu*, p. 536.

60. *Jiefang Xizang shi*, p. 391.

61. Ji Youquan, *Xizang pingpan jishi*, p. 218.

62. Wei Ke, at that time head of the mass work department of the Political Department of the TMC, writes that the Battle of Zone 2 deployed a total military force of around 18,000. Wei Ke, *Xizang wenshi ziliao xuanji*, 19, p. 267.

63. *Ibid.*, p. 269.

64. Ji Youquan, *Xizang pingpan jishi*, p. 219.

65. Ibid.; Ding Sheng, "Dingzhi budui de Xizang pingpan zuozhan," p. 309.

66. Ji Youquan, *Xizang pingpan jishi*, p. 219.

67. Ibid.

68. The specific location cannot be identified. Based on the information in the Chinese and Tibetan sources, this place is likely to be a prairie land surrounded by hills.

69. See Dawa Tsering, *Xueji xueyu*, p. 537; Ji Youquan, *Xizang pingpan jishi*, pp. 219–20; Ding Sheng, "Dingzhi budui de Xizang pingpan zuozhan," p. 310.

70. Ji Youquan, *Xizang pingpan jishi*, p. 220.

71. *Ibid.*, p. 221.

72. *Ibid.*, p. 225.

73. *Ibid.*, p. 227.

74. For a more detailed description of the battle from a Tibetan source, see Dawa Tsering, *Xueji xueyu*, pp. 533–54. For Chinese sources, see Pan Zhaomin, "Wuji zhi zhan," and Wei Ke, "Zhengzhan zai 'erhao' diqu," in *Xizang wenshi ziliao xuanji* 19, pp. 266–72.

75. *Zhongguo Renmin Jiefangjun di 18 jun ji Xizang junqu junshi*, p. 224.

76. Ding Sheng, "Dingzhi budui de Xizang pingpan zuozhan," p. 311.

77. *Ibid.*

78. Apart from dropping bombs, the air force also sent out 53 scouting missions and made 42 airdrops of provisions. See *Jiefang Xizang shi*, p. 393.

79. The specific location is unclear; probably Laktse La, a mountain pass between Tibet and Nepal.

80. Drongpa County was under the administration of Ngari Prefecture from 1960 to 1962. Since September 1962, it has been under the administration of Shigatsé Prefecture. Kunggyu Tso is in today's Purang County.

81. *Zhongguo Renmin Jiefangjun bubing dishiyishi junzhanshi*, pp. 246–47.

82. Ibid., p. 247.

83. Ju Youquan, *Xizang pingpan jishi*, p. 161.

84. In General Sir Sam Cowan's account, based on British diplomatic dispatches, the party had 17 members, including soldiers from the border security post and locals familiar with the terrain, and they were acting on orders to confirm reports of a large PLA presence north of Kora La, which had apparently caused concern in Kathmandu by then. See Cowan, "The Curious Case of the Mustang Incident."

85. For more details of the incident, see Ji Youquan, *Xizang pingpan jishi*, pp. 161–62.

86. *Zhongguo Renmin Jiefangjun bubing dishiyishi junzhanshi*, p. 250.

87. *Ibid.*

88. *Ibid.*

Chapter 22

1. The 5412 Special Group originated with the National Security Council Directive on Covert Operations signed by President Dwight Eisenhower on December 28, 1955 (NSC Document No. 5412/2). This document provided for a special committee composed of the president, secretary of state, secretary of defense, and assistant secretaries of designated departments to evaluate and authorize covert operations submitted by the CIA.

2. Conboy and Morrison, *The CIA's Secret War in Tibet*, p. 84.

3. "Coordination and Policy Approval of Covert Operations," FRUS 1964–1968, vol. 33, document 263.

4. Knaus, *Orphans of the Cold War*, pp. 137–38.

5. Conboy and Morrison, *The CIA's Secret War in Tibet*, p. 55. The CIA's Far Eastern Division used the prefix ST as a code name for China.

6. *Ibid.*

7. The first group of CIA trainees was airdropped into Tibet in the fall of 1957. See Li Jianglin, *Tibet in Agony*, pp. 136–38.

8. The training course later expanded to include anti-tank strategies.

9. Regarding the course of events in Lhasa in 1959, see Li Jianglin, *Tibet in Agony*.

10. Ngawang Wangyal (c. 1901–1983), usually referred to as Geshe Wangyal, was born in Astrakhan, Russia, and obtained a degree in Buddhist studies at the Drepung Monastery's Buddhist Institute. In 1955, he moved to the United States and settled in New Jersey; in 1958, he established the Labsum Shedrub Ling Monastery, and in the 1960s and 1970s he taught Tibetan language and Buddhism at Columbia University. He was one of the most important Tibetan Buddhist *émigrés* in the United States. See Conboy and Morrison, *The CIA's Secret War in Tibet*, pp. 48–52.

11. The full text of the cable was at one time available on the CIA website but may now have been deleted: https://www.cia.gov/library/readingroom/document/untitled-re-dalai-lama-and-officials-arrived-safely-india. Accessed August 31, 2010.

12. Conboy and Morrison, *The CIA's Secret War in Tibet*, p. 97.

13. Williams, "Camp Hale's Top Secret," p. 8.

14. Conboy and Morrison, *The CIA's Secret War in Tibet*, pp. 119–30. See also McCarthy, *Tears of the Lotus*, p. 5.

15. "Autobiography of Gompo Tashi," Bruce Walker papers, Box 3.

16. Conboy and Morrison, *The CIA's Secret War in Tibet*, p. 115.

17. *Ibid.*, pp. 115–18.

18. *Ibid.*, p. 118. There is little material on the third group, and therefore no way to ascertain whether all nine members left Tibet.

19. According to Lhamo Tsering, the fourth, fifth, and sixth groups were air-dropped into Pelbar on the 15th day of the 9th lunar month, 1959, in the Tibetan calendar, i.e, some time in November. See Tsongka, "Resistance," p. 132. See also Conboy and Morrison, pp. 120–21.

20. Information on the fourth, fifth, and sixth groups is drawn from my interview with Donyo Jagotsang on October 2, 2008. See also Conboy and Morrison, *The CIA's Secret War in Tibet*, pp. 120–23.

21. The Pelbar Monastery was in today's Pelbar (Bianba) Township, Pelbar County, the location of the former Pelbar Dzong, also known as Tar Dzong.

22. Dudul Choying, "Cong zong mishu dao Bianba diqu panfei siling."

23. Interview with Donyo Jagotsang, October 2, 2008.

24. For the PLA's battle plan, see chapter 21, section 1.

25. Conboy and Morrison, *The CIA's Secret War in Tibet*, pp. 122–23.

26. Dawa Norbu, *China's Tibet Policy*, p. 270. See also chapter 21, section 3.

27. Dawa Norbu, *China's Tibet Policy*, pp. 269–71.

28. The source for these figures is a document that the author obtained from the New York branch of Chushi Gangdruk in 2009 (a letter to Bruce Walker dated September 1, 2006, probably from Roger McCarthy, now in the private collection of Kelsang Gyadotsang). In 2006, the former leader of the CIA's Tibet Task Force, Roger McCarthy, and Chushi Gangdruk compiled a directory of the names and current situation of some of the trainees, and this document was an appendix to the directory. The figures include people later involved in training the guerrilla force in Mustang, Nepal.

29. Dawa Tsering, *Xueji xueyu*, 384–89.

30. Tsongka Lhamo Tsering, *bTsan rgol rgyal skyob*, pp. 59–63, 139–42, 159.

31. Dawa Tsering states that there were six airdrops of weapons to Pelbar, but the number of flights is unclear. Dawa Norbu records four airdrops in a total of

seven flights. Lhamo Tsering states that there were eight airdrops of weapons in total. See Dawa Tsering, *Xueji xueyu*, p. 501; Dawa Norbu, *China's Tibet Policy*, p. 270; Tsongka, "*Resistance.*"

32. Tsongka Lhamo Tsering, *bTsan rgol rgyal skyob*, pp. 139–42.

33. Dawa Tsering, *Xueji xueyu*, p. 534.

34. Liu Jun and Tang Huiyun, "Shixi Zhongguo dui Yuenan de jingji yu junshi yuanzhu," p. 15.

35. Shi Hongsheng, "Xizang pingpan zhong de houqin baozhang gongzuo," p. 238.

36. "Zai Guofang Weiyuanhui huiyi shang de baogao tigang" (Outline for report to the meeting of the National defense Council," in Huang Kecheng, *Huang Kecheng junshi wenxuan*.

37. Ji Jiansheng, "Niu Qian jiang shou hua 'gongniu.'"

38. The CIA's four airdrops to Pelbar occurred on October 16, 1959; November (day uncertain), 1959; December 15, 1959; and January 6, 1960. See Dawa Norbu, *China's Tibet Policy*, p. 270.

39. "Kongjun baogao yu jianyi (si)."

40. See *Qinghai shengzhi: junshi zhi*, pp. 532–34.

Chapter 23

1. Hu Liyan, *Zouguo xiaoyan*, p. 657.

2. For details about the Battle of Lhasa, see Li Jianglin, *Tibet in Agony: Lhasa 1959*, pp. 231–290.

3. Dong Zhanlin, *Junlü chunqiu*, pp. 179–80.

4. He Xicheng, "Xizang pingpan suoji," pp. 19–20.

5. *Ibid.*

6. Known in Tibetan as Domé Chikyap.

7. See Derong Tsering Dondrup, *Zangzu tongshi*, p. 29.

8. Wang Xiaobin, "Zhonghua Renmin Gongheguo Changdu diqu renmin jiefang weiyuanhui lishu guanxi de lishi yange," pp. 41–42. On April 20, 1959, the Chinese State Council announced the disbanding of the Changdu Liberation Committee and its subordinate structure. See *Zhonggong Xizang dangshi dashiji 1949–1994*, pp. 101–2.

9. Li Benxin, "Changdu diqu dashi tiyao."

10. See *Zhongguo Gongchandang Xizang Zizhiqu zuzhishi ziliao 1950–1987*, pp. 36–37.

11. This was the summer palace of the 7th to 10th Panchen Lamas near the Tashi Lhunpo Monastery. It was built in 1825 by the 7th Panchen Lama, swept away by the 1954 flood, and subsequently rebuilt (see Akester, *Jamyang Khyentse Wangpo's Guide to Central Tibet*, p. 515).

12. Xinhua News Agency *Neibu Cankao*, March 7, 1953, pp. 153–55.

13. Dudul Choying, "Cong zong mishu dao Bianba diqu panfei siling," p. 57.

14. Xinhua News Agency *Neibu Cankao*, March 7, 1953, pp. 153–55.

15. Hu Liyan, *Zouguo xiaoyan*, p. 657.

16. Today's Khargang (Kagong) Township, Jomda (Jiangda) County, Chamdo City.

17. Today's Terton (Dedeng) Township, Jomda County.

18. Today's Jomda (Jiangda) County.

19. Dong Zhanlin, *Junlü chunqiu*, p. 184.

20. Ibid.

21. Today's Tangpu (Tongpu), Khargang (Kagong), and Chunyedo (Qingnidong) townships in Jomda County and Topa (Tuoba) Township in Chamdo County, all on the Sichuan-Tibet highway.

22. Today's Dzigar (Zijia) Township, Jomda County.

23. Today's Khampa (Kangba) Village, Topa Township, Chamdo County.

24. Dong Zhanlin, *Junlü chunqiu*, p. 186.

25. The area of today's Douzha cattle ranch in Jomda County.

26. Dong Zhanlin, p. 188.

27. Ji Youquan, *Xizang pingpan jishi*, p. 260.

28. I have been unable to identify this person. According to Shirla Lhundrup Wangyel's memoir, *Mun nag khrod kyi bod mi zhig gi mi tshe*, pp. 199–200, the local incarnate lamas killed in the fighting in Jomda in the summer of 1959 included Lhamchog Dorjé and Pelga Tulku of Dzigar Monastery, Dorsem Tulku of Gyuné Monastery, Drupa Tulku of Kyabjé Monastery, and Yedor Tulku of Jopu Monastery.

29. Dong Zhanlin, *Junlü chunqiu*, p. 188.

30. *Ibid.*, p. 189.

31. Hu Liyan, *Zouguo xiaoyan*, p. 658.

32. *Hu Liyan, Baizhan jiangxing*, p. 358.

33. Ji Youquan, *Xizang pingpan jishi*, p. 270.

34. Dong Zhanlin, *Junlü chunqiu*, p. 192.

35. See chapter 21, section 2 for details on the Battle of Zone 1.

36. Now known as the Minzu University of China (MUC).

37. Tsering Dorjé's story is derived from the author's interview with Tsering Dorjé on December 4, 2010.

38. Ji Youquan, *Xizang pingpan jishi*, pp. 240–41. Fan Ming (*Xizang neibu zhi zheng*, p. 338) claimed that those soldiers defected, but this information cannot be confirmed.

39. Pangda Dorjé (1905–1974), a native of Markham, served as vice-chairman and chairman of the Chamdo Liberation Committee, as a member and deputy secretary general of the Tibet Autonomous Region Preparatory Committee, as commander of the Chamdo Garrison Command Changnan command post, and as vice-chairman of the first and second Tibet Autonomous Region Political Consultative Conference, as well as delegate to the first through third National People's Congress and to the second Chinese People's Political Consultative Conference.

40. There is no corroborating evidence of this incident in Chinese-language sources. This anecdote is drawn from the recollections of Tsering Dorjé.

41. For Mao's directive, see *Pingxi Xizang panluan*, p. 89.

42. Dawa Tsering, *Xueji xueyu*, pp. 370–71.

43. Ibid., p. 99.

44. Ji Youquan, *Xizang pingpan jishi*, p. 272. Li Benxin, "Changdu diqu dashi tiyao," p. 57, says that seven regiments of troops were deployed in this battle.

45. *Jiefang Xizang shi*, p. 400.

46. *Yunnan shengzhi*, p. 382.

47. Dawa Norbu, *China's Tibet Policy*, p. 270. Chinese sources give the last CIA mission drop as March 30, 1961. See Cheng Yue, *Zhongguo Gongchandang Changdu diqu lishi dashiji: 1949–2009*, p. 113.

48. *Jiefang Xizang shi*, p. 400.

49. For more details of the last battle, see Dawa Tsering, *Xueji xueyu*, pp. 384–88; Ji Youquan, *Xizang pingpan jishi*, p. 273.

50. Dawa Tsering, *Xueji xueyu*, p. 388.

51. Cheng Yue, *Zhongguo Gongchandang Changdu diqu lishi dashiji: 1949–2009*, pp. 117–18.

52. *Zhonggong Xizang dangshi dashiji 1949–1994*, p. 102.

53. *Ibid.*, p. 103. Furthermore, according to the former party secretary of Tengchen County, Li Benxin ("Changdu diqu dashi tiyao," p. 195), Chamdo Prefecture "carried out two suppressions of counterrevolutionaries in December

1959 and June 1960, all counties arrested rebel elements and put others in training camps, and some counties jailed as many as 700 to 800 people."

54. Dong Zhanlin, *Junlü chunqiu*, p. 195.

55. See "Xi Zhongxun, Li Weihan, deng tongzhi he Banchan tanhua jiyao," p. 36.

56. *Zhonggong Xizang dangshi dashiji 1949–1994*, p. 130.

57. "Xizang de jiben qingkuang" (The basic situation in Tibet), Xinhua News Agency *Neibu Cankao*, April 21, 1959, p. 2.

58. Based on figures in Dong Zhanlin, *Junlü chunqiu*, p. 182.

59. "Xi Zhongxun, Li Weihan deng tongzhi he Banchan tanhua jilu," p. 38.

60. *Jiefang Xizang shi*, p. 385, states that Zhang Aiping went to Chamdo on June 21, but he went in 1960, and not, as that book implies, in 1959.

61. Ibid.

62. See "Xi Zhongxun, Li Weihan deng tongzhi he Banchan tanhua jilu."

Chapter 24

1. For Aten's story in this chapter, see Jamyang Norbu, *Warriors of Tibet*, pp. 143–152.

2. *Ibid.*, pp. 140–41.

3. Translator's note: See chapter 1.

4. Cavalry troops from the Inner Mongolian Military Command took part in the PLA's military suppression of Tibetans in Qinghai and Central Tibet from 1958 to 1960. See Amulan, *Kong Fei fengyu kanke liushi nia*; see also Yang Haiying, *Menggu qibing zai Xizang huiwu Riben dao*.

5. The "four antis" are "anti-rebellion, anti-crime, anti-privilege, and anti-exploitation" (see also chapter 16, section 2). This campaign was one of the components of the "democratic reform movement" in Tibetan regions.

6. Interview with Lama Yetan, September 7, 2010.

7. Mount Kailash (Gangdisi), 6,638 meters above sea level, in Purang (Pulan) County, Ngari Prefecture, TAR.

Chapter 25

1. *Yunnan shengzhi*, p. 382.

2. *Sichuan shengzhi: junshi zhi*, p. 319.

3. Markham Dzong is in today's Markham County, and Sa-ngen Dzong is in today's Gonjo County, both under Chamdo City in the Tibet Autonomous Region.

4. *Jiefang Xizang shi*, p. 401.

5. *Zhongguo Renmin Jiefangjun bubing dishiyishi junzhanshi*, pp. 220–28.

6. *Sichuan shengzhi: junshi zhi*, p. 319.

7. In other words, the Battle of Lhasa; the Battle of Lhoka; the Battle of Namtso; the Battle of Mitikha; the Battle of northeastern Chamdo; the Battle of southeastern Chamdo; the battles of Zones 1, 2, 3, and 4; and the battles of Ngari and Markham.

8. Ji Youquan, *Xizang pingpan jishi*, p. 270.

9. *Qinghai shengzhi: junshi zhi*, p. 524.

10. *Zhongguo Renmin Jiefangjun bubing dishiyishi junzhanshi*, p. 227.

11. *Yunnan shengzhi*, p. 383.

12. *Qinghai shengzhi: junshi zhi*, p. 524.

13. *Sichuan shengzhi: junshi zhi*, p. 319.

14. Wang Zhongxing and Liu Liqin, *Guofang lishi*, p. 138. Compare the number given in a classified document of the TMC published on October 1, 1960, *Xizang xingshi he renwu jiaoyu de jiben jiaocai*, p. 6: "From March of last year to the present, around 87,000 of the enemies were exterminated."

15. The number for the Kanlho TAP comes from *Zhongguo Renmin Jiefangjun bubing dishiyishi junzhanshi*, pp. 221–22, 227. Furthermore, according to "Gannan Zangqu 'shuanggai' jingguo" (The course of the "dual reforms" in the Kanlho Tibetan region), a November 4, 1958 report in Xinhua News Agency *Neibu Cankao*, insurrections broke out in "all six counties of the autonomous prefecture. Some 29,700 people took part in the armed rebellions." This number doesn't include the number of people "annihilated" in the 1958 rebellion in the Linxia Hui Autonomous Prefecture.

16. This number is calculated from figures in the *Yunnan shengzhi*, p. 383.

17. According to another source, as of the end of 1961, around 500 "bandit remnants were scattered." See "1959: Xizang pingpan," p. 57.

18. "Zhongguo Renmin Jiefangjun zhongzhengzhibu guanyu panluan jiben pingxi hou zhu Zangzu diqu budui zhengzhi gongzuo de zhishi," p. 28.

19. *Jianguo sanshinian shaoshu minzu gongzuo tongji ziliao, 1949–1979*, p. 9.

20. *Minzu zongjiao gongzuo wenjian huiji 1949–1959*, vol. 2, p. 1093.

21. *Ibid.*

22. *Ibid.*, p. 1103.

23. *Qinghai Zangzu renkou*, p. 17.

24. Apart from the number killed, these numbers allow for the possibility of individuals being counted on multiple occasions.

25. *Qinghai shengzhi: junshi zhi*, p. 524.

26. Wang Zhongxing and Liu Liqin, *Guofang lishi*, p. 138. Also, according to the classified document *Xizang xingshi he renwu jiaoyu de jiben jiaocai (Shiyongben)*, p. 6, from February 1959 until the publication of that book in 1960 some 100,000 firearms had been seized, but in the Battle of Lhasa, most of the weapons seized had been looted from the Tibetan army's arsenal and had never been used.

27. *Qinghai shengzhi: Fulu*, pp. 777–78.

28. Wang Zhongxing and Liu Liqin, *Guofang lishi*, p. 131. The "commander" of the "Yushu Military Sub-command" must be the commander of the Yushu Rebellion Pacification Command Post, Sun Guang.

29. *Ibid.*

30. Wei Cong, *Xunhua Salazu Zizhixian zhi*, p. 468.

31. *Chengduo xianzhi*, chapter 8, section 5, "Pacification of Rebellion."

32. Interview with Damcho Pelsang, November 30, 2010.

33. Wang Zhongxing and Liu Liqin, *Guofang lishi*, p. 131.

34. The Tibetan name of this place has not been identified.

35. This location has not been identified.

36. Han Youren, *Yichang yanmo le de guonei zhanzheng*, pp. 105–6.

37. *Guinan xianzhi*, p. 19.

38. The former name of today's Guomaying Township in Guinan County. I have been unable to determine the original Tibetan name; Xiashituo is a Chinese transliteration.

39. Han Youren, *Yichang yanmo le de guonei zhanzheng*, p. 103.

40. A number of unverifiable Chinese sources claim that the Tibetans used "black magic" to kill Chinese government cadres.

41. Han Youren, *Yichang yanmo le de guonei zhanzheng*, pp. 103–4. The former deputy director of the Anhui Province Public Security Bureau in charge of day-to-day operations, Yin Shusheng, was working at that time in the Qinghai Province Public Security Bureau. In his later years he published an autobiographical essay that mentioned the "Guomaying incident." See Yin Shusheng, "Jinyintan zhi tong," p. 43.

42. *Akha* is a colloquial Amdo term for a monk.

43. Han Youren, *Yichang yanmo le de guonei zhanzheng*, p. 104.

44. Yin Shusheng, "Jinyintan zhi tong," p. 43.

45. *Minzu zongjiao gongzuo wenjian huiji 1949–1959*, p. 1000; for the report of the Hainan Rebellion Pacification Command Post, see pp. 1002–7 of that book.

46. *Qinghai shengzhi: junshi zhi*, p. 1138.

47. Jampel Gyatso, *Shishi Banchan Lama Zhuanji*, p. 92.

48. "Xi Zhongxun, Li Weihan deng tongzhi he Banchan tanhua jilu."

49. *Zhongguo Renmin Jiefangjun bubing dishiyishi junzhanshi*, pp. 252–53; *Yunnan shengzhi*, p. 379.

50. The son of the Ngulra headman, Kesang Rinpoché, for example, was arrested while returning from a pilgrimage to Tibet and was beaten and denounced in Golok and other places. Interview with Kesang Rinpoché, July 11, 2011.

51. Gyalthang County, Dechen Prefecture, Yunnan, today's Shangri-La City.

52. *Zhongdian xianzhi*, p. 25.

53. *Aba Zangzu Qiangzu Zizhizhou zhi*, p. 776.

54. *Zhonggong Xizang dangshi dashiji 1949–1994*, p. 127.

55. The article "Xizang jiben qingkuang" (Tibet's basic situation), published in the April 21, 1959, edition of Xinhua News Agency *Neibu Cankao*, states the population of Tibet as around 1 million. According to *Zhonggong Xizang dangshi dashiji 1949–1994*, p. 127, on October 22, 1960, the TWC issued the "Directive Regarding Strengthening and Improving Work to Suppress Counterrevolutionaries," which required each locality to make arrests that did not exceed the TWC's stipulated target of 2% of the population. Page 163 of the same book quotes a Xinhua report from August 20, 1965, as saying, "The population of Tibet had grown from more than 1,180,000 in 1959 to the present [1,321,500]." On May 10, 1959, Mao Zedong, while talking about Tibet to a delegation from the Volkskammer of the German Democratic Republic, said that the population of Tibet was 1.2 million.

56. *Zhongguo Gongchandang Gannan lishi (1921.7–2003.7)*, p. 240.

57. Han Youren, *Yichang yanmo le de guonei zhanzheng*, p. 45.

58. *Ibid.*

59. *Yushu Zangzu Zizhizhou zhi*, p. 536.

60. *Ibid.*, pp. 107–8.

61. *Gannan Zangzu Zizhizhou zhi*, vol. 2, pp. 1322–33; *Tianzhu xianzhi*, p. 496.

62. *Zhongguo Gongchandang Gannan lishi 1921.7—2003.7*, p. 233.

63. For details, see *Tianzhu xianzhi*, p. 495. The number of people arrested in Kanlho is calculated from material on p. 234 of *Zhongguo Gongchandang Gannan lishi 1921.7—2003.7*, and from population statistics on p. 216 of that book.

64. The number of arrested people in Garzê Prefecture is calculated from the percentage of rehabilitated persons among those arrested. The figure for Ngawa is the 1979 "corrected" figure for the number of people "dealt with" around the

time of the 1958 "pacification of rebellion." See *Ganzi zhouzhi*, p. 707; *Muli Zangzu Zizhixian zhi*, p. 693; Li Zhongkang and Li Ruiqiong, "1978–1992 nian Sichuan Abazhou gaige kaifang de huigu yu sikao," p. 193.

65. During the "pacification of rebellion" in Sichuan's Tibetan and Yi ethnic regions around 1958, a total of 17,541 people were sentenced. A total of 17,222 cases in Garzê, Ngawa, and Liangshan were reexamined in 1984, and in 48.5% of the cases, sentences were revised and redress was carried out; in 72% of the cases, the defendants were declared not guilty. These figures didn't distinguish between ethnic groups, so there is no way, on the basis of these statistics, of calculating precisely how many Tibetans were arrested. See *Sichuan shengzhi: jiancha shenpan zhi*, p. 256.

66. *Sanzhong quanhui yilai zhongyao wenxian huibian*, p. 960.

67. *Haixi Mengguzu Zangzu Zizhizhou zhi*, p. 40.

68. *Hainan Zangzu Zizhizhou zhi*, p. 32.

69. *Guoluo Zangzu Zizhizhou zhi* states that 8,735 people were arrested in the prefecture, but according to the figures published in the gazetteers of the prefecture's six counties, the total number is 9,262, and among these, the figure of 1,758 given for Darlag County is only for "wrongfully handled" cases and not the total number of people arrested. Furthermore, the figure for Matoe County is only for the year 1958. Consequently, the number of people arrested in Golok during the "pacification and prevention of rebellion" must be higher than this figure.

70. Calculated from statistics in the gazetteers of Malho TAP's Chentsa, Rebkong, and Tsekhok counties and Yulgen Mongol Autonomous County. See *Jianzha xianzhi*, p. 413; *Tongren xianzhi*, vol. 2, p. 661; *Zeku xianzhi*, p. 307; *Henan Menguzu Zizhixian zhi*, p. 710.

71. *Haibei Zangzu Zizhizhou zhi*, p. 83.

72. Han Youren, *Yichang yanmo le de guonei zhanzheng*, p. 47.

73. Tsoshar (Haidong) Prefecture became a Municipality in 2013.

74. *Dangdai Zhongguo minzu gongzuo dashiji*, p. 274; *Gannan Zangzu Zizhizhou zhi*, vol. 1, p. 131; *Zhongguo jin xiandai minzu shi*, p. 840; CCP *Zhonggong Xizang dangshi dashiji 1949–1994*, p. 219.

75. Han Youren, *Yichang yanmo le de guonei zhanzheng*, p. 42.

76. *Zhongguo Gongchandang Gannan lishi (1921.7–2003.7)*, p. 240.

77. *Jianzha xianzhi*, pp. 413, 520.

78. *Jiuzhi xianzhi*, pp. 20, 93.

79. *Maqin xianzhi*, pp. 50, 137.

80. *Sanzhong quanhui yilai zhongyao wenxian huibian*, p. 960.

81. Han Youren, *Yichang yanmo le de guonei zhanzheng*, p. 46.

82. Feng Haohua, *Qinghai renkou*, p. 32.

83. The source of this material is the unpublished manuscript of the *Chengduo xianzhi*.

84. Tashi Wangchuk (1913–2003) was one of the early Tibetan communists. He joined the Red Army in 1936 and became a CCP member in 1938. He was sent to Qinghai in 1949 and worked in a series of high-ranking positions. In 1958 he was criticized for trying to protect the grasslands. In 1959 he was dismissed from his position as deputy governor of Qinghai Province.

85. Puntsok Wangye, *Pindeng tuanjie lu manman*, p. 365.

86. Chos kyi dbang phyug, *A Poisoned Arrow*, p. 113.

87. Xinhua News Agency *Neibu Cankao*, February 2, 1962, p. 13.

88. *Xizang gongzuo wenxian xuanbian (1949–2005)*, p. 221.

89. These seven military commands were cited in the October 10, 1961, CMC general order commending the troops who had engaged in the "pacification of rebellion." For the full text, see the PLA General Political Department's *Gongzuo tongxun*, pp. 11–12.

90. The infantry divisions that took part in battle included the 4th, 11th, 42nd, 61st, 62nd, 1st, 130th, and 134th, as well as several independent regiments and frontier defense troops.

91. Air force divisions that took part in battle included the 13th, 23rd, and 25th, and the independent 4th and 5th Regiments.

92. Cavalry that took part in battle included the 1st Division; the 1st, 2nd, and 3rd Independent Cavalry Regiments of the Lanzhou Military Command, the 13th and 14th Regiments of the Inner Mongolian Military Command; the Lanzhou Military Command's infantry and cavalry brigade; and the Yulshul, Golok, Malho, Tsolho, Tsonub, and Tsaidam (Chaidamu) cavalry detachments in the Qinghai Military Command.

93. This included armored, motor, anti-chemical, demolition, communication, and other units.

94. Xu Yan, *Taojin bai zhan pingshuo gujin*, p. 283. Furthermore, according to Hua Qiang, Xi Jirong, et al. (*Zhongguo kongjun bainian shi*, p. 216), from March 1959 onward the PLA "assembled 69 infantry and cavalry regiments, totaling around 150,000 men, to do battle in pacifying rebellion," but the book errs in referring to "194 counties in Tibet." That number should refer to all of the Tibetan regions, not only to the TAR.

95. *Zhongguo Renmin Jiefangjun Chengdu junqu junshi jiaotong shi 1937–1990*, p. 128; *Sichuan shengzhi: junshi zhi*, p. 319.

96. Wang Zhongxing and Liu Liqin, *Guofang lishi*, p. 128. The troops that took part in this battle included the 11th and 62nd Infantry Divisions, the independent 1st and 2nd Infantry Regiments, and the 1st and 3rd Cavalry Regiments. The number of participants was calculated by the author.

97. The military units that took part in this battle at various times included the 61st, 62nd, 55th, and 134th Infantry Divisions; the 1st Cavalry Division; the Inner Mongolian Military Command's 13th and 14th Cavalry Regiments; and the independent 1st, 2nd, and 3rd Cavalry Regiments of the Lanzhou Military Command, along with motor, armored, airborne, communications, pontoon bridge, antichemical, and other units. See *Qinghai shengzhi: junshi zhi*, p. 518; *Yushu Zangzu Zizhizhou zhi*, p. 664.

98. *Qinghai shengzhi: junshi zhi*, p. 518; *Yushu Zangzu Zizhizhou zhi*, p. 664.

99. *Qinghai shengzhi: junshi zhi*, p. 524.

100. The figures for counties in Ngawa Prefecture come from *Aba Zangzu Qiangzu Zizhizhou zhi*, p. 786; the militia figures for Ngawa Prefecture come from p. 794. Furthermore, according to p. 790 of that gazetteer, in 1961, the prefecture had a total of 98,957 militiamen. The figures for the People's Armed Defense Force in Garzê Prefecture come from *Ganzi Zangzu Zizhizhou junshi zhi*, p. 186. The figures for the People's Armed Defense Force in the Mili Tibetan Autonomous County come from *Muli Zangzu Zizhixian zhi*, p. 28.

101. *Gansu shengzhi di 10 juan junshi zhi*, p. 805.

102. *Yunnan shengzhi*, p. 805.

103. The PLA's casualties in the Tibetan region included 1,551 dead and 1,987 wounded. For Yunnan there is only a figure of 824 total casualties; in Qinghai, casualties included 1,515 dead and 1,628 wounded; in Garzê, Sichuan Province, PLA casualties totaled 1,382 dead and 1,608 wounded. Figures for Ngawa and Kanlho prefectures are lacking. See *Jiefang Xizang shi*, p. 402; *Yunnan shengzhi*, p. 369; *Qinghai shengzhi: junshi zhi*, p. 525; *Ganzi Zangzu Zizhizhou junshi zhi*, pp. 189, 192, 196, 198. Furthermore, troops under the Yunnan Military Command suffered 963 casualties in Tibet. There is no way of ascertaining whether this figure is included in the total number of PLA casualties in Tibet.

104. *Qinghai shengzhi: junshi zhi*, p. 525.

105. Shi Hongsheng, "Xizang pingpan zhong de houqin baozhang gongzuo," p. 235.

106. For Mao Zedong's three directives regarding using the "pacification of rebellion in Tibet" to train troops, see Mao Zedong, *Jianguo yilai Mao Zedong wengao*, pp. 10–11, 12, 46.

107. There are many autobiographical essays and journals by PLA servicemen and cadres who were sent to Tibet to take part in "tempering through pacification of rebellion." For example, 333 young military officers and cadres from the Nanjing Military Command alone were sent to Tibet for this purpose in 1959. See Wang Guozhong, "Chuanqi jingli, qingchun muhui," p. 829. In the spring of 1960, the Guangzhou Military Command also transferred more than 300 primary-level officers and men and cadres with no battle experience to Tibet to "receive tempering and testing." See Liu Wenqiao, *Suiyue ruliu wei cuotuo*, p. 109.

108. Guan Shengzhi, "Zhuiyi hongzha hangkongbing ershiwushi lishi pianduan."

109. *Kongtian zhujian*, p. 115.

110. Hong Weiquan, "Xueyu jiaofei ji," pp. 14, 15.

111. *Zhongguo Renmin Jiefangjun Chengdu junqu junshi jiaotong shi 1937–1990*, p. 129.

112. *Ibid.*, p. 128.

113. *Ibid.*

114. *Qinghai shengzhi: junshi zhi*, p. 805.

115. *Ibid.*, p. 801.

116. Shi Hongsheng, "Xizang pingpan zhong de houqin baozhang gongzuo," p. 235.

117. *Zhongguo Renmin Jiefangjun Chengdu junqu junshi jiaotong shi 1937–1990*, p. 132.

118. *Qinghai shengzhi: junshi zhi*, p. 812; *Gansu shengzhi di 10 juan junshi zhi*, p. 806.

119. *Qinghai shengzhi: junshi zhi*, p. 806.

120. *Qinghai shengzhi: junshi zhi*, p. 803.

121. *Zhongguo Renmin Jiefangjun Chengdu junqu junshi jiaotong shi 1937–1990*, p. 129.

122. *Ibid.*, p. 132.

123. *Ibid.*

124. *Gansu shengzhi di 10 juan junshi zhi*, p. 806.

125. *Qinghai shengzhi: junshi zhi*, p. 813.

126. *Ibid.*, p. 806.

127. *Ibid.*, p. 804.

128. *Lanzhou wenshi zhiliao xuanji: Di 22 ji*, pp. 28–29.

129. *Diqing Zangzu Zizhizhou zhi*, p. 490.

130. *Zhongguo Renmin Jiefangjun Chengdu junqu junshi jiaotong shi 1937–1990*, p. 131.

131. Shi Hongsheng, "Xizang pingpan zhong de houqin baozhang gongzuo," p. 236.

132. *Ibid.*, p. 238.

133. *Ibid.*, p. 239.

134. *Zhongguo Renmin Jiefangjun Chengdu junqu junshi jiaotong shi 1937–1990*, p. 131.

135. Hua Qiang, Xi Jirong, et al., *Zhongguo kongjun bainian shi*, p. 218.

136. *Qinghai shengzhi: junshi zhi*, p. 802.

137. *Ibid.*, p. 812.

138. *Gansu Zangzu renkou*, pp. 34–35.

139. *Sichuan Zangzu renkou*, p. 24.

140. *Qinghai Zangzu renkou*, p. 17.

141. *Diqing Zangzu Zizhizhou zhi*, p. 221.

142. Figures for the Tibetan population of Qinghai in 1953 were "adjusted" downward by the government.

143. Li Jianglin, "Qinghai caoyuan shang xiaoshi de wangling," pp. 77–78. According to the population figures in *Yushu Zangzu Zizhizhou zhi*, p. 108, the population reached its lowest point in 1961, when the total population of the prefecture was 93,095, including Chinese cadres and a small number of Chinese migrants and soldiers. In 1963, the Chinese population of Yulshul was 4,930, so the population in 1961 was probably around 3,000, which means that the Tibetan population that year was around 90,000.

144. *Yushu Zangzu Zizhizhou zhi*, p. 108.

145. Darje, *Guoluo jianwen yu huiyi*, p. 34.

146. Feng Haohua, *Qinghai renkou*, p. 160.

147. The source of this material is *Chengduo xianzhi*, the 1985 pre-publication manuscript circulated for comment.

148. *Seda xianzhi*, pp. 6, 94.

149. "Introduction," *Tibetans in Exile, 1959–1969*.

150. *Zhongguo Gongchandang Xizang Zizhiqu zuzhishi ziliao 1950–1987*, p. 69, states, "During the pacification of rebellion and reform, in exceptional places there

occurred an enlargement of the scope of suppression of counterrevolutionaries, as well as premature recommendation of semi-cooperative pilot projects and other such problems. As of January 1961, around 20,000 frontier inhabitants crossed the border, and some 100,000 livestock were lost."

151. *Seda xianzhi*, p. 11. [Translator's note: The original Chinese measuring units have been converted into international measures for readers' convenience.]

152. *Muli Zangzu Zizhixian zhi*, pp. 90, 616.

153. *Aba Zangzu Zizhizhou gaikuang*, pp. 142–43.

154. *Ganzi Zangzu Zizhizhou minzu gaige shi*, p. 77.

155. *Zhongguo Gongchandang Gannan lishi 1921.7—2003.7*, p. 235.

156. *Ruoergai xianzhi*, p. 62.

157. *Heishui xianzhi*, p. 40.

158. *Zhongguo Gongchandang Gannan lishi 1921.7—2003.7*, p. 235.

159. *Aba Zangzu Zizhizhou gaikuang*, p. 143.

160. *Derong xianzhi*, p. 228.

161. *Aba Zangzu Zizhizhou gaikuang*, p. 143.

162. *Zhongguo Gongchandang Xizang Zizhiqu zuzhishi ziliao 1950–1987*, p. 67.

163. The following narrative was told to me by Lama Yetan in two interviews on September 7 and 8, 2010.

Afterword

1. Regarding the Dalai Lama's flight to India, see Li Jianglin, *Tibet in Agony*.

2. For details, see Jetsun Pema, *Tibet: My Story*, pp. 99–138.

3. Tsering Wangchuk, *Xinxiang ziyou*, pp. 160–61.

4. Jamyang Norbu, *Warriors of Tibet*, p. 7.

5. Han Youren, *Yichang yanmo le de guonei zhanzheng*, p. 121.

6. *Ganzi zhouzhi*, p. 707.

7. *Haixi Mengguzu Zangzu Zizhizhou zhi*, p. 40.

8. See *Yushu Zangzu Zizhizhou zhi*, p. 514; *Guoluo Zangzu Zizhizhou zhi*, p. 272; *Huangnan Zangzu Zizhizhou zhi*, p. 930.

9. *Haibei Zangzu Zizhizhou zhi*, p. 83.

10. *Zhongguo Gongchandang Gannan lishi (1921.7–2003.7)*, p. 357.

11. *Ibid.*, p. 356.

12. *Sanzhong quanhui yilai zhongyao wenxian huibian*, pp. 960, 963.

13. *Haibei Zangzu Zizhizhou zhi*, p. 83.

14. *Sanzhong quanhui yilai zhongyao wenxian huibian*, p. 963.

15. *Ibid.*, p. 964.

16. *Zhongguo Gongchandang Gannan lishi 1921.7—2003.7*, p. 359. The "five wrongs" refers to "wrong designation (class), wrongful arrest, wrongly labeled a rebel, wrongly controlled, and wrongly capped (labeled)."

17. See Wang Yan, *Peng Dehuai nianpu*, pp. 740–50.

18. Peng Dehuai died on November 29, 1974, and was rehabilitated in December 1978. *Ibid.*, pp. 745–46.

19. Liu Chongwen and Chen Shaochou, *Liu Shaoqi nianpu, 1898–1969*, p. 661.

20. Shen Zaiwang, *Qingshan wuyan*, pp. 222–23.

21. Wang Xitang and Xie Xienong, "Zhongyang tongzhanbu fubuzhang Zhang Jingwu zhi si," p. 13.

22. See Shao Guozheng, Wang Yunxiang, and Liu Shankui, "Wang Qimei zhuan," pp. 65, 73.

23. Ding Sheng, "Dingzhi budui de Xizang pingpan zuozhan," pp. 178–79.

24. "Zhangong zhuozhu Dong Zhanlin."

25. Hu Liyan, *Zouguo xiaoyan*, pp. 661–63.

26. "Zongli jiejian Banchan dengren de tanhua jiyao."

27. See Conboy and Morrison, *The CIA's Secret War in Tibet*, pp. 145–63; Knaus, *Orphans of the Cold War*, pp. 238–47.

28. Zhang Xiangming, *Zhang Xiangming 55 nian Xizang gongzuo shilu*, p. 106; Knaus, *Orphans of the Cold War*, p. 249.

29. *Xizang xingshi he renwu jiaoyu de jiben jiaocai*, p. 6.

30. *Ibid.*, p. 4. One *mu* is equivalent to about 0.0667 hectares. One catty is equivalent to 0.5 kilo.

31. "Xinjiang shengchan jianshe bingtuan yuanzhu Xizang shi jiemi."

32. "Xizang gengdi mianji he jiben nongtian dadao guojia guiding de baohu yaoqiu."

33. *Xizang xingshi he renwu jiaoyu de jiben jiaocai*, pp. 12, 13.

34. *Ibid.*, p. 29.

35. During the Cultural Revolution, the Chinese government considered two of the Tibetan regions to have experienced "new rebellions": one was Ngawa, Sichuan Province, and was related to the "Red Guard Chengdu Headquarters incident"; and the other was the "Nyemu (Nimu) incident" in the TAR. Both incidents were suppressed by the PLA. See Yangling Dorjé, "Yige minzu ganbu xinzhong de Zhao Ziyang," p. 77.

36. The people's communes were eradicated in 1984. For more on the people's

communes in the TAR, see Dhondub Choedon, *Life in the Red Flag People's Commune.*

37. Dan Zeng, *Dangdai Xizang jianshi,* p. 269. Other historic buildings partially exempted from destruction during the Cultural Revolution were the Drepung and Sera monasteries, the Tashi Lhunpo Monastery, the Gyantsé Monastery, the Sakya South Monastery, and the Chamdo Jampaling Monastery.

38. *Diqing Zangzu Zizhizhou zhi,* p. 44.

39. *Gansu wenshi ziliao xuanji di 31 ji,* p. 88.

40. See Jampel Gyatso, *Shishi Banchan Lama zhuanji,* pp. 73–74. See also Yang Shangkun, *Yang Shangkun riji,* vol. 2, p. 366.

41. Jampel Gyatso, *Shishi Banchan Lama zhuanji,* pp. 77–78.

42. Ibid., pp. 85–86.

43. Panchen Lama, *Qiwanyanshu,* p. 97.

44. "Peng Zhen tongzhi he Banchan, Apei de tanhua jiyao."

45. "Zhou Enlai jiejian Banchan dengren tanhua jiyao."

46. "Xi Zhongxun, Li Weihan deng tongzhi he Banchan tanhua jilu."

47. These four documents, which have not yet been officially declassified, are "Jiaqiang Zizhiqu Chouweihui gongzuo, gaijin hezuo gongshi guanxi (cao'an)" (Strengthen the work of the autonomous region preparatory committee, improve cooperation and working together [draft]), "Guanyu jixu guangche zhixing zongjiao xinyang ziyou zhengce de jixiang guiding (cao'an)" (Several provisions regarding continuing to implement and execute the policy of freedom of religious belief [draft]), "Jixu guanche zhixing chuli fan, panfenzi guiding de yijian (cao'an)" (Opinions on continuing to implement and execute the provisions for dealing with counterrevolutionaries and rebels [draft]), and "Peiyang he jiaoyu ganbu de juti banfa (cao'an)" (Specific measures to train and educate cadres [draft]).

48. Zhang Xiangming, *Zhang Xiangming 55 nian Xizang gongzuo shilu,* p. 193.

49. "Xi Zhongxun, Li Weihan deng tongzhi he Banchan tanhua jilu," p. 31.

BIBLIOGRAPHY

Major archival sources

Academia Historica, Taipei.

Bruce Walker Papers, Hoover Institution, Stanford University, USA.

CIA (United States Central Intelligence Agency) website, https://www.cia.gov/index.html.

C. V. Starr East Asian Library, Columbia University, USA.

FRUS (Foreign Relations of the United States) website, https://history.state.gov/historicaldocuments/frus1914Supp.

Library of Tibetan Works and Archives, Dharamsala, India.

National Central Library, Taipei

Universities Service Centre for China Studies, Chinese University of Hong Kong.

Series

Gazetteers of ten Tibetan autonomous prefectures and 83 counties in Gansu, Qinghai, Yunnan, and Sichuan (listed in detail below).

Jiefangjun zhanshi (PLA Soldier pictorial magazine), 1959.

Qinghai huabao (Qinghai Pictorial), 1958.

Qinghai ribao (Qinghai Daily), 1957–1961.

Qinghai zangwen bao (Qinghai Tibetan Daily [bilingual Chinese-Tibetan]), 1958.

Xinhua News Agency *Neibu Cankao* (Internal Reference), 1950–1962.

English-Language Sources

Akester, Matthew. *Jamyang Khyentsé Wangpo's Guide to Central Tibet.* Chicago: Serindia Publications, 2016.

Ali, S. Mahmud. *Cold War in High Himalayas: The CIA, China and South Asia in the 1950s.* New York: St. Martin's Press, 1999.

[Andrugtsang] Gompo Tashi. *Four Rivers, Six Ranges: Reminiscences of the Resistance Movement in Tibet.* Dharamsala, India: Information and Publicity Office of the Dalai Lama, 1973.

Ani Pachen and Adelaide Donnelley. *Sorrow Mountain: The Journey of a Tibetan Warrior Nun.* New York: Kodansha International, 2000.

Arjia Rinpoché. *Surviving the Dragon: A Tibetan Lama's Account of 40 Years Under Chinese Rule.* New York: Rodale, 2010.

Bageant, Joe. "CIA's Secret War in Tibet," originally published in the February 2004 issue of Military History. Historynet.com. http://www.historynet.com/cias-secret-war-in-tibet.htm. Accessed April 20, 2011.

Bapa Puntsok Wangyal, Tenzin Losel, and Jane Perkins. *Witness to Tibet's History.* New Delhi: Paljor Publications, 2007.

Barber, Noel. *From the Land of Lost Content.* Boston: Houghton Mifflin Company, 1970.

Barnett, Robert. *Resistance and Reform in Tibet.* Bloomington: Indiana University Press, 1994.

Bell, Charles Alfred. *Tibet: Past and Present.* Oxford: Clarendon Press, 1924.

Carrasco, Pedro. *Land and Polity in Tibet.* Seattle: University of Washington Press, 1959.

Chen, Jian. "The Tibetan Rebellion of 1950 and China's Changing Relations with India and the Soviet Union." *Journal of Cold War Studies* 8:3 (2006): 54–101.

Chieu, Vita, and James Zhu. *The Khmer Rouge and Red China: My Untold Story.* Taipei: Bookman Books, 2010.

Chogyam Trungpa. *Born in Tibet.* Boston: Shambhala, 1995.

Chos kyi dbang phyug [the 10th Panchen Lama]. *A Poisoned Arrow: The Secret Report of the 10th Panchen Lama.* London: Tibet Information Network, 1997.

Clarridge, Duane R., with Digby Diehl. *A Spy for All Seasons: My Life in the CIA.* New York: Scribner, 1997.

Conboy, Kenneth J., and James Morrison. *The CIA's Secret War in Tibet.* Lawrence: University Press of Kansas, 2002.

Concerning the Question of Tibet. Peking: Foreign language press, 1959.

Cowan, Sam. "The Curious Case of the Mustang Incident." *The Record*, January 17, 2016, .http://www.recordnepal.com/wire/curious-case-mustang-incident/.

Dalai Lama. *Freedom in Exile: The Autobiography of the Dalai Lama*. New York: HarperPerennial, 1991.

Dalai Lama. *My Land and My People: The Original Autobiography of His Holiness the Dalai Lama of Tibet*. New York: Potala Corp., 1983.

Dawa Norbu. *China's Tibet Policy*. London: Curzon Press, 2001.

[Dewatshang] Kunga Samten. *Flight at the Cuckoo's Behest: the Life and Times of a Tibetan Freedom Fighter*. New Delhi: Paljor Publications, 1997.

Dhondub Choedon. *Life in the Red Flag People's Commune*. Dharamsala: The Information Office of H. H. the Dalai Lama, 1978.

Dorji, Khandu-Om. "A Brief History of Bhutan House in Kalimpong." *Journal of Bhutan Studies* 19 (2008): 9–33.

Dunham, Mikel. *Buddha's Warriors: The Story of the CIA-Backed Tibetan Freedom Fighters, the Chinese Invasion, and the Ultimate Fall of Tibet*. New York: Jeremy P. Tarcher/Penguin, 2004.

Garver, John W. "The China-India-U.S. Triangle: Strategic Relations in the Post-War Era." *NBR Analysis* 5 (2002): 3–56.

Gelder, G. Stuart, and Roma Gelder. *The Timely Rain: Travels in New Tibet*. New York: Monthly Review Press, 1965.

Ginsburg, George, and Michael Mathos. *Communist China and Tibet: The First Dozen Years*. The Hague: Martinus Nijhoff, 1964.

Goldstein, Melvyn C. *A History of Modern Tibet, Volume 2, The Calm Before the Storm, 1951–1955*. Berkeley: University of California Press, 2007.

Goldstein, Melvyn C. *A History of Modern Tibet, Volume 3, The Storm Clouds Descend, 1955–1957*. Berkeley: University of California Press, 2013.

Goldstein, Melvyn C. "Taxation and the Structure of a Tibetan Village." *Central Asiatic Journal*, 15:1 (1971): 1–27.

Goldstein, Melvyn C. "The United States, Tibet, and the Cold War." *Journal of Cold War Studies* 8:3 (2006): 145–64.

Goldstein, Melvyn C., Dawei Sherap, and William R. Siebenschuh. *A Tibetan Revolutionary: The Political Life and Times of Bapa Phuntso Wangye*. Berkeley: University of California Press, 2004.

Gould, B. J. *The Jewel in the Lotus: Recollections of an Indian Political*. London: Chatto & Windus, 1957.

Grassdorff, Gilles Van. *Hostage of Beijing: The Abduction of the Panchen Lama*. Shaftesbury, Dorset: Element, 1999.

Gruber, Elmar. *From the Heart of Tibet: The Biography of Drikung Chetsang Rinpoché, the Holder of the Drikung Kagyu Lineage*. Boston: Shambhala, 2010.

Gyalo Thondup (Dhondrup) and Anne F. Thurston. *The Noodle Maker of Kalimpong, The Dalai Lama's Brother and His Struggle for Tibet*. New York: PublicAffairs, 2015.

Halper, Lezlee Brown, and Stefan A. Halper. *Tibet: An Unfinished Story*. Oxford and New York: Oxford University Press, 2014.

Huang , Philip C. C. "Rural Class Struggle in the Chinese Revolution: Representational and Objective Realities from the Land Reform to the Cultural Revolution." *Modern China*, vol. 21, no. 1, Symposium: Rethinking the Chinese Revolution. Paradigmatic Issues in Chinese Studies, IV (Jan. 1995), pp. 105–43.

"Huiyi Yushu pingpan douzheng pianduan" (Remembering parts of the struggle to pacify the rebellion in Yushu). http://blog.sina.com.cn/s/blog_61b56c560100edpo.html. Accessed August 17, 2011.

Hutheesing, Raja. *Tibet Fights for Freedom: A White Book: The Story of the March 1959 Uprising As Recorded in Documents, Despatches, Eye-Witness Accounts and World-Wide Reactions*. Bombay: Orient Longmans, 1960.

Jamyang Norbu. *Warriors of Tibet: The Story of Aten and the Khampas' Fight for the Freedom of their Country*. London: Wisdom Publications, 1986.

Jetsun Pema. *Tibet: My Story, an Autobiography*. London: Element Limited, 1996.

Johnson, Tim. *Tragedy in Crimson: How the Dalai Lama Conquered the World but Lost the Battle with China*. New York: Nation Books, 2011.

Knaus, John Kenneth. "Official Policies and Covert Programs: The U.S. State Department, the CIA and the Tibetan Resistance." *Journal of Cold War Studies* 8:3 (2003): 54–79.

Knaus, John Kenneth. *Orphans of the Cold War: America and the Tibetan Struggle for Survival*. New York: PublicAffairs, 1999.

Leeker, Joe, F. "Mission to Tibet." University of Texas at Dallas Special Collection. http://www.utdallas.edu/library/collections/speccoll/Leeker/history/Tibet.pdf. Accessed June 22, 2011.

Li Jianglin. *Tibet in Agony: Lhasa 1959*. Cambridge, Massachusetts: Harvard University Press, 2016.

Liu, Melinda. "When Heaven Sheds Blood." *Newsweek*, April 18, 1999, http://www.newsweek.com/when-heaven-shed-blood-164864. Accessed July 22, 2009.

Lobsang Gyeltso and Gareth Sparham (trans. & ed.). *Memoirs of a Tibetan Lama*. Ithaca, New York: Snow Lion Publication, 1998.

Mao Tsetung [Mao Zedong]. *Selected Works of Mao Tsetung, vol. 1.* Peking (Beijing): Foreign language press, 1965.

McCarthy, Roger E. *Tears of the Lotus: Accounts of Tibetan Resistance to the Chinese Invasion, 1950–1962.* Jefferson, North Carolina: McFarland & Co., 2006.

McGranaham, Carole. *Arrested Histories: Tibet, The CIA, and Memories of a Forgotten War.* Durham: Duke University Press, 2010.

McGranaham, Carole. "Tibet's Cold War: The CIA and the Chushi Gandrug Resistance 1956–1974." *Journal of Cold War Studies* 8:3 (2006): 102–30.

McMahon, Robert J. "U.S. Policy toward South Asia and Tibet during the Early Cold War." *Journal of Cold War Studies* 8:3 (2006): 131–44.

Miller, Beatrice D. "Last Rejoinder to Goldstein on Tibetan Social System." *The Tibet Journal*, 13:3 (1988): 64–67.

Moraes, Frank. *The Revolt in Tibet.* New York: The MacMillan Company, 1960.

Mullik, B. N. *My Years with Nehru: The Chinese Betrayal.* Bombay: Allied Publishers, 1971.

Naktsang Nulo and Angus Cargill. *My Tibetan Childhood: When Ice Shattered Stone.* Durham: Duke University Press, 2014.

Namgyal Lhamo Taklha. *Women of Tibet.* Derhadun, India: Songtsen Library, 2005.

Nehru, Jawaharlal, H. Y. Sharada Prasad, and A. K. Damodaran. *Selected Works of Jawaharlal Nehru*, series 2, vol. 35 (1 September–30 November 1956). Delhi: Jawaharlal Nehru Memorial Fund, 2005.

Nehru, Jawaharlal, H. Y. Sharada Prasad, and A. K. Damodaran. *Selected Works of Jawaharlal Nehru*, series 2, vol. 36 (1 December 1956–21 February 1957). Delhi: Jawaharlal Nehru Memorial Fund, 2006.

Patil, Sameer Suryakant. "India's China Policy in the 1950s: Threat Perceptions and Balances." *South Asian Survey* 14:2 (2007): 283–301.

Patterson, George N. *Requiem for Tibet.* London: Aurum Press, 1990.

Patterson, George N. *Tibet in Revolt.* London: Faber and Faber Limited, 1960.

Peissel, Michel. *Cavaliers of Kham: The Secret War in Tibet.* London: William Heinemann Ltd., 1972.

Richardson, Hugh. *A Short History of Tibet.* New York: Dutton, 1962.

Rinchen Sadutshang. *A Life Unforeseen: A Memoir of Service to Tibet.* Somerville, Massachusetts: Wisdom Publications, Inc., 2016.

Roberts, John B., and Elizabeth A. Roberts. *Freeing Tibet: 50 Years of Struggle, Resilience and Hope.* New York: AMACOM, 2009.

Sengupta, R. "The CIA Circus: Tibet's Forgotten Army." *Outlook*, February 15, 1999, http://www.friendsoftibet.org/databank/usdefence/usd7.html.

Smith, Warren W. Jr. *Tibetan Nation: A History of Tibetan Nationalism and Sino-Tibetan Relations*. New Delhi: Rupa & Co., 2010.

Sumner Carnahan. *In the Presence of My Enemies: Memoirs of Tibetan Nobleman Tsipon Shuguba*. Santa Fe, New Mexico: Clear Light Publishers, 1995.

Talty, Stephan. *Escape from the Land of Snows: The Young Dalai Lama's Harrowing Flight to Freedom and the Making of a Spiritual Hero*. New York: Crown Publishers, 2011.

Thomas, Lowell. *The Silent War in Tibet*. Garden City, New York: Doubleday, 1959.

Tibetans in Exile, 1959–1969: A Report on Ten Years of Rehabilitation in India. Dharamsala: Bureau of H. H. the Dalai Lama, 1969.

Tsering Shakya. *The Dragon in the Land of Snows: A History of Modern Tibet*. New York: Columbia University Press, 1999.

Tubten Khetsun. *Memories of Life in Lhasa under Chinese Rule*. Translated by Matthew Akester. New York: Columbia University Press, 2007.

W. D. Shakabpa. *One Hundred Thousand Moons: An Advanced Political History of Tibet*. Translated and annotated by Derek F. Maher. Boston: Brill, 2009.

White, David. *Himalayan Tragedy: The Story of Tibet's Panchen Lamas*. London: Tibet Society of the UK, 2002.

Wijer, Birgit van de. *Tibet's Forgotten Heroes: The Story of Tibet's Armed Resistance against China*. Stroud: Amberley, 2010.

Williams, Kristin Kenney. "Camp Hale's Top Secret: The CIA's Covert Operation to Save the Dalai Lama." *The Vail Trail*, vol. 32, no. 35, July 3, 1998, pp. 8–9.

Witness to Tibet: News Reports to Tibet. Beijing: New Star Publishers, 2003.

Yangdon Dondrup and Hildegard Diemberger. "Tashi Tsering: The Last Mongol Queen of 'Sogpo' (Henan)." *Inner Asia*, vol. 4, no. 2, pp. 197–224.

Yudru Tsomu. The Rise of Gönpo Namgyal in Kham: The Blind Warrior of Nyarong. Lanham: Lexington, 2015.

Zai Qiang. "Tibet and Chinese-British-American Relations in the Early 1950s." *Journal of Cold War Studies*, vol. 8, no. 3, Summer 2006, pp. 34–53.

Chinese-Language Sources

"1959: Xizang pingpan—Shijie wuji shang de qiangsheng" (1959: Pacification of rebellion in Tibet—Gunfire on the roof of the world). *Jingu Chuanqi* (On-the-spot Reporting Edition), no. 1, 2007, pp. 50–57.

Aba Zangzu Qiangzu Zizhizhou zhi (Aba Tibetan and Qiang Autonomous Prefecture Gazetteer). Sichuan Province Aba Tibetan and Qiang Autonomous Prefecture Gazetteer Editorial Committee (ed.). Beijing: Minzu chubanshe, 1994.

Aba Zangzu Zizhizhou gaikuang (Survey of Aba Tibetan Autonomous Prefecture). Survey of Aba Tibetan Autonomous Prefecture Editorial Committee (ed.). Chengdu: Sichuan minzu chubanshe, 1985.

Alo Chunzed. "Ale Qunze tan wei renmin huiyi qingkuang" (Alo Chunzed talks about the situation of the counterfeit people's assembly). *Xizang dangshi tongxun* (Tibet Party History Bulletin), no. 2, 1989, pp. 24–30. [Semiclassified].

Ama Ade (Adhe Tapontsang), as told to Joy Blakeslee. *Jiyi de shengyin* (The Voice of Memory). Translated by Yang Lili. Washington, D.C.: Laogai Research Foundation, 2006.

Amulan. *Kong Fei fengyu kanke liushi nian: Xin Zhongguo kaiguo Menguzu jiangjun Kong Fei zhuanji* (Kong Fei's 60 years of trials and hardship: The biography of Mongolian General Kong Fei at the founding of the New China). Hohhot: Neimenggu renmin chubanshe, 2010.

An Yucai. "Wo zai Naqu canjia pingpan" (My participation in pacifying rebellion in Naqu). Huanqiu wang, http://china.huanqiu.com/roll/2009-3/397403.html. Accessed December 17, 2009.

Bai Jingyuan, Ma Qicheng, and Li Zhuqing (eds.). *Zhou Enlai tongzhi dui minzu wenti yu minzu zhengce lunshu xuanbian* (Anthology of Comrade Zhou Enlai expounding on the question of ethnic minorities and ethnic minority policies). Beijing: Zhongyang minzu xueyuan keyan chu (for internal circulation), 1981.

Bingqi zhishi (Ordnance knowledge). Beijing: Guofang gongye chubanshe, 1979–.

Changdu zhanyi wenxian ziliao xuanbian (Selected documentary material on the Battle of Changdu). CCP Changdu Prefectural Party Committee and Changdu Prefectural Administrative Office (eds.). Lhasa: Xizang renmin chubanshe, 2000.

Chen Bing. "Panguo bi wang" (Treason deserves death), in Re Di et al. (ed.), *Xizang geming huiyilu* (Memoirs of the Tibetan Revolution Vol. 4), Jinian Xizang shixing minzhu gaige sanshi zhounian zhuanji (Collection commemorating the 30th anniversary of the implementation of democratic reform in Tibet). Lhasa: Xizang renmin chubanshe, 1989, pp. 18–31.

Chen Duxiu. "Ouxiang pohuai lun" (On the destruction of idols). *Xin qingnian* (New Youth), vol. 5, no. 2 (1918), pp. 89–91.

Chengduo xianzhi (Chengduo County Gazetteer). Unpublished 1985 version. Found at http://gfs2004052.blog.163.com/blog/static/43720022011111605626997/. Accessed January 26, 2012.

Chen Guansheng and An Caidan. *Han Ying Zang duizhao changjian Zangyu renming diming cidian* (Dictionary of common personal and place names in Chinese, English and Tibetan). Beijing: Waiwen chubanshe, 2004.

Chen Guoguang. *Qinghai Zangzu shi* (History of Qinghai's Tibetans). Xining: Qinghai minzu shubanshe, 1997.

Cheng Yue (ed.). *Zhongguo Gongchandang Changdu diqu lishi dashiji: 1949–2009* (Chronicle of the History of the Chinese Communist Party in Changdu Prefecture: 1949–2009). Beijing: Zhongguo Zangxue chubanshe, 2010.

Chen Jinshui. "Zedang qixiangzhan baowei zhan de huiyi" (Recollections of the battle to protect the Zedang weather station), in Zhongguo qixiang xuehui (ed.), *Wo yu xin Zhongguo qixiang shiye* (New China's meteorological undertaking and I). Beijing: Qixiang chubanshe, 2002, pp. 185–89.

Chen Qingying. *Zhongguo Zangzu buluo* (China's Tibetan tribes). Beijing: Zhongguo Zangxue chubanshe, 1990.

Damcho Pelsang (Danqu Baisang). *Guoluo lishi—Nianbuyuwuze zhi shenxiang* (History of Golok—The divine fragrance of Mt. Nyenbo Yutse). Translated by Xia'er Zongdedan, unpublished Chinese manuscript.

Dangdai Yunnan Zangzu jianshi (A concise history of the Tibetan people in contemporary Yunnan). Kunming: Yunnan renmin shubanshe, 2009.

Dangdai Zhongguo minzu gongzuo dashiji (Chronicle of major events in modern China's ethnic minority work 1949–1988), vol. 1. Beijing: Minzu chubanshe, 1989.

Dan Zeng. *Dangdai Xizang jianshi* (Brief history of contemporary Tibet). Beijing: Dangdai Zhongguo chubanshe, 1996.

Daofu xianzhi (Daofu County Gazetteer). Chengdu: Sichuan renmin chubanshe, 1997.

Dari xianzhi (Dari County Gazetteer). Xi'an: Shaanxi renmin chubanshe, 1993.

Darje (Dajie). *Guoluo jianwen yu huiyi* (Golok seen, heard, and remembered). Internal publication, Xining, 2008.

Dawa Tsering. *Xueji xueyu* (Blood sacrifice in the Land of Snows). Taipei: Xueyu chubanshe, 2012.

Dege xianzhi (Dege County Gazetteer). Chengdu: Sichuan renmin chubanshe, 1995.

Deng Jiahua. "Yi Litang pingpan" (Recalling pacifying rebellion in Litang), in *Fengyu zhengcheng: Xin Zhongguo qixiang shiye huiyilu Vol. 1 1949–1978* (Hard journey: A memoir of the meteorological undertaking in the New China, vol. 1, 1949–1978). Beijing: Qixiang chubanshe, 2006, pp. 405–7.

Deng Xiaoping junshi wenji di'er juan (Military writings of Deng Xiaoping, vol. 2). CCP Central Committee Documentary Research Office and China PLA Academy of Military Sciences (eds.). Beijing: Junshi kexue chubanshe, Zhongyang wenxian chubanshe, 2004.

Deng Xiaoping nianpu 1904–1974 (Chronology of Deng Xiaoping 1904–1974). Yang Shengqun and Yan Jianqi (eds.), vol. 3. Beijing: Zhonggong zhongyang wenxian yanjiushi, 2009.

Derong Tsering Dondrup (Derong Zerendengzhu). *Zangzu tongshi: Jixiang baoping* (A general history of Tibet: Auspicious treasure vase). Lhasa: Xizang renmin chubanshe, 2001.

Derong xianzhi (Derong County Gazetteer). Chengdu: Sichuan daxue chubanshe, 2000.

Diqing Zangzu Zizhizhou zhi (Diqing Tibetan Autonomous Prefecture Gazetteer), vol. 1. Lei'an Wangdui (ed.). Kunming: Yunnan minzu chubanshe, 2003.

Diqing Zangzu Zizhizhou zongjiao zhi (Diqing Tibetan Autonomous Prefecture Religious Gazetteer). Beijing: Zhongguo Zangxue chubanshe, 1994.

Ding Sheng, as told to Qi Xin. "Dingzhi budui de Xizang pingpan zuozhan" (The Ding Command Post's battles to pacify rebellion in Tibet), in Ding Sheng, *Luonan yingxiong—Ding Sheng jiangjun huiyilu* (Hero in Hardship: The Memoirs of General Ding Sheng), Jin Guang and Yu Ruxin (ed.). Hong Kong: Xingke'er chuban gongsi, 2008.

Dong Zhanlin. *Junlü chunqiu* (Army years). Lanzhou: Gansu renmin chubanshe, 1991.

Dorjé Tseten. "Kangnan Litang pingxi panluan he minzhu gaige qingkuang gaishu" (A summary of the pacification of the armed rebellion and democratic reform in Lithang, southern Kham), in *Ganzizhou wenshi ziliao*, vol. 12, compiled by Zhengxie Sichuansheng Ganzi Zangzu Zizhizhou weiyuanhui. Kangding (?): internal publication, pp. 82–90.

Dudul Choying. "Cong zong mishu dao Bianba diqu panfei siling" (From *dzong* secretary to bandit rebel commander in Bianba area). *Xizang dangshi tongxun* (Tibet Party History Bulletin), no. 1, 1989, pp. 57–62.

"Fangeming de chaoxue—Ta'er si" (Den of counterrevolutionaries—Kumbum Monastery). *Neibu cankao* (Internal Reference), Xinhua News Agency (ed.), March 10, 1959, pp. 10–13.

Fang Yangda and Huang Yaming. "Jijizhongliu" (Sworn to annihilate the rebels). http://blog.sina.com.cn/s/blog_4b50a1d30100gahr.html. Accessed August 22, 2011.

Fang Zhao. *Laobing Sun Fudi he tade zhanyoumen* (Veteran soldier Sun Fudi and his comrades-in-arms). Guilin: Guangxi shifan daxue chubanshe, 2010.

Fan Ming. *Xizang neibu zhi zheng* (Tibet's internal struggle). Hong Kong: Mingjing chubanshe, 2010.

Fan Shaoxian. "Huiyi wo jin Zang de zhandou shengya" (Recalling my combat career entering Tibet), *Erye Jun daren* (Great man of the 2nd Field Army), Chongqing eryejun daxiao shi yanjiuhui (ed.). Hong Kong: Zhongguo minzu wenhua chubanshe, 2009, pp. 953–56.

Feng Haohua. "Dui Qinghai yimin yu kenhuang dui lishi kaocha" (Historical observation of immigration and soil reclamation in Qinghai). *Jinji yanjiu*, no. 5, 1983.

Feng Haohua. *Qinghai renkou* (Qinghai population). Xining: Qinghaisheng jihua shengyu xuanchuan zhongxin, 1988 (for internal circulation).

Gannan Zangzu Zizhizhou zhi (Gannan Tibetan Autonomous Prefecture Gazetteer), vols. 1 and 2. Beijing: Minzu chubanshe, 1999.

Gansu liushi niandai da jihuang kaozheng: Lanzhou wenshi ziliao xuanji di 20 ji (Verification of the Great Famine in Gansu in the 1960s: Selection and compilation of Lanzhou literary and historical material, vol. 20) (for internal circulation), Zhongguo renmin zhengzhi xieshang huiyi Gansusheng weiyuanhui wenshi ziliao yanjiu weiyuanhui (ed.). Lanzhou: Lanzhoushi zhengxie, 2001.

Gansu shengzhi di 10 juan junshi zhi (Gansu Province Gazetteer, vol. 10, Military Gazetteer), part 1. Lanzhou: Gansu renmin chubanshe, 2011.

Gansu shengzhi di 71 juan zongjiao zhi (Gansu Province Gazetteer, vol. 71, Religious Gazetteer). Lanzhou: Gansu renmin chubanshe, 2005.

Gansu wenshi ziliao xuanji di 30 ji (Selection and compilation of Gansu literary and historical material, vol. 30). Zhongguo renmin zhengzhi xieshang huiyi Gansusheng weiyuanhui wenshi ziliao yanjiu weiyuanhui (ed.). Lanzhou: Gansu renmin chubanshe, 1989.

Gansu wenshi ziliao xuanji di 31 ji: Minzu zongjiao zhuanji (Selected Material on Gansu Literature and History, vol. 31: Ethnic minority religion). Zhongguo renmin zhengzhi xieshang huiyi Gansusheng weiyuanhui wenshi ziliao yanjiu weiyuanhui (ed.). Lanzhou: Gansu renmin chubanshe, 1989.

Gansu Zangzu renkou (Gansu's Tibetan population). Beijing: Zhongguo tongji chubanshe, 1994.

Ganzi Zangzu Zizhizhou junshi zhi (Ganzi Tibetan Autonomous Prefecture Military Gazetteer) (semi-classified). Sichuanshen Ganzi junfenqu bianyin, 1999.

Ganzi Zangzu Zizhizhou Litangsi, Dajinsi, Ganzisi, Babangsi diaocha cailiao (Survey material on the Litang, Dajin, Ganzi, and Babang monasteries in the Ganzi Tibetan Autonomous Prefecture). Beijing (?), Zhongguo kexueyuan minzu yanjiusuo, Sichuan shaoshu minzu shehui lishi diaocha zu (classified), 1963.

Ganzi Zangzu Zizhizhou Litangxian Maoya muqu shehui diaocha baogao (Social survey report on the Maoya pastoral region of Litang County, Ganzi Tibetan Autonomous Prefecture) (classified), compiled by Zhongguo hexueyuan minzu yanjiusuo, Sichuan shaoshu minzu shehui lishi diaochazu. Beijing (?), Zhongguo hexueyuan minzu yanjiusuo, Sichuan shaoshu minzu shehui lishi diaochazu, 1963.

Ganzi Zangzu Zizhizhou minzu gaige shi (History of democratic reform in the Ganzi Tibetan Autonomous Prefecture), CCP Ganzi Prefectural Party Committee Party History Research Room (ed.). Chengdu: Sichuan minzu chubanshe, 2000.

Ganzi Zangzu Zizhizhou minzu zhi (Ganzi Tibetan Autonomous Prefecture Ethnic Minority Gazetteer), compiled by Kangding minzu shizhuan bianxiezu. Beijing: Dangdai Zhongguo chubanshe, 1994.

Ganzi zhouzhi (Ganzi Prefecture Gazetteer), vol. 1. Chengdu: Sichuan renmin chubanshe, 1997.

Gao Wangling and Liu Yang. "Tugai de jiduanhua" (Extremism in land reform). *Ershiyi shiji* (Twenty-first century), no. 2, 2009, pp. 37–47.

Gelek (Gelei). "Zangdong mumin—Renleixue tianye kaocha biji" (The herders of Eastern Tibet: Notebook of an anthropological field study). http://www.cwru.edu/affil/tibet/booksAndPapers/Gelek/Gelek_east.pdf. Accessed April 5, 2009.

Gelek (Gelei) and Nancy Levine., "Waxu Seda: Dongbu Zanqu de yige youmu buluo" (Waxu Seda: A nomadic tribe in eastern Tibet), translated by Zhai Shengde. *Shijie minzu*, no. 2, 1998, pp. 44–52.

Gelek (Gelei) et al. (eds.). *Zangbei mumin—Xizang Naqu diqu shehui lishi diaocha baogao* (Nomads of northern Tibet: A survey report of the society and history of Tibet's Naqu Prefecture). Beijing: Zhonggou Zangxue chubanshe, 2004.

Gong Yin. *Zhongguo tusi zhidu* (China's headman system). Kunming: Yunnan minzu chubanshe, 1992.

Gongzuo Tongxun (Work Bulletin), *Zhongguo Renming Jiefangjun zong zhengzhibu bianyin* (Classified), no. 33: October 26, 1961.

Gou Xiaorong. "Zhaxi Wangxu yu Guoluo gongzuotuan" (Tashi Wangchuk and the Golok Work Team), in *Qinghai wenshi ziliao xuanji* (Selected literary and historical documents on Qinghai) (classified), vol. 24. Nanning: Qinghaisheng zhengxie xuexi he wenshi weiyuanhui, 1995, pp. 57–70.

Guan Shengzhi. "Zhuiyi hongzha hangkongbing ershiwushi lishi pianduan" (Fragmentary recollections of the history of the Bombardment Aviation 25th Division). http://kong25.bokee.com/297867158.html. Accessed August 28, 2011.

Guanyu Xizang wenti—1959 sanyue—wuyue de wenjian, ziliao (Regarding the Tibet problem—Documents and material March–May 1959). Beijing: Renmin chubanshe, 1959.

Guinan xianzhi (Guinan County Gazetteer). Xi'an: Sanqin chubanshe, 1996.

Guo Chaoren and Liu Hanjun. "Pingpan hou de Lasa" (Lhasa after the pacification of rebellion). *Xin Guancha*, no. 10, 1959, pp. 5–8.

Guoluo Zangzu Zizhizhou zhi (Guoluo Tibetan Autonomous Prefecture Gazetteer). Beijing: Minzu chubanshe, 2001.

Guo Yonghu and Li Ye. "Meiguo Zhongyang Qingbaoju dui Zhongguo Xizang de zhun junshi xingdong (1949–1969)" (The U.S. Central Intelligence Agency's paramilitary operations regarding China's Tibet [1949–1969]). *Shixue jikan*, no. 4 (October), 2005, pp. 75–81.

"Guxi laoren Zhang Chengzuo rudang 50 nian fengxian 50 nian yilu jianxin" (A tribute to 50 arduous years of the 70-year-old Zhang Chengzuo on his 50th anniversary of joining the party). *Wuling dushibao* (Wuling metropolitan daily), July 1, 2011. http://cq.qq.com/a/20110701/000301.htm. Accessed August 25, 2011.

Gyaltsen Norbu (Jiangcun Luobu) (ed.). *Huihuang de ershi shiji xin Zhongguo da jilu Xizang juan 1949–1999* (A great record of the twentieth century's new China, Tibet volume 1949–1999). Beijing: Honqi chubanshe, 1999.

Haibei Zangzu Zizhizhou zhi (Haibei Tibetan Autonomous Prefecture Gazetteer), vol. 1. Lanzhou: Gansu renmin chubanshe, 1999.

Hainan Zangzu Zizhizhou zhi (Hainan Tibetan Autonomous Prefecture Gazetteer). Beijing: Minzu chubanshe, 1997.

Hai Ning and Padmatsho (Baimacuo). "Qinghai Sajia gusha jiegusi" (The

Qinghai Sakya Jiegu Monastery). *Qinghai minzu yanjiu*, vol. 19, no. 4 (2008), pp. 101–4.

Haixi Mengguzu Zangzu Zizhizhou zhi (Haixi Mongolian and Tibetan Autonomous Prefecture Gazetteer), vol. 1. Xi'an: Shaanxi renmin chubanshe, 1995.

Haixi Menguzu Zangzu Zizhizhou junshizhi (Haixi Mongolian and Tibetan Autonomous Prefecture Military Gazetteer) (classified), 2004.

Han Youren. *Yichang yanmo le de guonei zhanzheng—ji 1958 nian Qinghai muqu pingpan kuodahua jiqi jiuzheng guocheng* (A vanished civil war—The whole story of the enlargement and correction of the pacification of rebellion in Qinghai's pastoral region in 1958). Hong Kong: Tianyuan shuwu, 2013.

Heishui xianzhi (Heishui County Gazetteer). Beijing: Minzu chubanshe, 1993.

Henan Menguzu Zizhixian zhi (Henan Mongolian Autonomous County Gazetteer), vol. 2. Lanzhou: Gansu renmin chubanshe, 1996.

He Xicheng. "Xizang pingpan suoji" (Fragmentary recollections of the pacification of rebellion in Tibet). *Wuhan wenshi ziliao* (Wuhan literary and historical materials), no. 3, 2011 (221), pp. 19–26.

Hong Weiquan. "Xueyu jiaofei ji—Jiefangjun Kongjun gaoyuan pingpan jishi" (Suppressing bandits in the Land of Snows: A true record of the PLA Air Force pacification of rebellion on the plateau). *Hangkongshi Yanjiu* (Aviation history research), no. 5, 2001, pp. 13–16.

Huang Kecheng. *Huang Kecheng junshi wenxuan* (Huang Kecheng's military writings). Beijing: Jiefangjun chubanshe, 2002.

Huangnan Zangzu Zizhizhou zhi (Huangnan Tibetan Autonomous Prefecture Gazetteer), vol. 2. Lanzhou: Gansu renmin chubanshe, 1999.

Huangzhong xianzhi (Huangzhong County Gazetteer). Xining: Qinghai renmin chubanshe, 1989.

Hua Qiang, Xi Jirong, et al. *Zhongguo kongjun bainian shi* (The hundred-year history of the Chinese Air Force). Shanghai: Shanghai renmin chubanshe, 2005.

Hu Liyan. *Baizhan jiangxing Huang Xinting* (A Battle-Hardened General Star: Huang Xinting). Beijing: Jiefangjun wenyi chubanshe, 2000.

Hu Liyan, *Zouguo xiaoyan—Huang Xinting chuan* (Passing by gunpowder smoke—The biography of Huang Xinting). Beijing: Biejing, Zhongguo Qingnian chubanshe, 1997.

Jampa Jiangba. "Zai panfei qiangjie wuqi de beihou" (Behind the plundering of weapons by rebel bandits). In *Xizang wenshi ziliao xuanji* (Selected literary and historical materials regarding Tibet), vol. 5, pp. 93–95.

Jampel Gyatso (Jiangbian Jiacuo). *Li Jue zhuan* (The biography of Li Jue). Beijing: Zhongguo Zangxue chubanshe, 2005.

Jampel Gyatso (Jiangbian Jiacuo). *Mao Zedong yu Dalai Banchan* (Mao Zedong and the Dalai Lama and Panchen Lama). Hong Kong: Xindalu chubanshe, 2008.

Jampel Gyatso (Jiangbian Jiacuo). *Shishi Banchan Lama Zhuanji* (The 10th Panchen Lama: A life). Hong Kong: Kaifang chubanshe, 2008.

Jiang Dasan. "Blog. 74 sui lao feixing renyuan de boke" (Jiang Dansan: blog of a 74-year old pilot." http://blog.sina.com.cn/s/blog_4bf5830401000a0z.html. Accessed November 11, 2009.

Jianguo sanshinian shaoshu minzu gongzuo tongji ziliao, 1949–1979 (Statistical data on ethnic minority work in the thirty years since the founding of the country, 1949–1979). State Nationalities Affairs Commission Second Department (ed.), Series: *Zhonggong zhongyao lishi wenxian ziliao huibian di sanshi ji, Xijian gongji ziliao zhuanji di 143 fence* (CCP important historical documentary material collection, vol. 30, scarce statistical data special collection fascicle no. 143). Los Angeles: Zhongwen chubanwu fuwu zhongxin, 2013.

Jianguo yilai zhongyao wenxian xuanbian: 1953.1–1953.12, vol. 4 (Selected important documents since the founding of the country: January–December 1953, vol. 4). Beijing: Zhongyang wenxian chubanshe, 1993.

Jianguo yilai zhongyao wenxian xuanbian: 1961.1–1961.12, vol. 14 (Selected important documents since the founding of the country: January–December 1961, vol. 14), CCP Central Documentary Research Room (ed.). Beijing: Zhongyang wenxian chubanshe, 2011, pp. 817–44.

Jian Jun. *Xueyuan gouhuo* (Campfire on the snowy plain), chapter 8, "Bingshang lamasi" (Tragic deaths of soldiers in lamaist temple). http://www.zigui.org/article.php?id=84195. Accessed April 20, 2011.

Jianzha xianzhi (Jianzha County Gazetteer). Lanzhou: Gansu renmin chubanshe, 2003.

Jiao Donghai. "Lasa pingpan er san shi" (Two or three things about the pacification of rebellion in Lhasa). *Zhongwai wenzhai*, no. 7, 2016, pp. 46–47.

Jiefang Xizang shi (History of the liberation of Tibet). History of the Liberation of Tibet Editorial Committee (ed.). Beijing: Zhonggong dangshi chubanshe, 2008.

Ji Jiansheng, as told to Lin Rusheng. "Niu Qian jiang shou hua 'gongniu'" (Bull's retired general talks about the Bull), *Bingqi zhishi* (Ordnance knowledge), no. 7, 2009, pp. 75–78.

Jindai Kangqu dang'an jiliao xuanbian (Selected archival materials on modern Kham history), Sichuan Provincial Archive, Sichuan Nationality Institute. Chengdu: Sichuan daxue chubanshe, 1990.

Jinri Pan'an (Pan'an Today). July 15, 2011. http://goo.gl/AaOoW. Accessed August 17, 2011.

Jiuzhi xianzhi (Jiuzhi County Gazetteer). Xi'an: Sanqin chubanshe, 2005.

Ji Youquan. *Bai xue—Jiefang Xizang jishi* (White snow: A true record of the liberation of Tibet). Beijing: Zhongguo wuzi chubanshe, 1993.

Ji Youquan. *Xizang pingpan jishi* (A True Record of the Pacification of Revolt in Tibet). Lhasa: Xizang renmin chubanshe, 1993.

Kesang Tseden (Gazang Caidan). *Qingzang gaoyuan youmu wenhua* (Nomadic culture on the Tibetan plateau). Lanzhou: Gansu minzu chubanshe, 2000.

"Kongjun baogao yu jianyi (si)" (Air Force report and recommendations). *Jiang Zhongzheng zongtong wenwu* (Writings of President Jiang Zhongzheng). Academia Historica, Diancanghao: 002-080-0096-016, registration no. 002000001097A.

Kongtian zhujian: Renmin kongjun tengfei he zhuangbei fazhan shilu (Forging a sword in the sky: A true record of the People's Air Force rapid rise and equipping). Air Force Equipping Department (ed.). Beijing: Lantian chubanshe, 2011.

Lai Zuozhong and Deng Junkang. "Dege tusi jiazu de youlai jiqi shehui zhidu jiankuang" (Brief introduction to origins and social system of the Dege headman clan), in *Sichuan wenshi ziliaon xuanji* (Selected literary and historical material on Sichuan). Chengdu: Sichuan renmin chubanshe, vol. 33 (1984), pp. 177–210.

Lamajiao de fandong mianmu (Lamaism's reactionary features). Qinghai Provincial Party Committee Primary Party School Teaching and Research Section (classified). Xining: Qinghai renmin chubanshe, 1959.

Lanzhou wenshi zhiliao xuanji: Di 22 ji: Zhongguo liushi niandai dajihuang kao (Selection of Lanzhou historical documents: vol. 22: The case of China's 1960s famine). Lanzhou Municipal People's Political Consultative Conference Humanities Materials and Study Committee (ed.). Lanzhou, 2002.

Lasa zai qianjin—Jinian Lasa heping jiefang he jianli dangzuzhi sishi zhounian xuanji (Lhasa advancing—Selected essays commemorating the 40th anniversary of the peaceful liberation of Lhasa and the establishment of the party organization). CCP Lhasa Municipal Party Committee Party History Material Compilation Leading Group. Lhasa: Zhonggon Lasa shiwei dangshi ziliao zhangji lingdao xiaozu, for internal circulation, 1991.

Liao Shuxin. "Xizang kangbao yundong de minzuguan" (The national viewpoint of Tibet's movement against tyranny). *Zhongguo bianzheng* (China's Frontier Administration) (Taiwan), No. 100, 1987.

Li Benxin. "Changdu diqu dashi tiyao" (Summary of major events in Changdu Prefecture). *Xizang dangshi tongxin* (Tibet Party History Bulletin), no. 2, 1984, pp. 45–59.

Li Guoqing. *Xizang dashiji 1949–1984* (Chronicle of Tibet 1949–1984). Lhasa: Xizang renmin chubanshe, 1984.

Li Jianglin. *1959 Lasa! Dalai Lama ruhe chuzhou* (Lhasa 1959! How the Dalai Lama escaped). Taipei: Lianjing chuban gongsi, 2010.

Li Jianglin. "Qinghai caoyuan shang xiaoshi de wangling" (Vanished specters on the Qinghai prairie). *Dongxiang*, no. 2, 2011. Author's blog. http://bloodundersnow.blogspot.com/2011/02/blog-post_16.html.

Li Lushan, as told to Liu Yingfu. "Zhandou zai Gannan he Xizang" (Combat in southern Gansu and Tibet). http://www.wangcang.gov.cn/html/article/view/1565.html. Accessed August 18, 2011.

Li Mingzhong, Li Kunbi, and Bai Yuzhen. "Zeng Quezha zhuan" (The biography of Zeng Quezha). *Batangxian wenshi ziliao* (Literary and historical material on Batang County), vol. 3 (semiclassified). Batang: Batangxian zhengxie wenshi zhuanmen weiyuanhui bangongshi, 2008, pp. 187–97.

Lin Xiaoting. "Lengzhan bianyuan: Erci Dazhan hou Meiguo zai Zhongguo bianjiang diqu de mimi huodong (1947–1951)" (Cold War border: America's secret activities in China's border regions after the Second World War [1947–1951]). *Zhongyang yanjiuyuan jindaishi yanjiusuo jikan* (Collected Papers of Academia Sinica's Modern History Research Institute), no. 53 (September 2006), pp. 103–48.

Lin Zhaozhen. *Lama sharen: Xizang kangbao sishinian* (Lama killers: Tibet's 40 years fighting against tyranny). Taipei: Lianhe wenxue chubanshe, 1999.

Li Ping and Ma Zhisun. *Zhou Enlai nianpu 1949–1976* (Chronology of Zhou Enlai 1949–1976), vols. 1 and 2. Beijing: Zhongyang wenxian chubanshe, 2007.

Li Qixian. "Qinghai gaoyuan bujian kongjiang tewu" (Seizing and annihilating air-dropped secret agents on the Qinghai Plateau). *Huanqiu Shiye* online, http://www.globalview.cn/ReadNews.asp?NewsID=3207. Accessed December 19, 2009.

Li Shu, Liu Peiyi, and Du Yanlin (eds.). *Shehuizhuyi Shehui zhuyi shiqi Zhongguo Renmin Jiefangjun biannianshi* (Chronicle of the Chinese People's Liberation Army during the socialist period). Beijing: Renmin chubanshe, 1993.

Litang xianzhi. Chengdu: Sichuan renmin chubanshe, 1996.

Liu Chongwen and Chen Shaochou (eds.). *Liu Shaoqi nianpu, 1898–1969* (xia), (Chronology of Liu Shaoqi 1898–1969 [vol. 2]). Beijing: Zhongyang wenxian chubanshe, 1996.

Liu Hengxun. "Chuanxi pingpan jishi" (Record of the pacification of the rebellion in western Sichuan). http://www.jnzx.gov.cn:8080/Html/81012006515170747-1.html. Accessed April 23, 2011.

Liu Hongkang (ed.). *Zhongguo renkou (Sichuan fence)* (China Population [Sichuan]). Beijing: Zhongguo caizheng jingji chubanshe, 1988.

Liu Jun and Tang Huiyun. "Shixi Zhongguo dui Yuenan de jingji yu junshi yuanzhu (1950–1978 nian)" (An analysis of China's economic and military aid to Vietnam [1950–1978]). *Dongnanya zongheng* (Southeast Asian review), no. 5, 2010, pp. 13–18.

Liu Rui (ed.). *Zhongguo renkou (Xizang fence)* (China Population [Tibet]). Beijing: Zhongguo caizheng jingji chubanshe, 1988.

Liu Shulin. "Gan Qing Chuan Zang bianjie diqu pingpan jiaofei huiyi" (Recollections of pacifying rebellion and suppressing bandits in the Gansu-Qinghai-Sichuan-Tibet border region). *Zhengzhou wenshi ziliao* (Zhengzhou literary and historical material), vol. 29, pp. 277–85.

Liu Wenqiao. *Suiyue ruliu wei cuotuo* (Time flies too fast to catch), vol. 1. Beijing: Zhonguo minzhu fazhi chubanshe, 2000.

Li Weihan. *Tongyi zhanxian wenti yu minzu wenti* (United Front problems and ethnic minority problems). Beijing: Renmin chubanshe, 1981.

Li Xiaowei and Liao Xinhua. "Wode Hongse chaoji baolei—Duli disituan feixingyuan Wang Shengwen de Tu-4 zhandou gushi" (My red super fortress—The story of Independent 4th Regiment aviator Wang Shengwen's Tupelov-4 battle). *Bingqi*, no. 12, 2007, pp. 48–53.

Li Xing. "Hongjun changzheng zai xueshan caodi de liangshi wenti" (The problem of food in the Red Army's long march in the snow-capped mountains and grasslands). *Xizang yanjiu*, no. 1, 2003, pp. 85–91.

Li Zhenyu. "Xizang wangshi" (Past events in Tibet), CCTV Online. http://www.cndfilm.com/special/jlysh/20110923/106419.shtml. Accessed December 2, 2011.

Li Zhongkang and Li Ruiqiong. "1978–1992 nian Sichuan Abazhou gaige kaifang de huigu yu sikao" (Review and reflections on reform and opening in Aba Prefecture, Sichuan Province, 1978–1992). In in *Minzu diqu de nongcun gaige yu fazhan* (Rural reform and development in ethnic minority regions), CCP

Central Committee Party History Research Room, Third Research Section (ed.). Beijing: Zhonggong dangshi chubanshe, 2008.

Li Zonghua and Li Yankai. *Anduo Zangzu shi* (The history of the Tibetans of Anduo). Xining: Qinghai minzu chubanshe, 1992.

Lodro Gyatso (Luo Jianzhong). "Yushu Xiuma, Bairimaima buluo canzao zhenya he fankang douzheng jishi" (A true record of the suppression inflicted on Yulshul's Shuma and Beri Méma tribes and their resistance and struggle). *Qinghai wenshi ziliao xuanji* (Selected literary and historical materials on Qinghai), vol. 13, pp. 134–40.

Luhuo xianzhi (Luhuo County Gazetteer). Chengdu: Sichuan renmin chubanshe, 2000.

Luo Yinjun. "Huiyi Xinlong xian de minzhu gaige" (Remembering the democratic reforms in Xinlong County). *Ganzizhou wenshi ziliao* (Literary and historical documents of Ganzi Prefecture), vol. 7, pp. 227–54.

Luo Wei. "Meiguo Zhongyang Qingbaoju chashou Xizang miwen" (The secret of the United States Central Intelligence Agency's involvement in Tibet). *Bainian Chao*, no. 3, 2001, pp. 17–24.

Luozhu Chodron. "Shisishi dalai xingong xiujian qingkuang" (About the construction of the 14th Dalai Lama's new palace), in *Xizang wenshi ziliao xuanji* (Selected historical and literary materials regarding Tibet), compiled and edited by Xizang Zizhiqu zhengxie wenshi ziliao yanjiu weiyuanhui, vol. 4. [semiclassified] [Lhasa?], 1985.

Luqu xianzhi (Luqu County Gazetteer). Lanzhou: Gansu wenhua chubanshe, 2006.

Lu Shoubiao. *Cong shusheng dao hujiang: Wei Tongtai jiangjun* (From bookworm to warrior: General Wei Tongtai). Beijing, Jiefangjun wenyi chubanshe, 2011.

Ma Hongchang. "Yingxiong de Jiefangjun qibing diyishi" (The heroic PLA 1st Cavalry Division). *Dangshi bocai (Jishi ban)* (Party history collection [on-the-spot reports]), no. 5, 2007, pp. 29–34.

Mai Qunzhong. "Shishi Banchan mengnan shimo" (The whole story of the demise of the 10th Panchen Lama). *Wenshi jinghua*, no. 6, 2005, pp. 27–35.

Mao Zedong. *Jianguo yilai Mao Zedong wengao: Yijiuwubanian yiyue—Yijiuwubanian shi'eryue / di qi ce* (Manuscripts of Mao Zedong since the founding of the country: January 1958–December 1958 / vol. 7), Zhonggong zhongyang wenxian yanjiushi (ed.). Beijing, Zhongyang wenxian chubanshe, 1992 (semiclassified).

Mao Zedong. *Jianguo yilai Mao Zedong wengao: Yijiuwujiunian yiyue—Yijiuwujiunian shi'eryue / di yi ce* (Manuscripts of Mao Zedong since the founding of the country: January 1959–December 1959 / vol. 1), Zhonggong zhongyang wenxian yanjiushi (ed.). Beijing: Zhongyang wenxian chubanshe, 1993 (semiclassified).

Mao Zedong. *Jianguo yilai Mao Zedong wengao: Yijiuwujiunian yiyue—Yijiuwujiunian shi'eryue / di ba ce* (Manuscripts of Mao Zedong since the founding of the country: January 1959–December 1959 / vol. 8), Zhonggong zhongyang wenxian yanjiushi (ed.). Beijing: Zhongyang wenxian chubanshe, 1993 (semiclassified).

Mao Zedong. *Jianguo yilai Mao Zedong wengao: Yijiuwuliunian yiyue—Yijiuwuqinian shi'eryue / di liu ce* (Manuscripts of Mao Zedong since the founding of the country: January 1956–December 1957 / vol. 6), Zhonggong zhongyang wenxian yanjiushi (ed.). Beijing: Zhongyang wenxian chubanshe, 1992 (semiclassified).

Mao Zedong. *Mao Zedong wenji* (Collected Works of Mao Zedong). Beijing: Renmin chubanshe, 1996.

Mao Zedong. *Mao Zedong xuanji* (Selected Works of Mao Zedong), vols. 4 and 5. Beijing: Renmin chubanshe, 1969 and 1977.

Mao Zedong nianpu 1949–1976 (Chronology of Mao Zedong 1949–1976). Vol. 3, Zhongyang wenxian yanjiushi, Pang Xianzhi, Feng Hui (eds.). Beijing: Zhongyang wenxian chubanshe, 2013.

Mao Zedong Xizang gongzuo wenxuan (Selected writings of Mao Zedong on Tibet work). CCP Central Committee Documentary Research Section, CCP Tibet Autonomous Region Party Committee and China-Tibet Studies Research Center (eds.), Zhongyang wenxian chubanshe, Zhongguo zangxue chubanshe, 2001.

Maqin xianzhi (Machen County Gazetteer). Xining: Qinghai renmin chubanshe, 2005.

Maqu xianzhi (Machu County Gazetteer). Lanzhou: Gansu renmin chubanshe, 2001.

Ma Wanli. *Jingjian: Qinghai minzu gongzuo ruogan zhongda lishi shijian huigu* (Mirror: Looking back at some major historical incidents in Qinghai's ethnic minority work). Xining: Qinghai renmin chubanshe, 2005.

Ma Wuji. *Gansu Xiahe Zangmin diaocha ji* (Survey of Tibetans in Xiahe, Gansu Province). Shanghai [?]: Wentong shuju, 1941.

Miao Piyi. *Miao Pi-yi huiyilu* (Memoir of Miao Pi-yi). Lhasa: Xizang renmin chubanshe, 2005.

Min Zengfu. *Qiangguo kongjun zhi lu* (The way to a powerful country's air force). Beijing: Jiefangjun chubanshe, 2013.

Minzu wenti wenxian huibian 1921.7–1949.9 (Compilation of documents on ethnic minority issues July 1921–September 1949) (semiclassified). CCP Central Committee United Front Department (ed.). Beijing: Zhonggong Zhongyang Dangxiao chubanshe, 1991.

Minzu zongjiao gongzuo wenjian huiji 1949–1959 (Collected documents on ethnic minority religious work 1949–1959). Compiled by the Qinghai provincial party committee United Front Department (for internal circulation). Xining (?), 1959, vols. 1 and 2.

Muli Zangzu Zizhixian zhi (Muli Tibetan Autonomous County Gazetteer). Chengdu: Sichuan renmin chubanshe, 1995.

Naidong xianzhi (Naidong County Gazetteer). Beijing: Zhongguo Zangxue chubanshe, 2006.

Neimenggu de tudi zhidu gaige (Land reform in Inner Mongolia), compiled by CCP Inner Mongolian Autonomous Region History Research Room., Beijing: Zhonggong dangshi chubanshe, 2008.

Palden Gyatso (Bandan Jiacuo), as told to Shakya Tsering (Xiajia Ciren). *Xueshan xia de huoyan* (Fire under the snow). Translated by Liao Tianqi. Washington, D.C., Laogai Research Foundation, 2003.

Panchen Lama. *Qiwanyanshu: Banchan Lama wenlun xuanji* (The seventy-thousand-word petition: Selected writings of the Panchen Lama). Dharamsala: Tibet Government in Exile Foreign Affairs and Information Department, 1998.

Pan Zhaomin. "Wuji zhi zhan—Yi Xizang erhao diqu pingpan zhanyi" (War on the roof of the world—Remembering the campaign to pacify rebellion in Tibet's Zone 2), in Tibet People's Publishing (ed.). *Xizang geming huiyilu* (Reminiscences of the Tibet revolution), vol. 4, Special commemorating the 30th anniversary of implementing democratic reform in Tibet, Redi et al. (eds.), pp. 87–97.

"Peng Zhen tongzhi he Banchan, Apei de tanhua jiyao" (Summary of conversation between Comrade Peng Zhen and the Panchen Lama and Ngapo Ngawang Jigmé). In *Zhonggong Xizang zhongyao lishi wenxian ziliao huibian: Di'er fence: Youguan Banchan yinyan huozui de ruogan xijian shiliao* (Compilation of important historical documentary materials of the CCP in Tibet: Fascicle No. 2: Certain scarce historical material regarding the Panchen Lama being punished for his speech), Document no. 3. Los Angeles: Zhongwen chubanwu fuwu zhongxin, 2010 (top secret).

Peng Zhiyao. "Yige laobing de pingpan riji" (An old soldier's diary of pacifying rebellion). Xinhua Online Military Channel. http://www.bingtuannet.com/2007-09/13/content_11141281.htm. Accessed October 5, 2009.

Pingpan yinxiong zhuan (Tales of rebellion pacification heroes). Vol. 1, Lanzhou Military Command Political Department Propaganda Department (ed.). Lanzhou: Lanzhou junqu zhengzhibu, 1960.

Pingxi Xizang panluan (Suppressing the armed rebellion in Tibet). Tibet Autonomous Region Party History Material Collection Committee, Tibet Military Command Party History Material Collection Leading Group (eds.). Lhasa: Xizang renmin chubanshe, 1995 (semiclassified).

Puntsok Wangye (Puntsok Wangyal, Pingcuo Wangjie). *Pindeng tuanjie lu manman: Dui woguo minzu guanxi de fanxi* (The slow road to equality and unity: Reflections on ethnic relations in my country). Hong Kong: Xinshiji chubanshe, 2014.

Pu Wencheng. *Ganqing Zanchuan fojiao siyuan* (Tibetan Buddhist monasteries in Gansu and Qinghai). Xining: Qinghai renmin chubanshe, 1990.

Pu Wencheng. "Qinghai Zangchuan Fojiao siyuan gaishu" (Overview of Qinghai's Tibetan Buddhist monasteries). *Qinghai shehui kexue* (Qinghai social sciences), no. 5, 1990, pp. 92–99.

Qian Jiang. *Mimi zhengzhan: Zhongguo junshi guwentuan yuan Yue kang Fa jishi* (Secret expedition: A true record of China's military advisor group in supporting Vietnam to resist France). Chengdu: Sichuan renmin chubanshe, 1999.

Qiao Cangyu. "Canjia jin Zang yunshu zongdui ji Qingzang zhulu gongcheng" (Participating in the transport unit entering Tibet and the Qinghai-Tibet highway construction project). *China's Tibet*, no. 1, 2005, pp. 58–59.

Qinghaisheng Zangzu Menguzu shehui lishi diaocha (Social and historical survey of the Tibetan and Mongolian ethnic minorities in Qinghai), Qinghai Province Editing and Compilation Group. Xining: Qinghai renmin chubanshe, 1985.

Qinghai shengzhi: junshi zhi (Qinghai Province Gazetteer: Military Gazetteer). Xining: Qinghai renmin chubanshe, 2001.

Qinghai shengzhi: Fulu (Qinghai Province Gazetteer: Appendix). Xining: Qinghai renmin chubanshe, 2003.

Qinghai Zangzu renkou (Qinghai's Tibetan population). Beijing: Zhongguo tongji chubanshe, 1993.

Qin Heping (ed.). "Guanyu Sichuan Ganzi Zangqu yu Xizang diqu minzhu gaige de renshi" (Understanding Sichuan's Ganzi Tibetan region and democratic reform in the Tibetan regions). *Zhongguo xinan minzu yanjiu xuehui jianhui 30 zhounian jingxuan xueshu wenku—Sichuan juan* (Selected academic library from the 30th anniversary of the Chinese Southwest ethnic minority research society—Sichuan volume), compiled by Yuan Xiaowen and Chen Guo-an. Beijing: Minzu chubanshe, 2013.

Qin Heping (ed.). *Sichuan minzu diqu minzhu gaige yanjiu—20 shiji 50 niandai Sichuan Zangqu Yiqu de shehui biange* (Research on democratic reform in Sichuan's ethnic minority regions—Social transformation in Sichuan's Tibetan and Yi regions in the 1950s). Beijing: Zhongyang minzu xueyuan chubanshe, 2011.

Qin Heping (ed.). *Sichuan minzu diqu minzhu gaige ziliaoji* (Collected materials on the democratic reforms in Sichuan's ethnic minority regions). Beijing: Minzu chubanshe, 2008.

Qin Heping and Ran Linwen (eds.). *Sichuan minzu diqu minzhu gaige dashiji* (Chronicle of democratic reforms in Sichuan's ethnic minority regions). Beijing: Minzu chubanshe, 2007.

Renmin huabao (China pictorial). Beijing: Renmin huabao she, 1950–.

Ren Zhiyi. "Xizang pingpan qinliji" (A record of my personal experience of the suppression of rebellion in Tibet). *Dangyuan wenzhai*, 2009, no. 3, pp. 38–41.

Ruoergai xianzhi (Ruoergai County Gazetteer). Beijing: Minzu chubanshe, 1996.

Sanzhong quanhui yilai zhongyao wenxian huibian (Compilation of important documents since the Third Central Committee). Vol. 2, CCP Central Committee Documentary Research Room (ed.). Beijing: Renmin chubanshe, 1982 (classified).

Seda xianzhi (Seda County Gazetteer). Chengdu: Sichuan renmin chubanshe, 1997.

Sha Na. "Zai Ganzi Zangzu Zizhizhou nongye xianjin danwei daibiaohui shang de zongjie baogao" (Summary report on the Ganzi Tibetan Autonomous Prefecture agricultural cash unit congress). *Minzu gongzuo ziliao yuebao* (Ethnic minority work data monthly), Southwest National Minorities Institute Scientific Research Committee (ed.), no. 12, 1958, pp. 48–52 (classified).

Shan Chao. "Lasa pingpan jianwen" (Seen and heard in the pacification of rebellion in Lhasa). *Xin Guancha*, no. 10, 1959, pp. 8–10.

Shan Chao. "Yuguo tianqing—Lasa pingluan liangzhou riji" (Clear skies after rain—A journal of two weeks during the suppression of rebellion in Lhasa). *Remin Ribao* (People's daily), April 25, 1959, p. 7.

Shao Guozheng, Wang Yunxiang, and Liu Shankui. "Wang Qimei zhuan" (The biography of Wang Qimei). *Xizang dangshi ziliao* (Tibet party history historical materials), no. 1, 1992, pp. 51–74.

Shen Zaiwang. *Qingshan wuyan: Huiyi fuqin Li Jingquan* (The silent hills: Remembering my father, Li Jingquan), in Wei Renzheng (ed.), *Dangdai Jiangxi shi yanjiu congshu: Huiwang* (Modern Jiangxi historical research series: Looking back). Beijing: Dangdai Zhongguo chubanshe, 2012.

Shi Hongsheng (ed.). "Xizang pingpan zhong de houqin baozhang gongzuo" (Logistical safeguard work in the pacification of rebellion in Tibet). *In Shijie wuji fengyun lu* (Storm on the roof of the world), vol. 3, 1991, pp. 235–39.

Shi Hongsheng, Zhang Jun and Liu Guangrun (eds.). *Shijie wuji fengyunlu* (Storm on the roof of the world), compiled by Sixang junqu zhengzhibu. Vol. 3. Chengdu [Publisher unknown]: 1998 (semiclassified).

Shiqu xianzhi (Shiqu County Gazetteer). Chengdu: Sichuan renmin chubanshe, 2000.

Sichuan Abazhou Zangzu shehui lishi diaocha (Historical survey of Tibetan society in Sichuan's Aba Prefecture). Chengdu: Sichuan shehui kexue chubanshe, 1985.

Sichuan Ganzizhou Zangzu shehui lishi diaocha (Historical survey of Tibetan society in Sichuan's Ganzi Prefecture). Chengdu: Sichuan shehui kexue chubanshe, 1985.

Sichuan shengzhi: Fulu (Sichuan Province Gazetteer: Appendix). Chengdu: Sichuan kexue jishu chubanshe, 2003.

Sichuan shengzhi: jiancha shenpan zhi (Sichuan Province Gazetteer: Procuratorial and Trial Gazetteer). Chengdu: Sichuan renmin chubanshe, 1996.

Sichuan shengzhi: junshi zhi (Sichuan Province Gazetteer: Military Gazetteer). Chengdu: Sichuan renmin chubanshe, 1999.

Sichuan shengzhi: Nongye zhi (Sichuan Province Gazetteer: Agricultural Gazetteer). Chengdu: Sichuan cishu chubanshe, 1996.

Sichuan shengzhi: Zongjiaozhi (Sichuan Province Gazetteer: Religious Gazetteer). Chengdu: Sichuan renmin chubanshe, 1998.

Sichuan Zangzu renkou (Sichuan's Tibetan population). Beijing: Zhongguo tongji chubanshe, 1994.

Southwest University for Nationalities, Nationalities Research Institute. *Caodi Zangzu diaocha cailiao* (Survey data for grassland Tibetans). Chengdu: Xinan minzu xueyuan minzu yanjiusuo, 1984.

Sun Jingxin (ed.). *Zhongguo Zangzu renkou* (China's Tibetan population). Beijing: Zhongguo tongji chubanshe, 1994.

Sun Zuobin. CCP Shaanxi Provincial Party Committee Party History Research Room (ed.), Liu Yunyue, Wu Chongxin (chief eds). Xi'an: Shanxi Renmin chubanshe, 1997.

Su Yu nianpu (Chronology of Su Yu). Zhonggong Jiangsu shengwei dangshi gongzuo bangongshi (ed.). Beijing: Dangdai Zhongguo chubanshe, 2012.

Su Yu wenxuan (1949.10–1984.1) (Selected essays of Su Yu [October 1949 to January 1984]), vol. 3, Su Yu Wenxuan Compilation Group (ed.). Beijing: Junshi kexue chubanshe, 2004.

Tianzhu xianzhi (Tianzhu County Gazetteer). Lanzhou: Gansu renmin chubanshe, 1994.

Tibet Autonomous Region Party Committee Party History Material Collection Committee. "Wei renmin huiyi shimo" (The whole story of the counterfeit people's assembly). *Xizang dangshi tongxun* (Tibet party history bulletin), no. 2, 1989, pp. 9–23.

Tongde xianzhi (Tongde County Gazetteer). *Beijing: Minzu chubanshe, 1999.*

Tongren xianzhi (Tongren County Gazetteer). Xi'an: Sanqin chubanshe, 2001.

Tongzhan zhengce wenjian huibian (Compilation of documents on the United Front policy). Vols. 1–4 (internal circulation), Zhonggong zhongyang tongyi zhanxian gongzuobu (ed.). Beijing (?): 1958.

Tsering Wangchuk (Ciren Wangjiu). *Xinxiang ziyou—Zhonggong paobing yingzhang toushen Xizang kangbao ji* (A mind toward freedom—Record of a Chinese artillery battalion commander joining the Tibetan resistance). Dharamsala: Government of Tibet in Exile Information Department, 1991.

Wang Gui. "Huiyi zai Xizang zhanwen jiaogen de jianxin suiyue" (Recalling the hard years gaining a firm foothold in Tibet). *Zhongguo Zangxue*, no. 2 (1991), pp. 94–109.

Wang Gui. "Xizang panluan shimo" (The whole story of the armed rebellion in Tibet), in *Jianzheng bainian Xizang: Xizang lishi jianzhengren fangtan lu* (Witnessing 100 years in Tibet: A record of interviews with witnesses of history in Tibet), vol. 1. Beijing: Wuzhou chuanbo chubanshe, 2003.

Wang Guozhen. "Pili tianjiang cheng xiongwan" (Fire bolts falling from the sky to punish the wicked), in *Xizang geming huiyilu disiji jinian Xizang shixing minzhu gaige sanshi zhounian* (Memoirs of the Tibetan revolution, vol. 4, the 30th anniversary of implementing democratic reform in Tibet). Lhasa: Xizang renmin chubanshe, 1989, pp. 38–45.

Wang Guozhong. "Chuanqi jingli, qingchun muhui—Ji canjia Xizang pingpan, xiafang duanlian de laojianyoumen" (Legendary experience, no regret of youth—Remember old comrades-in-arms who took part in the pacification of rebellion and tempering in Tibet), in *Wei zuguo: Zhangzhan de suiyue* (For the motherland: Years at war), vol. 2, Changzhou City New 4th Army History Research Room (ed.). Changzhou: 2005, pp. 829–33.

Wanglo et al. "Wo shi zenyang zai Yuke fadong panluan de" (How I launched the armed rebellion in Yukog). In Chinese People's Political Consultative Conference Sichuan Province Daofu County Committee (ed.), *Daofu wenshi zhiliao xuanji* (Selected literary and historical materials of Daofu), vol. 1 (1985), pp. 102–14.

Wang Qixiu. *Xueyu yixi* (Recollections of the snowy region). Lhasa: Xizang renmin chubanshe, 2004.

Wang Ruilian (ed.). *Lishi de kuayue: Qingzu Changdu jiefang liushi zhounian zhuanji* (History's great strides: Special collection commemorating the 60th anniversary of the liberation of Changdu). Beijing: Zhongguo Zangxue chubanshe, 2010.

Wang Shijin. "Chuan, Gan caodi zhujun shenghuo hen ku" (The life of troops garrisoned on the Sichuan and Gansu grasslands is very hard). Xinhua News Agency, *Neibu Cankao* (Internal Reference), January 18, 1957, pp. 351–53.

Wang Tingsheng. *Wangshi huimou* (A look back at past events). Beijing: Zhongguo renmin chubanshe, 2008.

Wang Xiaobin. "Zhonghua Renmin Gongheguo Changdu diqu renmin jiefang weiyuanhui lishu guanxi de lishi yange" (Historical evolution of the subordinate relations of the people's liberation committee of Changdu Prefecture in the People's Republic of China). *Zhongguo Zangxue*, no. 3, 2010, pp. 41–47.

Wang Xitang and Xie Xienong. "Zhongyang tongzhanbu fubuzhang Zhang Jingwu zhi si" (The death of the deputy director of the Central Committee United Front Department, Zhang Jingwu). *Yanhuang Chunqiu*, no. 10, 2003, pp. 10–13.

Wang Yan (ed.). *Peng Dehuai nianpu* (Chronology of Peng Dehuai). Beijing: Renmin chubanshe, 1998.

Wang Yan et al. (eds.). *Peng Dehuai zhuan* (The biography of Peng Dehuai). Beijing: Dangdai Zhongguo chubanshe, 1993.

Wang Yunfeng. *Huofo de shijie: Jin Xi Dashi Gongtangcang Danbeiwangxu zhuan* (The world of a living buddha: The biography of Gungthangtsang Rinposhe Tenpe Wangchug). Beijing: Minzu chubanshe, 1996.

Wang Zhongxing and Liu Liqin. *Guofang lishi* (National defense history), vol. 2. Beijing: Junshi kexue chubanshe, 2003.

Wei Cong (ed). *Xunhua Salazu Zizhixian zhi* (Xunhua Sala Autonomous County Gazetteer). Beijing: Zhonghua shuju, 2001.

Wei Ke. *Xizang wenshi ziliao xuanji, 19: Liu zai xueyu gaoyuan de jiaoyin* (Selected literary and historical materials on Tibet, 19: Footprints left on the snowy plateau), Xizang Zizhiqu Zhengxie wenshi ziliao weiyuanhui (ed.). Beijing: Minzu chubanshe, 2000.

Wei Ke and Tang Xueyuan. "Heping jinjun: Hongqi chashang Ximalaya Shan" (Peaceful occupation: The red flag planted in the Himalayas). *Wan Xia*, no. 9, 2010, pp. 14–15.

Weizhen changkong (Threat in the sky). Beijing: Kongjun zhengzhibu, 1980.

Woguo minzu quyu zizhi wenxian ziliao huibian disan ji disan fence (Compilation of documentary materials regarding our country's regional national autonomy, vol. 3, part 3). Chinese Academy of Social Sciences Institute of Nationality Studies Nationality Issues Theoretical Research Room. Beijing: Zhongguo shehui kexueyuan minzu yanjiusuo minzu wenti lilun yanjiushi (no date of publication).

Wu Lengxi. *Yi Mao zhuxi—Wo qinshen jingli de ruogan zhongda lishi shijian pianduan* (Remembering Chairman Mao—Fragments from my personal experience of certain major historical events). Beijing: Xinhua chubanshe, 1995.

Xiangcheng xianzhi (Xiangcheng County Gazetteer). Chengdu: Sichuan daxue chubanshe, 1997.

Xiang Yilei. "Boji zai mangmang caoyuan—Qinzang gaoyuan pingxi panluan zhandou shenghuo zhuiyi" (Fighting on the vast grasslands—Recollections of combat life pacifying rebellion on the Tibet-Qinghai Plateau), in *Junlü shengya: 21 jun Wenzhou zhanyou yijiu* (Army career: Wenzhou comrades-in-arms of the 21st Army recall the past) (no publisher), 1999.

Xie Shaoquan and Zhao Shukang. "Pingxi Kangba panluan" (Pacifying the Khampa rebellion*), in Ganzi zhou wenshi ziliao* (Literary and historical materials on the Ganzi Prefecture), vol. 18, Chinese People's Political Consultative Conference Ganzi Tibetan Autonomous Prefecture Committee (ed.). Kangding: Zhongguo renmin zhengzhi xieshang huiyi Ganzi Zangzu Zizhizhou weiyuanhui, 2000 (semiclassified).

Xie Youtian. *Xiangcun shehui de huimie* (The destruction of rural society). Carle Place, New York: Mingjing chubanshe, 2010.

Xinghai xianzhi (Xinghai County Gazetteer). Xi'an: Sanqin chubanshe, 2000.

Xing Haining. *Guoluo Zangzu shehui (Golok Tibetan society). Beijing: Zhongguo Zangxue chubanshe, 1994.*

Xinhuashe xinwengao (Xinhua News Agency press releases). Xinhua News Agency (ed.). Beijing, Xinhua tongxunshe, vol. 2133 (April 8, 1956).

"Xinjiang shengchan jianshe bingtuan yuanzhu Xizang shi jiemi" (The declassified history of the Xinjiang Production-Construction Corps aiding Tibet). Xinjiang bingtuan chengzhen boke wang, http://hi.baidu.com/phoenix296/blog/item/a1c2af02993cb5e508fa93b4.html. Accessed November 2, 2011.

Xinlong County Literary and Historical Materials Editorial Committee. *Xinlong xian wenshi zhiliao diyiji: Jianguo 50 nian Xinlong zhi bianhua zhuanji* (Xinlong County literary and historical materials vol. 1: Special issue on changes in Xinlong in the 50 years since the founding of the country). Zhongguo Renmin Zhengzhi Xieshang Huiyi Xinlong xian weiyuanhui chuban, 1999.

Xinlong xianzhi (Xinlong County Gazetteer). Chengdu: Sichuan renmin chubanshe, 1992.

Xin Yuchang (ed.). *Ganzi shihua* (Historical narrative of Ganzi). Lanzhou: Gansu wenhua chubanshe, 2012.

Xin Zhongguo guofang dashiji 1955–1960 (Chronical of major events in national defense in the new China). Shanghai National Defense Strategy Research Institute. http://www.gf81.com.cn/index.html. Accessed November 20, 2010.

Xizang de minzhu gaige (Tibet's democratic reforms). CCP Tibet Autonomous Region Party History Data Collection Committe (ed.). Lhasa: Xizang renmin chubanshe, 1995 (semiclassified).

Xizang diming jianbian (cugao) (Concise Tibetan place names [first draft]). Tibet Autonomous Region Revolutionary Committee Survey and Mapping Bureau, Tibet Military Command Headquarters Reconnaissance Division (eds.), 1979 (classified).

"Xizang gengdi mianji he jiben nongtian dadao guojia guiding de baohu yaoqiu" (Tibet's cultivated area and basic farmland meet the demand of state protection regulations). Renmin wang, http://xz.people.com.cn/GB/13941406.html. Accessed February 3, 2011.

Xizang geming huiyilu (Reminiscences of the Tibet Revolution). Vol. 4, (Special commemorating the 30th anniversary of implementing democratic reform in Tibet), Redi et al. (eds), Tibet People's Publishing (ed.). Lhasa: Xizang renmin chubanshe, 1989.

Xizang geming shi (History of the revolution in Tibet). CCP Tibet Autonomous Region Party Committee Party History Material Collection Committee (ed.). Lhasa: Xizang renmin chubanshe, 1991.

"Xizang gongwei xuanchuanbu dui Renmin Ribao fabiao 'Yuguo tianqin' yigao de yijian" (Tibet Work Committee's views regarding *People's Daily* publishing "Clear skies after rain"). *Neibu Cankao* (Internal reference), Xinhua News Agency (ed.), May 31, 1959, pp. 19–23 (classified).

Xizang gongzuo wenxian xuanbian (1949–2005) (Selected documents on Tibet Work [1949–2005]). CCP Central Committee Documentary Research Section, CCP Tibet Autonomous Region Party Committee (eds.). Beijing: Zhongyang wenxian chubanshe, 2005.

Xizang renwu jieshao (Who's who in Tibet). CCP Central Military Commission Liaison Department Reference Room (ed.). Los Angeles: Zhongwen chubanwu fuwu zhongxin, 1997 (top secret).

Xizang wenshi ziliao xuanji (Selected literary and historical materials on Tibet), vol. 4. (Lhasa?): Xizang Zizhiqu zhengxie wenshi ziliao yanjiu weiyuanhui, 1985 (semiclassified).

Xizang wenshi ziliao xuanji (Selected literary and historical materials on Tibet), vol. 9. Lhasa: Xizang Zizhiqu zhengxie wenshi ziliao yanjiu weiyuanhui, 1986 (semiclassified).

Xizang xingshi he renwu jiaoyu de jiben jiaocai (Shiyongben) (Basic teaching materials for education on Tibet's situation and tasks [trial edition]). Zhongguo renmin jiefangjun Xizang junqu zhengzhibu, 1960 (classified).

Xizang Zizhiqu junshi zhi (Tibet Autonomous Region Military Gazetteer). Beijing: Zhongguo Zangxue chubanshe, 2007 (semiclassified).

Xizang Zizhiqu Zhengxie Wenshi Ziliao Yanjiu Weiyuanhui (ed.). *Xizang wenshi ziliao xuanji* (Selected literary and historical materials on Tibet), vol. 9. Lhasa: Xizang zizhiqu zhengxie wenshi ziliao yanjiu weiyuanhui, 1986 (semiclassified).

"Xi Zhongxun, Li Weihan deng tongzhi he Banchan tanhua jilu" (Record of a conversation between comrades Xu Zhongxun, Li Weihan, and others and the Panchen Lama). In *Zhonggong Xizang zhongyao lishi wenxian ziliao huibian* (Compilation of important historical documents of the CCP in Tibet), *Di'er fence: Youguan Panchan yinyan huozui de ruogan xijian shiliao* (Fascicle no. 2: Certain rare historical materials regarding the Panchen Lama being punished for his speech). Los Angeles: Zhongwen chubanchubanwu fuwu zhongxin, 2010, pp. 24–43 (top secret). English translation available at author's blog: http://historicaldocs.blogspot.com/2016/01/achievements-are-predominant-mistakes.html.

Xu Donghai. "Pingxi Lasa wuzhang panluan mudu ji" (Eyewitness account of the pacification of the armed rebellion in Lhasa), *Xizang dangshi ziliao*, no. 2, 1999, pp. 9–23 (semiclassified).

Xu Hongsen. "1958 qi-ba yue Zhang Jingwu tong galunmen de jici tanhua jianlu" (A brief record of several conversations between Zhang Jingwu and the *kalons* in July and August 1958), in *Xizang wenshi ziliao xuanji* (Selected historical and literary materials regarding Tibet), vol. 24, pp. 196–207.

Xu Mingde. *Wo zhe yibeizi* (My life) (no publisher given), 2006.

Xu Yan. *Taojin baizhan pingshuo gujin* (Dredging up 100 battles commenting on the past and present). Beijing: Changzheng chubanshe, 2013.

Xu Yan. "Zangqu pingpan de wunian jianku suiyue" (Five hard years pacifying rebellion in the Tibetan regions). *China Tibet News*, http://www.chinatibetnews.com/xizang/lishi/2008-2/12/content_181416.htm. Accessed February 19, 2010.

Xu Yanbo. "Wo suo jingli de Xizang pingpan wangshi" (My past experience of pacifying rebellion in Tibet). *Hongya Chunqiu*, no. 5, 2008, p. 73.

Xu Zhengyu. *Xizang keji zhi* (Tibet Scientific Gazetteer). Lhasa: Xizang renmin chubanshe, 1995.

Yang Haiying. *Menggu qibing zai Xizang huiwu Riben dao: Meng-Zang minzu de shidai beiju* (Mongolian cavalry brandishing Japanese swords in Tibet: The epochal tragedy of the Mongolian and Tibetan people). Taipei: Dakuai wenhua, 2017.

Yangling Dorjé (Yangling Duojie). "Yige minzu ganbu xinzhong de Zhao Ziyang" (Zhou Ziyang in the heart of an ethnic cadre), in *Zhao Ziyang in Sichuan (1975–1980)*, Cai Wenbin (ed.). Hong Kong: New Century Media & Consulting Co, Ltd., 2011. pp. 74–91.

Yang Shangkun. *Yang Shangkun riji* (The journals of Yang Shangkun). Beijing: Zhongyang wenxian chubanshe, 2001.

Yang Yizhen (ed.). *Xizang jiyi—Jinjun Xizang jiefang Xizang huiyi wenxuan* (Remembering Tibet—Collected recollections of advancing into Tibet and liberating Tibet), vols. 1 and 2. Fuzhou: Haifeng chubanshe, 2011.

Yan Zhengde and Wang Yiwu. *Jinghai baike dacidian* (Encyclopedia of Qinghai). Beijing: Zhongguo caizheng jingji chubanshe, 1994.

Yin Shusheng. "Dayuejin qianhou de shehui kongzhi" (Social control before and after the Great Leap Forward). *Yanhuang Chunqiu*, no. 4, 2011, pp. 8–12.

Yin Shusheng. "Gong'an gongzuo dayuejin" (Great Leap Forward in public security work). *Yanhuang Chunqiu*, no. 1, 2010, pp. 17–23.

Yin Shusheng. "Jinyintan zhi tong" (Suffering on the gold and silver shoal). *Yanhuang Chunqiu*, no. 3, 2012, pp. 41–45.

Yin Shusheng. "Wo canjia luoshi minzu zhengce de jingli" (My experience implementing the ethnic minority policy). *Yanhuang Chunqiu*, no. 7, 2012, pp. 5–9.

Yixijunmin. "Bu pingfan de zuji: ji Ganzizhou Zangmintuan de zhandou licheng" (The marvelous battle history of the Tibetan Regiment). In *Ganzizhou wenshi ziliao dijiu ji, jinian Ganzi jianzhou sishi zhounian zhuanji* (Literary and historical materials of Garzê Prefecture), vol. 1, 1950–1990. Kangding (?): Zhengxie Sichuansheng Ganzi Zangzu Zizhizhou weiyuanhui, 1990 (semiclassified).

Yongqingbamu, Wang Juong, and Zhang Hong (comps. and eds.). *Zang shi yaowen (1949–2011)* (Headline events in Tibet [1949–2011]). Beijing: Zhongguo Zangxue chubanshe, 2011.

Youguan Xizang wenti de wenjian he cailiao huibian (guonei bufen), 1949–1959 (Compilation of documents and materials regarding the Tibet problem [domestic portion], 1949–1959). Xinhua News Agency (internal publication). Los Angeles: Zhongwen chubanwu fuwu zhongxin, 2001.

Yunnan bianjiang minzu diqu minzhu gaige (Democratic reform in the ethnic minority border areas of Yunnan). CCP Yunnan Provincial Party Committee Party History Research Room (ed.). Kunming: Yunnan daxue chubanshe, 1996.

Yunnan shengzhi: junshi zhi (Yunnan Province Gazetteer: Military Gazetteer). Kunming: Yunnan renmin chubanshe, 1997.

Yushu Zangzu Zizhizhou zhi (Yushu Tibetan Autonomous Prefecture Gazetteer). Vol. 1. Xi'an: Sanqin chubanshe, 2005.

Zeku xianzhi (Zeku County Gazetteer). Beijing: Zhongguo xianzhen nianjian chubanshe, 2005.

Zhai Songtian (ed.). *Zhongguo renkou (Qinghai fence)* (China population [Qinghai]). Beijing: Zhongguo caizheng jingji chubanshe, 1989.

Zhang Dingyi. *1954 nian Dalai, Banchan jinjing jilue, jianji Xizang Zizhiqu choubei weiyuanhui chengli* (Brief record of the Dalai Lama and Panchen Lama proceeding to the capital in 1954, and remembering the establishment of the

Tibet Autonomous Region Preparatory Committee). Beijing: Zhongguo Zangxue chubanshe, 2005.

Zhang Dingyi. "1954 nian Dalai, Banchan lianmei jinjing chuxi quanguo renda huiyi jishi" (A true record of the joint visit to Beijing in 1954 by the Dalai Lama and Panchen Lama to attend the National People's Congress), in *Xizang dangshi zhiliao* (Tibet party history materials) (classified), no. 3, 1991, pp. 42–51.

Zhang Guohua. "Xizang, huidaole zuguo de huaibao" (Tibet, returning to the embrace of the motherland), in *Xinghuo liaoyuan* (A single spark can start a prairie fire), vol. 10. Beijing: Zhongguo renmin jiefangjun zhanshi chubanshe, 1982, pp. 518–34.

Zhang Guoxiang and Sun Yong, as told to Lin Rusheng. "Zhongguo tu-4 chuanqi" (The legend of China's Tu-4), *Bingqi zhishi* (Ordnance knowledge), no. 5, 2008, pp. 32–35.

Zhang Lihe. "Chuanxibei gaoyuan de Zangchuan fojiao xianzhuang" (The situation of Tibetan Buddhism on Sichuan's northwestern plateau). *Zhongguo Xizang*, no. 1, 1998, pp. 44–45.

"Zhangong zhuozhu Dong Zhanlin" (Outstandingly meritorious military service, Dong Zhanlin). *Dangshi tiandi* (Party history world), no. 18, 2015, p. 38.

Zhang Peihui. "Yao guanxin gaoyuan bianfang budui de shenghuo" (We must care about the living conditions of the frontier defense troops on the plateau). *Houqin gongzuo ziliao* (Logistics work material), no. 30, 1957, pp. 8–9.

Zhang Pingzhi. "Gaoyuan hongying" (Red eagle on the plateau). http://kong25.bokee.com/275102689.html. Accessed August 15, 2011.

Zhang Xiangming. *Zhang Xiangming 55 nian Xizang gongzuo shilu* (A true record of Zhang Xiangming's 55 years of Tibet work). Beijing (?) (for internal circulation), 2006.

Zhang Zhengming. "Ganzi Zangqu shehui xingtai de chubu kaocha" (A preliminary study of the social forms of the Ganzi Tibetan region), in *Ganzi Zangqu shehui diaocha huiji* (Ganzi Tibetan Region social survey collection), National People's Congress Ethnic Minorities Committee Office (ed.). Beijing: Quanquo Renmin Daibiao Dahui minzu weiyuanhui bangongshi, 1957, pp. 1–40.

Zhao Junwen. "Bei baowei de qishisi tian" (Surrounded for 74 days), in *Xizang geming huiyilu Vol. 4, Jinian Xizang shixing minzhu gaige sanshi zhounian zhuangji* (Memoirs of the revolution in Tibet, vol. 4, commemorating the

30th anniversary of implementing democratic reform in Tibet). Lhasa: Xizang renmin chubanshe, 1989, pp. 76–86.

Zhao Shenying. *Zhang Guohua jiangjun zai Xizang* (General Zhang Guohua in Tibet). Beijing: Zhongguo Zangxue chubanshe, 2001.

Zhao Shenying. *Zhongyang zhuzang daibiao Zhang Jingwu* (Zhang Jingwu the Central Committee's representative in Tibet). Beijing: Zhongguo zangxue chubanshe, 2001.

Zhao Xinyu and Qin Heping. *Kangqu Zangzu shehui lishi diaocha ziliao jiyao* (A Summary of Historical Survey Materials of Kang (Kham) Region Tibetan Society). Chengdu: Sichuan minzu chubanshe, 2004.

Zhao Xinyu, Qin Heping, and Wang Chuan. *Kangqu Zangzu shehui zhenxi ziliao jiyao, Shang.* (Summary of rare and valuable material on the Tibetan society of the Kang region), vol. 1. Chengdu: Bashu shushe, 2006.

Zhayi Rinpoché (Alak Tsayu). *Wo guxiang de beican shi* (The tragedy of my homeland). Dharamsala: Tibetan Writers' Association, 1994.

Zhi Bin, Sun Xiao, and Jiang Zhenshou (eds.). *Zhongguo "tiejun" chuanqi—wushisi jun zhengzhan shilu* (The legend of China's "Iron Army"—A true record of the campaigns of the 54th Army). Beijing: Zhongguo wenluan chubanshe, 1995.

Zhi Xiaomin. *Liu Shaoqi yu Jin-Sui tugai* (Liu Shaoqi and land reform in the Jin-Sui region). Taibei: Xiuwei zixun keji gufen youxian gongsi, 2008.

Zhongdian xianzhi (Zhongdian County Gazetteer). Duan Zhicheng (ed.). Kunming: Yunnan minzu chubanshe, 1997.

Zhonggong dangshi cankao ziliao (CCP party history reference material). Vols vols. 2 and 9, Beijing Zhongguo renmin jiefangjun zhengzhi xueyuan dangshi jiaoyanshi, 1979, (classified).

Zhonggong Lasa dangshi dashiji 1951–1966 (Chronicle of the CCP's party history in Lhasa 1951–1966). CCP Lhasa Municipal Party Committee Party History Material Compilation Leading Group. Lhasa: for internal circulation, 1991.

Zhonggong Xizang dangshi dashiji 1949–1966 (Chronicle of events in the history of the CCP in Tibet 1949–1966). CCP Tibet Autonomous Region Party Committee Party History Material Compilation Committee, ed. Lhasa: Xizang renmin chubanshe, 1990 (semiclassified).

Zhonggong Xizang dangshi dashiji 1949–1994 (Chronicle of events in the history of the CCP in Tibet 1949–1994). CCP Tibet Autonomous Region Party Committee Party History Material Compilation Committee (ed.). Lhasa: Xizang renmin chubanshe, 1995.

"Zhonggong zhongyang pizhuan Xibei diqu diyici minqu gongquo huiyi jiyao" (CCP Central Committee's endorsed transmission of the summary of the First Northwest Region Ethnic Minorities Work Conference). In *Jianguo yilai zhongyao wenxian xuanbian: 1961.1—1961.12, Vol. 14* (Selected important documents since the founding of the country: January—December 1961, vol. 14), CCP Central Documentary Research Room (ed.). Beijing: Zhongyang wenxian chubanshe, 2011, pp. 817–44.

Zhongguo Gongchandang Gannan lishi 1921.7—2003.7 (History of the Chinese Communist Party in Gannan July 1921 to July 2003). CCP Gannan Prefecture Party History Research Room. Lanzhou: Gansu minzu chubanshe, 2003.

Zhongguo Gongchandang Xizang Zizhiqu zuzhishi ziliao 1950–1987 (Materials on the organizational history of the Chinese Communist Party in the Tibet Autonomous Region 1950–1987). CCP Tibet Autonomous Region (TAR) Party Committee Organization Department, CCP TAR Party Committee Party History Material Compilation Committee and TAR Archive (eds.). Lhasa: Xizang renmin chubanshe, 1993 (semiclassified).

Zhongguo Gongchandang zuzhishi ziliao: di 5 juan: Guodu shiqi he shehui zhuyi jianshe shiqi (1949.10–1966.5) (Historical material on the organization of the Chinese Communist Party: vol. 5: The transition period and socialist construction period (October 1949–May 1966). CCP Central Committee Organization Department, CCP Central Committee Party History Research Section, Central Archives (ed.). Beijing: Zhonggong dangshi chubanshe, 2000.

Zhongguo jin xiandai minzu shi (History of China's ethnic minorities in recent modern times). Chen Liankai et al. (eds.). Beijing: Zhongyang minzu daxue chubanshe, 2011.

Zhongguo minzu tongji 1949–1990 (China ethnic minority statistics 1949–1990). State Ethnic Affairs Commission Economics Department, State Bureau of Statistics (eds.). Beijing: Zhongguo tongji chubanshe, 1991.

Zhongguo Renmin Jiefangjun bubing dishiyishi junzhanshi (Military history of the Chinese People's Liberation Army 11th Infantry Division). Military History of the Chinese People's Liberation Army 11th Infantry Division Editorial Committee (ed.). Urumqi (?): Xinjiang chubanshe, 1987.

Zhongguo Renmin Jiefangjun Chengdu junqu junshi jiaotong shi 1937–1990 (Military transportation history of the Chinese People's Liberation Army Chengdu Military Command, 1937 to 1990). Chengdu: Chengdu junqu houqin jushi yunshu bu, 1992.

Zhongguo Renmin Jiefangjun di 18 jun ji Xizang junqu junshi, Zhonggong zhongyao lishi wenxian ziliao huibian di 31 ji bianjiang minzu lishi zhuangji di 43 fence (Compilation of important historical documentary materials, collection 31, special collections on frontier nationalities, fascicle no. 43). Los Angeles: Zhongwen chubanwu fuwu zhongxin, 2014.

Zhongguo Renmin Jiefangjun qishinian dashiji (Seventy-year chronicle of the People's Liberation Army). PLA Academy of Military Science Military History Research Department (ed.). Beijing: Junshi kexue chubanshe, 2000.

Zhongguo Renmin Jeifangjun quanshi. Di'erjuan. Zhongguo Renmin Jiefangjun qishinian dashiji (Complete history of the Chinese People's Liberation Army. Vol. 2: Major events in 70 years of the People's Liberation Army). Beijing: Junshi kexue chubanshe, 2000.

"Zhongguo Renmin Jiefangjun zhongzhengzhibu guanyu panluan jiben pingxi hou zhu Zangzu diqu budui zhengzhi gongzuo de zhishi" (People's Liberation Army General Political Department directive regarding the political work of troops stationed in the Tibetan regions after the basic pacification of rebellion). *Gongzuo Tongxun*, no. 37, November 21, 1961, pp. 28–33 (classified).

Zhonghua Renmin Gongheguo renkou tongji ziliao huibian 1949–1985 (Compilation of population statistical material for the People's Republic of China 1949–1985). State Bureau of Statistics Population Statistics Department, Ministry of Public Security Third Bureau (eds.). Beijing: Zhongguo caizheng jingji chubanshe, 1988.

Zhonghua Renmin Gongheguo rishi 1958 nian (Chinese People's Liberation Army daily history 1958). Chengdu: Sichuan renmin chubanshe, 2003.

Zhonghua Renmin Gongheguo tudi gaigefa (Land reform law of the People's Republic of China). Beijing: Renmin chubanshe, 1952.

"Zhongyang junwei tongling jiajiang zhixing pingpan renwu de budui" (Central Military Commission notice commending the troops carrying out the task of pacifying rebellion). *Gongzuo Tongxun*, no. 33, October 26 1961, pp. 11–12 (classified).

Zhongyang renmin zhengfu zhengwuyuan guanyu huafen nongcun jieji chengfen de jueding (Chinese People's Government state administrative council decision regarding rural class composition). Beijing: Xinhua shudian, 1950.

Zhou Enlai. *Zhou Enlai tongyi zhanxian wenxuan* (Selected United Front writings of Zhou Enlai), compiled by the CCP Central Committee United Front Work

Department and CCP Central Committee Documentary Research Room. Beijing: Renmin chubanshe, 1984.

Zhou Enlai yu Xizang (Zhou Enlai and Tibet), Tibet Autonomous Region Party History Office (ed.). Beijing: Zhonggon Zangxue chubanshe, 1998.

"Zhoujin Zangmintuan de guangrong lishi" (The glorious history of the civil corps in Tibet). *Ganzi Ribao* (Ganzi daily) online. July 27, 2011. http://www.gzznews.com/content.asp?id=38496. Accessed August 15, 2011.

Zhu De nianpu (Chronology of Zhu De). CCP Central Documentary Research Room. Beijing: Renmin chubanshe, 1986.

"Zongli jiejian Banchan dengren de tanhua jiyao" (Summary of conversation between the premier and the Panchen Lama and others). In *Zhonggong Xizang zhongyao lishi wenxian ziliao huibian: Di'er fence: Youguan Banchan yinyan huozui de ruogan xijian shiliao* (Compilation of important historical documentary materials of the CCP in Tibet: Fascicle No. 2: Certain scarce historical material regarding the Panchen Lama being punished for his speech), Document no. 4. Los Angeles: Zhongwen chubanwu fuwu zhongxin, 2010 (top secret).

Zou Qiyu and Miao Wenjun (eds.). *Zhongguo renkou (Yunnan fence)* (China population [Yunnan]). Beijing: Zhongguo caizheng jingji chubanshe, 1989.

Tibetan-Language Sources

Athar Norbu, *bsTan srung dang blangs dpa' bo Li thang A thar nor bu'i mi tshe lo rgyus* (The Life-story of Athar Norbu of Litang, warrior of the Volunteer Defence Army). Kathmandu: privately published, 2004.

Dochö Tenzin Wangyal, ed. *Bar khams Po ti dgon pa gtsos Sho star lho gsum khul gyi rang gi dngos myong dang mthong thos ji byung bden gtam shul bzhag Tshangs pa'i thig shing Po ti dgon pa'i grva zur Badzra yi mi tshe'i lo rgyus* (A true account for posterity of my experiences at Poti monastery and in the Sho-tar-lho-sum region, entitled "Brahma's Measuring Stick," being the life-story of former Poti monk Badzra). Dharamsala: Tibetan Centre for Human Rights and Democracy, 2006.

Kargyal Dondrup. *mDo khams cha phreng kyi lo rgyus gser gyi snye ma* (A history of Kham Chatreng entitled The Golden Grain). Dharamsala: Library of Tibetan Works and Archives, 1992.

Ke'utsang Tulku Jampel Yeshe. *Ma bltas kun gyis mthong ba skyid sdug gi myong bya* (The unseen seen by all). Bylekuppe: Sera Mey monastery, 1990.

mDzad rnam rgya chen rnying rje'i rol mtsho (Vast ocean of compassionate activity), vol. 4. Dharamsala: Norbulingka Institute, 2009.

Ratuk Ngawang. *mDo khams spo 'bor sgang gi Li thang dgon yul gnyis kyis btsan 'dzul par ngo rgol gyis rang sa srung skyob byas pa'i skor* (On the defence of the Litang monastery and community against invaders 1936–59–vol. 2 of Litang Historical Records). Dharamsala: Amnye Machen Publications, 2006.

rGya dmar gyis bod nang mi spyod las 'das pa'i bya ngan ji byas dngos byung gnas lugs rags bsdus gSal bar mthong ba'i me long (1959–84) (A Clear Mirror, being a collection of real accounts of the inhumane crimes of the Red Chinese in Tibet (1959–84). Dharamsala: Tibetan Government in Exile, Department of Security, 1991.

Shirla Lhundrup Wangyal. *Mun nag khrod kyi bod mi zhig gi mi tshe* (Life of a Tibetan caught up in darkness). Dharamsala: Privately published, 2004.

Tarawa Tenzin Choenyi. *Rang nyid ngo sprod* (Introducing Myself). Dharamsala: Library of Tibetan Works and Archives (Oral History Series, vol. 18), 2005.

Tsongkha Lhamo Tsering. *bTsan rgol rgyal skyob (vol. 2): Bod nang du drag po'i 'thab rtsod byas skor 1957–62* (Resistance, vol. 2: The armed struggle inside Tibet 1957–62). Dharamsala: Amnye Machen Publications, 1998.

List of Interviewees (in Chronological Order)

Dondrup Dorjé (monk, Yulshul), October 28, 2007, Majnu-ka-tilla Tibetan Refugee Settlement, India.

Dondrup Norbu (monk, Nagchu), November 5, 2007, Dharamsala Home for the Elderly, India.

Sonam Puntsok (Tibetan Army officer, Lhasa), November 5, 2007, Dharamsala Home for the Elderly, India.

Drolkar (tradeswoman, Pagri), November 11, 2007, Majnu-ka-Tilla Tibetan Refugee Colony, India.

Tsering Yangzom (tradesman, Pagri), November 11, 2007, Majnu-ka-Tilla Tibetan Refugee Colony, India.

Puntsok (monk, Sershul), November 13, 2007, Sera Monastery, India

Tsering Wangdu (tradesman, Shigatsé), November 14, 2007, Bylakuppe Tibetan Refugee Settlement, India.

Jigmé Woeser (herder, Dergé), September 30, 2008, Bir Tibetan Refugee Settlement, India.

Nyima Tsering (herder, TAR), October 1, 2008, Bir Tibetan Refugee Settlement, India.

Donyo Jagotsang (son of Jagö Topden [1898–1960], the minister of Dergé Gyalpo), October 2, 2008, Bir Tibetan Refugee Settlement, India.

Drakyang (herder, Dergé), October 7, 2008. Jawalakhel Tibetan Handicraft Center, Nepal.

Jampa (son of a headman, Yulshul), October 7, 2008, Kathmandu, Nepal.

Pema Wangchen (farmer, Garzê), October 13, 2008, Gangtok, Sikkim, India.

Tashi (herder, Tengchen), October 14, 2008,Ravangla Tibetan Refugee Settlement, Sikkim, India.

Kelsang Gyadotsang (monk, Lithang), May 10, 2009, New Jersey, USA.

His Holiness the Dalai Lama, June 27, 29, 30, 2009; December 3, 2010, Dharamsala, India.

Ngari Rinpoché (younger brother of His Holiness the Dalai Lama), July 18, 21, 2009, Dharamsala, India.

Lobsang Kungpo (monk, Garzê), September 10, 2009, Dalhousie Tibetan Refugee Settlement, India.

Lobsang Yeshe (monk, Garzê), September 11, 2009, Dalhousie Tibetan Refugee Settlement, India.

Ngawang Tsering (monk), September 11, 2009, Dalhousie Tibetan Refugee Settlement, India.

Jampa Tenzin (monk, Lhasa), September 12, 2009, Dharamsala, India.

Wangmo (herder, Purang), September 12, 2009, Dalhousie Tibetan Refugee Settlement, India.

Juchen Tubten(farmer, Dergé), September 22, 2009, Dharamsala, India.

Ratuk Ngawang (merchant, Lithang), December 3, 2009, Majnu-Ka-Tilla Tibetan Refugee Colony, India.

Pema Yungdrung (herder, Ngari), September 3, 2010, Mundgod Tibetan Refugee Settlement, India.

Jigmé Paljor (son of former Nedong *dzongpon*), September 4, 2010, Mundgod Tibetan Refugee Settlement, India.

Pema Tsering (farmer, Ngari), September 4, 2010, Mundgod Tibetan Refugee Settlement, India.

Tenzin Woeser (monk, Chentsa), September 5, 2010, Drepung Monastery, India.

Tubten Nyima (monk,Tsikorthang), September 6, 2010, Drepung Monastery, India.

Yetan (monk, Garzê), September 7, 8, 2010, Drepung Monastery, India.

Khotse Jinpa (nomad, Labrang), October 19, 2010, Dondrupling Tibetan Refugee Settlement, Dehradun, India.

Lobsang Sherab (merchant, Barkham), October 20, 2010, Dondrupling Tibetan Refugee Settlement, Dehradun, India.

Ngolo (herder, Golok), October 20, 2010, Dondrupling Tibetan Refugee Settlement, Dehradun, India.

Pema Tharchin (herder, Garzê), October 20, 2010, Dondrupling Tibetan Refugee Settlement, Dehradun, India.

Drolkar Gye (herder, Sangchu), October 20, 24, 2010, Dondrupling Tibetan Refugee Settlement, Dehradun, India.

Lhakpa (herder, Sangchu), October 22, 2010, Dondrupling Tibetan Refugee Settlement, Dehradun, India.

Gyalrong Tenzin (farmer, Barkham), October 23, 2010, Dondrupling Tibetan Refugee Settlement, Dehradun, India.

Tenkyong (monk, Chikdril, Golok), November 21, 2010, Dharamsala, India.

Damcho Pelsang (monk, Chikdril, Golok), November 21, 2010, Dharamsala, India.

Tsering Dorjé (son of Markham chieftain Phupa Pon Tsering Gyaltsen), December 4, 2010, Dharamsala, India.

Yangdrup (monk, Golok), June and July, 2011, many telephone interviews.

Kesang Rinpoché (monk, Machu), July 11, 2011, Washington, D.C.

Kirti Rinpoché (monk, Ngawa), November 16, 2011, New York.

Darje (cadre, Golok), August 22, 24, 2012. Xining, Qinghai, China.

INDEX